THE ROUTLEDGE COMPANION TO EARLY CHRISTIAN THOUGHT

The shape and course which Christian thought has taken over its history is largely due to the contributions of individuals and communities in the second and third centuries. Bringing together a remarkable team of distinguished scholars, *The Routledge Companion to Early Christian Thought* is the ideal companion for those seeking to understand the way in which early Christian thought developed within its broader cultural milieu and was communicated through its literature, especially as it was directed toward theological concerns.

Divided into three parts, the *Companion*:

- asks how Christianity's development was impacted by its interaction with cultural, philosophical, and religious elements within the broader context of the second and third centuries;
- examines the way in which early Christian thought was manifest in key individuals and literature in these centuries;
- analyses early Christian thought as it was directed toward theological concerns such as God, Christ, redemption, scripture, and the community and its worship.

D. Jeffrey Bingham is Department Chair and Professor of Theological Studies at Dallas Theological Seminary, USA. He is editor of the Brill monograph series, *The Bible in Ancient Christianity*, as well as author of *Irenaeus' Use of Matthew's Gospel in Adversus Haereses* and several articles and essays on the theology and biblical interpretation of early Christianity.

THE ROUTLEDGE COMPANION TO EARLY CHRISTIAN THOUGHT

Edited by D. Jeffrey Bingham

Routledge
Taylor & Francis Group

LONDON AND NEW YORK

First published 2010
by Routledge
2 Park Square, Milton Park, Abingdon, Oxon OX14 4RN

Simultaneously published in the USA and Canada
by Routledge
270 Madison Ave., New York, NY 100016

Routledge is an imprint of the Taylor & Francis Group, an informa business

© 2010 D. Jeffrey Bingham for selection and editorial materials; the contributors for their
contributions

Typeset in Goudy Oldstyle Std 10.5/13pt
By Fakenham Photosetting Ltd, Fakenham, Norfolk, NR25 8NN
Printed and bound in Great Britain by CPI Antony Rowe, Chippenham, Wiltshire

British Library Cataloguing in Publication Data
A catalogue record for this book is available from the British Library

Library of Congress Cataloging in Publication Data
The Routledge companion to early Christian thought / edited by D. Jeffrey Bingham. p. cm.
Includes bibliographical references and index.
ISBN 978-0-415-44225-1 (hardback : alk. paper) – ISBN 978-0-203-86451-7 (ebook) 1.
Christianity–Philosophy–History–Early church, ca. 30-600. I. Bingham, D. Jeffrey (Dwight Jeffrey)
II. Title: Companion to early Christian thought.
BR100.R67 2009
230.09'015–dc22
2009026872

ISBN10: 0-415-44225-7 (hbk)
ISBN10: 0-203-86451-4 (ebk)
ISBN13: 978-0-415-44225-1 (hbk)
ISBN13: 978-0-203-86451-7 (ebk)

For Pamela and Marti,
and in memory
of my Father,
Dwight Hemenway Bingham, Jr.
(12 April 1926–28 May 2009)

CONTENTS

CONTRIBUTORS

D. Jeffrey Bingham is Department Chair and Professor of Theological Studies at Dallas Theological Seminary in Dallas, Texas.

Lynn H. Cohick is Associate Professor of New Testament in the Biblical and Theological Studies department at Wheaton College in Wheaton, Illinois.

Geoffrey D. Dunn is currently an Australian Research Council-funded Australian Research Fellow in the Centre for Early Christian Studies, Australian Catholic University.

Mark J. Edwards is Tutor in Theology at Christ Church, Oxford and Lecturer in Patristics in the Theology Faculty of Oxford University.

J. K. Elliott is Emeritus Professor at the University of Leeds, UK. He has recently retired from the personal chair of New Testament Textual Criticism.

James D. Ernest is an Academic Acquisitions Editor for Baker Publishing Group and Adjunct Instructor in Historical Theology at Calvin Theological Seminary in Grand Rapids, Michigan.

Everett Ferguson is Distinguished Scholar in Residence at Abilene Christian University in Abilene, Texas.

Henny Fiskå Hägg is Associate Professor at the Department of Religion, Philosophy and History at the University of Agder, Norway.

Paul Hartog is an Associate Professor of New Testament and Early Christian Studies at Faith Baptist Theological Seminary in Ankeny, Iowa.

Ronald E. Heine is Professor of Bible and Theology at Northwest Christian University in Eugene, Oregon.

Clayton N. Jefford is Professor of Scripture at the St Meinrad School of Theology in St Meinrad, Indiana.

Peter W. Martens is an Assistant Professor in the Department of Theological Studies at Saint Louis University in St Louis, Missouri.

J. A. McGuckin is Ane Marie and Bent Emil Nielsen Professor in Late Antique and Byzantine Christian History at Union Theological Seminary as well as Professor of Byzantine Christian Studies at Columbia University, New York.

Anne McGuire is the Kies Family Associate Professor in the Humanities and Associate Professor of Religion at Haverford College in Haverford, Pennsylvania.

Pheme Perkins is Professor of New Testament in the Theology Department at Boston College in Boston, Massachusetts.

Oskar Skarsaune is Professor of Church History at the MF Norwegian School of Theology, Oslo.

M. C. Steenberg is Chair and Professor of Theology at Leeds Trinity University College in Horsforth, Leeds, UK.

George H. van Kooten is Dean of Faculty and Professor of New Testament and Early Christianity in the Faculty of Theology and Religious Studies of the University of Groningen, The Netherlands.

PREFACE

In the second and third centuries, as Christianity continued its movement outward and westward from its early urban centers into the larger Roman world, the challenge of relating to Greco-Roman socio-political, philosophical, and religious forces intensified. Christians – increasingly of pagan rather than Jewish background – struggled to discern whether and how to reject or adapt commonplace Greco-Roman philosophical ideas. Conversely, their pagan neighbors were formulating their own judgments regarding Christianity, some more generous than others. Meanwhile, Jews and Christians were also reading each other and defining themselves by way of a hermeneutical struggle for the inheritance of the Hebrew scriptures. Part I of this volume therefore treats the interaction between these overarching, problematic categories: Christian, Greco-Roman, Jew.

Early Christian thought is complex, not amenable to simple description. The era was fraught with conflicting definitions of the pairings catholic and heretic, Christian and Jew, Christian and Roman. Enculturated in various social and geographical settings, early Christianity sometimes exhibited dizzying diversity; at other times it demonstrated surprising continuity in thought and practice. Sacred writings were being identified and collected; in some cases they were being written. Always they were being interpreted. These interpretations spawned various rites, ideas, manners of life, and inevitably, additional literature, some of it pastoral, some of it expositional, some of it adversarial, some of it defensive. Within this literature and within their patterns of living, worshipping, and dying, Christians manifested peculiar ways of thinking and formulated distinctive theological ideas. Part II of this book therefore discusses diverse writers and literatures of those early years and their theological concerns, and part III surveys selected theological topics that are particularly prominent in texts from the whole period.

The chapters are written by an international group of experts who aim to serve the needs both of beginners and of those who are continuing their study of early Christian thought. For those who require an initial orientation to understand the cultural context and theological contributions of early Christian literature, these essays will point out the prominent defining features of the period. Those already initiated will find further insight into Christianity's early complexity and simplicity. Both will find helpful suggestions for further reading.

I am very grateful for the tireless and conscientious efforts of Christopher Graham, who, at the end of the project, provided essential aid, and to Stephen Bagby, and Stephen Presley, my generous and careful research assistants at various stages of this work. Their devotion to the study of early Christian thought has enriched and sharpened the book. I must also offer heartfelt thanks to Lesley Riddle, senior publisher for religion and anthropology at Routledge, and to Amy Grant, editorial assistant in religion, for their professionalism, patience, and charity throughout the entire process.

Part I
WORLD

1

CHRISTIANITY IN THE GRAECO-ROMAN WORLD

Socio-political, philosophical, and religious interactions up to the Edict of Milan (CE 313)[1]

George H. van Kooten

In this essay I present a framework situating early Christianity within the geographical and cultural context of the Graeco-Roman world. I examine how Christianity interacted with the socio-political, philosophical, and religious forces in the Graeco-Roman world in the second and third centuries. How did these forces set the stage for developments within Christianity, especially its ideology (theology) in the second and third centuries? Firstly, I shall comment on Christianity in relation to Hellenistic-Roman "philosophy" and "religion." What exactly was the difference between philosophy and religion in this age, and how did Christianity relate to them? In a companion to early Christian *thought*, it is particularly worthwhile to reflect on the question of how Christianity appeared to the interested onlooker in antiquity: as a religion, or rather as a philosophy? Secondly, I will focus on the interaction of Christianity with the socio-political, philosophical, and religious forces, commenting on its organization, its ethics, its criticism of sacrifice and pagan idols, and its disparagement of mere sophistic rhetoric. Through this picture, I will portray Christianity as involved in a deep-seated rivalry with other religious and philosophical competitors on the market of antiquity. Thirdly and finally, I shall further illustrate this competition between Christianity and paganism by commenting on the antagonism between the followers of Christ and those of one of those other demigods of antiquity, Heracles.

Christianity, "philosophy," and "religion"

A note on the historiography of early Christianity

Before stipulating the relation between Christianity on the one hand, and the philosophy and religion of the Hellenistic-Roman environment on the other, it is important to clarify how I understand the Christian movement of the second and third centuries (the prime focus of the present volume) vis-à-vis its origins in the first century CE. To my mind, it is not fruitful to distinguish too strongly between the first century and the following second and third centuries; rather, one should regard these centuries as equally part of ante-Nicene Christianity. In the course of these three centuries, the partings of the ways between Christianity and Judaism gradually became visible. At the same time, Christianity was largely regarded as an illicit movement until the Edict of Milan in 313, when Christianity was first allowed religious freedom. It makes no sense to regard the Christianity of the first century as still "Palestinian," in contrast to the Christianity which became embedded throughout the Mediterranean world in the second and third centuries. First of all, together with Judea, Galilee, the homeland of Jesus of Nazareth, was a region of the Roman province of Syria, and, as we know from Josephus, the region itself saw major developments in the first centuries BCE and CE, when new cities such as Tiberias and Sepphoris were founded and were also partly inhabited by Greeks.[2] Secondly, it is – for that reason – scarcely surprising that "even in Galilee" Justus of Tiberias, the son of a first-century-CE Jewish faction leader, could entertain a lively interest in Socrates and Plato, and could be deemed by Josephus to be very proficient in Greek.[3] And thirdly, the Gospel of Mark emphasizes Jesus' activity among Jewish-Galilean settlements in the milieu of the Hellenistic cities and his journeys from Galilee into the Gentile territory of the Greek Decapolis, Phoenician Tyre and Sidon, and Roman Caesarea Philippi.[4] All these features suggest that it would be wrong to regard Galilee as an exception to the rule that the ancient world had become thoroughly Hellenized.[5] Moreover, already in the 30s and 40s of the first century CE, Christian communities existed outside Galilee and Judea in Syria, notably in Antioch, the third largest city of the Eastern Mediterranean. And in the 50s Christianity spread through other important cities there, with Paul founding communities in cities such as Thessalonica, Corinth, and Ephesus.

This is important to realize, as the myth of a simple first-century Christianity as opposed to the Hellenized Christianity of the subsequent centuries is still prevalent. This seems to be the fruit of ideological historiographies of the nineteenth century, such as that of Adolf von Harnack, according to whom first-century Christianity was a moralized version of a simple-minded Judaism.[6] It was only in the second century, according to von Harnack, that Christianity became exposed to the full force of Hellenism. This led to the emergence of Christian Gnosticism, which combined Hellenistic philosophy with the Gnostic conviction that the world was the product not of the highest God, but of an ignorant or malevolent creator god. In attempting to express their convictions, the Christian Gnostics drew on Hellenistic philosophy, thus causing the first radical Hellenization of Christianity. The Hellenization of Christianity then became complete when the church fathers of the second and third centuries, who saw themselves obliged to refute the Gnostic movement within Christianity, also drew on Hellenistic philosophy in their efforts to combat the Gnostics effectively. As a result, the simple, highly moral essence of the original form of Christianity became contaminated with Greek metaphysics. In this way, von Harnack succeeded in distinguishing an original, "biblical" Christianity from the later secular-Greek and early catholic encrustations, which were removed through the reforming endeavours of Augustine and Luther, which went back to the theology of Paul. Although the Protestant interests of this historiography are clearly visible (and though his understanding of Paul is highly questionable), von Harnack's paradigm has been very influential. Even Keith Hopkins, in his best-selling *A World Full of Gods: Pagans, Jews and Christians in the Roman Empire* (1999), reinforces this interpretation: "Gnostics used a transcendental language, which united the thought-worlds of Judaism, Christianity and pagan Neo-Platonism. Gnostics in the second century moved Christianity out of Palestine, and out of the restricted world of Judaeo-Christian myth, on to a cosmic stage."[7] This is far from the historical truth, as first-century Christianity was already firmly embedded in the Mediterranean world. Even Judaism, from which Christianity only gradually parted, was not restricted to Palestine but dispersed throughout the ancient world, participating in, and inter-acting with, its culture.[8] Moreover, Palestine, too – as I already briefly suggested with reference to Galilee – was firmly part of the Hellenistic world.[9] As Christianity only gradually emancipated itself from Judaism during the first two centuries, mainly as a result of its distancing itself from the Jewish revolts against Rome in CE 66–70 and 132–5, it was in fact largely part of the phenomenon which we call Hellenistic Judaism. This started with the advent of Alexander the Great to the Ancient Near East, and constituted a pluriform and yet in many respects coherent movement which, in a variety of ways, had to come to terms with the Hellenistic movement and, at a later stage, Rome, too.[10] The exposure of Christianity to Hellenism is not an issue which only emerged in the second and third centuries, in a secondary development of Christianity; rather, Hellenism already preceded Christianity, inasmuch as Judaism, of which Christianity was part, had already been interacting with Hellenism for over three centuries.

Christianity is a profoundly Jewish movement of the Hellenistic-Roman era. The designation "Christianity" is still very rare in the New Testament, and the result of the outsiders' perspective of the Romans.[11] Moreover, it is early Christianity, and not post-CE-70 rabbinical Judaism, which preserved the Septuagint, the writings of Philo of Alexandria and Josephus, as well as the so-called Jewish pseudepigrapha.[12] And like the Judaism of the Hellenistic-Roman period, it was in interaction with its Graeco-Roman environment.

For all these reasons, I shall closely link the Christianity of the second and third centuries with its manifestation in the first century and regard it as a continuum, uninterrupted by a new cultural epoch, rather than viewing it from a Harnackian perspective of progress, degeneration, and (a need for) reformation. First-century Christianity does not enjoy a separate standing as "biblical." Even the decision about what should be regarded as the authoritative "New Testament writings" was an organic process which spanned the first centuries: the four Gospels and the Pauline Epistles were recognized as authoritative around 150.

"Religion" and "philosophy" in antiquity

The question I shall address now is how, in the first three centuries, Christianity presented itself within the Graeco-Roman world. Was it a (new) religion, or rather a philosophy? This question, awkward as it seems in the ears of those used to the fixed form of modern definitions of religion and philosophy, is essential for us to understand the way in which early Christian thought was communicated on the religious market of antiquity. This market was not just "religious" in the modern sense, but rather religio-philosophical. This is also clear when one looks at the ancient understanding of "religion," "superstition," "philosophy," and "atheism," taking care that our inter-pretation is not influenced by an anachronistic understanding. According to particular ancient Jewish, early Christian, and ancient philosophical perspectives, Judaism and Christianity are philosophical movements, and pagan religion is regarded as providing access to "ancient" wisdom as a source for philosophy.[13]

This observation is confirmed by lexicographical and conceptual analysis of the term "religion" in recent research that questions a modern, anachronistic definition of "religion" and "philosophy" when applied to antiquity. Jan Bremmer, for instance, asks himself,

> What does the term "religion" mean and what does that meaning imply for a contemporary study of Greek religion? The first part of this question may occasion surprise, but the present meaning of religion is the outcome of a long process. ... In the time of Cicero, Lucretius and Virgil, *religio* was not equivalent to our notion of "religion" but contained a strong ritualistic aspect and was often connected with active worship according to the rules.[14]

Against this background, Paul's definition of Christianity (although he still does not use that term) as "a logical [i.e., non-ritualistic] way of worshipping God" (Rom. 12:1–2), which is characterized by ethical deliberations, is most interesting. Through its stress on "logical" worship, Christianity is presented more in terms of a(n) (ethical) philosophy, and not as a ritualistic religion. The same holds true for Christ's view in the Gospel of John that true worship no longer consists in worshipping God in accordance with ancestral Samaritan or Jewish custom, in temples either on Mt Gerizim or in Jerusalem: "the true worshippers will worship the Father in spirit and truth. ... God is spirit, and those who worship him must worship in spirit and truth" (John 4:20–24).[15] Temple worship, which is of a locative and ritualistic nature, is replaced with the worship of God through the rather philosophical medium of spirit and truth. As we shall see, this view is manifest in Origen's criticism of the pagan philosopher Celsus, who still embraces a locative understanding of religion.

Consequently, we should exercise caution in using the term "religion," as Bremmer reminds us: "the use of the term 'religion' for certain Greek ideas and practices is an etic term, which reflects the observer's point of view, not that of the actor: the Greeks themselves did not yet have a term for 'religion'."[16] If we apply not an etic (general, modern, "objective") but an emic perspective, describing early Christianity in terms of its internal elements and their functioning in the ancient world at large, Christianity is not so much a religion, in the Graeco-Roman sense of the word, but rather a philosophy. This is rightly highlighted by Loveday Alexander, who follows the now classic views on Christianity put forward by Arthur Darby Nock in the 1930s:

> To the casual pagan observer the activities of the average synagogue or church would look more like the activities of a school than anything else. Teaching or preaching, moral exhortation, and the exegesis of canonical texts are activities associated in the ancient world with philosophy, not religion.[17]

These developments substantiate Nietzsche's intuitive view of early Christianity as a particular type of Graeco-Roman philosophy, as "Platonismus für's Volk."

At the same time, what is called "ancient philosophy" should not be understood to be devoid of religion. Classicists such as David Sedley have hinted at the religious nature of ancient philosophy. This is shown in the following analysis, which Sedley puts forward in his work on the allegiance of ancient philosophers to a particular founding figure:

> In the Graeco-Roman world, specially during the Hellenistic and Roman periods, what gives philosophical movements their cohesion and identity is less a disinterested common quest for the truth than a virtually religious commitment to the authority of a founder figure.[18]

Philosophy has certain "religious" overtones. The commitment to a particular founder figure manifests itself in reverence for his texts:

> For the vast majority of thinkers in this period … , the revered text was either that of Plato, commonly regarded as divine, or of course the Old and/or New Testament, which were taken to represent, most prominently, the authority of Moses and St Paul, respectively.[19]

These remarks could be further supported with references to the representation of Plato as divine. In Platonism in antiquity, Plato came to be regarded as a divine man (vir divinus), and his writings as divine scriptures (scripta divinitus: Cicero, On the Orator 1.49, 3.15; Laws 1.15, 2.14, 3.1). Such views are matched by similar stories about the divine gift of Plato's philosophy (Cicero), legendary and miraculous tales about Plato's birth under the protection of Apollo (Plutarch, Apuleius, Diogenes Laertius), and several historiographies that link Plato's philosophy with the ancient wisdom of the East, including that of Moses (Numenius).[20]

It is highly relevant to note that Plato was not accorded high status because he was a philosopher, but because his philosophy was considered to confer access to ancient wisdom. This is stressed by Michael Frede in his work on the figure of the philosopher in antiquity:

> One did not primarily think that Plato had been such an excellent philos-
> opher that he must have known the truth; one thought, rather ... that there
> was an ancient wisdom that Plato, being the person he was and the excellent
> philosopher he was, had access to. ... In the light of this, Plato's writings came
> to have a status rather like Scripture.[21]

The religious features of ancient philosophy are also visible in the way philosophy and the religious phenomenon of the oracles were brought together. From the second century CE, oracles were regarded as a source of philosophical reflection. One example of this is provided by the so-called *Chaldean Oracles*, which contain doctrines that are based upon Platonic and Pythagorean speculation, cult, and magic.[22] Another example is the oracles of Apollo at Claros, which are also of a philosophical nature.[23] Reference to Plato's writings, with the aim of reconstructing the ancient wisdom, and philosophical interpretation of the oracles could coexist and reinforce one another. As Frede puts it:

> One believed that Plato's writings were merely a means toward attaining
> the truth that, once attained, would make reference to Plato redundant.
> One could even believe this if, in reconstructing the true philosophy, one
> also relied, for instance, on the Chaldean Oracles, which one took to be
> divinely inspired.[24]

A similar role to that of oracles is played by hymns. They too are both "religious" and applied by philosophers to express their philosophical reflections on the gods. This practice already existed in the *Hymn to Zeus* written by the third century BCE Stoic philosopher Cleanthes, and the genre, continued to be used.[25] This is clearly related to the remarkable phenomenon that important philosophers, such as the first-century-CE Middle Platonist Plutarch, were at the same time priests in a particular cult. Plutarch was a priest of Apollo at Delphi.

Finally, the religious nature of philosophy is also revealed in the practice of *converting* to philosophy.[26] The role of conversion in the lives of ancient philoso-
phers proves very important and also attests to the close resemblance between ancient philosophy and Christianity. Philostratus, for instance, relates that the sophist Isaeus "had devoted the period of his early youth to pleasure. ... But when he attained manhood he so transformed himself as to be thought to have become another person," indicating that "all pleasures are a shadow and a dream."[27] Similar conversion stories are found in Dio Chrysostom, Lucian, Diogenes Laertius, Maximus of Tyre, and Galen.[28] They also employ the vocabulary of conversion, such as the terms *epistrophè*, *conversio*, and *metanoia*. This vocabulary is identical with that of Christians, both in the New Testament writings and in authors such as Justin Martyr.[29]

Having looked briefly at the philosophical self-portrayal of Christianity, already by Paul and John, and at religious features of ancient philosophy, we are in a better position to appreciate how early Christian thought was contextualized in, and interacted with, the Graeco-Roman world. We shall now study this interaction in more detail, and differentiate interactions with the socio-political, philosophical, and religious forces which Christianity entered into competition with.

Christianity in competition

Christianity's organization: interaction with the socio-political forces

The blending of "religion" and "philosophy" in Christianity, Judaism, and pagan philosophy is facilitated by the sociological structure of the religio-philosophical market of antiquity. Apart from the State, and the State-controlled civic religion, over which the emperor presided as its *pontifex maximus*, religio-philosophical life took place in the so-called "private," voluntary associations and the philosophical "schools."[30] Judaism, Christianity, and pagan philosophy all find their natural habitat in the same types of networks, those of associations and (pseudo-) schools whose vague boundaries provided ample room for competition, as long as public order was maintained. If not, the State did not hesitate to intervene, as the frequent expulsions from Rome of Jews, philosophers, and adherents of mystery cults illustrate. But outside Rome, too, in the more distant regions of the empire, private associations could be suppressed, as the correspondence between Trajan and Pliny the Younger shows. Pliny, Trajan's direct representative in the province of Bithynia-Pontus (*c.* CE 110–12), writes to the emperor about an "edict, issued on your instructions, which banned all *hetaeriae*," i.e. all (political) societies and (religious) brotherhoods and fraternities.[31] As far as Judaism was concerned, its adherents were reminded not only of the need to respect the public order, for which the State was responsible, but also, more specially, "not to set at nought the beliefs about the gods held by other peoples but to keep their own laws."[32] This, as we shall see, increasingly caused a problem for Christianity, as it actively engaged in criticizing ancestral religious customs, whether Jewish or pagan. The more Christianity was distinguished from Judaism, the more it became vulnerable as a new association which did not respect existing religious traditions.

An important common denominator between these associations is that, probably with the exception of the synagogue, they organized their meetings around a meal, followed by a symposium. Jews did not necessarily share a meal in their synagogues because of differing views on ritual purity. Yet Christians did, and Paul's description of the way in which the Christian community in Corinth gathered and celebrated the meal of the Lord (see 1 Cor. 11:17–34) closely resembles the meal practices of the associations.[33]

The model of the association is certainly very fruitful for understanding early Christianity's social structures, but it has its limitations and needs to be supplemented with the model of the philosophical school, which only partly overlaps with that of the associations. This was already noted by Alexander in her exploratory work on Christianity as a philosophical school. In this she adduces the remarks by the second-century philosopher and physician Galen, who explicitly referred to Judaism and Christianity as "the schools of Moses and Christ." According to Alexander, the associations only partly account for the social outlook of Christianity:

> In terms of social structure ... , the school has distinct advantages over the more familiar models of the household or the association, neither of which normally produces literature, or sees itself as part of a worldwide movement: there are a number of potentially valuable comparisons to be made in this area.[34]

Alexander herself has made a further contribution to this research by showing that the way in which authorities are cited in Paul's writings is very similar to the use of citations in the Hellenistic schools.[35] This model of the school is also fruitful because, whereas associations often used buildings of their own, neither philosophers nor Christians had such buildings. The latter could meet out-of-doors, but tended to use houses of wealthy Christians, shops, workshops, hired dining rooms, storehouses, or baths for their meetings. The earliest purpose-built churches probably date from the third century.[36] The pagan philosopher Porphyry (234 to c. 305), for instance, writes: "Moreover the Christians also imitate the building of temples by building the greatest houses in which they gather for prayer, although nothing prevents them from doing this in their own houses, since God clearly hears from everywhere."[37] This passage shows that although, as Porphyry acknowledges, Christians had no religious need for specific holy places and could use their own houses, they did in fact build special meeting-places in the third century. This is confirmed by excavations of churches in Dura Europos and Qirqbize in Belus, to the East of Antioch.[38]

Both models, that of the associations and that of the schools, are applied by second-century Christians such as Justin Martyr and Tertullian. They offer some of the earliest reflections about how Christianity was to be socially organized. Justin's Christianity takes the form of a school.[39] And Tertullian, despite his much quoted phrase "What indeed has Athens to do with Jerusalem?,"[40] explicitly compares his allegiance to Christ with that of the philosophers to Pythagoras, Socrates, or Plato.[41] In his *Apology*, however, Tertullian employs the other organizational model, urging his contemporaries to grant Christians the rights of an association.[42]

The self-understanding of Christianity as a philosophical school is not mirrored only by Galen's depiction of Christianity as the school of Christ. Plotinus, too, in his third-century criticism of Christian Gnosticism, likewise portrays it not as a religion, but a philosophical movement in which Plato is misunderstood.[43] This is not to say, however, that Christianity was a formal, organized, institutionalized school. In addition to the formal schools, there were a plethora of other, less formal schools. As Tiziano Dorandi puts it in his overview of the organization and structure of the philosophical schools:

Beside this kind of organized and institutionalized school (*scholai*, *diatribai*), there were also groups of people who got together to practise philosophy in an apparently less rigidly structured form, which could be defined as a "pseudo-school" or, better, "philosophical tendency" (*agōgai* or *haereseis*).[44]

Apart from the terminology of schools and associations, Christianity, starting with Paul, also defines itself in what we might call para-political language as "the assembly of God," the *ekklèsia tou theou*. Unfortunately this term is commonly mistranslated, in idiosyncratic language only applicable to Christianity, as "the church of God." There is reason to believe, however, that Paul, who employs the phrase frequently, deliberately paralleled the Christian assembly, "the assembly of God," with the political assembly of the Greek cities, most explicitly so in his address to the Christian community of Corinth: "To the assembly of God that is in Corinth" (1 Cor. 1:2; 2 Cor. 1:1). Although "assembly" is the term in the Septuagint which depicts the Jewish congregation, the phrase "assembly of God" occurs only once and does not seem to be the exemplar on which Paul modelled his depiction of the Christian congregation.[45]

Rather, as the addresses of the Corinthian correspondence make particularly clear, "the assembly of God that is in Corinth" offers an alternative for the political assembly of Corinthians. It is, I believe, no mere word play on the double meaning of *ekklèsia* (as the political assembly and as "the Church") when Origen, following Paul, contrasts the Christian and the political assembly in this way. Rather it is an important statement of Christian self-understanding which offers an interesting insight into how Christianity defines itself vis-à-vis the political forces of its time. According to Origen,

> everywhere in the world in order that men might be converted and reformed He [i.e. God] made the gospel of Jesus to be successful, and caused assemblies ("churches") to exist in political opposition to the assemblies (*genesthai pantachou ekklèsias antipoliteuomenas ekklèsiais*) of superstitious, licentious, and unrighteous men. For such is the character of the crowds who everywhere constitute *the assemblies of the cities*. And *the assemblies of God* which have been taught by Christ, when compared with *the assemblies of the people* where they live, are "as lights in the world." ... The *assembly of God*, say, at Athens is meek and quiet, since it desires to please God. But *the assembly of the Athenians* is riotous and in no way comparable to *the assembly of God* there. You may say the same of *the assembly of God at Corinth* and *the assembly of the people of the Corinthians*, and of *the assembly of God*, say, at Alexandria and *the assembly of the people of Alexandria*. If the man who hears this has an open mind, and examines the facts with a desire to find out the truth, he will be amazed at the one who both planned and had the power to carry into effect the establishment of *the assemblies of God* in all places, living beside *the assemblies of the people* in each city. And so also, if you compare *the council of the assembly of God* with the council in each city, you may, in the future, find

that some council members of the assemblies [of the Church] are worthy, if there exists a city of God in the universe, to hold public office in it.

(Origen, *Against Celsus* 3.29–30)[46]

Here, and elsewhere, Origen, following Paul, draws the full consequences of the view that Christianity is an assembly of God, parallel to the political assembly of the Greek cities of the ancient world.[47] In Paul's understanding, Christianity is not an apolitical organization but offers a better alternative, although it does certainly not envisage the subversion of the existing political authorities: "Let every person be subject to the governing authorities; for there is no authority except from God, and those authorities that exist have been instituted by God" (Rom. 13:1). Yet Paul's language is deliberately cast in political terminology, thus rendering the "church," "the assembly of God," a para-political institution; the Christian assembly is deliberately styled as an alternative to the normal, political assemblies. This is confirmed by the fact Paul also describes this assembly in terms of an organic body, in the same way as the State was described as a coherent body in Graeco-Roman authors (1 Cor. 12:12–27).[48] Moreover, in line with his depiction of the Christian community as "the assembly of God," Paul speaks of the citizenship of Christians, not of the earthly cities, but a citizenship which is of a heavenly nature. Instead of setting their mind on earthly things, Christians possess a citizenship which is in heaven (Phil. 3:20), and are consequently encouraged to live as free citizens of that heavenly government (Phil. 1:27). Paul's understanding of the Christian assembly and the heavenly citizenship it implies is in fact very similar to the Stoic notion of the cosmic city. This, too, is expressed in political language, and entails the idea that God, the cosmos, and the Stoic sages constitute a cosmic city, which is distinct from a particular political citizenship.[49] It is this notion that Origen seems playfully to allude to when he refers to the existence of a city of God "in the universe." Like the Stoics, Paul and Origen cling to the ideal of dual-citizenship: the exercise of citizenship in heaven, accessible through the assemblies of God on earth, as well as the concomitant submission to the governing authorities that have been instituted by God.

I have one final remark with regard to the way in which early Christians gathered. From a fairly early stage, their place of gathering seems to have been oriented towards the sun. This seems to be implied already in Pliny's description of their habit of meeting "regularly before dawn on a fixed day to chant verses alternately among themselves in honour of Christ as if to a god."[50] The orientation to the light is very understandable, given the repeated association of Christ with the light in the New Testament writings. Especially the identification of Christ with "the true light which enlightens everyone" (John 1:9) may have given rise to this practice.[51]

Christianity's ethical tenor: philosophical ethics and popular myths – interaction with philosophical and religious forces

As we have already seen, in Paul's definition of Christianity as "a logical [i.e., non-ritualistic] way of worshipping God" (Rom. 12:1–2) which involves firm ethical deliberations, Christianity is presented as a fully ethical philosophy and not as a ritualistic religion. This logical worship of God, in which the human mind is renewed, enables man to "discern what is the will of God – what is good and acceptable and perfect."[52] This strong ethical tenor of the Christian religion is in marked contrast with the highly mythologically charged nature of pagan popular cults. As we have seen, Graeco-Roman religion itself "was not equivalent to our notion of 'religion' but contained a strong ritualistic aspect."[53] And, as Peter Brunt has pointed out with regard to the pagan religious cults: "The cults themselves comprised no moral teaching."[54] Christianity thus competed with philosophical ethics on the one hand, and on the other hand religio-mythological cults which were devoid of ethics. This can be illustrated by focusing on an important ethical notion such as philanthropy. According to (Pseudo-)Paul's letter to Titus, who is at that moment on the island of Crete (Titus 1:5), with the birth of Christ mankind was challenged to end the era of human disobedience and to be saved, precisely because God's philanthropy manifested itself:

> We ourselves were once foolish, disobedient, led astray, slaves to various passions and pleasures, passing our days in malice and envy, despicable, hating one another. But when the goodness and philanthropy of God our Saviour appeared, he saved us.
>
> (Titus 3:3–5)

It is no coincidence that Paul writes about the manifestation of God's philanthropy in this letter to Crete, as, according to Diodorus of Sicily, a large number of Greek gods had their origin in Crete and extended their *philanthropy* to the Cretans;[55] from there they set out "to visit many regions of the inhabited world, conferring benefactions upon the races of men."[56] In particular, the Cretan cults and myths included the cult of Zeus. As B. C. Dietrich summarizes:

> Legend placed his birth in a Cretan cave on Mt. Ida or Dicte (Psychro). He also died in Crete, and from Hellenistic times his tomb was shown on the island (Diodorus Siculus 3.61.2), prompting Callimachus's outburst that all Cretans are liars (*Hymn* 1.8).[57]

Callimachus's criticism shows the tension which arose between philosophy and mythology. It seems as though Paul deliberately challenges the view that the gods of the myths were indeed philanthropic, as their behaviour was rather an incitement to foolishness, disobedience, and subjection to passions and pleasures, instead of acting as a role-model for philanthropy. Paul's attitude is typical of the way in which Christians interacted with the religious forces of that time, and we shall explore this issue further in the final section, in which Christ and Heracles are compared. Callimachus's philosophical disapproval of the Cretans' belief in the death of Zeus also became a topic in Christian authors. Christians borrowed arguments from the philosophers to drive a wedge between philosophy and mythological religion. The pagan philosopher Celsus, however, became so angered by these Christian polemics that he complained, as Origen reports, that "we ridicule those who worship Zeus because his tomb is shown in Crete, without knowing how and why the Cretans do this."[58] Celsus's reaction is proof not only that Christians did interact with the pagans, but also that this interaction was a two-way process.

Although Christians would strongly object to the claim of the gods' philanthropy as professed in the myths, they did agree with many of the philosophical schools in their views on the philanthropic nature of God. The Platonists agreed with the Stoics that God is philanthropic and beneficent, and they both disagreed with the Epicureans, according to whom the gods take no heed of this cosmos. The Platonist philosopher Plutarch, for instance, grants that the Stoic philosopher Chrysippus is right to fight "especially against Epicurus and against those who do away with providence," and regards Stoics and Platonists like himself as drawing on the same conception of the gods "in thinking of them as beneficent and philanthropic." Like Chrysippus, Plutarch criticizes Epicurus for believing that the gods are not provident and philanthropic.[59] Plutarch thus clearly sides with the Stoics against the Epicureans, because the former say "that God is preconceived and conceived to be not only immortal and blessed but also philanthropic."[60] When Christianity entered the ancient world with its own propagation of God's philanthropy, the philosophical forces which it met were rather diverse and formed changing allegiances, depending on the topic discussed. Even despite his basic agreement with the Stoics on God's philanthropy, Plutarch complains that the Stoics' views were inconsistent and in certain respects as absurd as those of the Epicureans.[61] Plutarch criticizes Chrysippus, for instance, because the deeds which Chrysippus imputes to God are sometimes harsh, barbarous, and "Galatian," although his epithets for God are always fair and philanthropic.[62] Plutarch is an ardent proponent of the idea of God's philanthropy, and strongly emphasizes that it is God's nature to bestow favour and give assistance, and that it is not his nature to be angry and do harm.[63] This conviction is also found in other philosophers.[64]

Among early Christians, the topic of God's philanthropy was also emphasized in the growing internal polemics against the Gnostics, who denied the beneficent providence and philanthropy of the creator God. In an anti-Marcionite chapter of his Christ the Educator, Clement of Alexandria reminds his readers of

> the supreme proof God has given of his philanthropy, in that he has become man. ... Out of the excess of his philanthropy, he has himself experienced the sufferings which are common to every man by his nature.
> (Clement of Alexandria, Christ the Educator 1.8.62)

In line with Paul's view, God becoming man is seen as the most radical manifestation of his love of man. This radical view on God's philanthropy is not the only difference between Christians and pagan philosophers. Despite the similarities mentioned above, the Graeco-Roman notion of philanthropy retained a very elitist character, which is

14

particularly obvious in two aspects. Philanthropy was thought of as primarily practised by the king (although, admittedly, the king served as an exemplary model), and it was often restricted in its application to the worthy, the good, and the noble, whereas Christianity was concerned with the needy and the poor.[65]

The same radicalism of Christian ethics can be observed in the thorough way the notion of assimilation to God was propagated by Christians. The notion arose in Platonism, where Plato's definition of assimilating to God as "becoming righteous and holy, with wisdom" was, from the first century BCE on, construed as the goal of ethics.[66] This Platonic definition was so powerful that it was appropriated not only by Stoics, but also by Jews and Christians. The latter two, however, considerably widened access to the process of assimilation to God. Whereas many philosophers restricted this access to those involved in the contemplative life, according to Jews such as Philo of Alexandria, and early Christians, one could also pursue assimilation to God in an active life in the world, through virtue.[67]

Both in its extensive reflections on God's philanthropy and in its thorough appropriation of the Platonic doctrine of assimilation to God as the model of righteousness and holiness, Christianity showed itself radically committed to an ethical life. In the brief pagan restoration under emperor Julian (361–3) some decades after Constantine's rule, this was recognized even by the pagan rulership, as Julian's letter to a pagan high-priest in Galatia shows.[68] Contrasting pagan Hellenic religion with that of Judaism and Christianity, Julian emphasizes that "it is disgraceful that, when *no Jew ever has to beg*, and the impious Galilaeans support *not only their own poor but ours as well*, all men see that our people lack aid from us."[69] To change this, Julian argues that Homer's myths contain already clear incitements to philanthropy.

Criticism of pagan sacrifice, idols, and polytheism

Christianity's propagation of an ethical–logical religion accords well with its criticism of ritualistic religion. On the one hand, this concerns its relation to the Jewish temple and its cult. On the other hand, and perhaps even more strongly, this criticism also relates to the sacrifices of the pagan cults, the idols displayed in these cults, and the many gods to which they refer. This is not to say that Christianity's espousal of non-sacrificial and monotheistic religion was without analogy in the Graeco-Roman world. As we know, particular strands of Greek philosophy, such as those of Pythagoras and Empedocles, were known for their criticism of animal sacrifices (Diogenes Laertius, Sextus Empiricus). Moreover, Plato and Platonic philosophers such as Plutarch and notably Porphyry (*On Abstinence from Killing Animals*) held critical views on sacrifices.[70] As regards monotheism, it has now come to be recognized that this was also a strong trend within pagan philosophy, as Athanassiadi and Frede's programmatic collective volume on pagan monotheism (1999) has shown. They argue against the misconception "that in the Graeco-Roman world ... Christianity, in the tradition of Jewish monotheism, succeeded in replacing invariably polytheistic systems of religious belief with a monotheistic creed." Rather, "monotheism was increasingly widespread by the time of late antiquity" and "the success of Christianity in that world [should be attributed] to its advocacy of a way of seeing things, of thinking and acting, which it shared with a growing number of pagans."[71] Christianity was part of a broader movement of growing monotheism, which encompassed the mainstream philosophies.

Yet, within this general monotheism, differing views were present, and especially the relation between monotheism and civic religion was perceived differently in Christianity and in paganism. According to the pagan Roman historian of religion, Varro, religion could be differentiated into three different types: (1) philosophical religion, which is monotheistic and without cult images; (2) mythical religion, which is reprehensible from a philosophical perspective; and (3) civic religion, which does have images and is advocated by the State.[72] This brings to light an important divergence between pagan philosophers and Christians. As Brunt has indicated, according to pagans such as Varro, "'the natural theology' of philosophers, even if it might present a truer conception of the divine than that commonly entertained, was superfluous for the masses. It was therefore to be confined to the schools, not ventilated in the forum."[73] This attitude seems to differ greatly from Christian missionary activities, which did ventilate such views in public. Christians recognized that their monotheism was preceded by Plato, but also pointed out his limitations; they referred to the passage in Plato's *Timaeus* (28c) where Plato considers it possible to discover the one God, the "Maker and Father of this universe," but impossible to instil this monotheistic insight into the masses.[74] Plato's assertion became much debated between philosophers and Christians, as Philo, Josephus, Justin, Celsus, and Origen indicate. Jews and Christians took Plato's statement and turned it against paganism, in favour of the Jewish-Christian "true philosophy" which, they claimed, was embraced by the masses, too. Again, it was Christianity's popularizing radicalism which distinguished it from ancient philosophy.

The same holds true for Christianity's identity as a non-sacrificial religion. Although there were pagan precursors, as has just been indicated, the combination of Jewish and Greek-philosophical anti-sacrificial traditions in Christianity reinforced its criticism to such an unprecedented degree that it is justifiable to label this development a revolution.[75] Already at the beginning of the second century CE, pagans complained that the meat of sacrificed animals was not in demand.[76] Both vis-à-vis Judaism and paganism, Christianity entailed "the end of sacrifice."[77]

The early Christians' disapproval of sacrifice and the polytheistic worship of idols went together with a deep sense of developing a universal religion, which was no longer dependent on the concepts of holy places and religious customs which differed from place to place and were, in this sense, ethnically determined. This is exactly the criticism which ancient philosophers such as Celsus levelled against Christianity. According to Origen's reply, the pagan cults "are localized in a particular place."[78] Celsus's criticism, however, is that Christians pay no heed to such places. According to Celsus, at least the Jews "behave like the rest of mankind, because each nation follows its traditional customs. ... In fact, the practices done by each nation are right when they are done in the way that pleases the [divine] overseers; and it is impious to abandon the customs which have existed in each locality from the beginning."[79] Origen, however, from his universalistic perspective, questions the view that "because of the overseers that have been allotted to the parts of the earth the practice done by each nation is right."[80]

According to Origen, Celsus's view would imply that "piety will not be divine by nature, but a matter of arbitrary arrangement and opinion";[81] in this way, "piety and holiness and righteousness are reckoned to be relative, so that one and the same thing is pious and impious under differing conditions and laws."[82] Quite the contrary view should be taken, Origen asserts:

> it is pious to break customs which have existed in each locality from the beginning and to adopt better and more divine laws given us by Jesus, as the most powerful being, "delivering us from this present evil world" (Gal. 1:4), and from "the rulers of this world who are coming to nought" (1 Cor. 2:6).
> (Origen, *Against Celsus* 5.32)

In this way Origen expresses a universal, non-localized Christian view which we have already identified in Paul's exhortation to logical worship, and in John's plea for worshipping God, not in specific holy places, but in spirit and truth.[83] It is this fundamental criticism of ancestral religious customs which causes problems for Christianity, as it is not confined to the Christian "school," but ventilated in the forum. Unlike Judaism, which was tolerated as long as it did not set "at nought the belief about the gods held by other peoples,"[84] and which was first and foremost an ethnic religion, Christianity spoke out, also outside its meeting places, and offered full membership to everybody, regardless of ethnic background, in "the assembly of God." For this reason, Christianity increasingly differentiated itself from Judaism, all the more when it declined to participate in the Jewish revolts against Rome in 66–70 and 132–5. This abstinence, however, was not appreciated. It was its outspoken public criticism of religious customs that placed Christianity under suspicion. The problem for the Christians was that their attitude brought them close to an atheistic philosophy. Christianity's non-ritual character and Christians' refusal to participate in the rites of pagan religion led pagans to consider the Christian movement as "atheism."[85] Moreover, the Christians' attitude differed notably from that of pagan "atheists,"[86] insofar as the latter at least continued to participate in the cults.[87] Other philosophers, too, such as Cicero and Celsus, though they were critical of the cults to some extent, had no problem with outward conformity. In this respect, the Christian movement differed greatly from the pagan philosophies.

Criticism of Sophistic rhetoric – interaction with the contemporary movement of the Second Sophistic

Christianity not only interacted with the socio-political, philosophical, and religious forces of the time, but was also confronted with the movement known as the Second Sophistic.[88] Its ideas revolved around the basic conviction that truth is secondary to rhetorical presentation, and that speakers should have the ability to improvise, to invent new themes, to impress their audience with their strong bodily presence and, in so doing, to earn praise, honour, and fame. Sophists manifest themselves everywhere. Apart from their declamation and competitions in houses, lecture halls, libraries, council-chambers, and theatres, they, as Ewen Bowie summarizes, "were influential in their cities and even provinces, intervening to check civic disorder or inter-city rivalry ... , or dispatched as envoys to congratulate emperors on their accession or to win or secure privileges for their cities (and often themselves)."[89] The philosopher Plutarch greatly dislikes them. In his view, "public speakers and sophists ... are led on by repute and ambition ... to competition in excess of what is best for them."[90] Plutarch is particularly concerned about the pseudo-learned, sophistic after-dinner disputations, "which have as their goal an ostentatious or stirring rivalry."[91] He fears discussions that deteriorate "into an unpleasant squabble or a contest in sophistry" and into the type of strife going on in the *ekklèsia*, the political assembly.[92] No wonder then that this fashionable movement also exerts its influence within the Christian assembly and here, too, determines the standards for what is considered to be appropriate rhetoric. Such a situation occurs in the Christian assembly of Corinth, and it is in this context that Paul writes to the Corinthians: "Consider your own call, brothers: not many of you were wise by common human standards, not many were powerful, not many were of noble birth" (1 Cor. 1:26). Often these words are taken to point to the low-class background of the first Christians. Yet, the "wise," "powerful" and "those of noble birth" constitute a typical sophistic audience, so that Paul is in fact combating the influence of the Sophistic movement in the Corinthian Christian assembly.[93] His criticism of "the wisdom of the world" and his plea for "the wisdom of God" in this context (1 Cor. 1–4) do not reflect an anti-philosophical attitude. Rather, this differentiation between two types of wisdom is characteristic of the philosophical criticism of the Second Sophistic, and is also found in philosophers such as Dio Chrysostom and Plutarch.[94]

Paul's anti-sophistic strategy was recognized and taken up by Christians such as Clement of Alexandria and Origen. The latter counters Celsus's objection that the Christians "want and are able to convince only the foolish, dishonourable and stupid, and only slaves, women, and little children."[95] This view, Origen suggests, derives from a misunderstanding of Paul:

> It is probably the words written by Paul in the first Epistle to the Corinthians, where he is addressing Greeks who prided themselves on Greek wisdom, which have led some people to imagine that the Gospel does not want wise men. But let the man who imagines this understand that the passage is an attack upon bad men, saying that they are not wise concerning intelligible, invisible, and eternal things, but only interest themselves in things of sense, and that because they put everything into this last category, they become wise men of the world.
>
> (Origen, *Against Celsus* 4.38)[96]

As Henry Chadwick notes, "Celsus shuts his eyes to the fact of a rational Christian theology. There is an emotional heat apparent in his dogged insistence on the anti-cultural nature of Christianity."⁹⁷ Celsus's underestimation of Christianity can also be proven wrong by other pagan reports. In his description of the composition of Christianity in the province of Bithynia-Pontus at the beginning of the second century, Pliny remarks that the Christian movement consists of "a great many individuals of every age *and class* (*omnis ordinis*), both men and women."⁹⁸ The least one can say is, as Origen does, that the higher, intellectual classes are not under-represented in Christianity:

> It was inevitable that in the great number of people overcome by the word [of God], because there are many more vulgar and illiterate people than those who have been trained in rational thinking, the former class should far outnumber the more intelligent. But as Celsus did not want to recognize this fact, he thinks that the philanthropy shown by the word of God, which even extends to every soul from the rising of the sun, is vulgar, and that it is successful only among the uneducated because of its vulgarity and utter illiteracy. Yet not even Celsus asserts that only vulgar people have been converted by the gospel to follow the religion of Jesus; for he admits that among them there are some moderate, reasonable, and intelligent people who readily interpret allegorically. (Origen, Against Celsus 1.27)

Against Celsus's charge that Christianity is anti-cultural, Origen reveals his own intention to let "the assembly of Christians" consist of "the cleverer and sharper minds because they are able to understand the explanation of problems and of the hidden truths set forth in the law, the prophets, and the gospels."⁹⁹ Consequently, he attempts "to convert philosophers to Christianity."¹⁰⁰ This clearly underlines the competitive nature of Christianity, for which there are so many indications.

Christianity's engagement in cosmological and historiographical debates

Cosmology

Although important instances have been given of Christianity engaging in competition with the socio-political, religious, and philosophical forces, this overview is not exhaustive. The field of cosmology, the view on the origins, constitution, and future of the cosmos, also provided a setting for early Christians to explore which ancient philosophical models were most suitable to elucidate their own views. To give an example, Edward Adams has convincingly shown that the author of 2 Peter took fault with a static Platonic cosmology, which encouraged believers to state: "ever since our ancestors died, all things have continued as they were from the beginning of creation" (2 Pet. 3:4). Instead, the author regards a Stoic cosmology, which reckons with the fiery destruction of the cosmic elements (3:11–13), as far more compatible with his Christian world-view.¹⁰¹ This illustrates that from an early stage Christians looked for compatible cosmologies which best fitted their own views. To that end they contrasted existing Graeco-Roman cosmologies. The same issue might underlie a debate within the Pauline school: the cosmology of the author of the Letter to the Ephesians is Stoic in outlook, enabling him to stress the cosmic process; whereas, the cosmology of the author of the Letter to the Colossians is more Platonizing, in accordance with his wish to stress the current coherence and stability of the cosmos, held together in Christ, its body tied with bonds.[102] In a similar way John, in the opening of his gospel, re-narrates the creation account of Genesis 1–2. John – like Philo of Alexandria before him, and early Christian authors such as Clement of Alexandria after him – understands these opening chapters as the account of a double creation: the first being the creation of the invisible paradigm (supported by the Septuagint translation of Genesis 1:2 as "the earth was *invisible and unformed*"), whereas the second is the subsequent creation of the visible universe. This Platonic understanding becomes apparent when he identifies Christ as "the true light" (1:9; cf. Plato, *Phaedo* 109e), which is the source of all visible, physical light. This application by John of the Platonic notion of the true, intelligible light is recognized by Christian authors such as Origen and Augustine.[103]

The Christian debate about the cosmos became very intense in the second century because of the emergence, within Christianity, of a Gnostic dualism which viewed the cosmos as essentially evil and the product of an inferior malevolent or ignorant creator-god. It is this cosmological dualism that dominates the Christian agenda from the mid-second century onwards. The first signs of this debate within the New Testament writings are the assertion in 1 Timothy 4:4 that "everything created by God is good, and nothing is to be rejected, provided it is received with thanksgiving," and the emphatic stress in both 1 Timothy 3:16 and 1 John 4:2 that Jesus Christ has appeared "in the flesh."[104] The challenge which Gnosticism posed to both early Christianity and pagan philosophy was in many senses new. As Jaap Mansfeld has argued, despite some limited Greek antecedents of the Gnostic position, this radical dualism – which holds that the world is not good, because there is an evil creator-god – is unprecedented, and "filled a lacuna in the grid of possible options" in Greek cosmology. According to Mansfeld,

> the original Gnostic dualistic impulse cannot be fully derived from Greek antecedents, although, to a certain extent, it may perhaps be explained as a critical response to Greek ideas. … Enough resemblances of a partial nature, however, can be indicated to make the fact that the Gnostic religion was capable of flourishing in a Graeco-Roman environment somewhat more understandable.[105]

For this reason both (orthodox) Christianity and pagan philosophy were obliged to deal *in extenso* with the emerging Gnostic cosmology.

One of Plotinus's main objections against the Gnostics' radical rejection of the visible cosmos and its complete segregation from the supreme God is his concern that they effectively deny the relation between the supreme God's providence and this world, so that there is no reason to develop an ethics which relates to this world: "this doctrine censures the lord of providence and providence itself still more crudely [than the Epicurean belief that the gods take no thought for this cosmos], and despises all the laws of this world."[106] Plotinus's charge of immorality against the Gnostics is partly correct, as their dualistic doctrine was indeed not only compatible with the extreme of asceticism, at one end of the spectrum, but also with that of antisocial and self-destructive antinomianism, at the other.[107] It is important to note that the church's polemics against Gnosticism were not a matter of the repression of a minority by an institution but, as Plotinus's attack on the Gnostics shows, rather an engagement with a competing position within the process of the formation of a school. Plotinus views Gnosticism as a distorted form of Platonism.[108]

Historiography

Apart from these competing cosmological views, and the debate as to which of them is compatible with Christianity as a whole, I shall briefly mention another important area of competition between Christians and pagans, the field of historiography. Already Jews such as Josephus felt the need to reply to particular pagan claims, made by Apion and others, that Judaism was irrelevant and lacked a distinguished history. In his *Against Apion*, Josephus drew an alternative history, in which the standing of "barbarian" history, and especially the Jewish type, was defended and portrayed as superior to Greek history.[109] Apion's anti-Semitic historiography, however, was by no means the rule among Greeks, as there were also positive Greek views on the figure of Moses.[110] And the Greek philosopher Numenius accorded the Jews, and Moses in particular, pride of place in the quest for ancient wisdom, the retrieval of which was regarded the objective of ancient philosophy; Plato is none other but Moses talking Attic.[111]

It is this kind of historiographical competition which continues to exist between early Christians and pagans. Celsus, for instance, exhibits the same critical view of Judaism and its breakaway-movement Christianity. Although Celsus states that "there is an ancient doctrine which has existed from the beginning, which has always been maintained by the wisest nations and cities and wise men," he deliberately omits the Jews.[112] He does so, Origen replies, by deviating from the position of Numenius and others.[113] In order to counterbalance Celsus's views, Origen gives multiple examples in which "the antiquity of Moses" is clearly contrasted with that of the Greeks.[114] The latter are regarded as being dependent on Moses for several of their views, which they, however, have often misunderstood. In fact, Origen purports, "Moses was more ancient than Homer" and "is proved to have lived long before the Trojan war."[115] Because "Moses and the prophets ... are not only earlier than Plato but also than Homer and the discovery of writing among the Greeks," it is impossible that they – Moses and the prophets – "misunderstood Plato," as Celsus had suggested. "How could they have heard a man who had not yet been born?" Origen counters.[116] This type of historiography is widespread among early Christian authors and is also found in, for instance, Justin, Tatian, and Clement of Alexandria.[117]

Christianity's competitive nature

All the examples given in this paper provide sufficient proof for the highly competitive, enquiring nature of early Christianity. Its language and ideas were fully inscribed in the Greek discourse, even if, through this competition, Christians developed a critical stance against particular Greek views. For this reason I have reservations about the modern term "Christian apologists," which is applied to Christian authors who engaged fully in debate with their contemporaries. As Wolfram Kinzig notes, "The modern collective term appears to go back to F. Morel (*Corpus Apologetarum*, 1615) and P. Maran (1742; cf. *Patrologiae Cursus, series Graeca* 6)."[118] But the term carries the connotation of defensiveness, as if this mode of thinking merely applies an apologetic veneer, like an additional coating, onto an underlying Christian faith.[119] The implied suggestion seems to be that this way of reasoning is only a secondary translation of a religious belief into philosophical categories, often brought together in an eclectic way, as long as these categories suit the Christian belief. The term is then applied first and foremost to those who defended Christianity against contemporary pagan attacks: Quadratus, Aristides, Justin Martyr, Tatian, Melito, Athenagoras, and Theophilus of Antioch, on the Greek side; Minucius Felix and Tertullian, on the Latin side. And, as Kinzig indicates, in a wider sense also to "later writers such as Hermias, the author of the Epistle to Diognetus, Clement of Alexandria, Ps-Justin, Commodianus, Arnobius, Lactantius, and Firmicus Maternus."[120]

To be sure, there are writings which are clearly meant to respond to particular charges and are in that sense defensive. One could refer, for instance, to the chief representatives of the genre "Against the Nations": Tertullian, Minucius Felix, Arnobius, and his pupil Lactantius. The latter's work, entitled *The Divine Institutes*, was completed in the year of the Edict of Milan (CE 313), the end of Constantine's pagan, pre-Christian era.[121] Yet the label, "Christian apologists," suggests that their reasoning was not an authentic expression of an integral Christian world-view, as if it was only applied to render Christianity acceptable to the elite. I agree with Chadwick that apologists such as Justin

> must be asserted to have some measure of genuinely independent status as a thinker. It is a naïve mistake to suppose that because the diffused philosophy of his time was eclectic … , Justin is *merely* reflecting this popular synthesis. … Precisely what one means by the misty term "eclecticism" it is never very easy to say. There is no philosophy that does not draw together elements from diverse sources.[122]

As John Dillon has pointed out, the term eclecticism – defined as "an approach to philosophy which consists in the selection and amalgamation of elements of different systems of thought" – "has been much misused in relation to ancient philosophy, however, little account being taken of the historical perspectives of the individuals concerned."[123] This despite the fact that "all these men considered themselves faithful adherents of one school or another, and as merely utilizing formulations developed in another school for the elucidation of their own positions."[124] Similarly, with regard to Origen, Chadwick reminds us that the "penetration of his thought by Platonism is no merely external veneer of apologetic. Platonic ways of thinking about God and the soul are necessary to him if he is to give an intelligible account of his Christian beliefs."[125]

It would be better then to drop the term "Christian apologists" altogether and to recognize that in the Graeco-Roman period, Christianity profiled itself as a competitor on the religio-philosophical market, confident of being able to show its distinct added value.[126] That the nature of this market was highly competitive may be clear from the descriptions above, but also comes to the fore particularly vividly in the second-century belletrist Lucian's portrayal of the daily competition between philosophers, pseudo-philosophers, Christians, and religious entrepreneurs. Lucian operated in the context of the Second Sophistic, and earned his living as an itinerant lecturer on literary and philosophical themes.[127] In his eighty works, he shows himself to be a lively and important commentator on his cultural and religious environment. He reveals that Christianity was perceived by pagans as a competitor. According to Lucian, for example, Christ himself was a sophist (if a crucified, unsuccessful one) and he mentions that Peregrinus, a philosophical convert to Christianity for some period of his life, is styled by the Christians "the new Socrates."[128] At the same time, Lucian puts this into the general picture of a competition which is ongoing in the public domain. Peregrinus, for instance, converts again to Cynic philosophy, and becomes an adherent of Heracles. His biography shows how pagans could switch their allegiance from Christ to Heracles; both demigods, as we shall see in the last section below, attracted much attention.

Lucian's detailed depictions of relations between religious and philosophical movements make his work an invaluable source for studying the daily life of Christians within antiquity. Lucian also likens Christians to atheists and Epicureans because of their refusal to participate in the cults. In *Alexander the False Prophet*, for instance, he portrays the polemical stance of this charlatan against atheists, regardless of whether they were Christians or Epicurean philosophers:

> When at last many sensible men, recovering, as it were, from profound intoxication, combined against Alexander, especially all the followers of Epicurus ... , he issued a promulgation designed to scare them, saying that Pontus was full of Atheists and Christians who had the hardihood to utter the vilest abuse of him.
>
> (Lucian, *Alexander the False Prophet* 25)

This gives a very vivid picture of how Christians could be conceived of as atheist philosophers. When Alexander established a mystery cult, according to Lucian, "On the first day ... , there was a proclamation, worded as follows: 'If any atheist or Christian or Epicurean has come to spy upon the rites, let him be off'."[129]

Lucian himself is reported to have converted to Epicurean philosophy. This raises interesting points. On the one hand, Lucian is very critical about Christians.[130] On the other hand, he shows no hesitation in linking Christians with Epicureans, to whom he himself belonged, and he indicates that both were equally resented by a religious entrepreneur such as Alexander the False Prophet. Also, even if critical about Christians, he still treats them as counterfeit Cynics.[131] In other words, even in portraying them as pseudo-Cynics, Lucian still depicts them in philosophical terms. Lucian's works, thus, provide a deep insight into the dialectics that operate between competing religio-philosophical groups in antiquity.

In the present introduction to second- and third-century Christian thought, it is important to emphasize that this full and successful engagement of Christianity in the daily competition on the religio-philosophical market, reinforced by the deep impact made by the Christian martyrs, seems to have led to the gradual growth of Christianity, up to an estimated 10 per cent of the population of the Roman Empire around CE 300, at the end of the period before Constantine the Great.[132] Christianity was clearly already on the rise before Constantine. His conversion was probably not so much the cause – as the traditional perspective on Constantine would have it – but rather the result of the growth of Christianity.[133] Such is the view of ancient historians who represent the new perspective on Constantine, such as Tim Barnes, Robin Lane Fox, and the late Keith Hopkins.[134]

This all seems to confirm the validity of the economics-of-religion approach, as undertaken by the sociologist Rodney Stark. His theoretical views are also applicable to antiquity and the rise of Christianity in the first three centuries. Stark defines a religious economy in terms of a "market" (the adherents), "firms" (the organizations which seek to attract adherents), and the "products" of religious culture they offer. The basic principle of his theory is that "competition among religious organizations in any society stimulates effort, thus increasing the overall level of religious commitment and causing the demise of faiths lacking sufficient market appeal."[135]

Before I briefly summarize what we have seen in terms of this economics of religion theory, I wish to point out that the perspective of competition is not just an outsider's view, but that some "insiders," who lived in antiquity, were also aware of the usefulness of such a perspective for understanding what was going on. In the period immediately after Constantine, the pagan philosopher Themistius, political adviser and spokesman of several Christian emperors in the East, argued "that it was appropriate to encourage healthy competition between people of different religious persuasions, to avoid falling into indolence and lethargy,"[136] so that all men should compete in virtue.[137] The importance of the concept of competition in religio-philosophical matters is thus fully justified, both from a modern theoretical outsider's perspective and from a contem-porary insider's perspective.

It does indeed seem to be the case that "competition among religious organizations in any society stimulates effort," and that this applies equally to antiquity. As a result, "the overall level of religious commitment [increased] and caus[ed] the demise of faiths lacking sufficient market appeal." As we have seen, from the outset Christianity became engrained in the networks of antiquity because its social appearance matched the organizational form in which the religio-philosophical market was organized: the form of voluntary organizations, distinguished from the State, and of the philo-sophical schools. The added competitive value of early Christianity on the market was its radical monotheism, its anti-sacrificial nature, its universalism and concomitant criticism of localized religion, and its development of an ethical religion. Whereas ethics was mainly an issue for philosophers, and cults involved no moral teaching, Christianity offered the ancient world a logical, non-ritualistic, ethical religion.[138] This ethical nature of Christianity seems to be linked with its founder and the way he was understood, as I shall argue in the final section. As we shall see, despite heavy philosophical "upgrading," the mythological figure of Heracles remained too ambiguous to prove a successful competitor against Christ.

The competition between Christ and Heracles

Christianity's role as a competitor on the religio-philosophical market of the first three centuries can be nicely illustrated by the rivalry between Christ and Heracles. I shall first briefly narrate the myth of Heracles' life in the version which the second-century-CE author, Pseudo-Apollodorus, gives in his *Library*.[139] Heracles is born as a demigod because Zeus, after deceiving Heracles' human mother by assuming the likeness of her husband, fathers Heracles. The goddess Hera, Zeus's wife, desires the destruction of Zeus's bastard son. She drives Heracles mad so that he kills his children, whom he had by Megara. Heracles condemns himself to exile, and on his request receives from the oracle at Delphi the order "to dwell in Tiryns, serving Eurystheus for twelve years and to perform the ten labours imposed on him, and so, she said, when the tasks were accomplished, he would be immortal."[140] And so Eurystheus sets Heracles impossible tasks, such as bringing the skin of the Nemean lion, an invincible beast, killing the Lernaean hydra, a nine-headed water snake, and carrying out the dung of the cattle of Augeas in a single day. Heracles, however, fulfils them all. His labours bring him over the whole world, and on the Caucasus he frees Prometheus, after shooting the eagle that daily devoured his liver, which was renewed each night. After the successful completion of his labours, Heracles does indeed become immortal when he is accidentally killed by his wife Deianira, who smears his tunic with poison which she believes to be a love-potion, but which corrodes Heracles' skin. Tortured by the poisoned robe, Heracles proceeds to Mount Oeta, constructs a pyre and has it kindled: "While the pyre was burning, it is said that a cloud passed under Heracles and with a peal of thunder wafted him up to heaven. Thereafter he obtained immortality."[141]

During the centuries the Heracles myth was appropriated by Greek and Roman philosophers, who interpreted it in an allegorical, philosophical way. Plato, in the *Euthydemus*, his educational manifesto, already understands Heracles in such a way, and portrays him as the one who defeats each of the heads of the hydra, "that female sophist who was so clever that she sent forth many heads of debate in place of each one that was cut off."[142] This portrayal of Heracles as a philosopher who engages in battle with the sophists also occurs in the Greek orator and popular philosopher, Dio Chrysostom (CE c. 40/50 to after 110), who puts a eulogy to Heracles in the mouth of the fourth-century-BCE Cynic philosopher, Diogenes. The latter is said to remind the visitors to the Isthmian games of the far more impressive moral endeavours of Heracles, the true athlete, who completed his labours in sorry circumstances, unnoticed by the masses.[143] As a true philosopher, Heracles turns against the deception of public opinion by freeing Prometheus from its ruinous effects: "And Prometheus, whom I take to have been a sort of sophist, he [i.e. Heracles] found being destroyed by popular opinion; for his liver swelled and grew whenever he was praised and shrivelled again when he was censured. So he took pity on him."[144] Heracles himself is pictured as very concerned not to appeal to public opinion, but to combat it: "to avoid creating the opinion that he did only impressive and mighty deeds, he went and removed and cleaned away the dung in the Augean stable, that immense accumulation of many years. For he considered that he ought to fight stubbornly and war against opinion as much as against wild beasts and wicked men."[145]

This positive, philosophical image of Heracles is shared by many Cynic and Stoic philosophers. Cynics regard Heracles as "an interpreter of truth and free speech."[146] And Stoics such as Cicero, Seneca, and Epictetus emphasize the deeds which Heracles performed "pro salute gentium," for the salvation and well-being of humankind,[147] and exhort people to follow his example.[148] Unlike Alexander the Great, according to Seneca, Heracles "conquered nothing for himself; he traversed the world, not in coveting, but in deciding what to conquer, a foe of the wicked, a defender of the good, a peacemaker on land and sea."[149] Characteristic of him, in Epictetus's view, is his obeisance to God's will:

> how many acquaintances and friends did he have with him as he went up and down through the whole word? Nay, he had no dearer friend than God. That is why he was believed to be a son of God, and was. It was therefore in obedience to his will that he went about clearing away wickedness and lawlessness.
> (Epictetus, *Discourses* 2.16.44–45)[150]

It is exactly this point, the extreme perseverance in fulfilling God's will and the accomplishment of deeply moral deeds, that provides a point of comparison between Heracles and Christ. According to David Aune, already within the New Testament writings Christian authors show themselves to be aware of this parallel, and the author of the Letter to the Hebrews seems to be drawing on this philosophical interpretation of the Heracles myth when he emphasizes with regard to Christ that, "Although he was a Son [of God], he learned obedience through what he suffered" (Hebrews 5:8). As Aune concludes, "the similarities between Heracles imagery and the Christology of Hebrews ... suggest that many of the important and vital functions attributed to Heracles as a Hellenistic saviour figure were understood by some early Christians as applicable to Jesus to an even greater extent than they were to Heracles."[151]

This competition between Christ and Heracles was also noticed on the pagan side. Celsus, in his writing against the Christians, puts forward the irritated, and somewhat desperate question of why Christians are not satisfied with Heracles. It would have been better, Celsus tells the Christians, "to have addressed your attentions to some other man among those who have died noble deaths and are sufficiently distinguished to have a myth about them like the gods," and then holds up Heracles as an example.[152] Celsus's question as to why Heracles is no successful alternative to Christ can probably best be answered by reference to the ambiguous portrayal of Heracles, despite the philosophers' attempts to interpret his myth in a philosophical manner. It is no surprise when Origen answers Celsus by pointing to negative features in these myths:

> Since he [i.e. Celsus] refers to Heracles, let him show us records of his teaching, and give an explanation of his undignified slavery with Omphale. Let him show whether a man was worthy of divine honour who took the ox of a farmer by force like a thief, and feasted on it, delighting in the curses

which the farmer swore at him while he was eating, so that even to this day
the daemon of Heracles is said to receive the sacrifice with certain curses.

(Origen, *Against Celsus* 7.54)

Not only the Christians, but also the pagan mythographers, the poets and comedians,[153]
and, despite pagan philosophers' idealization of him, they too were aware of the darker
side of Heracles,[154] for instance when he impulsively killed the three sons of Eurystheus
because he himself received a smaller portion at dinner. The troubling ambiguity of
Heracles becomes clear when Athenaeus, having narrated this last incident, remarks:
"Well, then, we have no such temper ourselves, though we are emulators of Heracles
in all things."[155] Sometimes the philosophers make an unconvincing attempt at
defending Heracles' behaviour. Epictetus, for instance, commenting on the trail of
children engendered by Heracles during his travels around the world, says:

He was even in the habit of marrying when he saw fit, and begetting children,
and deserting his children, without either groaning or yearning for them, or as
though leaving them to be orphans. It was because he knew that no human
being is an orphan, but all men have ever and constantly the Father, who
cares for them.

(Epictetus, *Discourses* 3.24.14–16)

It is this ambiguity of Heracles' character to which early Christians call attention in
their competition with the pagans. On the one hand, many Christians, such as Justin
Martyr, Theophilus of Antioch, Clement of Alexandria, and Origen, are not blind to
Heracles' bright side and are willing to acknowledge the similarities between him and
Christ.[156] On the other hand, however, they emphasize his dark side. Some of them,
such as Athenagoras and Tertullian, also referred explicitly to negative pagan views
on Heracles in support of their own criticism.[157] Others compared his positive and
negative features.[158]

It is noteworthy that among these fierce critics of Heracles there are also a number
of pagan intellectuals who converted to Christianity. Justin, for instance, accused
Heracles of merely mimicking the truth.[159] Clement of Alexandria, too, criticizes the
figure of Heracles, points out his unethical behaviour, and concludes, in allusion to
Homer: "It is not, then, without reason that the poets call him a cruel wretch and
a nefarious scoundrel."[160] A similar opponent of Heracles is Arnobius of Sicca, a
teacher of rhetoric who suddenly converted to Christianity at the end of the third
century, and within a few years, wrote his *Against the Heathen* at the request of his
bishop.[161] His pupil Lactantius, too, is very critical of Heracles. Lactantius lost his
position as a teacher of rhetoric in Nicomedia when he converted to Christianity,
and after Diocletian's persecution of the Christians in 303 he composed, among other
writings, the *Divine Institutes* (303–13). This work was framed as a reply to attacks on
Christianity by the Neo-Platonist philosopher Sossianus Hierocles, who was a major
inspiration behind the persecution and the author of an anti-Christian disputation.[162]
The heat of this confrontation is mirrored in Lactantius's attitude towards Heracles in

his *Divine Institutes*, when he makes the following observation: "Heracles is renowned for his virtues; he is seen as a sort of Africanus [the conqueror of Hannibal] among the gods. Yet his rapes and adulteries and other sexual exploits fouled the very earth that his travels are said to have cleansed."[163]

In these passages by pagan converts to Christianity, the fierce competition between Christ and Heracles is evident. The widespread coverage of this topic in early Christian literature is also noteworthy. Gradually Heracles lost ground. As Marcel Simon puts it,

> Here again we hit upon the drama of late paganism. ... The inability of Heracles ... to hold the first rank for any length of time simply reflects the inability of the old religion which – still partly caught in the paralysing trammels of polytheism – cannot reorganise and rejuvenate itself around a central figure. ... After having in some sort opened the way to Christianity by lending it a vocabulary and some concepts to define itself, paganism was reduced to a pale copy of the rival cult.[164]

Or as Karl Galinsky phrases it, Heracles "became paganism's last, desperate choice to head off the appeal of Christianity."[165]

It seems that what was decisive for Heracles' defeat was the fact that his moral image was too ambiguous to allow for an ethics to be based on him. Myths, as Christian authors let their pagan public know, are not simply an innocent pastime for the authors who write about them, but have an impact on society. Tertullian gives an ironic description of the religious flavour of the gladiatorial games in the amphitheatres, where criminals are forced to re-enact the myths and identify with the gods, including Heracles:

> You are, of course, possessed of a more religious spirit in the show of your gladiators, when your gods dance, with equal zest, over the spilling of human blood, (and) over those filthy penalties which are at once their proof and plot for executing your criminals, or else (when) your criminals are punished personating the gods themselves. ... A wretch burnt alive has personated Heracles.
>
> (Tertullian, *To the Heathen* 1.10)

Kathleen Coleman has shown how these "fatal charades" were particularly popular in the first and second centuries CE.[166] Similarly, according to Lactantius, the widespread popularity of the myths of Heracles and others, in the plays in the theatre and in popular songs, is bad for morals:

> How will they curb their sex-drive when they venerate Jupiter, Heracles, Bacchus, Apollo and all those others whose rapes and adulteries against men and women are not just known to scholars but are acted out in theatres and put into songs, so that everybody knows them all the better? How can they

possibly be just people amid all this? Even if they were born good, they would be brought up to injustice, precisely by those gods. To please the god you worship you need what you know makes him happy and joyful. Thus it is that a god shapes the life of his worshippers after the nature of his own spirit; the most devoted worship that exists is imitation.

(Lactantius, *The Divine Institutes* 5.10)

The above case-study on Heracles touches on the general link between the myths and lack of morals. This relation was also suggested by pagan authors. Philostratus, for instance, puts the following words in the mouth of Agathion, the purer lookalike of Heracles: "the wise Greeks were doing an immoral thing when they listened with delight to the criminal deeds of the houses of Pelops and Labdacus; for when myths are not discredited they may be the counsellors of evil deeds."[167] In a similar mode Lucian describes the wish of Menippus to descend into Hades to find out the right way to live, because he is perplexed that the myths of his boyhood appear to be contradicted by the laws which he is expected to uphold as an adult:

While I was a boy, when I read in Homer and Hesiod about wars and quarrels, not only of the demigods but of the gods themselves, and besides about their amours and assaults and abductions … , I thought that all these things were right, and I felt an uncommon impulsion toward them. But when I came of age, I found that the law contradicted the poets and forbade adultery, quarrelling, and theft.

(Lucian, *Menippus* 3)

Or, as Lucian puts it in a different writing: "The general herd, whom philosophers call the laity, trust Homer and Hesiod and the other mythmakers in these matters, and take their poetry for a law unto themselves."[168] It is this rift between the philosophers and the laity which Christians claimed to bridge. They fully engaged with the philosophical and religious forces of their time on the religio-philosophical market of antiquity. The secret of their added competitive value was the unambiguous trustworthiness and moral character of Christ.

Further reading

P. Athanassiadi and M. Frede, *Pagan Monotheism*, Oxford: Clarendon, 1999. (Groundbreaking book on the monotheistic nature of pagan philosophy.)

R. M. Berchman, *Porphyry Against the Christians*, Leiden: Brill, 2005. (Important anti-Christian polemic.)

A. Bowen and P. Garnsey (trans., intro., and notes), *Lactantius: Divine Institutes*, Liverpool: Liverpool University Press, 2003. (Very important text of a pagan teacher of rhetoric who converted to Christianity.)

G. R. Boys-Stones, *Post-Hellenistic Philosophy: A Study of Its Development from the Stoics to Origen*, Oxford: Oxford University Press, 2001. (Shows common discourse between pagan and Christian philosophers.)

H. Chadwick, *Origen: "Contra Celsum," Translated with an Introduction and Notes*, Cambridge: Cambridge University Press, 1953. (One of the most important examples of the controversy between Christianity and pagan philosophy: pagan criticism, followed by Origen's counter-arguments.) *Early Christian*

Thought and the Classical Tradition: Studies in Justin, Clement, and Origen, Oxford: Clarendon, 1966. (Sensitive introduction to three Christian key figures.)

G. Clark, *Christianity and Roman Society*, Cambridge: Cambridge University Press, 2004. (Excellent brief introduction.)

M. Edwards, M. Goodman, S. Price, and C. Rowland (eds), *Apologetics in the Roman Empire: Pagans, Jews, and Christians*, Oxford: Oxford University Press, 1999. (Important collection of papers on apologetics.)

M. M. Mitchell and F. M. Young (assistant editor K. Scott Bowie) (eds), *The Cambridge History of Christianity*, vol. 1: *Origins to Constantine*, Cambridge: Cambridge University Press, 2006. (The authoritative overview of early Christianity.)

A. D. Nock, *Conversion: The Old and the New in Religion from Alexander the Great to Augustine of Hippo*, Oxford: Clarendon, 1933. (Classic book on conversion as a common feature of Christianity and pagan philosophy.)

D. Sedley, "The Ideal of Godlikeness," in G. Fine (ed.), *Plato*, vol. 2: *Ethics, Politics, Religion, and the Soul*, Oxford: Oxford University Press, 1999, pp. 309–28. (Ground-breaking paper on the religious nature of Graeco-Roman ethics.), *Creationism and Its Critics in Antiquity*, Berkeley, CA: University of California Press, 2007. (Shows that the majority of ancient philosophers were creationists.)

R. Stark, *The Rise of Christianity: A Sociologist Reconsiders History*, Princeton, NJ: Princeton University Press, 1996. (Provocative study on the competitive nature of early Christianity.)

G. H. van Kooten, *Paul's Anthropology in Context: The Image of God, Assimilation to God, and Tripartite Man in Ancient Judaism, Ancient Philosophy, and Early Christianity*, Tübingen: Mohr Siebeck, 2008. (Detailed study about the common discourse on man in ancient Judaism, early Christianity and Graeco-Roman philosophy.)

R. L. Wilken, *The Christians as the Romans Saw Them*, New Haven, CT/London: Yale University Press, 1984. (Excellent book on how the Christians were perceived.)

F. Young, L. Ayres, and A. Louth (assistant editor A. Casiday) (eds), *The Cambridge History of Early Christian Literature*, Cambridge: Cambridge University Press, 2004. (The necessary complement to *The Cambridge History of Christianity*.)

Notes

1 I wish to devote this piece to the memory of Michael Frede (ob. 11 August 2007), out of gratitude for his inspirational guidance in the subject matter of this essay. All flawed interpretations remain my responsibility.

2 See, e.g., Josephus, *Jewish Antiquities* 18.37 and *The Life* 67, on the Greek residents of Tiberias.

3 On Justus of Tiberias, see G. H. van Kooten, "The 'True Light which Enlightens Everyone' (*John* 1:9): John, *Genesis*, the Platonic Notion of the 'True, Noetic Light', and the Allegory of the Cave in Plato's *Republic*," in G. H. van Kooten (ed.), *The Creation of Heaven and Earth: Re-interpretations of Genesis 1 in the Context of Judaism, Ancient Philosophy, Christianity, and Modern Physics*, Leiden: Brill, 2005, pp. 149–94 (esp. 170–1, 173–4).

4 T. Schmeller, "Jesus im Umland Galiläas: Zu den markinischen Berichten vom Aufenthalt Jesu in den Gebieten von Tyros, Caesarea Philippi und der Dekapolis," *Biblische Zeitschrift* 38, 1994, pp. 44–66; D. E. Aune, "Jesus and the Romans in Galilee: Jews and Gentiles in the Decapolis," in A. Y. Collins (ed.), *Ancient and Modern Perspectives on the Bible and Culture: Essays in Honor of Hans Dieter Betz*, Atlanta: Scholars, 1998, pp. 230–51; K. R. Iverson, *Gentiles in the Gospel of Mark: "Even the Dogs Under the Table Eat the Children's Crumbs,"* London: T&T Clark, 2007.

5 For a different view, cf. M. A. Chancey, *The Myth of a Gentile Galilee*, Cambridge: Cambridge University Press, 2002; *Greco-Roman Culture and the Galilee of Jesus*, Cambridge: Cambridge University Press, 2005.

6 See E. P. Meijering, *Die Hellenisierung des Christentums im Urteil Adolf von Harnacks*, Verhandelingen der Koninklijke Nederlandse Akademie van Wetenschappen, Afd. Letterkunde, Amsterdam: North-Holland, 1985.

7 K. Hopkins, *A World Full of Gods: Pagans, Jews and Christians in the Roman Empire*, London: Phoenix, 1999, p. 256.

8 For Jews in the Mediterranean Diaspora, see J. M. G. Barclay, *Jews in the Mediterranean Diaspora: From Alexander to Trajan (323 BCE–117 CE)*, Edinburgh: T&T Clark, 1996.

9 On Hellenization and Judaism, see M. Hengel, *Judaism and Hellenism: Studies in their Encounter in Palestine during the Early Hellenistic Period*, London: SCM, 1974; *The "Hellenization" of Judaea in the First Century after Christ*, London: SCM, 1989.

10 On Rome and Jerusalem, see M. Goodman, *Rome and Jerusalem: The Clash of Ancient Civilizations*, London: Penguin, 2007.

11 On the name "Christians," see D. G. Horrell, "The Label Christianos: 1 Peter 4:16 and the Formation of Christian Identity," *Journal of Biblical Literature* 126, 2007, pp. 361–81; J. N. Bremmer, "Appendix 1: Why Did Jesus' Followers Call Themselves 'Christians'?" in *The Rise and Fall of the Afterlife: The 1995 Read – Tuckwell Lectures at the University of Bristol*, London: Routledge, 2002, pp. 103–8.

12 For a translated collection of the pseudepigrapha, see J. H. Charlesworth (ed.), *The Old Testament Pseudepigrapha*, 2 vols, Garden City, NY: Doubleday, 1983–5.

13 G. R. Boys-Stones, *Post-Hellenistic Philosophy: A Study of its Development from the Stoics to Origen*, Oxford: OUP, 2001; M. F. Burnyeat, "Platonism in the Bible: Numenius of Apamea on Exodus and Eternity," in G. H. van Kooten (ed.), *The Revelation of the Name YHWH to Moses: Perspectives from Judaism, the Graeco-Roman World, and Early Christianity*, Leiden: Brill, 2006, pp. 139–68.

14 J. N. Bremmer, "'Religion', 'Ritual' and the Opposition 'Sacred vs. Profane'," in F. Graf (ed.), *Ansichten griechischer Rituale*, Stuttgart/Leipzig: Teubner, 1998, pp. 9–32.

15 Translations from the Bible are normally taken from the New Revised Standard Version, with alterations where necessary, and those from classical authors from the Loeb Classical Library, again with occasional changes.

16 Bremmer, "'Religion', 'Ritual' and the Opposition," p. 10.

17 L. Alexander, "Paul and the Hellenistic Schools: The Evidence of Galen," in T. Engberg-Pedersen (ed.), *Paul in His Hellenistic Context*, Edinburgh: T&T Clark, 1994, pp. 60–83. Cf. A. D. Nock, "Conversion to Philosophy," in *Conversion: The Old and the New in Religion from Alexander the Great to Augustine of Hippo*, London: Oxford University Press, 1933, pp. 164–86.

18 D. Sedley, "Philosophical Allegiance in the Graeco-Roman World," in M. Griffin and J. Barnes (eds), *Philosophia Togata: Essays on Philosophy and Roman Society*, Oxford: Clarendon, 1989, pp. 97–119.

19 Sedley, "Philosophical Allegiance," p. 100.

20 Many relevant texts have been collected in H. Dörrie and M. Baltes, *Der Platonismus in der Antike: Grundlagen, System, Entwicklung*, 5 vols, Stuttgart: Bad-Cannstatt, 1987ff. For Numenius, cf. also Boys-Stones, *Post-Hellenistic Philosophy*.

21 M. Frede, "The Philosopher," in J. Brunschwig, G. E. R. Lloyd (eds), with the collaboration of P. Pellegrin, *Greek Thought: A Guide to Classical Knowledge*, trans. under the direction of C. Porter, Cambridge, MA/London: Belknap, 2000; trans. of *Le Savoir Grec*, 1996, pp. 3–19.

22 R. Majercik, *The Chaldaean Oracles: Text, Translation and Commentary*, Leiden: Brill, 1989.

23 A. Busine, *Paroles d'Apollon: Pratiques et traditions oraculaires dans l'Antiquité tardive (IIe–VIe siècles)*, Leiden: Brill, 2005.

24 Frede, "Philosopher," p. 16.

25 Cf. G. Zuntz, *Griechische philosophische Hymnen*, Tübingen: Mohr Siebeck, 2005.

26 Cf. also Nock, *Conversion*.

27 Philostratus, *Lives of the Sophists* 512–13.

28 On Lucian, see H. Cancik, "Lucian on Conversion: Remarks on Lucian's Dialogue Nigrinos," in Collins, *Ancient and Modern Perspectives*, pp. 26–48; J. Schwartz, "La 'conversion' de Lucien de Samosate," *L'Antiquité Classique* 33, 1964, pp. 384–400.

29 Justin, *Dialogue with Trypho* 2–3.

30 J. S. Kloppenborg and S. G. Wilson (eds), *Voluntary Associations in the Graeco-Roman World*, London: Routledge, 1996; O. M. Van Nijf, *The Civic World of Professional Associations in the Roman East*, Amsterdam: J. C. Gieben, 1997; P. A. Harland, *Associations, Synagogues, and Congregations*, Minneapolis: Fortress, 2003; R. S. Ascough, *Paul's Macedonian Associations*, Tübingen: Mohr Siebeck, 2003.

31 Pliny the Younger, *Letters* 10.96.7.

32 Josephus, *Jewish Antiquities* 19.290.

33 D. E. Smith, *From Symposium to Eucharist*, Minneapolis: Fortress, 2003.

34 Alexander, "Paul and the Hellenistic Schools," p. 82.

35 L. Alexander, "IPSE DIXIT: Citation of Authority in Paul and in the Jewish and Hellenistic Schools," in T. Engberg-Pedersen (ed.), *Paul Beyond the Judaism-Hellenism Divide*, Louisville: Westminster John Knox, 2001, pp. 103–27; cf. S. Mason, "*Philosophiai*: Graeco-Roman, Judean and Christian," in Kloppenborg and Wilson, *Voluntary Associations*, pp. 31–58.

36 On the development of church buildings, see L. M. White, *The Social Origins of Christian Architecture*, 2 vols, Valley Forge, PA: Trinity Press International, 1996–7.

37 Porphyry, *Against the Christians*, frg. 76, = frg. 207 in A. von Harnack, *Porphyrius: Gegen die Christen*, Abhandlungen der preussischen Akademie der Wissenschaften, Philosoph.-hist. Kl. 1, Berlin: Königliche Akademie der Wissenschaften, 1916; trans. R.M. Berchman, *Porphyry Against the Christians*, Leiden: Brill, 2005, pp. 216–17, = Macarius, *Apocriticus seu Monogenès*, book 4, edn Blondel, p. 201.

38 C. Markschies, *Das antike Christentum: Frömmigkeit, Lebensformen, Institutionen*, München: C. H. Beck, 2006, p. 177.

39 P. Lampe, *From Paul to Valentinus: Christians at Rome in the First Two Centuries*, London: Continuum, 2003, pp. 276–9.

40 Tertullian, *Prescription against Heretics* 7.9.

41 Tertullian, *To the Heathen* 1.3–4.

42 Tertullian, *Apology* 38–39.

43 Plotinus, *Ennead* 2.9.6.

44 T. Dorandi, "Organization and Structure of the Philosophical Schools," in K. Algra, J. Barnes, J. Mansfeld, and M. Schofield (eds), *The Cambridge History of Hellenistic Philosophy*, Cambridge: Cambridge University Press, 1999, pp. 55–62.

45 The phrase "assembly of God" only occurs in 2 Esdras 23:1. The phrase "assembly of the Lord" does occur seven times in the LXX, notably in Deuteronomy, but this phrase is not applied in the NT.

46 Origen, *Against Celsus* 3.29–30; trans. H. Chadwick, *Origen Contra Celsum*, Cambridge: Cambridge University Press, 1953, p. 147, with alterations.

47 See further Origen, *Against Celsus* 8.5; 8.74–75.

48 G. Strecker, U. Schnelle, with the cooperation of G. Seelig, *Neuer Wettstein: Texte zum Neuen Testament aus Griechentum und Hellenismus*, vol. 2.1: *Texte zur Briefliteratur und zur Johannesapokalypse*, Berlin: Walter de Gruyter, 1996, pp. 357–66.

49 See M. Schofield, *The Stoic Idea of the City*, Cambridge: Cambridge University Press, 1991; C. J. Rowe and M. Schofield (eds), *The Cambridge History of Greek and Roman Political Thought*, Cambridge: Cambridge University Press, 2000, pp. 556, 606–7, 611, 613, 648–9.

50 Pliny the Younger, *Letters* 10.96.7. M. Wallraff, *Christus verus Sol: Sonnenverehrung und Christentum in der Spätantike*, Münster: Aschendorffsche, 2001.

51 Cf. van Kooten, "'True Light which Enlightens Everyone' (John 1:9)."

52 Cf. G. H. van Kooten, *Paul's Anthropology in Context: The Image of God, Assimilation to God, and Tripartite Man in Ancient Judaism, Ancient Philosophy, and Early Christianity*, Tübingen: Mohr Siebeck, 2008, ch. 7.3 (pp. 388–92).

53 Bremmer, "'Religion', 'Ritual' and the Opposition," p. 10.

54 P. A. Brunt, "Philosophy and Religion in the Late Republic," in Griffin and Barnes, *Philosophia Togata*, pp.178–9.

55 Diodorus of Sicily, *The Library of History* 5.46.3; cf. 5.64.2.

56 Diodorus of Sicily, *The Library of History* 5.77.4. On "philanthropy," in Titus 3:4, see also C. Spicq, "La philanthropie hellénistique, vertu divine et royale (à propos de Tit. III,4)," *Studia Theologica* 12, 1958, pp. 169–91; cf. C. Spicq, *Notes de lexicographie néo-testamentaire*, vol. 2, Fribourg/Göttingen: Éditions Universitaires/Vandenhoeck & Ruprecht, 1978, pp. 922–7; R. Le Déaut, ΦΙΛΑΝΘΡΩΠΙΑ dans la littérature grecque jusqu'au Nouveau Testament (Tite III, 4)," in E. Tisserant (ed.), *Mélanges Eugène Tisserant*, vol. 1, Vatican City: Biblioteca Apostolica Vaticana, 1964, pp. 255–94; A. Pelletier, "Ce n'est pas la sagesse, mais le Dieu sauveur qui aime l'humanité," *Revue Biblique* 87, 1980, pp. 397–403.

57 B. C. Dietrich, "Cretan Cults and Myths," in S. Hornblower and A. Spawforth (eds), *Oxford Classical Dictionary*, 3rd edn, Oxford: Oxford University Press, 1996, p. 408.

58 Origen, *Against Celsus* 3.43. For references to this argument in Christian authors, see Chadwick, *Origen Contra Celsum*, 1953, p. 157, n. 2.

59 Plutarch, *Stoic Self-Contradictions* 1051D–1052B.

60 Plutarch, *On Common Conceptions* 1075E–F.

61 Plutarch, *Stoic Self-Contradictions* 1051D–1052B.

62 Plutarch, *Stoic Self-Contradictions* 1049A–B.

63 Plutarch, *A Pleasant Life Impossible* 1102A.

64 On pagan, Jewish, and Christian philanthropy in antiquity, see further G. H. van Kooten, "Pagan, Jewish, and Christian Philanthropy in Antiquity: A Pseudo-Clementine Keyword in Context," in J. N. Bremmer (ed.), *The Pseudo-Clementines*, Louvain: Peeters 2009, pp. 36–58.

65 See van Kooten, "Pagan, Jewish, and Christian Philanthropy in Antiquity", pp. 37–47.

66 Plato, *Theaetetus* 176b. See D. Sedley, "The Ideal of Godlikeness," in *Ethics, Politics, Religion, and the Soul*, vol. 2 of G. Fine (ed.), *Plato*, Oxford: Oxford University Press, 1999, pp. 309–28; J. Annas, *Platonic Ethics, Old and New*, Cornell Studies in Classical Philology 57, Ithaca, NY: Cornell University Press, 1999, esp. ch. 3 (pp. 52–71); van Kooten, *Paul's Anthropology in Context*, ch. 2 (pp. 92–219).

67 Van Kooten, *Paul's Anthropology in Context*, pp. 128, 154–7, 179, 190–1, 211, 372.

68 On the conflict between paganism and Christianity in the fourth century, see A. Momigliano (ed.), *The Conflict between Paganism and Christianity in the 4th Century*, Oxford: Clarendon, 1963.

69 Julian, *Letters* 22, "To Arsacius, High-Priest of Galatia," 430D; cf. 363A–B; cf. also Juvenal, *Satires* 3.296.

70 G. Clark, *Porphyry: On Abstinence from Killing Animals*, Ithaca, NY: Cornell University Press, 2000.

71 P. Athanassiadi and M. Frede (eds), *Pagan Monotheism in Late Antiquity*, Oxford: Clarendon, 1999, p. 1; see esp. in this volume M. Frede, "Monotheism and Pagan Philosophy in Later Antiquity," pp. 41–67.

72 Y. Lehmann, *Varron: Théologien et philosophe romain*, Brussels: Latomus, 1997; H. Cancik and H. Cancik-Lindemaier, "The Truth of Images: Cicero and Varro on Image Worship," in J. Assman and A. I. Baumgarten (eds), *Representation in Religion*, Leiden: Brill, 2001, pp. 43–61.

73 Brunt, "Philosophy and Religion in the Late Republic," p. 195; see Varro *apud* Augustine, *The City of God* 6.5.

74 Cf. A. D. Nock, "The Exegesis of Timaeus 28C," *Vigiliae Christianae* 16, 1962, pp. 79–86. For Graeco-Roman creationism, see D. Sedley, *Creationism and Its Critics in Antiquity*, Berkeley, CA: University of California Press, 2007.

75 G. G. Stroumsa, *La fin du sacrifice: Les mutations religieuses de l'Antiquité tardive*, Paris: Odile Jacob, 2005; English translation, *The End of Sacrifice: Religious Transformations in Late Antiquity*, trans. S. Emanuel, Chicago: The University of Chicago Press, 2009. For different views on this issue, cf. G. Heyman, *The Power of Sacrifice: Roman and Christian Discourses in Conflict*, Washington, DC: The Catholic University of America Press, 2007; M.-Z. Petropoulou, *Animal Sacrifice in Ancient Greek Religion, Judaism, and Christianity, 100 BC–AD 200*, Oxford: Oxford University Press, 2008.

76 Pliny the Younger, *Letters* 10.96.10. For Pliny's report about the Christians, cf. R. L. Wilken, "Pliny: A Roman Gentleman," in *The Christians as the Romans Saw Them*, New Haven, CT: Yale University Press, 1984, pp. 1–30.

77 Cf. Stroumsa, *La fin du sacrifice*.

78 Origen, *Against Celsus* 3.34.

79 Origen, *Against Celsus* 5.25.

80 Origen, *Against Celsus* 5.32.

81 Origen, *Against Celsus* 5.27.

82 Origen, *Against Celsus* 5.28.

83 For the antithesis between "locative" and "utopian" forms of religion, see J. Z. Smith, *Map is Not Territory: Studies in the History of Religions*, Leiden: Brill, 1978, pp. xi–xv, 67–207; *Drudgery Divine: On the Comparison of Early Christianities and the Religions of Late Antiquity*, Chicago: University of Chicago Press, 1990, pp. 116–43.

84 Josephus, *Jewish Antiquities* 19.290.

85 P. F. Beatrice, "L'accusation d'athéisme contre les chrétiens," in M. Narcy and É. Rebillard (eds), *Hellénisme et christianisme*, Villeneuve d'Ascq: Presses Universitaires du Septentrion, 2004, pp. 133–52; G. Feige, "Der Atheismus-Vorwurf gegen die frühen Christen," in E. Coreth (ed.), *Von Gott reden in säkularer Gesellschaft: Festschrift für Konrad Feiereis*, Leipzig: Benno, 1996, pp. 61–73; D. W. Palmer, "Atheism, Apologetic, and Negative Theology in the Greek Apologists of the Second Century," *Vigiliae Christianae* 37, 1983, pp. 234–59; N. Brox, "Zum Vorwurf des Atheismus gegen die Alte Kirche," *Trierer Theologische Zeitschrift* 75, 1966, pp. 274–82; E. Fascher, "Der Vorwurf der Gottlosigkeit in der Auseinandersetzung bei Juden, Griechen und Christen," in O. Betz, M. Hengel, and P. Schmidt (eds), *Abraham unser Vater: Juden und Christen im Gespräch über die Bibel*, Leiden: E. J. Brill, 1963, pp. 78–105; A. von Harnack, *Der Vorwurf des Atheismus in den drie ersten Jahrhunderten*, Leipzig: J. C. Hinrichs, 1905.

86 A. B. Drachmann, *Atheism in Pagan Antiquity*, London: Gyldendal, 1922; J. N. Bremmer, "Atheism in Antiquity," in M. Martin (ed.), *The Cambridge Companion to Atheism*, Cambridge: Cambridge University Press, 2006, pp. 11–26.

87 Cf. Brunt, "Philosophy and Religion in the Late Republic," p. 191.

88 T. Whitmarsh, *The Second Sophistic*, Oxford: Oxford University Press, 2005; B. E. Borg (ed.), *Paideia: The World of the Second Sophistic*, Berlin: Walter de Gruyter, 2004; G. Anderson, *The Second Sophistic: A Cultural Phenomenon in the Roman Empire*, London: Routledge, 1993; G. W. Bowersock, *Greek Sophists in the Roman Empire*, Oxford: Clarendon, 1969.

89 E. L. Bowie, "Second Sophistic," in Hornblower and A. Spawforth (eds), *Oxford Classical Dictionary*, pp. 1377–8.

90 Plutarch, *Advice about Keeping Well* 131A.

91 Plutarch, *Advice about Keeping Well* 133E.

92 Plutarch, *Table-Talk* 713F.

93 B. W. Winter, *Philo and Paul Among the Sophists: Alexandrian and Corinthian Responses to a Julio-Claudian Movement – Second Edition*, Grand Rapids, MI/Cambridge: Eerdmans/Cambridge University Press, 1997; van Kooten, *Paul's Anthropology in Context*, ch. 4 (pp. 245–68).

94 Van Kooten, *Paul's Anthropology in Context*, ch. 4.5 (pp. 262–7).

95 Origen, *Against Celsus* 3.44.

96 Cf. Origen, *Against Celsus* 3.47, 3.73, 6.12–14, 7.44.

97 H. Chadwick, *Early Christian Thought and the Classical Tradition: Studies in Justin, Clement, and Origen*, Oxford: Clarendon, 1966, p. 24.

98 Pliny the Younger, *Letters* 10.96.9.

99 Origen, *Against Celsus* 3.74.

100 Origen, *Against Celsus* 3.75.

101 E. Adams, *The Stars Will Fall From Heaven: Cosmic Catastrophe in the New Testament and its World*, London: T&T Clark, 2007, ch. 6 (pp. 200–35).

102 G. H. van Kooten, *Cosmic Christology in Paul and the Pauline School: Colossians and Ephesians in the Context of Graeco-Roman Cosmology*, Tübingen: Mohr Siebeck, 2003.

103 Origen, *Against Celsus* 5.10–11; Augustine, *The City of God* 10.1–2. Van Kooten, "'True Light which Enlightens Everyone' (John 1:9)." For other cosmological debates, see, e.g., the second-century Christian authors Hermogenes (K. Greschat, *Apelles und Hermogenes: Zwei theologische Lehrer des zweiten Jahrhunderts*, Leiden: Brill, 2000) and Hippolytus, *Liber adversus Graecos, seu contra Platonem de causa universi*.

104 For the debate in 1 Tim., see B. Dehandschutter, "The History-of-Religions Background of 1 Timothy 4.4: 'Everything that God has Created is Good'," in van Kooten, *Creation of Heaven and Earth*, pp. 211–21.

105 J. Mansfeld, "Bad World and Demiurge: A 'Gnostic' Motif from Parmenides and Empedocles to Lucretius and Philo," in R. van den Broek and M. J. Vermaseren (eds), *Studies in Gnosticism and Hellenistic Religions Presented to G. Quispel on the Occasion of his 65th Birthday*, Études Préliminaires aux Religions Orientales dans l'Empire Romain 91, Leiden: Brill, 1981, pp. 261–314.

106 Plotinus, *Ennead* 2.9.15.

107 On gnostic ethics, see E. M. Yamauchi, *Gnostic Ethics and Mandaean Origins*, Cambridge, MA: Harvard University Press, 1970.

108 Plotinus, *Ennead* 2.9.6. See Boys-Stones, *Post-Hellenistic Philosophy*, ch. 8 (pp. 151–75), on the process of the formation of orthodoxy as a characteristic of school formation.

109 For commentary see J. M. G. Barclay, *Against Apion*, vol. 10, in *Flavius Josephus: Translation and Commentary*, Leiden: Brill, 2007. Cf. also M. Goodman, "Josephus' Treatise against Apion," in M. Edwards, M. Goodman, S. Price, and C. Rowland (eds), *Apologetics in the Roman Empire: Pagans, Jews, and Christians*, Oxford: Oxford University Press, 1999, pp. 45–58.

110 J. G. Gager, *Moses in Greco-Roman Paganism*, Nashville: Abingdon, 1972; G. H. van Kooten, "Moses/ Musaeus/Mochos and his God YHWH, Iao, and Sabaoth, Seen from a Graeco-Roman Perspective," in van Kooten, *Revelation of the Name YHWH to Moses*, pp. 107–38.

111 For Numenius see Burnyeat, "Platonism in the Bible." For Plato and ancient wisdom see Boys-Stones, *Post-Hellenistic Philosophy*, ch. 1 (pp. 3–27, esp. pp. 8–14).

112 Origen, *Against Celsus* 1.14.

113 Origen, *Against Celsus* 1.15.

114 Origen, *Against Celsus* 4.11–12.

115 Origen, *Against Celsus* 4.21; 4.36.

116 Origen, *Against Celsus* 6.7. See further also 4.33; 6.13, 19, 43, 80; 7.28, 30, 59.

117 Cf. A. J. Droge, *Homer or Moses? Early Christian Interpretations of the History of Culture*, Tübingen: Mohr Siebeck, 1989; and Boys-Stones, *Post-Hellenistic Philosophy*, ch. 9 (pp. 176–202).

118 W. Kinzig, "Apologists, Christian," in Hornblower and Spawforth, *Oxford Classical Dictionary*, pp. 128–9.

119 Cf. also A. Klostergaard Petersen, "The Diversity of Apologetics: From Genre to a Mode of Thinking," in J. Ulrich and A.-C. Jacobsen (eds), *Critique and Apologetics*, Frankfurt: Peter Lang, 2009, pp. 15–41.

120 Kinzig, "Apologists, Christian," p. 128.

121 For a treatment of Arnobius's competition with ancient philosophy, see M. B. Simmons, *Arnobius of Sicca: Religious Conflict and Competition in the Age of Diocletian*, Oxford: Clarendon, 1995.

122 Chadwick, *Early Christian Thought and the Classical Tradition*, pp. 21–2.

123 J. Dillon, "Eclecticism," in Hornblower and Spawforth, *Oxford Classical Dictionary*, p. 502; J. Dillon and A. A. Long (eds), *The Question of "Eclecticism": Studies in Later Greek Philosophy*, Berkeley: University of California Press, 1988.

124 Dillon, "Eclecticism," p. 502.

125 Chadwick, *Early Christian Thought and the Classical Tradition*, p. 122.

126 For an excellent overview of "apologetics" in the debate between Jews, Christians, and pagans, see Edwards *et al.*, *Apologetics in the Roman Empire*, and especially contributions by Michael Frede on Origen and Eusebius in the volume.

127 On Lucian, see C. P. Jones, *Culture and Society in Lucian*, Cambridge, MA: Harvard University Press, 1986; G. Anderson, "Lucian: A Sophist's Sophist," *Yale Classical Studies* 27, 1982, pp. 61–92; *Lucian: Theme and Variation in the Second Sophistic*, Leiden: Brill, 1976; B. I. Galerkina, "Les conceptions philosophiques de Lucien," *Vestnik Drevnej Istorii* 98, 1966, pp. 166–72; and Schwartz, "La 'conversion' de Lucien de Samosate."

128 Lucian, *The Passing of Peregrinus* 11–13. On Peregrinus's Christian career, see J. N. Bremmer, "Peregrinus' Christian Career," in A. Hilhorst, É. Puech, and E. Tigchelaar (eds), *Flores Florentino: Dead Sea Scrolls and Other Early Jewish Studies in Honour of Florentino García Martínez*, Leiden: Brill, 2007, pp. 729–47.

129 Lucian, *Alexander the False Prophet* 38. For the way in which Christians are portrayed in Lucian, see H. D. Betz, "Lukian von Samosata und das Christentum," *Novum Testamentum* 3, 1959, pp. 226–37; H. D. Betz, "Lukian von Samosata und das Neue Testament: Religionsgeschichtliche und paränetische Parallelen. Ein Beitrag zum Corpus Hellenisticum Novi Testamenti," in H. D. Betz, *Hellenismus und Urchristentum*, Tübingen: J. C. B. Mohr, 1990, pp. 10–21; L. Varcl, "Lucien et les chrétiens," *Studii Clasice* 3, 1961, pp. 377–83; A. M. Rot'ko, "L'historiographie étrangère sur la critique par Lucien de la religion préchrétienne et du haut christianisme," in *Voprosy istorii drevnego mira i srednikh vekov* 1977, pp. 82–9; M. J. Edwards, "Satire and Verisimilitude: Christianity in Lucian's Peregrinus," *Historia* 38, 1989, pp. 89–98.

The portrayal of philosophers is discussed in A. S. Alexiou, "Philosophers in Lucian," PhD diss., Fordham University, New York, 1990; D. Clay, "Lucian of Samosata: Four Philosophical Lives (Nigrinus, Demonax, Peregrinus, Alexander Pseudomantis)," in W. Haase and H. Temporini (eds),

Aufstieg und Niedergang der römischen Welt 2.36.5, Berlin: Walter de Gruyter, 1992, pp. 3406–50; A. D. Papanikolaou, "Pythagoras nach den Zeugnissen des Lukianos," in G. W. Most, H. Petersmann, and A. M. Ritter (eds), *Philanthropia kai eusebeia: Festschrift für Albrecht Dihle*, Göttingen: Vandenhoeck & Ruprecht, 1993, pp. 341–54; C. P. Jones, "Cynisme et sagesse barbare : le cas de Pérégrinus Proteus," in M.-O. Goulet-Cazé and R. Goulet (eds), *Le cynisme ancien et ses prolongements*, Paris : Presses Universitaires de France, 1993, pp. 305–17.

And for pseudo-philosophers see L. Romeri, "Idiotai et philosophoi à la table de Lucien," *Revue des Études Grecques* 114, 2001, pp. 647–55; W. Fauth, "Pseudophilosophen bei Lukian: Iatromagie und Teratologie in den 'Lügenfreunden'," *Würzburger Jahrbücher für die Altertumswissenschaft* 26, 2002, pp. 113–33.

130 Betz, "Lukian von Samosata und das Christentum," Rot'ko, "L'historiographie étrangère sur la critique par Lucien de la religion préchrétienne et du haut christianisme."

131 Edwards, "Satire and Verisimilitude." On Lucian and the Cynics, see H.-G. Nesselrath, "Lucien et le cynisme," *L'Antiquité Classique* 67, 1998, pp. 121–35; "Kaiserlicher Skeptizismus in platonischem Gewand: Lukians Hermotimos," in Haase and Temporini, *Aufstieg und Niedergang der römischen Welt* 2.36.5, pp. 3451–82.

132 R. Stark, *The Rise of Christianity: A Sociologist Reconsiders History*, Princeton, NJ: Princeton University Press, 1996, p. 7, table 1.1.

133 For a critical review of the traditional view on Constantine, see Bremmer, "Vision of Constantine," in A. Lardinois, M. van der Poel, V. Hunink, A. H. M. Kessels (eds) *Land of Dreams: Greek and Latin Studies in Honour of A. H. M. Kessels*, Leiden: Brill, 2006, pp. 57–79.

134 T. D. Barnes, "Constantine and Christianity: Ancient Evidence and Modern Interpretations," *Zeitschrift für antikes Christentum* 2, 1998, pp. 274–94; R. Lane Fox, *Pagans and Christians*, Harmondsworth: Viking, 1986; K. Hopkins, "Christian Number and Its Implications," *Journal of Early Christian Studies* 6 (1998), pp. 185–226.

135 R. Stark, "Economics of Religion," in R. A. Segal (ed.), *The Blackwell Companion to the Study of Religion*, Oxford: Blackwell, 2006, pp. 47–67; cf. R. Stark and R. Finke, *Acts of Faith: Explaining the Human Side of Religion*, Berkeley: University of California Press, 2000.

136 Themisitus, *Orations* 567b–70c. Cf. S. Mitchell, *A History of the Later Roman Empire*, Blackwell History of the Ancient World, Oxford: Blackwell, 2007, pp. 246–7.

137 Themisitus, *Orations* 6.77a–c.

138 For an interesting discussion of religious rivalries in the early Roman Empire, and for a critical assessment of Rodney Stark's view on the rise of Christianity, see L. E. Vaage, *Religious Rivalries in the Early Roman Empire and the Rise of Christianity*, Waterloo, Canada: Published for the Canadian Corporation for Studies in Religion by Wilfrid Laurier University Press, 2006.

139 Apollodorus, *Library* 2.4.8–2.7.8. For the interpretation of the Heracles myth through the centuries, see G. K. Galinsky, *The Herakles Theme*, Oxford: Blackwell, 1972.

140 Apollodorus, *Library* 2.4.12.

141 Apollodorus, *Library* 2.7.7.

142 Plato, *Euthydemus* 297c. For Plato's *Euthydemus*, see D. Hitchcock, "The Origin of Professional Eristic," in T. M. Robinson and L. Brisson (eds), *Plato: Euthydemus, Lysis, Charmides: Proceedings of the V Symposium Platonicum*, Sankt Augustin, Germany: Academia Verlag, 2000, pp. 59–67.

143 Dio Chrysostom, *Orations* 8.27–28, 30.

144 Dio Chrysostom, *Orations* 8.32.

145 Dio Chrysostom, *Orations* 8.35. Cf. *Orations* 47.4; 4.28–32.

146 Lucian, *Philosophies for Sale* 8.

147 Cicero, *On Moral Ends* 2.118–19.

148 Cicero, *On Offices* 3.25.

149 Seneca, *On Benefits* 1.13.1–3.

150 Cf. Epictetus, *Discourses* 1.6.30–36; 3.26.31.

151 D. E. Aune, "Heracles and Christ: Heracles Imagery in the Christology of Early Christianity," in D. L. Balch, E. Ferguson, and W. A. Meeks (eds), *Greeks, Romans and Christians*, Minneapolis: Fortress, 1990, pp. 3–19 at p. 19.

152 Origen, *Against Celsus* 7.53.

153 See, e.g., the references to them in Dio Chrysostom, *Orations* 32.94–95; 66.23.

154 See, e.g., Dio Chrysostom, *Orations* 15.5, 64.19, 60.1–8; Cicero, *The Nature of the Gods* 3.39, 41–2; Seneca, *The Madness of Hercules* 918–19, 955–75, 1315–16; Plutarch, *On the E at Delphi* 387D, *On the Obsolescence of Oracles* 413A, *On the Delays of Divine Vengeance* 557C, 560D; Athenaeus, *The Sophists at Dinner* 9.411a–10.412b, 13.556f.

155 Athenaeus, *The Sophists at Dinner* 4.157f–158a.

156 Justin, *Second Apology* 11; Theophilus of Antioch, *To Autolycus* 1.13; Clement of Alexandria, *Miscellanies* 5.14.103; Origen, *Against Celsus* 3.66; Pseudo-Clement, *Homilies* 6.16.1–2; Arnobius, *Against the Heathens* 1.38, 1.41, 2.74. Cf. also C. H. Talbert, "The Concept of Immortals in Mediterranean Antiquity," *Journal of Biblical Literature* 94, 1975, pp. 419–36.

157 Athenagoras, *Plea on Behalf of Christians* 29.1; Tertullian, *Apology* 14 and *To the Heathen* 1.10; Pseudo-Clement, *Recognitions* 10.24.2.

158 For a comparison of Heracles' negative and positive character traits, see Pseudo-Justin, *Oration to the Greeks* 3; Origen, *Against Celsus* 3.42.

159 Justin, *Dialogue with Trypho* 69; *Apology* 54.

160 Clement of Alexandria, *Exhortation to the Greeks* 2.33.4, with allusion to Homer, *Odyssey* 21.28ff.; cf. 7.76.5, with reference to Euripides.

161 See Arnobius, *Against the Heathen* 4.25, 4.26, 4.35.

162 Cf. Eusebius's treatise *Against Hierocles*. For Eusebius's anti-pagan polemics, see A. Kofsky, *Eusebius of Caesarea Against Paganism*, Leiden: Brill, 2000. For the rivalry between Neoplatonism and Christianity, see N. Siniossoglou, *Plato and Theodoret: The Christian Appropriation of Platonic Philosophy and the Hellenic Intellectual Resistance*, Cambridge: Cambridge University Press, 2008.

163 Lactantius, *The Divine Institutes* 1.9; trans. A. Bowen and P. Garnsey, *Lactantius: Divine Institutes – Translated with an Introduction and Notes*, Liverpool: Liverpool University Press, 2003.

164 M. Simon, "Early Christianity and Pagan Thought: Confluences and Conflicts," *Religious Studies* 9, 1973, pp. 385–99 at p. 398. Cf. M. Simon, *Hercule et le christianisme*, Paris: Belles Lettres, 1955.

165 Galinsky, *Herakles Theme*, p. 106.

166 K. M. Coleman, "Fatal Charades: Roman Executions Staged as Mythological Enactments," *Journal of Roman Studies* 80, 1990, pp. 44–73.

167 Philostratus, *Lives of the Sophists* 554.

168 Lucian, *Funerals* 2; cf. Lucian, *Sacrifices* 5.

2

EARLY CHRISTIANITY AND PHILOSOPHY

Mark J. Edwards

For a century and a half at least, it has generally been assumed, by its defenders and by its detractors alike, that ecclesiastical thought in the age that separates Paul from Constantine was not a mere blossoming of the primitive gospel but a kind of oleaster, the result of a studious grafting of mundane philosophies on to the biblical stem. There are those who maintain that it had to be so, that God could not have spoken to every people through the words of Christ had he not prepared them already by communicating truth to them in their own idiom; others protest that Paul denounces the wisdom of this work, that Christ was avowedly the bearer of a new commandment, that his advent was anticipated only in the preaching of the Hebrew prophets, and even they were misunderstood by those who had only nature's ears to hear them. On either view, philosophy is an importation into Christian teaching, and, because it is widely held that the philosopher in the Roman world was not a man who thought for himself but the mouthpiece of a dead master, it has been natural to assume that the Christian too would not devise his own philosophy, but would attach himself to the creed already promulgated by an established school. Thus an author will be classified as a Platonist or a Stoic if he airs a doctrine that reminds the modern critic of those sects, and all the more so if his own citations lead us to his source. The author adduced most frequently, and with the least reproach, in Christian texts is Plato; Platonism, therefore, is supposed to have been the dominant philosophy of the church fathers, and the reason for this is commonly said to be not so much that they chose to make it so as that its influence in the world from which they received their education was irresistible. The adoption of philosophy, then, is presented at best as a wise passivity to circumstance, which cajoled the intelligence and dispelled the enmity of pagans, while enabling the Christian neophyte to eke out the teachings of the infant church with answers to questions that the apostles and Jesus never thought to ask.

Yet if accommodation had been the aim of the first apologists, they ought to have done anything sooner than take up philosophy. The philosopher was one who abstained from sacrifice, who baited the pride of tyrants, who denied himself the ties of matrimony and procreation, and who taught the young to disobey their parents (Plato, *Meno* 91c–92c). In return the world mocked his isolation, his moroseness, his ostentatious ineptitude in worldly matters: even if he were not cruising the air in a basket or hurling himself into a volcano, we have it on Plato's authority that a philosopher is a hermit abroad, who knows the heavens better than his own street.[1] The philosopher, then as now, was a marginal figure, and for this reason alone, we could never speak of Platonism, or any of its rivals, as a dominant philosophy, as we might speak of the dominance of Islam or Marxism in a modern culture. Christian apologetic, which is polemical or hortatory more often than it is defensive, was designed not so much to illustrate the conformity of the church to the world as to justify its defiance; the virtue of the philosophers, in Christian eyes, was that at their best they had set an example of overt defiance which was tolerated not so much despite, but because of, its intractability. The nonconformity of the philosopher, like that of the Jew, was acceptable to the government because it was not a solvent to the conformity of others; if Christianity too could take its place among the philosophies (as Judaism had already done), it would be possible for the believer to proclaim his faith without dilution and without dying for it. To accredit this claim, the Christian had not only to don a cloak and differ conspicuously from the ambient population; he had also to show that his creed possessed its own axioms, which differed from those of any other school, and that these axioms, together with a cogent system of glosses and deductions, had passed down from one generation of authorized teachers to another. The same principle which led pagans of this epoch to set up half-fictitious dynasties for the transmission of ideas led Jews to manufacture equally fictitious chains of rabbinic tradition and churchmen to construct invidious pedigrees for heretics; but it made it equally necessary for churchmen to advertise their own genealogies, to be able to say "I had it from a presbyter, who had it from an apostle, who was with Christ." Against the cults of the ancient world, but in common with the philosophical schools, both Jew and Christian held religious tenets that determined all belief and conduct, proving themselves philosophers by the singleness of aim in life and fortitude in death; but Christians also urged, in contrast to both, that their immutable doctrines were founded upon the teachings of a single man, who was literally infallible because he was identical with the word of God himself, and that this word in turn was identical with the written text or group of texts that the church had adopted as its norm of faith.

In the following discussion, we must remember that this subordination of every human word to the word of God was a notorious trait of Christian thought, and one that pagan philosophers adduced as a proof that Christians were not of their fraternity. We must remember again that the purpose of representing Christianity as a philosophy was partly to justify martyrdom and partly to forestall it, so that pagan controversialists seemed all the more culpable in Christian eyes when instead of applauding the martyrs they colluded with their murderers and supinely conformed to religious practices which they openly derided in books and lectures. Finally we must remember that, both in commending the philosophers and in denouncing them, a Christian was apt to assume that every sect was answerable only to its founder, and hence to ascribe a changeless uniformity to its teachings. The failure of the apologists to notice the philosophers of their own time is partly a symptom of that antiquarianism which is characteristic of all Greek writing of the Roman era; at the same time, it indicates that the marriage of the gospel to philosophy was palatable only when the pagan school had come to be perceived as a kind of church.

The majority of those who knew what an ancient philosopher said will not have read him, in the Roman world or in ours. The aims of the present study require us to ascertain not what any distinguished thinker of antiquity may have said, but what his name represented to cultivated minds in (what we now call) the second century. Such knowledge will have been derived in the first place from compendia – like those ascribed to Aetius, Galen, and Plutarch – which proceeded topic by topic, briefly adumbrating the doctrines of the principal schools in series under each head, or from a biographical digest such as the *Lives of the Philosophers* by Diogenes Laertius, in which lesser names are appended in temporal sequence to that of the real or putative founder of the school, and the account of the latter includes a systematic inventory of his leading doctrines. As in our time, such manuals governed the common understanding of a thinker even in readers who had made their own perusal of his writings. It has been maintained that the frequency with which the same quotations recur in Christian authors betokens the use of a different resource, a florilegium of pagan testimonies to the gospel.[2] No such collection is known, however, and a survey of modern books on ancient philosophy will show that an informal florilegium tends to evolve within the scholarly tradition, merely because the repeated canvassing of the same difficulties sends one commentator after another to the same small quorum of texts. In addition to the handbook and the conjectural florilegium, we may be sure of another influence which would modify even an independent reading of the authorities – the consensus of a dead philosopher's latter-day interpreters, which we know only from desultory citations, though in the intellectual atmosphere of those times it was the oxygen of all study and debate.

Platonism

The majority of Plato's works are too playful or gladiatorial in form, too abrupt or tentative in their results, to be kneaded without duress into a coherent system. Nevertheless, the conventions of doxography, or history of opinions, in antiquity, demanded that every philosopher should build with purpose upon a few fixed principles, and, since the *Timaeus* was much the most celebrated of his dialogues, his system was conceived as a cosmology whose principles were God, the ideas, and matter. The term "God" denotes the Demiurge, or father and maker of all, whose superabounding goodness prompted him to frame the earth and the spheres that circle it in imperishable harmony, to entrust the orchestration of these motions to a benevolent soul, and to delegate the creation of sentient beings to lesser deities. The ideas, which in the *Timaeus* are said to constitute the paradigm of which the material world is an image, appear in other dialogues as the immutable and universal archetypes of virtues, qualities, natural kinds, and mathematical properties, which transcend the flux and change of the sensible world but are predicated of objects in this world which participate in them; it is the presence of these archetypes, when correctly apprehended, that imparts validity to our judgments of rectitude, beauty, equality, and the like. "Matter" is not a term employed by Plato, but was used after Aristotle to denote the space or receptacle whose disorderly motions the demiurge subjects to form, but with incomplete success, so that the universe which this substrate upholds is not only distinct from the paradigm but prone to ills, vicissitudes, and frailties that are unknown in the higher realm.

Christian authors espoused the most literal reading of the *Timaeus*, according to which the paradigm is eternal, whereas the sensible world has an origin in time. This tenet they could cite in corroboration of the opening chapter of Genesis, where God is said to create the heaven and earth a mere five days before the creation of the first man, and thus deflect the ridicule of those philosophers who maintained that the world was eternal, or that world follows world in perpetual succession. On the other hand, the similarity enabled them to subordinate Plato to Moses, as it could not be denied that the Hebrew philosopher antedated the Greek by a thousand years. As to the ideas, no Christian could endorse the view (which the dialogue seemed to inculcate when literally construed) that these inhabited a plane independent of, and indeed superior to, that which the demiurge occupied; if these archetypes could be said to exist eternally, it could only have been as prescient thoughts in the mind of a God who knew what he intended to create. The postulation of matter as the raw stuff of creation seemed warranted by the statement in Genesis 1:2 that the earth remained "without form and void" until the spirit moved upon its waters. No Christian, on the other hand, could allow that this primordial turbulence was uncreated, or that the evils of the world proceeded from its invincible enmity to the will of the Creator.

Both in what they affirmed and in what they denied, the Christian readers of the *Timaeus* were anticipated, and in some respects guided, by the Jewish apologist and exegete Philo of Alexandria. While he is often ranked with the middle Platonists – a purely taxonomic label embracing all writers between 350 BCE and CE 250 who read Plato's works with sympathy and attention – his Platonism is circumscribed by his loyalty to the Torah as the infallible and sufficient word of God.[3] It is God's injunction "let there be light" at Genesis 1:3, together with variants and glosses on this verse in the later Israelite tradition, that accounts for his use of Logos as an appellative for the intermediate deity, or divine power, through which God creates the world without any sacrifice of his own transcendence or simplicity. But, whereas in the Mosaic text and its echo at John 1:1 this term denotes the creative act of speech, Philo takes it also to signify "reason" (as it often does in Greek), so that his Logos is at once the dynamic and almost personal author of a temporal creation and an eternal archetype in the mind of God. In short, this Logos is at once the paradigm of Plato and his Demiurge; whether Philo held that he makes use of a material substrate in this latter capacity seems not to have been securely ascertained. The belief in Jewish circles that the cosmos was formed from "things that are not" is attested in 2 Maccabees 7:28 and endorsed in Hebrews 11:2; Christians, to whom both texts were authoritative, had still to decide whether "out of nothing" meant from an absolute void, from the indeterminate possibilities which lay before the creator at the outset, or from an inchoate materiality which God himself produced as the foundation of all that he purposed to bring into being.

Coincidences between Christian and Philonic exegesis are common enough to suggest that his work was widely known in the church at first or at second hand, though Clement of Alexandria is unusual in citing him by name. To Clement he is not a Christian but a Pythagorean, that is a member of the sect which professed to cherish and interpret the cryptic teachings of Pythagoras of Samos. Born perhaps a century before Plato, Pythagoras is supposed to have discovered the mathematical proportions which defined both the notes of the octave and the intervals between the orbits of the celestial spheres. He was thought to have anticipated one of the most arcane of Plato's doctrines by making the monad and the dyad (reified forms of the numbers 1 and 2) the progenitors of all things, both in the intellectual and in the sensible cosmos. The Pythagorean tradition surpasses Plato in its ascription of mystical properties to numbers and in its testimonies to the inscrutability of the first principle, which it characterizes only by the negation of every predicate, including the most dignified of those that we apply to objects in the present world. The practical counsels handed down in the name of Pythagoras, outwardly trifling or superstitious, were understood in the Roman age as esoteric precepts for the discipline of the soul. Philo could pass for a Pythagorean because he celebrated the properties of the number seven, held that God could be spoken of only in privative terms, and urged that the ordinances of the Mosaic law were designed to be applied literally to the flesh and symbolically to the outward man.

Roman Pythagoreanism and Roman Platonism coalesce in modern scholarship; what early Christians knew of either we can hardly say.[4] We do not know if they were conscious of the tendency, represented in the *Handbook* of Alcinous, to treat the ideas as thoughts in the mind of God. We do not know when they first learned of a shift from the naïve interpretation of the *Timaeus* to a more artificial reading, first attested by the grammarian Calvenus Taurus, who argues that the sensible world, like the paradigm, is eternal, and that the former is generated in the sense that it depends upon the latter for its existence, not in the sense of having an origin in time. The one middle Platonist cited in Christian texts of the first three centuries, Numenius of Apamea, could also be called a late Pythagorean. As a Platonist he conflated the *Timaeus* with the *Republic*, in which the highest principle is the Good – that is, the unsurpassed measure of value and the terminus of all rational endeavour. Numenius arrives at a theory of two gods, the first corresponding to the Good, the second to the Demiurge, while the paradigm takes shape in the second through its contemplation of the first.[5] Some early Christian writers found the relation between these two gods analogical to that between the Father and the Son. But the parallel is not exact, and the most anomalous teaching of Numenius – that this world results from the schism which the second god incurred when a lapse of concentration embroiled it in matter – could not have been entertained by any Christian whom we should now think orthodox.

Philosophies of the Roman world[6]

Aristotle's lectures to his students were assembled as a corpus by Andronicus of Rhodes, about thirty years before the start of the Christian era. Two centuries were to elapse before detailed commentaries on these esoteric works were undertaken by Alexander of Aphrodisias, and in the meantime they are not so widely cited as the "exoteric" treatises which Aristotle himself prepared for general circulation. In the latter, the existence of a benevolent creator was deduced from the pulchritude and harmony of the visible cosmos, and a fifth element, or quintessence, was added to earth, air, fire, and water, though authorities are divided as to whether this was conceived as the stuff of God, the soul, or the circumambient ether. It is in his esoteric disputations that Aristotle asserts, against his erstwhile tutor Plato, that the world has no beginning in time, that essences and ideas do not exist except insofar as they are instantiated in matter, that God is the final cause or end of all but not the efficient cause of anything, and that the soul (or at least the irrational soul in contrast to the intellect) is as mortal as the body that it informs. It did not occur to Christians in the age before Constantine that this last tenet could be turned into a proof of the resurrection, or that a man who gives the name God to the highest principle might be a more durable ally than one who set the Good above the Demiurge; it is possible, indeed, that it was only from Platonic controversialists that most Christians learned anything of Aristotle's defection from his master.[7] Some profess an acquaintance with his logic, though most often to deride and misrepresent it. Clement of Alexandria owes to Aristotle the title, but not the tenor, of his *Exhortation to the Greeks* (*Protrepticus*), or summons to conversion, while Alexander of Aphrodisias may have furnished a model for commentary to those who required any other model than Philo.[8] For the most part, it cannot be said that Christian knowledge of Aristotle's teachings was profound.

Whereas Aristotle taught that the soul cannot flourish without some measure of good repute and material comfort, Plato equated happiness with the uncompounded pleasure of contemplation. The most rigorous of all sects in their moral teaching were the Stoics, whose three authorities – the caustic Zeno, the pious Cleanthes, and the subtle Chrysippus – wrote successively in the fourth century BCE. They urged that the end of human life is to live with the frugality and integrity that nature prescribes; the good they located not so much in the achievement of this end as in the virtuous pursuit of it, and the unbending zeal which many of the followers displayed in the teeth of mockery and oppression could not fail to impress the first Christians. On the other hand, their doctrine that all existence is corporeal, which entailed the identification of God himself with a tenuous fire that pervades the universe, could not be endorsed by anyone who wished to uphold the liberty and omnipotence of God. The Stoic god does not create, but comes into being as the logos or informing principle of each new world, surviving only until that world is swallowed up in its appointed *ekpyrosis* or combustion to be succeeded by another in which the same cycle of events will be reproduced to the last particular. Still more repugnant to Christian faith was the cold theology of Epicurus, a contemporary of the earliest Stoics, who taught that the world and its gods arise from the chance collision and confluence of atoms. The end of life, according to this philosopher, is simply to be free from pain; the gods are the lofty exemplars of this imperturbability, and for that reason exercise no providential government below. The Stoics rejoined that a natural affinity between the human intellect and the divine guarantees that the world is ordered for our sake and that the future can be revealed by divination. It followed that what is ordained cannot be evaded, a corollary that to other schools (though not to the Stoics themselves) appeared to rob humanity of that moral freedom which permits the allocation of praise and blame.

The odium which the world had hitherto reserved for the Epicureans fell upon the Christians who proclaimed that the gods of myth and the civic cults were helpless idols. They were also assimilated to the Cynics, who on the plea that whatever is merely customary is unnatural, made a duty of denouncing common goals and flouting public norms of conduct. The likeness was not even superficial for the Cynics lived under no law, impugned their founder Diogenes as freely as they upbraided one another, and preached autonomy rather than the service of any superhuman power as the goal of life. It was alleged that certain Christians had imposed on the mob by a showy imitation of Cynic fortitude; intellectual churchmen were more likely to seek their allies among the skeptics who, while entertaining no creed of their own, set out to explode whatever was taught in other schools as more than a probable approximation to truth. Christians could deploy the skeptic's arsenal against the shams of magic and astrology; at the same time, they could urge, against the skeptic and the dogmatist alike, that the authority of the Bible is established by the uniqueness of its own claim to authority, now that reason itself has demonstrated the vanity of the philosopher's promise to build on reason alone.

First steps[9]

It is hard to say when Christian thought began to sport the colors of philosophy. The first chapter of John's Gospel represents Christ as the embodiment of the Word, or creative utterance, that was "with God in the beginning"; the epistle ascribed to Barnabas gives a figurative turn to the superannuated rites and ordinances of the Mosaic covenant, sometimes applying them to the inner man, sometimes construing them as mystical adumbrations of the gospel. The first apologist, Aristides of Athens, apes the doxographers by dividing peoples rather than men according to their first principles; rather than canvass the fashionable question, whether philosophy was invented by the Greeks or by the barbarians, he asks which race has held the worthiest notions of the divine and awards the palm to those who are not Chaldaeans, Greeks or Egyptians, neither polytheists nor Jews. The *First Apology* of Justin Martyr, who wore his philosopher's cloak with ostentation until his death in CE 165, informs the Greeks that the best of their philosophers merely eavesdropped on the truth that had been vouchsafed to the barbarians. In his *Dialogue with Trypho* he relates that, having spurned three other teachers as soon as he met them, he became an ardent Platonist, until he was robbed of his faith in the capacities of the soul by an encounter with an old man. The latter waylaid him with arguments derived from Aristotle, but his medicine for perplexity was submission to the words of a single book, to which the classics of the pagan world were children both in age and in profundity.[10]

Justin has been credited with the view that what Israel received through oral prophecy was imparted by inspiration to a handful of philosophers; what he says, however, is only that the philosophers excelled in logos, not that they were acquainted with that Logos whom Justin celebrates as the architect of the heavens, the author and subject of all true Scriptures, and in latter days the embodied Son of God. Independent knowledge of him was granted to the Sibyl and Hystaspes,[11] but the philosophers trained their wits on a revelation gleaned by stealth from the Greek translation of the Torah.[12] Platonists partook of this Logos fully enough to recognize him in Hermes, the ambassador of Zeus,[13] and Plato himself had even framed the soul in the image of the cross in his *Timaeus*;[14] the Stoic belief that the Logos is born and extinguished with the universe is a specimen of the errors that result from a false presumption of affinity between the soul and God. Popular lampoons on the founders of all schools are revived in a coarse *Oration to the Greeks* by Justin's pupil Tatian, whose image of the Logos leaping forth from the Father after a stage of latency is too violent for the Platonists, too fissiparous for the Stoics. For Christian apologists of the second century, reason and speech are two successive determinations of the Logos, and not merely contiguous senses of the same term as in Philo. Theophilus, Bishop of Antioch, writing about 170, borrows Stoic terms to discriminate the *logos endiathetos*, or immanent word, from the *logos prophorikos*, or word enunciated; Stoics, however, used these terms to contrast articulate thought with the din of brutes, not to delineate two stages in human utterance.[15] Theophilus may also be the first to say expressly that the world was made from nothing, taking matter to be the void and formless earth of Genesis 1:2 and hence the first product of God's will.[16]

Disenchantment

Secular philosophies are epitomized in the manner of the handbooks, but with sustained and polemical rancor, by Hippolytus, a disaffected prelate of the Roman church at the end of the second century. Conscious no doubt, that *hairesis*, or "choice," was the technical term for a philosophical sect, he undertakes to prove, in his *Refutation of all Heresies*, that every "choice" which deviates from the teaching of the church is underwritten by some stealthy appropriation of pagan thought. The libel is eclectic if not erudite: Pythagoras inspired the numerology of the gnosticizing heretic Valentinus;[17] his disciple Empedocles bequeathed to Marcion a false dichotomy between the just creator and the benevolent redeemer, while an older sage,[18] Heraclitus, was the true father of that protean speculation which the first heretic, Simon Magus, published as his own discovery, in the hope of being taken for a God.[19] Basilides, a pioneer of apophatic or negative theology, is said to have found his "non-existent deity" in Aristotle, whose *Categories* are paraphrased with the shrewd burlesque that characterizes adversarial writings by the Platonists of this era.[20] Much of this is fallacious and defamatory, but not all, for we possess two Gnostic tractates of the third century, the *Allogenes* and the *Zostrianus*, in which motifs from Plato were handled deftly enough to vex his pagan followers into composing long replies.[21]

Equally contumelious, though far more energetic in style, is a Latin contemporary of Hippolytus, Tertullian of Carthage, who, in his philippic against the use of philosophy by heretics, produced the famous epigram, "What is Athens to Jerusalem, the academy to the church?"[22] Nevertheless, Tertullian is perhaps the earliest Christian to have mastered not only the tenets but the controversial arts of the pagan schools. Knowing that he cannot produce a decisive text from the Scriptures to support his view that the soul is a kind of body, he threatens his adversaries with paradox. Why should we deny corporeality to a being simply because it lacks the traits of other bodies?[23] How can the soul be innocent of corporeal affections when the body itself would not feel these affections but for the presence of a soul?[24] Can it be said to inhabit any place after death,[25] can it even be said to quit its carnal tenement,[26] unless is possesses some shape and dimension? No Christian hitherto had fenced so nimbly with the weapons of the Stoa, and yet Tertullian is no Stoic but a biblical Christian, urging strenuously that God and the human soul are not of a piece.[27] It is not clear that the Stoics could differentiate corporeality from materiality, but in Tertullian's day, a Latin speaker could assert that God is a *corpus* and mean only to credit him with discrete existence, without subjecting him to the frailty and impermanence of matter.[28] It is spirit, not matter, that constitutes the substance of Tertullian's God, who is not the immanent *logos* of creation, but has projected his eternal thought as the sempiternal Logos to bring creation out of nothing. Stoics may be the janitors of truth, but not its guardians: the locution *dixit Seneca saepe noster* should not be rendered "as our Seneca often says" (as though Tertullian and the Stoic teacher were of the same school[29]) but rather "as Seneca says, who is often on our side."[30]

New approaches

The libraries of Alexandria bred a scholasticism in philosophy that resembled Christian handling of the Scriptures. The author whom we call Clement of Alexandria received a pagan education in Athens before he took up residence in the Egyptian capital. Pantaenus, his instructor in Christianity, is frequently alleged to have been a Stoic, though we do not learn this from Clement. Both were later said to have presided over the Catechetical School in Alexandria, but in Clement's first surviving work, the *Exhortation to the Greeks* (*Protrepticus*), the philosopher is more in evidence than the theologian. The text derives its name from a famous work by Aristotle, and its denunciation of pagan cults as marts of imposture and lechery finds an echo in harangues against the populace by Platonists, Cynics, Stoics, and Epicureans. Yet Clement leaves these forebears behind him in his denunciation of idolatry, his allusions to the fall, his refusal to palliate myth by allegory, and his castigation of philosophers who scoff at the cults but are afraid to shun them.[31] That Christians and philosophers can be intellectual allies he sets out to prove in his *Miscellanies* (*Stromateis*), where philosophers are said to have arrived at correct opinions on many topics, the Logos is discovered to be the seat of the Platonic ideas, and the principles of Pythagorean symbology are adopted not only to dissipate obscurities in the Scriptures but to buttress the claim that deeper truths are hidden even in the more lucid passages.[32] In the eighth book,

Clement shows off his proficiency in logic; in the first, he commends the acquisition of an "eclectic" wisdom, which is common to all philosophies, as a means to the perfection of Christian faith.[33] It is the knowing or gnostic Christian who obeys the commandments truly, discerning (for example) that the "noetic" sense of Christ's injunction to give away one's riches can be applied to the inner man without any outward loss to the wealthy benefactors of the church. Unsympathetic commentators surmise that Clement's true philosophy is his "eclecticism," from which he makes a procrustean bed for the gospel, lopping away the unpalatable elements which had made the world afraid of Christ and formidable to his saints.[34]

This judgment is unlikely to survive a thorough reading of Clement's works. The knowledge that he inculcates entails the recognition of humility as a virtue, though the philosophers had no word for it; admonishing the rich that they are debtors in spirit to those who receive their alms,[35] it requires a woman to dress without ornament and a man to dispense with footwear.[36] So much a philosopher might also do, but if he is guided in this by a true apprehension of God, he derived this (Clement argues) from the Hebrew prophets, not from any deposit of common truth. It is in their theology that philosophers differ, and it is not they but the Sibyl and Hystaspes (as in Justin) who have imbibed their knowledge of God by inspiration.[37] Clement's inventory of pagan thefts from Scripture takes up half of the fifth book in the *Miscellanies*, and he has twice as many citations from St Paul as from the more voluminous Plato.[38] Pythagorean maxims are adopted to forestall the literal exposition of passages that we too would consider metaphorical; and while the Logos seems to represent a diffuse and universal teaching at some points in the *Miscellanies*, we must not forget that this is only one of his works, designed not so much to propagate a systematic theology as to reconcile the gospel with those elements in philosophy which admitted of harmonization. We cannot tell what we have lost in Clement's *Outlines* (*Hypotyposes*), where he proceeds by exegesis of the New Testament; we can observe, however, that in his *Christ the Educator*, or *Schoolmaster*, the Logos is incarnate and attired in a crown of thorns.[39]

Origen is reputed to have been a pupil of Clement and the next leader of the Catechetical School. Disappointed in his early hope of martyrdom, he became a noted expositor of the Scriptures, and in his celebrated treatise *On First Principles* he endeavors to build a system from this source alone, dispelling superficial contradiction and absurdities, vindicating the harmony of the two testaments and laying down canons for profitable reading. Yet he also alludes to his schooling with an unnamed master, whose name is agreed in ancient sources to have been Ammonius.[40] This man or a namesake also taught Plotinus, the founder of Neoplatonism, and the epithet "Platonist" sticks like a burr to Origen in modern criticism, though he cannot have read Plotinus, expressly repudiates the theory of ideas, and differs from every known representative of Platonism in using "God" as the proper, rather than merely honorific, name of the highest principle. His equation of God with mind and his adoption of the terms *monad* and *henad* to illustrate God's simplicity are authorized by the practice of Philo and previous Christian writers; they are also exemplifications of that process which, in a letter to a disciple, he called "spoiling the Egyptians" – that is, enriching the church from the treasuries of the nations who oppress her, or, in plainer terms, availing oneself of all that Greek philosophy and philology can contribute to the elucidation of Scriptures (*Philokalia* 13, citing Exodus 3:22). Philosophy may suggest, but Scripture judges: thus at *On Prayer* 27, Origen has to explain the otherwise unattested compound *epiousios* in the Lord's Prayer (Luke 11:3), which he takes to mean supersubstantial. In imitation of Plato's *Sophist*, he notes that the Greeks are divided into two parties, one contending that whatever truly is must be immune to change, and therefore incorporeal, while the other asseverates that nothing exists unless that is not apprehensible to the senses.[41] The first are of course the Platonists and the others the Stoics, but in siding with the former Origen argues not from his schooling or the consensus of divines in Alexandria, and not even from those premises which were endorsed by all philosophers, but solely from other passages in Scriptures. If a Platonist is one who rests his beliefs on the authority of Plato, Origen does not qualify for the designation.

Plato is the Greek most often praised in the one surviving work that Origen dedicated to philosophy. The eight books of his apology *Against Celsus* were written towards the end of his life to rebut an attack on the Christians which had been current for seventy years. Its author is characterized in modern scholarship as a rhetorician with Platonic sympathies, though Origen repeatedly taunts him as an Epicurean. This imputation allows him to draw promiscuously on all the schools opposed to Epicurus in his vindication of providence and the immateriality of God. He calls on the Stoics to expose the faults of his interlocutor's logic, and to corroborate his Christian belief that the world is governed in the interests of humanity. On the other hand, the *Symposium* of Plato affords a parallel to the superficial obscenities of the Old Testament,[42] an echo of Numenius is detectable when Christ is acclaimed as a second god,[43] and a shopworn passage from the *Timaeus* illustrates the difficulty of obtaining or publishing knowledge of the Father.[44] But none of this makes Origen a Platonist, and his defense of all three positions is designed not so much to reconcile the philosophers as to reprove them. He will not allow that the vices of any Greek text can be wholly purged by allegory,[45] and his own assiduity in this practice struck the Platonists as an innovation, reminiscent of the Stoics.[46] His second God is subordinated to God the Father only on biblical grounds, and enters the human realm by condescension, not by an inadvertent shift of vision.[47] As for the impediments to our knowledge of God, they are barely observed by Plato, who pronounces difficult that which Christians know to be impossible without special revelation.[48] Origen holds that Christians have a duty to answer the cavils of philosophers in language that will command their esteem, but at the same time he admonishes the Greeks that it is not the sublimation of the intellect, but the voluntary abasement of the Word, that spans the gulf between the infinite God and the objects of his love.

Aftermath

Origen's pupil and panegyrist Gregory Thaumaturgus records that he devised his own conspectus of the chief schools as an introduction to theological studies. His writing marks a caesura in relations between the church and the Greeks, not only because so little Christian literature on any topic survives from the next half century, but because, when the apologists once again took up the case against the pagans, it was no longer possible for them simply to spurn the philosophers even when they pretended to knowledge of God without revelation. Eusebius, though he endorses and embellishes the charge of plagiarism, blames the philosophers primarily for their failure to perceive that the works of their greatest predecessors anticipated or confirmed the Christian preaching of three hypostases and one God. Arnobius and Lactantius, taking the common Roman view that the test of philosophy is conduct, holds up Christ as the exemplar of those virtues which have been eclipsed in Rome by love of conquest or collusion with the vices of the conquered. For Arnobius the enemy is religion, while for Lactantius it is rhetoric; philosophy, as the latter intimates, can lead the Christian not only away from error but home to truth.[49]

Further reading

H. Chadwick, *Early Christianity and the Classical Tradition*, Oxford: Clarendon, 1966 and 1984.
C. N. Cochrane, *Christianity and Classical Culture*, Oxford: Clarendon, 1940.
J. Daniélou, *Gospel Message and Hellenistic Culture*, London: Darton, Longman & Todd, 1973.
J. Pelikan, *Christianity and Classical Culture*, New Haven, CT: Yale University Press, 1995.
J. M. Rist, *Eros and Psyche*, Toronto: University of Toronto Press, 1965.
R. Sorabji, *Emotion and Peace of Mind*, Oxford: Clarendon, 2000.
G. C. Stead, *Philosophy in Christian Antiquity*, Cambridge: Cambridge University Press, 1994.

Notes

1 Plato, *Theaetetus* 173c–176a. See Hermias, *Satire des philosophes Païens*, ed. R. P. C. Hanson, Paris: Cerf, 1993.
2 J. Daniélou, *Gospel Message and Hellenistic Culture*, London: Darton, Longman & Todd, 1973, p. 112.
3 See H. A. Wolfson, *Philo: Foundations of Religious Philosophy in Judaism, Christianity, and Islam*, 2 vols, Cambridge, MA: Harvard University Press, 1947.
4 The usual cicerone is J. M. Dillon, *The Middle Platonists: A Study of Platonism, 80 B.C. to A.D. 220*, London: Duckworth, 1996.
5 See, above all, Numenius of Apamea, *Fragments* 11 and 16; *Fragments*, ed. E. Des Places, Paris: Budé, 1973.
6 See generally G. C. Stead, *Philosophy in Christian Antiquity*, Cambridge: Cambridge University Press, 1994.
7 On the controversies of the second century see G. Karamanolis, *Plato and Aristotle in Agreement? Platonists on Aristotle from Antiochus to Porphyry*, Oxford: Clarendon, 2006.
8 G. Bendinelli, *Il commentario a matteo di origene: l'ambito dell metodologia scolastica dell' antichità*, Rome: Institutum patristicum Augustinianum, 1997.
9 For convenience of reference, I have used the chapter divisions found in the series A. Roberts and J. Donaldson (eds), *The Ante-Nicene Fathers*, 10 vols, Edinburgh: T&T Clark, 1885–7; repr. Grand Rapids, MI: Wm. B. Eerdmans, 1987; repr. Peabody, MA: Hendrickson, 1994.
10 Justin, *Dialogue with Trypho* 3–8. See further J. M. C. Van Winden, *An Early Christian Philosopher: Justin Martyr's Dialogue with Trypho. Chapters 1–9*, Leiden: Brill, 1971.
11 Justin, *First Apology* 44.
12 Justin, *First Apology* 59.
13 Justin, *First Apology* 21.
14 Justin, *First Apology* 60.

15 Theophilus, *To Autolycus* 2.10.
16 Theophilus, *To Autolycus* 2.10; cf. G. May, *Creatio ex Nihilo: The Doctrine of "Creation Out of Nothing" in Early Christian Thought*, Edinburgh: T&T Clark, 1994. The utility of matter as a concept is denied by the author of *Philokalia* 24: see J. A. Robinson, *The Philocalia of Origen*, Oxford: Clarendon, 1911.
17 Hippolytus, *Refutation of all Heresies* 6.17–18.
18 Hippolytus, *Refutation of all Heresies* 6.17.
19 Hippolytus, *Refutation of all Heresies* 6.4; 12.
20 Hippolytus, *Refutation of all Heresies* 6.4–6.
21 Porphyry, *Life of Plotinus* 16. On the representation of Greek philosophy in Hippolytus see C. Osborne, *Rethinking Early Greek Philosophy: Hippolytus of Rome and the Presocratics*, Ithaca, NY: Cornell University Press, 1993; J. Mansfeld, *Heresiography in Context: Hippolytus' Elenchos as a Source for Greek Philosophy*, Leiden: Brill, 1992.
22 Tertullian, *Prescription against Heretics* 7.9. In contrast to Hippolytus he labels Valentinus a Platonist and Marcion a Stoic – proof enough that he himself was no Stoic, and no historian.
23 Tertullian, *On the Soul* 8.3–5.
24 Tertullian, *On the Soul* 17.
25 Tertullian, *On the Soul* 7.3, 57.12.
26 Tertullian, *On the Soul* 5.3.
27 Tertullian, *On the Soul* 11.3.
28 Tertullian, *Against Praxeas* 7.8; cf. Augustine, *Letter* 166, and Tertullian, *Against Hermogenes*, on the creation of matter by God.
29 J. Daniélou, *The Origins of Latin Christianity*, London: Darton, Longman & Todd, 1974, p. 380.
30 Tertullian, *On the Soul* 20.1.
31 Clement of Alexandria, *Exhortation to the Greeks* 6.
32 Clement of Alexandria, *Miscellanies* 5.5.
33 Clement of Alexandria, *Miscellanies* 1.7. In chapters 4 and 5 he follows Philo in interpreting Hagar and Sarah as representatives of secular and divine wisdom.
34 H. F. Hägg (*Clement of Alexandria and the Origins of Christian Apophaticism*, Oxford: Clarendon, 2006) agrees with S. Lilla (*Clement of Alexandria: A Study in Christian Platonism*, Oxford: Clarendon, 1971) in tracing Clement's theology to the Platonists. The position taken here accords more closely with that of E. Osborn, *Clement of Alexandria*, Cambridge: Cambridge University Press, 2005.
35 See Clement of Alexandria, *Christ the Educator* 3.6–7, as well as *Salvation of the Rich*.
36 Clement of Alexandria, *Christ the Educator* 2.8–12.
37 Clement of Alexandria, *Miscellanies* 6.5.42.
38 Clement of Alexandria, *Miscellanies* 5.14.
39 Clement of Alexandria, *Christ the Educator* 2.8.
40 Eusebius, *Ecclesiastical History* 6.19, disputing the identity of Ammonius with Porphyry, who may have thought him identical with Ammonius in *Life of Plotinus* 3, but cannot have confused him with the pagan Origen, who figures there as a contemporary of Plotinus. The case for Origen's Platonism is learnedly and eloquently defended by C. H. Bigg, *The Christian Platonists of Alexandria: The 1886 Bampton Lectures*, Oxford: Clarendon, 1886. Since then it has gone by default until the appearance of M. J. Edwards, *Origen against Plato*, Aldershot, UK: Ashgate, 2002, then P. Tzamalikos's *Origen: Cosmology and Ontology of Time*, Leiden: Brill, 2006, and *Origen Philosophy of History and Eschatology*, Leiden: Brill, 2007.
41 Plato, *Sophist* 245e–246e.
42 Origen, *Against Celsus* 4.39.
43 Origen, *Against Celsus* 5.39.
44 Origen, *Against Celsus* 7.42, citing Plato, *Timaeus* 28c.
45 Origen, *Against Celsus* 4.38.
46 Porphyry, in Eusebius, *Ecclesiastical History* 6.19.
47 Origen, *Against Celsus* 4.15.
48 Origen, *Against Celsus* 7.42.
49 See M. Frede, "Eusebius' Apologetic Writings," and M. J. Edwards, "The Flowering of Latin Apologetic," in M. J. Edwards, M. D. Goodman, and S. R. F. Price (eds), *Apologetics in the Roman Empire*, Oxford: Clarendon, 1999, pp. 223–50, 197–222.

3

GRECO-ROMAN UNDERSTANDING OF CHRISTIANITY

Paul Hartog

How did early Christianity appear to pagan observers within its Greco-Roman cultural context? Such a question underscores the difference between "insider" and "outsider" perspectives. As Robert Wilken notes, "The Christians 'read' themselves quite differently than their contemporaries 'read' them." On the one hand, "insider" texts "present the life of Jesus and the beginning of the church as the turning point of history." On the other hand, "outsider" texts view "the Christian communities as small, peculiar, anti-social, irreligious sects, drawing their adherents from the lower strata of society."[1]

This present essay will trace the literature written by "outsiders," individuals loyal to Greco-Roman society and its ideology that directly engaged and challenged Christianity in the second and third centuries. Such a task is not without its difficulties. The pagan perceptions of Christianity that survive are often found in offhand references or fragmentary sources. Many of them are extant only because they were "quoted (selectively) and paraphrased (tendentiously) by Christian authors."[2] Moreover, both Christianity and pagan philosophy were "moving targets," since both "were in continuous change and development throughout the period."[3]

Furthermore, most of these pagan materials are found in literature addressed to upper-class readers. Thus one senses that a certain "social prejudice" frequently characterizes the polemics.[4] On the other hand, one should not assume that a "hard-and-fast" boundary fell between intellectual critics and popular perceptions. Sometimes the cultural elite adapted the simplistic prejudices of their social milieu, and at other times they shaped popular opinion. As a Christian apologist, Justin Martyr felt compelled to insist that judgment be given only "after an exact and searching enquiry, not moved by prejudice or by a wish to please superstitious people, nor by irrational impulse or long prevalent rumors."[5]

Before the Decian suppression of Christianity, persecutions were usually prompted by popular opposition.[6] Christian sources recognized this role of public opinion, and they frequently decried the role of the *famae*, the *rumores*, and the *suspiciones*.[7] The *acta martyria* often highlight the decisive role played by hostile crowds. Popular opposition linked with official persecution, due to the wide latitude permitted to the provincial governors in sentences *extra ordinem*, as well as the function of *delatores* in the Roman legal system.[8] The cases (below) of Marcus Cornelius Fronto and Sossianus Hierocles demonstrate that such popular opposition could be aggravated by those deemed to be intellectual elites. During this period the "outsider" views embodied in intellectual critiques, state policies, and popular prejudices were inseparably intertwined.

One should not assume that these "outsider" perspectives are irrelevant to the study of early Christianity as it "really" was or came to be. Wilken explains, "For the attitudes of outsiders not only defined the world Christians inhabited; they were also a factor in making Christianity what it eventually became. What is said critically by pagans in one generation will be mirrored positively by Christians in the next."[9] Christian apologists often felt compelled to define themselves in a manner that responded to an agenda set by "outsiders."[10] Pagan critiques served as dams that altered the flow of Christian development, thereby changing the terrain of Christian self-identity. For example, pagan opposition caused second-century apologists to portray Christianity as a philosophy comparable to other philosophical schools. "There is no doubt," comments Marta Sordi, "that the apologists' decision to present Christianity in these terms was also dictated by the historical situation of the times."[11] Pagan and Christian apologists participated in an intergenerational chess match that spread from Justin Martyr to Celsus to Origen to Porphyry. In turn, Porphyry's polemic provoked rejoinders from a wide company of Christian defenders.[12] This ideological debate never checkmated the progress of Christian apologetics, but it did change the defensive strategy.[13]

Furthermore, early Christian doctrines frequently developed in direct response to pagan critiques, and (in turn) the classical tradition was transformed by Christian influence.[14] For example, philosophical criticisms sometimes prompted the further integration of Platonism into Christianity.[15] Wilken argues that the pagan opponents caused Christians "to grasp the implications of Christian belief earlier than would have been possible if they had talked only among themselves – in short, to understand the very tradition they were defending."[16] Pagan critics forced Christians to find "their authentic voice," and without them "Christianity would have been the poorer."[17] Wilken lists the following examples of tenets forged within the furnace of pagan opposition: the relationship of faith and reason, the relation of God to the world, creation *ex nihilo*, the relation of Christianity to Judaism, the status of Jesus and his relation to God, the historical reliability of the Scriptures, the role of civil religion and the civil position of Christianity, and the revelation of God in history.[18] One might append the Christians' discussions of free will and divine impassibility. In addition, Christianity clarified its relationship to Judaism partly in response to pagan criticisms.[19]

Early Greco-Roman references

While glancing back to the reign of Nero, Suetonius (a second-century *equestrian* and biographer) narrates that "Punishment was inflicted on the Christians, a class of men given to a new and mischievous superstition (*superstitio nova ac malefica*)."[20] While discussing the reign of Claudius, Suetonius asserts, "Since the Jews constantly made disturbances at the instigation of Chrestus, he expelled them from Rome."[21] The word *Chrestus* in this passage is sometimes interpreted as an alternative spelling (or corruption) of *Christus* ("Christ").[22] This *Christus–Chrestus* debate shows no signs of abating, although the burden of proof appears to lie upon those who read Christianity into the passage.[23]

Tacitus, another early second-century Roman historian, narrates how Nero used Christians as scapegoats when he was accused of setting fire to Rome.[24] It is noteworthy that this accusation of incendiarism seemed credible to many Roman residents, who seemed convinced that Christians were capable of various "abominable vices" or "atrocities" (*flagitia*).[25] Christians were known for their "hatred of the human race" (*odio humani generis*).[26] The pernicious superstition (*exitiabilis superstitio*) was plaguing Rome, "where all things horrible or shameful in the world collect and find a vogue."[27] Tacitus had already leveled this accusation of *superstitio* against the Jews, and he seems to have viewed Christianity as a "superstition" of Jewish origin.[28]

Around the year 112, Pliny the Younger sent a letter to the emperor Trajan, asking advice concerning the proper treatment of Christians. At the time, Pliny was the governor of Pontus and Bithynia.[29] He complained that Christianity, as a "contagious superstition," had spread beyond the cities to the villages and rural districts.[30] Pliny had never been involved in the *cognitio* (legal investigation) of a Christian, so he posed a series of questions.[31] Should age be taken into account? Could one be pardoned by recanting the Christian faith? Were Christians to be punished merely for the sake of the name itself (*nomen ipsum* = "Christian"), or was it necessary to find them guilty of affiliated offenses (*flagitia cohaerentia nomini*)?

For his part, Pliny ordered the accused to worship the gods, offer sacrifices, and curse Christ.[32] Those who publicly recanted were summarily discharged. But if they disregarded his thrice-repeated threats and persisted in their Christian commitments, Pliny executed them or sent them on to Rome (in the case of Roman citizens). "For whatever the nature of their creed might be," Pliny did not doubt that "pertinacity and inflexible obstinacy (*pertinacia et inflexibilis obstinatio*) deserved punishment."[33] Upon further investigation, Pliny could find no proof of criminal or conspiratorial activity within the Christian assemblies. Rather, the Christians sang hymns to Christ "as to god," took an oath (*sacramentum*) not to commit crimes, and shared an innocent, common meal. He discovered "nothing more than depraved and excessive superstition" (*superstitio prava et immodica*).[34] Both Trajan's reply to Pliny and the later rescript of Hadrian sought to curb the abuses of *delatio* (informing) against Christians.[35]

Some philosophically minded writers of the second century appreciated the courage manifested by Christian martyrs in the face of death. Among these authors were Epictetus, Marcus Aurelius, and Galen. Epictetus maintained that someone who was not improperly attached to life or material possessions would not manifest fear.[36] He contended that the antidote to fear was a mental framework which allows one to "set the will neither upon dying nor upon living at any cost, but only as it is given one to live."[37] Epictetus noted that the same mindset can be produced by "madness" (μανίας) or by "habit" (ἔθους), as with "the Galileans." Many scholars have interpreted Epictetus's "Galileans" as a reference to Christians.[38]

Eusebius's *Ecclesiastical History* includes a letter purportedly written by Marcus Aurelius to the Council of Asia.[39] The letter states,

> But you drive them into tumult, for you confirm them in the opinion which they hold by accusing them as atheists (ἀθέων), and they too when so accused might well prefer apparent death rather than life for the sake of their own God.

(Eusebius, *Ecclesiastical History* 4.13.3)

This same material is found in Justin Martyr's *Apology*, but he ascribes it to Antoninus Pius.[40] Benko notes, "Whether the letter is a complete Christian forgery or whether Christian interpolators have altered an originally genuine text is still a subject of scholarly debate."[41]

The extant text of Marcus Aurelius's *Meditations* includes an offhand reference to Christians.[42] The emperor admired the soul which is "ready and resolved" to "be released from the body." This readiness must "arise from a specific decision, not out of sheer opposition like the Christians."[43] For his part, Marcus Aurelius espoused "reflection and dignity" rather than "histrionic display." While he valued certain traits found among Christian martyrs, he still viewed their final moments as too emotional and melodramatic. One should stalwartly face death but not play the stage-heroics of a theatrical martyr.

Galen, the famous Roman physician and philosopher, praised "the people called Christians" for their contempt of death, restraint in cohabitation, self-control in food and drink, and keen pursuit of justice. In these matters, they were not inferior to "genuine philosophers."[44] On one level, Galen treated Christians as adherents of a philosophical school, as when he compared "the followers of Moses and Christ" with "physicians and philosophers who cling fast to their schools."[45] Galen sympathetically admired the Christian conduct of a life, since they acted in the same way "as those who philosophize." Nevertheless, they were merely playing the part, since they lacked a rational foundation.[46]

According to Galen, Christian virtue rested upon parables, miracles, and tales of rewards and punishments in a future life. In "the school of Moses and Christ," one hears talk of "undemonstrated laws, and that where it is least appropriate."[47] Galen grumbled that the "followers of Moses and Christ" order their pupils "to accept everything on faith."[48] For him, "Christians were neither dangerous conspirators nor abominable cannibals, but were rather adherents of an inferior philosophical school."[49] Although they did not pose a serious threat to society, they had been hoodwinked by a simplistic belief system.

The brunt of speeches and satires

In his public speeches, Crescens attacked Christians as "impious" and as "atheists."[50] According to the reconstruction of many scholars, Crescens's contemporary, Marcus Cornelius Fronto, delivered a speech accusing Christians of incestuous banqueting and of infanticide.[51] Fronto's tirade may provide a backdrop to the persecution of Christians in Lyons and Vienne c. 177, as well as the response embodied in Athenagoras's *Plea*.[52]

In one of his speeches, the orator Aelius Aristides referred to "those impious people of Palestine." They "do not believe in the higher powers" but have "defected from the Greek race, or rather from all that is higher." "But they are cleverest of all at housebreaking, in upsetting those within and bringing them into conflict with one another, and in claiming that they can take care of everything. They have never spoken, discovered, or written a fruitful word; they have never added adornment to the national festivals, never honored the gods."[53]

Benko wavers in his assessment of this material from Aristides, which "may or may not refer to Christians."[54] The charges of antisocialism and disturbing family life certainly parallel common perceptions of Christians. According to pagan censures, Christians were affiliated with "the repudiation of pleasure, the breaking of home and family ties, the ruining of business, the abandonment of religion, and the avoidance of civic duties."[55] From the pagan perspective, Christian commitment subverted familial bonds and preyed on the emotionally vulnerable.[56] Pagans resented the disruptive force of Christianity upon the Roman commonwealth and upon traditional family values.[57] "Many a pagan first heard of Christianity as the disintegrating force that had wrecked a neighbor's home."[58]

Apuleius's *Metamorphoses* is a comic tale of the protagonist's alteration into a donkey by magic, his adventures as an ass, and his eventual transformation back into a human through the benevolence of Isis. While living as a donkey, Lucius was sold to a baker and his wife. Apuleius wrote that this woman did not lack "a single fault," but "her soul was like some muddy latrine into which absolutely every vice had flowed." She was "cruel, and perverse, crazy for men and wine, headstrong and obstinate, grasping in her mean thefts and a spendthrift in her loathsome extravagances, an enemy of fidelity and a foe to chastity." Furthermore, "she scorned and spurned all the gods in heaven, and, instead of holding a definite faith, she used the false sacrilegious presumption of a god, whom she would call 'one and only'." In this god's honor she invented "meaningless rites to cheat everyone and deceive her wretched husband, having sold her body to drink from dawn and to debauchery the whole day."[59] This passage may disparage Christian women (or perhaps Jewish women), yet its contemptuous tenor reveals an uncritical adaptation and satirical exploitation of popular prejudice.[60]

In his *Apology*, Apuleius describes a certain Aemilianus who mocked divine matters and despised the gods:

> For I learn from certain men of Oea who know him, that to this day he has never prayed to any god or frequented any temple, while if he chances to pass

any shrine, he regards it as a crime to raise his hand to his lips in token of reverence.

(Apuleius, *Apology* 56)[61]

Whether this "atheist" was a Christian cannot be established with certainty, although V. Hunink argues that "much is to be said" for this theory.[62]

Lucian of Samosata was another famous literary wit who ridiculed Christians, along with many others who came within the cross-hairs of his satirical sights.[63] Peregrinus Proteus, the protagonist and namesake of one of Lucian's satires, was a huckster and a swindler. After murdering his father, Peregrinus slipped away to Palestine to learn "the wonderful wisdom of the Christians," and he quickly rose among their ranks. Lucian mocked the "credulity" of the Christians, yet he also satirized "the fanatical masses who wanted to see the Christians sentenced to death for atheism."[64] When Peregrinus was imprisoned, his fellow believers visited him and luxuriously supported their "new Socrates."[65] Peregrinus was able to amass a sizeable fortune through Christian beneficence, but he was finally excommunicated from the church when he ate meat sacrificed to idols. He eventually became a Cynic philosopher and wandering teacher before his dramatic demise via self-immolation.

In one passage, Lucian characterizes the Christians as follows:

> The poor wretches have convinced themselves, first and foremost, that they are going to be immortal and live for all time, in consequence of which they despise death and even willingly give themselves into custody, most of them. Furthermore, their first lawgiver persuaded them that they are all brothers of one another after they have transgressed once for all by denying the Greek gods and by worshipping that crucified sophist himself and living under his laws. Therefore, they despise all things indiscriminately and consider them common property, receiving such doctrines traditionally without any definite evidence. So if any charlatan and trickster, able to profit by occasions, comes among them, he quickly acquires sudden wealth by imposing upon simple folk.

(Lucian, *Peregrinus* 5)[66]

Lucian briefly returns to the subject of Christians in his account of Alexander of Abonoteichus. "Pontus was full of atheists and Christians who had the hardihood to utter the vilest abuse of [Alexander]."[67] Within the narrative, "death to the Epicureans" and "death to the Christians" are interchangeable exclamations with "death to the atheists," because of a shared disregard for the traditional gods.[68] Lucian manifests a surface-level understanding of Christianity, which he merely employs as a foil within his satirical caricaturizations.[69] As M. J. Edwards surmises, "Satire seeks, not truth, but the characteristics and the probable: it depicts living creatures, not as individuals, but as representative[s]."[70]

Celsus, Porphyry, and Hierocles

Most of the pagan critics described above did not make "a serious effort to study Christian teachings or to observe Christians in action."[71] All this changed with Celsus, who wrote an entire treatise against Christianity in *True Doctrine*, probably composed in the 160s or 170s.[72] Although the work is now lost, much of it can be reconstructed from Origen's reply in *Against Celsus*. The *True Doctrine* reveals that Celsus was a traditional conservative who believed that "religion was inextricably bound to the unique customs of a people," that behind all the traditional religions was "an ancient doctrine that has existed from the beginning," and that the "old doctrine" was the "true doctrine."[73] Christianity was dangerous because it unraveled the social fabric of traditional piety that wove together religion, society, and politics. Celsus raised anti-Christian polemic to a whole new level, since he personally examined the Jewish and Christian scriptures and even recognized internal quarrels among Christians.[74]

Celsus castigated the Christians for their unsocial behavior and for practicing their religion in secret.[75] "They wall themselves off and break away from the rest of mankind."[76] They rejected Hellenic *paideia* and culture by turning to "barbarian" beliefs.[77] They shirked their civil responsibilities, such as cooperating with the emperor and fighting as his "fellow-soldiers" and "fellow-generals."[78] They were like ungrateful tenants who gave nothing back for the use of property.[79]

Celsus opposed the fideistic gullibility and incredulous dogmatism he alleged was among Christians. They "vulgarly discuss fundamental principles and make arrogant pronouncements about matters of which they know nothing."[80] Therefore, claimed Celsus, adherents represented "wool-workers, cobblers, laundry-workers and the most illiterate and bucolic yokels." They convinced "only the foolish, dishonourable and stupid, and only slaves, women, and little children."[81] Instead of giving "a reason for what they believe," Christian teachers repeated stock expressions such as "Do not ask questions, just believe!"[82]

Celsus argued that Jesus was a magician and could not have been divine.[83] Why, asked Celsus, would a god need to eat, as Jesus did? Why would a god, who should be unafraid of death, need to flee to Egypt as a child? Why would a god permit himself to be arrested? How could an immortal god suffer and die? Why would the Son of God require an angel to move the tomb stone? If Jesus were God, why would the men who tortured him go unpunished?[84] Celsus concludes that "the Christians are the losers, since they worship neither a god nor even a demon, but a dead man!"[85]

Celsus attacked the biblical writings as fables. He maintained that the original belief in Jesus' resurrection was based upon sorcery-formed delusion, wishful thinking, and female hysteria.[86] The disciples later fabricated Jesus' prophecies of his death and resurrection to make it appear that the entire plot was foretold. Celsus argued that Christians also foisted Jesus upon the Hebrew prophecies, since "the prophecies could be applied to thousands of others far more plausibly than to Jesus."[87] In addition, the idea of a virgin birth was borrowed from pre-existing myths.[88]

Celsus claimed that Christian theology was riddled with internal contradictions. Why was an omnipotent, sovereign God unable to control his creatures?[89] How could humans be made in the image of an incorporeal God? Why would an omnipotent God need a day of rest after creation?[90] How could God create the world, leave it to evil, and only return to its rescue centuries later?[91] Why would he come to an out-of-the-way corner of the earth like Palestine? How could an immutable God change and take on human form?[92]

Celsus complained that Christianity was unoriginal and yet had the brazenness to claim exclusivity. While the Jewish religion could rightfully claim ancient roots, Christians freely picked their teachings and rituals from other sources.[93] Not only did the Christians refuse to admit their free borrowing, they even claimed that "they alone know the right way to live."[94] But the multiplicity of Christian schisms raised an epistemological specter. How could all of the schismatic groups claim exclusive truth?

Porphyry of Gaza, who had been tutored by Origen, later became a pupil of Plotinus, a Neoplatonic philosopher whose lectures criticized "Christians of many kinds" (and especially Gnostics).[95] Porphyry's *Philosophy from Oracles* included various anti-Christian pieces. For instance, Augustine preserved Porphyrian oracular materials concerning a pagan husband's concern for his Christian wife.[96] "Let her go as she pleases, persisting in her vain delusions, singing in lamentation for a god who died in delusions, who was condemned by right-thinking judges, and killed in hideous fashion by the worst of deaths."[97] Porphyry also composed a multi-volume work (or collection of works) eventually known as *Against the Christians*.[98] Modern scholars have attempted to reconstruct some of the contents, based upon secondary excerpts.[99] T. D. Barnes has described *Against the Christians* as "the largest, most learned and most dangerous of all the ancient literary attacks on Christianity."[100] Porphyry "could not be laughed off as an ignorant and ill-informed critic."[101]

Porphyry derided Christianity as "an irrational and unexamined *pistis*," and he called Christians "impious" and "atheists" for throwing aside their ancestral gods.[102] He portrayed the apostles and evangelists as "poor country bumpkins (*rusticani et pauperes*) who performed second-rate magic merely 'for profit'."[103] He maintained that the evangelists manipulated and misquoted the prophecies of the Hebrew scriptures,[104] that the Gospels contradicted one another,[105] and that Paul was erroneous and incon-sistent in his own writings.[106] Porphyry argued that the book of Daniel was written as *prophecy ex eventu* in the second century BCE.

Lactantius reports hearing two anti-Christian polemicists speak at Diocletian's court immediately before the outbreak of the "Great Persecution," and some modern scholars believe that one of the pair was Porphyry.[107] The other was most probably Sossianus Hierocles, governor of Bithynia.[108] Scholars debate the dating of Hierocles' work, *Lover of Truth*, although Michael Simmons argues that an edition was circu-lating in the Eastern provinces by c. 303.[109] Hierocles depicted Apollonius of Tyana (a pagan wonder-worker) as a holy-man possessed with divine qualities, while he portrayed Jesus as a brigand, and a leader of low-class disciples. Hierocles contrasted pagan "well-established judgment" with "the easy credulity of Christians."[110] "For whereas we reckon him who wrought such feats not a god, but only a man pleasing to the gods, they on the strength of a few miracles proclaim their Jesus a god."[111] Simmons notes how the *Lover of Truth* reveals significant information concerning the background of the pagan–Christian conflict leading into the Great Persecution, the relationship between pagan intellectuals and the religious policies of the Tetrarchy, the polemical focus upon miracles and prophecy, and the development of the apologetic genre in the late Roman Empire.[112]

Celsus, Porphyry, and Hierocles embodied the "increasingly hostile attack upon Christianity by some of the best representatives of the cultured classes of the Roman Empire."[113] These opponents caused Christians to clarify the issues, refine many arguments, and take positive corrective measures. One should not assume that "this response would have been formulated in the absence of the challenge."[114]

Recurring themes

Intellectual opponents caricatured Christianity as appealing to those deemed as social inferiors.[115] In the words of Celsus, Christianity appealed to women, slaves, and children.[116] Critics also highlighted the "barbarian" character of Christianity, in contrast with the cultural achievements of the Greeks.[117] As a corollary to such "social prejudice," pagans frequently looked down upon the Christian Scriptures, which seemed "uncouth and barbaric" and "grated on the sensibilities" of the educated.[118] "It is difficult," explains A. H. M. Jones, "for us to appreciate how serious an obstacle this was."[119] Christian authors sought to ease the tension by employing allegorical interpretation.[120] And when pagan polemicists insisted upon the superiority and antiquity of Greco-Roman culture, Christian apologists countered that the classical Greek writings borrowed from Moses.[121]

At the same time, there was no hard-and-fast boundary between the clamor of the ignorant masses and the intellectual critiques of the literary elites. The intellectual critics were not immune to adopting (or even inciting) popular accusations. For instance, Marcus Cornelius Fronto accused Christians of incest and cannibalism. Pliny asked Trajan whether the Christians were to be punished merely for the sake of the name itself ("Christian"), or was it necessary to find them guilty of affiliated offenses (*flagitia cohaerentia nomini*)? Pliny, it is true, made the effort to investigate Christian meetings before jumping to rash conclusions, and he found no evidence of such *flagitia*. But his question still manifests that he was a man of his times.

Christians often felt persecuted merely for the sake of the name, the *nomen Christianum*.[122] Justin Martyr protested, "By the mere statement of a name, nothing is decided, either good or evil, apart from the actions associated with the name."[123] But the name "Christian" was often associated with the undesirable traits of *superstitio* and *obstinatio*, as well as a wider "complex of guilt," including the purported *flagitia* of incest and cannibalistic infanticide ("Oedipean intercourse" and "Thyestean banquets").[124] Tertullian complained, therefore, that the only thing necessary to incite public hatred was "the confession of the name of Christian, not an investigation of the charge."[125]

Like the pagan masses, the pagan literary figures were suspicious of Christian secrecy. According to Celsus, Christians conducted their business and instruction "in secret."[126] Pagans spoke of the Christians' "mysterious intimacy," including their nocturnal gatherings.[127] Their lack of altars, images, and temples within worship was a telltale sign of a secret society.[128] Minucius Felix's pagan interlocutor insisted that Christians are "a furtive race which shuns the light, mute in the open but garrulous in the corners."[129] Secrecy was cousin to conspiracy, and although the Christians were secretive, they were well-organized.[130]

The Greco-Roman critique often focused upon six recurring themes – Christianity as a *superstitio*, as "atheism," as a novel sect, as a "blind faith," as a magical movement pandering supernatural wonders, and as the source of scandalous doctrines. First, we have seen that Pliny, Suetonius, and Tacitus all agreed that Christianity was a *superstitio*.[131] Among the educated, the term *superstitio* designated irrational, fanatical, exotic, idiosyncratic, or degenerate religion.[132] "Superstition" was associated with irreligion and impiety (*asebia*).[133] True *religio* "promoted and engendered virtue, justice, public morality, whereas superstition did not."[134] Therefore, in the Greco-Roman world, impiety carried political undertones of sedition. As Cicero explained, "In all probability the disappearance of piety towards the gods will entail the disappearance of loyalty and social union among men as well, and of justice itself, the queen of all the virtues."[135]

Second, pagan critics such as Crescens, Lucian, and Porphyry accused Christians of "atheism."[136] Minucius Felix's pagan interlocutor exclaims, "They despise the temples as no better than sepulchers, abominate the gods, sneer at our sacred rites."[137] Faithful Christians also refused to participate in the imperial cult, a central facet of public ritual.[138] They would not take an oath by the emperor's Genius, nor sacrifice to the gods on his behalf.[139] Tertullian repeats a common anti-Christian accusation in his *Apology*: "You do not worship the gods … and you do not offer sacrifice for the emperors."[140]

Third, critics came to view Christianity as a novel sect. Galen closely associated Christianity with Judaism ("the followers of Moses and Christ"), and he merged criticisms common to both. Other pagan authors, however, began to discriminate between the two, and they used the schismatic origin of Christianity to their argumentative advantage. Judaism was "vindicated by its antiquity," even if it exhibited some of the same exclusivistic, antisocial tendencies as Christianity.[141] Christianity, however, was a religious upstart recently founded by a seditious leader, and Christians possessed neither an ethnic identity nor a national history.[142] Celsus disparaged Christianity as a rebellious sect from a people who themselves were rebels (the Jews).[143]

Fourth, Greco-Roman critics attacked Christianity as a blind faith.[144] Galen complained that Christianity relied upon faith and revelation rather than upon proof, logic, and demonstrable laws. Celsus "had no respect for religions that were based on faith alone, because in his opinion faith was a poor substitute for experienced truth."[145] Porphyry likewise condemned the Christians' "mindless and unexamined faith."[146] Hierocles ridiculed "the easy credulity of the Christians."[147] From the pagan perspective, Christians naively adopted the "stupid fables" of the Jewish scriptures and then added their own fantastic fabrications.

Fifth, pagan "outsiders" depicted Christianity as a magical movement.[148] Certain Christian rites such as exorcisms, *glossolalia*, healings, praying "in the name of Jesus," and making the sign of the cross could all be viewed as magic.[149] Celsus depicted Jesus himself as a magician who had learned his trade in Egypt.[150] Since both Christians and pagans conceded supernatural wonders, the debate centered upon the source of power. Porphyry concluded that Christians "have performed some wonders by their magic arts," but adds that "to perform wonders is no great thing."[151]

Sixth, pagan intellectuals critiqued the scandalous nature of specific Christian beliefs. For example, the Christian doctrines of incarnation, crucifixion, and atonement were "ludicrous" to Porphyry, who maintained absolute divine transcendence, immutability, and impassibility.[152] Pagan philosophers considered "resurrection in the flesh" to be "a startling, distasteful idea, at odds with everything that passed for wisdom among the educated."[153] According to Porphyry, the soul could not be saved until it was liberated from the body with its sensations and passions.[154] "Platonism," notes Simmons, "could teach a final salvation *in* and *from* the body, but never, as Christians professed, *of* the body."[155]

Christian apocalyptic material that predicted the fall of Rome (and sometimes gleefully) would have been an automatic affront to Roman officials.[156] The Christian doctrine of eternal punishment was also scandalous, and divine wrath was "held to be monstrous by the educated pagan."[157] Celsus mocked the belief that "God applies the fire like a cook," so that "all the rest of mankind will be thoroughly roasted and they alone will survive."[158] Celsus reasoned that if all religions claimed the exclusive route to salvation, how would the earnest seeker ever choose? "Are they to throw dice in order to divine where they may turn, and whom they are to follow?"[159]

Pagans also opposed the notion of the particularity of God's revelation in Jesus of Nazareth.[160] Porphyry was willing to grant that Jesus was a devout man, but he recoiled when Christians claimed Jesus as "the sole and universal source of salvation."[161] Porphyry hunted for a soteriological *via universalis*, and he recommended living in accordance with the *nous*, participating in theurgical purifications, and rejecting bodily passions. Christian authors could borrow aspects of this philosophical program, but they still emphasized God's redemptive works in history and particularity in Jesus Christ and thereby downplayed argumentation based upon human reason confined to the abstract.[162] But this Christian response lies beyond the purview of this essay.

Further reading

Primary sources

R. M. Berchman, *Porphyry Against the Christians*, Leiden: Brill, 2005. (An introduction to Porphyry and his polemical material against Christianity, followed by translations of fragments and testimonia.)

Celsus, trans. R. J. Hoffmann, *Celsus: On the True Doctrine: A Discourse against the Christians*, New York: Oxford University Press, 1987. (A lively rendition of Celsus's arguments that attempts to restore his original tenor and style, an admittedly subjective endeavor.)

Secondary sources

T. D. Barnes, "Pagan Perceptions of Christianity," in Ian Hazlett (ed.), *Early Christianity: Origins and Evolution to A.D. 400*, London: SPCK, 1991, pp. 231–44. (A brief survey of the pagan social attitudes directed toward Christians, ranging from hostile contempt to intellectual acceptance.)

S. Benko, "Pagan Criticism of Christianity During the First Two Centuries," *Aufstieg und Niedergang der römischen Welt* 2.23.2, Berlin: Walter de Gruyter, 1980, pp. 1055–1118. (A compilation and critical analysis of the primary source critiques of Christianity from Suetonius to Galen, as well as a synopsis of Celsus's polemic.)

G. Clark, *Christianity and Roman Society*, Cambridge: Cambridge University Press, 2004. (A concise yet rich study that includes a chapter on "Christians and Others," which discusses how pagans viewed early Christianity.)

C. De Vos, "Popular Graeco-Roman Responses to Christianity," in P. F. Esler (ed.), *The Early Christian World*, London: Routledge, 2000, pp. 869–89. (An evaluation of the popular resentment arising from Christianity's threat to traditional Greco-Roman society.)

R. L. Fox, *Pagans and Christians*, New York: Knopf, 1987. (An extensive yet engaging portrait of the vigor of pagan religiosity and the eventual triumph of Christianity.)

A. Meredith, "Porphyry and Julian against the Christians," *Aufstieg und Niedergang in der römischen Welt* 2.23.2, Berlin: Walter de Gruyter, 1980, pp. 1119–49. (A critical review of the anti-Christian polemic of Porphyry and Julian, accompanied by an assessment of relevant modern scholarship.)

M. B. Simmons, "Graeco-Roman Philosophical Opposition," in P. F. Esler (ed.), *The Early Christian World*, vol. 2, London: Routledge, 2000, pp. 840–68. (An examination of the "increasingly hostile" and refined attack upon Christianity represented by Celsus, Porphyry, Hierocles, and Julian.)

R. L. Wilken, *The Christians as the Romans Saw Them*, New Haven, CT: Yale University Press, 1984. (A fascinating interpretation of the pagan descriptions and critiques of early Christianity, grounded in scholarly expertise but targeting a wide audience.)

Notes

1 R. L. Wilken, "Toward a Social Interpretation of Early Christian Apologetics," *Church History* 39, 1970, pp. 438–9.

2 G. Clark, *Christianity and Roman Society*, Cambridge: Cambridge University Press, 2005, p. 17.

3 E. R. Dodds, *Pagan and Christian in an Age of Anxiety*, New York: Cambridge University Press, 1965, p. 103.

4 R. MacMullen, *Christianizing the Roman Empire: A.D. 100–400*, New Haven, CT: Yale University Press, 1984, pp. 38; 135, n. 24.

5 Justin, *First Apology* 2; trans. L.W. Barnard, *St. Justin Martyr: The First and Second Apologies*, New York: Paulist, 1997, p. 23. One notes how Justin turned the charge of "superstition" back upon his opponents.

6 E. C. Colwell, "Popular Reactions against Christianity in the Roman Empire," in J. T. McNeill, M. Spink, and H. R. Willoughby (eds), *Environmental Factors in Christian History*, Chicago: University of Chicago Press, 1939, pp. 53–71; J. Engberg, *Impulsore Chresto: Opposition to Christianity in the Roman Empire c. 50–250 AD*, Frankfurt am Main: Peter Lang, 2007.

7 Cf. Tertullian, *Apology* 7.8–14.

8 A. N. Sherwin-White, "The Early Persecutions and Roman Law Again," *Journal of Theological Studies* 3, 1952, p. 212. The standard procedure against Christians was "accusatory" rather than "inquisitorial," and therefore required a formal denunciation by a *delator* (G. E. M. Ste Croix, "Why Were the Early Christians Persecuted?" *Past and Present* 26, 1963, p. 15).

9 R. L. Wilken, "Christians as the Romans (and Greeks) Saw Them," in E. P. Sanders (ed.), *Jewish and Christian Self-definition*, vol. 2, London: SCM, 1980, p. 101.

10 R. L. Wilken, *The Christians as the Romans Saw Them*, New Haven, CT: Yale University Press, 1984, p. xv.

11 M. Sordi, *The Christians and the Roman Empire*, trans. A. Bedini, Norman, OK: University of Oklahoma, 1986, p. 161.

12 See M. B. Simmons, "Graeco-Roman Philosophical Opposition," in P. F. Esler (ed.), *The Early Christian World*, vol. 2, London: Routledge, 2000, p. 851.

13 On Christian assemblies as *collegia* (clubs) or burial societies, see Pliny, *Letters* 10.33–34, 10.96; Wilken, *Christians as the Romans Saw Them*, pp. 31–47.

14 See C. N. Cochrane, *Christianity and Classical Culture*, Oxford: Oxford University Press, 1957; H. Chadwick, *Early Christian Thought and the Classical Tradition*, Oxford: Oxford University Press, 1966.

15 Cf. C. Andresen, "The Integration of Platonism into Early Christian Theology," *Studia Patristica* 15.1, 1984, pp. 399–413.

16 Wilken, *Christians as the Romans Saw Them*, p. 200.

17 Wilken, *Christians as the Romans Saw Them*, p. 205.

18 Wilken, *Christians as the Romans Saw Them*, p. xvi.

19 See H. Remus, "Outside/Inside: Celsus on Jewish and Christian *Nomoi*," in J. Neusner *et al.* (eds), *New Perspectives on Judaism*, vol. 2, Lanham, MD: University Press of America, 1987, pp. 133–50.

20 Suetonius, *Life of Nero* 16.2, cf. 19.3; trans. J. C. Rolfe, *Suetonius*, vol. 2, Loeb Classical Library, London: Heinemann, 1939, p. 111.

21 Suetonius, *The Deified Claudius* 25; trans. Rolfe, *Suetonius*, p. 53.

22 For evidence, see S. Benko, "Pagan Criticism of Christianity during the First Two Centuries A.D.," in *Aufstieg und Niedergang der römischen Welt* 2.23.2, Berlin: Walter de Gruyter, 1980, pp. 1057–8.

23 D. Slingerland, "Chrestus: Christus?," in A. J. Avery-Peck (ed.), *The Literature of Early Rabbinic Judaism: Issues in Talmudic Redaction and Interpretation*, vol. 4 of J. Neusner, E. S. Frerichs, W. S. Green, G. Porton *et al.* (eds), *New Perspectives on Ancient Judaism*, Studies in Judaism, Lanham, MD: University Press of America, 1989, pp. 133–44.

24 Tacitus, *Annals* 15.44. E. Laupot further argues that the reference to *Christiani* in the piece known as "Tacitus' Fragment 2" (Sulpicius Severus, *Chronicles* 2.30.6–7) is genuine (E. Laupot, "Tacitus' Fragment 2: The Anti-Roman Movement of the *Christiani* and the Nazoreans," *Vigiliae Christianae* 54, 2000, pp. 233–47).

25 Ste Croix, "Why Were the Early Christians Persecuted?," p. 8.

26 Tacitus, *Annals* 15.44.2–4.

27 Tacitus, *Annals* 15.44; trans. J. J. Jackson, in *Tacitus: The Histories and The Annals*, vol. 4, Loeb Classical Library, London: Heinemann, 1937, p. 283.

28 Tacitus, *Histories* 5.5.

29 According to R. MacMullen, Pliny's trouble with Christians concerned only Pontus (see MacMullen, *Christianizing the Roman Empire*, p. 135, n. 26).

30 Pliny the Younger, *Letters* 10.96.

31 Recent studies include A. Reichert, "Durchdachte Konfusion: Plinius, Trajan und das Christentum," *Zeitschrift für die neutestamentliche Wissenschaft und die Kunde der älteren Kirche* 93, 2002, pp. 227–50; K. Thraede, "Noch Einmal: Plinius d. J. und die Christen," *Zeitschrift für die neutestamentliche Wissenschaft und die Kunde der älteren Kirche* 95, 2004, pp. 102–28.

32 See Benko, "Pagan Criticism of Christianity," pp. 1073–4.

33 Pliny the Younger, *Letters* 10.96; adapted from trans. W. Melmoth, *Pliny: Letters*, vol. 2, London: Heinemann, 1927, pp. 401–3.

34 Ibid.

35 Pliny the Younger, *Letters* 10.97; Eusebius, *Ecclesiastical History* 4.8.6, 4.9.1–3, 4.26.10; Justin, *First Apology* 68. See Benko, "Pagan Criticism of Christianity," pp. 1079–80.

36 Epictetus, *Discourses* 4.7.4–6.

37 Epictetus, *Discourses* 4.1.3; adapted from trans. W. A. Oldfather, *Epictetus: The Discourses as Reported by Arrian, the Manual, and Fragments*, vol. 2, Loeb Classical Library, London: Heinemann, 1946, p. 361.

38 Some have deemed the text to be a reference to Galilean Zealots, but compare Lucian, *Peregrinus* 13; Marcus Aurelius, *Meditations* 11.3; cf. Origen, *Against Celsus* 8.65; R. Walzer, *Galen on Jews and Christians*, London: Oxford University Press, 1949, p. 15. Julian "the Apostate" reused the label "Galileans" as a reference to Christians. Clark theorizes that Epictetus may have confused Jews and Christians in *Discourses* 2.9.20–21 (see Clark, *Christianity and Roman Society*, p. 27).

39 Eusebius, *Ecclesiastical History* 4.13.1–7; trans. K. Lake, *Eusebius: The Ecclesiastical History*, vol. 1, Loeb Classical Library, London: Heinemann, 1965, p. 333.

40 Justin, *First Apology* 68.

41 Benko, "Pagan Criticism of Christianity," p. 1093.

42 Marcus Aurelius, *Meditations* 11.3. Some maintain that the words referring to Christians have been interpolated. See P. A. Brunt, "Marcus Aurelius and the Christians," in C. Deroux (ed.), *Studies in Latin Literature and Roman History*, vol. 1, Brussels: Latomus, 1979, pp. 483–519.

43 Marcus Aurelius, *Meditations* 11.3; trans. A. S. L. Farquharson, *The Meditations of Marcus Aurelius Antoninus*, Oxford: Oxford University Press, 1989, p. 102.

44 Galen's commentary on Plato's work; trans. Walzer, *Galen on Jews and Christians*, p. 15. Cf. S. Gero, "Galen on the Christians: A Reappraisal of the Arabic Evidence," *Orientalia Christiana Periodica* 56, 1990, pp. 371–411.

45 Galen, *On the Differences of Pulses* 3.3; trans. Walzer, *Galen on Jews and Christians*, p. 14.

46 Galen's commentary on Plato's work; trans. Walzer, *Galen on Jews and Christians*, p. 15.

47 Galen, *On the Differences of Pulses* 2.4; trans. Walzer, *Galen on Jews and Christians*, p. 14.

48 Galen's commentary on Plato's work; trans. Walzer, *Galen on Jews and Christians*, p. 15.

49 S. Benko, *Pagan Rome and the Early Christians*, Bloomington, IN: Indiana University Press, 1986, p. 144.

50 Benko, "Pagan Criticism of Christianity," p. 1078.

51 Minucius Felix, *Octavius* 9.6; 31.2; cf. Sordi, *Christians and the Roman Empire*, pp. 197–98. Minucius Felix may have preserved a fragment of this oration in *Octavius* 8–9 (Benko, "Pagan Criticism of Christianity," pp. 1081–9). Barnes argues that Fronto more probably attacked Christianity in the lost work *Against Pelops* (T. D. Barnes, "Pagan Perceptions of Christianity," in I. Hazlett [ed.], *Early Christianity: Origins and Evolution to A.D. 400*, London: SPCK, 1991, pp. 233–4). Cf. C. P. Hammond Bammel, "Die erste lateinische Rede gegen die Christen," *Zeitschrift für Kirchengeschichte* 104, 1993, pp. 295–311.

52 See Sordi, *Christians and the Roman Empire*, pp. 195, 198.

53 Aelius Aristides, *Orations* 3.671; trans. C. A. Behr, *Aelius Aristides: The Complete Works*, vol. 1, Leiden: Brill, 1986, p. 275.

54 Benko, "Pagan Criticism of Christianity," p. 1098.

55 Colwell, "Popular Reactions against Christianity in the Roman Empire," p. 61.

56 Origen, *Against Celsus* 3.55. From the Christian standpoint, the local assembly (ἐκκλησία) functioned as an alternative family, offering practical aid, spiritual community, and mutual support (see Clark, *Christianity and Roman Society*, p. 21).

57 Cf. *Acts of Paul and Thecla* 8–15, 20.

58 Colwell, "Popular Reactions against Christianity in the Roman Empire," p. 62.

59 Apuleius, *The Golden Ass* 9.14; trans. J. A. Hanson, *Apuleius: Metamorphoses*, vol. 2, Loeb Classical Library, Cambridge, MA: Harvard University Press, 1989, pp. 151–3.

60 T. D. Barnes overstates the case when he argues that the baker's wife is "unambiguously and unmistakeably depicted as a Christian" (Barnes, "Pagan Perceptions of Christianity," p. 233).

61 Trans. H. E. Butler, *The Apologia and Florida of Apuleius of Madaura*, Oxford: Clarendon, 1909, p. 97.

62 V. Hunink, "Apuleius, Pudentilla, and Christianity," *Vigiliae Christianae* 54, 2000, p. 90.

63 H. V. Schmidt, "Reaktionen auf das Christentum in den *Metamorphosen* des Apuleius," *Vigiliae Christianae* 51, 1997, pp. 51–71.

64 Sordi, *Christians and the Roman Empire*, p. 161.

65 Lucian, *Peregrinus* 12; cf. Justin, *Second Apology* 10; Athenagoras, *Plea on Behalf of Christians* 8.2.

66 Trans. A. M. Harmon, *Lucian*, vol. 5, Loeb Classical Library, London: Heinemann, 1936, p. 15.

67 Lucian, *Alexander* 25; adapted from trans. Harmon, *Lucian*, vol. 4, p. 209.

68 Lucian, *Alexander* 38. See Sordi, *Christians and the Roman Empire*, p. 162. "Death to the ... " is a dynamic translation of ἔξω.

69 Benko argues that Lucian viewed the Christian movement as a philosophical school or a new oriental mystery, or perhaps a blend of both (Benko, "Pagan Criticism of Christianity," p. 1097).

70 M. J. Edwards, "Satire and Verisimilitude: Christianity in Lucian's *Peregrinus*," *Historia* 38, 1989, p. 89.

71 Benko, *Pagan Rome and the Early Christians*, p. 140.

72 R. J. Hoffmann, *Celsus: On the True Doctrine*, New York: Oxford University Press, 1987; M. Frede, "Origen's Treatise *Against Celsus*," in M. Edwards, M. Goodman, and S. Price (eds), *Apologetics in the Roman Empire: Pagans, Jews and Christians*, Oxford: Oxford University Press, 1999, p. 132.

73 Wilken, *Christians as the Romans Saw Them*, pp. 201–2; Origen, *Against Celsus* 1.14.

74 Frede, "Origen's Treatise *Against Celsus*," p. 133.

75 Origen, *Against Celsus* 1.1.

76 Origen, *Against Celsus* 8.2; trans. Benko, *Pagan Rome and the Early Christians*, p. 155.

77 Origen, *Against Celsus* 1.2.

78 Origen, *Against Celsus* 8.73; trans. H. Chadwick, *Origen: Contra Celsum*, Cambridge: Cambridge University Press, 1965, p. 509.

79 Origen, *Against Celsus* 8.55

80 Trans. Benko, *Pagan Rome and the Early Christians*, p. 153; based on Origen, *Against Celsus* 3.68; 1.27; 3.44, 50, 55, 59, 74–5; 6.7ff., 11–14, 65; 7.42, 45.

81 Origen, *Against Celsus* 3.55, 3.44; trans. Chadwick, *Origen*, p. 158.

82 Origen, *Against Celsus*, 1.9; trans. Chadwick, *Origen*, p. 12.

83 See E. V. Gallagher, *Divine Man or Magician? Celsus and Origen on Jesus*, Chico: Scholars, 1982; M. Choi, "Christianity, Magic, and Difference: Name-Calling and Resistance between the Lines in *Contra Celsum*," *Semeia* 79, 1997, pp. 75–92.

84 See Hoffmann, *Celsus*, pp. 59–62, 90, 107, 119.

85 Origen, *Against Celsus* 7.68; trans. Hoffmann, *Celsus*, p. 115.

86 Origen, *Against Celsus* 2.55.

87 Origen, *Against Celsus* 2.28; trans. Chadwick, *Origen*, p. 91.

88 Origen, *Against Celsus* 1.37.

89 Origen, *Against Celsus* 4.40.

90 Origen, *Against Celsus* 6.61.

91 See A. Stötzel, "Warum Christus so spät erschien: Die apologetische Argumentation des frühen Christentums," *Zeitschrift für Kirchengeschichte* 92, 1981, pp. 147–60.

92 Origen, *Against Celsus* 4.14.

93 R. J. Hoffmann, *Celsus*, pp. 67, 89, 95, 98; See M. Fédou, *Christianisme et religions païennes dans le Contre Celse d'Origène*, Paris: Beauchesne, 1988.

94 Origen, *Against Celsus* 3.55; trans. Hoffmann, *Celsus*, p. 73.

95 Porphyry, *On the Life of Plotinus* 16. See D. T. Runia (ed.), *Plotinus amid Gnostics and Christians*, Amsterdam: Netherlands Free University Press, 1984; C. Evangeliou, "Plotinus's Anti-Gnostic Polemic and Porphyry's Against the Christians," in R. T. Wallis and J. Bregman (eds), *Neoplatonism and Gnosticism*, Studies in Neoplatonism: Ancient and Modern 6, Albany, NY: SUNY Press, 1992, pp. 111–28.

96 See J. J. O'Meara, *Porphyry's Philosophy from Oracles in Augustine*, Paris: Études Augustiniennes, 1959.

97 Augustine, *City of God* 19.23; trans. H. Bettenson, *Saint Augustine: City of God*, London: Penguin, 2003, pp. 884–5.

98 See R. M. Berchman, *Porphyry Against the Christians*, Leiden: Brill, 2005, pp. 1–6. Berchman argues that *Against the Christians* was originally a "collection of several works," perhaps including *Philosophy from Oracles*.

99 A. Meredith, "Porphyry and Julian against the Christians," in *Aufstieg und Niedergang der römischen Welt*, 2.23.2, pp. 1119–49; J. G. Cook, "A Possible Fragment of Porphyry's *Contra Christianos* from Michael the Syrian," *Zeitschrift für Christentum* 2, 1998, pp. 113–22.

100 Barnes, "Pagan Perceptions of Christianity," p. 238.

101 Barnes, "Pagan Perceptions of Christianity," p. 239.

102 See Dodds, *Pagan and Christian in an Age of Anxiety*, p. 121; Eusebius, *Preparation for the Gospel* 1.2.2.

103 Porphyry, *Against the Christians* frg. 4; trans. J. M. Schott, "Porphyry on Christians and Others: 'Barbarian Wisdom', Identity Politics, and Anti-Christian Polemics on the Eve of the Great Persecution," *Journal of Early Christian Studies* 13, 2005, p. 303. The numbering system of the fragments is taken from A. Harnack. For a recent edition of Porphyrian fragments, see Berchman, *Porphyry Against the Christians*. Scholars have debated whether materials embedded in Macarius Magnes should be attributed to Porphyry's *Against the Christians*. T. D. Barnes concludes negatively in "Porphyry, *Against the Christians*: Date and the Attribution of Fragments," *Journal of Theological Studies* 24, 1973, pp. 424–42. R. J. Hoffmann argues affirmatively in *Porphyry's Against the Christians: The Literary Remains*, Amherst: Prometheus, 1994. See also E. DePalma Digeser, "Porphyry, Julian, or

Hierocles? The Anonymous Hellene in Makarios Magnes' *Apokritikos*," *Journal of Theological Studies* 53, 2002, pp. 466–502.

104 Porphyry, *Against the Christians* frgs 9–10.

105 Porphyry, *Against the Christians* 12, 15, 16.

106 Porphyry, *Against the Christians* 21, 30–33.

107 Lactantius, *Divine Institutes* 5. See Schott, "Porphyry on Christians and Others," pp. 285–7.

108 Lactantius, *On the Deaths of Persecutors* 11, 16.

109 Simmons, "Graeco-Roman Philosophical Opposition," p. 848.

110 Eusebius, *Against Hierocles* 2; trans. Simmons, "Graeco-Roman Philosophical Opposition," p. 849.

111 Ibid.

112 Simmons, "Graeco-Roman Philosophical Opposition," p. 849.

113 Simmons, "Graeco-Roman Philosophical Opposition," p. 861.

114 Benko, *Pagan Rome and the Early Christians*, p. 158, referring specifically to Celsus.

115 According to Tertullian, *Apology* 37.4, Christians could be observed in the imperial palace and the senate. A Valerian edict of 257 suggests that Christians were found among senators and *equites Romani* (Cyprian, *Letters* 80.2). Of course, Christian apologists naturally emphasized such examples to improve the overall social reputation of Christianity. On the "socially mixed character of the early Christian communities," see E. A. Judge, "The Social Identity of the First Christians: A Question of Method in Religious History," *Journal of Religious History* 11, 1980, pp. 201–17.

116 Cf. Tatian, *Oration* 33.

117 See J. M. Schott, "Porphyry on Christians and Others."

118 A. H. M. Jones, "The Social Background of the Struggle between Paganism and Christianity," in A. Momigliano (ed.), *The Conflict between Paganism and Christianity in the Fourth Century*, Oxford: Clarendon, 1963, p. 20; cf. Origen, *Against Celsus* 4.87, 6.2.

119 Jones, "Social Background of the Struggle," p. 20.

120 This approach was criticized by pagan opponents. See P. Sellew, "Achilles or Christ: Porphyry and Didymus in Debate over Allegorical Interpretation," *Harvard Theological Review* 82, 1989, pp. 79–100; cf. Eusebius, *Ecclesiastical History* 6.19.4.

121 Simmons, "Graeco-Roman Philosophical Opposition," pp. 844–7.

122 *Martyrdom of Polycarp* 12.2; Irenaeus, *Demonstration of the Apostolic Preaching* 97; Justin, *First Apology* 1; *Second Apology* 2. See G. E. M. Ste Croix, "Why Were the Early Christians Persecuted? – A Rejoinder," *Past and Present* 27, 1964, pp. 28–33; D. Horrell, "The Label Χριστιανός: 1 Peter 4:16 and the Formation of Christian Identity," *Journal of Biblical Literature* 126, 2007, pp. 361–81.

123 Justin, *First Apology* 4; trans. Barnard, *St. Justin Martyr*, p. 24.

124 *Acts of Paul and Thecla* 15, 20; Athenagoras, *Plea on Behalf of Christians* 3.31; Justin, *First Apology* 26; *Second Apology* 12; *Dialogue with Trypho* 10; Tertullian, *Apology* 6–8; Minucius Felix, *Octavius* 8–9, 28, 30–31; Origen, *Against Celsus* 6.27, 40; Eusebius, *Ecclesiastical History* 4.7.11; 5.1.14–26; 9.5.2.

125 Tertullian, *Apology* 2.3; trans. R. Arbesmann, E. J. Daly, and E. A. Quain, *Tertullian: Apologetical Works and Minucius Felix: Octavius*, New York: Fathers of the Church, 1950, p. 10.

126 Origen, *Against Celsus* 1.3. Cf. the reappearance of "secrecy" in Origen, *Against Celsus* 1.1, 7; 8.17, 39.

127 Dodds, *Pagan and Christian in an Age of Anxiety*, p. 111.

128 Origen, *Against Celsus* 8.17.

129 Minucius Felix, *Octavius* 8; trans. Arbesmann *et al.*, *Tertullian*, p. 335.

130 Clark, *Christianity and Roman Society*, pp. 20, 24.

131 Tacitus, *Annals* 15.44; Suetonius, *Deified Claudius* 25.3; *Life of Nero* 16.3; Pliny the Younger, *Letters* 10.96–97. Cf. Origen, *Against Celsus* 3.29, 79; 4.5.

132 See L. F. Janssen, "'Superstitio' and the Persecution of Christians," *Vigiliae Christianae* 33, 1979, pp. 131–59. *Religio deos colit, superstitio violat* (Seneca, *On Clemency* 2.3.1).

133 Wilken, "Toward a Social Interpretation," 440. Philo, however, distinguishes between superstition and impiety (Philo, *On the Special Laws* 5.147–48).

134 Wilken, "Toward a Social Interpretation," 439.

135 Cicero, *On the Nature of the Gods* 1.3–4; trans. Wilken, "Christians as the Romans (and Greeks) Saw Them," p. 107.

136 Lucian, *Alexander* 25, 38; Apuleius, *The Golden Ass* 9.14. See the charge of "atheism" as found in *Martyrdom of Polycarp* 3.2; 9.2; 12.2; *Epistle to Diognetus* 2.6; Justin, *First Apology* 5–6, 13; Eusebius, *Ecclesiastical History* 5.1.9; Athenagoras, *Plea on Behalf of Christians* 1, 3, 4–30; Clement of Alexandria, *Miscellanies* 7.1.1; Tertullian, *Apology* 6.10, 10.1–28.2; Arnobius, *Against the Gentiles* 1.29, 3.28, 5.30, 6.27. Cf. W. R. Schoedel, "Christian 'Atheism' and the Peace of the Roman Empire," *Church History* 42, 1973, pp. 309–19; J. J. Walsh, "On Christian Atheism," *Vigiliae Christianae* 45, 1991, pp. 255–77.

137 Minucius Felix, *Octavius* 8; trans. Arbesmann *et al.*, *Tertullian*, p. 335.

138 See D. L. Jones, "Christianity and the Roman Imperial Cult," in *Aufstieg und Niedergang der römischen Welt* 2.23.2, pp. 1023–54.

139 Ste Croix downplays the role of emperor-worship proper in "Why Were the Early Christians Persecuted?," p. 10.

140 Tertullian, *Apology* 10.1; trans. Arbesmann, *et al.*, *Tertullian*, p. 35.

141 Origen, *Against Celsus* 5.25–26, 5.34–35; cf. Tacitus, *Histories* 5.5.

142 See P. Stockmeier, "Christlicher Glaube und antike Religiosität," in *Aufstieg und Niedergang der römischen Welt* 2.23.2, pp. 871–909.

143 This turn of phrase comes from Wilken, "Christians as the Romans (and Greeks) Saw Them," p. 120. See Origen, *Against Celsus* 3.1, 4.31.

144 See J. Bregman, "Logismos and Pistis," in R. C. Smith and J. Lounibos (eds), *Pagan and Christian Anxiety: A Response to E. R. Dodds*, Lanham, MD: University Press of America, 1984, pp. 217–31.

145 Benko, *Pagan Rome and the Early Christians*, p. 142.

146 See E. A. Judge, "Christian Innovation and Its Contemporary Observers," in B. Croke and A. M. Emmett (eds), *History and Historians in Late Antiquity*, Sydney: Pergamon, 1983, p. 17.

147 Eusebius, *Against Hierocles* 2; trans. Simmons, "Graeco-Roman Philosophical Opposition," p. 849.

148 Origen, *Against Celsus* 1.9; Minucius Felix, *Octavius* 11.6. See A. B. Kolenkow, "A Problem of Power: How Miracle-Doers Counter Charges of Magic in the Hellenistic World," *Society of Biblical Literature Seminar Papers*, 1976, pp. 105–10; H. Remus, *Pagan–Christian Conflict over Miracle in the Second Century*, Cambridge, MA: Philadelphia Patristic Foundation, 1983.

149 See Tertullian, *To His Wife* 5.

150 Origen, *Against Celsus* 2.52–53; 8.9.

151 Porphyry, *Against the Christians* frg. 4; trans. Dodds, *Pagan and Christian in an Age of Anxiety*, p. 125.

152 M. B. Simmons, "Porphyry of Tyre's Biblical Criticism: A Historical and Theological Appraisal," in C. A. Bobertz and D. Brakke (eds), *Reading in Christian Communities*, Notre Dame: University of Notre Dame Press, 2002, pp. 96–7.

153 MacMullen, *Christianizing the Roman Empire*, p. 12; cf. H. Chadwick, "Celsus and the Resurrection of the Body," *Harvard Theological Review* 41, 1948, pp. 83–102.

154 Simmons, "Porphyry of Tyre's Biblical Criticism," p. 100.

155 Simmons, "Graeco-Roman Philosophical Opposition," pp. 857–8.

156 See A. Momigliano, "Some Preliminary Remarks on the 'Religious Opposition' to the Roman Empire," in *On Pagans, Jews, and Christians*, Middletown, CT: Wesleyan University Press, 1987, pp. 120–41.

157 A. Cameron, "Palladas and Christian Polemic," *Journal of Roman Studies* 55, 1965, p. 26.

158 Origen, *Against Celsus* 5.15–16; trans. Chadwick, *Origen*, pp. 275–6.

159 Origen, *Against Celsus* 6.11; trans. Chadwick, *Origen*, p. 324.

160 See M. Fédou, "L'unicité du Christ selon le *Contre Celse* d'Origène," *Studia Patristica* 36, 2001, pp. 415–20.

161 Schott, "Porphyry on Christians and Others," 312; cf. Porphyry's oracle in Augustine, *City of God* 19.23.

162 Simmons, "Porphyry of Tyre's Biblical Criticism," pp. 99–100. See also L. Alexander, "'Foolishness to the Greeks': Jews and Christians in the Public Life of the Empire," in G. Clark and T. Rajak (eds), *Philosophy and Power in the Graeco-Roman World*. Oxford: Oxford University Press, 2002, pp. 229–49.

4
JEWS AND CHRISTIANS
Lynn H. Cohick

Perhaps more than for most issues, one's starting point in speaking about Christian–Jewish relations sets the course for one's conclusions. To begin with stories about Paul's rejection by Jews in the book of Acts leads often to an expectation of conflict between Jews and Christians in the second- and third-century sources. Focus on theological statements about Christology or the church often propels the reader to conclude that Christians did not interact a great deal with "real" Jews, but were engaged in an intense struggle to define Christianity. If one proposes at the outset that Christianity should be understood as a sect of Judaism, the sociological tools from this kit will suggest rivalry (between parent and child or between siblings) as the natural course, and conflict between the groups in their literature and in society becomes the accepted course of growth. Assumptions about the nature of the literary evidence – dialogues, theological treatises, rabbinic texts, *Adversus Iudaeos* writings, sermons – and the place of archaeological remains, Roman imperialism, and pagan authors' accounts significantly impact the argument. Moreover, scholars often examine the early engagement between Jews and Christians with an apologetic eye to explaining current Jewish–Christian dialogue or suggesting paths of reconciliation. This essay will trace the history of modern examination of second- and third-century Christian–Jewish relations, paying special attention to the underlying presuppositions which motivate and shape the analysis. A word about terminology; I am choosing to label this study as "Christian–Jewish" relations rather than the more normal "Jewish–Christian" relations. My purpose in this is to distinguish the broad category from the narrower group of Christians who were either Jews by birth or who affiliated with Judaism, and thus are called "Jewish Christians." This group plays a critical role in some scholars' reconstruction of the relationship between Jews and Christians.

Modern history of interpretation

Analysis of the Christian–Jewish relationship often begins with a nod to, if not a discussion of, Adolf von Harnack's historical reconstruction.[1] Harnack assumed it to be normal that Christianity would supersede Judaism and assume prominence in the Roman Empire. He argued that the "Jew" found in Christian writings was a literary construct exploited in an intra-Christian debate about the nature of Christianity. In

Justin's *Dialogue with Trypho the Jew*, he admitted that perhaps there lurks a real figure behind the text, but for the most part, Harnack did not believe that he could recover historical Jews from Christian texts. Additionally, he did not think it mattered to do so, for ancient Judaism was dead or dying, having deteriorated socially and religiously after losing to Rome in several revolts and succumbing to forces of syncretism in its interactions with Hellenism. The Jewish missionary attitude, once pulsating, grew listless due to its failure to accept as full members the gentile converts; Christianity put right the weakness and soon surpassed its rival in numbers of adherents. Judaism became inwardly focused and Christianity had no substantive interaction with Jews from the end of the first century.

Reacting strongly against Harnack's reconstruction, Marcel Simon found a vibrant Jewish interlocutor engaged in direct, lively debate with Christians.[2] Writing in 1948, Simon argued that Jews had a compelling missionary stance which put them at odds with the emerging Christian church's efforts to win converts. The two groups struggled against each other for pagan converts, as brothers might over an inheritance, using whatever means possible to win as many to their side; some label this the "conflict theory."[3] Moreover, rabbinic Judaism did not emerge immediately after the destruction of the temple; Judaism in its variety continued to engage with the Greco-Roman culture as a vital force. Simon cautioned that "the split [between Christianity and Judaism] came into being gradually, and at different rates in different places."[4] He located the beginning of a hardening between the groups in the second century, with the rise of ecclesial structures and Talmudic writings. The Second Revolt and the increase of anti-Jewish literature by Christian authors is a significant signpost on the way to full separation in the fourth century with the triumph of the church.

Simon's theory has held sway for the last quarter century, even as parts of his analysis have come under review. While the assumption, that conflict to one degree or another reflects the historical situation for Jews and Christians, has taken root in historians' imaginations, certain key aspects of the theory have been called into question, including the contention that Judaism was a missionary religion in the first few centuries CE. Rather than compete for pagan converts, as the theory argues, Jews seemed to have welcomed gentiles interested in Judaism, while not actively proselytizing.[5] The antagonism of some Christian texts against Jews and Judaism is explained as part of the intra-Christian debate over who defines Christianity. This raises a central issue in understanding Christian–Jewish relations, namely how to interpret Christian anti-Jewish rhetoric. Does it hold any connection to historical circumstances, or does it reflect only a constructed, symbolic Jew? Do we find social reality encoded in the rhetoric, or are we reading a theological argument detached from actual contemporary Jews? If the former is chosen, then the way is opened for allowing a concrete basis for Christian vitriol against Jews, who apparently harassed and persecuted Christians. If the latter is chosen, a symbolic portrayal of Jews is privileged, and historical Jews are erased from the landscape. For most, the response lies somewhere in the middle, determined by the specific passage analyzed.

Recently the phrase, "parting of the ways," has been used to describe Christian–Jewish relations, wherein two religions, Christianity and Judaism, separated and began establishing their own identities. Some suggest this separation occurred in CE 70 or 135, with the failed revolts and the destruction of the Temple, while others locate it in the period of Constantine. Some argue the separation took an uneven course, transpiring at different times in various locales.[6] The division between Judaism and Christianity is described as involving conflict, revealing an underlying historical interchange between Christians and Jews, often for a place within the city and the spoils of gentile converts. Representative of this position is the work edited by James D. G. Dunn, *Jews and Christians: The Parting of the Ways*.[7] In response to this model, Adam Becker and Annette Yoshiko Reed edited a volume provocatively titled *The Ways That Never Parted*.[8] These essays recommend that Jews and Christians maintained dynamic social interactions. Additionally, Daniel Boyarin argues that boundaries between Christians and Jews are artificial and imposed; thus he speaks of partitions.[9] Rather than "parting of the ways" he proposes that similarities might be the result of convergence of differences based on proximity. In a similar vein, Andrew Jacobs suggests understanding identity-building as involving dialogue, not conflict. Group identity-building occurs as it negotiates with the other, with each group's identity being less solid, less rigid, especially near the periphery.[10]

Defining and describing Christian and Jew

A significant problem faces any student of Christian–Jewish relations – what constitutes a Christian? One possible answer is to identify Christian with the Apostolic Fathers, church fathers, and related Christian literature preserved in the main streams of the Christian tradition. This will be our approach, given the purpose of this volume. Another tactic would be to accept self-definition; however, this would be too broad, in terms of potential textual and theological contact points between Jews and Christians, to serve our analytical purpose. In our period of the second and third centuries CE, the church lives under Roman imperialism and Greco-Roman religion, much as do the Jews, with both groups negotiating this reality. Unlike Jews, however, who at least in theory were protected under Roman law, gentile Christians faced initially sporadic and later systematic persecution by the Roman government. Questions of proper belief and practice become highly focused in such an environment, as apologists and bishops sought to shore up the faithful, deal with the lapsed, and defend Christianity against charges of antisocial crimes such as incest, infanticide, and cannibalism.

Another key difficulty in describing Christian–Jewish relations is imagining what a particular Jewish community would look like that might engage a Christian congregation, or vice versa. We cannot assume a fully functioning and dominant rabbinic Judaism in Palestine and the Diaspora during the late second and third centuries. Nor does the evidence suggest a withdrawn, segregated Jewish community. For example, a Jewish funerary inscription from the Imperial period identifies a father with the title *archiatros*, an honorary position bestowed by the city, given to a personal physician of a ruler. This inscription is representative of a significant number, indicating that (at least some) Jews integrated fully with the "Graeco-Roman society and the ethos of the Hellenic *polis*."[11] The Jewish community's political standing is more difficult to sort out. Josephus and Philo speak of Diaspora Jewish communities in major cities such as Alexandria, Syrian Antioch, and major centers in Asia Minor, as having their own *politeia* (citizenship or commonwealth), and being granted *isotimia* (equal honor) or *isonomia* (equality under the law). What exactly these terms denote continues to be debated by scholars, but a general consensus recommends, not that Jews were citizens of the city in a technical sense of having representation on the city council, but rather that they had certain rights relative to their own community. In general, Jews were able to govern themselves according to their laws, but it is unclear how these laws were understood or implemented. Roman imperial behavior seems to have taken a benign view of Jews overall; however, tensions between Greeks and Jews flared periodically. While Rome insisted on the *fiscus Iudaicus* tax (replacing the half-shekel Temple tax) after the Temple's destruction, Rome respected Jewish customs, making special exemption for Jews to practice circumcision. At the turn of the third century, Rome ruled that Jews could serve on city councils without having to take part in the Greco-Roman religious ceremonies attached to those offices. Caracalla, in 212, granted citizenship to all in the Empire, including Jews. In any case, Christian *Adversus Iudaeos* material hardly does justice to the extant evidence of Jewish vitality and robust engagement with their social milieu.

Focusing on Roman Palestine, the key question is the manner in which Jews recovered from the two devastating revolts. One argument contends that from the ashes quickly sprang rabbinic Judaism as the majority expression of Judaism. An alternative position suggests that the archaeological remains indicate that for many Jews, the defeat by the Romans shattered their faith.[12] In their daily activities, many Jews became indistinguishable from their Gentile neighbors. Local fledgling rabbinic groups had little influence outside of their limited circles in Palestine, and virtually no influence in the wider Diaspora. The reconstruction of a particular Jewish community is important, not only in its own right, but also when considering anti-Jewish rhetoric or comments by Christians about Judaism and Jews. For example, we might ask what sort of Judaism Tertullian might have encountered, considering that the revolt in CE 115–17 decimated Jewish communities for several generations in North Africa.[13] The same question can be raised concerning the possible interaction between Origen and Jewish teachers, including rabbis, in his Roman Palestine setting. We do well to ask when Chrysostom spoke against Christians attending the local synagogue, what sort of Jewish practices were followed. At this point (fourth-century Antioch) did it follow rabbinic teachings? Or was it closer to a Greco-Roman association served by patrons who offered political and economic aid to the members? Because the evidence is sparse as to how quickly rabbinic Judaism became dominant outside of Palestine (and even within Palestine) we should be cautious in assuming a specific form of Jewish worship against which Chrysostom warns. Similar questions could be asked of the Jewish community engaged by Melito of Sardis or Polycarp of Smyrna, figures discussed below.

Before we turn to individual authors, a summary picture of religion in the ancient *polis* is in order. Today we in the West segregate religion from the public sphere, understanding religious convictions to be private matters. In the ancient world, however, religion infused politics, education, and recreation, not simply at the level of intellectual assent, but in terms of public behavior. Judaism similarly held an open-door policy for its synagogues. The Apostle Paul imagines the Christian community's worship to be open to all (1 Cor. 14:23). The average Gentiles, then, were acclimatized to attend civic festivals, processions, theater productions, as well as, if they so desired, stopping in at the synagogue or dropping by the Christian service. These events had a religious component, but were also viewed as part of the social and cultural fabric of Roman life. After all, Christians (and Jews) were also Romans.[14]

A brief look at the Greco-Roman authors shows that in the early second century, Tacitus speaks of Nero blaming Christians for Rome's great fire; the emperor sentenced many to horrific deaths.[15] Interestingly, in his recounting, everyone in Rome knew who the Christians were. This implies that Christians were a discernible group, at least to Tacitus. The implications for identity formation and boundary construction are intriguing – for it suggests that Romans who followed their ancestral rites discerned the difference between Jews and Christians at this date. A similar confidence is displayed by Pliny the Younger in his communication with Trajan.[16] He understands Christians to share a few characteristics, the predominant one being the refusal to pay homage to Caesar, but to give exclusive allegiance to their god Christ. From the Jewish side, the *fiscus Iudaicus* instituted after the failed First Revolt heightened the identity issue. Scholars disagree as to whether gentile Christians would want to pay the tax and assume the protection of the synagogue, and whether the Jewish synagogue would permit such action. Domitian's intense enforcement of the tax may suggest that Rome was fairly certain it could isolate and identify Jews from their Gentile neighbors.[17]

Ancient sources

In the first or second decade of the second century, Ignatius, bishop of Antioch, sent six letters to churches in Asia Minor and Rome instructing them on matters of faith and explaining his own journey to martyrdom in Rome. In two letters he speaks directly about Judaism. In his letter *To the Philadelphians*, he warns readers, "But if anyone expounds Judaism to you, do not listen to him. For it is better to hear about Christianity from a man who is circumcised than about Judaism from one who is not. But if either of them fails to speak about Jesus Christ, I look on them as tombstones and graves of the dead."[18] In the letter *To the Magnesians*, he writes, "For if we continue to live in accordance with Judaism, we admit that we have not received grace. For the most godly prophets lived in accordance with Christ Jesus."[19] In the next chapter he continues, "If, then, those who had lived according to ancient practices came to the newness of hope, no longer keeping the Sabbath but living in accordance with the Lord's day … ."[20] And in chapter ten he urges, "It is utterly absurd to profess Jesus Christ and to practice Judaism. For Christianity did not believe in Judaism, but Judaism in Christianity."[21] These statements form the basis for discussion about Ignatius's interaction with Jews.

For some, these texts highlight the tension between the Christians in these communities and their Jewish counterparts. But the question is, which communities? It may be that Ignatius is assuming or imposing his own Syrian Antioch context onto the churches in Asia Minor. Some draw a straight line from Ignatius's views as representing early second-century Antioch to Chrysostom in fourth-century Antioch; in the intervening 250 years, Christians remained interested in Judaism and the synagogue.[22] Others suggest that Ignatius dealt with what he observed in Philadelphia and Smyrna (the two cities he visited), and used that information to address a similar situation in Magnesia.[23] If the latter is assumed, the phrase in *To the Magnesians* 8.1 "if we continue to live according to Judaism" might indicate that Gentile god-fearers from the synagogue have migrated to the church, and are encouraging practices and beliefs similar to those they followed in the synagogue. Those include following Sabbath, but also teaching a docetic Christology.[24] By attacking these former god-fearers' judaizing, Ignatius is reasserting Christianity's superiority over Judaism, including the local synagogue. Perhaps some in this church are visiting the synagogue to access scriptures, and Ignatius views this as dangerously close to Judaism.

Those unconvinced by the conflict model suggest that overall in his letter *To the Magnesians*, Ignatius is responding to aberrant theology espoused by Docetists, rather than attacking judaizing practices (11.1). By drawing on an anti-Judaic corpus to make analogies about what a true Christian life looks like, Ignatius reinforces a Christian identity. Judaism is described as both living apart from grace (8.1) but also as that which, through the prophets, accurately foretold and professed Christianity (9.2, 10.3). These prophets knew the Son, who was the Word (8.2); this theological conviction is aimed at those who would deny the "birth and the suffering and the resurrection that took place during the time of the governorship of Pontius Pilate."[25] A similar conclusion could be drawn from assessing the statement which leads to *To the Philadelphians* 6.1, wherein Ignatius praises the prophets whose messages point to the gospel. Thus the Christians are urged to close their ears to anyone propounding Judaism, because they will not present the prophets' teaching correctly. Additionally, 6.1 can be read in light of 8.2:

> For I heard some saying, "If I do not find it in the archives, I do not believe in the gospel" and when I said to them, "it is written," they replied, "That is just the issue." But for me "the archives" are Jesus Christ; the inviolable archives are his cross and death and his resurrection and the faith which comes through him.
>
> (Ignatius, *To the Philadelphians* 8.2)[26]

Ignatius is not making a judgment on the ethnic background of the speaker as much as he is commenting on the proper interpretation of the scriptures.

Shortly after Ignatius's letters, we encounter Justin Martyr's *Dialogue with Trypho the Jew*. Justin wrote his *Dialogue* in Rome, c. 155–60, after he composed his *First Apology*. Yet the setting of the *Dialogue* is twenty-five years earlier, shortly after the Bar Kokhba revolt.[27] Eusebius claims the debate occurred in Ephesus.[28] The most immediate question raised by this genre is whether or to what extent the dialogue represents historical interaction between Jews and Christians. Do the issues and scriptures discussed reflect a living, lively exchange between at least one group of Jews and

Christians, or is the dialogue a vehicle whereby Christians clarify their own identity in an intra-Christian debate? The dominant position holds to the former assessment: Justin's *Dialogue* to one degree or another displays actual contact between Jews and Christians.

Reasons given for seeing this dialogue as capturing real exchange between Jews and Christians include the fact that Trypho is presented favorably overall. This is no straw man; even though he is presented as a bit weak, he carries some flesh on his bones. The debate is staged as a two-day event, but probably Justin includes conversations which occurred with many Jews over time. Justin's statements of Jewish exegesis and practice are judged to be generally on the mark, suggesting a decent level of knowledge and understanding of Judaism. In this case, Trypho's interpretations often are similar to what we find in rabbinic or Palestinian sources. Moreover, Justin's own interpretations often parallel those he speaks of as Jewish, which suggests exchange between Christians and Jews. Such contact would be possible in Samaria, Justin's home area. Though he shows an awareness of Jewish thought, Justin's rhetoric reverses meaning as it overturns Jewish understanding when he announces that the promises of God's blessing to Jews (for example circumcision) turn out instead to be curses or punishment. Justin declares that circumcision served as a marker of a disobedient people who were set apart for punishment – punishment meted out in the failed Bar Kokhba revolt. Justin's attempt at differentiation reveals historical reality as Trypho expresses that Jews can still be faithful to the law even with the loss of the Temple.[29] Though Justin seems to have the Jewish reader at least in part in mind, by addressing the pagan/Gentile audience, Justin is targeting those who might be inclined to join the synagogue. Overall, those who see real interaction between Jews and Christians in his presentation note the reality of a vibrant compelling Judaism that has successfully defended its interpretation of the law to anyone interested.

While the dominant approach to Justin's *Dialogue* sees the text revealing, to one degree or another, historical evidence of exchange between Jews and Christians, some argue that Justin's enterprise is focused on creating Christian identity.[30] Boyarin identifies Justin as the first Christian author to define *hairesis* as a group outside normative tradition, moving from its earlier meaning as a party which held definable beliefs and practices. This fits with Justin's overarching concern to identify Christianity as independent of Judaism, and to distinguish true from false Christians. For Boyarin, Justin defines Christianity theologically, and Trypho also in the *Dialogue* admits that some Jews are heretics.[31] Such conviction is found as well in rabbinic texts, where the term *minut* signifies "other" (not equivalent to Christian) as outside the true body of Israel. Thus even as Christians argued about the theological limits of their group, so too did the rabbis. For example, according to Mishnah *Sanhedrin* 10, Sadducees are heretics because they deny the resurrection of the dead, a theological marker that determines who is "in" and "out" of the community. Both the Temple's destruction and the rise of Gentile Christianity opened the possibility of establishing heresy and orthodoxy as effective boundary markers. Rabbis did not mimic Christians in using these categories, rather the historical situation pushed for this response. A dialogical relationship and an intertextuality that drew from a shared pool of ideas informed second-century Jewish and Christian authors.

Andrew Jacobs examines Justin's *Dialogue* as well as Origen's *Against Celsus* and later dialogues with an eye to the inherent multiplicity of voices present in the texts. Jacobs sees the Christian arguments surrounding Judaism/Jews arising not from direct pressure from Jewish sources or specific historical events, but from an urgent pursuit of Christian identity which nonetheless internalizes its "necessary" Jewishness.[32] By making the other an internal and indispensable part of one's self definition, one creates an ambivalent identity, which relies upon continued dialogue to maintain its distinctiveness. Thus for Jacobs, we should not read the dialogues or *Adversus Iudaeos* literature as reflecting a gradual hardening of boundaries, but rather as witnessing to the multiple cultural and religious voices which are juxtaposed creatively to render a social identity. In the case of the *Dialogue*, Jacobs argues that Justin's irresolution, finally, of Christian identity vis-à-vis Judaism is not due to a failure on Justin's part, but is precisely where Justin wants to end up.

To pursue his point, Jacobs focuses on the role of Jesus' circumcision in these dialogues. As in Justin's *Dialogue*, he finds in Origen's *Against Celsus* a seemingly counter-intuitive stance: though Christianity transcends the law, this was realized at precisely the point where Jesus submitted to the law in his circumcision. In both accepting and repudiating the law, Origen creates porous borders between Judaism and Christianity. Jacobs suggests that the genre of these Christian texts, dialogue and apology, are hardly accidental. The choice highlights the decision to incorporate multivalent voices, for to speak in the voice of the "other" suggests "a dialogics of identity that inscribes and destabilizes difference."[33] The robust Jewish character painted by Justin and Origen could, but need not, reflect any particular Jewish community or social reality; it rather underscores the Christian author's attempt to manage or control the irreducible Jewish voice that is part of the former's identity. The pay-off for Justin, as Jacobs sees it, is that it allows him to maintain communication with Judaism, even if it is to say that his understanding is superior.

In *Dialogue to Trypho* 47 Justin discusses those Christians who follow Jewish law. This section probably reflects historical reality because this Christian group does not further Justin's argument; in many ways it has the potential to weaken it. Justin declares that he would welcome those Jews who turned to Christ but continued observing the law – so long as they did not insist that others also followed the law. More grudgingly, he also allows for Gentile Christians who had previously followed the law to continue to do so, with a similar caveat. Justin reveals the historical turmoil within the church over acceptable levels of adherence to the law. The argument suggests a fluid boundary between synagogue and church at least in some locations, and a willingness to allow for personal choice in matters of adhering to the law. Justin might feel obligated to make such concessions so that Gentiles who choose the church would not turn later to the synagogue. Within fifty years, Irenaeus will speak of the Ebionites, Jewish Christians who observed the law but held a faulty Christology, according to the bishop.[34] These Christians are arguably distinguishable from the Nazarenes, an ethnic Jewish Christian group which held a Christology similar to the wider Gentile orthodox community and also practiced key elements of the Jewish law. Jewish Christianity presents its own challenges in terms of historical reconstruction;

I mention it here to say that Gentile Christians, to one degree or another, seem to make room for continued practice of the law by ethnic Jews who declare themselves Christian. Whether this group was integrated well into the larger Gentile church, and whether the group served as a bridge between the Christian and Jewish communities in specific areas is a question whose definitive answer lies beyond our sources.[35]

In the *Dialogue*, Justin levels serious charges against Jews concerning aggression against Christians. He claims that Jews are turning public opinion against Christians (117.3), telling people not to talk with Christians (38.1). He declares that Jews hate Christians (39.1), they curse them (16.14), and even kill them (95.4, 122.2, 133.6).[36] Moreover, they say a prayer, after which they scorn Jesus (137.2). This prayer is often identified as the *Birkath ha-minim*, which was reportedly introduced under Gamaliel II (c. CE 90–130).[37] Justin connects it with Pharisee teachers. This reference to Pharisees might suggest that he is drawing on material from the New Testament for his information, and is less concerned in presenting a historical picture than in buttressing his theological argument. However, Justin also notes that local synagogue leadership played a role in confronting Christians, which could indicate that at the community level, Jewish leaders engaged Christians, though perhaps not with the malice alleged by Justin.

One question raised by the information is whether this possible interaction between Christians and Jews occurred at the level of learned writers and community leaders, or between average members of each group. Said another way, even if we grant that Justin's *Dialogue* indicates historical interaction between Jews and Christians about serious theological and social matters, does this exchange take place at all levels of society, or within a small social group? A reconstruction of the relationship between Jews and Christians at this time must be sensitive to the realities of a stratified social order which shaped all societal interactions. A second, similar question revolves around the level of theological and intellectual sophistication which one can assume was held by average group members compared with their leaders. Unfortunately the evidence to answer these questions is lacking, but recognition that both Jews and Christians would have included in their numbers some from an elite social status as well as numerous average members cautions scholars from drawing monochromatic images of each community.

From Justin's *Dialogue*, we turn to the *Martyrdom of Polycarp*. In the 160s Bishop Polycarp of Smyrna was martyred, and the account of his death includes brief references to Jewish collusion. The focus of this work is hagiographic; the purpose is instruction for the faithful. Many details in the martyrdom suggest the story is best understood as an *imitatio Christi*, which necessitates that Jews should appear in at least one scene. Similarities to the Gospels include that the arresting officer's name is Herod; moreover, Polycarp is betrayed by one from his own household. He is arrested on a Friday, and rides to the city on a donkey.[38] The crowd cries for his blood, even though the chief magistrate does not want to convict him.[39] Polycarp is pierced in his side.[40] The Jews are able to convince the officers not to release the body to the Christians.[41] The parallels to Jesus' crucifixion are noteworthy, but that does not immediately rule out the possibility that the story also has historical information. However, in terms of Jewish complicity, the reader is asked to believe that Jews would gather wood on the Sabbath and to cry out that Polycarp is a destroyer of our gods (plural); neither action is generally attributed to Jews at this time.[42] Moreover, one wonders whether Jews would want to make themselves known at a time of such religious fervor amongst the Gentile townsfolk.[43] Thus the *Martyrdom of Polycarp* does not reflect a social world of second-century Christianity and Judaism, but rather only the theological identity construction of Christianity. Given the pedagogical purpose of the text, however, its social ramifications might include Christians distancing themselves in their everyday lives from their Jewish neighbors.[44]

While theological factors clearly drive the author's views on Jews, some hold historical information may still be mined from the text.[45] For example, the detail about wood-gathering on Sabbath might reveal a Jewish community well integrated with its Gentile neighbors, and thus not opposed to attending events in the stadium. Even more, though we do not have conclusive evidence that Jews participated in persecution of Christians, rivalry for pagan converts might escalate to persecution.

A third important genre that plays a role in interpreting Christian–Jewish relations is the Christian sermon. Perhaps none is so famous (or infamous) as Melito of Sardis's paschal homily, which has the dubious distinction of being the earliest extant writing to charge the Jews with deicide. A typical interpretation suggests that Melito, as a member of the small Christian group, is reacting against the large, vibrant Jewish community in Sardis.[46] Initially this thesis was supported by an archaeological discovery of a sizeable synagogue adjacent to the city's gymnasium. Later reconsideration of the synagogue's dating, however, moves the structure's function as synagogue to the late third or fourth century. Nonetheless, many scholars extrapolate that conditions were similar in the century and a half before the present synagogue, pointing to evidence in Josephus of a flourishing Jewish community in the Hellenistic period.[47] Thus a fairly continuous line is drawn between the first century BCE and the fourth century CE in terms of the vibrancy and vitality of the Jewish community, which maintained its exclusive identity but also adapted to the changing pagan environment. With this reconstruction of the Jewish community as a backdrop, Melito's *On Pascha* is evaluated as the fierce, yet ironically pathetic, outburst of a marginalized voice seeking social and political clout for his group.

An alternative view argues that the theological language and categories used by Melito do not reflect directly a social reality of Jews and Christians in Sardis. Questioned is the assumption that the Jewish community of the fourth century is reliably the same as the Jewish community which preceded it by 150 years. Even if this historical continuity is granted, must we assume that the Christians in Sardis were a small, oppressed group led by an overwhelmed pastor? Tertullian praises Melito as an elegant preacher, suggesting a level of education that implies some wealth which is not the sort of profile that would be easily intimidated.[48] Indeed, even if we were to allow both the large Jewish community and the small Christian one, we need not assume that the social "inferiors" would hold animosity against the larger group. For example, from the same period, Theophilus of Antioch (a city with a large Jewish population), in his apology *To Autolycus*, does not attack Jews; indeed, he praises both the law[49] and the "Hebrews" as the Christians' ancestors.[50] Theophilus's posture concerning Jews or Judaism cautions against assuming that Christian apologists were, by default, antagonistic towards the synagogue. The rhetoric against Jews in the *On Pascha* should not be softened by suggesting a battered minority group striking out at its oppressors. Instead, its theological claims should be taken at face value, and by arguing that its descriptions of Jews come from the first century (details which are found in New Testament writings), the force of the anti-Jewish argument is accentuated. That is, rather than suggest this homily is an isolated, unrepeated tirade against a large social group this approach gives full weight to the implications for Christian anti-Jewish claims and identity-making in the second century and beyond.

By the end of the second century, *Adversus Iudaeos* literature is produced by key figures such as Tertullian from North Africa and Irenaeus in Gaul. The anti-Jewish arguments share similarities with the condemnation of heresy, leading some to conclude that the attacks against Jews are essentially a veiled assault against Christians with whom the author disagrees. For example, in Tertullian's *Antidote for the Scorpion's Sting* 10, we find the phrase "synagogues of the Jews, founts of persecution."[51] Does this descriptor reflect a historical context wherein Jews in at least some locales harassed Christians? While some cite this phrase as evidence for aggression by Jews against Christians, others note that Tertullian finishes this line with "before which the apostles endured the scourge." He defines this synagogue as that of the first century, even more, a synagogue described to serve his theological point that martyrdom is to be praised (this against the Gnostics). A similar argument can be made about Irenaeus's claims of Jews plotting against Christians and persecuting them.[52] The charge is found in his argument describing the transfer of blessing from Esau to Jacob, which is understood to speak about reassigning the blessing of the Jews to the church. As Jacob suffered the anger of his brother, so too the church experiences suffering from the Jew – the theological claim is not elaborated upon with any specific historical details. Such silence reinforces the sense that Irenaeus is not thinking of actual aggression by Jews against Christians, but is rather filling out his typological schema.

Irenaeus's reaction against the heretics was in part driven by larger historical forces. The sporadic, localized, but nonetheless intense, Roman persecutions that had taken his teacher, Polycarp, resulted in the migration of many Christians of Asia Minor, including Irenaeus, to Gaul and elsewhere. In the persecutions of CE 177, his predecessor, Pothinus, bishop of Lyons, was killed. Additionally, the failed Bar Kokhba revolt created a new reality in Judea. Jerusalem was off limits to Jews (it was renamed Aelia Capitolina), and many fled not to Alexandria, the city which experienced its own Jewish uprising a few decades earlier, but to the villages of Galilee, where rabbinic Judaism was developing. This expression of Judaism reflected a social, political, and philosophical milieu different from that of the early second-century Trypho, or Celsus's Jew.

Into this new environment steps Origen, born and educated in Alexandria, but who moved to Caesarea Maritima to spend his last twenty years (CE 185–254). He claims that he engaged with Jews in discussions of scriptural exegesis, and that he was competent in Hebrew.[53] His work, *On First Principles*, written in Alexandria, sets out a method for reading Scripture that establishes a higher, spiritual sense beyond the fleshly or literal sense.[54] The latter is a legitimate starting point, but the reader is encouraged to seek deeper, spiritual meanings. Origen draws on Paul's letters for support of the higher sense, and accuses "the Jews" of failing to recognize a spiritual interpretation. His indictment is ironic, given his willingness to draw on the allegorical insights of Philo of Alexandria, whom he identifies not as a Jew, but as one of "our predecessors." His work on the versions of the Septuagint, the *Hexapla*, points to a scholar interested in the underlying Hebrew text (i.e., the Jewish text), and his encyclopedic knowledge of the Scriptures, together with his hermeneutical interest in the details of the biblical text, could be seen to reflect interaction with Jewish learning.

With Origen we have what appears to be concrete evidence of interaction between a Christian and Jews, and most identify these interlocutors as rabbinic Jews.[55] In several places in *Against Celsus*, Origen states that he has either disputed with Jews or has engaged with their exegesis. Origen asserts that his first-hand knowledge of local Jewish history, local culture, and language – over against Celsus's fictitious Jew – provides a solid basis for refuting Celsus's critique of Christianity.[56] His letter to the Christian Africanus (*To Africanus*) includes several claims about his interaction with Jews. In promoting the Septuagint as the church's Scriptures, Origen claims to have learned the differences between it and the Jewish Scriptures so that he can debate with Jews on an equal footing, rather than have them mock him for not knowing the texts. He also professes to have spoken with several Jews, including a very learned man, the son of a Sage. From other evidence we know that rabbis were expanding their influence in the region, so conversations between such academics is not outside the realm of possibility. How reliable are Origen's comments about Jews' opinions and positions? This question is complicated both by the polemical nature of Origen's appeals to Jews and by the difficulties involved in establishing historical contexts for rabbinic writings.

Although Origen's works are important for the study of Christian–Jewish relations, some scholars are perhaps too eager to see rapprochement between Origen and his rabbinic compatriots, viewing it as an ancient model for modern dialogue. Presenting Origen's thought as influenced predominately by his interactions with developing rabbinic thought may lead to painting a double-faced Origen – in public antagonistic towards Jews, but in private, much more sympathetic. Instead, one might argue that Origen found his theological inspiration, not in his dialogue with Jewish interlocutors, but from the Apostle Paul's works.[57] Finally, if Origen knew at least a bit of Hebrew, it is possible, and perhaps even likely, that his teachers were Jewish Christians. This raises the possibility that Origen's primary information concerning Jewish exegesis was acquired from those Jews who embraced the church.

Those who study Christian–Jewish relations in the second and third centuries generally agree on at least one point: both Judaism and Christianity, regardless of their actual numbers, included vibrant local communities within many Roman cities. They each interacted with the dominant Greco-Roman cultures in ways that sought to preserve their distinct identity and yet negotiate as a minority group in the commerce and politics of the day. We must also take into account the highly stratified Roman culture, recognizing that wealthy Christians or Jews would have a different social experience relative to their Greco-Roman neighbors than would poor or average members of the congregation. The protected legal status of the Jews and the intermittent persecution of Christians by Rome certainly played a part in how Christians and Jews interacted socially. It is not surprising, then, given the numerous contingencies and the paucity of our information, that numerous theories as to the interaction (direct and indirect) between these two groups have generated a range of diverse opinions.

Further reading

W. Bauer, *Orthodoxy and Heresy in Earliest Christianity*, R. A. Kraft and G. Krodel (eds), Philadelphia: Fortress, 1971; originally published as W. Bauer, *Rechtgläubigkeit und Ketzerie im ältesten Christentum*, Beiträge zur historischen Theologie 10, Tübingen: Mohr/Siebeck, 1934.

P. Blowers, "Origen, the Rabbis, and the Bible: Towards a Picture of Judaism and Christianity in Third-Century Caesarea," in C. Kannengeisser and W. L. Petersen (eds) *Origen of Alexandria: His World and Legacy*, Notre Dame, IN: Notre Dame Press, 1988, pp. 96–116.

G. Bowersock. *Hellenism in Late Antiquity*. Cambridge: Cambridge University Press, 1990.

S. J. D. Cohen, "'Those Who Say They Are Jews But Are Not': How Do You Know a Jew in Antiquity When You See One?," in S. J. D. Cohen and E. Frerichs (eds) *Diasporas in Antiquity*, Atlanta: Scholars, 1993, pp. 1–45.

T. Horner, *Listening to Trypho: Justin Martyr's Dialogue Reconsidered*, Leuven: Peeters, 2001.

J. Neusner, *Introduction to Rabbinic Literature*, New York: Doubleday, 1999.

D. T. Runia, *Philo in Early Christian Literature: A Survey*, Minneapolis: Fortress, 1993.

C. Setzer, *Jewish Responses to Early Christians: History and Polemics, 30–150 C.E.*, Minneapolis: Fortress, 1994.

B. L. Visotzky, *Fathers of the World: Essays in Rabbinic and Patristic Literatures*, Wissenschaftliche Untersuchungen zum Neuen Testament 80, Tübingen: J. C. B. Mohr (Paul Siebeck), 1995.

A. L. Williams, *Adversus Judaeos: A Bird's-Eye View of Christian 'Apologiae' until the Renaissance*, Cambridge: Cambridge University Press, 1935.

Notes

1 A. Harnack, *The Mission and Expansion of Christianity in the First Three Centuries*, 2 vols; trans. and ed. J. Moffatt, New York: Putnam, 1908.

2 M. Simon, *Versus Israel: A Study of the Relations between Christians and Jews in the Roman Empire (A.D. 135–425)*, trans. H. McKeating, Oxford: Oxford University Press, 1986.

3 M. Taylor, *Anti-Judaism and Early Christian Identity: A Critique of the Scholarly Consensus*, Leiden: Brill, 1995, p. 24. She uses this label, but argues against the approach.

4 Simon, *Versus Israel*, p. xii.

5 S. McKnight, *A Light to the Gentiles: Jewish Missionary Activity in the Second Temple Period*, Minneapolis: Fortress, 1991; M. Goodman, *Mission and Conversion: Proselytizing in the Religious History of the Roman Empire*, Oxford: Clarendon, 1994. For a defense of Jewish proselytizing, see L. Feldman and M. Reinhold (eds), *Jewish Life and Thought among Greeks and Romans*, Minneapolis: Fortress, 1996, pp. 124–35.

6 J. Lieu, *Christian Identity in the Jewish and Graeco-Roman World*, Oxford: Oxford University Press, 2004. See also *Image and Reality: The Jews in the World of the Christians in the Second Century*, Edinburgh: T&T Clark, 1996.

7 J. D. G. Dunn (ed.), *Jews and Christians: The Parting of the Ways*, Tübingen: J. C. B. Mohr (Paul Siebeck), 1992; 2nd edn, Grand Rapids, MI: William B. Eerdmans, 1999.

8 A. H. Becker and A. Y. Reed (eds), *The Ways That Never Parted: Jews and Christians in Late Antiquity and the Early Middle Ages*, Minneapolis: Fortress, 2007.

9 D. Boyarin, *Border Lines: The Partition of Judaeo-Christianity*, Philadelphia: University of Pennsylvania Press, 2004.

10 A. S. Jacobs, "Dialogical Differences: (De-) Judaizing Jesus' Circumcision," *Journal of Early Christian Studies* 15.3, 2007, pp. 291–335.

11 G. Kalantzis, "Ephesus as a Roman, Christian, and Jewish Metropolis in the First and Second Centuries C.E.," *Jian Dao* 8, 1997, p. 115.

12 S. Schwartz, *Imperialism and Jewish Society: 200 B.C.E to 640 C.E.*, Princeton, NJ: Princeton University Press, 2001, p. 175, writes "in the wake of the revolts, Jewish society disintegrated." An alternative perspective comes from F. Millar, *Roman Near East 31 B.C.–A.D. 337*, Cambridge: Cambridge University Press, 1993. For a critique, see T. Rajak, "Jews, Semites and Their Cultures in Fergus Millar's *Roman Near East*," in T. Rajak, *The Jewish Dialogue with Greece and Rome: Studies in Cultural and Social Interaction*, Leiden: Brill, 2001, pp. 503–9.

13 Dunn offers a careful discussion of the evidence. He concludes that "for Tertullian, the Jews he discovered in the pages of the Scriptures were the same Jews (in his mind) he encountered in Carthage; for him their thinking had not changed at all." G. D. Dunn, *Tertullian*, New York: Routledge, 2004, pp. 47–51 (esp. 51).

14 For a discussion of this topic in Chrysostom's Antioch, see C. Shepardson, "Controlling Contested Places: John Chrysostom's *Adversus Iudaeos* homilies and the Spatial Politics of Religious Controversy," *Journal of Early Christian Studies* 15.4, 2007, pp. 483–516.

15 Tacitus, *Annals* 15.37–41.

16 Pliny the Younger, *Letters* 10.96–97.

17 S. E. Porter and B. W. R. Pearson, "Ancient Understandings of the Christian-Jewish Split," in S. E. Porter and B. W. R. Pearson (eds), *Christian–Jewish Relations through the Centuries*, Journal for the Study of the New Testament Supplement Series 192, Sheffield: Sheffield Academic, 2000, pp. 36–51 (esp. 47).

18 Ignatius, *To the Philadelphians* 6.1; trans. M. Holmes, *The Apostolic Fathers: Greek Texts and English Translations*, 3d edn, Grand Rapids, MI: Baker Academic, 2007, p. 241.

19 Ignatius, *To the Magnesians* 8.1; trans. Holmes, *Apostolic Fathers*, pp. 207–8.

20 Ignatius, *To the Magnesians* 9.1; trans. Holmes, *Apostolic Fathers*, p. 209.

21 Ignatius, *To the Magnesians* 10.3; trans. Holmes, *Apostolic Fathers*, p. 209.

22 P. van der Horst, "Jews and Christians in Antioch at the End of the Fourth Century," in Porter and Pearson, *Christian–Jewish Relations through the Centuries*, pp. 228–38.

23 S. Wilson, *Related Strangers: Jews and Christians 70–170 C.E.*, Minneapolis: Fortress, 1995, p. 164.

24 Ignatius, *To the Magnesians* 9.1; *To the Philadelphians* 3.3, 4.1.

25 Ignatius, *To the Magnesians* 11; trans. Holmes, *Apostolic Fathers*, p. 211.

26 Trans. Holmes, *Apostolic Fathers*, p. 243.

27 Justin, *Dialogue with Trypho* 9.3.

28 Eusebius, *Ecclesiastical History* 4.18.6.

29 Justin, *Dialogue with Trypho* 46.2–4.

30 Boyarin, *Border Lines*. See also Taylor, *Anti-Judaism and Early Christian Identity*; T. Rajak, "Talking at Trypho: Christian Apologetic as Anti-Judaism in Justin's *Dialogue with Trypho the Jew*," in *The Jewish Dialogue with Greece and Rome: Studies in Cultural and Social Interaction*, Leiden: Brill, 2001, pp. 511–33. Rajak writes, "The *Trypho* goes to the heart of the problem ... what today we would call supersessionism. ... This is a struggle on both the intellectual and emotional plane; its practical consequences, in his own time or later, may not have concerned Justin in the least" (p. 513).

31 Justin, *Dialogue with Trypho* 62.2.

32 A. Jacobs writes, "If Christians persist in defining themselves in contradistinction to some other – pagan, heretic, or Jews – they make the other an indispensable part of 'Christianness'" (Jacobs, "Dialogical Differences," p. 295).

33 Jacobs, "Dialogical Differences," p. 317.

34 Irenaeus, *Against Heresies* 1.26.2; 3.21.1; 5.1.3; more fully discussed by Epiphanius.

35 R. Bauckham discusses the Ebionites in "The Origin of the Ebionites," in P. J. Tomson and D. Lambers-Petry (eds), *The Image of the Judaeo-Christians in Ancient Jewish and Christian Literature*, Wissenschaftliche Untersuchungen zum Neuen Testament 158, Tübingen: J. C. B. Mohr (Paul

Siebeck), 2003, pp. 162–81. See also A. F. J. Klijn and G. J. Reinink, *Patristic Evidence for Jewish-Christian Sects*, Supplements to Novum Testamentum 36, Leiden: Brill, 1973; O. Skarsaune, *The Proof from Prophecy: A Study in Justin Martyr's Proof-Text Tradition: Text-Type, Provenance, Theological Profile*, Supplements to Novum Testamentum 66, Leiden: Brill, 1987; O. Skarsaune and R. Hvalvik, *Jewish Believers in Jesus: The Early Centuries*, Peabody, MA: Hendrickson, 2007. An important text in this discussion is the *Pseudo-Clementine* corpus.

36 For a discussion of Jesus through the charges of his opponents in the first several centuries, see S. McKnight and J. Modica (eds), *Who Do My Opponents Say that I Am?*, London: T&T Clark, 2008.

37 *b. Ber.* 28b–29a. Boyarin, *Border Lines*, rejects the suggestion that in Justin's day the *birkat hamminim* (a later Jewish liturgical prayer) reflected expulsion of Christians by Jews. He doubts the attribution to Gamaliel II at Yavneh (*b. Ber.* 28b–29a), and concludes that "once the evidence of a so-called curse of the heretics before the third century is removed from the picture, there is no warrant at all to assume an early Palestinian curse directed at any Christians" (p. 71). W. Horbury, *Jews and Christians in Contact and Controversy*, Edinburgh: T&T Clark, 1998, argues for the centrality of the Benediction of the *minim* in Christian–Jewish encounters, pp. 43–110.

38 *Martyrdom of Polycarp* 8.

39 *Martyrdom of Polycarp* 12.

40 *Martyrdom of Polycarp* 16.

41 *Martyrdom of Polycarp* 17.

42 *Martyrdom of Polycarp* 12–13.

43 P. Fredriksen, *Augustine and the Jews: A Christian Defense of Jews and Judaism*, New York: Doubleday, 2008, suggests that they would have kept their heads down and tried to be inconspicuous, p. 93. Alternatively, perhaps the Jewish community believed that such participation would highlight their loyalty to the city, although the capriciousness of mob violence suggests that the prudent course would be to stay out of sight.

44 D. Boyarin, *Dying for God: Martyrdom and the Making of Judaism and Christianity*, Stanford: Stanford University Press, 1999, argues that martyrology and the martyrdom tradition of the second through fourth centuries shows evidence of ongoing contact and interaction between Jewish and Christian groups.

45 Lieu, *Image and Reality*, "the theme of Christian imitation of Christ brought Jewish participation in persecution into the theological tradition. As study of the texts has shown, actual evidence of Jewish instigation of persecution ('stirring up trouble') is hardly to be found. This is separate from the question whether Jews shared in the spreading of calumnies against the Christians" (pp. 91–2).

46 L. H. Cohick, *The Peri Pascha Attributed to Melito of Sardis: Setting, Purpose and Sources*, Brown Judaic Studies 327, Providence, RI: Brown University Press, 2000. I suggest that Melito, second-century bishop of Sardis described by Eusebius, is not the author of our *On Pascha*, thus decoupling the text from the Sardis provenance.

47 Josephus, *Jewish Antiquities* 14.10.17 [235]; 10.24 [259–61]; 16.6.6 [171].

48 Jerome, *On Illustrious Men* 24.

49 Theophilus, *To Autolycus* 3.9.

50 Theophilus, *To Autolycus* 3.20, 21.

51 Latin of *Scorpiace* 10: "synagogas Judaeorum fontes persecutionum."

52 Irenaeus, *Against Heresies* 4.21.2–3.

53 This claim is disputed by scholars; most believe he had a rudimentary knowledge of Hebrew only.

54 For a discussion of Origen's exegetical method, see E. A. Dively Lauro, *The Soul and Spirit of Scripture within Origen's Exegesis*, Leiden: Brill, 2005.

55 N. de Lange, *Origen and the Jews: Studies in Jewish-Christian Relations in Third-century Palestine*, Cambridge: Cambridge University Press, 1976, writes, "Origen's reliance on the living Jewish tradition is one of the most distinctive features of his exegesis and serves to mark him out from all earlier and contemporary Greek fathers. It is no exaggeration to say that there is not a single aspect of his biblical writings that is not touched by it to a greater or lesser degree" (p. 134).

56 A. S. Jacobs, *Remains of the Jews: The Holy Land and Christian Empire in Late Antiquity*, Stanford: Stanford University Press, 2004, notes that Origen does not seek knowledge of the Jews to dominate them, but to defend Christianity against the pagan Celsus, pp. 60–7. Origen's knowledge is a form of resistance against the more powerful Jews, who when he bests them in argument (as he claims)

he reinforces Christianity's superiority. A century later, Jerome learns Hebrew initially from a Jewish Christian, as the dynamics of power have shifted after Constantine, see M. Graves, *Jerome's Hebrew Philology*, Leiden: Brill, 2007, p. 88.

57 J. A. McGuckin, "Origen on the Jews," in D. Wood (ed.) *Christianity and Judaism*, Oxford: Blackwell, 1992, pp. 1–13 (esp. 10).

Part II
LITERATURE

5

IMITATIONS IN LITERATURE AND LIFE

Apocrypha and martyrdom

J. K. Elliott

Now when Severus also was stirring up persecution against the churches splendid martyrdoms of the champions of piety were accomplished everywhere, but especially frequently in Alexandria. God's champions were taken there as to a grand arena from Egypt and the whole of Thebes. They, through their most steadfast endurance, were wreathed with the crowns that come from God.

Thus begins the sixth book of the *Ecclesiastical History* by Eusebius (260–340). That work is filled with tales of martyrs' deaths, often told in gruesome detail. Stories of early martyrdoms are to be found in a variety of sources:

1 There exist separate accounts of martyrdoms based on what on the face of it seem to be authentic law-court transcripts. These are the *acta* of Christians martyrs.[1]
2 Within that amorphous body of early non-canonical literature commonly called the Apocryphal New Testament are the apocryphal Acts, telling of the deeds and deaths of famous apostles. Many writers on early martyrdoms ignore these quasi novels, although Eusebius knew of some of them. *Ecclesiastical History* 3.25.6 refers to the *Acts of Andrew* and the *Acts of John*. Eusebius fails to use their contents, probably because he branded them unorthodox.
3 Elsewhere, accounts of the martyrdoms of pagan noblemen have also survived in extant manuscripts; those are generally known as *The Acts of Pagan Martyrs*.
4 Jewish martyrdoms are described in the books of Maccabees.

This varied literature has, as a common theme, the extolling of those who died for their faith or principles, whose example is to be followed and whose memory is hallowed.

A *formgeschichtliche* approach to the *acta* of the Christian martyrs and to the apocryphal Acts shows common characteristics – beatings and imprisonments, conventional *dramatis personae* (including wealthy tyrants and women converts) and the theatrical stage-settings of arena or law court, and, usually, a judicial sentence. An analysis of similarities, such as the reactions of onlookers or the inclusion of visions, is presented by H. Musurillo.[2] But many of the parallels and similarities in this type of literature are inevitable, given the traditions behind the subject matter.[3]

Martyrdom stories were important, inspirational, and popular. In Christian tradition the *Te Deum* can include the "noble army of martyrs" alongside the glorious company of the Apostles and the goodly fellowship of the Prophets. Such was their reputation.

This survey will examine the apocryphal Acts and the possible influences, sources, and background to such writings. We shall then turn to the *acta* of the Christian martyrs, before looking at the relevance and importance of these and the apocryphal Acts for subsequent generations of Christians. A concluding section looks at the pagan martyrdom stories. But, first, the term "martyr" needs clarifying.

The word "martyr"

The *Oxford English Dictionary* defines a martyr as "A person who voluntarily undergoes the death penalty for refusing to renounce the Christian faith or a Christian doctrine, for persevering in a Christian virtue or for obeying a law of the church." It is thus, specifically Christian, although the dictionary allows a broader definition: "A person who undergoes death or great suffering on behalf of any religious or other cause or as a consequence of devotion to some object."

We shall concentrate on the original Christian definition which derives from μαρτυς, who in Acts 1:8, 22 is a *witness* to the life and resurrection of Jesus. (In classical literature a μαρτυς was a witness in a court of law and in many of the apocryphal Acts and the accounts of Christian martyrdom more generally that legal context is often present.)

By the time the book of Revelation was written the μαρτυς was being remembered for having made the ultimate sacrifice in a time of persecution. Revelation 16:6 and 17:6 is alert to the blood of the saints and the martyrs. These were singled out for special rewards during the millennial rule of Christ (see Rev. 20:4–6, with its reference to those beheaded δια την μαρτυριαν Ιησου, which is particularly significant if Ιησου is an objective genitive here). Revelation 2:13 refers to a named but otherwise unknown martyr, Antipas.

A martyr is therefore a Christian believer who gives his or her life or allows his or her life to be taken specifically in times of persecution. The death in itself thereby then becomes the *witness* and is a testimonial.

Whereas Voltaire claims that a punishment may be inflicted *"pour encourager les autres"* (*scil.* from behaving badly), the aim of the death of the Christian martyr is not to dissuade others from a forbidden course of action but, rather, precisely to encourage them to fight the good fight and to follow this model.

The death of the Christian martyr is not a suicide, which is negative. Martyrdom has to be presented and succeed as a positive act, a willing acceptance of fate for the purpose of maintaining and promoting one's faith. And it is obviously different from modern military use, where a fallen combatant fighting a totalitarian regime, for example, may be described as having made the ultimate sacrifice – in effect as a martyr – and where heroes may be poignantly described on headstones and on war memorials as dying for a higher cause than self, such as for King and Country, *Vaterland*, or for *la république*. (Those references may be allied to the language used in pagan sources such as those in which fallen heroes are brought to Walhalla by the Valkyre to have an honourable final resting place amidst fellow heroes.) Unlike such cases Christian martyrdom requires a choice to have been available: death itself could have been avoided, albeit only at a price the Christian was unwilling to pay.

The apocryphal Acts[4]

Readers of that genre of ancient Christian literature known as the apocryphal Acts find that the conclusion of each of the legends about the eponymous apostolic figure is a detailed account of his death, usually by execution. Four of the main five second-century Acts (those of Andrew, Paul, Peter and of Thomas) have their heroes die as a martyr at the hands of the imperial authorities. (The conclusion to the *Acts of John* is exceptional, in that John merely lies in his grave and dies.)

The *Acts of Thomas* has survived virtually complete in extant manuscripts, so that its second-century contents can be relatively easily restored. But the other four are very fragmented: large portions of the original writings have been lost and it is only with difficulty that modern scholars can reconstruct much of the remainder from fragments, later rewritings, and citations. But despite this fragmentation and destruction, it is noteworthy that it is the concluding sections of all these books, telling of the apostle's death, that have survived virtually intact.

Several church fathers objected to the contents of these apocryphal texts, partly because of their relatively recent composition, compared with the books that eventually were promoted as canonical and accepted to form the New Testament, and partly because of their contents being magical, superstitious, uncritical or (occasionally) tinged with Gnostic or other "unorthodox" ideologies. Those objections encouraged the destruction of many such texts or their rewriting in expurgated and catholicized versions (called réchauffés by M. R. James) or their being circulated in clandestine copies.[5] However, their conclusions seem to have enjoyed a degree of acceptance based on their survival. Eventually the tales of the deaths of the apostles as separate accounts in their own right became part of the growing hagiographical writings of the church.

A typical example of a martyrdom story in the apocryphal Acts is in the *Acts of Andrew*. In the scene of Andrew's death we read:

> And when Aegeates again attempted to approach the wood to untie Andrew, the entire city was in an uproar at him. The apostle Andrew shouted: "O Master, do not permit Andrew, the one tied to your wood, to be untied again. O Jesus, do not give me to the shameless devil, I who am attached to your mystery. O Father, do not let your opponent untie me, I who am hanging upon your grace. May he who is little no longer humiliate the one who has

known your greatness. But you yourself, O Christ, you whom I desired, whom I loved, whom I know, whom I possess, whom I cherish, whose I am, receive me, so that by my departure to you there may be a reunion of my many kindred, those who rest in your majesty." When he had said these things and further glorified the Lord, he handed over his spirit, so that we wept and everyone grieved his departure.

(*Acts of Andrew* 63[9])

Another telling example occurs in the *Acts of Paul*. Prior to the account of Paul's beheading we read:

And among the many Paul also was brought in fetters. Those who were imprisoned with him looked at him, so that the emperor observed that he was the leader of the soldiers. And he said to him, "Man of the great king, now my prisoner, what induced you to come secretly into the Roman Empire and to enlist soldiers in my territory?" But Paul, filled with the Holy Spirit, said in the presence of all, "Caesar, we enlist soldiers not only in your territory but in all lands of the earth. For thus we are commanded to exclude none who wishes to fight for my king. If it seems good to you serve him, for neither riches nor the splendours of this life will save you; but if you become his subject and beseech him you shall be saved. For in one day he will destroy the world." Having heard this Nero commanded all the prisoners to be burned with fire, but Paul to be beheaded according to the law of the Romans.

(*Acts of Paul*, Martyrdom 3)

Paul's example in this second-century account spawned many imitators.[6] The confession found in this last extract above is comparable to the witness given in many of the *acta* of Christian martyrs (see below). Another parallel between the apocryphal *Acts* and the *acta* is the judgement of the women onlookers in the *Acts of Paul* 27 "impious judgment, evil judgment" which corresponds to comparable words in one of Christian *acta*, *The Martyrdom of Carpus, Papylus and Agathonice* 45. There are many other similarities between the two corpora.

In the *Acts of Peter*, the famous *Quo Vadis?* scene is an exception to the normal theme of the apostle's unswerving constancy, in that Peter is about to desert his duty until he is strengthened by an appearance of the risen Christ, whose words shame Peter into returning to Rome to face death by crucifixion.[7] Possibly that episode was occasioned by a reminiscence of Peter's vulnerable character known from the New Testament. Peter's death for "godlessness" then results in his request to be crucified head downwards. The title for this final part of the *Acts of Peter* is "The Martyrdom of Peter" found before chapter 33 in the Patmos manuscript 48 and before chapter 30 in the Athos manuscript Vatopedi 84. Such headings are found *mutatis mutandis* in manuscripts of most of the early Acts, showing that these final chapters were ready for separation from what precedes, and acknowledging them as detachable units.

Peter's acceptance that he is to die results in this statement to the sorrowing brethren: "I will not object so long as the Lord will keep me alive; and again if he will take me away I shall be glad and rejoice."[8] That represents the dominant attitude to death and martyrdom promulgated by the church – one should not court death but, should the need arise, then a willing acceptance is to be encouraged if it is in the cause of faith. We shall encounter that message elsewhere, below.

These second-century apocryphal stories of the apostles gave rise to later secondary versions. In the cases of Peter and/or Paul, for example, we have Pseudo-Linus, *Passion of Peter* and *Passion of Paul*; Pseudo-Marcellus, *Passion of Saints Peter and Paul*.

The climaxes to "biographies" of the early apostles were obviously sympathetically received, and certainly were officially welcomed more than the bulk of the original contents, particularly in a Christian society that regularly found solace and encouragement in reading of the founding fathers of the church being subjected, as they themselves occasionally were, to persecution and prosecution. We note below when some of those times of persecution actually occurred.

Although it was obviously the death by martyrdom of these apostolic heroes that was particularly inspirational, many of their earlier deeds, tribulations, and experiences would also have struck a chord with persecuted Christians too. That would explain the occasional survival of stories in which, for instance, Thecla, a rare example of a female apostle (in the *Acts of Paul*), is miraculously saved from burning on a pyre (see here below). She is saved from death itself, even when she is confronted by a lioness, then by wild beasts in the arena, and later exposed to seals in a pool (also abstracted below); she has to endure humiliations such as these (and was willing to accept martyrdom) in her progress as a Christian:

> And the boys and girls brought wood and straw in order that Thecla might be burned. And when she came in naked the governor wept and admired the power that was in her. And the executioners arranged the wood and told her to go up on the pile. And having made the sign of the cross she went up on the pile. And they lighted the fire. And though a great fire was blazing it did not touch her. For God, having compassion upon her, made an underground rumbling, and a cloud full of water and hail overshadowed the theatre from above, and all its contents were poured out so that many were in danger of death. And the fire was put out and Thecla saved.
>
> (*Acts of Paul* 22)

> Then they sent in many beasts as she was standing and stretching forth her hands and praying. And when she had finished her prayer she turned around and saw a large pit full of water and said, "Now it is time to wash myself." And she threw herself in saying, "In the name of Jesus Christ I baptize myself on my last day." When the women and the multitude saw it they wept and said, "Do not throw yourself into the water!"; even the governor shed tears because the seals were to devour such beauty. She then threw herself into the water in the name of Jesus Christ, but the seals, having seen a flash of lightning, floated

dead on the surface. And there was round her a cloud of fire so that the beasts could neither touch her nor could she be seen naked.

(Acts of Paul 34)

The background to these stories, though not their details, may well lie ultimately in actual court transcripts of those accused of religious beliefs that were inimical to Roman society and its laws (and we shall look later at some possible protocols) and in eyewitnesses' reminiscences of killings in an arena; but, obviously, it was the accounts of Christ's sufferings and passion that would have been uppermost in the storytellers' minds. They would also be alert to scriptural, that is Old Testament, tales in which the hero accepts death. As always, it is worth investigating Jewish antecedents for Christian stories, beliefs, and theology. We shall first examine Jewish texts before turning to pagan and Christian influences on the writers of these apocryphal tales.

Jewish precedents

The Old Testament

There are six characters that are often put forward as examples of voluntary death in the Old Testament: Abimelech (Judg. 9:50–57); Saul and his armour-bearer (1 Sam. 31:1–13, but cf. 1 Chron. 10:4; 2 Sam. 1:1–16); Samson (Judg. 16:28–31); Ahithophel (2 Sam. 17:23); Zimri (1 Kings 16:15–20).[9] Droge and Tabor, throughout their book on suicide and martyrdom among Christians and Jews in antiquity, are determined to emphasize the lack of condemnation in these examples from the Hebrew Bible, as is also the case for the examples they cite from other ancient literatures.[10] Further Old Testament examples of characters seeking death are Jonah, who is thrown overboard at his own request (Jon. 1:12; 4:3, 8); Moses and Elijah, who pray for death (Exod. 32:32; Num. 11:15; 1 Kings 19:4); and Zebah and Zalmunna, who desire Gideon to kill them in Judges 8:18–21. Such examples show that the desire for death is not condemned in these stories – the intention heightens the theatricality of the narratives, comparable as these are to similar scenes found in classical drama. But even where the hero does in fact achieve his ambition for voluntary death, these Old Testament stories are hardly on a par with the martyr literature of later times. They are seldom public events; the deaths are publicized only in the sense that they occur in a subsequent storytelling.

Nevertheless, the motive for most of the voluntary deaths in these Old Testament examples is consistent with the later stories of martyrdom. Abimelech, though wounded, kills himself to avoid the indignity of a woman killing him. The choice for him was an honourable death at once and an unbearably disgraceful one in the immediate future. Saul and the armour-bearer fall on their swords to prevent the uncircumcised killing them. The deaths are tragic and noble. Samson's pulling down the temple which kills him and his adversaries is again explained as an inevitable and unavoidable way of averting humiliation.

There is therefore a noble cause that is espoused or, rather, the avoidance of a dishonourable ending for the hero. The death is no reckless or self-indulgent act. The stories are exemplary, as the later martyrdom stories were to be. They are intended to encourage and hearten the reader to put a noble cause above self. In all cases (even when the main character is a traitor) the events are seen as divinely ordered.

A change in Hebrew writing occurred once belief in an afterlife developed and took hold. Whereas in earlier times the desire was for deliverance from the troubles of this life (as in books like Job or Ecclesiasticus, which caution against voluntary death by emphasizing the value of life), in Hellenistic times we observe that a belief in immortality carries with it the promise of a better future beyond death. A transformed universe is thus envisaged and self-sacrifice becomes possible and is even a desirable goal.

The Old Testament Apocrypha and pseudepigrapha

It is later in the Old Testament apocryphal texts that the concept of martyrdom and the efficacy of such behaviour is advocated. The persecutions related in the books of Maccabees are comparable to the onslaughts on Christianity in its early centuries, and they provide the context for stories in which heroes withstand dreadful tortures and death rather than surrender their beliefs. Thus we read in 1 Maccabees 6:44 of Eleazar Avaran who gave his life to save his people and to win for himself an everlasting name. His death is therefore no selfish act: it results in positive benefits. 2 Maccabees 6:10–12 details punishments and martyrdoms designed "not to destroy but to discipline our people."

A different Eleazar appears in 2 Maccabees 6:18–31; he refuses to eat swine's flesh and welcomes death with honour "rather than life with pollution" and "he went up to the rack of his own accord." We compare this with the early Christian martyrs' refusal to sacrifice to Roman gods (see below). In the case of Razis (2 Macc. 14:37–46), his particularly gory end is self-inflicted because he is accused by the Romans of Judaism "for which he had with all zeal risked life and limb" (2 Macc. 14:38). Razis prefers to kill himself rather than surrender, and, in so doing, he is alert to his own imminent bodily resurrection (14:46). The story of the mother and her seven sons in 2 Macc. 7:1–41 again starts as a refusal to eat pork. Each of her seven sons in turn is tortured and killed.

In 4 Maccabees 17:1 the mother of the seven sons kills herself. Fourth Maccabees 5–17:1 repeats the stories of Second Maccabees 6:18–7:41 in even more lurid detail, showing the ongoing relevance of the original tales for the edification of later generations. In these rewritings, the deaths now bring vicarious atonement for sinful Israel. Fourth Maccabees is usually dated to the first century CE.[11] The stories were retold at annual commemorations to celebrate the martyr's death at his supposed death site (as may be seen from clues in 4 Macc. 1:10; 3:19; 17:7–10).

These accounts of Maccabean martyrs were clearly more of an influence on Christian writers than the earlier Old Testament stories of voluntary deaths. The stories of Eleazar and of the mother and her seven sons are recalled in two Christian *acta: The Martyrdom of Marian and James* 13.1 and *The Martyrdom of Montanus and Lucius* 16.4. Origen in his *Exhortation to Martyrdom* (written to persecuted Christians in Caesarea in 235) cites the examples of these Maccabean martyrs. For Origen martyrdom was seen as a second baptism and as a means of achieving forgiveness of sins (*Exhortation* 30; cf. *Homilies on Leviticus* 2.4). Fourth Maccabees influenced Gregory of Nazianzus, John Chrysostom, Ambrose, and Augustine. These Fathers read it as a Christian text, the Jewish martyrs being portrayed as Christian proto-martyrs. Gregory's oration on the martyrs says that these Jews lived according to the cross even though they lived before Jesus![12] Augustine in *City of God* 18.36 explains that the books of Maccabees were preserved by the church because of their stories about martyrdom.[13] The heroic actions of the main characters show that their deaths were to have vicarious benefits. The martyrs were eager to die in the face of opposition to their beliefs – and they are thus worthy precursors to Christians who shared those attitudes.

Josephus

Josephus (37–100) certainly belongs to a similar school of thought. He retells the stories of the six Old Testament examples of suicides, noted above, branding their deaths as honourable.[14] Those deaths were portrayed as examples for posterity's sake. To die by one's own hand here shows a noble escape from intolerable conditions and that message was especially relevant for those martyred under Antiochus IV "Epiphanes."[15]

It is, of course, Josephus to whom we turn for details of the Masada episode, when 960 volunteers died rather than succumb to capture by Rome.[16] Contrary to Josephus's speech condemning suicide by his surviving forty troops at Jotapata, when he judged the situation worth overcoming in order to effect subsequent change, at Masada circumstances were such that voluntary death is accepted as inevitable and thus approved of.[17] The creation of martyrs then was deemed to be efficacious.

Rabbinic writings

Similar attitudes to martyrdom are also found within Jewish writings from later Christian centuries. Even though the teachings of the Rabbis strongly preserve the sanctity of human life, nonetheless even in some Rabbinic texts the benefits of martyrdom for one's faith are found; these are similar to Christians' warnings that one must not deliberately put one's life in danger, but that occasionally martyrdom is to be encouraged. See for instance *Leviticus Rabbah* 32.1, extolling the virtuous deaths of Jewish martyrs at Roman hands, and the reasons for their martyrdom:

> What is the reason that you go forth to be stoned? Because I circumcised my son. What is the reason that you go forth to be burned? Because I have kept the Sabbath. What is the reason that you go forth to be killed? Because I have eaten unleavened bread.

Pagan literature

Jewish literature would have been supplemented by the tales of heroic deaths told in Greek and Roman sources. For example, the philosophic schools of the Stoics, the Cynics, and the Epicureans encouraged voluntary death if the circumstances for such an action were present. Pagan examples often refer to the death of Socrates, as idealized by Plato. Also Plato in *Phaedo* allows for voluntary death when God brings compulsion to bear on an individual. Divine initiative in the form of a sign was looked for. That was why Cato's suicide was approved of by Cicero.

First-century Christian precedents

Above all, it was Christ's example of giving his own life that needed to be followed. Although Christians may have taught that Jesus' self-sacrifice was uniquely redemptive and a once-and-for-all act that left no need for any subsequent comparable action by believers, nonetheless his followers were expected to emulate his career. (See 1 Pet. 3:18, regardless of which of the principal textual variants are accepted as original, and 1 Pet. 2:21 where Christians are enjoined to follow Jesus' footsteps and to suffer.) Martyrdom was recognized and extolled as compatible with Christ's vicarious sacrifice. Despite the teaching that those who were united in Christ through baptism (Rom. 6:4) were *already* sharing in the benefits of his resurrection and were confident in their assurance of eternal life, the urge and urgency to pass over prematurely to join the risen Christ became dominant at certain stages in the first two Christian centuries, precisely because death was believed *not* to be final.

Jesus dies not by his own hand but because of his own decision to surrender his life. He is portrayed as having an awareness that he is following the divine plan which, inevitably, he is destined to complete, as is seen in John 10:18: "No one takes my life from me. I give it up of my own free will. I have the right to give it up, and I have the right to take it back. That is what my Father has commanded me to do" (cf. John 8:21–29).

As the primary participant in the divine plan, Jesus could not have avoided his death, as the Gethsemane incident in the Synoptic Gospels makes plain (Mark 14:36 and parallels). Christians therefore wanted to follow his example and his teaching, in which the saying about the taking up of one's cross (Matt. 10:38, 16:24, and parallels) was interpreted literally. The mission of the twelve (Matt. 10:18; Luke 12:11) and the prophecies in the eschatological discourse (Luke 21:12; Mark 13:9) have their consequence and fulfilment in Luke's second volume, Acts, where the apostles are indeed arraigned before governors, councils, and kings on several occasions. That milieu and comparable scenes are continued and developed in the *acta* of the Christian martyrs and the apocryphal Acts.

Apart from Jesus himself, the other principal early Christian precedence for martyrdom before the emergence of the apocryphal Acts is Stephen, the prototype Christian martyr.[18] In the New Testament Stephen is arrested and called before the Council. His death is clearly modelled on comparable details in the account of Jesus' death.[19] Stephen's martyrdom is described as having been beneficial in one particular regard: Saul was an onlooker at Stephen's death, and that experience of observing a Christian suffer for his faith influenced his subsequent post-conversion career as Paul.

Paul in the New Testament lists the hardships he endures for the gospel. He is a sufferer, as are all the other apostles in the later apocryphal Acts. Although the canonical Acts does not retail Paul's death, his afflictions, grief, and punishments are triumphantly paraded by him in various of his letters (e.g. Phil. 1:17, 2:27, 4:11–14; 2 Cor. 1:8–9, 6:4–5, 11:24–29). If we accept the variant *kauthesomai* ("that I may burn") in 1 Corinthians 13:3 it seems as if Paul was prepared to face death as a martyr. These privations and Paul's glorying in them acted as strong spurs for later Christians to emulate his example, and of course served to inspire tales in the apocryphal Acts. But it is Philippians 1:21 where his words on his attitude to death may be found: "For to me, living is Christ and dying is gain."[20] The interpretation of this verse as his seeming intention to achieve release from earthly troubles and to continue to live with Christ in death was to serve as a powerful impetus to subsequent generations of Christians and to those prepared to undergo martyrdom. That teaching served to impress constancy, especially among new converts, but, of course, within the context in Philippians Paul rejects the solution posed in that verse for the sake of helping the church there.

Origin of the martyrdom stories

The early Christian stories about martyrdom seem to have originated in times of general or localized persecution.[21] We know of several periods when Christians suffered such persecution. From its earliest days Christians were marked out. Tacitus *Annals* 15.44 describes the deaths of Christians under Nero in 64. They were scapegoats at a time of social unrest; merely admitting to being a Christian was a capital offense. Christians were seen as antisocial because they separated from society, abandoning their public religious duties. Tacitus even reports the pity the martyrs evoked (cf. Suetonius, *Life of Nero* 16).

Two centuries later, following many times of persecutions in-between times, Decius *c*.249 required all citizens, but especially Christians or those suspected of embracing Christianity, to sacrifice and to obtain certificates, *libelli*, showing that they had done so. Valerian in 257–8 likewise required Christians to produce certificates to prove they had sacrificed. Also, Christians could not assemble at this time. Diocletian's great persecution (303–5) revived the edict of Valerian. This was a major time for persecution and martyrdoms as churches were razed, and Christians killed. Troubles persisted for several more years until respite was found in the Edict of Toleration in 311, but it was Constantine and the Edict of Milan in 313 that put an end to officially inspired persecution.

We turn now to stories of Christian martyrdom in the *acta*. Many of these were produced in the third century, precisely when the earliest apocryphal Acts were being composed. Some of these *acta* may be pre-Decius.

Acta sanctorum[22]

There is a vast Christian hagiographical corpus among which are the *acta* of the martyrs. The earliest *acta sanctorum*, or *acta martyrum*, unlike the apocryphal Acts, have a certain freshness and immediacy, suggesting a closeness to the facts, free from fanciful elements and relatively unadorned. Their historicity has been frequently questioned, but, in general, they contain a high degree of verisimilitude, as T. D. Barnes attempted to show in the case of the nine *acta* that seem to be pre-Decian.[23] He investigated the allegedly historical details within these, and concluded that not all should be regarded as accurately reporting the trials of Christians:

> The *Acts of Apollonius* ... must be rejected. ... The *Acts of Carpus, Papylus and Agathonice*, even if they are based on a genuine substratum, are inadmissible in their extant recensions and perhaps belong to the Decian persecution rather than the second century. The stories of Ptolemaeus and Lucius and of Potemiaena and Basidides may have been refashioned for literary genres. The accuracy of the *Acts of the Scillitan Martyrs* has been defended, as has that of the short recension of the *Acts of Justin and his Companions*. The *Martyrdom of Polycarp*, the *Martyrs of Lugdunum* [Lyons] and the *Passion of Perpetua and Felicitas* have all been argued to be contemporary with the events they describe.[24]

The martyrdoms at Vienne and Lyons, for instance, are said to have taken place originally at the festival of the three provinces of Gaul in 177. Polycarp's death occurs during the public games in Smyrna. By contrast, no scholar would try or be able to defend the historicity of the apocryphal Acts, although as we shall see, those stories did give rise to vigorous traditions, especially regarding geographical features such as burial places which adherents accepted as historically accurate.

The Martyrdom of Polycarp is the oldest account of a Christian martyrdom outside the New Testament. It seems to have been composed around the middle of the second century when the church was at variance with Rome. The central concern was the irreconcilable difference between those who refused to acknowledge any Lord bar Christ and those who required its citizens to demonstrate their loyalty to the state by their devotion to Caesar. Polycarp's martyrdom, *c*.167 (or maybe a decade earlier), is presented as a model worthy of emulation (in contrast to the overenthusiastic example of Quintus in *Martyrdom of Polycarp* 4 – especially as he ultimately rescinded). There are striking parallels between Jesus' death and Polycarp's, but the significant emphases are that Polycarp is acting in accordance with the divine will and that his death is no self-indulgence but an example to be followed for the good of the Christian community. It has a public significance and relevance. The seven extant manuscripts that contain the martyrdom in Greek are dated from the tenth through thirteenth centuries, which shows how popular the story was, being copied and repeated over eight centuries after the event. The death itself is described in terms that would not be out of place in a near contemporary apocryphal Acts:

When the lawless men eventually realized that his body could not be consumed by the fire, they ordered an executioner to go up to him and stab him with a dagger. And when he did this, there came out a dove and a large quantity of blood, so that it extinguished the fire; and the whole crowd was amazed that there should be so great a difference between the unbelievers and the elect. This man was certainly one of the elect, the most remarkable Polycarp, who proved to be an apostolic and prophetic teacher in our own time, bishop of the catholic church in Smyrna. For every word that came from his mouth was accomplished and will be accomplished.

(*The Martyrdom of Polycarp* 16)

The centurion, therefore, seeing the opposition raised by the Jews, set Polycarp's body in the middle and cremated it, as is their custom. And so later on we took up his bones, which are more valuable than precious stones and finer than refined gold, and deposited them in a suitable place. There, when we gather together as we are able, with joy and gladness, the Lord will permit us to celebrate the birthday of his martyrdom in commemoration of those who have already fought in the contest and also for the training and preparation of those who will do so in the future.

(*The Martyrdom of Polycarp* 18)

Such is the story of the blessed Polycarp. Although he (together with those from Philadelphia) was the twelfth person martyred in Smyrna, he alone is especially remembered by everyone, so that he is spoken of everywhere, even by pagans. He proved to be not only a distinguished teacher but also an outstanding martyr whose martyrdom all desire to imitate since it was in accord with the pattern of the gospel of Christ. By his endurance he defeated the unrighteous magistrate and so received the crown of immortality; now he rejoices with the apostles and all the righteous, and glorifies the almighty God and Father, and blesses our Lord Jesus Christ, the Saviour of our souls and Helmsman of our bodies and Shepherd of the catholic church throughout the world.

(*The Martyrdom of Polycarp* 19)

Note the teaching, requiring the *imitation* of the martyr's example.

A first-person narrative is found in the *Martyrdom of Perpetua and Felicitas*. The martyrdoms described here occurred in Carthage at the very beginning of the third century. At *Martyrdom of Perpetua and Felicitas* 7.9 and 16.3 we see that the deaths were related to Geta's birthday – such a detail gave the story verisimilitude. Prior to her actual fight with beasts Perpetua had a vision (one of several in the account):

My clothes were stripped off, and suddenly I was a man. My seconds began to rub me down with oil (as they are wont to do before a contest). Then I saw the Egyptian on the other side rolling in the dust. Next there came forth a man of marvellous stature, such that he rose above the top of the amphitheatre. He was clad in a beltless purple tunic with two stripes (one on either side) running down the middle of his chest. He wore sandals that were wondrously made of gold and silver, and he carried a wand like an athletic trainer and a green branch on which there were golden apples. And he asked for silence and said: "If this Egyptian defeats her he will slay her with the sword. But if she defeats him, she will receive this branch." Then he withdrew. We drew close to one another and began to let our fists fly. My opponent tried to get hold of my feet, but I kept striking him in the face with the heels of my feet. Then I was raised up into the air and I began to pummel him without as it were touching the ground. Then when I noticed there was a lull, I put my two hands together linking the fingers of one hand with those of the other and thus I got hold of his head. He fell flat on his face and I stepped on his head. The crowd began to shout and my assistants started to sing psalms. Then I walked up to the trainer and took the branch. He kissed me and said to me: "Peace be with you, my daughter!" I began to walk in triumph towards the Gate of Life. Then I awoke.

(*Martyrdom of Perpetua and Felicitas* 10)[25]

Of the contest we read:

For the young women, however, the Devil had prepared a mad heifer. This was an unusual animal, but it was chosen that their sex might be matched with that of the beast. So they were stripped naked, placed in nets and thus brought out into the arena. Even the crowd was horrified when they saw that one was a delicate young girl and the other was a woman fresh from child birth with the milk still dripping from her breasts. And so they were brought back again and dressed in unbelted tunics. First the heifer tossed Perpetua and she fell on her back. Then sitting up she pulled down the tunic that was ripped along the side so that it covered her thighs, thinking more of her modesty than of her pain. Next she asked for a pin to fasten her untidy hair: for it was not right that a martyr should die with her hair in disorder, lest she might seem to be mourning in her hour of triumph. Then she got up. And seeing that Felicitas had been crushed to the ground, she went over to her, gave her her hand, and lifted her up. Then the two stood side by side. But the cruelty of the mob was by now appeased, and so they were called back through the Gate of Life.

(*Martyrdom of Perpetua and Felicitas* 20)[26]

See also *The Acts of Justin and his Companions*. Justin Martyr's death is normally dated as 165 in Rome.

The prefect Rusticus said: "You do admit, then, that you are a Christian?" "Yes, I am," said Justin. To Chariton the prefect Rusticus said: "Tell me further, Chariton: are you a Christian, too?" "I am," said Chariton, "by God's command." The prefect Rusticus turned to Charito and asked her: "What say you, Charito?" "I am a Christian," said Charito, "by the gift of God." The prefect Rusticus said to Evelpistus: "And what are you, Evelpistus?" Evelpistus, one of the emperor's slaves, answered: "I too am a Christian. I have been freed by Christ and I share in the same hope by the favour of Christ." The prefect Rusticus turned to Hierax: "Are you a Christian, too?" "Yes, I am," said Hierax; "I adore and worship the same God." "Did Justin convert you to Christianity?" asked the prefect Rusticus. "I have long been a Christian," said Hierax, "and ever shall be." Paeon arose and spoke: "I am a Christian also." "Who instructed you?" asked the prefect Rusticus. "I received this good faith from my parents," said Paeon. "I listened gladly to the teaching of Justin," said Evelpistus, "but I also received my faith from my parents."

(*The Acts of Justin and his Companions* Recension B.3–4)[27]

The Prefect turned to Justin: "You are said to be learned. You think you know the true doctrine. Tell me: if you are scourged and beheaded, do you suppose that you will ascend to heaven?" "I have confidence," said Justin, "that if I endure all this I shall possess his mansions. Indeed, I know that for all those who live a just life there awaits the divine gift even to the consummation of the whole world." The prefect Rusticus said: "You think, then, that you will ascend to heaven to receive certain worthy rewards?" "I do not think," said Justin, "but I have accurate knowledge and am fully assured of it." "Well then," said the prefect Rusticus, "let us come to the point at issue, a necessary and pressing business. Agree together to offer sacrifice to the gods." "No one of sound mind," said Justin, "turns from piety to impiety." The prefect Rusticus said: "If you do not obey, you will be punished without mercy." Justin said: "We are confident that if we suffer the penalty for the sake of our Lord Jesus Christ we shall be saved, for this is the confidence and salvation we shall have at the terrible tribunal of our Saviour and Master sitting in judgement over the whole world." Similarly the other martyrs said, "Do what you will. We are Christians and we do not offer sacrifice to idols." The prefect Rusticus passed judgement, saying: "Those who have refused to sacrifice to the gods and to yield to the emperor's edict are to be led away to be scourged and beheaded in accordance with the laws."

(*The Acts of Justin and his Companions* Recension B.5)[28]

The martyrdoms recounted in *The Acts of the Scillitan Martyrs* occurred in North Africa c. 180.[29] This work is the earliest dated document from the Latin church in North Africa. J. A. Robinson's edition is based on three Latin manuscripts dating from the ninth through thirteenth centuries, and one Greek manuscript of the ninth century. Many consider the account authentic. One example suffices:

Speratus said: "We have never done wrong; we have never lent ourselves to wickedness. Never have we uttered a curse; but when abused, we have given thanks, for we hold our own emperor in honour." Saturninus the proconsul said: "We too are a religious people, and our religion is a simple one: we swear by the genius of our lord the emperor and we offer prayers for his health – as you also ought to do." ... "If you begin to malign our sacred rites," said Saturninus, "I shall not listen to you. But swear rather by the genius of our lord the emperor." Speratus said: "I do not recognize the empire of this world. Rather, I serve that God whom no man has seen, nor can see, with these eyes. I have not stolen; and on any purchase I pay the tax, for I acknowledge my lord who is the emperor of kings and of all nations."

(The Acts of the Scillitan Martyrs 1–6)[30]

The Martyrdom of Apollonius occurred between 180 and 185 in Rome and represents a philosopher's defence of Christianity:

Apollonius answered: "I have been glad to live, Perennis, but I have not been afraid of death because of my love of life. There is nothing more precious than life – that is, eternal life – which is the immortality of the soul that has lived a good life on earth."

(The Martyrdom of Apollonius 30)[31]

Most of these accounts maintained their popularity and importance. Some of the Christian *acta* read like trial transcripts supplemented by dialogue, including a confession and death sentence. However, although most post-Constantinian accounts are pure fiction, even the earlier *acta* were literary creations written for and used in the liturgies of communities, especially on the anniversary of the martyrdom. As we saw earlier, the anniversary of Polycarp's death is referred to in the *Martyrdom of Polycarp* 18.3 – that date then became the anniversary date when believers would honour his memory and example. Accounts of martyrdom were known to have been read in Carthage and a calendar of the deaths of martyrs was established there under Cyprian in the second century. All apostles, with the possible exception of John, were remembered as martyrs from the second century onwards. The example of the North African churches in additionally remembering liturgically the pagan Alexandrian *acta* based on the court protocols was followed. (See below on the Alexandrian martyrs.)

The separate *acta* of these Christian martyrs' stories reminded Christianity of its historical roots and served as memorials of its faithful dead; but they were also primarily intended to strengthen communities. The emphasis is on the Christian's death; there is no interest in his earlier career. That marks them out from the original second-century apocryphal Acts which, in their entirety, gave a high priority to the acts, miracles, speeches, prayers, and travels of the eponymous hero.

Influence of the Acts and *acta*

Although the original five apocryphal Acts were composed in the second century, copies and rewritings can be found from many centuries thereafter. This shows they were bestsellers. The fact also that many of these Acts were translated into different languages betrays the geographical spread of these popular tales. The manuscripts of the Christian *acta* tell a similar textual story. Most of the texts edited in Musurillo's *Acts of the Christian Martyrs* are based on medieval manuscript copies. Among the major common features are the following related topics. These show the abiding significance of the stories and the reasons why many were preserved:

The reappearance of the martyr beyond death

From the apocryphal Acts we read that Paul reappears, and as a consequence Nero ceases to punish the brethren.

> Paul came about the ninth hour, and in the presence of all he said, "Caesar, behold, here is Paul, the soldier of God; I am not dead but live in my God. But upon you, unhappy one, many evils and great punishment will come because you have unjustly shed the blood of the righteous not many days ago." And having spoken this Paul departed from him. When Nero had heard he commanded that the prisoners be released, Patroclus as well as Barsabas with his friends. And, as Paul had told them, Longus and Cestus, the centurion, came in fear very early to the grave of Paul. And when they drew near they found two men in prayer and Paul with them, and they became frightened when they saw the unexpected miracle, but Titus and Luke, being afraid at the sight of Longus and Cestus, turned to run away. But they followed and said to them, "We follow you not in order to kill you, blessed men of God, as you imagine, but in order to live, that you may do to us as Paul promised us. We have just seen him in prayer beside you." Upon hearing this Titus and Luke gave them joyfully the seal in the Lord, glorifying God and the Father of our Lord Jesus Christ to whom be glory for ever and ever. Amen.
>
> (*Acts of Paul*, Martyrdom 6–7)

We see elsewhere that a martyrdom account can contain a similar story showing that martyr's enduring influence. The story of Potamiaena occurs in Eusebius, *Ecclesiastical History* 6.5; here her reappearance after death causes the conversion of Basilides, the soldier, to Christianity. The efficacy of the dead martyr is proof of the positive benefit of that death, and, as such, doubtless encouraged the preservation and dissemination of these stories for centuries thereafter.

Relics

Coupled with the above, the stories fuelled (and maybe already reflected) a belief in the efficacy of a martyr's relics, which became a tradition that has continued in many parts of Christianity. Relics emphasized in a tangible way the theological point that these Christian martyrs' deaths were influential even after death. Like Jesus himself, their active influence continued beyond the grave.

One of the earliest such stories is in the *Acts of Thomas*, where Thomas's continuing influence manifests itself through the remains in his tomb:

> Now it came to pass after a long time that one of the children of Misdaeus the king was a demoniac and no one could cure him, for the devil was extremely fierce. And Misdaeus the king took thought and said, "I will go and open the sepulchre, and take a bone of the apostle of God and hang it upon my son, and he shall be healed." But while Misdaeus thought about this, the apostle Thomas appeared to him and said to him, "You did not believe in a living man, and will you believe in the dead? Yet fear not, for my Lord Jesus Christ has compassion on you and pities you of his goodness." And he went and opened the sepulchre, but did not find the apostle there, for one of the brethren had stolen him away and taken him to Mesopotamia but from that place where the bones of the apostle had lain Misdaeus took dust and put it about his son's neck, saying, "I believe in you, Jesus Christ, now that he has left me who troubles men and opposes them lest they should see you." And when he had hung it upon his son, the boy became whole.
>
> (*Acts of Thomas* 170)

The place of burial

The legends of the apostles continued not only in literary forms or in theological beliefs but were also celebrated geographically. The tombs of many of them became places of pilgrimage. The events leading to the death were rooted to a site, and that doubtless encouraged belief in the historicity of these tales. The location of St John's burial place in Ephesus was known to Justin, Clement of Alexandria, and Irenaeus. Peter's and Paul's deaths are firmly rooted in Rome in the apocryphal traditions. Thecla in the *Acts of Paul* dies in Seleucia, although in later traditions Egypt also claimed her, as too did Ephesus, Milan, and Tarragona. Thomas's original burial was believed to have been in Mylapore near Madras according to the *Acts of Thomas* 170, before his body was removed to Edessa. Philip was believed to have been buried in Heliodorus.[32]

Summary

The existence, popularity, and distribution of the apocryphal Acts and of the *acta* prove the lively interest in and influence of these characters' deaths. The apocryphal Acts had all originated in the second century – a period when most persecutions occurred and before Constantine's establishment of Christianity as the state religion ended officially inspired persecutions of Christians. But, obviously, the stories continued to be popular for centuries afterwards, showing that the value of stories which told of the deaths of apostles as martyrs was maintained. Even where their examples of role models showing how the persecuted needed to stand firm was less immediately relevant, nonetheless the fact that Christians from the beginning were prepared to die for their faith was intended to send the message that this was indeed a faith proudly to uphold. Many of the Christian martyrdoms were known to and repeated by Eusebius.[33] His *Ecclesiastical History* is the principal source for the *Letter of the Churches of Lyons and Vienne*, *The Martyrdom of Potamiaena and Basilides*, *The Martyrdom of Marinus*, and *The Letter of Phileas*. He, writing after Constantine had established himself at the head of a Christian empire, was still finding it valuable to retail these stories about martyrdom, not only to show us the reality of being a Christian during the bad old days (in contrast to a now peaceful present and hopefully a stable future), but for the precise purpose of indicating that this faith was, and always had been, a worthwhile and enduring set of principles to hold.

Appendix: pagan Acts

The Acts of the Pagan Martyrs (*Acta Alexandrorum*) is a compilation of Egyptian papyrological collections concerned with the relationship of Alexandrians (notably Jews) to Rome.[34] Alexandrian Greeks received harsh treatment at the hands of the Romans and their experiences were not dissimilar to those of Christians. Many were martyred. They, like the Christian *acta*, were originally court transcripts supplemented later by speeches and other reports. Many are incomplete or fragmentary. Again, the flowering of such documents occurred in the first through third centuries CE and they may be described as semi-literary creations. Many are described by Musurillo as "reworked protocols." We select two:

The Acts of Isidorus is possibly based on accusations against Jews that occurred in the mid-first century:

> Isidorus: "My Lord Augustus, with regard to your interests, Balbillus indeed speaks well. But to you, Agrippa, I wish to retort in connexion with the points you bring up about the Jews. I accuse them of wishing to stir up the entire world. ... We must consider the entire mass. They are not of the same temperament as the Alexandrians, but live rather after the fashion of the Egyptians. Are they not on a level with those who pay the poll-tax?" Agrippa: "The Egyptians have had taxes levied on them by their rulers. ... But no one has levied taxes on the Jews." Balbillus: "Look to what extremes of insolence either his god or ... ."
>
> (*The Acts of Isidorus* Recension C [P. Berol. 8877])[35]

Acts of Paulus and Antoninus is possibly referring to events in 117–20:

> Paulus: "My only concern is for the grave in Alexandria which I expect to have. Advancing as I am towards this, I shall have no fear of telling you the truth. Listen to me then, Caesar, as to one who may not live beyond the morrow." Antoninus: "My Lord Caesar, I swear by your genius he speaks the truth as one who may not live another day. For when we were in such pressing circumstances and so many letters had been sent you saying that (the prefect)

had ordered the impious Jews to transfer their residence to a place from which they could easily attack and ravage our well-named city – if not a line on this matter fell into your beneficent hands, then the reason for your august words is clear. It is obvious that this has been perpetrated against you, to prevent you from having any evidence of the woes that have befallen us." Caesar: "Let Paulus go; but have Antoninus bound … ."

(*Acts of Paulus and Antoninus* Louvre 2376*bis* cols vi–vii)[36]

Tertullian, somewhat uniquely among Christian writers, in his pre-Montanist period extolled the examples of pagan martyrs. In his *Apology* I.5–9, he names several examples, such as C. Mucius Scaevola, Anaxarchus, and Zeno of Elea.[37] Similar lists occur in his *To The Heathen* i.18 and *To the Martyrs* 4. Clement of Alexandria is the only other notable early Father to see benefit in pagan martyrdoms: *Miscellanies* 4.17.1–3 draws Christians' attention to the examples of pagans.

Further reading

J. H. Charlesworth (ed.), *The Old Testament Pseudepigrapha*, London: Darton, Longman & Todd, 2 vols, 1982 and 1985.

A. J. Droge and J. D. Tabor, *A Noble Death*, New York: HarperCollins, 1992. (A well-documented discussion on voluntary death in pagan, Jewish, and early Christian sources.)

J. K. Elliott, *The Apocryphal New Testament*, Oxford: Clarendon, 1993. (A major collection containing English translations of apocryphal Acts and other early non-canonical Christian writings.)

W. H. C. Frend, *Martyrdom and Persecution in the Early Church*, Oxford: Blackwell, 1965. (A respected and classic study of biblical and patristic teachings about the conflicts from the Maccabees to Donatus.)

H. J. Lawlor and J. E. L. Oulton, *Eusebius: The Ecclesiastical History and the Martyrs of Palestine*, 2 vols, London: SPCK, 1954. (Vol. 1: Translation; vol. 2: Introduction and Notes.)

P. Middleton, *Radical Martyrdom and Cosmic Conflict in Early Christianity*, Library of New Testament Studies 307, London: T & T Clark, 2008. (A thesis that promotes the argument that volitional martyrdom was a significant form of devotion in the earliest Christian cultures.)

H. Musurillo, *The Acts of the Christian Martyrs*, Oxford: Clarendon, 1972. (Introductions to and the English text of twenty-eight early martyrdom accounts.), *The Acts of the Pagan Martyrs: Acta Alexandrinorum*, Oxford: Clarendon, 1954. (The Greek fragments, English translations, notes, and commentary on about twenty-one texts or dubious fragments.)

W. Whiston (trans.), *The Works of Josephus: New Updated Edition*, Peabody, MA: Hendrickson. (Despite its having been translated by Whiston in the early eighteenth century, the translation has been regularly updated. The 1994 [9th reprint] by Hendrickson is a convenient and serviceable one-volume collection.)

Notes

1 A. Hilhorst recommends our reserving *acta* for accounts based on the court records and *actūs* for the deeds of the famous apostles (πραξεις), which are found in the apocryphal literature. A. Hilhorst, "The Apocryphal Acts as Martyrdom Texts: the Case of the Acts of Andrew," in J. N. Bremmer (ed.), *The Apocryphal Acts of John*, Kampen, Netherlands: Kok Pharos, 1995, pp. 1–14.

2 H. Musurillo, *The Acts of the Christian Martyrs*, Oxford: Clarendon, 1972, pp. lii–liii.

3 I. Czachesz, "The Gospel of Peter and the Apocryphal Acts of the Apostles," in T. J. Kraus and T. Nicklas (eds), *Das Evangelium nach Petrus: Text, Kontexte, Intertexte*, Texte und Untersuchungen 158, Berlin and New York: de Gruyter, 2007, pp. 235–62. Czachesz tries to show on that, because of oral traditions, common features became the blueprint to which all these differing genres of martyrdom

stories adhere, thereby creating many points of agreement, on both a literary and compositional, as well as a conceptual, level (see esp. "Martyrdom Texts in Cognitive Perspective," pp. 256ff.).

4 See J. K. Elliott, *The Apocryphal New Testament*, Oxford: Clarendon, 1993.

5 See, for example, M. R. James, *Apocryphal New Testament*, Oxford: Clarendon, 1924, p. xix.

6 For more on Paul see H. W. Tajra, *The Martyrdom of St. Paul*, Wissenschaftliche Untersuchungen zum Neuen Testament 2.67, Tübingen: Mohr (Siebeck), 1994.

7 *Acts of Peter* 35(6).

8 *Acts of Peter* 36(7).

9 See D. Daube, "Death as a Release in the Bible," *Novum Testamentum* 5, 1962, pp. 82–104.

10 A. J. Droge and J. D. Tabor, *A Noble Death*, New York: HarperCollins, 1992.

11 H. Anderson in his introduction to 4 Macc. in J. H. Charlesworth (ed.), *The Old Testament Pseudepigrapha*, vol. 2, London: Darton, Longman & Todd, 1982, pp. 533–4.

12 Charlesworth, *Old Testament Pseudepigrapha*, pp. 541f.

13 Augustine was against voluntary death (*City of God* 1.19): his teaching influenced Christian teaching on suicide thereafter for many centuries.

14 Josephus, *Antiquities of the Jews* 5.251–53, 317; 6.370–73; 7.229; 8.311.

15 Josephus, *Antiquities of the Jews* 12.256, 274, 373. Jews are encouraged to face death in defence of their law in Josephus, *Against Apion* 2.233–34. Death is seen as freedom from slavery and torture by Herod in *Jewish War* 1.311ff. Cf. the example of the priests in the Temple in *Jewish War* 1.150–51.

16 Josephus, *Jewish War* 7.252–407.

17 Josephus, *Jewish War* 3.375, cf. 3.331.

18 Jesus is described as a martyr in Rev. 1:5, 3:14, although that is not a common designation by later Christian writers. Discussion of Judas's death is not relevant here. His death (in Matthew's account) is related to his repentance and in any case is seen both in Matthew and Acts as a fitting end for a deicide. The New Testament does not condemn his suicide. There is similarly no condemnation for Paul's gaoler's would-be suicide in Philippi (Acts 16:27–30). Neither of these is of course a martyr, prepared to die for faith.

19 Surprisingly, unlike the apocryphal tales of Peter or of Paul written in the second century, it was much later when Christians concocted further stories about Stephen. François Bovon has been active recently researching this material. See his "Beyond the Book of Acts: Stephen, the First Christian Martyr, in Traditions outside the New Testament Canon of Scripture," *Perspectives in Religious Studies* 32, 2005, pp. 93–107; "The Dossier on Stephen, the First Martyr," *Harvard Theological Review* 96, 2003, pp. 279–305; (with B. Bouvier) "Étienne le premier martyr: Du livre canonique au récit apocryphe," in C. Breytenbach and J. Schröter, with D. S. Du Toit (eds), *Die Apostelgeschichte und die hellenistische Geschichtsschreibung*, Ancient Judaism and Early Christianity 57, Leiden: Brill, 2004, pp. 19–31; "La révélation d'Étienne ou l'invention des reliques d'Étienne, la saint premier martyr (Sinaiticus Graecus 493)," in Albert Frey and Rémi Gounelle (eds), *Poussières de christianisme et de la judaïsme antiques*, Prahins: Éditions de Zèbre, 2007, pp. 79–105.

20 See D. W. Palmer, "To Die is Gain (Philippians 1 21)," *Novum Testamentum* 17, 1975, pp. 203–18.

21 See W. H. C. Frend, *Martyrdom and Persecution in the Early Church*, Oxford: Blackwell, 1965.

22 H. Musurillo, *The Acts of the Christian Martyrs*, Oxford: Clarendon, 1952, gathers together twenty-eight such *acta*.

23 T. D. Barnes, "Pre-Decian Acta Martyrum," *Journal of Theological Studies* 19, 1968, pp. 509–31.

24 Barnes, "Pre-Decian Acta Martyrum," p. 527.

25 Trans. Musurillo, *Acts of the Christian Martyrs*, p. 119.

26 Trans. Musurillo, *Acts of the Christian Martyrs*, p.129.

27 Trans. Musurillo, *Acts of the Christian Martyrs*, p. 51.

28 Ibid.

29 J. A. Robinson, "Appendix: The Scillitan Martyrs," in *The Passion of S. Perpetua*, Texts and Studies 1.2, Cambridge: Cambridge University Press, 1891, pp. 106–21.

30 Trans. Musurillo, *Acts of the Christian Martyrs*, p. 87.

31 Trans. Musurillo, *Acts of the Christian Martyrs*, p. 99.

32 See S. J. Davis, *The Cult of St Thecla*, Oxford: Oxford University Press, 2001.

33 Eusebius wrote *The Martyrs of Palestine* – an account of the Diocletian persecution which he had witnessed.

34 H. A. Musurillo, *The Acts of the Pagan Martyrs: Acta Alexandrinorum*, Oxford: Clarendon, 1954. Musurillo helpfully lists characteristics common to the *Acta Alexandrinorum* and roughly contem-

poraneous Hellenistic Greek novels by Heliodorus, Achilles Tatius of Alexandria, and Chariton the author of *Aithiopika*, whose works are now recognized (thanks to recently discovered papyrus finds) as having been written centuries earlier than at one time thought (pp. 252ff). Characteristics include travelogues, imprisonments, torture, court trials, piety, Hellenistic patriotism as well as anti-Roman and anti-Jewish features.

35 Trans. Musurillo, *Acts of the Pagan Martyrs*, pp. 25–6.

36 Trans. Musurillo, *Acts of the Pagan Martyrs*, p. 58.

37 Significantly, given the context, it is in the conclusion to *Apology* 1 where we find the famous tag "*semen est sanguis Christianorum*," often rendered "The blood *of martyrs* is the seed of Christianity."

6

IGNATIUS AND THE APOSTOLIC FATHERS

Clayton N. Jefford

The collection of early patristic writings that historians now classify under the title of Apostolic Fathers offers us a unique glimpse into the early church as it came to identify itself as a community of faith after the passing of the apostles.[1] These assorted texts represent a variety of Christian voices that spoke throughout the Roman world for almost a hundred years, beginning in the last quarter of the first century. We are fortunate to know some of their authors by name (Papias of Hierapolis, Clement of Rome, Polycarp of Smyrna, and Ignatius of Antioch) and to recognize them in their role as leaders of the earliest post-apostolic church. At the same time, the identity of other authors has been lost, though it is clear from their contributions that they too added prominently to the ecclesiastical deliberations that shaped the evolving framework of the institutional church.

In any discussion of the primary themes and concerns of the Apostolic Fathers, we find that the breadth and variety of materials hamper our efforts. For example, these writings do not speak to a common concern. They are diverse in nature, mostly featuring letters that address an assortment of issues, but also a handbook of liturgical and religious teachings, a homily, a martyrology, an apology, and other sundry works. Furthermore, our authors represent a rich diversity of views within the second-century church that spanned from Italy to Syria and Asia Minor, from Greece to Egypt. They reflect training and insights borrowed from local traditions and instruction. We can hardly expect that they were in essential agreement on every aspect of the budding Christian faith or that their individual attitudes were uniformly accepted everywhere throughout the Roman world. Finally, it remains unclear as to whether the views that our authors espoused always reflect the tried and tested teachings of an ancient faith tradition, particularly as we recall that the church was still in the infancy of its development. The memory of later orthodoxy has largely accepted the wisdom of these authors as the foundation of subsequent doctrinal and ecclesiastical order. Yet it is difficult to distinguish the extent to which their views incorporated the principles of a general community faith, a so-called *regula fidei* (rule of faith), like that which guided the work of Irenaeus of Lyons and his theological heirs, or are instead better attributed to the genius of their individual faith experience.

Thus, with the difficulties that arise when we excavate a diverse and eclectic collection of writings for common themes and views, our survey seeks to measure its remarks against the work of a single, primary figure within the Apostolic Fathers, that is, Ignatius of Antioch. The bishop of a prominent church in an eastern, provincial capital at the beginning of the second century, Ignatius leaves us with the most extensive set of materials from a single mindset that dominates our collection. His seven authentic letters address a variety of issues from the late first-century and early second-century church, concerns that we now consider typical of the period. We turn, then, to the witness of the Apostolic Fathers and the transitional church of the post-apostolic period, measuring our insights by the standard of Bishop Ignatius and the views that he believed to be of primary concern to the institutional church.

Unity and liturgy

Even the most casual of readers will immediately notice that an axial concern within the Apostolic Fathers is the drive for unity. As the church shaped itself into a conventional blend of religious beliefs at the close of the first century, the need for generally acceptable standards and norms quickly became evident. The desire for unity is certainly evident throughout the larger corpus of the Apostolic Fathers, yet it is nowhere more overt than in the writings of Ignatius.[2] For the bishop of Antioch, several factors come into play in the quest for Christian unity and it is within these elements that the community of faith finds its core: church leadership, proper teaching, and correct liturgy.

With respect to ecclesiastical leadership, subsequent Christian tradition is largely dependent upon Ignatius for its vision of a three-tiered hierarchy of offices: bishop, presbyter, and deacon.[3] God's anointed who serve in these roles stand at the center of life and faith within the larger community. Most vital of these positions for Ignatius is the bishop, who embodies the presence of God among the people. A steady motif as he writes to successive communities in Asia Minor, Ignatius insists that all Christians must be in harmony with the singular authority of the local bishop.[4] His power in prayer suffices for all the church;[5] within the congregation he presides in the place of God;[6] to honor him is to be honored by God.[7] As Ignatius observes, worthy are those presbyters who are "in tune with the bishop as strings on a harp."[8]

Other authors among the Apostolic Fathers are not as clear about a similar hierarchy of leadership, though tradition has read between the lines to assume its presence. The author of 1 Clement, for example, refers to "bishops and deacons" without mention of "presbyters" as the first fruits of what the apostles appointed.[9] At the same time, however, the author of this letter focuses upon the managerial role of presbyters in the church at Corinth without mention of any particular bishop in residence there. Much like 1 Clement, the author of the Didache instructs readers to "appoint for yourselves bishops and deacons," again without any specific mention of presbyters within the community.[10] In each instance, both with 1 Clement and the Didache, the term "bishop" may refer to someone who acted as the head of a local presbytery, thus signifying the presence of presbyters behind each text, but this remains uncertain.[11]

The early church's concern for leadership closely relates to a second element of unity, that of proper teaching. Indeed, correct teaching and instruction is seen to help a bishop to verify the identity of those who are "catholic" and are thus allied with certain guidelines of faith inherited from authentic apostolic preaching.[12] For Ignatius himself, the primary threats against proper teaching are twofold: so-called "Judaizers," who seek to keep Christianity within the fold of the synagogue, and Docetists, who insist that Christ did not come in the flesh.

With respect to Judaizers, the apostle Paul had already refuted such teachings in his epistle to the Galatians, arguing that God in Christ has superseded any particular need to adhere to the scrupulosity of Jewish cult and ritual. The threat of this sort of conservatism, while certainly real both to Ignatius and his contemporaries, was destined to evaporate during the second century via the church's separation from the synagogue and rabbinic Judaism.

With respect to Docetism, yet another New Testament writer, the author of 1 John, addresses those who argue that Christ has not come in the flesh but in spirit alone, identifying them as speaking in the spirit "of the antichrist."[13] This threat is particularly poignant in the late first and second centuries, ultimately leading to the deliberations of later church councils concerning the nature of Jesus of Nazareth as the Christ, whether divine or human in form, or both. Ignatius categorizes views such as those of the Judaizers and Docetists as "heresies" and classifies them under the rubrics of "evil teaching,"[14] "ancient fables,"[15] "strange teachings,"[16] and "strange plants."[17] For Ignatius, to claim such unconventional perspectives is to stand in opposition to the bishop and to disrupt the harmony of God's faithful assemblies.

A key way in which Ignatius bolsters the confessing church against such false teachings is through his insistence upon creeds. Prior to his letters, there is no such emphasis upon this confessional tool in Christian literature. The Ignatian creed takes many forms, but typically includes the acknowledgement that Jesus Christ came both in flesh and in spirit, was both from the seed of David and from the Holy Spirit, suffered and received crucifixion under Pontius Pilate, and was raised from the dead.[18] Individual elements of these creeds maintain the divine nature of Christ's mission on earth, thus to remove the Christian confession beyond the parameters of Jewish thought. At the same time, an emphasis upon the authentically physical aspects of the life of Jesus Christ seeks to refute the claims of contemporary Docetists.

Issues associated with proper teaching surface elsewhere throughout the Apostolic Fathers, of course. Polycarp of Smyrna, for instance, reminds the Philippians that the apostle Paul taught "the word of truth" and that they should teach themselves to follow "the command of the Lord."[19] Likewise, the *Shepherd of Hermas* identifies hypocrites who instruct with "strange teachings" and warns against following the evil instruction of the angel of wickedness.[20] The clear identification of such teachings typically does not parallel the efforts of Ignatius. Instead, our authors tend to employ more general approaches to training, perhaps best illustrated by the popular use of the "two ways" philosophy. This motif appears variously in writings like *Hermas*, the *Didache*, and *Barnabas* and reflects the ancient idea that there are two courses in life, a correct path and a false path.[21] Our authors usually employ a variety of contemporary virtue and vice lists to populate their descriptions of these two ways, sometimes associating the paths with light and darkness (*Barnabas*), at other times with life and death (*Didache*), and on occasion with righteousness and wickedness (*Shepherd of Hermas*).[22] There does not tend to be a specific "teaching" that necessarily characterizes either path[23] but, instead, a series of instructions that encourage the faithful Christian to live an ethical lifestyle that is worthy of the Lord.[24] Ultimately, as with Ignatius, the intention of such teachings is to guide the faith community toward a unity of spirit and conformity.

Finally, the idea of correct liturgy and worship serves as a foundational pillar around which communal unity seeks to fashion itself. Few writings in the Apostolic Fathers speak specifically to the question of liturgical practice, but those that do so clearly hold it as a primary concern. Once again, Ignatius provides our best evidence for this consideration.

Throughout the letters of Ignatius, we find that the bishop offers constant comment upon the need for a unified liturgical approach to worship. On the one hand, he clearly assumes that all Christians unite through their common understanding of worship as ritual. At the same time, it is largely for the safe control of worship practices that each bishop sits as a unifying force within their respective communities and serves as a common link between churches in an association of orthodoxy.

Within the common experience of worship, the ritual of baptism receives much of the bishop's attention. Baptism "serves as a shield" for each Christian, who in turn functions as a soldier in the army of their bishop.[25] The common bonds of faith unite all believers into a close association of warriors for Christ. Ignatius observes that Jesus Christ himself was born and received baptism so that by suffering he might "cleanse the water" for those who believe in him.[26] In this way, all believers share, not only in the human experience of Christ, but also in the salvation that his divine activity affords. The faithful are authentic both to Christ and to one another.

Ultimately, the ritual of Eucharist forms the central framework upon which Ignatius reflects about the common worship experience. In this act, each believer participates in the one flesh of Jesus Christ and the unity that results through the blood of his one cup.[27] In his letter to Rome, the bishop insists that he himself only wants to eat the bread of God that comes through the flesh of Christ, and for drink, he only wants Christ's blood.[28] To "break one bread" as a worshipping community is both to "take the medicine of immortality"[29] and to acknowledge the authority of the bishop, without which no Eucharist or "love feast" is valid.[30] Indeed, the Docetists, who refuse to accept that participation in the Eucharist is to partake of the flesh of Jesus Christ, refrain from this liturgical ritual and thus distance themselves from the unity of the orthodox faithful.[31]

Apart from Ignatius, the Apostolic Fathers offer a variety of perspectives about the act of common Christian worship. The author of the *Didache*, for example, speaks of baptism and the exact manner by which a baptismal event should occur, from the use of "living" or running water to the ritualistic blessing that is given in the name of the Trinity.[32] In addition, Christians are instructed to fast and to pray three times daily, using the Lord's Prayer according to the form that appears in Matthew 6:9–13.[33]

Otherwise, the author offers several ancient prayers for use in the celebration of the Eucharist.³⁴ While the words of institution known from the New Testament and typical of modern practices do not appear in the *Didache*, it is surely conceivable that worshippers spoke these prayers in conjunction with such words. In either case, the prayers of the *Didache* are most noteworthy for their request that God gather the church by the four winds in order to sanctify it for the kingdom that has been prepared.³⁵ This is truly an example of worship ritual that leads to intentional unity.

Apart from the *Didache*, Hermas offers a variety of parables about the necessary unity of the church. One recalls the elm and vine, a parable that portrays the rich as the economic support by which the poor of the church may live, while the poor, through their confessions and prayers in worship, intercede with God on behalf of the wealthy.³⁶ This is a sentiment with which the author of *1 Clement* firmly agrees.³⁷ The author of the epistle to Diognetus likewise reflects a common conviction that what a person worships is what they themselves eventually become, accusing those who worship false gods of becoming false themselves.³⁸ The drive for a common and valid source of worship thus becomes central to the early Christian vision. The author of the *Martyrdom of Polycarp* insists that Christians must worship the Son of God alone, while simply loving the martyrs as "disciples and imitators of the Lord."³⁹

Thus, we find that Christians of the late first and second centuries found their various experiences of worship to reflect a universal quest for unity. As reflected by Ignatius, this was a unity of leadership, teaching, and liturgical practice. The common task of learning to confess Christ together through the shared structure of worship and fellowship undeniably went far toward drawing the early post-apostolic church away from its Jewish roots.

Between Christians and Jews

One of the more prickly issues of the early second century was the struggle of the early church to define itself over against the Jewish moorings that it eventually abandoned. The perspectives of the Apostolic Fathers run the full spectrum here, from a close association with Jewish ideals and teachings to a virtual break with Christianity's ancestral background.

In many respects, the most "Jewish" of the Apostolic Fathers is the *Didache*. In the first portion of this text, the author endorses an ethic that finds its basis in the traditional teachings of the Decalogue.⁴⁰ The reader is instructed in prohibitions against murder, adultery, false witness, and so forth, but also in those practices that lead to such sins – sorcery, being double-minded and arrogant, lying, etc. In this way, the *Didache* espouses an oral teaching that serves as a fence to protect written scripture, much like the oral and written Torah of developing rabbinic Judaism. Likewise, the liturgical teachings of the *Didache* reflect a certain Jewish sensitivity, endorsing a traditional Jewish flavor to baptism and prayer and perhaps incorporating Jewish meal prayers into the celebration of the Eucharist. Perhaps most telling here is that the *Didache* never overtly equates the figure of Jesus Christ with God, preferring instead to refer to the "Lord" throughout and leaving the reader with the choice of a strict monotheistic perspective. In all of these ways, the author of the *Didache* appears to endorse a very Jewish approach to Christianity, undoubtedly assuming the same for the audience.

Apart from the *Didache*, only *1 Clement* seems to offer any particularly Jewish view of early Christian faith. The author encourages the church at Corinth to avoid jealousy and to embrace obedience, faith, piety, hospitality, humility, and peace as aspects of a virtuous lifestyle.[41] A variety of scriptural passages surface as the basis for such teaching, including texts from the Pentateuch, as well as passages from the Prophets and Writings. Most interesting in *1 Clement*, though, is the author's appeal to Moses as a prototype of what a true Christian leader should be. It was through Moses that the tribe of Levi became priests.[42] So too, it was Moses who pleaded for God's people when they strayed from the divine will.[43] An appeal to the figure of Moses is especially important since our author makes no similar claim for any specific apostle as a model for faithful leadership. This is especially intriguing in light of the Roman origin of the letter, a community that is well familiar with the figures of Peter and Paul.[44]

In clear contrast to the *Didache* and *1 Clement* are the writings of *Barnabas* and the *Martyrdom of Polycarp*, two texts that speak poorly of Judaism. The letter of *Barnabas* is adamant in its insistence that, because of their infidelity to the divine covenant, the Jews have forfeited their claim to be God's people in favor of the church. This perspective appears to be a clear extension of the claims by early Christians who came to define themselves as the "new Israel." Indeed, Christianity's new reading of scripture in light of the coming of Christ led the church to supersede those rituals that Jews have traditionally observed as part of their devotion to God. For this perspective, a new people of faith now receive Israel's divine promise.

The *Martyrdom of Polycarp* takes an even harder stance toward the Jews. In its portrayal of the death of Polycarp, the reader discovers that the local Jews of Smyrna, through the inspiration of the "evil one," ultimately act to encourage the trial and persecution of the bishop.[45] As in a well-choreographed theater production, they push the crowds and Roman authorities to kill Polycarp in a stark rehearsal of the death of Jesus of Nazareth in the New Testament Gospels. Abundant parallels are evident. The resulting anti-Semitic rhetoric of the author is indeed typical of numerous regions of Asia Minor. In such locations, the synagogue comes to stand as an adversary to the very existence of the church,[46] and complete alienation of the church from its Jewish heritage is both assumed and encouraged.

The perspective of Ignatius stands firmly between polar opposites (the *Didache*, *1 Clement* versus *Barnabas*, the *Martyrdom of Polycarp*) and very much represents what subsequent Christian tradition ultimately came to accept as a suitable understanding for its Jewish heritage. For Ignatius, there is no need for Christianity to embrace its Jewish roots. As observed above, he follows the Apostle Paul quite strenuously in denouncing so-called "Judaizers" who seek to return to the restrictions of a Jewish perspective. While Paul found those who endorsed such a return among the apostles of the Jerusalem church, Ignatius undoubtedly finds them among the "God fearers" of his day, that is, non-Jews who come to their newfound faith during contact with messianic

Jews while worshipping in the synagogue. Ignatius offers precious little to suggest that he himself holds any particular inclination toward Jewish practices. He bases neither his teachings nor his theology upon Jewish principles and, within his seven letters, only quotes from the Old Testament on three occasions.[47] Jewish traditions clearly do not shape his faith world.

This much now said, however, Ignatius does not launch vindictive rhetoric against Judaism itself, but only against those who would have Christianity return to its Jewish heritage. He freely admits that the Jews persecuted the prophets of old, who lived in accordance with Christ, and yet themselves lived in disobedience to the spirit of God that came into the world as the divine Word. So, too, he insists that it is senseless to profess Jesus Christ while at the same time practicing Judaism, for the latter is actually "bad yeast" that has soured and gone stale, while Christ himself provides the "new yeast" that causes every tongue to confess.[48] To mix the two is absurd. As Ignatius observes, "it is better to hear about Christianity from a circumcised man than about Judaism from an uncircumcised man."[49] For him, there is no necessary connection between the old faith of Judaism and the new faith of the church.

Ultimately, Judaism stands as something of a failed enterprise of faith for Ignatius. Those Jews whose confidence in God is truly righteous and pure find the option of the church to be the only logical solution. It is clear that, as bishop of Antioch in Syria, Ignatius works within a large, cosmopolitan city that features a large Jewish community and, as such, necessarily encounters the sway of Judaism that influences many within his own church community.[50] So, too, these are the days when Jewish leaders regularly identify messianic believers within their midst and usher them from the safety of the synagogue and its legal protection under Roman law. Nevertheless, at no point do we hear Ignatius attack the Jews themselves. Instead, his concern, like that of many Christians early in the second century, is to rally believers in Christ around a new faith, not to call them back to an old "failed" allegiance. As the bishop readily notes, "Christianity did not believe in Judaism, but Judaism in Christianity."[51]

Christology

As with the question of the church's relationship to Judaism, the issue of christological perspectives runs the gamut of our literature.[52] At one extreme, scholars often find a particularly low Christology within the text of the *Didache*. The author makes no direct appeal to the authority of Jesus of Nazareth as God,[53] for example, preferring to call him "servant."[54] So, too, even though *Didache* 9–10 includes prayers that presumably are associated with the rite of Eucharist, no association is made between that event and the suffering of the cross. While it is entirely likely that the *Didache* is an "evolved" or composite document and thus may represent several theological perspectives, nevertheless, there clearly is no concern to emphasize the divinity of Jesus of Nazareth throughout the text.

The author of *2 Clement* offers a noteworthy advancement over the *Didache*, beginning this ancient homily with the comment "we should think of Jesus Christ as God, as judge of the living and dead."[55] This marks a significant step of theological development with respect to the traditional Jewish claim that one God alone is the judge of humanity's destiny. No longer are Christians to see Christ merely as an advocate for sinners before the divine throne of justice, but actually as the very judge before whom pleas for mercy must be offered. The ramifications of this expression are widespread, since Christ himself comes to bear responsibility for human salvation. In reflection of Paul's own kenotic hymn, we hear that Christ, though formerly spirit, became flesh in order to effect the deliverance of humanity.[56] It is through the flesh of Christ that the spiritual church reveals itself. The living church of history, being a reflection of the first spiritual church, forms the body of Christ.[57] As our author notes, God sent Christ to be our "savior and founder of immortality."[58]

While 2 Clement undoubtedly stands as a somewhat advanced expression of Christology within the Apostolic Fathers, other writers reflect parallel ideas, at least in part. The author of Barnabas, for instance, notes that God speaks to the Son when scripture declares, "Let us make humankind according to our image and likeness."[59] Here we find a typical patristic reading of scriptural imagery through the eyes of the divine Christ as its author. In another text, 1 Clement, Christ is called "the majestic scepter of God" who came in humility and is the "high priest" of human offerings, the guardian and defender of human weaknesses.[60] Finally, the author of the epistle to Diognetus identifies Christ as both the "child" and "only son" of God who served as a ransom for humanity: "the holy for the lawless, the innocent for the guilty, the just for the unjust, the imperishable for the corrupt, the immortal for the mortal."[61] Such descriptions reflect a perspective that identifies the Son with the Father in function, if not always in essence.

It is appropriate, then, that we turn to Ignatius to provide the christological insight that serves as the norm for early second-century theology.[62] Throughout his seven letters, Ignatius makes reference to the name of Jesus Christ, Christ Jesus, Jesus, or Christ over 130 times.[63] On the one hand, he speaks of Jesus Christ as divine, distinctly identifying the Messiah with God in a sense that far exceeds the monotheistic confession of Judaism.[64] This is very much in keeping with the parallel confession of 2 Clement, as seen above, and with the evolving tendency of later Christians to think of Jesus Christ as the second person of the Trinity. At the same time, though, he is careful to guard the human nature of Christ, as is perhaps best illustrated throughout the Ignatian creeds. It is in the creeds that we hear the confession that Jesus Christ is "both flesh and spirit,"[65] "from the seed of David,"[66] "was truly born, both ate and drank,"[67] and "was truly nailed up by Pontius Pilate."[68] Thus, we witness the multifaceted character of Christ as seen through the eyes of Ignatius, though it remained for later church councils to determine how those two natures – the divine and the human – were ultimately to be conjoined.

Ignatius becomes a pivotal point for early confessions about the nature of Jesus Christ. He reflects a Christology that in many respects parallels that of the Gospel of John, incorporating such Johannine themes as "bread of God"[69] and "living water,"[70] in addition to Jesus being "the door to the Father"[71] who does "nothing without the Father."[72] Continuing in that same tone, he envisions the true Christian lifestyle as a direct reflection of the relationship between Father and Son that typifies the

Johannine vision. Hence, for Ignatius, the opportunity to suffer and die at the hands of Rome is the most cherished expression of complete discipleship in Christ. It is the manifestation of the human spirit purely joined with the divine will; it is the re-enactment on earth of what it means to be "in Christ" as first recorded by Paul. Ultimately, what Ignatius perceives about Jesus Christ – the human activity united with the divine nature – is both a reflection of the foundational faith of the New Testament and the evolving confession of the institutional church as expressed by succeeding theologians of the patristic period.

The living voice of scripture

Those texts that the Apostolic Fathers consider "scripture" are in essence the same ones that the writers of the New Testament used, that is, our present Old Testament.[73] In both instances, the Greek version of the Old Testament (the Septuagint) tends to be the preferred edition. At the same time, many authors among the Apostolic Fathers recognize the authority and value of certain early Christian writings that have evolved into our present New Testament, and they employ portions of these works into the structure of their arguments. There is broad variety in the use of scriptural texts and biblical themes, the extent of which exceeds the scope of our survey. Nevertheless, it is possible to give some illustration of the concern for scripture here.

Ignatius refers to the Old Testament as the "archives" and observes that certain Christians use these texts as the basis for determining the validity of the gospel. The bishop offers a rejoinder here that is appropriate for the arguments of later patristic authors: "for me, the archives are Jesus Christ; the enduring archives are his cross, death, resurrection, and faith in him."[74] We thus see both the reverence that early Christians hold for their scriptures as a collection of authoritative teachings and the ways in which these texts serve as a standard by which their faith is measured. Of course, as seen above, Ignatius himself makes only tentative use of the archives in his arguments, preferring instead to align his thought with New Testament authors.

The Gospel of Matthew, themes from the Johannine tradition, and the person and letters of Paul are among the most important Christian sources both for Ignatius and various other authors among the Apostolic Fathers. There is little evidence that Ignatius knows the Gospels of Mark or Luke. This holds true for the Gospel of John as well, though, as shown above, a range of Johannine themes populate the language of the bishop. Ignatius rarely quotes from Matthew directly, yet employs the Matthean text as a platform for his arguments.[75] A clear demonstration of this process is evident in the Ignatian explanation for the baptism of Jesus of Nazareth, where we are told that Jesus was baptized in order to "cleanse the water" for the subsequent baptism of those who follow.[76] Here we see Ignatius attempting to clarify the way in which the baptism of Jesus can "fulfill all righteousness," as Jesus himself explains to John when the latter objects that "I need to be baptized by you."[77] Such a sophisticated use of Scripture indicates the degree to which Ignatius is familiar with the Gospel text. Elsewhere, the Ignatian use of Matthew appears in the bishop's diverse references to the coming wrath of God,[78] the tree that is known by its fruit,[79] and the presence of wolves within the community of faith.[80]

Perhaps most important for Ignatius is his allegiance to Paul and to Pauline themes. His letters incorporate numerous Pauline words and phrases, including apostolic ideas that pepper his views of the church and its theology. While it is indeed true that the bishop's primary devotion is to the life and passion of Christ, he envisions that the best realization and expression of this fidelity comes as he seeks to "imitate" the apostle Paul, his hero in faith.[81] There is little question that succeeding generations of Christian thinkers have anchored much of their theological allegiance to Paul based upon the Ignatian reverence for the Pauline ideal.

Beyond Ignatius, the Apostolic Fathers reveal a variety of approaches to scripture. The *Shepherd of Hermas*, for example, makes virtually no use of scriptural texts, apart from certain general allusions that Jewish literature broadly reflects, such as the image of vineyards and vines.[82] At the other extreme, texts like *1 Clement*, *Barnabas*, and the *Didache* are rife with scriptural citations and allusions. It is only natural that the Old Testament supplies the grand majority of these references, since its writings served as the literary authority for Jewish tradition out of which the church sprang. For the most part, however, these Jewish sources appear within the framework of New Testament thought, largely employing the phraseology of the early evangelists and Paul, and occasionally making specific quotation of early Christian sources.[83] Further, it is not always clear that our authors are quoting from precise literary texts but, instead, are making use of oral versions of scripture.[84] The Apostolic Fathers operate within a society that is largely oral in nature, a culture that reflects the living reality of God's voice at work within the scriptural tradition. Already by the early second century, early Christianity's most prominent thinkers are firmly entrenched in a belief that the authority of Old Testament texts is only correctly understood within the outline of the early church's messianic faith.

Conclusion

The writings now preserved for us in the secondary collection of texts of the Apostolic Fathers clearly form a bridge between the apostolic witness of the New Testament and the post-apostolic faith of the patristic period. Diverse voices speak within this compilation. In many respects, they echo the vast diversity of Christian views that thrived within the Mediterranean world of the late first and second centuries. They paint a colorful picture of assorted theological and ecclesiological perspectives, of checkered encounters with Jewish and Hellenistic culture, and of the evolving structure of the institutional church in its manifold forms. At the same time, however, they articulate a growing recognition of the need for unity. As is best demonstrated within the letters of Ignatius of Antioch, a unified culture of faith is only possible when there is common respect for authority, a universal appreciation for liturgy, and a regular confession of belief.[85] The subsequent tradition of Christianity's evolution and growth is indeed indebted to those early bishops and theologians who first fashioned a common view of the universal church and the foundational elements upon which it has been constructed.

Further reading

Primary sources

B. Ehrman (ed.), *The Apostolic Fathers*, Cambridge, MA: Harvard University Press, 2003.

M. W. Holmes (ed.), *The Apostolic Fathers*, 3d edn, Grand Rapids, MI: Baker Academic, 2007.

Secondary sources

A. Brent, *Ignatius of Antioch and the Second Sophistic*, Tübingen: Mohr Siebeck, 2006. (Thorough examination of the thought of Ignatius within his cultural context.)

P. Foster (ed.), *The Writings of the Apostolic Fathers*, London: T&T Clark, 2007. (Introduction to the literature from contributing authors.)

J. P. Lotz, *Ignatius and Concord*, New York: Peter Lang, 2007. (Provides an intriguing focus on the issue of unity for Ignatius.)

H. O. Maier, *The Social Setting of the Ministry as Reflected in the Writings of Hermas, Clement and Ignatius*, Waterloo, Canada: Wilfrid Laurier University Press, 1991. (Solid survey of sociological implications behind the writings.)

W. R. Schoedel, *Ignatius of Antioch*, Philadelphia: Fortress, 1985. (Useful and readable commentary on the life and letters of Ignatius.)

C. Trevett, *A Study of Ignatius of Antioch in Syria and Asia*, Lewiston, NY: Edwin Mellen, 1992. (Solid investigation of the role of Ignatius among the churches of Asia Minor and Syria.)

S. Tugwell, *The Apostolic Fathers*, London: Geoffrey Chapman, 1989. (Broad introduction to the literature from a singular perspective.)

Notes

1 Typically included among these texts are *1–2 Clement*, epistles written under the names of Ignatius, Polycarp, and Barnabas, the *Martyrdom of Polycarp*, the *Didache*, the *Epistle to Diognetus*, the *Shepherd of Hermas*, fragments by Papias, and the *Apology of Quadratus*.

2 As Schoedel correctly notes, "The theme of unity may well represent the central concern of the letters of Ignatius"; W. R. Schoedel, *Ignatius of Antioch*, Philadelphia: Fortress, 1985, p. 21.

3 Such offices reflect specific roles for Ignatius – the bishop (for God), the presbyters (for the apostolic council), and the deacons (for Jesus Christ); so *To the Magnesians* 6.1.

4 See, e.g., Ignatius, *To the Ephesians* 5.3; *To the Magnesians* 7.1; *To the Trallians* 7.1; *To the Philadelphians* 3.2.

5 Ignatius, *To the Ephesians* 5.2.

6 Ignatius, *To the Magnesians* 6.1.

7 Ignatius, *To the Smyrnaeans* 9.1.

8 Ignatius, *To the Ephesians* 4.1.

9 Clement, *1 Clement* 42.4–5.

10 *Didache* 15.1.

11 Polycarp refers to "presbyters and deacons" only in *To the Philippians* 5.3, once again perhaps only implying a bishop among the presbytery.

12 Ignatius is the first to use the term "catholic" in Christian literature; see *To the Smyrnaeans* 8.2; cf. *Martyrdom* Proem.

13 1 John 4:2–3.

14 Ignatius, *To the Ephesians* 9.1.

15 Ignatius, *To the Magnesians* 8.1.

16 Ignatius, *To Polycarp* 3.1.

17 Ignatius, *To the Trallians* 6.1.

18 For specific creeds, see *To the Ephesians* 7.2 and 18.2, *To the Magnesians* 11.1, *To the Trallians* 9.1–2, and *To the Smyrnaeans* 1.1–2.

19 *To the Philippians* 3.2 and 4.1, respectively.
20 *Shepherd of Hermas, Similitudes* 8.6.5 and *Shepherd of Hermas, Mandates* 6.2.7, respectively.
21 See *Shepherd of Hermas, Mandates* 6.1–2, *Didache* 1–6, and *Barnabas* 18–20.
22 The two ways are often identified with angels (so *Shepherd of Hermas, Barnabas,* and Qumran's *Rule of the Community* 3.13–14.26), but sometimes with human figures (so the *Tabula of Cebes;* see J. T. Fitzgerald and L. M. White, *The Tabula of Cebes,* Chico, CA: Scholars, 1983, pp. 14–15).
23 Though *Didache* 2.1 identifies love of God and neighbor as the primary teachings; cf. Matt. 22:37–38 and 7:12.
24 See C. N. Jefford, *The Apostolic Fathers and the New Testament,* Peabody, MA: Hendrickson, 2006, pp. 73–106.
25 A Christian is also clad with the helmet of faith, the spear of love, and the armor of endurance; see Ignatius, *To Polycarp* 6.2.
26 Ignatius, *To the Ephesians* 18.2.
27 Ignatius, *To the Philadelphians* 4.
28 Ignatius, *To the Romans* 7.3.
29 Ignatius, *To the Ephesians* 20.2.
30 Ignatius, *To the Smyrnaeans* 8.1–2.
31 Ignatius, *To the Smyrnaeans* 6.2.
32 *Didache* 7.1–4.
33 *Didache* 8.1–3.
34 *Didache* 9.1–10.7. See especially J. A. Draper, "Ritual Process and Ritual Symbol in *Didache* 7–10," *Vigiliae Christianae* 54, 2000, pp. 121–58.
35 *Didache* 10.5; see Mark 13:27.
36 *Shepherd of Hermas, Similitudes* 2.1–10.
37 Clement, *1 Clement* 38.1–2.
38 *Diognetus* 2.5.
39 *Martyrdom of Polycarp* 17.3.
40 *Didache* 1–6.
41 *1 Clement* 4–20.
42 *1 Clement* 43 (see Num. 17).
43 *1 Clement* 53 (see Exod. 32; Deut. 9).
44 These figures are indeed mentioned (*1 Clement* 5), though no appeal is made to their leadership styles.
45 *Martyrdom of Polycarp* 13.1, 17.1–2.
46 See, e.g., Rev. 2:8–11, 3:7–13.
47 See *To the Ephesians* 5.2 (Prov. 3:34), *To the Magnesians* 12 (Prov. 18:17), and *To the Trallians* 8.2 (Isa. 52:5) with some few scattered allusions to Scripture elsewhere (*To the Ephesians* 15.1; *To the Magnesians* 10.3; 13.1; 14.1; *To the Smyrnaeans* 1.2; *To Polycarp* 1.2; 3.1).
48 See Ignatius, *To the Magnesians* 8–10.
49 Ignatius, *To the Philadelphians* 6.1.
50 The dialogue between synagogue and church in Antioch continues with the bishops Serapion and Theophilus at the end of the second century.
51 Ignatius, *To the Magnesians* 10.3.
52 The classifications of A. R. Stark over a century ago still serve as a guideline: *1 Clement, Didache,* and Papias (Group One) subordinate Christ to God; *2 Clement,* Polycarp, and Ignatius (Group Two) extend the authority of Christ, who is actually called God and to whom prayer is offered; and Hermas, *Barnabas,* and *Diognetus* (Group Three) attribute a cosmological function to Christ as creator and sustainer of the universe. See A. R. Stark, *The Christology of the Apostolic Fathers,* Chicago: University of Chicago Press, 1912.
53 At the same time, however, the author insists upon use of the classic Trinitarian formula in baptism; see *Didache* 7.1, 3.
54 See *Didache* 9.2–3 and 10.3. The Coptic text, which begins in the middle of 10.3, provides the phrase "Jesus your Son" at 10.3 and 10.7.
55 *2 Clement* 1.1.
56 *2 Clement* 9.5 (for Paul, see Phil. 2:5–11).

57 *2 Clement* 14.
58 *2 Clement* 20.5.
59 *Barnabas* 6.12 (see Gen. 1:26).
60 *1 Clement* 16.1 and 36.1, respectively.
61 *Diognetus* 9.1–4.
62 See P. Foster (ed.), *The Writings of the Apostolic Fathers*, London: T&T Clark, 2007, pp. 98–100.
63 See R. M. Grant, *Ignatius of Antioch*, vol. 4 of R. M. Grant (ed.), *The Apostolic Fathers*, Camden, NJ: Thomas Nelson & Sons, 1966, p. 7.
64 See, e.g., Ignatius, *To the Ephesians* 7.2 and *To the Romans* 6.3.
65 Ignatius, *To the Ephesians* 7.2.
66 Ignatius, *To the Ephesians* 18.2.
67 Ignatius, *To the Trallians* 9.1–2.
68 Ignatius, *To the Smyrnaeans* 1.1–2.
69 Ignatius, *To the Ephesians* 5.2 and *To the Romans* 7.3 (see John 6:33).
70 Ignatius, *To the Romans* 7.2 (see John 4:10; 7:38).
71 Ignatius, *To the Philadelphians* 9.1 (see John 10:7, 9).
72 Ignatius, *To the Magnesians* 7.1 (see John 5:19, 30; 8:28).
73 Though the parameters of this collection remain uncertain; so L. M. McDonald, *The Biblical Canon*, Peabody, MA: Hendrickson, 2007, pp. 150–69.
74 Ignatius, *To the Philadelphians* 8.2.
75 Massaux notes two references, seven cases of "literary contact," and five more probable contacts with Matthew; see É. Massaux, *The Influence of the Gospel of Saint Matthew on Christian Literature before Saint Irenaeus*, vol. 1, Leuven, Belgium: Peeters; Macon, GA: Mercer University Press, 1990, pp. 85–120.
76 Ignatius, *To the Ephesians* 18.2.
77 Matt. 3:14–15; John the Baptist's objection appears only in Matthew and not its Gospel parallels.
78 Ignatius, *To the Ephesians* 11.1 (see Matt. 3:7).
79 Ignatius, *To the Ephesians* 14.2 (see Matt. 12:33).
80 Ignatius, *To the Philadelphians* 2.2 (see Matt. 7:15).
81 This seems evident in the life of Polycarp as well; see E. A. Castelli, *Imitating Paul*, Louisville, KY: Westminster John Knox, 1991.
82 See Hermas, *Similitudes* 5.5 (cf. Ps. 80:8–16; Isa. 5:1–7; Ezek. 19:10–14; Matt. 20:1–16; John 15:1–11).
83 See, e.g., *Didache* 9.5; *Martyrdom of Polycarp* 2.3; *2 Clement* 2.4.
84 See already the work of Helmut Köster, *Synoptische Uberlieferung bei den apostolischen Vätern*, Berlin: Akademie-Verlag, 1957.
85 As Behr observes, this "was a period of struggle for survival and the crucible in which the basic elements of Christian identity and organization were forged." See J. Behr, "Social and Historical Setting," in F. Young, L. Ayres, A. Louth (eds), *The Cambridge History of Early Christian Literature*, Cambridge: Cambridge University Press, 2004, pp. 55–70 (esp. 55).

7

JUSTIN AND THE APOLOGISTS

Oskar Skarsaune

Introductory remarks on "apologists" and "apologies"

The term *apologists* – used in order to single out a distinct group of Christian authors of the second century – is of modern provenance. J. C. Th. von Otto was the first to use it as a term for the authors of a specific set of second-century works.[1] If we leave out those authors from whom only a few fragments are extant, von Otto's "apologists" comprise the following listed with the titles of their apologetic works, and approximate dates:

Aristides of Athens	*Apology*	*c.* 125–150?
Justin Martyr of Nablus	*1* and *2 Apology*	*c.* 150–5
Tatian of Syria	*Oration to the Greeks*	*c.* 170
Athenagoras of Athens	*Plea on Behalf of Christians*	*c.* 177
Theophilus of Antioch	*To Autolycus*	*c.* 180
Diognetus		*c.* 180?

Von Otto's criterion for calling these authors "apologists" seems to have been that these authors in some way or other wrote works in which they *defended* Christians or the Christian faith against attacks from outsiders. To some extent this is true about all the authors enumerated, but this common feature conceals great differences among them, especially as to the genre of their works.

While "apologist" is of modern provenance, the term "apology" as name for a certain kind of book is not modern. It was probably coined by someone during the late second or the third century, and was used by Eusebius of Caesarea in his *Ecclesiastical History* around 310.[2] Eusebius's criterion for calling a book an "apology" (in Greek: *apologia*) is simple and straightforward: these books were "handed over" to named Roman emperors. That such was the case is something Eusebius concludes from these books' beginnings: they are *addressed to Roman emperors* (or other Roman authorities). Eusebius names the following writers as authors of apologies:

Tertullian
(Quadratus)
Aristides
Justin
(Melito; Apollinarius; and Miltiades).[3]

Compared with von Otto's list above, only Aristides and Justin qualify as "apologists" according to Eusebius's terminology, but so does also Tertullian, who was not included in von Otto's edition. Eusebius's criterion would also have made Athenagoras's book an apology, but apparently Eusebius did not know it, or its author. On the other hand, he knew the works of Tatian and Theophilus, but calls them *logoi*, orations, not apologies. They were not addressed to Roman authorities.

In the following essay I shall argue that among preserved apologies, only Justin's so-called *First Apology* really meets Eusebius's criterion for an apology. Only Justin's book was actually handed in to the Imperial administration as a formal *petition*, with the expectation of being answered by the emperor. (Whether this expectation was realistic or not, is another matter.) Some of the non-preserved apologies mentioned by Eusebius may also have qualified as real petitions, but this we cannot know. This leaves us with Aristides as the only one to challenge Justin's position as the great pioneer in the genre of apology. But Aristides' so-called *Apology* is clearly not a real *petition*, in spite of its two titles marking it as such (see more on this below).[4] In the following, I shall therefore treat Justin as the pioneer among the "real" apologists, and, according to Eusebius's criterion, perhaps the only real apologist there was. At the same time I will also point out the considerable continuity there was between Justin, on the one hand, and some predecessors and several successors, on the other. This continuity is seen more in the contents than in the genre of their writings, and gives von Otto's grouping together of these authors some justification. One should only add Tertullian's *Apology* to his list.

Justin's so-called first apology: creating something new

Before Justin, most Christian literature had been written for internal consumption among Christians. They were small and marginal groups in a society mostly hostile towards them. They had, in a sense, more than enough with keeping up their faith, solidifying their identity, and fighting the tendency to increased fragmentation that often threatens such marginal groups. These concerns are dominant in the group of writings commonly called the Apostolic Fathers, stemming from CE c. 100 to c. 150, the period preceding Justin and the other apologists. In these writings, you speak *about* the world outside the Church rather than *to* it.

When Polycarp was led to martyrdom in the arena, and was offered the opportunity to defend his faith publicly before the crowd gathered there, he simply refused.

> The Pro-Consul said: "Persuade the people." And Polycarp said: "You I should have held worthy of discussion, for we have been taught to render honour ...

to princes and authorities appointed by God. But as for those, I do not count
them worthy that an *apologia* should be made to them."

(*Martyrdom of Polycarp* 10.2)[5]

The willingness of Polycarp to discuss his faith with the Roman officer was not
rewarded by the latter – he was simply not interested. And this was the general
impression among early Christians as far as the Roman world around them was
concerned. The Roman Empire, when persecuting Christians, had been seen as the
demonic or satanic enemy of God's church, not susceptible to any form of argument,
only to be resisted and paradoxically conquered by the endurance to the end shown
by the Christian martyrs.

Justin chooses a radically different approach. For the first time, a Christian dares
to address in public the highest Roman authorities: the emperor, the senate, and the
Roman people – making a rational appeal to them to stop the unlawful and irrational
persecutions of Christians. It was a daring approach, and it would hardly have been
possible but for the fact that in Justin's time there was a new type of emperor.

It is here that the genre, the *form* of Justin's book, becomes important, and also
its address. In order to show this point more clearly, a few words must be said about
the practice of *libelli* (public petitions) in the Roman Imperial administration. If one
individual or several, like the inhabitants of a village, had some complaint to make
about the procedures followed by some local Roman official, they could hand in a
complaint to the emperor. This was technically called a *libellus* in Latin and a *biblidion*
in Greek (both words meaning "small scroll"). Literally, this name indicated the
small size of the scrolls containing the complaint or request. Functionally, the correct
translation is no doubt "petition." This term would correspond more closely to Greek
enteuxis, however, and the latter Greek term is sometimes used to characterize the
contents of a *biblidion*. When *a city* addressed the emperor with a similar request, it was
called a *presbeia* in Greek and a *supplicatio* or *legatio* in Latin; in English best rendered
as "plea."[6] The emperor was obliged to answer such complaints. At the end of the
scroll containing the petition or plea there would be some blank space, and here the
emperor's answer – which became imperial law in this and similar cases – was written
in. Such answered *libelli* were then posted in public at certain places in Rome, so that
anyone could be updated on the latest news in imperial legislation.

Justin's so-called *First Apology* exhibits several formal characteristics of being a real
libellus; even more so if a recently launched theory is correct, namely that the so-called
Second Apology is really a collection of cut-out material that was originally part of the
original *libellus*.[7] In this case, 2 *Apology* 14.1 contains Justin's own characterization of
his writing as being a formal petition: "And now we request of you to publicly post this
petition (*biblidion*), with your answer appended, so that others may know our customs
and be released from the bonds of false beliefs and of ignorance of good."[8] This corresponds perfectly with the opening address:

To the Emperor Titus Aelius Hadrianus Antoninus Pius Augustus Caesar; to
his son Verissimus the philosopher; to Lucius the philosopher, by birth son

of Caesar and by adoption son of Pius, an admirer of learning; to the sacred
Senate and to the whole Roman people; in behalf of those men of every
race who are unjustly hated and mistreated: I, one of them, Justin, the son
of Priscus and grandson of Bacchus, of the city of Flavia Neapolis in Syria-
Palestine, do present this address and *petition* (*enteuxis*).

(Justin, *First Apology* 1)[9]

These formal characteristics correspond perfectly with Justin's first point of substance
in the writing: he complains that the legal proceedings against Christians are not up to
the standards that one would expect of an empire led by self-proclaimed *philosophers*.
Christians are condemned and executed simply by admitting to being Christians, not
because they have been convicted of any crime in each case. Roman judges proceed
on the assumption that the crimes commonly attributed to Christians have actually
been committed by each and every person admitting to be a Christian, but this is an
irrational and illegal procedure, unworthy of rational men, let alone philosophers.[10]

This is a formal complaint about Roman malpractice in courts of law, a typical
example of what petitions were about. And this element in Justin's writing, taken
together with its genre, is what defines it as an "apology" in Eusebius's sense. On this
background it is easy to see that the only so-called apology that *may* antedate Justin's –
that of Aristides – does not belong to the same category: there is no formal complaint
about Roman legal proceedings against Christians in it, no accusation of malpractice,
and no petition that current practice be changed. The defining element of Justin's
Apology is missing.

Justin and his successors

Justin had more than one successor in employing this format: Athenagoras's *Plea on Behalf
of Christians* (unknown to Eusebius) is in many ways a revised, improved, and strategi-
cally shortened version of Justin's petition, containing much the same legal argument
but more cogently stated. For Athenagoras, however, the genre of "plea" may be no
more than a literary fiction, using Justin's pioneering writing as model for a new literary
genre.[11] The same seems to have been true about Melito's lost writing; the few fragments
preserved by Eusebius seem to indicate that Melito leaned heavily on Athenagoras as
well as Justin.[12] Finally, this genre culminated in Tertullian's *Apology*. Here the book's
pretence of being a petition is shown to be fictional by Tertullian himself:

Rulers of the Roman Empire ... if the extreme severities inflicted on our
people in recently private judgments, stand in the way of our being permitted
to *defend ourselves before you*, you cannot surely forbid the truth to reach your
ears by *the secret pathway of a noiseless book* (*occulta via tacitarum litterarum*).

(Tertullian, *Apology* 1.1)[13]

Tertullian not only perfects the literary genre, he also ends it. After him, no more
apologies in petition style were written.[14]

What we have seen here provides us with important clues to unlock the message and meaning of Justin's pioneering work and of the works of his successors. The choice of addressing the emperors by a formal petition, appealing to their respect for rational argument, their honouring rationality as such, would have been unthinkable to earlier generations of Christians, say under Domitian's reign. Rationality would be the last thing they associated with the empire and its leader – recall the portrayal of the beast in Revelation! Justin's literary and argumentative strategy is so startlingly new and different because he had to do with a new and different brand of emperors. Antoninus Pius (138–61), the ruling emperor to whom Justin addressed his petition, was perceived as a new type of emperor – more humane than his predecessors. His adoptive son and successor, Marcus Aurelius (161–80 – the Verissimus of Justin's address), was already co-ruler at the time Justin wrote his *Apology*. He made no secret of his ambition of being "the Philosopher on the throne," authoring a full-blown Stoic philosophical treatise, the *Meditations*. The probably fictive petitions by Athenagoras and Melito were addressed to him.[15] Tertullian, on the other hand, writes his *Apology* (probably 197) *after* the time of the "philosophical" Antoninus, under the first years of the Severian dynasty (Septimius Severus 193–211). Tertullian no longer calls his imperial addressees philosophers – he had no reason to.

The political context here outlined is of the highest relevance for understanding the flow of argument in Justin's and later apologies. The first common denominator in these works is the complaint that Roman legal procedure in court proceedings against Christians is illegal and irrational. In Justin's, in Athenagoras's, and in Tertullian's apologies this is the first point made.[16] But none of these authors were satisfied in making this legal point. All of them went further, and used by far the greater part of their books to make a more general point: Christian faith was not only politically and legally harmless and unobjectionable; it was actually true – in fact, the *only* true doctrine about "things human and divine," the very subject matter of philosophy.

When they embark on the demonstration of this, the three writers are by no means saying only new and original things. On the contrary, they all draw on a well-established tradition of Jewish and Christian polemic against pagan worship, pointing out the irrationality of the latter, and often calling upon Greek philosophers as allies in this battle. And this more general "apologetic" agenda is what unites the works of these three authors with those of the two or three others who are often called "apologists" in modern scholarship: Tatian, *Oration to the Greeks*;[17] Theophilus, *To Autolycus*;[18] and the anonymous author of *Diognetus*. Since these writers in several aspects argue very similarly to Justin, I shall refer briefly to their works in our discussion primarily when they add significantly to Justin's argument, or emphasize other dimensions of the Christian–Roman encounter.

The argumentative strategy of Justin's *Apology*

After what has been said, it hardly needs any explanation that *philosophy*, and an appeal to the *rationality* advocated by philosophy, loom large in Justin's work. It could hardly be otherwise. Christians were persecuted as "atheists" simply because they refused to take any part in the official Roman cult of the Roman gods and the cult of the emperor's genius.

When Justin and his colleagues wanted to counter this accusation, it was not sufficient just saying that Christians, like other people, should be judged on an individual basis and not according to general rumours about the whole group. The general accusations against Christians had to be addressed head-on. Christians were not irrational atheists; on the contrary, Christians were the only ones to worship the true God in full accordance with reason. It is here that Justin and his successors could tap into a set of arguments others had used before them, Jewish as well as Christian writers. And in rehearsing these arguments, the apologists were confident they would catch the hearing of philosophers.

Already in the Jewish Scriptures it is a stock accusation against pagan worship that it is utterly irrational. This is most clearly seen in the ironical descriptions of idol production and idol worship that we find in the books of Isaiah (44:9–20) and Jeremiah (10:2–16), and which is carried on in the apocryphal Wisdom of Solomon (13:10–15:19). Common to these texts is the view that praying to something oneself has produced, the maker bowing down before that which he has made, and expecting help from something that is helpless itself – this is the apogee of irrationality. In the New Testament writings, this polemic is continued, for example, by Paul in Romans 1:18–32; and by the Paul of Acts, especially in Acts 17:22–31. "Since we are God's offspring, we ought not to think that the deity is like gold, or silver, or stone, an image formed by the art and imagination of mortals" (Acts 17:29).[19]

In saying this, Luke's Paul is no doubt also aligning himself with the theological ideas already entertained by some in his Gentile audience – especially, perhaps, some of "the Stoic philosophers" (17:18) who had debated with him. They would to a large extent agree with Paul in this criticism of idol worship. And it is of great relevance in our context that Luke in Acts 17:16–34 actually portrays Paul in Athens and before the Areopagos court as a second Socrates. Like Socrates, he proclaims *the God unknown* to the Athenians; like Socrates he does this in the marketplace, talking with people; like Socrates, he is accused of introducing strange gods, and is brought before a court to investigate the matter. In this indirect, allusive way, Luke calls in Socrates as a predecessor of Paul.[20]

In Justin, Athenagoras, Tatian, Theophilus, and *Diognetus*, this ridicule of idolatry is continued, and the references to philosophy as an ally become more explicit, especially in Justin and Athenagoras. We shall look at Justin's arguments more closely, pointing out parallels in the other writers as we go along.

To his philosophical addressees on the imperial throne Justin points out that one of the greatest heroes of philosophy had done exactly the same as Christians were now doing, and had been accused in exactly the same way!

> Everything that the philosophers and legislators discovered and expressed well, they accomplished through their discovery and contemplation of some part of the Logos (Reason). ... [Among these,] those who were born before Christ ... were dragged into law courts as irreligious and meddling

persons. ... Socrates, the most ardent of all in this regard, was accused of the very crimes that are imputed to us. They claimed that he introduced new deities [Cf. Plato, *Apology of Socrates* 14] and rejected the state-sponsored gods. But what he did was to ostracize Homer and the other poets [Plato, *Republic* books 2 and 10], and to instruct men to expel the evil demons and those who perpetrated the deeds [of the gods] narrated by the poets; and to exhort men by meditation to learn more about God who was unknown to them, saying: "It is not an easy matter to find the Father and Creator of all things, nor, when he is found, is it safe to announce him to all men." [Plato, *Timaeus* 28c] Yet, our Christ did all this through his own power. There was no one who believed so much in Socrates as to die for his teaching, but not only philosophers and scholars believed in Christ, of whom even Socrates had a vague knowledge, ... but also workmen and men wholly uneducated, who all scorned glory, and fear, and death.

(Justin, Second Apology 10.2–8)²¹

In this one text Justin has stated almost all the major points he wanted to impress on the minds of the ruling emperors. He was not satisfied just to point out that Roman practice in the legal proceedings against Christians was irrational. The emperors being philosophers, he wanted to discuss with them the whole question of *truth* with regard to religion and God.

Beginning with Socrates (in Plato's *Republic*), several philosophers had criticized quite severely the stories told about the gods in Homer and Hesiod.[22] These stories or "myths" were found to be inappropriate, unworthy of divine beings, and utterly unfit as stories about divine conduct to be emulated by human beings. Or, in Justin's words, Socrates "ostracize[d] Homer and the other poets." But then Justin places this within a larger framework with which every philosopher ought to be familiar: the great divide there was in antiquity between *reason* and *passion*. Reason, *Logos*, stood for true knowledge of reality as it really is, stood also for knowledge of the deep moral principles that contribute to a good life and happiness, stood for everything true and profitable, and encapsulated the essence of divinity. *Pathos*, passion(s), stood for the opposite, for the irrational emotions that lead human beings astray and extinguish every rational insight.[23] Reason and passion are contrary and antagonistic forces in human beings, and the Homeric gods were found to be on the wrong side in this great confrontation.

So far, the "historical" Socrates would probably have gone along with Justin, and many of Socrates' philosophical followers as well. But Justin probably goes beyond what Socrates himself could have said when he makes him claim that the Homeric gods were really demons in disguise. When he says that Socrates "instruct[ed] men to expel the evil demons and those who perpetrated the deeds [of the gods] narrated by the poets," it is not really Socrates we hear speaking, but someone expounding an old topic in Jewish criticism of pagan worship.

It is said already in the Septuagint, the Greek Bible of the Jews of Alexandria, that "all the gods of the Gentiles are [in reality] *demons*" (Ps. 96:5; LXX 95:5). Paul presupposes the same idea in 1 Corinthians 10:20: "what pagans sacrifice [when they bring sacrifices to their gods], they sacrifice to demons and not to God." In fact, Paul is here echoing another Septuagint text: "they sacrificed to demons and not to God." Another Jewish writer, certainly prior to Paul, took the idea one step further by identifying the story told in Gen. 6:1–4 with the story of the origin of the pagan gods. In *1 Enoch* 12–19 it is told how some angels – "the sons of God" – left their heavenly abode and had sexual relations with the daughters of men. From these unions the giants were born; when the giants died, their spirits lived on as *demons*. The fallen angels thereupon terrified men and seduced them into sacrificing to the demons as if the latter were gods.

Justin was entirely familiar with these Jewish ideas, and spells them out very clearly as follows: God had set high angels as rulers over mankind, but some of them

> violated their charge, fell into sin with women and begot children who are called demons. Moreover, they subsequently subjected the human race to themselves, partly by magic writings, partly by the fear they instilled into them ... and partly by instructing them in the use of sacrifices, incense, and libations, which they [the spirits] really needed after becoming slaves of their lustful *passions* [*pathe*]; and among men they engendered murders, wars, adulteries, all sorts of dissipation, and every species of sin.
>
> (Justin, *Second Apology* 5.3–4)[24]

The poets, however, believed all this was done by their gods, not by demons, and therefore ascribed to their gods this most irrational behaviour. Pagan religion is therefore decidedly not on the side of reason in the great struggle that is always going on between passions and rationality. And the true philosopher, the spokesman of reason, should have no doubt as to what his calling is with regard to this type of religion. He should take Socrates as his model:

> When Socrates attempted ... to draw men away from the demons *by true reason* [*logo alethei*] and judgment, then these very demons brought it about, through men delighting in evil, that he be put to death as an atheist and impious person, because, they claimed, he introduced new divinities. And now they endeavour to do the very same thing to us. And not only among the Greeks were these things through Socrates condemned *by reason* [*hypo logou*] but also among the Barbarians by the *Logos Himself*, who assumed a human form and became man, and was called Jesus Christ.
>
> (Justin, *First Apology* 5.3–4)[25]

Through this portrayal of Socrates, Justin is presenting his philosophical audience with quite a challenge. The emperors were portraying themselves as philosophers, but who were now really the true philosophers? Philosophers should be the defenders of reason, *logos*, they should never side with reason's enemies, the passions, *ta pathe*. The very embodiment of irrational passions was Greco-Roman religion. Accordingly the true philosopher had no choice but to break decisively with traditional religion – just as Socrates had done. The only ones who now followed Socrates' example, however, were in fact the Christians! Even without a philosophical education they opposed irrational religion and stood up for reason. They even paid the same price for it as Socrates had once done. In persecuting Christians, the empire aligned itself with Socrates' enemies and the demoniacal forces working through them, not with reason and philosophy.

This is poignant polemic on Hellenism's own terms. The great conflict between *reason* and *passion* (*logos* versus *pathos*), so deeply perceived and analyzed in the classical Greek philosophical traditions, is seen by Justin as concretely acted out in the conflict between pagan religion (based on passion) and philosophy's severe *criticism* of it (based on reason). At the same time, Justin's polemic is also aimed at philosophers in Justin's own time: they had worked out a practical compromise with official religion, and were able to live harmoniously with it.[26] Socrates and Christians were not! (One strategy in this compromise was the Stoic allegorical exegesis of Homer's myths. In Plato's *Republic*, Socrates rejects this strategy, like Justin and other Christian apologists.) Thus, not only were Christians philosophers like Socrates; they were, in Justin's days, the *only* true philosophers around! This equation could also be reversed: if Christians were philosophers, then Socrates was some sort of Christian.[27] Calling Socrates a Christian was extremely effective rhetoric with regard to the philosophical audience at which it was aimed.

But all this was no mere rhetorical strategy for Justin. He was deeply convinced of the truth of this perspective. For him, Jesus Christ was not only a teacher of reason, like Socrates. Christ was more than that. He was Reason Himself, reason in person. He was, from the beginning, the *Logos* who later became incarnate. In developing this point, Justin is largely expounding traditional Jewish and Christian ideas, and in so doing, he had predecessors as well as successors.

Some basic tenets of apologetic theology, mainly Justin's

First, as God's own *Logos*, Christ took part in creation, and especially in the creation of humanity. When God said: "Let us make man in our image," the Father was dialoguing with his *Logos*, the Son.[28] As the only one among the creatures, the human being was endowed with *logos*, the capacity for rational thinking. Justin can therefore call this capacity in human beings "seeds of the Logos,"[29] and he can call the Logos Himself "The Sowing Logos," *Logos spermatikos*.[30] In creating human beings in God's and the *Logos*'s image, God's *Logos* sowed a seed of himself, a *logos*-seed, a seed of rationality, in human beings. If so, there ought to be some manifestation of this God-given rationality also outside the circle of those who had knowledge of God's revelation in the Scriptures. And this proves to be the case, as we have seen, although clear manifestations among the Gentiles prove to be exceedingly rare. Apart from Socrates, Justin in one place adds Heraclitus and Musonius Rufus and a more general reference to the Stoic philosophers[31] and in another the ancient lawgivers.[32] Those who gave good laws curbed the raging passions of men. The philosophers were in part excellent teachers of morals (as were the Stoics), but their crowning achievement, as in Socrates, was their severe criticism of traditional religion. One should carefully note that Justin – unlike some modern theologians who refer to him – never saw the *Logos spermatikos* active in pagan religion. It is not Christ who is the hidden power behind them, but demons. No, the Sowing Logos is active in non-Christian *criticism* of pagan religion![33]

Basically the same point of view recurs in Athenagoras. Christians are not atheists, since they believe in the one God there is, defining him in much the same way as do the best of Greek poets, and also Plato and Aristotle.[34]

> Now, if Plato is no atheist when he understands the Creator of all things to be the one uncreated God, neither are we atheists when we acknowledge him by whose Logos all things were created and upheld by his Spirit and assert that he is God.
>
> (Athenagoras, *Plea on Behalf of Christians* 6.2)[35]

Even Tertullian – known for his brisk denial of any positive relationship between "Athens and Jerusalem"[36] – is willing, in his *Apology*, to enlist Socrates as a witness of truth:

> I do not dwell on the philosophers, contenting myself with a reference to Socrates, who, in contempt of the gods, used to swear by an oak, and a goat, and a dog. In fact, for this very thing Socrates was condemned to death, that he overthrew the worship of the gods. Plainly, at one time as well as another, that is, always truth is disliked.
>
> (Tertullian, *Apology* 14.8)[37]

In denying your gods, says Tertullian to the Romans, Socrates "had a glimpse of the truth."[38]

In Tatian[39] and Theophilus[40] we encounter again Justin's concept of the one God and his creating the world through his Logos (Theophilus adds: and through his Wisdom, apparently equating Wisdom with the Spirit),[41] but these writers are more reticent in calling philosophy to their aid as a witness of truth. In Tatian this has to do with his overall polarization of anything Greek over against the "barbarian" truth of Christian doctrine.[42] Theophilus admits that Plato said many good things about "the sole rule of God and about the human soul, saying that the soul is immortal," but on the other hand he contradicts these good things by teaching bad sexual morals and other depravities, and the transmigration of souls.[43] In another place he again recognizes that Plato's concept of God is adequate, but Plato destroys it by also according eternity, hence divinity, to matter.[44]

Looking back on the ideas presented here, one notices that the usual dichotomy between "Jewish" and "Hellenistic" – with which scholars have long approached these matters – is inadequate. There is no doubt that in talking about God and his Logos, and the latter as a mediating entity in God's dealings with the created world, Justin and his successors were using concepts, terms, and ideas that philosophically educated people could easily recognize as their own. At the same time we have seen that there are biblical and Jewish precedents for almost everything Justin says. And on the decisive point – branding pagan religion as the very expression of irrationality, and every attempt at criticism and abandonment of pagan religion as glimmering manifestations of Logos – Justin and his successors were thinking in biblical terms rather than Hellenistic. For them, this conflict was not a purely intellectual matter; it was a life-and-death battle – dramatically demonstrated in Christian martyrdom. This leads us on to the next point.

Second, for Justin, the seeds of reason implanted in all human beings are, to all practical purposes, entirely powerless. What really dominates the life of human beings is the overwhelming power of Satan and demons.[45] Against this power human beings are really helpless, they are held captive by the evil powers and the sins they have committed under the influence of these powers. This means that it was not sufficient that God's Logos merely informed human beings of some relevant truths about themselves and the divine. This was insufficient, even if this truth was communicated by the Logos in person.

It is here that Justin – and the tradition of which he is part – decisively parts company with Platonism and also with the Gnostics. For these, the highest element of human beings was of the same nature as the divine. "Salvation" therefore basically meant to recognize and realize one's own true nature. This was within the capacity of human beings, or at least some of them. Justin was thinking in completely different terms. The breaking of the power of Satan, demons, and sin was not something merely noetic, something gained by new insight. It was not enough that the Son of God was a teacher of new knowledge. In order to be the saviour, he had to *do* something. He had to share our sufferings, die, and rise again. It was by this *act* that he conquered man's enemies; it was by something he *did* that he liberated human beings. "For we worship and love, after God the Father, the Logos who is from [him] … , since he even became man for us, so that by sharing in our sufferings he also might heal us [cp. Isa. 53:5]."[46]

Justin knew well that on this point he could no longer rely on Platonic philosophy to support him – quite the contrary. Therefore he does not elaborate this point in any great detail in his Apologies. His immediate successors – Athenagoras, Tatian, and Theophilus – are almost silent about it. But this silence should not be taken to imply that they had nothing to say about the incarnation and the saving act of the Son of God. In the case of Justin and Melito, we have preserved other of their works, not in the genre of apology, that clearly demonstrate that the apologetic genre did not allow these writers to say everything they had to say.

In Justin's *Dialogue with Trypho* we see him presenting extensively and emphatically two points that are only briefly hinted at in his Apologies: *first*, a deep-going criticism of Plato and his teaching concerning the nature of the human soul.[47] This criticism is stated by "a very old man" portrayed as a Christian Socrates. The Platonic position is defended by Justin, as he was before his conversion to Christ. In the philosophical dialogue between himself and the old man – written according to the best Platonic models – Justin negates the basic Platonic premise; namely, that the human soul can know God because it is of the same nature. But if so, asks "Justin" the Platonist, to whom should we then turn for reliable knowledge about God? The old man answers: to those who had direct experience with God because they had actually met and heard and seen him. These men we call prophets. Because of this immediate encounter with God, their words are far superior to anything said by philosophers.[48]

And what did they say? This brings us to Justin's *second* point, which is polemical with regard to Judaism.[49] The prophets said that there would come to earth the Son of God, that he would die to redeem men from their slavery to Satan, sin, and death, and that he would rise again and be seated on God's throne as the Father's co-regent. In the *Dialogue*, this creed-like summary of the prophets' message is defended against the Jewish objections of Trypho, but – as the only one among the apologists – Justin also finds it worthwhile to present a shorter version of this "proof from prophecy" in his *First Apology*.[50] How should he make this narrative about the incarnate Son of God credible to a philosophical audience?

> Lest anyone should object and ask, "What prevents us from supposing that he whom we call Christ was a man born of men, and has worked what we term miracles through the art of magic, and thus [only] appeared to be the Son of God," we now present proof that such was not the case. We shall do so not by trusting in mere claims, but by necessarily believing those who predicted these things before they happened, for we are actual eyewitnesses of events that have happened and are happening [now] in the very manner in which they were foretold. This, we are sure, will appear *to you [philosophers] too*, the greatest and truest proof.
>
> (Justin Martyr, *First Apology* 30)[51]

That is, not only to an audience already believing the prophets and being familiar with their prophecies, but also to a philosophical audience unfamiliar with the Bible, would the "proof from prophecy" appear rationally convincing. How could anyone predict centuries in advance something that actually happened, unless the Spirit of God had revealed these later events to him?

Athenagoras has much the same admiration for the superiority of the prophets over any purely human wisdom, but grounds it more in the inspired account of creation in the first chapters of Genesis than on the messianic prophecies.[52] The same is true of Tatian, who also emphasizes the chronological priority of the "barbaric" prophets.[53] Both aspects are then elaborated in great detail by Theophilus – he has an extensive and apologetic exegesis of Genesis 1–4,[54] a defence of the superior teaching of the biblical prophets,[55] as well as a learned proof of the greater antiquity of the biblical prophets, compared with Homer and the other Greek writers.[56]

Justin is thus alone in setting forth in considerable detail – in the genre of a *petition!* – the messianic prophecies, portraying a Messiah dying and rising and being enthroned for the redemption of human beings. I do not think he did it merely to demonstrate the correspondence between prophecy and fulfilment of prophecy. I believe he also wanted his readers to get the flavour of what the story of Jesus was all about. As when he expounds the meaning of Genesis 49:11 ("washing his robe in the blood of the grape"): this was "a forewarning of the passion he was to endure, purifying with his blood those who believe in him."[57] "His robe" is a metaphor used by the Spirit of prophecy to signify the community of believers, Justin explains.

Conclusion

I have been trying in this essay to portray Justin and the other apologists not only as *thinkers* – a well-deserved name. They were educated men; they had a current knowledge of the philosophy, science, and general learning of their time, and made intelligent and sometimes innovative use of this knowledge. But I have also tried to portray them as *Christian* thinkers. This is most easily seen in Justin, but once you have seen it here, it also shines through in the others. They have much to say about God, meaning God the Father. But it is when they come to speak of his *Logos* that things really warm up. They believed they had met the *Logos*, the very *reason* of God, in the person of Jesus. This conviction made them bold and confident in their encounter with philosophy – in agreement as well as in criticism. And it made them brave in their encounter with irrational *pathos*, embodied in pagan worship, not least in the obligatory worship of the Roman pantheon. According to Justin[58] and later Tertullian[59] it often made a deep impression on heathen spectators to observe Christian martyrdom for truth. Christians were there to remind all self-professed thinkers that thinking rightly about God and his Logos was no child's play. It could have serious consequences – witness Justin, the Martyr.

Further reading

Primary sources

L. W. Barnard, St. Justin Martyr: The First and Second Apologies Translated with an Introduction and Notes, Ancient Christian Writers 56, New York: Paulist, 1997.
T. B. Falls, St. Justin Martyr: Dialogue with Trypho, rev. by T. P. Halton, ed. by M. Slusser, Selections from the Fathers of the Church 3, Washington, DC: The Catholic University of America Press, 2003.

Secondary sources

L. W. Barnard, Athenagoras: A Study in Second Century Christian Apologetic, Théologie historique 18, Paris: Beauchesne, 1972, Justin Martyr: His Life and Thought, Cambridge: Cambridge University Press, 1967.
R. M. Grant, Greek Apologists of the Second Century, Philadelphia: Westminster, 1988. (The best and most comprehensive introduction to all the second-century apologists.), The Early Christian Doctrine of God, Charlottesville: University Press of Virginia, 1966. (Good discussion of the adoption of philosophical terms in Jewish and early Christian theology.)
E. J. Hunt, Christianity in the Second Century: The Case of Tatian, London: Routledge, 2003.
A. D. Nock, Conversion: The Old and the New in Religion from Alexander the Great to Augustine of Hippo, London: Oxford University Press, 1933, paperback edn 1961. (By now a classic, describes in a superb way the religious and philosophical milieu in which early Christian thought was formed.)
E. F. Osborn, Justin Martyr, Beiträge zur historischen Theologie 47, Tübingen: Mohr, 1973. (Despite the series title, the book is in English, a modern classic on Justin.)
S. Parvis and P. Foster (eds), Justin Martyr and His Worlds, Minneapolis: Fortress, 2007. (A comprehensive collection of cutting-edge papers read at a conference in Edinburgh 2006.)

Notes

1 The authors included in his *Corpus apologetarum christianorum saeculi secundi*, 9 vols, 1st edn, Jena: Mauke, 1847–72, were, enumerated according to the dates traditionally ascribed to their writings, the following: *Quadratus (of Asia Minor? c. 125?); Aristides of Athens (contemporary with Quadratus); *Aristo of Pella (Jason and Papiscus, c. 140?); Justin of Nablus (c. 155–65 [including Pseudo-Justinian works of a later date]); *Miltiades of Asia Minor (c. 165?); Tatian of Syria (c. 170?); *Melito of Sardis (172); *Apollinarius of Hierapolis (172); Athenagoras of Athens (c. 177); Theophilus of Antioch (c. 180); Letter to Diognetus (c. 180?); Hermias (c. 200?). Among these, Hermias is ordinarily left out in recent treatments of the apologists, since his book is not considered a real apology. From the authors marked with an asterisk we have only a few fragments left, so there is very little we can say about them. An instructive review of the historical process culminating in von Otto's edition of "Christian Apologists" is given in S. Parvis, "Justin Martyr and the Apologetic Tradition," in S. Parvis and P. Foster (eds), *Justin Martyr and His Worlds*, Minneapolis: Fortress, 2007, pp. 115–27 (esp.116–17).

2 "Apology" was not the name by which the second-century authors themselves would have called their books. Concerning the somewhat later choice of this name, see P. Parvis, "Justin, Philosopher and Martyr: The Posthumous Creation of the Second Apology," in S. Parvis and P. Foster (eds), *Justin Martyr and His Worlds*, Minneapolis: Fortress, 2007, pp. 22–37 (esp. 30–7).

3 The works of those within parenthesis are not preserved. See Eusebius, *Ecclesiastical History* 2.2.4 (Tertullian's Apology); 4.3.1–3 (Quadratus and Aristides); 4.18.2 (Justin's two apologies); 4.26.1–2 and 4–11; 4.27 (Melito and Apollinaris); 5.17.5 (Miltiades).

4 According to its first title it was addressed to Emperor Hadrian (117–38), according to its second title it was addressed to Antoninus Pius (138–61 – making it roughly contemporary with Justin's). But there is a suspicion that both of these titles may have been added during a later revision, styling Aristides' book into something it originally was not. It may not have been addressed to any emperor at all, as its content clearly indicates. As for Quadratus, the only other possible contender, his time and identity are quite uncertain, and the one sparse fragment preserved from his book allows of no conclusion as to its general content or genre. See, for Aristides and Quadratus, S. Parvis, "Justin Martyr and the Apologetic Tradition," pp. 117–22.

5 Trans. and ed. K. Lake, *The Apostolic Fathers*, vol. 2, Loeb Classical Library, Cambridge, MA: Harvard University Press, 1913, p. 327; slightly altered.

6 On the function and meaning of these terms, see S. Parvis, "Justin Martyr and the Apologetic Tradition," p. 125, and P. Parvis, "Justin, Philosopher and Martyr," pp. 25–30.

7 See P. Parvis, "Justin, Philosopher and Martyr."

8 Trans. T. B. Falls, *Writings of Justin Martyr*, The Fathers of the Church: A New Translation 6, Washington, DC: Catholic University of America Press, 1948, p. 134; slightly altered.

9 Trans. Falls, *Writings of Justin Martyr*, p. 33.

10 Justin, *First Apology* 2–4.

11 See W. R. Schoedel in the Introduction to his *Athenagoras: Legatio and De Resurrectione*, Oxford Early Christian Texts, Oxford: Clarendon, 1972, pp. xi–xiii; S. Parvis, "Justin Martyr and the Apologetic Tradition," pp. 123–5.

12 See S. G. Hall's remarks in his *Melito of Sardis: On Pascha and Fragments*, Oxford: Clarendon, 1979, p. xxix. Greek and English text of Melito's Apology fragments in the same book, pp. 62–5.

13 Trans. S. Thelwall, *Apology*, in A. Roberts and J. Donaldson (eds), *Latin Christianity: Its Founder, Tertullian*, vol. 3 in *The Ante-Nicene Fathers*, 10 vols, Edinburgh: T&T Clark, 1885–7; repr. Grand Rapids, MI: Wm. B. Eerdmans, 1987; repr. Peabody, MA: Hendrickson, 1994, pp. 17–55 (p. 17).

14 See especially S. Parvis, "Justin Martyr and the Apologetic Tradition," pp. 126–7.

15 On the philosophical pretensions of the Antonine Emperors and their effect on Christian apologetics, see H. H. Holfelder, "*Eusebeia kai philosophia*: Literarische Einheit und Politischer Kontext von Justins Apologie," *Zeitschrift für die neutestamentliche Wissenschaft und die Kunde der älteren Kirche* 68, 1977, pp. 48–66 and 231–51 (esp. 48–51).

16 Justin, *First Apology* 2–4; Athenagoras, *Plea on Behalf of Christians* 1–2; Tertullian, *Apology* 1–4.

17 Tatian's book is not addressed to a ruling emperor, but quite simply to "you men of Greece." It is most commonly called by the title given it by Eusebius: *Logos pros hellenas, Oration to the Greeks*. It is referred

to in this essay according to the edition of M. Whittaker, *Tatian: Oratio ad Graecos and Fragments*, Oxford Early Christian Texts, Oxford: Clarendon, 1982.

18 The title of this book is also taken from Eusebius, *Ecclesiastical History* 4.24: *Tria pros Autolykon*. In the first book there is only the anonymous address "my friend." In the second and third books, however, the addressee is named Autolycus. Eusebius probably formed his title according to this. Quotations in this essay are from R. M. Grant, *Theophilus of Antioch: Ad Autolycum*, Oxford Early Christian Texts, Oxford: Clarendon, 1970.

19 In the early second century this line of rational attack on pagan religion and a rational defense of Christian worship of the one and only God is continued in the preserved fragments of an otherwise lost writing, the so-called *Preaching of Peter* (the fragments are found in Clement of Alexandria). Here again pagan religion is branded as irrational, while Christian worship is described as based on reason. This argument is carried further in Aristides' so-called *Apology*, and gets its fullest and most eloquent statement in *Diognetus*. In all three writings there is also an argument against the Jewish way of life: Jewish worship also contains irrational elements. The classic study of this Jewish and Christian tradition of rational criticism of pagan religion is B. Gärtner, *The Areopagus Speech and Natural Revelation*, Uppsala: Almquist & Wiksell, 1955.

20 See O. Skarsaune, "Judaism and Hellenism in Justin Martyr, Elucidated from His Portrait of Socrates," in H. Cancik, H. Lichtenberger, and P. Schäfer (eds), *Geschichte – Tradition – Reflexion: Festschrift für Martin Hengel zum 70. Geburtstag*, vol. 3: *Frühes Christentum*, Tübingen: Mohr, 1996, pp. 585–611.

21 Trans. Falls, *Writings of Justin Martyr*, pp. 129–30; slightly altered.

22 For a good review, see R. A. Norris, *God and World in Early Christian Theology: A Study in Justin Martyr, Irenaeus, Tertullian and Origen*, London: A&C Black, 1966 (esp. pp. 8–32).

23 For this somewhat simplified picture, see nuance and details in J. Brunschwig and M. Nussbaum (eds), *Passions and Perceptions: Studies in Hellenistic Philosophy of the Mind*, Cambridge: Cambridge University Press, 1993. The Stoics had developed a whole theory of how reason could discipline passions, to the point of man achieving *apatheia*. This was also the ideal espoused by Emperor Marcus Aurelius in his Stoic *Meditations*. In exploiting this theme, Justin is therefore right on target with regard to his addressees.

24 Trans. Falls, *Writings of Justin Martyr*, p. 125; emphasis mine.

25 Trans. Falls, *Writings of Justin Martyr*, p. 39; slightly altered.

26 See O. Skarsaune, "Judaism and Hellenism in Justin Matyr, Elucidated From His Portrait of Socrates," pp. 595–6; R. M. Grant, *Gods and the One God: Christian Theology in the Graeco-Roman World*, London: SPCK, 1986 (esp. pp. 75–83).

27 Justin, *First Apology* 46.3.

28 Justin, *Dialogue with Trypho* 61.

29 Justin, *Second Apology* 8.1; 13.5.

30 Justin, *Second Apology* 8.3; 13.3.

31 Justin, *Second Apology* 8.1.

32 Justin, *Second Apology* 10.2.

33 There are many studies of Justin's *Logos* and *Logos spermatikos* concepts, perhaps the most important being R. Holte, "Logos Spermatikos: Christianity and Ancient Philosophy according to St Justin's Apologies," *Studia Theologica* 12, 1958, pp. 109–68. See also Skarsaune, "Judaism and Hellenism in Justin Matyr, Elucidated From His Portrait of Socrates," pp. 594–607.

34 Athenagoras, *Plea on Behalf of Christians* 5–7.

35 Trans. Schoedel, *Athenagoras*, pp. 13–15; slightly altered.

36 "What indeed has Athens to do with Jerusalem? What concord is there between the Academy and the Church?" Tertullian, *Prescription against Heretics* 7; trans. P. Holmes, *The Prescription against Heretics*, A. Roberts and J. Donaldson (eds), *Latin Christianity: Its Founder, Tertullian*, vol. 3 in *The Ante-Nicene Fathers*, 10 vols, Edinburgh: T&T Clark, 1885–7; repr. Grand Rapids, MI: Wm. B. Eerdmans, 1987; repr. Peabody, MA: Hendrickson, 1994, pp. 243–65 (p. 246).

37 Trans. Thelwall, *Apology*, p. 30.

38 Tertullian, *Apology* 46.5; trans. Thelwall, *Apology*, p. 51.

39 Tatian, *Oration to the Greeks* 4–7.

40 Theophilus, *To Autolycus* 2.2–7; 2.9–10.

41 See the review of this motive in Jewish and early Christian tradition in O. Skarsaune, "Jewish Christian Sources Used by Justin Martyr and Some Other Greek and Latin Fathers," in O. Skarsaune and R. Hvalvik (eds), *Jewish Believers in Jesus: The Early Centuries*, Peabody, MA: Hendrickson, 2007, pp. 379–416 (esp. 402–8).

42 In Tatian, *Oration to the Greeks* 2–3 and 19 there is a rather abrasive attack on the most famous luminaries of Greek philosophy. But significantly, Socrates is not criticized. He is mentioned only once (*Oration* 3), and then quite positively as a righteous man.

43 Theophilus, *To Autolycus* 3.6–7; trans. Grant, *Theophilus of Antioch*, p. 109.

44 Theophilus, *To Autolycus* 2.4.

45 Justin, *First Apology* 5; *Second Apology* 5.

46 Justin, *Second Apology* 13.4; trans. Falls, *Writings of Justin Martyr*, p. 134; slightly altered.

47 Justin, *Dialogue with Trypho* 1–9.

48 An excellent commentary on *Dialogue* 1–9 is J. C. M. van Winden, *An Early Christian Philosopher: Justin Martyr's Dialogue with Trypho Chapters One to Nine*, Philosophia Patrum 1, Leiden: Brill, 1971.

49 Justin, *Dialogue with Trypho* 10–142.

50 Justin, *First Apology* 30–53. For a detailed analysis of Justin's scriptural proof in the *Dialogue* as well as in the *Apology*, see O. Skarsaune, *The Proof from Prophecy: A Study in Justin Martyr's Proof-Text Tradition*, Supplements to Novum Testamentum 56, Leiden: Brill, 1987.

51 Trans. Falls, *Writings of Justin Martyr*, p. 66; slightly altered.

52 Athenagoras, *Plea on Behalf of Christians* 7–9.

53 Tatian, *Oration to the Greeks* 29; 31; 36–41.

54 Theophilus, *To Autolycus* 2.11–29.

55 Theophilus, *To Autolycus* 2.33–38; 3.11.

56 Theophilus, *To Autolycus* 3.16–29.

57 Justin, *First Apology* 32.7; trans. Falls, *Writings of Justin Martyr*, p. 69; slightly altered.

58 Justin, *Second Apology* 12.1.

59 Tertullian, *Apology* 50.13–16.

8

IRENAEUS OF LYONS

D. Jeffrey Bingham

The man, the bishop

In the year 177, Pothinus, the bishop of Lyons, was ninety years old. He died that summer after two days of beatings at the hands of the Romans for his insistence that Christ was the Christian God. A terrible persecution had come upon the Christians of Lyons (Lugdunum to the ancient Romans), in modern France, and those of its neighboring city, Vienne, some sixteen miles south on the east bank of the Rhône. We are fortunate to have a selective record of this trial in the *Letter of the Churches of Lyons and Vienne* preserved for us by Eusebius in his *Ecclesiastical History*.[1] To the name of Pothinus, among others, we may add that of Attalus, who was burned alive in the amphitheater which lies nestled on the gentle and shaded slopes of the Croix-Rousse hill in Lyons. Maturus and Sanctus, too, were tormented there by the flames, and Blandina, after many tortures, was finally gored to death by a bull. Each sacrificed themselves in imitation of the true fleshly passion of Christ, their Incarnate-God, in hope of the bodily resurrection. So fundamental and pervasive was their resurrection-faith, that the Romans cremated the martyrs' corpses and dispersed the ashes in the river in hopes of defeating any notion of Christians being raised bodily from their graves.

The man who would follow Pothinus into the episcopacy of Lyons, knowing full well the fate of his predecessor and who was, quite likely, the author of the *Letter* which tells of his martyrdom, was Irenaeus.[2] According to Jerome, he flourished under the Roman Emperor, Commodus (180–92), son of Marcus Aurelius.[3] Probably born sometime between 125 and 140, Irenaeus died perhaps as a martyr some sixty or seventy years later during the persecution brought upon Christians by the Roman emperor Septimius Severus in the early years of the third century, but the precise time and circumstances surrounding his death are unknown.[4]

Irenaeus's native city was the present-day Turkish city, Izmir, "the pearl of the Aegean," known in the ancient world as Smyrna. Modern life has limited excavation of ancient Smyrna and few remnants of the boyhood city of Irenaeus can be seen today. Remains of the Agora, the market place and center for all commercial, political, and religious life, rebuilt in 178 with its impressive colonnades, however, may still be enjoyed. As one strolls through the Agora, it is not hard to imagine the boy Irenaeus walking by the Zeus altar or observing Polycarp, the bishop of Smyrna, in theological discussion with the Roman presbyter, Florinus, who would embrace ideas worrisome to Irenaeus's concept of orthodoxy.[5] In his youth, Irenaeus had been a disciple of Polycarp and learned key components of the Christian faith from this man who had been taught by the Apostle John and others who had seen Christ.[6] This pedigree places Irenaeus within that line of Christianity which flows, in his understanding, unbroken from the Apostle to the bishop. As Johannes Quasten wrote, according to Irenaeus's own testimony, "it is evident that through Polycarp Irenaeus was in touch with the Apostolic age."[7] It has recently been argued that the importance of Polycarp's teaching for Irenaeus can be seen explicitly in his argument that the Old Testament was a prophecy of the New Testament in the fourth book of *Against Heresies*. Charles Hill claims that the unnamed presbyter of *Against Heresies* 4.27–32 is Polycarp.[8]

Martyrdom seems never to have been far from Irenaeus. Polycarp, too, was martyred in February of 155 or 156. His pupil, Irenaeus, knew the tragic tale of his death, and an account from the church of Smyrna is available to us in the *Martyrdom of Polycarp*. It provides a window into the faith of the early Christians of Asia Minor through the steadfastness of an old man, who, in the face of death, hoped for the immortality of body and soul in resurrection and who saw himself as a partaker in the sufferings of Christ.

By the time of the persecution in Lyons, some twenty years after Polycarp's martyrdom, Irenaeus was already a presbyter within that diocese serving under Pothinus, having moved from Smyrna some time before. He was a trusted emissary of peace and on at least two occasions represented the believers in Lyons and in Asia in doctrinal and liturgical controversies. Just prior to the persecution of 177 he was chosen by those who would be martyrs to serve as courier of a letter to Pope Eleutherius in Rome concerning Montanism.[9] Around thirteen years later, during the Paschal controversy, he wrote a letter to Pope Victor I, requesting that peace be made with the Christians of Asia.[10] It was during his mission to Eleutherius in Rome that he was absent from Lyons during the persecutions. This explains his survival and positioned him to succeed Pothinus.

What we have in Irenaeus is one man, one bishop, in whom resided the expression and faith of Christianity from a breadth of geographical and cultural locations. In particular, his life demonstrates a connection between Gaul, the Roman region, which among other parts of modern-day western Europe, included France, in which Lyons is located, and the eastern part of the empire. Lyons was the converging point for all traffic and trade within Gaul, and Eusebius names it and its neighboring city of Vienne as the capital cities of the region.[11] Such a connection between Christians in Rome and the East is already evident early on, for example, in the letter of Clement of Rome to the church of Corinth (*1 Clement*) and in Ignatius's epistle to Rome. But here, in Irenaeus and the Christianity of Gaul, the early continuity and kinship between the East, Rome, and Gaul is shown. The bond becomes even more apparent when we consider that the account of the persecution that took place in Lyons (177) and included Christians from there as well as from Vienne was communicated by the survivors to the churches in Asia and Phrygia in a letter. The account also names some of the martyrs who were natives of the East, for instance, Attalus from Pergamum, and Alexander, a Phrygian.[12] The letter emphasizes, as well, that this connection is not just one of commerce and migration. The Christians of Gaul and the East share a common confession and expectation: "The servants of Christ at Vienne and Lyons in Gaul to our brothers in Asia and Phrygia who have the same faith and hope of redemption as we: peace, grace, and glory from God the Father and Christ Jesus our Lord."[13]

Irenaeus was well-traveled, well-mentored, and well-thought of. But his uniqueness rests largely in his representation of an observable confessional unity among disparate Christian communities:

> In his own person he united the major traditions of Christendom from Asia Minor, Syria, Rome, and Gaul, although his acquaintance with Palestine, Greece, and Egypt was minimal. We cannot say that he represents the whole of second-century Christianity, but he does represent the majority views outside Alexandria, where Christian speculative thought was closer to the Gnosticism he fought. He represents the literary categories of his predecessors as well as the areas through which he had passed.[14]

His writings

Eusebius, the church historian, honored Irenaeus as a peacemaker, in keeping with the meaning of his name.[15] It may be surprising to some that this irenic churchman, this diplomat, this representative Christian, was also the second century's most informed, prolific, and theologically structured polemicist against Gnosticism. His great literary work of five books, written around 180 from Lyons, is known as *Against Heresies*. It is still valued, not only for its example of early Christian biblical interpretation, theological argumentation, and anti-Gnostic and anti-Marcionite polemic, but also for its account of a variety of Gnostic beliefs. In it, Irenaeus claims to break new ground as he bases his account on his own reading of some of the literature of the Valentinians and even his discussions with some of their teachers.[16] Although some of his descriptions show stereotyping, polemical exaggeration, and faithfulness to rhetorical strategy, and although we may allow for some misunderstanding of his sources, Irenaeus's representations have been judged quite accurate and largely substantiated by our access to the Nag Hammadi library, discovered in the mid-twentieth century.[17] For example, Pheme Perkins has argued that Irenaeus was a good student of the Gnostic sources at his disposal, freeing him, somewhat, from reliance upon earlier heresiologists.[18] He demonstrated his ability to use his sources with originality, and to distinguish between works that were Valentinian and those which the Valentinians recognized as sources for their own systems. She suggests that some critics of Irenaeus's credibility may fail to account for his rhetoric and skilful handling of some Gnostic sources.[19]

One important insight provided by the Nag Hammadi find, however, which Irenaeus's polemical discussions do not always allow us to fully appreciate, is the amazing diversity of Gnostic teaching in Christianity's early years. Contemporary scholars prefer to speak of an early diversity of "particular approaches to Gnostic spirituality or even particular Gnostic schools of thought."[20] The texts from Nag Hammadi are typically classed within four "groups" or "expressions" of gnosis: Thomas Christianity, the Sethian school of Gnostic thought, the Valentinian school of Gnostic thought, and Hermetic religion.[21] In Irenaeus's descriptions of his opponents there is relation to only two of the four. *The Nag Hammadi Scriptures: The International Edition* (2007) puts it this way: "The texts of the Sethian and Valentinian schools of thought illumine the Gnostic forms of religion addressed by the heresiologists Irenaeus of Lyons, Hippolytus of Rome, Epiphanius of Salamis, and others, and they serve to clarify the teachings understood – or misunderstood – by the heresiological authors in their highly polemical writings."[22]

Christoph Markschies, while recognizing the variety of groups and currents within early Christian fascination with gnosis (knowledge), nevertheless points us to what he regards as an eight-component model of Gnosis, reflecting a consensus in contemporary study:

(1) the experience of a supreme, other-worldly god; (2) the inclusion of additional divine figures closer to human beings than the distant god; (3) the valuation of world and matter as evil and alienating; (4) the introduction of a (ignorant/evil) creator, craftsman (demiurge); (5) the explanation of alienation by means of a myth in which a divine element falls and is trapped within human beings of an elite class, longing for its ultimate freedom; (6) the definition of Gnosis as knowledge about this state which can only be provided by a descending redeemer from the other world; (7) the redemption of human beings by means of the knowledge of the distant god and/or divine element within them; and (8) a tendency towards dualism in concepts of the divine, spirit and matter, and human beings.[23]

These eight components, as we shall see, are not very different from what Irenaeus presents, within *Against Heresies*, as some of the central features of the ideologies of his opponents. In his polemic, Irenaeus may not pay the full diversity of Gnosis its due, as reflected in Nag Hammadi, but his model, informed by his own contextual experience and not exhaustive, has parallels with the contemporary consensus. Furthermore, it must be allowed that what, at a cursory glance, may appear as inaccuracies in Irenaeus's work may actually be a reliable reflection of variants in the expressions of Gnosis to which he was exposed and which were due at least in part to the diversity that existed among the Valentinian and other Gnostic groups which produced them.[24] Sometimes, close examination will reveal that what at first is seen as distortion of an expression of Gnosis or a school's thought actually shows an alternative within that school or only minor variation with it.[25]

Against Heresies, as the main five-book tome authored by Irenaeus is known (in both ancient and modern shorthand), was written while Eleutherius was bishop of Rome (174–89). Its longer title, *Refutation and Overthrow of Knowledge Falsely so Called*, is influenced by the language of 1 Timothy 6:20. Unfortunately, it is available now in the original Greek of Irenaeus only in selected parts preserved within the works of other early Christian writers and in some papyrus fragments.[26] Fortunately, however, there exists a very strict Latin translation of the work (probably done in the fourth or fifth century and certainly before 421 when Augustine quoted from it) and a literal Armenian translation of *Against Heresies* 4 and 5 (which even supplements the partially incomplete Latin translation), perhaps done in the sixth century and available to us in a thirteenth-century manuscript (discovered in Yerevan, Armenia, in 1904).[27] At the time, the most convenient, full, yet dated, English translation is that of A. Roberts and W. H. Rambaut.[28] There is a very good contemporary translation of *Against Heresies* 1 by D. Unger and J. J. Dillon in the Ancient Christian Writers series and a handy selection of texts by Robert Grant.[29] Other volumes of *Against Heresies* in the Ancient Christian Writers series are currently in process. The best critical edition is available in the French series, Sources chrétiennes.[30]

The first book of *Against Heresies* begins with a preface which introduces the bishop's understanding of the nature of heresy and the approach of his reply (1.Pref.).[31] His discussion then divides into three parts: (1) his exposure of the theses of the Valentinian Ptolemy (1.1–9); (2) his exposure of the diversity within the systems of his opponents contrasted with the unified faith of the church (1.10–22); and (3) his exposure of the roots of Valentinianism through discussion of its ancestors, both remote and immediate (1.23–31.2). Irenaeus's conclusion states his belief that he had succeeded in exposing the heretics (1.31.3–4). *Against Heresies* 2 opens with a preface that summarizes the accomplishments of his first book (exposure of the heresy) and informs the reader that the task at hand is now refutation (2.Pref.). This refutation takes place in five segments: (1) his refutation of the Valentinian notion of a Pleroma superior to the one, true Creator-Father (2.1–11); (2) his refutation of the Valentinian ideas concerning the Aeons, Sophia's passion, and their understanding of their true identity as the pneumatic seed (2.12–19); (3) a refutation of the numerology of his opponents (2.20–28); (4) a refutation of the Valentinian ideas concerning final consummation and the Demiurge (2.29–30); and (5) his refutation of erroneous ideas prior to the Valentinian myth (2.31–35). With a short conclusion Irenaeus states his confidence that his second book has demonstrated the unity between his refutation and Scripture's witness to the one God who is both Creator and Father (2.35.4).

The preface to the next book of *Against Heresies* summarizes the content of the first two books and quickly introduces the third volume: it is a proof from Scripture (3.Pref.). Following an argument for its truth and reliability (3.1–5), Irenaeus provides proof from the apostolic teaching within the Scriptures for the Church's faith in the one and only God, Creator, in contrast to the heretics' opinions (3.6–15). He then develops the apostolic witness to the one and only Son of God, Christ, and his recapitulative incarnation (3.16–23). He concludes by addressing the misfortune awaiting those who do not join the Church in faith (3.24–25). *Against Heresies* 4, after a preface which introduces Irenaeus's project against his opponents (4.Pref.), divides into three main parts. In part one he argues from the clear sayings of the Lord that there exists only one God who created all things and who oversees both covenants of redemption, new and old (4.1–19). In the second part, also from the clear sayings of the Lord, he provides proof that the New Testament was prophesied by the Old Testament (4.20–

35). Part three presents his argument, from the parables, that one God administrates both covenants, as well as blesses, and judges (4.36–41.3). His conclusion (4.41.4) summarizes the witness of the Lord's words to the one God, and promises the further polemic to come in the fifth volume from the words of Paul and other words of the Lord. Some earlier source criticism had argued that *Against Heresies* 4 was a work of disjointed borrowing which lacked both literary and theological harmony. The work of Phillippe Bacq has put such arguments to rest and has demonstrated the book's unity.[32] Antonio Orbe has also written a thorough commentary on book four.[33]

Irenaeus's fifth book continues his agenda demonstrating the church's faith from Scripture. Here, in addition to other words of the Lord, he brings to the table the apostolic epistles. The preface briefly summarizes the contributions of the four previous books and promises to continue the refutation in this final book (5.Pref.). Part one treats the resurrection of the flesh largely from the epistles of Paul (5.1–14). The second part argues for the one God, both Creator and Father, from different aspects of the life and teaching of Christ (5.15–24). Part three proves the unity of the Creator and Father from scriptural material he understands as Christ's eschatological teaching (5.25–36.2). It is within this portion of his argument that Irenaeus describes his thoughts, read with great interest by some and strong disagreement by others, on the eschatological figure of the antichrist and chiliasm. The bishop's conclusion to both *Against Heresies* 5 and the whole work sees him teaching that there exists only one God, one Son of God, and one humankind (5.36.3). Antonio Orbe has written an extensive commentary on book five.[34]

In addition to *Against Heresies*, which he sets forth both as a manifestation of the teachings of his Valentinian opponents and as a vehicle which refutes them, Irenaeus also composed several other works. Eusebius, the fourth-century church historian, set forth a list:

> In opposition to those at Rome who were falsifying the sound precepts of the Church, Irenaeus composed various letters, entitling one *To Blastus, On Schism*, another *To Florinus, On the Sole Sovereignty* or *That God is not the Author of Evil* – a notion which Florinus seemed to be defending. Again when Florinus was inveigled by the error of Valentinus, Irenaeus composed his masterpiece *The Ogdoad*, in which he also makes it clear that he himself was in the unbroken succession from the apostles. ... In addition to the letters and other works of Irenaeus already quoted, there is extant a very succinct and highly convincing essay directed against the Greeks and entitled *Scientific* [or *Concerning*] *Knowledge*; another, dedicated to a fellow-Christian named Marcian on the *Exposition* [or *Demonstration*] *of the Apostolic Preaching*; and a collection of addresses on various subjects, in which he mentions the Epistle to the Hebrews and the "Wisdom of Solomon," quoting several passages from them. That completes the list of works by Irenaeus that have come to my cognizance.
>
> (Eusebius, *Ecclesiastical History* 5.20.1; 5.26)[35]

In addition to listing these works, Eusebius also provides a glimpse into a few of the words from the conclusion of *The Ogdoad*, reproduces a lengthy passage from Irenaeus's letter *To Florinus, On the Sole Sovereignty*, and gives excerpts from his letter to Pope Victor concerning Easter.[36] Regrettably – apart from these few lines preserved by Eusebius, some scattered fragments, and *The Demonstration of the Apostolic Preaching* – all the other writings are lost.

Scholars debate whether the *Demonstration* was written before or after *Against Heresies* and even whether the last two chapters (99–100) are a later addition to the original text (1–98).[37] It was only in 1904 that, along with the Armenian translation of *Against Heresies* 4 and 5, the Armenian text of the *Demonstration* – a thirteenth-century manuscript of a sixth-century translation from the Greek – came into modern hands.[38] J. Behr has published a very good and handy English translation.[39] The critical edition is available in the series Patrologia orientalis.[40]

Irenaeus stated the purpose of the *Demonstration* upfront. He had taken up pen to write to Marcianus and thereby to provide him with a handbook, a summary, of the apostolic teaching. He informs Marcianus that

> We are sending you, as it were, a summary memorandum, so that you may find much in a little, and by means of this small [work] understand all the members of the body of the truth, and through a summary receive the exposition of the things of God so that, in this way, it will bear your own salvation like fruit, and that you may confound all those who hold false opinions and to everyone who desires to know, you may deliver our sound and irreproachable word in all boldness.
>
> (Irenaeus, *Demonstration* Pref. 1)[41]

Within the *Demonstration*, after an introduction (1–3a), Irenaeus composes the first part (3b–42a), which he begins by presenting the truth regarding God and human beings (3b–16).[42] In the first place is God, the Father, uncreated, who created all things by his Word, the Son of God, and who adorned all things by his wisdom, the Spirit of God. The Son became human among humans in order to join humans to God. The Spirit, the means of prophecy and guidance in the old economy, was poured out in newness in the last days to renew humanity to God. These three are the three articles of the church's faith. The Creator, he goes on to explain, created humanity so that in both "inspiration" and "formation" (materiality) humanity "was like God."[43] However, this blessing was not to lead humanity to think that it was autonomous. Rather, humanity "had as lord the Lord of all," and its immortality was conditional upon an obedience from which humanity wandered. So God placed humanity "far from His face, making him dwell by the road into Paradise, since the Paradise does not receive sinners."[44]

The second section (17–30), treats the history of salvation within the old economy.[45] Here we see God preparing humanity for Jesus Christ, God's Son, in his redemptive flesh and blood, through the promises and anticipation resident within the patriarchs, the Passover, the Law, the Tabernacle, the kings, the temple and the prophets. Section three (31–40a) and the conclusion (40b–42a) of part one describe the fulfillment in Jesus of what had previously been prophesied and expected. In order to reverse sin's mastery of Adam's flesh, brought about through disobedience, the obedient Son of God joined humanity with its flesh to God so that humanity might be released from the oppression of the flesh to incorruptibility. In order to reverse Eve's disobedience and the transgression at the tree, in the same way that Adam had been recapitulated in Christ, Eve was in Mary and the tree in the cross, "virginal obedience" replacing "virginal disobedience" and the one "hanging upon the tree" undoing the transgression "through the tree."[46] All of this, Jesus' actual birth, death, resurrection, and ascension, fulfilled promises to Abraham and David and provided for the dispensing of the Holy Spirit upon the Gentiles, the means of their own bodily resurrection.

The second part of the *Demonstration* (43–100) begins with Irenaeus's treatment of the eternality of Christ, the Son of God (43–52). He was with the Father in the beginning, prior to creation, and he was redemptively active and present in the old economy before his birth. He spoke with Abraham, Jacob, and Moses. David and Isaiah spoke of both Father and Son and portrayed the Son as the Lord, who existed prior to creation and was active in history. All of this is to show that he

> is before the whole world, is with the Father and with men, and King of all, since the Father has subjected all things to Him, and that He is the Saviour of those who believe in Him – these are demonstrated by such [passages of] Scripture.
>
> (Irenaeus, *Demonstration* 52)[47]

Next, Irenaeus demonstrates the anticipation of the birth, entry into Jerusalem, and resurrection of Jesus Christ, the Son of God, in Isaiah, Moses, Amos, Micah, David, and Zechariah (53–66). Then he demonstrates how Isaiah, David, Hosea, Jeremiah, and Zechariah prophesied the righteous Son of God's healings, his raising the dead, his trial, his substitutionary sufferings and passion on the cross which release believers from judgment, his divine lineage, his burial, his descent into hell, resurrection, and ascension to the Father's right hand (67–85). In the last section of the *Demonstration* (86–97), Irenaeus shows how Isaiah, David, Joel, Jeremiah, Ezekiel, Hosea, and Moses prophesied concerning the inclusion of the Gentiles by faith within the new covenant gospel blessings accomplished by Christ. He mentions the internalization of the law of love by the indwelling of the Spirit, the giving of a new name, and the pointing of the nations towards a new way separate from the old law and letter of Moses. In these it might be seen that in his ministry Christ was "mixing and blending the Spirit of God the Father with the handiwork of God, [so] that man might be according to the image and likeness of God."[48] The conclusion of this work (98–100) deserves to be read in the bishop's own words:

> This, beloved, is the preaching of the truth, and this is the character of our salvation, and this is the way of life, which the prophets announced and

Christ confirmed and the apostles handed over and the Church, in the whole world, hands down to her children. ... So, error, concerning the three heads of our seal, has caused much straying from the truth, for either they despise the Father, or do not accept the Son – they speak against the economy of His incarnation – or they do not accept the Holy Spirit, that is, they despise prophecy.

(Irenaeus, *Demonstration* 98–100)[49]

His polemical theology

Although Eusebius characterized Irenaeus as a man of peace, he remained a fierce opponent of the Gnostics, particularly of the Ptolemaeans, whom he understood as an offshoot of the Valentinians.[50] He saw them as threats to his own community, for, after they had infiltrated it disguised in the very words used by the community, they seduced and led astray the simple and the novices. In his mind, they cunningly disguised their error in scriptural, apostolic garb, for if it were not camouflaged, even the simple would reject it. Therefore they always presented their system as an authentic work of art or a priceless jewel, but through their rearrangement of the Scriptures, their wares ultimately proved to be counterfeit.[51] Irenaeus engaged the Gnostics, he said, for reasons of pastoral care and salvation of souls. He desired to "turn them back to the truth" and wished "to bring them to a saving knowledge of the one true God."[52] He was a shepherd concerned for his flock. His opponents were enticing members of his community away from orthodoxy with an erroneous but true-sounding message. He saw the Gnostics as false teachers who had cleverly and artfully placed an unorthodox theological system in a deceitful and seductive costume. He notes that:

Error, in fact, does not show its true self, lest on being stripped naked it should be detected. Instead it craftily decks itself out in an attractive dress, and thus, by an outward false appearance, presents itself to the more ignorant, truer than Truth itself, ridiculous as it is even to say this.

(Irenaeus, *Against Heresies* 1. Pref. 2)[53]

As he wrote these words the biblical text he had in mind was Matthew 7:15. There Jesus had warned the Christian community about false prophets who come cloaked in sheep's clothing, but who were inwardly, in truth, ravenous wolves. In his mind, the Gnostics exemplified a seductive duplicity. They sounded, and frequently acted, just like orthodox Christians, but their religious perspective was quite different. They read the Bible, used the Bible, and cited the Bible. The way they understood the Bible, the way they put its pieces together, however, differed dramatically from his perspective, as well as from that of his predecessors: Pothinus, Polycarp, and John. This is significant for Irenaeus since it was only through these individuals and those associated with them by their membership through baptism into the church – from the Apostles, to those they mentored, and eventually down to him, his community, and other communities throughout the world – that the one faith, the apostolic teaching, the Rule of Faith and of Truth, had been preserved.[54] This Rule involved giving a particular fit and arrangement to all the various parts of the Bible. The Gnostics made connections between Scriptures guided by their own rules, their own traditions. In doing so, however, Irenaeus explained, "they disregard the order and connection of the Scriptures and so far as it is possible, they dismantle the truth."[55] So while their biblical theology may at first appear to be the precious jewel of orthodoxy, it would actually be found to be an imitation in glass; and while their teaching may to the novice seem to be pure silver, it would be shown to be an alloy; and while the one who glanced quickly may see the familiar pieces of Scripture as in a mosaic in which the gems or tiles had originally been arranged to form the portrait of a king, upon second glance the observer would be horrified to see that the tiles have been rearranged into the form of a dog or fox![56]

As a pastor, then, Irenaeus composed *Against Heresies* in order to describe the component parts of the heresies which were threatening his flock and to present the apostolic, orthodox theological arrangement of the Scriptures. There had certainly been earlier defenders of the apostolic tradition against false teaching which certainly had Gnostic elements, such as Ignatius of Antioch and Justin Martyr. Irenaeus's work was unprecedented, however, because of the degree of attention he gave both to describing the Gnostic myths, particularly in its Valentinian variety, and then in replying to it with an immense and detailed exposition of the orthodox faith. In his work he revealed the cloaked deception for what it was and displayed the elements of the Rule of Truth as a saving reminder to the baptized faithful.

The heretics who threatened Irenaeus's community taught a myth, a religious perspective on reality, which in his mind always defaulted into dualism, a view which divides substances into two. In response to such Gnostic dualism, Irenaeus presented the apostolic faith of unity. It is at this point that we can see an important way in which Irenaeus's association with martyrdom shaped him. His opponents, he argued, teach that Christ must be divided from death. In general, though some variation exists within the accounts he knew, the pleromatic Christ-savior was a divine spirit-being from the heavenly realm (the *Pleroma*, the "fullness") that did not become really incarnate, enfleshed, so he could not really suffer.[57] He was not truly human, but either only appeared or seemed to be human or merely descended into, temporarily, a human receptacle named "Jesus." "Christ" and "Jesus," therefore, were divided. The real, bloody death of the incarnate Christ was a fundamental element of Christian faith. Martyrdom imitated it, and early creedal forms, or expressions of the Rule of Faith, included it:

> The Church ... received from the apostles and their disciples the faith in ... the one Jesus Christ, the Son of God, who was enfleshed for our salvation ... the coming, the birth from a virgin, the passion, the resurrection from the dead, and the bodily ascension into heaven of the beloved Son, Christ Jesus our Lord.
>
> (Irenaeus, *Against Heresies* 1.10.1)[58]

Irenaeus could not let such dualism deceive his flock. He responded with a biblical presentation of the oneness of Jesus Christ and the reality of his humanity and bloody crucifixion, and the propriety of martyrdom as imitation of Christ's suffering:

> [Christ] knew, therefore, both those who should suffer persecution, and He knew those who should have to be scourged and slain because of Him; and He did not speak of any other cross, but of the suffering which He should Himself undergo first, and His disciples afterward.
>
> (Irenaeus, *Against Heresies* 3.18.5)[59]

At the root of the Gnostic (Valentinian) myth known by Irenaeus was a view of God and creation. There were two gods: First, there existed the supreme spiritual, transcendent Father: "They claim that in the invisible and unnameable heights there is a certain perfect Aeon that was before all, the First-Being, whom they also call First-Beginning, First-Father, and Profundity. He is invisible and incomprehensible."[60] He exists with his heavenly world of spiritual beings, "Aeons," which emanated from him.[61] Second, there existed the offspring of Achamoth, brought forth as a result of her unfortunate pride and passion, the Demiurge, the creator of the physical, material world who was ignorant of the Father and arrogant.[62] He was identified with the Old Testament God, the God of the Jews and was "Father and God of all things outside the Fullness, inasmuch as he is the Maker of all the ensouled and material beings."[63] In the thought of his opponents there were three types of substances ranked in order of value: the spiritual, associated with the Father; the material, formed by the impostor Demiurge out of fear, grief, and perplexity; and the soulish (or ensouled), midway between the spiritual and the material.[64] This conception resulted in two dualisms: the Father versus the creator and the heavenly, spiritual world (*Pleroma*) versus the material world (and the soulish substance) of trees, rocks, earth, flesh, and blood. In contrast, Irenaeus declared one God, both Father and Creator of the material world:

> But there is one only God, the Creator – He who is above every Principality, and Power and Dominion, and Virtue: He is Father, He is God, He the Founder, He the Maker, He the Creator, who made those things by Himself, that is, through His Word and His Wisdom – heaven and earth, and the seas, and all things that are in them: He is just; He is good; He it is who formed man, who planted paradise, who made the world, who gave rise to the flood, who saved Noah; He is the God of Abraham, and the God of Isaac, and the God of Jacob, the God of the living: He it is whom the law proclaims, whom the prophets preach, whom Christ reveals, whom the Apostles make known to us, and in whom the church believes.
>
> (Irenaeus, *Against Heresies* 2.30.9)[65]

In these words we witness another Irenaean theme, that of unity between different economies within different periods of redemptive history: there is harmony between the Old and New Testaments, between the Prophets and Apostles. The Creator declared by Moses is the Father revealed in Christ. There are obviously differences between the old economy and the new, between the economy of creation, Israel, Law, and the prophets and the economy of Christ, salvation, Church, and the apostles. However, contrary to the Valentinians, it is a difference of degree, of greater and lesser, of promise and fulfillment, of part and whole, of progress towards the perfect, of prolepsis and consummation, but not one of substance.[66] These economies are different stages within a singular, united agenda of the one, true God: "All things therefore are of one and the same substance, that is, from one and the same God."[67] There is not one god who designs the first and another god who structures the second. The one God does not abandon his creation. Instead, through the recapitulative ministry of his Son he corrects the faults within human history and perfects under the lordship of his incarnate Son all of his creation. Through recapitulation God inaugurates in his Son a new order of life, a new community and brings that newness to consummation at the return of his ascended Son to the creation.[68] This one God manifests himself in the economies, however, within a Trinitarian structure.[69] The Father has two hands, the Son and the Spirit, and all divine activity is of the Father himself through the Son and Spirit.[70] With this construct Irenaeus is setting the church's faith against the thesis of his opponents. Their Father, as he sees it, needs additional spiritual forces, angels or other gods, to assist in the accomplishment of his will for he is weak, needy, and fragmented in his being.[71] But in Irenaeus's confession the Father stands in need of nothing for he is self-sufficient, the God, Father, and Lord of all, in indivisible unity with the Son and Spirit.[72]

Along with this view of two gods and two worlds the Valentinians taught that since the material world was created by an impostor, an ignorant deity, it and its components, including the human body, were void of value and must perish, for they cannot receive incorruption or immortality.[73] This was why, in their view, Christ did not become flesh in reality, did not die a true, bloody death, and why, for them, there would be no bodily resurrection or redemption of the created, material order. Irenaeus, in response, taught the redemption of creation, the salvation of the material by means of the material, flesh and blood by flesh and blood. For Irenaeus, salvation included the flesh, the creation of the one true Creator and Father, which by the Spirit of God would be resurrected incorruptible and immortal.[74] The earth and the flesh would undergo redemption and renewal:

> Those who reject the whole "economy" of God deny the salvation of the flesh and reject its regeneration, saying that it is not capable of receiving imperishability, are absolutely vain. If this flesh is not saved, the Lord did not redeem us by his blood (Col. 1:14) and the cup of the Eucharist is not communion with his blood and the bread we break is not communion with his body (1 Cor. 10:16). For blood comes only from veins and flesh and the rest of the human substance, which the Word of God became when he redeemed us by his blood.
>
> (Irenaeus, *Against Heresies* 5.2.2)[75]

And again,

For God is rich in all things, and all things are His. It is fitting, therefore, that the creation itself, being restored to its primeval condition, should without restraint be under the dominion of the righteous. ... For as God is really the one who raises man, so man will really rise from the dead, and not allegorically, as we have shown by so many examples [e.g., Isa. 65:17–22; Rev. 21:1–4]. ... Since men are real, their transformation must also be real, since they will not go into non-being but on the contrary will progress in being. For neither the substance nor the matter of the creation will be annihilated – true and solid is the one who established it – ...

(Irenaeus, *Against Heresies* 5.32.1; 5.35.2–36.1)[76]

For his opponents, salvation was for those who were of Achamoth and the Pleroma, those who were spiritual, not by behavior, but by nature: "They themselves [the Valentinians], however, so they dogmatize, are spiritual, not by conduct, but by nature, and so they will be saved entirely and in every case."[77] The spiritual ones, in their view, are eventually perfected by knowledge (*gnosis*): "The consummation will take place when every spiritual element has been formed and perfected by knowledge."[78] The spiritual person, according to Irenaeus, however, is not spiritual in a mere incorporeal, immaterial manner as the Valentinian thinks. Neither is one spiritual by nature or knowledge. Instead, "the union of flesh [the material] and [the human] spirit, receiving the Spirit of God makes up the spiritual person."[79] Against the Valentinians, Irenaeus emphasized the supernatural, redemptive ministry of the Holy Spirit in making a person spiritual in both body and spirit. For Irenaeus, salvation is not by nature of original substance but by God's transformation of the original substance. This is the faith of the church: God bestows on the faithful "as a grace the gift of incorruption," it is not something bestowed by nature.[80] What the Holy Spirit touches becomes alive, spiritual, incorruptible: "The flesh, therefore, when destitute of the Spirit of God, is dead, not having life and cannot possess the kingdom of God. But where the Spirit of the Father is, there is a living man."[81] The corruptible creature must receive the excellence of putting on incorruptibility from the Creator's powerful intervention.[82] It is this ministry of the Holy Spirit upon the flesh of the martyrs which strengthened them to bear witness unto death in hope of fleshly resurrection. On this very point of the connection between the powerful act of the Spirit and martyrdom, our Bishop wrote "Thus it is, therefore, that the martyrs bear their witness, and despise death, not after the infirmity of the flesh, but because of the Spirit."[83] It is on this note that Irenaeus joins his Christology to his pneumatology in support of his doctrine of salvation. Christ's incarnation promises the salvation of the believer's flesh through bodily resurrection: "For if the flesh were not to be saved, the Word of God would not have become flesh."[84]

So we see in Irenaeus the church's doctrines of unity: One God, who is the Father, Lord, and Creator of all things, immaterial and material, and who through his Son and Spirit orchestrates one harmonious history of creation, revelation and redemption, of anticipation and fulfillment; one Son and Savior, who is both divine spirit and human flesh, both Christ and Jesus; one Spirit of the prophets and apostles, of creation and redemption; one human nature, which is both immaterial and fleshly, and capable of receiving incorruption through the incarnate ministry of the Son and the transforming act of the Spirit; one salvation of both the immaterial and material, of both believing humans and the groaning creation, for the one Spirit can cause any aspect of the creature to be spiritual. Here are foundational doctrinal teachings in the faith of Irenaeus, received from those who passed the apostolic teaching down to him. Here are components of that orthodoxy which gave his flock protection from the wolves of heresy and which had given to Polycarp, as well as to the martyrs of Lyons and Vienne, the faith to endure even to the end.

Further reading

M. A. Donovan, *One Right Reading? A Guide to Irenaeus*, Collegeville, MN: Liturgical, 1997, "Irenaeus in Recent Scholarship," *Second Century* 4, 1984, 219–41.

D. Farkasfalvy, "Theology of Scripture in Irenaeus," *Revue Bénédictine* 78, 1968, 319–33.

F. R. M. Hitchcock, *Irenaeus of Lugdunum: A Study of His Teaching*, Cambridge: Cambridge University Press, 1914.

J. Lawson, *The Biblical Theology of Saint Irenaeus*, London: Epworth, 1948.

D. Minns, *Irenaeus*, Washington, DC: Georgetown University Press, 1994.

J. T. Nielsen, *Adam and Christ in the Theology of Irenaeus of Lyons: An Examination of the Function of the Adam–Christ Typology in the Adversus Haereses of Irenaeus, against the Background of the Gnosticism of His Time*, Assen: Van Gorcum, 1968.

J. Ochagavia, *Visible Patris Filius: A Study of Irenaeus' Teaching on Revelation and Tradition*, Rome: Pontificium Institutum Orientalium Studiorum, 1964.

J. Quasten, *The Beginnings of Patristic Literature Patrology*, vol. 1 of *Patrology*, 4 vols, Westminster, MD: Newman, 1950; repr. Westminster, MD: Christian Classics, 1986.

M. C. Steenberg, *Irenaeus on Creation: The Cosmic Christ and the Saga of Redemption*, Leiden: Brill, 2008.

G. Wingren, *Man and the Incarnation: A Study in the Biblical Theology of Irenaeus*, trans. R. Mackenzie, Philadelphia: Muhlenberg, 1959.

Notes

1 Eusebius, *Ecclesiastical History* 5.1–3.

2 Eusebius, *Ecclesiastical History* 5.5.8; P. Nautin, *Lettres et écrivains chrétiens des IIe et IIIe siècles*, Paris: Cerf, 1961, pp. 54–61.

3 Jerome, *On Illustrious Men* 35.

4 A. Benoît, *Saint Irénée, introduction à l'étude de sa théologie*, Paris: Presses universitaires de France, 1960, p. 50; J. van der Straeten, "Saint-Irénée fut-il martyre?," in J. Rougé and R. Turcan (eds), *Les martyrs de Lyon* (177), Colloques internationaux du Centre national de la recherche scientifique 575, Paris: Éditions du CNRS, 1978; Jerome, *Commentary on Isaiah* 64.

5 Irenaeus, *To Florinus* in Eusebius, *Ecclesiastical History* 5.20; Irenaeus, *Against Heresies* 3.3.4.

6 Irenaeus, *To Florinus*; *Against Heresies* 3.3.4.

7 J. Quasten, *The Beginnings of Patristic Literature*, vol. 1 of *Patrology*, 4 vols, Westminster, MD: Newman, 1950; repr. Westminster, MD: Christian Classics, 1986, p. 287.

8 C. Hill, *From the Lost Teaching of Polycarp: Identifying Irenaeus' Apostolic Presbyter and the Author of* ad Diognetum, Wissenschaftliche Untersuchungen zum Neuen Testament 186, Tübingen: Mohr Siebeck, 2006.

9 Eusebius, *Ecclesiastical History* 5.4.2.

10 Eusebius, *Ecclesiastical History* 5.24.17.

11 Eusebius, *Ecclesiastical History* 5.1.1.

12 Eusebius, *Ecclesiastical History* 5.1.17, 49.

13 Eusebius, *Ecclesiastical History* 5.1.3; trans. G. A. Williamson, rev. and ed. A. Louth, *Eusebius, The History of the Church from Christ to Constantine*, London: Penguin, 1989, p. 139.

14 R. M. Grant, *Irenaeus of Lyons*, London: Routledge, 1997, p. 1.

15 Eusebius, *Ecclesiastical History* 5.24.18.

16 Irenaeus, *Against Heresies* 1.Pref.1.

17 *The Nag Hammadi Scriptures: The International Edition*, ed. M. Meyer, New York: HarperCollins, 2007; *The Gnostic Scriptures*, ed., trans., and annot. B. Layton, New York: Doubleday, 1987; *The Nag Hammadi Library*, rev. and ed. J. Robinson, Leiden: Brill, 1988.

18 P. Perkins, "Irenaeus and the Gnostics: Rhetoric and Composition in Adversus Haereses Book One," *Vigiliae Christianae* 30, 1976, pp. 103–200.

19 Perkins, "Irenaeus and the Gnostics," p. 193, n. 1.

20 *Nag Hammadi Scriptures*, 778.

21 Ibid.

22 Ibid.

23 C. Markschies, *Gnosis: An Introduction*, trans. J. Bowden, London: T&T Clark, 2003; D. J. Bingham, Review of C. Markschies, *Gnosis: An Introduction*, *Journal of Early Christian Studies* 13, 2005, pp. 387–8.

24 Cf. Perkins's remark concerning G. Quispel, "Origen and the Valentinian Gnosis," *Vigiliae Christianae* 28, 1974, pp. 33–5, in Perkins, "Irenaeus and the Gnostics," p. 193, n. 1.

25 Cf. R. Grant's comments in his review of E. Pagels's works on Gnostic exegesis in *Religious Studies Review* 3, 1977, p. 32.

26 Irenaeus, *Against Heresies* 2.Pref.1; 4.Pref.1; 3.3.3; 5.Pref.; Irenaeus, *The Demonstration of the Apostolic Preaching* 99; Eusebius, *Ecclesiastical History* 2.13.5; 3.28.6; 5.5.9; 5.7.1; Basil, *On the Holy Spirit* 29.72; Jerome, *On Illustrious Men* 35; Photius, *Codex* 120.

27 Augustine, *Against Julian* 1.3.5; J. Chapman, "Did the Translator of St Irenaeus use a Latin New Testament?," *Revue Bénédictine* 36, 1924, pp. 34–51; K. T. Scäfer, "Die Zitate in der lateinischen Irenäus Übersetzung ihr Wert für die Textgeschichte des Neuen Testamentes," in N. Adler (ed.), *Vom Wort des Lebens*, Münster: Aschendorffsche, 1951, pp. 50–9; *Irénée de Lyon: Contre les Hérésies, Livre 4*, ed., trans., and annot. A. Rousseau, B. Hemmerdinger, L. Doutreleau, and C. Mercier, vol. 100.1, Paris: Cerf, 1965, pp. 89–92, 107–57, and for a thorough discussion on versions and manuscript traditions, pp. 15–191.

28 *Against Heresies, Books 1–5 and Fragments*, in A. Roberts and W. H. Rambaut (trans. and ed.), *The Apostolic Fathers with Justin Martyr*, rev. edn, vol. 1 in *The Ante-Nicene Fathers*, 10 vols, Edinburgh: T&T Clark, 1885–7; repr. Grand Rapids, MI: Wm. B. Eerdmans, 1987; repr. Peabody, MA: Hendrickson, 1994, pp. 315–578.

29 *Against the Heresies, Book 1*, trans. and annot. D. Unger and J. J. Dillon, Ancient Christian Writers 55, New York: Paulist, 1992; R. Grant, *Irenaeus of Lyons*, London: Routledge, 1997.

30 *Irénée de Lyon: Contre les Hérésies, Livres 1–5*, ed., trans., and annot. by A. Rousseau, L. Doutreleau, B. Hemmerdinger, and C. Mercier, Sources chrétiennes 263, 264 [Livre 1], 293, 294 [Livre 2], 210, 211 [Livre3], 100.1, 100.2 [Livre 4], 152, 153 [Livre 5], Paris: Cerf, 1979 [Livre 1], 1982 [Livre 2], 1974, 2002 [Livre 3], 1965 [Livre 4], 1969 [Livre 5].

31 For the outline of *Against Heresies 1* I am indebted to the analysis of the editors of the critical edition of Irenaeus's work in the Sources chrétiennes series. I also have referred to my own account (also informed by the editors of the critical edition) in D. J. Bingham, *Irenaeus's Use of Matthew's Gospel in Adversus Haereses*, Leuven: Peeters, 1998.

32 P. Bacq, *De l'ancienne à la nouvelle Alliance selon S. Irénée: Unité du livre IV de l'Adversus Haereses*, Paris: Éditions Lethielleux, 1978.

33 A. Orbe, *Teología de San Ireneo IV: Traducción y comentario del Libro IV del "Adversus haereses,"* Madrid: Biblioteca de Autores Cristianos, 1996.

34 A. Orbe, *Teología de San Ireneo: Comentario al Libro V del "Adversus haereses,"* 3 vols, Madrid: La Editorial Catolíca, 1985–8.

35 Trans. Williamson and Louth, *Eusebius, The History of the Church*, pp. 168, 174.

36 Eusebius, *Ecclesiastical History* 5.20.1; 5.20.4–8; 5.23.3; 5.24.11–17.

37 A reference to the longer title of *Against Heresies* can be found in *Demonstration*.
   This reference has been used as a clue to the relative dating of these two works.

Some, such as A. Rousseau, believe that the *Demonstration* was composed as a single work of one hundred chapters after Irenaeus wrote *Against Heresies*. Others, such as Y. Blanchard, believe that the final two chapters (99–100) of the *Demonstration* are a later addition to the first ninety-eight, and therefore place the composition of *Against Heresies* between the two components of the *Demonstration*. Y. M. Blanchard, *Aux sources du canon: Le témoignage d'Irénée*, Paris: Cerf, 1993, p. 113, n. 2. For an orientation to the debate see *St Irenaeus of Lyons on the Apostolic Preaching*, trans. and intro. J. Behr, Crestwood, NY: St Vladimir's University Press, 1997, p. 118, n. 229.

38 For a convenient and helpful English introduction to the issue of the text and translations of the *Demonstration* see Behr's discussion in his *St Irenaeus of Lyons on the Apostolic Preaching*, pp. 27–37.

39 *St Irenaeus of Lyons on the Apostolic Preaching*. One could consult also the work of I. M. MacKenzie, *Irenaeus's Demonstration of the Apostolic Preaching: A Theological Commentary and Translation*, Aldershot/Burlington: Ashgate, 2002. The translation in the MacKenzie volume is that of J. A. Robinson, *The Demonstration of the Apostolic Preaching*, London: SPCK, 1920.

40 *S. Irenaeus: The Proof of the Apostolic Preaching with Seven Fragments*, ed. and trans. K. Ter-Měkěrttschian and S. G. Wilson, Patrologia orientalis 12.5, Paris: Firmin-Didot et Cie, 1919; repr. Turnhout, Belgium: Brepols, 1989.

41 Trans. Behr, *St Irenaeus of Lyons on the Apostolic Preaching*, p. 39.

42 I follow here, the valuable synopsis of Behr, *St Irenaeus of Lyons on the Apostolic Preaching*, pp. 17–23.

43 Irenaeus, *Demonstration* 11; trans. Behr, *St Irenaeus of Lyons on the Apostolic Preaching*, p. 47.

44 Irenaeus, *Demonstration* 15–16; trans. Behr, *St Irenaeus of Lyons on the Apostolic Preaching*, pp. 49–50.

45 Behr, *St Irenaeus of Lyons on the Apostolic Preaching*, pp. 19–20, 50–60.

46 Irenaeus, *Demonstration* 33–34; trans. Behr, *St Irenaeus of Lyons on the Apostolic Preaching*, pp. 61–2.

47 Trans. Behr, *St Irenaeus of Lyons on the Apostolic Preaching*, p. 74.

48 Irenaeus, *Demonstration* 97; trans. Behr, *St Irenaeus of Lyons on the Apostolic Preaching*, p. 100.

49 Trans. Behr, *St Irenaeus of Lyons on the Apostolic Preaching*, pp. 100–1.

50 Irenaeus, *Against Heresies* 1.Pref.2.

51 Irenaeus, *Against Heresies* 1.Pref.1–2; 1.3.6; 1.8.1; 1.9.4; 1.13.1–6.

52 Irenaeus, *Against Heresies* 3.2.3, 25.7.

53 Trans. Unger and Dillon, *Against the Heresies, Book 1*, p. 21.

54 Irenaeus, *Against Heresies* 1.9.4–10.2, 22.1; 3.3.1–4.3.

55 Irenaeus, *Against Heresies* 1.8.1.

56 Irenaeus, *Against Heresies* 1.Pref.2; 1.8.1; 1.9.4; 3.16.4.

57 For the Christology of Irenaeus's opponents see *Against Heresies* 1.6.1; 1.7.1; 1.8.2–9.3; 1.15.1–3; 1.25.1; 1.26.1–2; 1.29.1; 1.30.1–2, 11–14; A. Houssiau, *La christologie de saint Irénée*, Louvain: Publications Universitaires de Louvain, 1955, pp. 145–62. For discussion of the view of his opponents and his own response see *Against Heresies* 3.16–23.

58 Trans. Unger and Dillon, *Against the Heresies, Book 1*, pp. 48–9.

59 Trans. Roberts and Rambaut, *Against Heresies, Books 1–5 and Fragments*, p. 447. I have chosen to use the published translations, even the outdated one of Roberts and Rambaut, rather than my own, in order to provide some level of continuity for readers without Latin skills who wish to consult the broader contexts of Irenaeus himself.

60 Irenaeus, *Against Heresies* 1.1.1; trans. Unger and Dillon, *Against the Heresies, Book 1*, p. 23.

61 Irenaeus, *Against Heresies* 1.1.1–3.

62 Irenaeus, *Against Heresies* 1.5.3–6.

63 Irenaeus, *Against Heresies* 1.5.3; trans. Unger and Dillon, *Against the Heresies, Book 1*, 14.

64 Irenaeus, *Against Heresies* 1.5.1–6.4.

65 Trans. Roberts and Rambaut, *Against Heresies, Books 1–5 and Fragments*, p. 406.

66 Irenaeus, *Against Heresies* 4.9.1–2.

67 Irenaeus, *Against Heresies* 4.9.1; trans. Roberts and Rambaut, *Against Heresies, Books 1–5 and Fragments*, p. 472.

68 I have briefly summarized here the helpful discussion on recapitulation in Irenaeus provided in E. Osborn, *Irenaeus of Lyons*, Cambridge: Cambridge University Press, 2001, pp. 97–140.

69 Cf. J. Fantino, *La théologie d'Irénée: Lecture des écritures en réponse à l'exégèse gnostique, une approche trinitaire*, Paris: Cerf, 1994, pp. 203–392.

70 See Irenaeus, *Against Heresies* 1.22.1; 2.2.4–6; 3.8.3; *Demonstration* 5. Cf. Osborn, *Irenaeus of Lyons*, pp. 38–42, 52–55, 89–93; D. J. Bingham, "Himself within Himself: The Father and His Hands in Early Christianity," *Southwestern Journal of Theology* 47, 2005, pp. 137–51. The biblical texts of John 1:3 and Eph. 4:6 are pivotal to his concept. For treatments of Irenaeus's use of John and Paul see: B. Mutschler, *Irenäus als johanneischer Theologe*, Tübingen: Mohr-Siebeck, 2004; R. Noormann, *Irenäus als Paulusinterpret: Zur Rezeption und Wirkung der paulinischen und deuteropaulinischen Briefe im Werke des Irenäus von Lyon*, Tübingen: Mohr-Siebeck, 1994; R. A. Norris, "Irenaeus' Use of Paul in His Polemic Against the Gnostics," in W. S. Babcock (ed.), *Paul and the Legacies of Paul*, Dallas: Southern Methodist University Press, 1990, pp. 79–98; D. L. Balás, "The Use and Interpretation of Paul in Irenaeus's Five Books, *Adversus Haereses*," *Second Century* 9, 1992, 27–39.

71 Irenaeus, *Against Heresies* 2.2.3; 2.5.1–4; 2.12.1; 2.13.3–9; 2.15.2–17.10; 2.31.1.

72 Irenaeus, *Against Heresies* 1.12.1; 1.22.1; 2.2.4; 2.10.4; 2.11.1; 2.13.3, 8; 2.28.4; 2.30.9; 2.31.1; 4.11.2.

73 Irenaeus, *Against Heresies* 1.6.1.

74 On the themes of incorruptibility and divinization in Irenaeus see Y. de Andia, *Homo Vivens: Incorruptibilité et divinisation de l'homme selon Irénée de Lyon*, Paris: Études Augustiniennes, 1986.

75 Trans. Grant, *Irenaeus of Lyons*, p. 164.

76 Irenaeus, *Against Heresies* 5.32.1; trans. Roberts and Rambaut, *Against Heresies, Books 1–5 and Fragments*, p. 561; *Against Heresies* 5.35.2–36.1; trans. Grant, *Irenaeus of Lyons*, p. 184.

77 Irenaeus, *Against Heresies* 1.6.2; trans. Unger and Dillon, *Against the Heresies, Book 1*, p. 37.

78 Irenaeus, *Against Heresies* 1.6.1; trans. Unger and Dillon, *Against the Heresies, Book 1*, p. 36.

79 Irenaeus, *Against Heresies* 5.8.2; trans. Roberts and Rambaut, *Against Heresies, Books 1–5 and Fragments*, p. 534.

80 Irenaeus, *Against Heresies* 1.10.1; trans. Unger and Dillon, *Against the Heresies, Book 1*, p. 49.

81 Irenaeus, *Against Heresies* 5.9.3; trans. Roberts and Rambaut, *Against Heresies, Books 1–5 and Fragments*, p. 535. Cf. *Against Heresies* 5.9.2.

82 E. Peretto, *La Lettera ai Romani cc. 1–8 nell' Adversus Haereses d'Ireneo*, Bari: Istitutio di Letteratura Cristiano Antica, 1971, p. 209.

83 Irenaeus, *Against Heresies* 5.9.2; trans. Roberts and Rambaut, *Against Heresies, Books 1–5 and Fragments*, p. 535.

84 Irenaeus, *Against Heresies* 5.14.1; trans. Grant, *Irenaeus of Lyons*, p. 168.

9

ROMAN AND NORTH AFRICAN CHRISTIANITY

Geoffrey D. Dunn

This chapter seeks to explore the second- and third-century history of Christian thought in the two major centers of the western Mediterranean: Rome and Carthage. The types of Christianity that were evident in these cities differed from each other, shaped by particular circumstances and events. Furthermore, it must be kept in mind that the thinking expressed in the writings of the outstanding individuals to be surveyed in this chapter, while it was forged in these cities, did not express necessarily the thinking of the whole Christian community in that city, but often only the individual attitude of the writer concerned. In the sections of this chapter I shall consider two authors from each city – Tertullian and Cyprian from Carthage and Hippolytus and Novatian from Rome – to outline their thinking about God, human nature, the church, and Christian living.

Tertullian

In the Severan age of the late second and early third centuries, a married layman in Carthage, who had converted to Christianity, emerged to become the first Latin-writing Christian thinker whose works survive. We do not know much about Christianity in North Africa before Tertullian, besides a couple of martyr Acts (*Acts of the Scillitan Martyrs, Passion of Perpetua and Felicitas*). There has been debate about the origins of Christianity in North Africa. Some think it emerged from local Jewish communities, and others think it arrived from Rome, following what Tertullian himself seems to suggest.[1] The argument of Telfer, that African Christianity did not have a single parentage but was formed out of the coalescing of originally separate communities, makes most sense, particularly in a major port city like Carthage, where there were people from all sorts of ethnic backgrounds.[2] By the time of Tertullian there seems to have been a single bishop supported by presbyters and deacons.

A growing number of scholars disbelieve many of the biographical elements of Jerome's *On Illustrious Men*, that Tertullian was a presbyter who left the church when he became a Montanist, and that we are to identify him with the Roman jurist of the same name.[3] He was rhetorically trained, and his literary ability shines through many pithy aphorisms and sharp comments.[4] He used his skills to combat theological opponents and to advocate a rigorist and uncompromising Christianity. Tertullian sought to win arguments more than to present coherent and consistent theological positions.[5] No one statement of Tertullian's necessarily represents his true thinking, for, like any half-decent orator, he could argue for or against something as the occasion demanded.[6] This is evident in his interpretation of the Scriptures. Together with logic and custom or practice, forming the basis of much of his argumentation, we find him endorsing allegory on the one hand, while advocating literalism on the other, making sure he rejected whatever method his opponent employed in order to argue his position.[7]

Tertullian's starting-point in talking about God was with God's unity: the very definition of God as supreme means there can be only one.[8] In his largest work, he argued against his dualist opponent Marcion. In the middle of the second century Marcion had gone to Rome from his native Pontus. His articulate theology attracted adherents, the Marcionites, and their views challenged Tertullian to explain his belief in the unity of God from the Scriptures more persuasively. Marcion could not integrate the paradox of goodness and justice into one divine being.[9] As Tertullian saw him, Marcion believed there were two gods revealed in the Scriptures: one harsh and belligerent, recorded in the Old Testament as the creator of evil (Isa. 45:7) and of the world, and the other totally good and superior, unknown until revealed by Christ.[10] Tertullian would admit no dichotomy between creation and salvation in God, because for him God's goodness is shown even in divine anger, which has a healing effect.[11] The proof that God's judgment is about love is the fact that God died.[12] Jesus reveals the Creator, not Marcion's until-then unknown god,[13] just as the Creator long announced the coming of the Christ who came.[14]

This unity of God was defended by Tertullian against Gnostic writers also. While there are some similarities between Marcion and the Gnostics, particularly in Tertullian's mind, we would do well to distinguish them.[15] Hermogenes, a contemporary of Tertullian and probably a fellow Carthaginian, under the influence of Stoicism argued that matter is eternal.[16] For Tertullian this amounted to an admission of two gods, with matter being superior.[17] Like Marcion, Hermogenes was concerned to absolve God from any responsibility for evil by investing it in matter. Instead, Tertullian argued that if God created using this matter, then God was responsible for evil. What Tertullian would do to resolve the dilemma, of course, would be to redefine the meaning of evil, as well as argue that God created all things out of nothing.[18]

God's unity also raised problems for some Christians when they came to explain the relationship between Jesus and God. Praxeas (perhaps a pseudonym for someone who, according to Tertullian, came from Asia to Rome, since Hippolytus fails to mention this name),[19] convinced that Jesus truly was God and that there was but one God, argued (as Tertullian presents it) that it was the Father who was born of the virgin and who died as Jesus.[20] According to Praxeas, the Father became the Son in the incarnation.[21] Behind this is John 10:30 about the Father and Son being one. This blurring of any real distinction between them (the Spirit is of less concern in the debate) is known theologically as modalist monarchianism or patripassianism.

Tertullian's response was to argue from the rule of faith (*regula fidei*) found in the Scriptures that in the economy of salvation there were distinctions in the Godhead: the Son proceeds from the Father, the Father sent the Son, the Son was both man and God, the Son was born of the virgin and died, the Father raised the Son, the Son sent the Spirit from the Father, and the Spirit proceeds from the Father through the Son. There is a distinction of person (*persona*) or a trinity (*trinitas*), while there is one God because there is one substance (*substantia*), one condition (*status*), and one power (*potestas*).[22] Out of this one God are the degrees (*gradus*), forms (*formae*), and aspects (*species*) of the Father, Son, and Spirit.[23] Yet, distinction is not diversity or division.[24]

The Son could be described as *logos*, God's Word or Reason or Thought, and *sophia*, God's Wisdom, the only-begotten of God before all things, but of the same substance as the Father.[25] Yet, although the Son is second to the Father (a derivation of the Father's whole substance[26] – not a phrase that would sit comfortably in a later orthodox theology suspicious of subordinationism) because the begetter is greater than the begotten (John 14:28), and the Spirit is third,[27] this is not some Gnostic form of emanation, as Valentinus held, where a hierarchy of beings existed between an ineffable god and creation, because Son is not separated from Father.[28] Tertullian found the Stoic notion of relative disposition helpful to explain the distinctions (since *persona* was not used substantively by Tertullian), but the analogy of father and child or husband and wife is imperfect because the relation is located within two separate existent beings, which is not how Tertullian understood God's *substantia*.[29] Even the organic images of root and tree, source and fountain, sun and ray, are limited in that the unifying substance seems to break into constituent elements, although one must be careful not to read too much into the imagery.[30] Defining what *substantia* and *persona* were (and relating them to Greek thinking) was not Tertullian's concern.[31]

Tertullian's anthropology focused on the question of the relationship between body and soul, flesh and spirit. For Tertullian, dependent upon Stoic thought but opposed to Platonic and other philosophical insights from which the various Gnostics derived their thinking, the human person is comprised of body and soul, the latter being created with each successful generative act (traducianism) and thereafter everlasting, and corporeal, in the sense of real and capable of experiencing. The human soul is possessed of free will yet develops differently in different people, is the home of the mind, and is the supreme principle of the human person.[32] We find in Tertullian a belief in original sin in that, because of Adam's sin, each soul is unclean until reborn in Christ (through baptism).[33] Unlike the Gnostics, Tertullian accepted the goodness of the body, while stressing the need for purity.[34]

One of the major implications of Tertullian's anthropology was for Christology. The notion of some that within the incarnate Word the flesh was the Son, the human person Jesus, while the spirit was the Father, the divine person Christ, was countered by Tertullian, who believed that what his opponents postulated separated, and not merely distinguished, Son from Father. Further, the divine spirit born of the Virgin was not changed into flesh, as Praxeas and Valentinus believed, nor mixed with flesh but was clothed with flesh, one person with two substances.[35] He also countered Marcion's docetic notion that Christ only appeared to have flesh.[36] For Tertullian, Christ needed real flesh in order to be born and die, events which Marcion accepted as real.[37] So real is Jesus having flesh that, although Mary conceived him through the Spirit as a virgin, she gave birth, not as a virgin, but as a woman.[38]

One of the other implications of his anthropology concerns Christian life. If baptism is the regeneration of the soul necessary for salvation and for the remission of sins committed in one's lifetime, then people should not be eager to receive baptism too early, particularly because so many people seemed to be unable to continue to live in that pure state.[39] Yet, Tertullian could also be critical of those who put off baptism because they knew they would sin after it, urging them instead to greater resolve rather than fatalism.[40] For those who did sin after baptism, he was prepared to concede that their sins could be forgiven once more, but only after an onerous period of public penance.[41] However, in later life, under the influence of Montanism and his own rigorist personality, he argued that major sins like adultery and fornication could not be forgiven repeatedly because God is not only merciful but just as well.[42]

In Tertullian's understanding of the church we find the full flowering of his rigorism. At some point he had come into contact with Montanists. This movement from Phrygia (south-west Turkey), which called itself New Prophecy, can be characterized by its belief in the outpouring of the Spirit (the Paraclete), prophetic and ecstatic utterances that called its adherents to a more committed, demanding, and disciplined living of the Christian life, and by its perceived threat to the authority of the church's nascent leadership structures, especially by having women as prophetic leaders. The type of New Prophecy Tertullian knew in Africa was different from that in Asia or in Rome (and it is difficult to tell when Tertullian reports Montanist views and when he is just expressing his own natural hard-line ones), but though charismatic and elitist, neither the group nor Tertullian was considered to be heretical or schismatic, and the idea that Tertullian left the church ought to be abandoned.[43] Tertullian distinguished between "spiritual" Christians of the New Prophecy and other "sensual" Christians (On Monogamy). Second marriage after the death of one's spouse was forbidden[44] (a hardening of the views he had expressed in To His Wife and On Exhortation to Chastity), rigorous fasting was customary (On Fasting), and sinners were to be excluded from the community not reconciled with it.[45] All of this was revealed by the Spirit for the new age in which Tertullian believed he was living.

Even before he found a home among the Montanist Christians within the broader Christian community of Carthage, Tertullian had looked upon reality in clear-cut terms. Although in Apology he could find much to praise in the Roman political system, this was because he was addressing that system asking for an end to the persecution of Christians (To Scapula).[46] Yet, when he wrote for a Christian readership, as Evans notes, he was more prepared to be critical, rejecting Christian participation in the military (On The Military Crown) and public entertainment (On Idolatry) because of its connection with idolatry.[47] Martyrdom was an opportunity to demonstrate commitment to the faith and was to be embraced, and its avoidance, which earlier he could understand (To His Wife and On Patience), was something he rejected in later life (On Flight in Persecution). With regard to the Jews, while Tertullian defended the Hebrew Scriptures against Marcion's dismissal of them, he did believe that with the coming of Christ the Jews had been supplanted as God's people by the Christians (*Against the Jews*).[48]

Hippolytus

The traditional view is that Hippolytus was a Roman presbyter of the early third century, roughly contemporary with Tertullian, who came from the East, possibly Alexandria. Accusing the Roman bishop Callistus (217–22) with being an adherent of Noetus (a modalist monarchian from Asia whose ideas were spread to Rome by Epigonus and Cleomenes and embraced by Sabellius) and morally corrupt, Hippolytus set himself up as a rival bishop (the first so-called antipope, although this is an anachronistic and unhelpful term) until reconciled with the church when he and Pontian, a later bishop, were both exiled in 235.[49] This view has been revised radically in recent years.[50]

Now increasingly it is argued that Christianity in Rome continued to exist as independent communities, each with their own leader, although with some leaders perhaps exercising particular functions on behalf of all the Roman Christian communities.[51] It was perhaps not until Victor, at the end of the second century at the time of the Quatrodeciman controversy over whether Easter should be 14 Nisan (the Jewish Passover) or a Sunday, or perhaps not until Pontian, that Rome had a single bishop. On this reading, Callistus and Hippolytus would have been leaders of different Christian communities in Rome, such that Hippolytus should not be seen as schismatic, but by the time of the death of Pontian one community had emerged, to which Hippolytus belonged as presbyter.[52]

What works did this Hippolytus write? The idea that one individual was responsible for *Refutation of All Heresies*, *Against the Heresy of One Noetus*, a number of biblical commentaries (including *Commentary on Daniel*), and *Apostolic Tradition*, as well as a number of other works, is today rejected by leading scholars. It is to be noted that all the works survive in Greek (*Apostolic Tradition* in a number of languages), perhaps indicating that at least one of the Christian communities in Rome was Greek-speaking and, given the absence of Christian literature from Rome at this time in Latin, was seemingly the center of Christian intellectual activity in the city. Some see the author of *Refutation of All Heresies* and *Against the Heresy of One Noetus* as being two distinct individuals.[53] Brent, for one, sees both works coming out of the same school, with *Refutation of All Heresies* written by someone while the community led by Hippolytus was still in dispute with that led by Zephyrinus and Callistus, while *Against the Heresy of One Noetus* was written by Hippolytus as a means of reconciliation between the two communities.[54] Simonetti, however, argues that *Against the Heresy of One Noetus* could have been written first (and he argues that there were two men called Hippolytus whose works were confusedly listed on the statue as being by one man).[55] The biblical commentaries could be of Eastern origin and written by the author of *Against the Heresy of One Noetus*.[56]

Brent and Stewart-Sykes accept that *Apostolic Tradition* was a composite third-century Roman document from the Hippolytan school, written in Greek, revealing the influence of the authors of *Refutation of All Heresies* and *Against the Heresy of One Noetus* and possibly, according to Stewart-Sykes, an even earlier layer of material.[57] Bradshaw, Johnson, and Phillips argue that *Apostolic Tradition* was never a single document but a variety of documents from different locations across the Mediterranean up until the middle of the fourth century based on second-century material, for no translation we have now (neither the fifth-century Latin version nor the later Coptic, Arabic, and Ethiopic versions) contains exactly the same version as any other.[58] As Baldovin points out, all of this presents a serious challenge to the attempt of reconstructing Roman liturgy with regard to things like initiation, ordination, and the celebration of the Eucharist in early third-century Rome if *Apostolic Tradition* cannot properly be called a Roman document.[59] What we do know is that no manuscript of what today we call *Apostolic Tradition* bears that title, and that the association of that text with a work entitled *Apostolic Tradition* – known from list of works on a statue discovered in the middle of the sixteenth century and now in the Vatican Library (now known not to be a statue of Hippolytus) – is educated guesswork and not necessary in the considered opinion of some. There seems to be something in Brent's idea that the list of works on the statue represents the products of a school, with which an Hippolytus was associated. This makes it impossible to posit a single set of ideas about God, human nature, the church, and Christian living for Hippolytus, given that we are looking at the works of several different authors.

Refutation of All Heresies is not listed on the statue, and so it may well not have been by Hippolytus (the longest-known manuscript of book one attributed it to Origen, not surprising given that he spent some time in Rome in the early decades of the third century and heard Hippolytus),[60] although other works of Hippolytus (or the Hippolytan school) are mentioned in the text as the author's own, and the author claims to be a high priest and teacher in the church and was an opponent of Callistus in Rome.[61] The work aims to show that heretics base themselves not on the Scriptures but upon pagan philosophy. The first four books (books two and three are missing) outline Greek philosophical, astrological, and magical systems, while the remaining six books deal with linking Gnostic heresies (including Simon Magus, Marcion, Valentinians, and Montanists) with Greek philosophy (books five to nine) – heavily dependent upon Irenaeus's *Against Heresies* – and a presentation of Jewish chronology (book ten). The author of *Refutation of All Heresies* was the presbyter in conflict with Zephyrinus and Callistus, accusing them of adopting the modalism of Noetus, which was supposedly derived from Heraclitus and which included the Spirit as another manifestation of the undifferentiated God.[62]

The author of *Refutation of All Heresies* described Christ as the Logos, the pre-existent first principle of creation, begotten from the Father, of the Father's substance, knowing and agreeing with the Father's will.[63] Modalists in Rome had accused the author of being ditheist (the belief in two gods). The Logos received a body in the incarnation from a virgin as a model for all people about how to live according to God's will. Humankind was created by God with self-determination, which includes the power to commit evil, and a slave to the passions.[64] In terms of church organization, it would seem that the author of this work defended the notion of the independence of individual house churches in opposition to any move for a single bishop.

The author of *Against the Heresy of One Noetus* refers to the Logos as *Nous* (Mind), a term generally avoided because of its Gnostic connotations,[65] and refers to the Logos in a more depersonalized way than does the author of *Refutation of All Heresies* as the power of God who only became Son with the incarnation – the unincarnate Logos became the incarnate Son.[66] The language used is that of two *prosopa* (actually three with a brief mention of the Spirit) but one God.[67] Brent's argument is that there is a degree of accommodation with the modalism of Callistus, with the depersonalized Logos, in this text that is not found in *Refutation of All Heresies*. The Modalists would have found the subordinationism of *Against the Heresy of One Noetus* less objectionable than *Refutation of All Heresies*. It is argued that what is found in this treatise reflects a belief in a church order of single bishop with a college of presbyters.[68] While *Against Noetus* 1 does refer to the presbyters summoning Noetus and examining his teaching, no mention is made, however, of a bishop, and so Brent's argument does not seem quite so strong here.

Apostolic Tradition may or may not represent something about the Roman liturgy in the third century, and it probably reflects the differing views about the nature of the church of several different hands. The efforts of Brent and Stewart-Sykes to associate chapter three of *Apostolic Tradition* (the ordination prayer for a "bishop" with its references to Aaron) with the author of *Refutation of All Heresies* and chapter seven (the ordination prayer for a presbyter as part of a college under the leadership of a bishop with its references to Moses) with the author of *Against the Heresy of One Noetus*, has not escaped criticism.[69] Whatever its origins and literary developments, *Apostolic Tradition* reflects an interest in the ritual life of the Christian community, with its directives about the liturgical practices for celebrating liturgies involving the Eucharist, the designation of ministers – like bishop, presbyter, and deacon – and initiation.

What we may say by way of conclusion to this section is that who Hippolytus was and what he wrote is now a highly debatable issue in early-Christian scholarship, and that much of what has been written in the past about the Roman church, its organization and liturgy, may well have to be revised radically.

Cyprian

The letters and treatises (homiletic essays may be a better term for most of these other works) of Cyprian, bishop of Carthage between 249 and 258, do not reveal great concern for speculative theology but for the practical application of the principles of ecclesiology and sacramental theology in the life of Christian communities coping with persecution. Cyprian had a very clear sense of who belonged to the church – although we may trace some modification over time – which can be characterized as restrictive and narrow.

Originally a wealthy and educated pagan, Cyprian became bishop in the second half of 248 or first half of 249, not long after his conversion to Christianity,[70] probably without having been a presbyter first.[71] While this election might have been popular with lay Christians who benefited from the patronage of a wealthy Christian bishop, there were a number of his clergy who were opposed to him, quite possibly because they had been overlooked.

Late in 249 or early 250 the emperor Trajan Decius ordered universal sacrifice to the gods in an effort to protect a threatened empire. Although those who refused to comply with the edict were to be punished, it may be fair to say that it was not directed against the Christians in particular.[72] While some Christians resisted the call to sacrifice and were imprisoned and died, like Fabian, the bishop of Rome, in early 250 (and he was not to be replaced for another fourteen months), many others either obtained the certificate affirming that they had sacrificed (*libellatici*) or were prepared to offer incense (*turificati*) or did offer the sacrifice (*sacrificati*) willingly or reluctantly. All of these Christians who had lapsed from their faith (*lapsi*) presented Cyprian with problems for the rest of his episcopate. He himself had avoided the demands of the imperial edict by going into hiding. A Christian who lapsed was excluded from the church. The question was whether such former Christians could be readmitted to the church if repentant.

Cyprian wanted the question to wait until he returned to Carthage, but some of the *lapsi* approached imprisoned confessors, those who refused to comply with the edict and who were held in high esteem because of it. They wrote to Cyprian in support of the readmission of the repentant *lapsi*. Behind this we can see the activity of those clergy in Carthage who were disgruntled with Cyprian's episcopacy, and they began to admit some of the *lapsi* back into communion.[73] This usurpation of the bishop's prerogatives threatened ecclesial cohesion.[74] As the crisis continued Cyprian made some concessions: those *lapsi* in danger of death and who held a certificate from a confessor could confess before a presbyter or deacon and be readmitted to communion by the clergy,[75] and in agreement with the practice put in place in Rome by the presbyters who were administering the bishopless church there, Cyprian then agreed that even *lapsi* without such a certificate but who were in danger of death could likewise be readmitted to communion.[76] With the hostility of many of his own clergy, Cyprian was wise to seek the support of the Roman church, which he received in their responses.[77] He criticized those *lapsi* who demanded immediate reconciliation not so much for their ideas about reconciliation as for their arrogance in asserting that this could be decided apart from the bishop, for authority in the church had been given to Peter and his successors, and each bishop was the successor of Peter in his own church.[78]

Cyprian began to appoint new clergy for Carthage who would be loyal to him.[79] Felicissimus a Carthaginian deacon and five presbyters who were leading the revolt against Cyprian were eventually excommunicated early in 251.[80] Not long after this Cyprian returned to Carthage and held a synod in which the matter of the readmission of the *lapsi* to communion was discussed.[81] Just before the synod met Cyprian wrote his treatise *The Lapsed*, in which he maintained the position he had held in the latter part of his time in hiding. However, the decision of the synod was to continue to readmit repentant *lapsi* in danger of death to communion, to readmit all repentant *libellatici* immediately, and to reconcile repentant *sacrificati* just before their death. Unrepentant *lapsi* were to be denied any readmission.[82] Cyprian accepted and then defended this compromise between a rigorist refusal to readmit any lapsed Christian and a laxist willingness to offer ready forgiveness to all was a healthy and moderate position. Support for Felicissimus, Novatus, and the other rebellious clergy, who formed their own community, quickly dwindled as Cyprian reincorporated the *libellatici* into the Christian community over which he presided.

Meanwhile in Rome an election had been held and Cornelius was elected bishop instead of the more fancied Novatian. Encouraged by Novatus, who had left Carthage for Rome, Novatian refused to accept Cornelius's election and had himself proclaimed bishop. The matter of which Roman bishop to recognize seems to have become a dominant one to the African bishops gathered in synod. After some time investigating, the Africans decided to support Cornelius's legitimacy largely on the basis that he had been elected first.[83] The support of the Africans helped Cornelius cement his position. The Italian bishops also met in synod and reached an identical position as the Africans about the readmission of the *lapsi*. Novatian, who wanted to maintain the more rigorist approach that the Italians had been following, had all the more reason to continue his schism.[84]

Much interest in Cyprian centers on his pastoral letter *The Unity of the Catholic Church* and the two versions of section four. This pamphlet was written just before the African synod and almost certainly addressed the African situation.[85] At its heart was the importance of maintaining ecclesial unity centered on the bishop in spite of theological differences within the church. In one version (the Primacy Text) the emphasis is on the one chair and primacy of Peter, while in the other version (the Received Text) there is greater emphasis on the apostles having equal power and dignity as Peter and the oneness of the church. The questions are whether Cyprian wrote both versions, in what order, what was he addressing in the first version, and what made him alter it. Scholarship on this is extensive. The argument of a number of scholars (including Bévenot, most notably), that the Primacy Text came first and was later rewritten as the Received Text because of misinterpretation, seems now well accepted.[86] His view that the Primacy Text version, *The Unity of the Catholic Church*, addressed the situation both in Carthage and Rome has, as I noted above, been put aside for one that sees it as addressing primarily the local African situation, but which was sent to Rome as well.[87] I would consider that the second edition of *The Unity of the Catholic Church* (the Received Text) was written after the 252 synod in Africa, again addressing the local situation.[88]

With this in mind it can be noted that when Cyprian wrote about the primacy of Peter and the chair of Peter he was not referring to the church of Rome. Each bishop in his own church was the successor of Peter. Unity in the church was achieved by the bishops acting as one. While Cyprian recognized the right of each bishop to administer his own church and follow his own decisions in being faithful to the Gospels, frequent synodal gatherings of bishops, especially when they could achieve unanimity of purpose, and the maintenance of communion with bishops in other regions, preserved that unity. Rome was important because of its apostolic foundation, size, and prestige, and its support was often vital and its influential views were to be respected, but that did not give it any jurisdictional primacy over the African churches.

In 252 another synod of African bishops met.[89] Privatus, the long-excommunicated bishop of Lambaesis, wanted his case retried, but when the synod refused he ordained

Fortunatus, one of Cyprian's rebellious clergy, as an alternative bishop in Carthage to head the laxest community (those who wanted the *sacrificati* readmitted immediately). Felicissimus and some of the others went to Rome to find support for this move (one is not to interpret *Letter* 59 as indicating that Felicissimus was appealing to Rome's greater authority), but with the formation of a breakaway church it became evident that the issue was no longer about the readmission of the *lapsi* to communion but opposition to Cyprian himself, and support for Fortunatus quickly dwindled.[90] Novatian himself sent over Maximus, as yet a third bishop in Carthage, to head the rigorist community who opposed the readmission of any lapsed Christian to communion, although we hear nothing further about him. In 253, afraid of fresh persecution, perhaps to be demanded in the light of a fierce outbreak of plague (Cyprian wrote *On the Deadly Plague* and *To Demetrian* at this time, the first to encourage Christians to face death bravely), the African bishops decided to readmit all remaining penitent *lapsi* (the *sacrificati*) to communion.[91] There was some opposition to this move, both in Africa and in Italy, where one should locate the anonymous *To Novatian* at this time.[92] The Italians seem to have decided to readmit *sacrificati* when they withstood new demands for sacrifice.[93] It was around this time that Cornelius of Rome was put to death, and by early 254 his successor Lucius was dead as well.

It must be remembered that not all those who lapsed had joined a breakaway community, but with the more liberal policy in place in Africa and Italy for the readmission of the *lapsi* the question arose as to what to do with those who had, if they wanted to rejoin mainstream churches, like the one over which Cyprian presided in Carthage. They could undergo penance and receive reconciliation. But what about those whose only initiation had been in a schismatic community? This gave rise to an issue that would dominate Cyprian's final years.

His position was that breakaway communities could in no way be described as churches and that any sacrament celebrated in them was completely void of any effectiveness. The boundary between church and non-church was clear-cut.[94] The purity, status, and faith of the minister celebrating the sacraments were important. This is the basis of Cyprian's assertion that there could be no salvation outside the church.[95]

In the spring of 256, after a second synod of African bishops discussed this matter, Cyprian informed Stephen, the Roman bishop, of this position with regard to initiation and ordination.[96] A laying-on of hands to impart the Spirit (as Cyprian chose to interpret this action; some who performed such hand-laying to receive people into the church saw it as a penitential gesture) on people who had been baptized in a breakaway community was ineffective, because either all of schismatic initiation (baptism and laying-on of hands) was effective or, as Cyprian believed, it was not; one could not have half of it valid and half of it invalid.[97] Such people who had experienced initiation in a breakaway community and who wished to join the church needed to undergo baptism (and Cyprian refused to call it rebaptism, because that would imply some degree of validity in the first baptism).[98] As Burns points out, Cyprian insisted that only a real bishop, one in apostolic succession, had the power to forgive sins in baptism, and anything else compromised the authority of the church.[99]

GEOFFREY D. DUNN

From Cyprian[100] and Eusebius[101] we are told that Novatianists too "rebaptised" those who joined their community, yet Stephen of Rome reports that heretics do not require "rebaptism."[102] Either the Novatianists were being distinguished from heretics by Stephen since (like Cyprian) they did require "rebaptism"[103] or Novatianist practice differed between Africa and Italy, with those in Africa rebaptizing while those in Italy did not.[104] The Roman practice, as affirmed by Stephen, was to accept the validity of baptism performed in all sects and to require only a penitential laying-on of hands (he made no mention of imparting the Spirit, although this was how Cyprian interpreted his statement) if a person initiated in a schismatic/heretical community wanted to join the church.[105] We know from the anonymous *On Rebaptism* that there were some, presumably in Africa, who were laying-on hands for the imparting of the Spirit rather than for reconciliation.[106]

Stephen broke off communion with the African bishops and with a number of Asian churches as well. In September 256 a large synod of African bishops was held, which upheld Cyprian's position.[107] The Africans and Asians thought that Stephen was claiming for himself an authority over bishops in their regions, something they rejected. The split between Rome and Carthage was not to last for Stephen was martyred in 257 and Cyprian was exiled, being martyred himself late in 258.

Novatian

Much of our knowledge of Novatian comes from the information contained in Cyprian's letters and from a letter written by Cornelius – his rival as bishop in Rome – which is preserved in Eusebius.[108] We have already noted above in the material on Cyprian how Novatian was one of the leading presbyters in the Roman church at the time of Fabian's death, and it was he who wrote *Letters* 30, 31, and 36 on behalf of his fellow presbyters to Cyprian. An adult convert to Christianity, his initiation by affusion (a sprinkling with water), rather than immersion, was pointed to as suspect by Cornelius – his rival for the office of Roman bishop – as was his presbyterial ordination.[109] Novatian was literate and literary and must have considered himself the favorite to succeed Fabian, when an election could at last be held in Rome. A number of works, some previously attributed to Cyprian, are now recognized as being by Novatian: *Jewish Foods*, *The Spectacles* (which demonstrates a knowledge of Tertullian and Cyprian), and *In Praise of Purity* (again dependent upon Tertullian and Cyprian). There is a natural rigorism in Novatian's thinking.

He was the author of the Latin treatise now called *The Trinity*. In reaction to the modalism of those like Noetus, Novatian set out to explain the Scriptures about the Father,[110] Son,[111] and Spirit,[112] in order to demonstrate, from the ancient Roman baptismal symbol of faith, the threeness of God.[113] The last two chapters consider the relationship between Father and Son.[114] In the first eight chapters Novatian considered the Father as creator, in which little attention is paid to any role of Son and Spirit in that process. Marcion's notion that the creator was not the God of the New Testament is clearly Novatian's target, for he emphasizes that there is only one God and that the Son had been promised throughout the Hebrew Scriptures.[115] The

Son was truly human, in opposition to the Docetists who argued that he only seemed to be human, and that he was also truly divine, in opposition to the Adoptionists, who believed that Jesus was only human, though adopted as divine by God.[116]

The bulk of the treatise is, in fact, a refutation of several christological views. At the same time he was also opposed to the modalism of those like Noetus, Praxeus, and Sabellius, who merged the Father and Son into one.[117] For Novatian, the Son is one with the Father by being from the Father, although this is not explained further.[118] Yet, there is more than a hint of the subordination of the Son to the Father in Novatian's interpretation of Philippians 2:6–11, even though the inequality between Father and Son is not one of essence (*forma*) but one of dignity or function.[119] There is also the subordination of the Spirit to the Son.[120] While the Son and Father share the same divinity there are distinctions, a point that needed to be emphasized against Modalists, in that it was the Son who joined or even mixed (a term that would not have been liked at Chalcedon) divine nature with human.[121] Each was a separate *persona*, a term not applied to the Spirit, it is to be noted.[122] Yet, whether the Son and Father shared the same *substantia* is not clear from Novatian.[123] Although the Son is pre-existent Novatian cannot help but use temporal language in asserting that the Son comes after the Father.[124] What distinguishes Father from Son is that the first is unoriginated and the second originated. In the light of later developments in Trinitarian theology, Novatian's work appears naive and undeveloped, but given the limited nature of his investigation this is not surprising.

With regard to humanity, Novatian taught the immortality of the soul and the perishability of the flesh.[125] As with Tertullian, Cyprian, and even Cornelius, sin was such a major issue that it excluded one from the membership of the church. The purity and perfection of the church was because of the activity of the Spirit in the church poured into the lives of believers in baptism.[126] It was this consideration that underpinned Novatian's high standards of Christian living. Unlike Cyprian and Cornelius, who compromised their positions, he held constantly that none but the dangerously ill could be readmitted to the communion of the church after having been excluded.[127]

Without clear evidence that Cornelius was elected bishop because he proposed a more moderate policy on the readmission of the healthy *lapsi* to communion, we are left with the position that Novatian was prepared to break the unity of the church by having himself ordained bishop in opposition to Cornelius out of pique at not having been elected.[128] Certainly Novatian's rigorist position with regard to the readmission of healthy *libellatici* gained him initial support from the hard-line Roman confessors at a time when Cornelius must have been proposing change to the policy to enable that to happen. As Burns points out, Novatian's attitude was exclusivist, with concern for the church's purity overriding any concern for its unity.[129]

Conclusion

As well as being concerned with how to interpret the seemingly contradictory statements in the Scriptures about God and about Jesus, early Christian thinkers in Rome and Carthage in the second and third centuries were concerned with the realities of church life at a time when persecution made Christianity a dangerous religion to adopt. Boundaries between people were considered important, whether between Christians and polytheists, Christians and Jews, or between Christians and followers of aberrant forms of Christianity, like Marcionism and Christian forms of Gnosticism. Tertullian became increasingly intolerant of those who did not take the demands of Christianity seriously enough, yet probably without experiencing any sharp break between his Montanist form of Christianity and that held by the rest of the Christian community in Carthage. Cyprian, although he was prepared to readmit penitent *lapsi* to communion after a lengthy period of penance, was not prepared to accept that other communities not in communion with him were in any way Christian. The Hippolytan authors too were very much concerned with heretical belief about God and what that meant for ecclesial membership. Novatian's rigorism and schism also reveal the tendency of much western pre-Nicene Christianity to elitism and clear differentiation between peoples. In terms of a contrast between Roman and Carthaginian Christianity, perhaps the size of Rome made it difficult to achieve the kind of centralized structure that seems to be in place in Carthage from the beginning. While in the middle of the third century both centers could call together synods of bishops to discuss matters of serious concern, Africa seemed to have a more developed network of consultation among churches than Italy.

Further reading

Primary sources

Cyprian, trans. G. W. Clarke, *The Letters of St. Cyprian of Carthage*, 4 vols, Ancient Christian Writers 43–4, 46–7, New York: Paulist, 1984–9. (English translation with excellent detailed notes.)

Secondary sources

J. P. Burns, *Theological Anthropology*, Sources of Early Christian Thought, Philadelphia: Fortress, 1981. (Introduction to views about the human person in early Christianity with selected texts.)
J. N. D. Kelly, *Early Christian Doctrines*, London: A&C Black, 1958; 5th rev. edn, 1977; repr. London: Continuum, 2007. (Survey of early Christian doctrines.)
R. A. Norris, *The Christological Controversy*, Sources of Early Christian Thought, Philadelphia: Fortress, 1980. (Introduction to Christology in early Christianity with selected texts.)
J. Quasten, *Patrology*, 4 vols, Westminster, MD: Newman, 1950; repr. Westminster, MD: Christian Classics, 1986. (Still standard introduction to early Christian literature, though in need of revision.)
B. Ramsey, *Beginning to Read the Fathers*, New York: Paulist, 1985; repr. London: Darton, Longman & Todd, 1986. (Survey of early Christian doctrine.)
W. G. Rusch, *The Trinitarian Controversy*, Sources of Early Christian Thought, Philadelphia: Fortress, 1980. (Introduction to Trinitarian theology in early Christianity with selected texts.)

Notes

1 Tertullian, *Prescription against Heretics* 36.3–4. G. D. Dunn, "Peter and Paul in Rome: The Perspective of the North African Church," in *Pietro e Paolo. Il loro rapporto con Roma nelle testimonianze antiche: XXIX Incontro di studiosi dell'antichità cristiana, Roma, 4–6 maggio 2000*, Studia ephemeridis Augustinianum 74, Rome: Institutum patristicum Augustinianum, 2001, pp. 408–11;

G. D. Dunn, *Tertullian*, The Early Church Fathers, London and New York: Routledge, 2004, pp. 13–18.

2   W. Telfer, "The Origins of Christianity in Africa," *Studia Patristica* 4, 1961, p. 516.

3   T. D. Barnes, *Tertullian: A Historical and Literary Study*, rev. edn, Oxford: Clarendon, 1985, pp. 3–29; D. I. Rankin, "Was Tertullian a Schismatic?," *Prudentia* 18, 1986, pp. 73–9; C. Trevett, *Montanism: Gender, Authority and the New Prophecy*, Cambridge: Cambridge University Press, 1996, p. 69; W. Tabbernee, *Montanist Inscriptions and Testimonies: Epigraphic Sources Illustrating the History of Montanism*, North American Patristic Society Patristic Monograph Series 16, Macon, GA: Mercer University Press, 1997, pp. 54–5; D. I. Rankin, "Was Tertullian a Jurist?," *Studia Patristica* 31, 1997, pp. 335–42; Dunn, *Tertullian*, pp. 3–11.

4   R. D. Sider, *Ancient Rhetoric and the Art of Tertullian*, Oxford: Oxford University Press, 1971; Jean-Claude Fredouille, *Tertullien et la conversion de la culture antique*, Collection des Études Augustiniennes Série Antiquité 47, Paris: Institut des Études Augustiniennes, 1972.

5   A. J. Guerra, "Polemical Christianity: Tertullian's Search for Certitude," *Second Century* 8, 1991, pp. 109–23.

6   Dunn, *Tertullian*, pp. 25–9.

7   G. D. Dunn, "Tertullian's Scriptural Exegesis in *De praescriptione haereticorum*," *Journal of Early Christian Studies* 14, 2006, 141–55.

8   Tertullian, *Against Marcion* 1.3–4.

9   E. Osborn, *Tertullian: First Theologian of the West*, Cambridge: Cambridge University Press, 1997, pp. 88–115.

10   Tertullian, *Against Marcion* 1.2, 1.6.

11   Tertullian, *Against Marcion* 1.17.

12   Tertullian, *Against Marcion* 2.14–16.

13   Tertullian, *Against Marcion* 1.19.

14   Tertullian, *Against Marcion* 3.2

15   On the difficulties of using Gnosticism as a term see M. A. Williams, *Rethinking "Gnosticism": An Argument for Dismantling a Dubious Category*, Princeton, NJ: Princeton University Press, 1996; K. L. King, *What is Gnosticism?*, Cambridge, MA: Harvard University Press, 2003.

16   Tertullian, *Against Hermogenes* 2.

17   Tertullian, *Against Hermogenes* 4–9.

18   Tertullian, *Against Hermogenes* 10–16; Osborn, *Tertullian*, pp. 183–91.

19   Barnes, *Tertullian*, pp. 278–9. See E. Evans, *Tertullian's Treatise Against Praxeas. The Text Edited, with an Introduction, Translation and Commentary*, London: SPCK, 1948.

20   Tertullian, *Against Praxeas* 1.

21   Tertullian, *Against Praxeas* 10.

22   On Tertullian and *potestas* see R. Kearsley, *Tertullian's Theology of Divine Power*, Rutherford Studies in Historical Theology, Carlisle, UK: Paternoster, 1998.

23   Tertullian, *Against Praxeas* 2, 4.

24   Tertullian, *Against Praxeas* 9.

25   Tertullian, *Against Praxeas* 5–7.

26   Tertullian, *Against Praxeas* 9.

27   Tertullian, *Against Praxeas* 3.

28   Tertullian, *Against Praxeas* 7–8.

29   Tertullian, *Against Praxeas* 10.

30   Tertullian, *Against Praxeas* 8.

31   Osborn, *Tertullian*, pp. 120–43; G. C. Stead, "Divine Substance in Tertullian," *Journal of Theological Studies* 14, 1963, pp. 46–63.

32   Tertullian, *The Soul* 1–22.

33   Tertullian, *Soul* 39–41; Osborn, *Tertullian*, pp. 163–75.

34   Tertullian, *The Resurrection of the Flesh* 11.

35   Tertullian, *Against Praxeas* 27.

36   Tertullian, *Against Marcion* 3.8–11.

37   Tertullian, *The Flesh of Christ* 1–5.

38 Tertullian, *On the Flesh of Christ* 23. See W. Otten, "Christ's Birth of a Virgin Who Became a Wife: Flesh and Speech in Tertullian's *De carne Christi*," *Vigiliae Christianae* 51, 1997, pp. 247–60; G. D. Dunn, "Mary's Virginity *in partu* and Tertullian's Anti-Docetism in *De carne Christi* Reconsidered," *Journal of Theological Studies* 58, 2007, pp. 467–84.

39 Tertullian, *Baptism* 18.

40 Tertullian, *Repentance* 5–6.

41 Tertullian, *Repentance* 7–10.

42 Tertullian, *Modesty* 1–2.

43 D. Rankin, *Tertullian and the Church*, Cambridge: Cambridge University Press, 1995, pp. 27–38; Trevett, *Montanism*, pp. 66–76; Dunn, *Tertullian*, pp. 6–7; W. Tabbernee, *Fake Prophecy and Polluted Sacraments: Ecclesiastical and Imperial Reactions of Montanism*, Supplements to Vigiliae Christianae 84, Leiden: Brill, 2007.

44 Tertullian, *Monogamy* 2.

45 W. Tabernee, "To Pardon or Not to Pardon? North-African Montanism and the Forgiveness of Sins," *Studia Patristica* 36, papers presented at the 13th International Conference on Patristic Studies, Oxford, 1999, Leuven: Peeters, 2001, pp. 375–86.

46 Tertullian, *Apology* 30–3.

47 R. F. Evans, "On the Problem of Church and Empire in Tertullian's *Apologeticum*," *Studia Patristica* 14, papers presented at the 6th International Conference on Patristic Studies, Oxford, 1971, Berlin: Akademie-Verlag, 1976, pp. 21–36 (esp. 25). See S. Gero, "*Miles Gloriosus*: The Christian and Military Service according to Tertullian," *Church History* 39, 1970, pp. 285–98.

48 See G. D. Dunn, *Tertullian's* Aduersus Iudaeos: *A Rhetorical Analysis*, Patristic Monograph Series 19, Washington, DC: Catholic University of America Press, 2008.

49 Hippolytus, *Refutation of All Heresies* 9.5–7, 10.23.

50 It is defended by M. Marcovich, *Hippolytus:* Refutatio omnium haeresium, Patristische Texte und Studien 25, Berlin: Walter de Gruyter, 1986, pp. 10–17.

51 G. La Piana, "The Roman Church at the End of the Second Century," *Harvard Theological Review* 18, 1925, pp. 201–77; J. F. Baldovin, *The Urban Character of Christian Worship: The Origin, Development and Meaning of Stational Liturgy*, Orientalia Christiana Analecta 228, Rome: Pontifical Oriental Institute, 1987, p. 145.

52 E. G. Jay, "From Presbyter-Bishops to Bishops and Presbyters," *Second Century* 1, 1981, pp. 125–62; P. Lampe, *From Paul to Valentinus: Christians at Rome in the First Two Centuries*, trans. M. Steinhauser, English edn, Minneapolis: Fortress, 2003; A. Brent, *Hippolytus and the Roman Church in the Third Century: Communities in Tension before the Emergence of a Monarch Bishop*, Supplements to Vigiliae Christianae 31, Leiden: Brill, 1995, pp. 398–457; A. Stewart-Sykes, *Hippolytus: On the Apostolic Tradition*, Popular Patristics Series, Crestwood, NY: St Vladimir's Seminary Press, 2001, pp. 12–16. Cf. M. Simonetti, "Una nuova proposta su Ippolito," *Augustinianum* 36, 1996, pp. 13–46.

53 P. Nautin, *Hippolyte et Josipe: contribution à l'histoire de la littérature chrétienne du troisième siècle*, Études et textes pour l'histoire du dogme de la Trinité 1, Paris: Cerf, 1947 (and the "real" Hippolytus wrote *Against the Heresy of One Noetus*, while Josephus wrote *Refutation of All Heresies* and the works listed on the statue); M. Simonetti, *Ippolito: Contra Noeto*, Bologna: Dehoniana, 2000, pp. 130–6; Brent, *Hippolytus and the Roman Church in the Third Century*, pp. 256–367.

54 Brent, *Hippolytus and the Roman Church in the Third Century*, pp. 109–14.

55 Simonetti, "Una nuova proposta su Ippolito," 17–33; Simonetti, *Ippolito*, pp. 61–8, 121–4.

56 J. Cerrato, *Hippolytus between East and West: The Commentaries and the Provenance of the Corpus*, Oxford: Oxford University Press, 2002, pp. 250–8.

57 Brent, *Hippolytus and the Roman Church in the Third Century*, p. 306; Stewart-Sykes, *Hippolytus*, pp. 25, 29.

58 P. F. Bradshaw, M. E. Johnson, and L. E. Phillips, *The Apostolic Tradition: A Commentary*, Hermeneia, Minneapolis: Fortress, 2002, pp. 7–15.

59 J. F. Baldovin, "Hippolytus and the Apostolic Tradition: Recent Research and Commentary," *Theological Studies* 64, 2003, pp. 532–42.

60 Jerome, *On Illustrious Men* 61.

61 Hippolytus, *Refutation of All Heresies* Proem.

62 Hippolytus, *Refutation of All Heresies* 9.5–6.

63 Hippolytus, *Refutation of All Heresies* 10.29.

64 Ibid.

65 Hippolytus, *Against the Heresy of One Noetus* 11.

66 Hippolytus, *Against the Heresy of One Noetus* 4; 10–11; Brent, *Hippolytus and the Roman Church in the Third Century*, pp. 208–58. The argument is that this was a rapprochement with Callistus's supposed modalism.

67 Hippolytus, *Against the Heresy of One Noetus* 14.

68 Brent, *Hippolytus and the Roman Church in the Third Century*, pp. 305–6, 471–5; Stewart-Sykes, *Hippolytus*, pp. 25–6.

69 Bradshaw, Johnson, and Phillips, *Apostolic Tradition*, pp. 33–4.

70 Cyprian, *To Donatus* 3–4; Pontius, *Life and Passion of St. Cyprian* 2–3.

71 M. Bévenot, "'Sacerdos' as Understood by Cyprian," *Journal of Theological Studies* 30, 1979, pp. 413–29 (esp. 414); C. A. Bobertz, "Cyprian of Carthage as Patron: A Social Historical Study of the Role of Bishop in the Ancient Christian Community," PhD diss., Yale University, 1988, p. 119; G. D. Dunn, "The White Crown of Works: Cyprian's Early Pastoral Ministry of Almsgiving in Carthage," *Church History* 73, 2004, pp. 715–40 (esp. 722). Cf. Jerome, *On Illustrious Men* 67; P. J. Fitzgerald, "A Model of Dialogue: Cyprian of Carthage on Ecclesial Discernment," *Theological Studies* 59, 1998, pp. 236–53 (esp. 243).

72 J. B. Rives, "The Decree of Decius and the Religion of Empire," *Journal of Roman Studies* 89, 1999, pp. 135–54. For a review of the literature on Decius's edict see G. D. Dunn, *Cyprian and the Bishops of Rome: Questions of Papal Primacy in the Early Church*, Early Christian Studies 11, Sydney: St Pauls, 2007, p. 23.

73 Cyprian, *Letters* 15, 16, 17. A. Brent's argument that the confessors themselves were readmitting the *lapsi* to communion is one that cannot be supported. See A. Brent, "Cyprian's Reconstruction of the Martyr Tradition," *Journal of Ecclesiastical History* 53, 2002, pp. 241–68; and "Cyprian and the Question of *ordinatio per confessionem*," in M. F. Wiles and E. J. Yarnold (eds), *Studia Patristica* 36, papers presented at the 13th International Conference on Patristic Studies, Oxford, 1999, Leuven: Peeters, 2001, pp. 323–37.

74 J. P. Burns, *Cyprian the Bishop*, Routledge Early Church Monographs, London: Routledge, 2002, pp. 23–34.

75 Cyprian, *Letters* 18–19.

76 Cyprian, *Letter* 20.

77 Cyprian, *Letters* 30–1.

78 Cyprian, *Letter* 33.

79 Cyprian, *Letter* 29.

80 Cyprian, *Letters* 34, 41, 42, 43.

81 G. D. Dunn, "The Carthaginian Synod of 251: Cyprian's Model of Pastoral Ministry," in *I concili della cristianità occidentale secoli III–V, XXX Incontro di studiosi dell'antichità cristiana, Roma 3–5 maggio 2001*, Studia ephemeridis Augustinianum 78, Rome: Institutum patristicum Augustinianum, 2002, pp. 235–57.

82 Cyprian, *Letter* 55.

83 Cyprian, *Letters* 44, 45, 48.

84 On Cyprian's understanding of schism and heresy see G. D. Dunn, "Heresy and Schism According to Cyprian of Carthage," *Journal of Theological Studies* 55, 2004, pp. 551–74.

85 M. M. Sage, *Cyprian*, Patristic Monograph Series 1, Cambridge, MA: Philadelphia Patristic Foundation, 1975, pp. 241–8; C. A. Bobertz, "The Historical Context of Cyprian's *De unitate*," *Journal of Theological Studies* 41, 1990, pp. 107–11; S. G. Hall, "The Versions of Cyprian, *De unitate*, 4–5: Bévenot's Dating Revisited," *Journal of Theological Studies* 55, 2004, pp. 138–46; Dunn, *Cyprian and the Bishops of Rome*, pp. 71–90.

86 M. Bévenot, *St. Cyprian's De unitate Ch. 4 in the Light of the MSS*, Analecta Gregoriana 11, Rome: Gregorian University Press, 1937; "'Primatus Petro datur': St. Cyprian on the Papacy," *Journal of Theological Studies* 5, 1954, pp. 19–35; "St. Cyprian and the Papacy: Musings on an Old Problem," *Dublin Review* 228, 1954, pp. 161–8; "'Hi qui sacrificaveunt': A Significant Variant in St. Cyprian's

De unitate," *Journal of Theological Studies* 5, 1954, pp. 68–72; *St. Cyprian: The Lapsed, The Unity of the Catholic Church*, Ancient Christian Writers 25, New York: Paulist, 1957, pp. 3–8.

87 Cyprian, *Letter* 54.

88 Dunn, *Cyprian and the Bishops of Rome*, pp. 101–2. Burns, *Cyprian the Bishop*, pp. 159–65, considers the second edition of *The Unity of the Catholic Church* to be written in 256 in conjunction with the baptismal controversy.

89 Cyprian, *Letters* 59–64. G. D. Dunn, "Cyprian and his *Collegae*: Patronage and the Episcopal Synod of 252," *Journal of Religious History* 27, 2003, pp. 1–13 (esp. 4).

90 G. D. Dunn, "Cyprian's Rival Bishops and their Communities," *Augustinianum* 45, 2005, pp. 61–93 (esp. 85).

91 Cyprian, *Letter* 57. G. D. Dunn, "*Censuimus*: Cyprian and the Episcopal Synod of 253," *Latomus* 63, 2004, pp. 672–88.

92 Dunn, *Cyprian and the Bishops of Rome*, pp. 104–5.

93 Cyprian, *Letter* 60.

94 J. P. Burns, "Social Context in the Controversy between Cyprian and Stephen," in E. A. Livingstone (ed.), *Studia Patristica* 24, papers presented at the 12th International Conference on Patristic Studies, Oxford, 1991, Leuven: Peeters, 1993, pp. 38–44 (esp. 41).

95 Cyprian, *Letter* 73.

96 Cyprian, *Letter* 72. G. D. Dunn, "Validity of Baptism and Ordination in the African Response to the 'Rebaptism' Crisis: Cyprian of Carthage's Episcopal Synod of Spring 256," *Theological Studies* 67, 2006, pp. 257–74.

97 It is important to note that the anonymous *On Rebaptism* 1 and 10 did demand rebaptism but did require a laying-on of hands to impart the Spirit, who had not been given in heretical baptism.

98 Cyprian, *Letters* 71, 73.

99 Burns, *Cyprian the Bishop*, pp. 103–4.

100 Cyprian, *Letter* 73.

101 Eusebius, *Ecclesiastical History* 7.8.

102 Cyprian, *Letter* 74.

103 S. G. Hall, "Stephen I of Rome and the Baptismal Controversy of 256," in B. Volger (ed.), *Miscellanea Historiae Ecclesiasticae* 8, Bibliothèque de la Revue d'histoire ecclésiastique 72, Brussels: Nauwelaerts, 1987, pp. 78–82 (esp. 78).

104 G. D. Dunn, "*Sententiam nostram non nouam promimus*: Cyprian and the Episcopal Synod of 255," *Annuarium Historiae Conciliorum* 35, 2003, pp. 211–21 (esp. 215).

105 Cyprian, *Letter* 74.

106 *On Rebaptism* 1.

107 G. D. Dunn, "*Nam quae foris exercentur nullum habent salutis effectum*: Cyprian and the Synod of Late 256," in *Pagani e cristiani alla ricerca della salvezza (I-III sec.): XXXIV Incontro di studiosi dell'antichità cristiana, Roma 5–7 maggio 2005*, Studia ephemeridis Augustinianum 96, Rome: Institutum patristicum Augustinianum, 2006, pp. 513–24.

108 Eusebius, *Ecclesiastical History* 6.43.

109 Ibid.

110 Novatian, *Trinity* 1–8.

111 Novatian, *Trinity* 9–28.

112 Novatian, *Trinity* 29.

113 For the structure of the treatise see R. J. DeSimone, *The Treatise of Novatian the Presbyter on the Trinity: A Study of the Text and the Doctrine*, Studia ephemeridis Augustinianum 4, Rome: Institutum patristicum Augustinianum, 1970, p. 53.

114 Novatian, *Trinity* 30–1.

115 G. D. Dunn, "The Diversity and Unity of God in Novatian's *De Trinitate*," *Ephemerides Theologicae Lovanienses* 78, 2002, pp. 385–409 (esp. 391–3).

116 Novatian, *Trinity* 11.

117 Novatian, *Trinity* 12.

118 Novatian, *Trinity* 23.

119 Novatian, *Trinity* 22.

120 Novatian, *Trinity* 16.
121 Novatian, *Trinity* 24.
122 Novatian, *Trinity* 27.
123 It seems to be in *Trinity* 24, but not 31.
124 Novatian, *Trinity* 31.
125 Novatian, *Trinity* 25.
126 Novatian, *Trinity* 29.
127 Cyprian, *Letter* 36; Dunn, *Cyprian and the Bishops of Rome*, pp. 51–3.
128 Dunn, "Cyprian's Rival Bishops," 61–93.
129 Burns, *Cyprian the Bishop*, p. 73.

10
CLEMENT AND ALEXANDRIAN CHRISTIANITY

Henny Fiskå Hägg

The Christian message spread from Jerusalem, a small but religiously important town in the Roman Empire. It was the center of Judaism, and in the early years of Christianity it also became the center for the new believers in Christ. From Jerusalem the message of Jesus as the Messiah was taken to many places of the empire, especially to the Greco-Roman cities of Asia Minor. In the New Testament book of Acts, cities like Damascus, Antioch, Sardis, Pergamum, Salamis, Corinth, Smyrna, Athens, and Rome are mentioned as places where there were Christian communities, and by the end of the first century even more are added.[1]

However, it is not until the beginning of the second century that we have evidence of the probable existence of Christian communities in Alexandria. Since it was the second largest city in the empire, historians of Christianity have devoted much effort to explaining the silence enveloping the origins of Alexandrian Christianity, and several hypotheses have been suggested. There has also been much discussion on the question of the existence of a so-called "catechetical school" in Alexandria, mentioned by the church historian Eusebius of Caesarea (*c.* 260 to *c.* 340). According to Eusebius, this was an institution of old custom (*ex archaiou ethous*) that still existed in his own time, and Clement of Alexandria (150–215) had been one of its leaders. These topics will be the focus of the first part of this essay. In the second part, I shall concentrate more specifically on Clement, the first important theologian of the city, with an emphasis on his views on Scripture, as well as perspectives on spirituality.

Origins of Christianity in Alexandria

It is still difficult to make up a clear picture of how the Christian movement found its way into Alexandria. Can it have existed there for more than a century without leaving clear traces? As a matter of fact, it is only towards the end of the second century that we find unambiguous evidence of the existence of a Christian community in Alexandria. The situation is more striking when one considers that during the first two centuries CE Alexandria was the largest Greek city in the Roman Empire, a leading center of learning and scholarship, and contained within its boundaries the largest Jewish community outside Palestine. The Alexandrian Jews were Greek-speaking and, prior to Roman rule (before 30 BCE), enjoyed considerable religious and political freedom.[2] By the middle of the first century CE, the number of Alexandrian Jews may have been as high as 150,000.[3] Under the Romans, however, their status deteriorated in relation to the Greeks of Alexandria. Unlike the Greeks, they were not considered Alexandrian citizens.[4] Alexandria was, nevertheless, the most important Jewish settlement of the Diaspora, and a community that one might have thought to have been a primary target for Christian mission.

The earliest extant historical source on Christianity in Alexandria is Eusebius, who, in his *Ecclesiastical History* (c. 312–23), conveys interesting, though highly controversial information on this early period. Since he was personally involved in the theological and political discussions of his own day, few scholars would argue that Eusebius presents an unbiased version of his material. The main points of disagreement are the origins and circumstances of Alexandrian Christianity up to Clement (180) and, related to this, questions concerning a so-called catechetical school. However, where it is possible to test the historical accuracy of his narrative by comparison with other sources (as is often the case concerning the churches in Rome, Jerusalem, and Antioch), Eusebius's account largely corresponds with these other sources.[5] With regard to the situation in Alexandria we have no such possibility. Despite the lack of evidence, scholars generally tend to believe that Christianity was established in Alexandria by the middle of the first century, either as a result of a mission from Jerusalem, or through Alexandrian Jews returning from the Pentecost celebration in Jerusalem. People from Egypt are among the many listed in Acts 2:7–12 as present in Jerusalem on this occasion.

What is it, then, that Eusebius writes about the Alexandrian church before 180? He is our earliest source for the tradition that the church was founded by Mark the evangelist, who was, according to Eusebius, the first bishop of Alexandria. Yet the New Testament contains no trace of this tradition. Additionally, the two prominent Alexandrian theologians, Clement and Origen (c. 185 to c. 254) – as well as Demetrius, bishop of Alexandria from 189 – never mention Mark as the founder of the Alexandrian church. Even more controversial than Eusebius's claim about Mark is his information about the Alexandrian episcopal succession, which is scattered throughout his account. He names the ten bishops who succeeded Mark up to the reign of the emperor Commodus (180–92), each with his exact years of office.[6] Whereas the eleventh, Bishop Demetrius (189–232), is well known from several other sources, the other ten remain mere names. Therefore, this construction too has been rejected by most scholars.[7]

Two alternative scenarios for early Alexandrian Christianity have been presented. For a long time the "Gnostic lead" was in favor, as it still is today in some quarters.[8] In this view the earliest Christianity in Alexandria (and Egypt) was heterodox, especially Gnostic, and there were no distinct boundaries between orthodox and non-orthodox

Christians until the end of the second century.[9] The majority of Christians in the city at an early stage adhered to a variety of Christianity that was predominantly Gnostic. The few "orthodox" Christians opposed their doctrine but did not win the upper hand until the end of the second century. Subsequently the Gnostics gradually became marginalized, they were condemned as heretics, and their writings disappeared.

This view has a certain inherent plausibility. There is no doubt that the Gnostic movement thrived in second-century Egypt. Texts defined today as Gnostic were quoted by Clement and Origen and were surely circulating in Egypt. As a matter of fact – except for Eusebius's assertion that Mark was the founder of the church, as well as some evidence for a few individual Christians[10] – the earliest Christian teachers in second-century Alexandria of whom we have any information were the Gnostics Basilides and Valentinus. According to Clement, Basilides was active in Alexandria at the time of the emperors Hadrian (117–38) and Antoninus Pius (137–61).[11] Valentinus received his education in Alexandria and, according to Bishop Epiphanius of Salamis (315–403), preached in Alexandria and other places in Egypt before he went to Rome (about 140).[12]

The theory, as most forcefully propounded by the German theologian Walther Bauer, provoked a critical reaction based upon papyrological evidence.[13] In his *Manuscript, Society, and Belief in Early Christian Egypt*, Colin H. Roberts shed important light on Christian origins in Egypt. His study of literary papyri found in the Egyptian sand provides no support for the view that Gnosticism was the earliest form of Christianity in Egypt. For one thing, of the fourteen extant Christian papyri dating from the second century, ten were canonical, and only one was Gnostic, the *Gospel of Thomas*.

Another important feature of Roberts's study is his discussion of *nomina sacra* in early Christian manuscripts. The *nomina sacra* are certain "sacred names" and religious terms that are given special treatment in writing by means of abbreviations and super-lineation, such as *Iesous*, *Christos*, *kyrios*, *theos*, and others. Roberts traces this scribal practice back to the Jerusalem church: it was invented by Jewish Christians in Jerusalem and from there brought to Alexandria.[14] Roberts's conclusion is that the earliest Christians in Alexandria were Jews, and there are so few traces of them because the Christians were an integral part of the Jewish community in Alexandria, hardly distinguishable from the Jews, at least from outside.[15]

There is, moreover, one important piece of evidence of Jewish (Greek-speaking) Christians in Alexandria: the so-called *Gospel of the Hebrews*, from the first decades of the second century,[16] of which several fragments are preserved in Clement, Origen, and Jerome. According to Jerome, Origen used it frequently.[17] Though it differs from the canonical gospels, to judge from the fragments it is not typically "Gnostic."[18] It has a clearly "life of Jesus" character, different from Gnostic gospels.[19]

According to the Jewish thesis, the Jesus-believing Jews (Judeo-Christians) stayed in the environment of the synagogues and prayed and worshipped with their fellow Jews for a longer time than at other places. The break between the group of Jesus-believing Jews and the rest of the Jewish population may not have come until after the Jewish revolt against the Romans in 115–17. For two years the Jews of Egypt, Cyrene, and Cyprus rebelled against Roman oppression. This ended in disaster and the Jews of Egypt suffered great losses, disappearing from sight.[20] Whether in the maelstrom of the revolt most of the Judeo-Christians of Alexandria were extinguished as well, is a matter of guesswork. The existence of the *Gospel of the Hebrews* suggests that at least some of them survived and formed an independent community. Evidence also suggests the existence of various groups of non-Jewish (Gentile) Christians in Egypt, of which some may have been Gnostic, apocalyptic, or Encratite in inclination.[21] Encratite Christians believed that it was sinful to engage in childbearing and sexuality, therefore rejecting marriage. The Greek *Gospel of the Egyptians* may be a witness to this group. Only fragments of the gospel survive, the chief source being Clement of Alexandria, who is mostly skeptical toward their negative views on marriage. It is also clear that he did not regard the gospel to be on a par with the "four gospels that have been handed down to us."[22]

Still another second-century work is connected with Alexandria, the *Epistle of Barnabas*. It has no explicit recipient (and no named author), but appears to be addressed to a Christian community in Egypt, probably Alexandria.[23] Clement is the earliest witness to its existence. It has a marked hostility to Judaism, and the author interprets the Old Testament in a way favourable to Christian claims. He holds that there has never been more than one covenant – the covenant that Moses offered the people of Israel was rejected, and through their idolatry they lost any claim to it. It was offered again through Christ and was received by Christians. Therefore, the Jews never had a covenant, and the Old Testament is the possession of the Christians. However, the ceremonial laws were never to be interpreted in a literal way; they are partly to be understood as prophecies about Christ, partly to be interpreted allegorically.[24] It may also be argued that the *Epistle* is marked by an anti-Jewish atmosphere that is not merely formalistic but may indicate a considerable Jewish presence in the city.[25]

Some reflections may be added, based on the research of the sociologist of religion Rodney Stark and the ancient historian Keith Hopkins, giving some indirect support to the Jewish character of Alexandrian Christianity. In his book *The Rise of Christianity* Rodney Stark investigates the question of Christian growth. He establishes an estimate of 40 per cent growth for every decade (an average growth rate similar to that of the Mormons during their first one hundred years). Starting with one thousand in CE 40, the resulting number of Christians in CE 350 would be thirty-three million, about half of the population of the Roman Empire.[26] That half of the empire's population may have been Christian in the middle of the fourth century is not very controversial. It is interesting to reflect on the fact that, if Christianity grew steadily at the rate of 40 per cent per decade, there would have been only about 7,000 Christians in the year CE 100, equal to barely 0.01 per cent of the empire's population, and 40,000 in the year CE 150, also a rather small percentage. Of course, the growth fluctuated; it probably grew faster in some periods, and in other periods, during persecutions, it even declined.[27] The regional differences will also have been great. Hopkins, following up on Stark's numerical experiment, draws the (obvious) conclusion that "in all probability, there were few Christians in the Roman world, at least until the end of the second century."[28] Consequently, the number of Jews was very high, compared with the number of (Judeo)-Christians, at least until the late third century.[29] Thus, during the period up to CE 180, which we are discussing, Christians were statistically insignificant, they were only small minority groups. If we relate this to the situation of first- and early second-century Alexandria, a city which had the greatest concentration of Jews in the Roman Empire, it is easy to imagine how groups of Jesus-believers would disappear amid its Jewish population.

Archaeological evidence too suggests that the Christians of the first two centuries were few everywhere and did not attract much attention. In terms of non-literary material, there are very few traces of them at all in any part of the Roman world. They did not build large churches; what we have of evidence points only to house churches, private homes that were not remodeled in any way. Not until after 300 is there evidence of larger places of meeting.[30]

Rodney Stark also challenges the widely held view that the first Christian mission to the Jews failed because the Jews rejected the Christian message. Rather, a very substantial conversion of Jews actually took place and continued well into the third and fourth centuries.[31] According to modern evidence, cult-groups usually expand within family and social networks, i.e., among relatives and friends. The local networks used by the early Christians were the local Jewish communities. In addition, there is the principle of cultural continuity. Modern evidence suggests that "people are more willing to adopt a new religion to the extent that it retains cultural continuity with conventional religion with which they already are familiar."[32] Stark argues that for the (mostly urban) Hellenized Jews of the Roman Empire, Christianity may have seemed more attractive than the Torah-observing "old-fashioned" Judaism of Israel.[33] Yet, it represented undoubtedly a continuity with their former beliefs.

The catechetical school and Christian organization

Eusebius's description in his *Ecclesiastical History* of a "school of sacred learning" in Alexandria, later commonly referred to as the catechetical school, has been much discussed.[34] At this point, a marked change occurs in his history of the Alexandrian church. The Eusebian narrative now becomes more than names and dates (cf. the list of bishops), and a rather detailed description of a certain Pantaenus[35] and his school emerges, a school with a succession of teachers who themselves had been the pupils of their predecessors:

> At that time a man very famous for his learning named Pantaenus had charge of the life of the faithful in Alexandria, for from ancient custom a school of sacred learning (*didaskaleiou ton hieron logon*) existed among them. This school has lasted on to our time, and we have heard that it is managed by men powerful in their learning and zeal for divine things, but tradition says that at that time Pantaenus was especially eminent, and that he had been influenced by the philosophic system of those called Stoics.
>
> (Eusebius, *Ecclesiastical History* 5.10)[36]

In a later passage, Eusebius claims that "Pantaenus was succeeded by Clement, who directed the instruction (*katekhesis*) at Alexandria up to such a date that Origen also was one of his pupils."[37] When Clement left Alexandria because of a persecution (*c.* 202/3), Origen took over the direction of the school, at the age of only eighteen.[38] This task, Eusebius writes, had been given to him by Demetrius, "the leader of the church."[39] Eusebius describes Origen as a highly successful teacher, and because of the many students, as well as their differing needs, he selected one of them, Heraclas, to assist him. He assigned to Heraclas "preliminary studies" while "reserving for himself the teaching of the experienced pupils."[40]

This traditional picture, based on Eusebius, of an official school under the control of the bishop and with a succession of teachers going far back in time, an institution of the church to prepare the catechumens for baptism, has long been challenged.[41] Following this older line of scholarship, to varying degrees scholars have regarded Eusebius's account as an unreliable reconstruction, based on sketchy evidence and bias. In this view, the catechetical school of Alexandria did not yet exist in the second century; it started only in CE 202/3 with Origen, when a monarchic episcopacy was in place with Demetrius.[42] The "school" before Origen, then – that of Pantaenus and Clement – was Christian, but private, and had nothing to do with the contemporary official school of the church, which was handled by humble catechists who prepared the catechumens for baptism. The school of Pantaenus was rather a parallel to that of Justin Martyr in Rome and, later on, that of Origen in Caesarea (which we know thanks to Gregory Thaumaturgos's description),[43] an independent private school of higher learning. And when persecution broke out, Clement left and this private school disappeared with him.[44]

Recently, however, a more positive assessment of the Eusebian account of the "school of Alexandria" and of Clement's and Origen's successive participation in catechetical instruction has emerged. In combination with the evidence we find in Clement's writings, a closer reading of Eusebius may give some new insights.[45] However, before we have a look at this new interpretation, a few words need to be said about Clement's life and works.

Unfortunately, Eusebius does not devote as much space to Clement's life as to Origen's. There is on the whole little extant information about Clement's life, much must therefore rest on mere assumptions. He was born around 150, of pagan parents, probably in Athens. After his conversion, presumably in his home town, he traveled through southern Italy, Palestine, and Syria, seeking out Christian teachers, and ended up in Egypt:

> I fell in with a final one – supreme in mastery. I tracked him down to his hiding-place in Egypt and stayed with him. He was the true Sicilian bee, culling out of the flowers from the meadow of prophets and apostles a pure substance of true knowledge in the souls of his hearers.
>
> (Clement of Alexandria, *Miscellanies* 1.11.2)

It is generally agreed that this "Sicilian bee" was Pantaenus, whom Clement, in his extant writings, mentions only once by name.[46] According to Eusebius who quotes a letter of CE 211 from Alexander, bishop of Caesarea in Cappadocia (later of Jerusalem), Clement was ordained a presbyter.[47] He has now, as Eusebius writes, arrived in Cappadocia. A statement by Jerome likewise refers to Clement as a presbyter in an Alexandrian community.[48] When persecution broke out under Septimus Severus, in 202 or 203, Clement left the city and went into exile.[49] In a second letter written from Jerusalem to Origen in CE 215, Alexander speaks of Clement as "one of those blessed fathers who has gone on before us."[50] The date of Clement's death may thus be fixed through these letters somewhere between 211 and 215. There is no evidence that he ever returned to Alexandria.

Clement seems to have written most of his works during the period of more than twenty years that he spent in Alexandria. Eusebius lists ten works by Clement, but not all of them have survived.[51] There are three major works extant: *Exhortation to the Greeks, Christ the Educator,* and *Miscellanies.* In addition we have three shorter collections of other people's writings, edited with a commentary by Clement (*Excerpts from Theodotus, Extracts from the Prophets,* and the "Eighth Book" of the *Miscellanies*) and one sermon (*Salvation of the Rich*). Of the lost works the most important seems to have been the *Outlines,* a commentary on the Scriptures, of which only scattered fragments remain.

Not all of Clement's works are meant for those already Christian. The *Exhortation to the Greeks* is an "exhortation" to conversion, addressed to educated Greeks with a knowledge of ancient philosophy as well as traditional religion and mythology. *Christ the Educator* and *Miscellanies* are both primarily addressed to Christians, *Christ the Educator* to those who are newly baptized or want to learn more about Christianity. It shows that he put much energy into the task of preparing candidates for baptism, or teaching those newly baptized. The *Miscellanies,* in eight books, is a witness to his involvement in a more advanced kind of teaching, to the benefit of those interested in a deeper understanding of Christianity. We see how Origen in a similar way divided his teaching into elementary and more advanced, taking on the latter himself and delegating the former to a pupil.[52] That there was no significant Jewish population in the city in Clement's time is visible from his writings. There are no signs there of any living contacts with Jewish scholars – his links with Jewish sources are all literary ones – or any teaching directed to Judeo-Christians specifically.[53]

Clement gives us insights into the organization of the Christian community at Alexandria. It has its priests (presbyters), deacons, and bishops, but he does not reveal any close connection with any local bishop.[54] Nor are there any signs of tension between priests and teachers. In *Miscellanies* 6.106.2 he writes:

> Such a one is in reality a presbyter of the church, and a true deacon of the will of God, if he do and teach what is the Lord's; not as being ordained by men, nor regarded righteous because a presbyter, but enrolled in the presbyterate because righteous.

Clement may well be speaking of himself here; it is probable that both he and Pantaenus were presbyters and that they both combined liturgical and teaching functions. Clement himself can use the term "presbyter" interchangeably with "bishop," indicating that there was still not a developed monarchic system in Alexandria.[55] As mentioned before, the first "bishop" of Alexandria about whom Eusebius records any information beyond a mere name is Demetrius, who "received the episcopate of the communities there."[56] It is after Demetrius has become the supreme bishop that tension develops, eventually causing Origen's departure from Alexandria in 231.

We now return for a moment to the question of the catechetical school. It has been common to argue for or against such a school in Alexandria, with reference to an actual school building. The *didaskaleion* of Eusebius may certainly denote such a building, but it may also mean a school tradition, Christian or non-Christian. This is the way the word is used in Justin, Irenaeus, and Epiphanius.[57] Clement himself never uses the word *didaskaleion*; by avoiding this term, he probably wants to dissociate his own activities from those of other "schools," whose opinions he believed were false.[58] Perhaps we may imagine that the "catechetical school" at Alexandria referred to one of several Christian communities in the city, an integration of "school" and "church" where Clement and Pantaenus were involved together in teaching the "divine scriptures."[59] When Pantaenus died, Clement was left in charge of it, and it was taken over by Origen when Clement left the city, as described by Eusebius.[60]

It is clear that Clement writes as a scholar with an extensive literary background, pagan as well as Christian. From a consideration of the varied literary sources that he employs in his writings, it has been suggested that he had access to a Christian library.[61] He is also the church father who most frequently cites from non-Christian authors. In addition to countless citations from the *Septuagint* and the New Testament, he very often refers to and quotes Greek poets, dramatists, philosophers, and historians. He may illustrate an argument with a passage from Plato or with a few lines from Homer, Euripides, Heraclitus, or Democritus. In addition to the more well-known authors, he mentions by name many writers whom we know next to nothing about because their works are lost. Some of these he certainly knew only through anthologies, but there is no doubt that he had read both Homer and Plato in the original. No Greek philosopher is as warmly praised by him as Plato, and Platonic expressions and ideas, including citations from his works, are spread throughout his works.[62] It was Clement's view that Greek philosophy and the Jewish law were two parallel covenants, so to speak, preparing the Greeks and the Jews, respectively, for the reception of the more perfect Christian message, the "true philosophy."[63]

Though Clement, and later Origen, regarded the *Septuagint* and the new Christian writings as superior to the Greek authors, their openness and curiosity in a novel way brought together Christianity and classical culture, and inaugurated what we today call Christian Hellenism. The diversity of opinions and the wide range of theological interpretations of the Scriptures that prospered in such a milieu did not last long. Origen's forced exile by Bishop Demetrius was a sign of a new ecclesiastical regime that was gradually enforced on Alexandrian Christianity.[64] It resulted in a severing of Christian theological speculation from pagan philosophy, until Christian Hellenism was reestablished in Alexandria and elsewhere under different conditions in the fourth century.

Views on Scripture

Clement was a Platonist and a biblical theologian. He was not a biblicist or an exegete. Was he an allegorist? Patristic interpretation of Scripture is often characterized in terms of literal, typological, and allegorical exegesis.[65] We must, however, be aware that the fathers may have meant different things by these concepts than we do. In fact, as Frances Young says, they did not even have a "single concept corresponding to our notion of literalness."[66] They distinguished wording from sense and the normal sense of the word from its use as a metaphor.[67] For Clement it was obvious that Scripture had a symbolic meaning, but he was also concerned with its historicity. In *Christ the Educator* he writes that there are some things in Scripture which are clear, and not symbolic – an example being moral instruction – while other things are obscure, enigmatic, and in need of interpretation.[68]

In a passage of the fifth book of *Miscellanies* Clement claims that all who have written about the highest or ultimate things, or Truth – be they Egyptians, Greeks, or barbarians – have veiled the truth in symbols, allegories, and metaphors, and he identifies four reasons for it. The first is ethical: the object is to conceal the truth from those who might pollute or misuse it. The second is didactic: veiled truth needs interpreters. The third is psychological: indirect statements make a stronger impression than direct ones. The fourth relates to complexity: symbolic interpretations allow more than one layer of meaning.[69]

It is central to Clement's view of the Scriptures that they are prophetic and contain God's plan of salvation. The prophets saw the noetic world, the world beyond the senses, but they spoke about it in metaphors and parables. In order for us to reach this world we must regard the text of the Bible as metaphorical, and with the help of Christ, who is not a metaphor, we may be led beyond. Christ who was not of this world but came in a worldly form, may by knowledge lead men to this other world. For those who are ignorant of the truth, the prophecies remain parables and even become stumbling blocks. But for those who have ears, the Scriptures will be opened up and the truth will be explained.[70]

There are strong links between Clement's concept of God and his views on language, and through his views on language, with his understanding of Scripture. In *Miscellanies* 2.72.4 he writes:

> It is not possible to speak of the divine in its actual nature. But even though we are fettered to flesh, it is possible for us to hear the Lord, accommodating himself to human weakness for our salvation, in the words of the prophets.

In a way, for Clement – as for many of the fathers of the later Orthodox tradition – the whole concept of language is God's self-accommodation to the limits and constraints of human existence.[71] Language is inadequate for expressing divine truths, and this creates a need for alternative, symbolic ways of writing. Clement also believes that the authors of the Scriptures employ a method of concealment.

However, to Clement the coming of Jesus to earth is no metaphor. He insists on the historicity and concreteness of the advent, life, and death of Jesus. He became flesh so that he could be seen,[72] and reveal who God is: "Hence the Son is said to be the Father's face, being the revealer of the Father's character to the five senses by clothing himself with flesh (*sarkoforos genomenos*)."[73]

For all Clement's talk of parables and metaphors and hidden truths, we find nowhere in his genuine writings any reference to a secret unwritten doctrine inaccessible to the reader whose only source of information is the author's written work.[74] It is for him rather a question of adapting the message to the needs and capacities of different categories of readers and not speaking in the same manner to everyone. As we have seen, some of Clement's work was obviously not directed to beginners, but rather to the more advanced student who had already received some instruction: "For only to those that often approach them, and have given them a trial by faith and in their whole life, will they supply the real philosophy and the true theology."[75]

As to the relationship between scripture and philosophy, Clement uses philosophy to explain and defend scripture. He holds Plato in particularly high regard, but he also speaks positively of philosophy in general terms:

> So, before the Lord's coming, philosophy was an essential guide to right-eousness to the Greeks. At the present time, it is a useful guide towards reverence for God. It is a kind of preliminary education for those who are trying to gather faith through demonstration.
>
> (Clement of Alexandria, *Miscellanies* 1.28.1)

Philosophy was given to the Greeks as a *paidagogos* to bring them to Christ. All good things come from God, some directly, like the Old and the New Testaments, and some in subsidiary ways, like philosophy. There is only one truth, and philosophy investigates this truth, which is Christ himself. Clement claims that a faith grounded in reason is preferable to simple faith. He confronts Christians who think they have no need of philosophy or science, who think they are "fully equipped by nature." "All they ask for is simply and solely faith."[76] It is important, he argues, for all Christians to engage in the training philosophy gives; it exercises the mind and produces a sharpness of intellect. It is necessary because knowledge of all kinds – mathematics, the fine arts, literary studies – may help us to defend the faith from those who want to destroy it.[77] For these purposes, experience and preparation are important; in the same way we choose the sea captain who has visited many places and the doctor who has treated many patients.[78]

Aspects of spirituality in Clement

A typical aspect of Clement's thought is the unity between the spiritual and the epistemological, between faith (*pistis*) and knowledge (*gnosis*). The foundation of *gnosis* is *pistis* and the two cannot be separated: "Now neither is knowledge without faith, nor faith without knowledge."[79] True knowledge is founded on faith.[80] Man's ultimate aim is the vision of God, the Platonic *theoria*, and in order to see God, you have to know him and become like him (*homoiosis to theo*).

To develop knowledge of God is to be part of a process, to grow in grace and advance in moral perfection; it is a process that leads from *pistis* via *gnosis* to the love (*agape*) of God.[81] Faith and love represent the beginning and the end of this process: "Knowledge added to faith and love to knowledge, and to love, the heavenly inheritance."[82] But the knowledge is not primarily intellectual, it is more of a spiritual, relational or intimate kind. In *Miscellanies* 7.57.4 he describes a process that leads from heathenism to faith, goes on to knowledge and then to love:

> As I mentioned before, there seems to me to be a first kind of saving change from heathenism (*ethnon*) to faith (*pistis*), a second from faith to knowledge (*gnosis*); and this latter, as it passes on into love (*agape*), begins at once to establish a mutual friendship between that which knows and that which is known.

Clement holds that love, faith, and knowledge are not like wisdom acquired by teaching; they are gained through training and practice, but also through communion with God.[83] Moreover, Clement describes a Gnostic as a person whose *gnosis* is demonstrated through his activities:

> The gnostic … being on the one hand not without a knowledge of God (or rather being known by him), and on the other hand showing the effects thereof. … For works (*ta erga*) follow knowledge, as the shadow the body.
> (Clement of Alexandria, *Miscellanies* 7.82.7)

It is, however, important to distinguish on the one hand between man's possibility to have knowledge (*gnosis*) of God, and on the other what Clement teaches about God being unknowable, unutterable, indescribable. When we say that man knows God, the focus is on man, and we are in the realm of spirituality. For as we saw, Clement also teaches that there is no knowledge (*gnosis*) without faith (*pistis*). But when we say (with Clement) that God is unknowable (*agnostos*), we express an epistemological fact – about God's apophatic nature.[84]

An important instance of the unity between the spiritual and the epistemological is Clement's doctrine of deification. The earliest Christian discussion of deification is concerned with a passage in Psalm 82, especially verse 6: "I said, You are gods, and are all sons of the most High." Who are they whom the Psalmist calls "gods"? About CE 160, Justin Martyr maintained that the people of God was the new Israel, and the "gods" were those who were obedient to Christ.[85] Irenaeus of Lyons, on the other hand, claimed that "gods" were those "who have received the grace of the 'adoption by which we cry Abba father.'"[86] In Clement, the idea is much more developed and he is the first of the church fathers who employs a technical terminology of deification, by using words such as *theopoieo* and *theazo*.[87] Psalm 82:6, however, is not the reference that occurs most often when Clement discusses the idea of deification. He does mention it a few times, but much more frequently he cites the famous Platonic paragraph of *Theaetetus*:

And to escape [from earth] is to become like God (*homoiosis theo*), so far as this is possible (*kata to dynaton*); and to become like God is to become righteous (*dikaion*) and holy (*hosion*) and wise (*meta froneseos*).

(Plato, *Theaetetus* 176b)[88]

In addition to Clement's fondness of Plato in general, I suspect that his preference for this passage to the scriptural one has to do with the expression *kata to dynaton*. This Platonic reservation is wholly in line with Clement's epistemological apophaticism in relation to God. Also when it comes to man's possibility of becoming like God, it is more compatible with his whole concept of God to add "as far as it is possible."[89]

It was man's goal to become "god," and this was made possible since Christ himself had become man. In *Exhortation to the Greeks* Clement writes: "The Word of God speaks, having become man, in order that such as you may learn from man how it is even possible for man to become a god."[90] Now, through baptism the image of God that was destroyed in the Fall is restored. This view, that the purpose of Christ's coming to earth was to deify man, runs like a scarlet thread through most of Greek theology in the early church, meaning that salvation is seen as an equivalent to deification.

So God, as he is in himself, cannot be known by man. He may, however, be reached by faith. Faith is central in Clement's theory of knowledge. It forms the basis for all kinds of knowledge, both for the specifically Christian *gnosis* and the logical *gnosis*.[91] Both types of truth or knowledge rest on the same indemonstrable first principles that cannot be proved, but must be accepted in faith.

Clement's understanding of faith is derived from Scripture. Referring to Paul he sees faith as opposed to the wisdom of the wise. Christ crucified is to those who believe the power and wisdom of God (1 Cor. 1:19–24).[92] Faith is something divine and has two sides: our decision and God's gift. As we have seen, we cannot know without faith. Why? Because truth is a gift of God, and until we are willing to receive it, we know nothing.[93]

With terms like *pistis*, *gnosis*, and *homoiosis*, Clement describes a human life of increasing knowledge and proximity to God. It is a life that possesses certain moral and spiritual qualities, such as justice, holiness and wisdom, love of God and love of man. Its end result is a vision of God who is beyond all knowledge, but has accommodated himself to human weakness by clothing himself with flesh.

Further reading

Primary sources

Clement of Alexandria, *Exhortation to the Heathen, The Instructor, The Stromata, or Miscellanies, Fragments, Who Is the Rich Man That Shall Be Saved*, vol. 2 in A. Roberts and J. Donaldson (eds), *Fathers of the Second Century*, in *The Ante-Nicene Fathers*, 10 vols, Edinburgh: T&T Clark,1885–7; repr. Grand Rapids, MI: Wm. B Eerdmans, 1979; repr. Peabody, MA: Hendrickson, 1994, pp. 165–605, *The Exhortation to the Greeks, The Rich Man's Salvation and the Fragment of an Address entitled To the Newly Baptized*, G. W. Butterworth (ed.), Loeb Classical Library, Cambridge, MA: Harvard University Press, 1982, *Christ the Educator*, trans. Simon P. Wood, The Fathers of the Church 23, Washington, DC: Catholic University of America Press, 1954, *Stromateis, Books 1–3*, trans. John Ferguson, The Fathers of the Church 85,

Washington, DC: Catholic University of America Press, 1991, *Stromateis*, Books 3 and 7, in H. Chadwick (ed.), *Alexandrian Christianity*, The Library of Christian Classics, Philadelphia: Westminster, 1954.

Secondary sources

C. Haas, *Alexandria in Late Antiquity: Topography and Social Conflict*, Ancient Society and History, Baltimore, MD: Johns Hopkins University Press, 1997.

K. Hopkins, *A World Full of Gods: Pagans, Jews and Christians in the Roman Empire*, London: Phoenix, 2000.

E. Osborn, *Clement of Alexandria*, Cambridge: Cambridge University Press, 2005.

O. Skarsaune and R. Hvalvik (eds), *Jewish Believers in Jesus: The Early Centuries*, Peabody, MA: Hendrickson, 2007.

R. Stark, *The Rise of Christianity: How the Obscure, Marginal Jesus Movement Became the Dominant Religious Force in the Western World in a Few Centuries*, San Francisco: HarperSanFrancisco, 1997.

E. J. Watts, *City and School in Late Antique Athens and Alexandria*, Berkeley, CA: University of California Press, 2006.

F. M. Young, *Biblical Exegesis and the Formation of Christian Culture*, Peabody, MA: Hendrickson, 2002.

Notes

1 R. Stark, *The Rise of Christianity: How the Obscure, Marginal Jesus Movement Became the Dominant Religious Force in the Western World in a Few Centuries*, San Francisco: HarperSanFrancisco, 1997, pp. 132ff.

2 J. Mélèze-Modrzejewski, *The Jews of Egypt: From Ramses II to Emperor Hadrian*, Philadelphia and Jerusalem: T&T Clark, 1995, pp. 161ff.

3 All such estimates must be regarded with caution; the suggested numbers for the whole population of Alexandria vary between 200,000 (C. Haas, *Alexandria in Late Antiquity: Topography and Social Conflict*, Baltimore, MD: Johns Hopkins University Press, p. 46) and 400,000 (Stark, *Rise of Christianity*, p. 131). Philo (*Against Flaccus* 43) claimed there were in his time at least a million Jews in Egypt and that two of the five districts of Alexandria were Jewish.

4 J. Mélèze-Modrzejewski, *The Jews of Egypt*, p. 163.

5 See R. Trevijano, "The Early Christian Church at Alexandria," *Studia Patristica* 12, 1971, p. 473.

6 Eusebius, *Ecclesiastical History* 2.24, 3.14, 3.21, 4.1, 4.4, 4.5.5, 4.19, 5.9.

7 B. A. Pearson, "Earliest Christianity in Egypt: Some Observations," in B. A. Pearson and J. E. Goehring (eds), *The Roots of Egyptian Christianity*, Philadelphia: Fortress, 1986, pp. 132–59; B. A. Pearson, "Egypt," in M. M. Mitchell and F. M. Young (eds), *The Cambridge History of Christianity*, vol. 1: *Origins to Constantine*, Cambridge: Cambridge University Press, 2006, pp. 336–7.

8 C. W. Griggs, *Early Egyptian Christianity: From its Origins to 451 C.E.*, Coptic Studies 2, Leiden: E. J. Brill, 1993, pp. 13–78. R. E. Heine, "The Alexandrians," in F. Young, L. Ayers, and A. Louth (eds), *The Cambridge History of Early Christian Literature*, Cambridge: Cambridge University Press, 2004, pp. 117–30, passes it on as the only view.

9 W. Bauer, *Orthodoxy and Heresy in Earliest Christianity*, ed. R. A. Kraft and G. Krodel, Philadelphia: Fortress, 1971, p. 58; originally published as W. Bauer, *Rechtgläubigkeit und Ketzerei im ältesten Christentum*, Beiträge zur historischen Theologie 10, Tübingen: Mohr Siebeck, 1934.

10 One is Apollos, an Alexandrian Jewish Christian, mentioned in Acts 18:24–25.

11 Clement of Alexandria, *Miscellanies* 7.106.4.

12 Epiphanius, *Refutation of All Heresies* 31.7.1–2.

13 Bauer, *Orthodoxy and Heresy in Earliest Christianity*.

14 C. H. Roberts, *Manuscript, Society, and Belief in Early Christian Egypt*, London: Oxford University Press, pp. 28–48.

15 Roberts, *Manuscript, Society, and Belief in Early Christian Egypt*, p. 71. See also Pearson, "Earliest Christianity in Egypt," p. 134; A. F. J. Klijn, "Jewish Christianity in Egypt," in Pearson and Goehring, *Roots of Egyptian Christianity*, pp.161–75.

16 R. van den Broek, "Juden und Christen in Alexandrien im 2. und 3. Jahrhundert," in *Studies in Gnosticism and Alexandrian Christianity*, Nag Hammadi and Manichaean Studies 39, Leiden: E. J. Brill, 1996, p. 184.

17 Jerome, *On Illustrious Men* 2.

18 This was the view of Bauer, *Orthodoxy and Heresy in Earliest Christianity*.

19 Van den Broek, "Juden und Christen in Alexandrien im 2. und 3. Jahrhundert," p. 184.

20 A. Fuks, "Aspects of the Jewish Revolt in 115–17," *Journal of Roman Studies* 51, 1961, pp. 98–104. Cf. O. Skarsaune and R. Hvalvik (eds), *Jewish Believers in Jesus: The Early Centuries*, Peabody, MA: Hendrickson, 2007, pp. 761–2: "When evidence of Jewish believers is forthcoming in the second century and later ... evidence from Alexandria, Cyrene and Cyprus is non-existent."

21 E. Osborn, *Clement of Alexandria*, Cambridge: Cambridge University Press, 2005, p. 84.

22 Clement of Alexandria, *Miscellanies* 3.93.1. Cf. further H. F. Hägg, "Continence and Marriage: The Concept of *Enkrateia* in Clement of Alexandria," *Symbolae Osloenses* 81, 2006, pp. 126–43.

23 See D. I. Rankin, *From Clement to Origen: The Social and Historical Context of the Church Fathers*, Aldershot: Ashgate, 2006, p. 115.

24 O. Skarsaune, "Barnabas brev," in E. Baasland and R. Hvalvik (eds), *De apostoliske fedre. I norsk overset-telse med innledning og noter*, Oslo: Luther, 1984, p. 163.

25 Rankin, *From Clement to Origen*, p. 116.

26 Stark estimates the population of the Roman Empire in the middle of the fourth century to be about sixty million (Stark, *Rise of Christianity*, pp. 3–27); other scholars suggest similar numbers.

27 K. Hopkins, "Christian Number and Its Implication," *Journal of Early Christian Studies* 6.2, 1998, p. 194. As Hopkins stresses, these are not truth statements, "they are numerical metaphors, good for thinking about Christians with" (p. 195).

28 Hopkins, "Christian Number and Its Implication," p. 185.

29 Hopkins, "Christian Number and Its Implication," p. 225.

30 G. F. Snyder, *Ante Pacem: Archeological Evidence of Church Life Before Constantine*, Macon, GA: Mercer University Press, 2003.

31 Stark, *Rise of Christianity*, pp. 49–71.

32 Stark, *Rise of Christianity*, p. 55.

33 Stark, *Rise of Christianity*, p. 57. We may see here a parallel to the so-called "god-fearers" of the New Testament. See also Skarsaune and Hvalvik, *Jewish Believers in Jesus*, pp. 768–71 who nuance some of the views of Stark, and reckon a figure of 2 per cent Jewish Christian believers in CE 250 not to be unrealistic.

34 Important studies include A. Knauber, "Katechetenschule oder Schulkatechumenat? Um die rechte Deutung des 'Unternehmens' der ersten grossen Alexandriner," *Trierer theologische Zeitschrift* 60, 1951, pp. 243–66; M. Hornschuh, "Das Leben des Origenes und die Entstehung der alexandrinischen Schule, 1–2," *Zeitschrift für Kirchengeschichte* 71, 1960, pp. 1–25, 193–214; J. Ferguson, *Clement of Alexandria*, New York: Twayne, 1974, p. 15; G. Bardy, "Aux origines de l'école d'Alexandrie," *Recherches de science religieuse* 27, 1937, pp. 65–90; A. L. Boulluec, "L'École d'Alexandrie: De quelques aventures d'un concept historiographique," in J. Pouilloux (ed.), *ALEXANDRINA: Hellénisme, judaïsme et christianisme à Alexandrie: Mélanges offerts au P. Claude Mondésert*, Paris: Cerf, 1987, pp. 403–17; U. Neymeyr, *Die christlichen Lehrer im zweiten Jahrhundert: Ihre Lehrtätigkeit, ihr Selbstverständnis und ihre Geschichte*, Leiden: Brill, 1989; A. Tuilier, "Les évangélistes et les docteurs de la primitive église et les origines de l'Ecole (*didaskaleion*) d'Alexandrie," *Studia Patristica* 17.2, 1982, pp. 738–49; R. L. Wilken, "Alexandria: A School for Training in Virtue," in P. Henry (ed.), *Schools of Thought in the Christian Tradition*, Philadelphia: Fortress, 1984, pp. 15–18; Pearson, "Earliest Christianity in Egypt"; D. Dawson, *Allegorical Readers and Cultural Revision in Ancient Alexandria*, Berkeley, CA: University of California Press, 1992, pp. 219–22; C. Scholten, "Die alexandrinische Katechetenschule," *Jahrbuch für Antike und Christentum* 38, 1995, pp. 16–37; van den Broek, "Juden und Christen in Alexandrien im 2. und 3. Jahrhundert."

35 Nothing from his hand has survived, but his historicity can hardly be doubted.

36 Trans. K. Lake, *Eusebius: The Ecclesiastical History*, vol. 1, Loeb Classical Library, Cambridge, MA: Harvard University Press, 1980, p. 463.

37 Eusebius, *Ecclesiastical History* 6.6; trans. J. E. L. Oulton, *Eusebius: The Ecclesiastical History*, vol. 2, Loeb Classical Library, Cambridge, MA: Harvard University Press, 1980, p. 27.

38 Eusebius, *Ecclesiastical History* 6.3.3.

39 Eusebius, *Ecclesiastical History* 6.3.8.

40 Eusebius, *Ecclesiastical History* 6.15; trans. Oulton, *Eusebius*, p. 51.

41 For the standard account see J. Quasten, *The Ante-Nicene Literature after Irenaeus*, vol. 2 of *Patrology*, 4 vols, Utrecht and Antwerp: Spectrum, 1950; repr. Westminster, MD: Christian Classics, 1983, pp. 2–4.

42 See e. g. Bardy, "Aux origines de l'école d'Alexandrie," p. 83.

43 Gregory Thaumaturgos, *Address of Thanksgiving to Origen*; R. Valantasis, "Chapter Two: The Spiritual Guide as Teacher and Revealer," in *Spiritual Guides of the Third Century: A Semiotic Study of the Guide-Disciple Relationship in Christianity, Neoplatonism, Hermetism, and Gnosticism*, Minneapolis: Fortress, 1991.

44 See e. g. C. Scholten, "Die alexandrinische Katechetenschule."

45 A. Méhat, *Étude sur les "Stromates" de Clément d'Alexandrie*, Patristica Sorbonensia 7, Paris: Seuil, 1966, pp. 62ff.; A. van den Hoek, "The 'Catechetical' School of Early Christian Alexandria and Its Philonic Heritage," *Harvard Theological Review* 90, 1997, pp. 59–87; Osborn, *Clement of Alexandria*, pp. 19–24.

46 Clement of Alexandria, *Extracts from the Prophets* 56.2.

47 Clement of Alexandria, *Miscellanies* 6.11.

48 Jerome, *On Illustrious Men* 38; quoted in O. Stählin (ed.), *Protrepticus und Paedagogus*, vol. 1 of *Clemens Alexandrinus*, Die griechische christliche Schriftsteller der ersten [drei] Jahrhunderte 12, Leipzig: Hindrichs, 1905, p. xii.

49 Alexander's letter was taken from Cappadocia to Antioch by Clement (*Miscellanies* 6.11). Some scholars have suggested that Clement left because of controversies with the bishop Demetrius.

50 Eusebius, *Ecclesiastical History* 6.14.9.

51 Eusebius, *Ecclesiastical History* 6.13.

52 Eusebius, *Ecclesiastical History* 6.15.1.

53 Van den Hoek, "The 'Catechetical' School of Early Christian Alexandria and Its Philonic Heritage," 82.

54 Osborn, *Clement of Alexandria*, p. 19.

55 In *Salvation of the Rich* 42.3–4, Clement describes the same person as "bishop" and then "presbyter."

56 Eusebius, *Ecclesiastical History* 6.2.2.

57 Van den Hoek, "The 'Catechetical' School of Early Christian Alexandria and Its Philonic Heritage," 63.

58 Osborn, *Clement of Alexandria*, p. 23; cf. also E. J. Watts, *City and School in Late Antique Athens and Alexandria*, Berkeley, CA: University of California Press, 2006, pp. 143–68.

59 Eusebius, *Ecclesiastical History* 5.11.1.

60 Eusebius, *Ecclesiastical History* 5.10.1.

61 A. van den Hoek, "How Alexandrian was Clement of Alexandria?: Reflections on Clement and his Alexandrian Background," *Heythrop Journal* 31, 1990, p. 190; "'Catechetical' School of Early Christian Alexandria and Its Philonic Heritage," pp. 81–2.

62 A standard account, though to be used with caution, is S. R. C. Lilla, *Clement of Alexandria: A Study in Christian Platonism and Gnosticism*, Oxford: Oxford University Press, 1971.

63 For Clement's views on Greek philosophy, see especially *Miscellanies* 1 and 6.

64 Eusebius, *Ecclesiastical History* 6.26.

65 F. M. Young, *Biblical Exegesis and the Formation of Christian Culture*, Peabody, MA: Hendrickson, 2002, p. 186.

66 Young, *Biblical Exegesis and the Formation of Christian Culture*, p. 187.

67 Young, *Biblical Exegesis and the Formation of Christian Culture*, p. 189.

68 Clement of Alexandria, *Christ the Educator* 3.97.1–98.1.

69 Clement of Alexandria, *Miscellanies* 5.56–66. An example is *Miscellanies* 5.32–40.

70 Clement of Alexandria, *Miscellanies* 6.127.1–2.

71 See Young, *Biblical Exegesis and the Formation of Christian Culture*, pp.140ff.

72 Clement of Alexandria, *Miscellanies* 5.16.5.

73 Clement of Alexandria, *Miscellanies* 5.34.1.

74 The letter's authenticity is doubted by many scholars in spite of Morton Smith, who regards as authentic a previously unknown letter of Clement which refers to a "secret Gospel of Mark," and who seems to endorse the concept of a hidden Christian doctrine. M. Smith, *Clement of Alexandria and a Secret Gospel of Mark*, Cambridge, MA: Harvard University Press, 1973; *The Secret Gospel: The Discovery and Interpretation of the Secret Gospel According to Mark*, London: Harper & Row, 1974.

75 Clement of Alexandria, *Miscellanies* 5.56.3.

76 Clement of Alexandria, *Miscellanies* 1.43.1.

77 Clement of Alexandria, *Miscellanies* 1.43.

78 Clement of Alexandria, *Miscellanies* 1.43.1–44.1

79 Clement of Alexandria, *Miscellanies* 5.1.3.

80 Clement of Alexandria, *Miscellanies* 2.12–14; 6.31.3; 5.15.1f.; 8.3.7.

81 See Clement of Alexandria, *Miscellanies* 7.84.1f.

82 Clement of Alexandria, *Miscellanies* 7.55.7.

83 Clement of Alexandria, *Miscellanies* 7.55–57. Cf. M. Kiley (ed.), *Prayer from Alexander to Constantine: A Critical Anthology*, London and New York: Routledge, 1997, pp. 296–303.

84 See further about Clement's apophaticism H. F. Hägg, *Clement of Alexandria and the Beginnings of Christian Apophaticism*, Oxford: Oxford University Press, 2006, pp. 153–79.

85 Justin, *Dialogue with Trypho* 123.

86 Irenaeus, *Against Heresies* 3.6.1; trans. A. Roberts and W. H. Rambaut, *Against Heresies, Books 1–5 and Fragments*, in A. Roberts and W. H. Rambaut (trans. and ed.), *The Apostolic Fathers with Justin Martyr*, rev. ed., in *The Ante-Nicene Fathers*, 10 vols, Edinburgh: T&T Clark, 1885–7; repr. Grand Rapids, MI: Wm. B. Eerdmans, 1987; repr. Peabody, MA: Hendrickson, 1994, p. 419.

87 M. D. Nispel, "Christian Deification and the Early *Testimonia*," *Vigiliae Christianae* 53, 1999, p. 292; see also N. Russell, *The Doctrine of Deification in the Greek Christian Tradition*, Oxford: Oxford University Press, 2004, pp. 121–40.

88 Trans. H. N. Fowler, *Plato*, vol. 7, Loeb Classical Library, Cambridge, MA: Harvard University Press, 1921, p. 129.

89 Cf. further H. F. Hägg, "Deification in Clement of Alexandria with a Special Reference to His Use of *Theaetetus* 176B," *Studia Patristica*, forthcoming.

90 Clement of Alexandria, *Exhortation to the Greeks* 8.4.

91 Cf. Clement of Alexandria, *Miscellanies* 8.7.2.

92 Clement of Alexandria, *Miscellanies* 5.8.1.

93 Clement of Alexandria, *Christ the Educator* 1.25. See E. Osborn, *The Philosophy of Clement of Alexandria*, Cambridge: Cambridge University Press, 1957, p. 128.

11

ORIGEN

Ronald E. Heine

Origen was born in CE 185 or 186 in Alexandria when Commodus ruled the Roman empire. He died, either as a martyr at Caesarea in the persecution of the emperor Decius, or at Tyre a year or so after Decius's death when Valerian was emperor.[1] His father was martyred in Alexandria during the persecution of Septimius Severus when Origen was a teenager.[2]

Origen had been educated in all the subjects of Greek education.[3] His use of Greek grammatical and rhetorical skills and his ability to think with the conceptual tools of Greek philosophy are evident throughout his works. The pages of his *Against Celsus* are dotted with citations of Greek authors. After his father's death Origen taught for some time as a *grammaticus*, teaching the basic subjects of Greek education.[4] He had also been instructed in the Bible as a child by his father.[5] We do not know what other Christian teachers may have influenced him. He seems to have been acquainted with the Jewish Christian teacher Pantaenus and probably also with Clement of Alexandria.[6] He refers several times to a Jewish Christian teacher that he designates simply as "the Hebrew."[7] According to Eusebius, Demetrius, the local bishop, put him in charge of catechetical instruction for the church in Alexandria when he was only eighteen years old.[8] Origen's fame for his understanding of the Christian faith and as a defender of it against both Greeks and heretics spread widely. The climax was perhaps the invitation from Mamaea, mother of the emperor Alexander Severus, to come to Antioch to tell her about the Christian faith.[9]

The catechetical school Origen instructed eventually became so large that he divided it between those needing instruction in the elements of the faith and those desirous and capable of advanced study. Origen took charge of the advanced group and appointed Heraclas to instruct the beginners.[10] Sometime in this period a rift began to develop between Origen and Demetrius, bishop of Alexandria. We do not know most of the details of the disagreement. It appears that Demetrius may have begun to be uncomfortable with some of Origen's theology. Ecclesiastical politics seem definitely to have been involved. Origen had been ordained as priest by the bishop of Caesarea during a visit there. Demetrius, for whatever reason, had not ordained Origen. He was convinced, however, that the decision about whether Origen should be ordained or not belonged to his jurisdiction as Origen's local bishop. Origen refers to the dispute in his *Commentary on John*, but his description is too allusive to allow any conclusions to be drawn beyond the obvious one that it was a severe dispute and Origen felt himself deeply wronged in the affair.[11] The result of the dispute was that Origen left Alexandria for good and moved to Caesarea where he preached almost all of his homilies, started a school of theology, and founded a Christian library. Caesarea became the center of his activities for the remainder of his life.

Origen was the most prolific author of all the Fathers of the church. His written works include the genres of commentary, textual criticism, theology, apologetics, and spiritual literature. Only a few of these works have been preserved entire in the Greek language in which Origen wrote them. Others have been partially preserved in Greek, and still others have been preserved either entire or in part in Latin translations. The bulk of Origen's writings, however, has perished.

I begin this discussion of Origen's thought with his work on Scripture because, for Origen, everything flowed from this source. He was the first Christian who might be called, in some sense at least, a systematic theologian but his theology arose from Scripture, as he understood Scripture. He was also a master of Christian spirituality, but like his theology, this too was rooted in his understanding of Scripture and expounded in its terminology. Origen lived in Scripture as perhaps no other has in the entire history of the church.

Origen as a biblical commentator

Commentaries were a staple part of the literary diet in Origen's time. The scholars at the Museum in Alexandria had been producing a steady flow of them on the writings of classical antiquity for at least three and a half centuries before Origen. There were commentaries on Homer, on the Greek dramas, and on the orations of the Attic orators. In Origen's time philosophers did philosophy by writing commentaries on the works of Plato and Aristotle, the recognized authorities of the past. Alexander of Aphrodisias, an older contemporary of Origen, had the position of state-funded professor of Aristotelian philosophy, probably in Athens, in the reigns of Septimius Severus and Caracalla.[12] He wrote numerous commentaries on the works of Aristotle. It was quite natural for Origen to undertake to set forth Christian theology in the form of commentaries on the authoritative books of the Christians.

We do not know exactly how many biblical commentaries Origen wrote. Eusebius refers to a complete list of Origen's works that he had made and included in his now lost *Life of Pamphilus*.[13] In a list provided by Jerome, who claims to have seen this catalogue drawn up by Eusebius,[14] there are references to commentaries on Genesis, Isaiah, Hosea, Joel, Amos, Jonah, Micah, Nahum, Habakkuk, Zephaniah, Haggai, Zechariah, Malachi, Ezekiel, the Psalms, Proverbs, Song of Songs, Lamentations, Matthew, John, Luke, Romans, Galatians, Ephesians, Philippians, Colossians, 1 and 2 Thessalonians, Titus, and Philemon.[15] None of these biblical commentaries has been preserved in its entirety, and many have been lost completely. In spite of the great loss, enough of Origen's work as a biblical commentator remains, whether in a direct Greek manuscript tradition, Latin translations, or fragments in the later catena commentaries, to gain an accurate impression of the way he approached the task of writing commentaries on Scripture.

While Origen's exegetical work is certainly our largest legacy of early Christian commentary literature, he was not the first to write commentaries on Scripture. There appear to have been commentaries produced on the Gospels by the Gnostic Basilides and Heracleon prior to Origen's work. Papias, bishop of Hierapolis in the mid-second century, may also have written commentaries on the Gospels. Eusebius relates that Clement of Alexandria had written up the scriptural exegesis of the Alexandrian Jewish Christian of the late second century named Pantaenus in his *Hypotyposeis*.[16] Hippolytus of Rome produced commentaries, including works on the Song of Songs and Daniel, in the early third century, prior to Origen. Ambrose, Origen's friend and patron, appears to have been the catalyst that set Origen on the path of writing biblical commentaries. Jerome asserts that Ambrose urged Origen to compose commentaries on Scripture as Hippolytus had done.[17]

Even before Christians began to write commentaries on Scripture, the Jews had already produced commentaries on the Hebrew Scriptures. The fragmentary biblical commentaries discovered at Qumran are the oldest known biblical commentaries. Those of the first-century-CE Jew, Philo of Alexandria, however, are writings that we know Origen was familiar with and which seem to have exercised considerable influence on him both in their theology and in their hermeneutical approach to Scripture.

Philo is the chief representative of what is called Hellenistic Judaism. He preceded Origen in Alexandria by approximately a century and a half but Origen clearly knew his works. He refers to Philo three times by name in his writings, once even citing the title of Philo's work and quoting a line from it.[18] Origen's more usual way of indicating his dependence on another scholar, however, was to make an anonymous reference to "someone," "some of those," or "who preceded us." David Runia has noted that in at least twenty of these "anonymous phrases" the reference is to Philo. Furthermore, Runia points out, there are more than four hundred additional passages in Origen where scholars have perceived the influence of Philo.[19]

When Origen began to write commentaries, therefore, he stepped into a large stream of established literary precedent flowing from Greeks, Jews, and Christians. He took over the techniques and style of the genre already long established. The Greek commentary literature had a definite format. Each book began with a rather stylized preface that addressed a set list of approximately six topics which included the aim of the treatise and its usefulness.[20] These topics were referred to with the phrase, "What comes before the study of … ." Jaap Mansfeld has called attention to the appearance of this phrase at the conclusion of the preface in the first book of Origen's *Commentary on John*.[21] Origen adopted most of these topics in the various prefaces that he wrote to the books of his commentaries. One of his most explicit discussions of these topics is in the preface to his *Commentary on the Song of Songs*. There he sets forth the list of topics he will discuss before he begins the actual discussion of the contents of the book. The topics to be discussed are the main theme of the book, the place this book holds in the order of the books of Solomon, why it has the title it has, and why it is presented in a dramatic dialogue.[22]

Origen provides a summary of his hermeneutic for interpreting the Bible in book 4 of his treatise *On First Principles*.[23] He begins by arguing that both the Old and New

Testaments are divine and that the Holy Spirit is their author.[24] He notes that the most common error which leads multitudes of people to misunderstand the Scriptures is that of understanding the text of Scripture literally as opposed to searching out its spiritual meaning. In this discussion he applies two of the technical terms found in the prefaces of the secular commentaries.

He begins with the "aim" of the Holy Spirit in what is recorded in Scripture. This aim was to meet the spiritual needs of humanity. The list Origen provides of the spiritual subjects treated in Scripture is a summary of the doctrines he sets forth in the preface of On First Principles as the basic doctrines that are to be discussed in the treatise.[25] Searching out these spiritual matters demands, however, a certain aptitude on the part of the reader of the Bible. Origen recognized that multitudes of people lacked this prerequisite and yet claimed a faith in Christ. There was, therefore, he argues, a secondary aim of the Holy Spirit in Scripture. That secondary aim was to conceal the spiritual doctrines in a historical narrative that would benefit those persons lacking the aptitude necessary for investigating the true spiritual meanings of Scripture. This latter is not, however, a disparaging view of the narrative of Scripture as we will see. Origen can, in fact, become quite defensive of the literal text of Scripture when he perceives it as being under attack.

When Origen discusses the story of the Samaritan woman in the Gospel of John, he identifies the well of Jacob as the Scriptures. The Scriptures serve as introductions to the higher understanding Jesus gives, referred to in the story as "a spring of water gushing up to eternal life."[26] Before one can partake of this spiritual meaning, however, one must first have drunk regularly and diligently from Jacob's well. Origen, then, notes that the Gnostic Heracleon had referred to the water from Jacob's well as "insipid, temporary, and deficient." Origen says he could agree with Heracleon if he had meant that the water from Jacob's well was a first or lower step to a more perfect level of understanding. But, he adds, Heracleon is to be blamed "if he does this to slander the ancient words."[27] Origen defends the literal meaning of Scripture again much later in his life to refute the arrogant arguments of the philosopher Celsus who ridiculed the stories in the Bible, including that of Jesus. Origen replied that it was because God cares for all people, not just those with a Greek education, that he employed a style that common people could understand in Scripture. Once they have taken their initial steps in the faith, these very people can be introduced to the doctrines hidden in the Bible. "For," he says, "it is obvious even to an ungifted person who reads them that many passages can possess a meaning deeper than that which appears at first sight." This perception of deeper meaning is not dependent on one's education, but depends on the energy and time one invests in studying the Bible and, a point which one must never neglect in trying to understand Origen, on the effort one makes to live as the Bible teaches.[28]

These two levels of meaning in Scripture are closely related to the second topic from the technical terminology of the secular commentaries that Origen adopted. This is the topic of "usefulness." Everything in Scripture must be useful for the Christian because it is all the work of the Holy Spirit. Some things are useful on the surface, such as the command for one to honor one's father and mother, or the prohibitions of murder, adultery, stealing, and bearing false witness.[29] Others, such as the prohibition to eat vultures, are unnecessary, seen in the best light, since no one has ever been so hungry as to attempt this, or irrational in the worst light.[30] Something which is not obvious, therefore, must be intended in commands such as these. What has been said of commandments applies to historical narrations as well. Some cannot be true in their literal or historical sense, such as the opening statements in Genesis in which light exists three days before the creation of the sun and other heavenly luminaries.[31] Origen uses the same approach in treating the discrepancies between the accounts of events in Jesus' life recorded in the four Gospels. In his discussion of the cleansing of the temple and the events narrated as preceding and following it in John's Gospel, for example, he notes the numerous disagreements with the similar narratives in the Synoptic Gospels. The answer to these difficulties, he asserts, is that the narrators used historical narratives to teach spiritual lessons. Some of the events, he suggests, did not happen at all historically while others did occur but not necessarily in exactly the way they have been narrated. Where it was possible the authors of the Gospels couched spiritual truth in accurate historical narratives but where that could not be done, historical accuracy was sacrificed for the sake of spiritual truth. Origen justifies this disregard for historical precision by appealing to both of the technical terms of the Greek commentators we have discussed. It was done, he says, to facilitate the "usefulness" of the author's "mystical aim."[32]

All of this leads Origen to posit his basic hermeneutical point: All Scripture has a spiritual meaning; not all Scripture has a literal or historical meaning.[33] Origen believes that this hermeneutic comes from Christ and has been handed down through the apostles.[34] He certainly considers himself to be following Paul in the way he reads Israel's history in the Old Testament. Paul, Origen asserts, understood the crossing of the Red Sea to point to baptism, the cloud leading the Israelites to be the Holy Spirit, and the rock which followed them to be Christ. Paul's interpretation should be a model applied to all Christian exegesis of Scripture.[35] Origen interprets the experience of the Israelites in Egypt using four primary symbols: Pharaoh represents the devil, Egypt stands for the world, the Israelite males represent the rational human faculty, and the Israelite females stand for the passionate side of human nature.[36] The last two symbols correspond with identifications Philo had made. Philo also treated Pharaoh and Egypt symbolically but did not give them precisely the same meaning that Origen gave them. Origen was working in the Alexandrian exegetical tradition in the way he understood the Old Testament.

Origen sees a kind of spiritual meta-narrative running throughout Scripture told sometimes in the narratives of things that happened and sometimes those that did not happen literally. If Paul, Origen argues, refers to an "Israel after the flesh," there must, then, also be an Israel after the spirit. The promises made to physical Israel must be spiritual and inapplicable to the historical Israelites. Paul's reference to a heavenly Jerusalem likewise suggests two Jerusalems. And if words referring to Israel and Jerusalem have a spiritual meaning, then so too must such words as Egypt, Babylon, and Tyre point to spiritual realities of a negative kind. The whole of Scripture narrates the spiritual drama of salvation in the symbols of the life of the physical Israel, Jesus, and the early Christians.[37]

One of the people who influenced Origen's manner of doing exegesis was a Jewish Christian in Alexandria whom Origen refers to simply as "the Hebrew." We do not know whether the man was someone under whom Origen studied formally, or whether he was simply someone Origen heard in the context of Christian discussions in Alexandria and who deeply impressed the young Origen. He appears to have been dead before Origen began his literary career, for Origen always refers to him in the past tense. Origen asserts, however, that it was from this man that he learned to apply to Scripture the principle of the scholars of the Museum that they called interpreting Homer by Homer. This principle meant that the way to understand an unclear passage in an author was to search in other passages in the same author's writings where he talked about the same subject or used the same vocabulary. This became a basic principle of Origen's exegetical method. Because he considered the Holy Spirit to be the author of all Scripture, Scripture's obscurities were to be solved by searching for similar topics and, especially, vocabulary in other passages throughout the Bible which could then be applied to the passage being studied. "The Hebrew," Origen tells us, taught this principle by means of a story about a house with many locked rooms. A key lies before each door but it is not the key to the adjacent door. To find the key to open Scripture's meaning one must search for similar words and ideas that are scattered throughout the Scriptures.[38]

How Origen ranged over Scripture using the "interpreting Homer by Homer" principle to weave a tapestry of spiritual meaning can be seen in the following example of his application of Zechariah 6:12 to a variety of texts. In the Septuagint the astronomical term *anatolē* (rising/the East) is applied to a person in Zechariah 6:12 in the words, "Behold a man, Rising (or the East) is his name." A common usage of this term in the Septuagint is to indicate the east, where the sun rises. Its application to a person in Zechariah 6:12 becomes the key to open the understanding of a number of Scriptures where reference is made to "the east." In the story of Gideon in Judges 6, where one of the nations is referred to as "the sons of the east," Origen suggests that the phrase must be understood in contrast to its opposite (which does not appear in the text of Judges), "sons of the west." The latter, he says, would have to mean "sons of darkness." Sons of the east, he suggests, would properly refer to those who have received the name of Christ for, he adds, "it is written of Christ, 'Behold a man, Rising (or the East) is his name.' Therefore, whoever has received the name of Christ is said to be a son of the East."[39] The appearance of the word 'east' in the Septuagint text of Judges led Origen's mind directly to Christ via Zechariah 6:12. In a homily in which he discusses Leviticus 16:14 – the Septuagint text refers to the priest sprinkling the blood of the sacrificial animal *eastward* on the mercy seat – Origen sees a reference to the mercy brought through Christ. It comes from the east, he says, "for there is a man from there whose name is Rising (or the East), who was made 'the mediator between God and humanity'."[40]

Origen's most celebrated commentary in antiquity, and perhaps ever, was his *Commentary on the Song of Songs*. Composed originally in ten books in the mid-third century when Origen was approximately fifty-five years old and master of his expositional techniques, his theological understanding, and spiritual discipline, it has been preserved in three books of Latin translation done by Rufinus in the early fifth century. Jerome praised the ten books of the original commentary in his well-known statement that Origen excelled all other authors in his other books, but in his *Commentary on the Song of Songs* he excelled even himself.[41] Origen reads the Song of Songs on three levels. At the literal level it is a drama about marriage written in the form of a wedding song sung by a bride to the groom. At the second level, the church is the bride, and at the third level the individual soul is the bride. Christ is the bridegroom on both of these levels of understanding, longed for corporately by the church and individually by the soul. A succinct example of the application of this approach to the text can be found in Origen's comments on the words of Song of Songs 1:4, "The King has brought me into his chamber." At the literal level the young woman is brought into the King's chamber and shown the royal treasures. At the other levels, and here Origen mentions both the church and the soul separately but joins them in the interpretation, it is the introduction of the soul or the church into what Paul called "the mind of Christ" where one experiences what "eye has not seen, nor ear heard."[42] This is what it means to be brought into the King's chamber.[43] The meaning Origen looks for and sets forth in his biblical commentaries is always the spiritual meaning of the text.

Origen's *On First Principles*

Origen's treatise *On First Principles*, or *Peri Archôn* in Greek, is the best known of all his numerous writings. It has been the basic text for the study of his thought since the fourth century and may be regarded as a convenient summary of his major teachings. It is, however, by no means a simple text.

On First Principles appears to have been an innovative departure so far as previous Christian writings are concerned. Earlier Christians had written letters, gospels, apocalypses, homilies, hymns, acts of apostles, treatises against heresies and against Jews, apologies, and commentaries on Scripture. While *On First Principles* sometimes attacks heresies and often engages in scriptural exegesis, it is neither an anti-heretical document nor is it a commentary. It attempts to set forth in a positive manner an understanding of what Origen considers to be the most important teachings of the Christian faith. Nevertheless, exactly how to classify it has been the subject of much modern scholarly debate.

Adolf Harnack considered Origen to have created Christian dogmatic theology in the *On First Principles*, constructed primarily "in opposition to the systems of the Greek philosophers and of the Christian Gnostics."[44] This view was perpetuated by the influential *Patrology* of Johannes Quasten who, following Harnack, called the *On First Principles* the first Christian systematic theology and said that "it stands in majestic isolation in the history of the early Church."[45] Berthold Altaner's equally well-known *Patrology* labeled the treatise "the first manual of dogmatics" but considered it to showcase "the erroneous doctrines" of Origen.[46] These discussions of *On First Principles* never questioned the four-book format in which we have the treatise today. The four books were considered to treat, respectively, the doctrines of God, the world, freedom, and revelation.[47]

A new approach to *On First Principles* was initiated by the work of Basilius Steidle who divided the work into three groupings each constructed around a discussion of the topics: Father, Son, Spirit, rational beings, and cosmos.[48] Marguerite Harl took up Steidle's suggestions and further refined them. She suggested that the *On First Principles* began as a series of independent lectures Origen had delivered and later brought together in a somewhat unified format.[49] The threefold division of Steidle, adopted by Harl, is followed in the Sources chrétiennes edition of the treatise edited by H. Crouzel and M. Simonetti.[50] On this plan the treatise is divided up as follows: the preface, which sets out the main topics of the apostolic preaching; a series of treatises (books 1.1–2.3); a second series of treatises (books 2.4–4.3); and a summary surveying the topics discussed in the two previous series (book 4.4).

While modern scholars differ on the precise genre to which *On First Principles* may belong and on the precise way to view the structure of its thought, there is no question concerning its importance for understanding either the mind of Origen or the history of Christian thought. Origen's *On First Principles* is a landmark in early Christian literature. It must be dealt with by anyone wanting to understand the development of early Christian theology.

On First Principles was written in Greek sometime between CE 220 and 231, before Origen left Alexandria for Caesarea.[51] The text is extant today only in a Latin translation produced by Rufinus in CE 397. The work was controversial from its inception. Some of the points set forth in the treatise may have been at the base of the dispute between Origen and the Alexandrian bishop Demetrius which resulted in Origen's move to Caesarea.

About 150 years after Origen's death many of the doctrines in *On First Principles* came under attack in the church. The first serious attack on *On First Principles* was made early in the fourth century by Methodius, bishop of Patara. In a treatise *On Things Created* he attacked Origen's cosmology, and in another work called *On the Resurrection* he attacked Origen's method of interpreting Scripture as well as his doctrine of the soul. Eustathius of Antioch also attacked Origen's biblical exegesis in the first quarter of the fourth century. Later in the fourth century the attack on Origen found new vigor in the work of Epiphanius, bishop of Salamis on Cyprus. Epiphanius took much of his early ammunition against Origen from Methodius. He went beyond Methodius, however, in attacking Origen's teachings about the nature of the Son and the Son's relation to the Father. In his old age Epiphanius took the battle to Palestine, a stronghold of those defending Origen's theology. There he encountered two friends, Rufinus, overseeing a monastery in Jerusalem, and Jerome, overseeing a monastery in Bethlehem. Both were admirers of Origen. Jerome yielded to Epiphanius's attack but Rufinus did not.

In CE 397 Rufinus returned to Italy, taking many Greek manuscripts with him. At the request of a friend, he translated Origen's *On First Principles* into Latin. In the preface to his translation Rufinus justifies his undertaking by citing the earlier translation of Origen's homilies on the Song of Songs into Latin by Jerome, and Jerome's indication that he wanted to translate more of Origen's works into Latin. Rufinus also noted that in translating some of Origen's other works which contained statements that would be offensive to the ears of fourth-century western orthodox Christians Jerome had emended these texts so that they would be in harmony with the later understanding of orthodoxy. Rufinus says that he followed Jerome in doing this, especially in those passages where Origen discusses the Trinity. In this same preface Rufinus also records his belief that disreputable persons had interpolated the writings of Origen with views that Origen himself had not held. Rufinus says that he has removed these interpolations and replaced them with Origen's true views which he has gleaned from other writings of Origen.

These remarks in Rufinus's preface infuriated Jerome who, by this time, under the influence of Epiphanius, had identified himself as an opponent of Origen's theology. Jerome then produced what he refers to as a literal translation of On First Principles into Latin to show how heretical the work really was in contrast to the way that Rufinus had presented it. This translation was sent to a friend, was never circulated, and, consequently, was lost. It would have been a valuable text to compare with the version we possess from Rufinus. All that remains of Jerome's translation are a few renderings in his letter to Avitus.[52]

There is no extant direct manuscript tradition of On First Principles in Greek. The fourth-century Cappadocian bishops, Basil of Caesarea and Gregory of Nazianzus, friends of Origen's theology, preserved Greek excerpts of On First Principles 3.1 and 4.1–3 in their treatise called the Philocalia. The only other reports of On First Principles in Greek are some brief statements in the more dubious sources of attacks made on Origen's theology by his enemies in the sixth century CE.

The text that we have to work with of this most important work of Origen must, consequently, be treated with some caution. Earlier scholars of the twentieth century were very skeptical about the trustworthiness of Rufinus's work as a translator.[53] The attitude today is more favorable to Rufinus and to the overall reliability of the text he produced. Perhaps the remark of Henry Chadwick at the conclusion of his comparison of the Greek fragments of Origen's Commentary on Romans with Rufinus's translation of those same passages can be applied to On First Principles as well: "The voice is the voice of Origen, even though the hands are the hands of Rufinus."[54]

What did Origen set out to do in his composition of On First Principles? Clues for an answer to that question have been searched for in the title and in the preface. It has been noted that On First Principles was a fairly common title of philosophical works in the Platonic schools, where it referred to the highest ontological principles. These principles were matter, ideas, and God. A corresponding series for Origen, it is suggested, may have been God, rational beings, and matter which correspond roughly to the subjects discussed in book 1 of On First Principles.[55] Some have attempted to understand On First Principles purely within the framework of the philosophical school traditions of the second and third centuries CE.[56] It has been noted, on the other hand, that Clement of Alexandria had planned, but never carried out, the composition of a work On First Principles. This has been used to argue that the title points to a theological rather than a philosophical basis for the book and to suggest that Origen may have seen his work as the completion of Clement's planned but unfulfilled theological program. On this approach to the understanding of the title, the principles are the three persons of the Trinity who are discussed in the first three chapters of *On First Principles* and referred to throughout the work.[57]

Origen's preface to the treatise holds more promise of pointing to what he wanted to accomplish in the work, though there is no unambiguous answer there either. We may be helped in this endeavor by considering the ancient rhetorical practice of putting the gist of a speech or drama in the first sentence or two of the document so that the hearer or reader would know the subject matter in advance and thus be enabled to follow the speech or drama better.[58] Origen begins *On First Principles* by emphasizing that truth resides in Jesus Christ. This truth has the practical goal of calling people to goodness and blessedness. The knowledge of this truth in Christ is found only in his words and teachings. These words and teachings, however, are not limited to the words of the incarnate Christ. They are also found in Moses and the prophets who preceded Christ because Christ, as the Word of God, was in them, and they are found in the teachings of the apostles in whom Christ continued to speak after his ascension.[59] This opening paragraph lays down the following base on which the treatise is founded: ultimate truth, which is the source of human goodness and blessedness, is to be found in Christ's teachings. These teachings are present in some very specific written documents: the writings of Moses and the prophets, the Gospels, and the epistles and, perhaps, acts of the apostles.

After setting forth the identification of Christ with the truth, Origen then poses the problem that he feels he must address. Many who profess to believe in this truth disagree with one another and with earlier Christians on major points of the Christian teaching: on God, Christ, the Holy Spirit, and created heavenly beings. Only that, he insists, can be considered to be the truth which has been handed down from the apostles and continues to be proclaimed in the churches.[60]

While the composition of *On First Principles* cannot be dated precisely, it is certain that it was begun after Origen had made the trip to Rome in the time of Zephyrinus to which Eusebius refers.[61] Eusebius relates that Origen made this trip because of his high regard for the antiquity of the Roman Church. The time of Zephyrinus, however, was the time of the intense disagreements in Rome over the modalistic monarchian issue involving Zephyrinus, Callistus, and Hippolytus.[62] This visit must have shaken any idealistic views Origen had about unanimity of Christian belief. His own home city of Alexandria with its numerous varieties of Christian faith would have also provided him with enough examples for his point about disagreement on major beliefs.

Origen proposes that, in light of all the disagreements, a "fixed boundary line and clear rule" (*certam lineam manifestamque regulam*) needs to be established in relation to the major teachings of the faith.[63] These major teachings of the faith were expressed, Origen says, clearly so that all could understand them. Origen then lists ten doctrines related to God, Christ Jesus, the Holy Spirit, the soul, the resurrection, free will, the existence of the devil and his angels, the beginning and end of this world, the Scriptures, and angels.[64]

The fact that Origen considers his list to represent the most basic teachings of the apostles that everyone should believe suggests something more than a private list of doctrines that he has decided on himself. This list of doctrines must represent the rule of faith used by the Alexandrian Church and, consequently, a significant part of the curriculum of the catechetical school in Alexandria with which Origen had been associated for some time before he wrote *On First Principles*. It is significantly more extensive than other rules of faith we know from the late second and early third centuries found in the works of Irenaeus and Tertullian. These are devoted primarily to the doctrines of God and of Christ. Occasionally the end, the resurrection of the flesh, and judgment are mentioned in these rules of faith.[65] In a later list of basic Christian beliefs which Origen includes in the last book of his *Commentary on John* written several years after he had left Alexandria, besides the three statements about the Father, Son, and Holy Spirit, he includes again statements about free will, and rewards and punishment as well.[66]

Origen closes his preface by asserting that anyone wanting to produce a coherent doctrinal system must use the points he has set forth as "first principles (*elementis*) and basic points (*fundamentis*)." In this manner

> he will discover the truth about each particular point and so will produce …
> a single body of doctrine, with the aid of such illustrations and declarations
> as he shall find in the holy scriptures and of such conclusions as he shall
> ascertain to follow logically from them when rightly understood.
>
> (Origen, *On First Principles* 1.Pref.10)[67]

The insistence on the coherence of the unified body of doctrine with the teachings of Scripture should be noted in light of what Origen said at the beginning of the preface concerning the truth residing in the teachings of Christ which are to be found in what we would call the Old and New Testament scriptures. The final words about the Scriptures being rightly understood point ahead to the fourth book of *On First Principles* where Origen discusses the hermeneutic by which the Scriptures are to be "rightly understood."[68] It would appear that Origen is indicating in these words that he intends, in the present work, to set forth this unified body of Christian doctrine based on the Scriptures "rightly understood."

In *On First Principles* 4.2.7, where he is discussing how to understand the Scriptures, he presents what is virtually a summary of the same doctrines set forth in the preface as the teachings the Holy Spirit has expressed figuratively in the narrative of Scripture. He notes, however, that his list here is not complete, for he says it was these "and similar topics" that the Holy Spirit wanted to teach.[69] The list of topics given in the preface is what is covered in the contents of the treatise, though not always in the order of their appearance in the preface nor always completely in one section. When Origen begins his final recapitulation section he indicates that his preceding discussions have not been completely systematic. He says he will now pull together what he has discussed "here and there" (*sparsim*) in the treatise.[70] Here again the general points discussed correspond with the list in the preface and with the contents of the treatise, but not perfectly.

The final sentence of the treatise echoes the closing words of the preface: "Our belief, therefore, on the questions dealt with herein, and on all that follows logically from them, must be framed in accordance with the principles (*formam*) explained above."[71] The evidence, it seems to me, suggests that by "first principles" Origen intended the basic points he enumerates in the preface as the main points of the apostolic preaching. In *On First Principles* he has attempted to unify the Christian understanding of these points by interpreting and illustrating them from Scripture read by means of the hermeneutic he sets forth in book 4.1–3, a hermeneutic which he also considers to have apostolic roots.

Origen and the spiritual life

Jean Daniélou once observed that Origen was "a man of deep spirituality," and noted that because Origen considered "the transition from the letter of Scripture to its spirit" to correspond to a similar transition in the reader of Scripture from carnality to spirituality, "history, theology, and spirituality are all interwoven in his work in a striking unity."[72] Origen would not have recognized the distinctions that we make between biblical study, theology, and spirituality. As Andrew Louth has said, "Understanding Scripture is not for Origen simply an academic exercise but a religious experience."[73] For Origen, biblical study and the theology that arises out of it translate directly into the life one lives. Origen read his own life and those of his fellow Christians into the biblical text.

He believed, following Paul, that the Christian is engaged in a cosmic struggle against "spiritual forces of evil."[74] These evil spiritual forces take on life in the stories of the Old Testament which speak of Israel's departure from Egypt, its struggles to survive in the wilderness, and its battles to capture and control the promised land. The enemies of Israel, the kings who opposed the people of God, and the fortified cities that had to be overcome are all interiorized in Origen's depiction of the Christian struggle. The Israelites' slaughter of all the inhabitants of Ai is understood as the Christian's annihilation of evil thoughts and words which, if left to live, will lead to sin.[75] Joshua's conquest of the numerous cities in southern Canaan speaks of the work of the Lord Jesus who casts out the hostile powers who previously ruled in our souls.[76] The stories of the wars in the Old Testament have been preserved for the sake of Christians because they are figures of the spiritual wars that the church must fight. Consequently,

> we may consider, by means of those nations that fought visibly against physical Israel, how great are the swarms of opposing powers from among the spiritual races that are called "spiritual wickedness in the heavens," and that stir up wars against the Lord's Church, which is the true Israel.
>
> (Origen, *Homilies on Joshua* 15.1)[77]

These "wars" between the Christian and the cosmic forces of evil could become more than mental and emotional struggles within the Christian in Origen's time. They could also take on physical manifestations in the efforts of the state to control or eliminate the Christian witness. Origen's spirituality embraced the willingness to die as a martyr if that should be necessary. When his friends Ambrose and Protoctetus were threatened in the persecution of the emperor Maximin, Origen wrote his *Exhortation to Martyrdom* to encourage them to faithfulness. In various places throughout the treatise he reads his friends into the text of Scripture. When they were still catechists, he says, they declared with the Israelites, "Far be it from us that we should forsake the Lord, to serve other gods. For the Lord our God, He is God, who brought us and our fathers out of Egypt … and preserved us in all the way that we went."[78] The actions of the emperor Maximin become those of Nebuchadnezzar who threatened to throw the three Hebrew young men into the furnace. "Even now Nebuchadnezzar says the same thing to us, the true Hebrews in exile from our homeland."[79] In the conclusion of his treatise Origen lifts the impending martyrdom of his friends up into the story of Jesus himself and suggests, on the basis of John's allusion to Jesus' death as an exaltation, that the martyr's death glorifies God.[80]

Origen did not, however, consider the spiritual life to be one continuous struggle against spiritual powers of evil. Victories won in these struggles do produce peace for the soul to advance to a love relationship with Christ. It is this relationship that Origen expounds in his commentary and homilies on the Song of Songs. The Song of Songs is not, however, for those at the beginning of the spiritual life. The study of the Song of Songs is to be taken up only by the advanced.[81] Here the spiritual life is depicted as the love and longing of the church or the individual Christian, the bride, for Christ, the bridegroom. The person who attains this level falls "deeply in love" with the Word of God and "receives from the Word Himself a … wound of love."[82]

This level of spirituality can only be reached by those who know how rightly to read the Scriptures. Commenting on Song of Songs 2:9, "Look, there he stands behind our wall, gazing in at the windows, looking through the lattice,"[83] Origen says that the wall is the Old Testament behind which Christ stood before he came to the church. He showed himself "through the windows of the Law and the Prophets." But now he calls the church to come forth from the house of the Old Testament and to advance "from the letter to the spirit," for unless she does this "she cannot be united with her Bridegroom, nor share the company of Christ. He calls her, therefore, … to come out from carnal things to spiritual, from visible to invisible, from the Law to the Gospel."[84] Origen certainly does not mean by this that the church should abandon the Old Testament and take up only the New Testament. He is referring to how the church must read both Testaments. All Scripture must be read spiritually, not literally. This spirituality is anchored in the hermeneutic and theology Origen laid out systematically in his *On First Principles*.[85] As Rowan Williams has said, in Origen's spirituality "[i]ntellect and heart are not separable."[86]

Further reading

Primary sources

Origen, *On First Principles*, trans. G. W. Butterworth, Gloucester, MA: Peter Smith, 1973, *Commentary on the Gospel According to John*, trans. R. E. Heine, The Fathers of the Church: New Series 80 (Books 1–10), 89 (Books 13–32), Washington, DC: Catholic University of America Press, 1989, 1993, *Contra Celsum*, trans.

H. Chadwick, Cambridge: Cambridge University Press, 1965, *The Song of Songs Commentary and Homilies*, trans. R. P. Lawson, Ramsey, NJ: Newman, 1956, *The Commentaries of Origen and Jerome on St. Paul's Epistle to the Ephesians*, trans. R. E. Heine, Oxford Early Christian Studies, Oxford: Oxford University Press, 2002.

Secondary sources

H. Crouzel, *Origen*, trans. A. S. Worrall, Edinburgh: T&T Clark, 1989.

C. Kannengieser and W. L. Petersen (eds), *Origen of Alexandria: His World and His Legacy*, South Bend, IN: University of Notre Dame Press, 1988.

J. A. McGuckin (ed.), *The Westminster Handbook to Origen*, Louisville: Westminster John Knox, 2004.

Notes

1   For the ambiguity see Eusebius's accounts in *Ecclesiastical History* 6.39.5; 7.1.

2   Eusebius, *Ecclesiastical History* 6.1–2.6.

3   Eusebius, *Ecclesiastical History* 6.19.1–9.

4   Eusebius, *Ecclesiastical History* 6.2.15–3.1.

5   Eusebius, *Ecclesiastical History* 6.2.7–11.

6   Eusebius, *Ecclesiastical History* 6.14.8–9; 6.19.11–14.

7   See Origen, *On First Principles* 1.3.4; 4.3.14; *Commentary on John* 1.215; *The Philocalia of Origen* 2.3. For a fuller list of texts where "the Hebrew" is mentioned see G. Bardy, "Les traditions juives dans l'oeuvre d'Origène," *Revue Biblique* 34, 1925, pp. 217–52.

8   Eusebius, *Ecclesiastical History* 6.3.1–3.

9   Eusebius, *Ecclesiastical History* 6.21.3–4.

10 Eusebius, *Ecclesiastical History* 6.15.

11 Origen, *Commentary on John* 6.8–11.

12 Alexander of Aphrodisias, *Alexander of Aphrodisias On Aristotle's* Metaphysics *1*, trans. W. E. Dooley, Ancient Commentators on Aristotle, London: Duckworth, 1989, p. 2.

13 Eusebius, *Ecclesiastical History* 6.32.3.

14 Jerome, *Apology against Rufinus* 2.22.

15 Jerome, *Epistle* 33.4.

16 Eusebius, *Ecclesiastical History* 6.13.2.

17 Jerome, *Lives of Illustrious Men* 61.

18 Origen, *Commentary on Matthew* 15.3; see also *Against Celsus* 4.51; 6.21. Texts cited by D. T. Runia, "Philo and Origen: A Preliminary Survey," in D. T. Runia (ed.), *Philo and the Church Fathers*, Supplements to Vigiliae Christianae 32, Leiden: Brill, 1995, pp. 117–25 (esp. 120).

19 D. T. Runia, "Philo of Alexandria," in J. A. McGuckin (ed.), *The Westminster Handbook to Origen*, Louisville: Westminster John Knox, 2004, pp. 169–71 (esp. 170).

20 See R. E. Heine, "The Introduction to Origen's *Commentary on John* compared with the Introductions to the Ancient Philosophical Commentaries on Aristotle," in G. Dorival and A. Le Boulluec (eds), *Origeniana Sexta*, Leuven: Peeters, 1995, pp. 3–12.

21 J. Mansfeld, *Prolegomena: Questions to be Settled before the Study of an Author, or a Text*, Leiden: Brill, 1994, pp. 26, 98; Origen, *Commentary on John* 1.88.

22 Origen, *Commentary on the Song of Songs*, Prologue 1.8.

23 This treatise will be discussed more generally in the next section.

24 Origen, *On First Principles* 4.1.1–7; 4.2.7, 9.

25 Origen, *On First Principles* 4.2.7; cf. 1.Pref.4–7.

26 John 4:14 (New Revised Standard Version).

27 Origen, *Commentary on John* 13.37–58, my italics; cf. 13.61; trans. R. E. Heine, *Origen Commentary on the Gospel according to John Books 13–32*, The Fathers of the Church: A New Translation 89, Washington, DC: The Catholic University of America Press, 1993, pp. 76–81.

28 Origen, *Against Celsus* 7.60; trans. H. Chadwick, *Origen: Contra Celsum*, Cambridge: Cambridge University Press, 1965, pp. 445–6.

29 Origen, *On First Principles* 4.3.4.
30 Origen, *On First Principles* 4.3.2.
31 Origen, *On First Principles* 4.3.1.
32 Origen, *Commentary on John* 10.18–20.
33 Origen, *On First Principles* 4.3.5.
34 Origen, *On First Principles* 4.2.2.
35 1 Cor. 10:1–4; Origen, *Homilies on Exodus* 5.1, *Commentary on John* 6.227.
36 See Origen, *Homilies on Exodus* 2.
37 Origen, *On First Principles* 4.3.6–14.
38 *The Philocalia of Origen* 2.3.
39 Origen, *Homilies on Judges* 8.1.
40 Origen, *Homilies on Leviticus* 9.10.
41 Jerome, Prologue to his translation of Origen, *Homilies on the Song of Songs.*
42 1 Cor. 2:16, 9.
43 Origen, *Commentary on the Song of Songs* 1.5.2–4.
44 A. Harnack, *History of Dogma*, vol. 2, translated from the third German edition by N. Buchanan, New York: Dover, 1961, pp. 332–4.
45 J. Quasten, *The Ante-Nicene Literature after Irenaeus*, vol. 2 of *Patrology*, 4 vols, Westminster, MD: Newman, 1950; repr. Westminster, MD: Christian Classics, 1986, p. 57.
46 B. Altaner, *Patrology*, 2nd edn, trans. H. C. Graef, New York: Herder & Herder, 1961, p. 228.
47 Paul Kübel, "Zum Aufbau von Origenes' De Principiis," *Vigiliae Christianae* 25, 1971, 31.
48 B. Steidle, "Neue Untersuchungen zu Origenes' Περὶ αρχῶν," *Zeitschrift für die neutestamentliche Wissenschaft und die Kunde der älteren Kirche* 40, 1941, pp. 236ff. summarized in P. Kübel, "Zum Aufbau von Origenes' De Principiis," p. 31.
49 M. Harl, "Recherches sur le περὶ αρχῶν d'Origène en vue d'une nouvelle édition," *Studia Patristica* 3, Texte und Untersuchungen 78, Berlin, 1961, pp. 57–67. See also M. Harl, "Structure et cohérence du Peri Archon," in H. Crouzel, G. Lomiento, and J. Rius-Camps (eds), *Origeniana: Premier colloque international des études origéniennes (Montserrat, 18–21 septembre 1973)*, Quaderni di "Vetera Christianorum" 12, Bari: Istituto di Letteratura Cristiana Antica, 1975, pp. 11–32.
50 H. Crouzel and M. Simonetti (eds), *Origène traité des principes*, 5 vols, Sources chrétiennes 252, 253, 268, 269, 312, Paris: Cerf, 1978, 1980, 1984.
51 L. Lies, *Origenes' "Peri Archon,"* Darmstadt: Wissenschaftliche Buchgesellschaft, 1992, p. 7; Eusebius, *Ecclesiastical History* 6.24.
52 Jerome, *Epistle* 124.
53 See, for example, E. de Faye, *Origène sa vie, son oeuvre, sa pensée*, 3 vols, Bibliothèque de l'école des hautes études 37, 43, 44, Paris: Éditions Ernest Leroux, 1923, 1927, 1928.
54 H. Chadwick, "Rufinus and the Tura Papyrus of Origen's Commentary on Romans," *Journal of Theological Studies* 10, 1959, p. 25.
55 H. Görgemanns and H. Karpp, *Origenes vier Bücher von den Prinzipien*, Darmstadt: Wissenschaftliche Buchgesellschaft, 1976, p. 79.
56 See, for example, H. Koch, *Pronoia und Paideusis*, Berlin and Leipzig: de Gruyter, 1932; R. M. Berchman, *From Philo to Origen*, Brown Judaic Studies 69, Chico, CA: Scholars, 1984.
57 C. Kannengiesser, "Divine Trinity and the Structure of Peri Archon," in C. Kannengiesser and W. L. Petersen (eds), *Origen of Alexandria: His World and His Legacy*, Notre Dame, IN: University of Notre Dame Press, 1988, pp. 239–46; see also Crouzel and Simonetti, *Origène traité*, vol. 1, pp. 13–14.
58 Aristotle, *Rhetoric* 3.14.6 (1415a); see R. E. Heine, *Gregory of Nyssa's Treatise on the Inscriptions of the Psalms*, Oxford: Clarendon, 1995, pp. 30–2.
59 Origen, *On First Principles* 1.Pref.1.
60 Origen, *On First Principles* 1.Pref.2.
61 Eusebius, *Ecclesiastical History* 6.14.10.
62 See R. E. Heine, "The Christology of Callistus," *Journal of Theological Studies* 49, 1998, pp. 56–91.
63 Origen, *On First Principles* 1.Pref.2.
64 Cf. Harl, "Structure et cohérence du Peri Archon," pp. 11–32, who lists nine doctrines. She omits the final point on angels.

65 The rules of faith are found in Irenaeus, *Against Heresies* 1.10.3, 1.21.1, 3.4.2; Tertullian, *The Veiling of Virgins* 1, *Prescription against Heresies* 13.1–6, and *Against Praxeas* 2.1–2.

66 Origen, *Commentary on John* 32.187–93.

67 Trans. G. W. Butterworth, *Origen On First Principles*, Gloucester, MA: Peter Smith, 1973, p. 6.

68 See the discussion of book 4 in the above section, "Origen as a Biblical Commentator."

69 Origen, *On First Principles* 4.2.8.

70 Origen, *On First Principles* 4.4.1. In the Greek fragment from Marcellus cited as a parallel to Rufinus's text of these opening words it says that a few things omitted in the discussion of the Father, Son, and Holy Spirit will be treated.

71 Origen, *On First Principles* 4.4.10; trans. Butterworth, *Origen On First Principles*, p. 328.

72 J. Daniélou, *Gospel Message and Hellenistic Culture*, trans. J. A. Baker, London: Darton, Longman & Todd; Philadelphia: Westminster, 1973, p. 274.

73 A. Louth, *The Origins of the Christian Mystical Tradition*, Oxford: Clarendon, 1981, p. 64.

74 Eph. 6:12 (New Revised Standard Version). See Origen, *On First Principles* 3.2; R. E. Heine, *The Commentaries of Origen and Jerome on St Paul's Epistle to the Ephesians*, Oxford: Oxford University Press, 2002, pp. 66–71.

75 Origen, *Homilies on Joshua* 8.7.

76 Origen, *Homilies on Joshua* 13.1.

77 Trans. B. J. Bruce, *Origen's Homilies on Joshua*, The Fathers of the Church: New Translation 105, Washington, DC: The Catholic University of America Press, 2002, pp. 138–9.

78 Josh. 24:16–17; Origen, *Exhortation to Martyrdom* 17; trans. R. Greer, *Origen: An Exhortation to Martyrdom, Prayer, First Principles: Book IV, Prologue to the Commentary on the Song of Songs, Homily XXVII on Numbers*, New York: Paulist, 1979, p. 53.

79 Origen, *Exhortation to Martyrdom* 33; trans. Greer, *Origen*, p. 63.

80 John 12:32; Origen, *Exhortation to Martyrdom* 50.

81 Origen, *Commentary on the Song of Songs* Prologue.1.4–6.

82 Origen, *Commentary on the Song of Songs* Prologue.2.17.

83 New Revised Standard Version.

84 Origen, *Commentary on the Song of Songs* 3.14.20–22; trans. R. P. Lawson, *Origen: The Song of Songs Commentary and Homilies*, Ancient Christian Writers 26, Ramsey, NJ: Newman, 1956, p. 235.

85 See the discussions above in the two preceding sections.

86 R. Williams, *Christian Spirituality*, Atlanta, GA: John Knox, 1979, p. 38. See also L. Brésard, H. Crouzel, and M. Borret, *Origène commentaire sur le Cantique des Cantiques* I, Sources chrétiennes 376, Paris: Cerf, 1991, pp. 51–2.

12

GNOSIS AND NAG HAMMADI

Anne McGuire

Introduction

Introductory remarks on "gnosis" and "Gnosticism"

"Gnosticism" is a modern European term that first appears in the seventeenth-century writings of Cambridge Platonist Henry More (1614–87). For More, "Gnosticism" designates one of the earliest Christian heresies, connected to controversies addressed in Revelation 2:18–29 and in his own day.[1] The term "gnosis," on the other hand, is one of several ancient Greek nouns for "knowledge," specifically experiential or esoteric knowledge based on direct experience, which can be distinguished from mere perception, understanding, or skill. For Plato and other ancient thinkers, "gnosis" refers to that knowledge which enables perception of the underlying structures of reality, Being itself, or the divine.[2] Such gnosis was valued highly in many early Christian communities,[3] yet the claims of some early Christians to possess gnosis came under suspicion and critique in the post-Pauline letter of 1 Timothy, which urges its readers to "avoid the profane chatter and contradictions of falsely so-called *gnosis*."[4] With this began the polemical contrast between "false gnosis" and "true faith."

It is this polemical sense of "false gnosis" that Bishop Irenaeus of Lyons took up in the title of his major anti-heretical work: *Refutation and Overthrow of Falsely So-Called Gnosis*, or *Against Heresies*, written c. CE 180.[5] Irenaeus used 1 Timothy's phrase not only to designate his opponents' gnosis as false, but, even more important, to construct a broad category of classification, a "Tree of Gnosis," which could be traced back to the "arch-heretic" Simon Magus.[6] In this sense, "Gnosis" refers to a wide variety of "false" thinkers and groups with a common parentage: the Simonians, as well as "a multitude of Gnostics," called "Barbelo-Gnostics, Ophites, and Cainites," Irenaeus regards as "the source and root," "the mothers, fathers, and ancestors" of his chief opponents, the Valentinians.[7] With this adaptation of "falsely so-called gnosis" into the "Tree of Gnosis," Irenaeus established the groundwork for both the pejorative and collective uses of "Gnosis" and its modern derivative, "Gnosticism."

For those who employ the category today, "Gnosticism" is most often defined as a religious movement that flourished from the second to fourth centuries CE in Jewish,

Christian, and pagan forms, and shared three essential features:[8] (1) a religious system of thought emphasizing the salvific power of *gnosis*, a secret knowledge about the divine, the cosmos, and/or the true self, conveyed by revelation, contemplation, and/ or ritual experience; (2) a radical dualism contrasting the superior realm of the divine to the lower realm of the cosmos and its creator; and (3) extensive and elaborate patterns of myth-making, or *mythopoeia*.

Serious challenges to such definitions of "Gnosticism" have been raised in recent years, most pointedly by Michael A. Williams and Karen L. King,[9] who point out that the diverse range of evidence does not fit into such definitions. While some individuals and groups undoubtedly claimed to possess "gnosis" and thus called themselves "knowers" or "*Gnostikoi*,"[10] the category of "Gnosticism" is an artificial construct, based on the anti-heretical writers' efforts to unify their opponents under a single pejorative category ("falsely so-called Gnosis"), that carries with it a set of misleading implications. These include the tendency to: generalize from a single element or sample to all representatives of the category; emphasize the negative, unattractive, immoral, or false characteristics the heresiologists sought to expose and refute; unify many varieties of thought into one mythological system; and think of "Gnosticism" almost exclusively as a "Christian heresy."[11]

As a result of these observations, several alternatives to traditional conceptions of "Gnosticism" have emerged in recent scholarship. These include: abandonment of the term altogether as a hopelessly outdated and distorting category;[12] redefinition of "Gnosticism" in a more narrow sense to designate a specific group whose members used the self-designation "*Gnostikoi*" ("knowers") and/or "*gnostike hairesis*" ("gnostic sect");[13] acceptance of "Gnosticism," "Gnostic," and/or "Gnosis" as heuristic categories designed to highlight shared patterns of thought across religious texts and traditions. I have chosen to avoid "Gnosticism," but to employ "Gnosis" and "Gnostic" in this third sense, as heuristic devices to designate not a single religious movement, but a broad range of religious systems with a shared emphasis on the saving significance of esoteric religious knowledge or "gnosis." In my view, it is crucial to recognize the variety of such "gnosis-centered" traditions, but equally important to consider individual examples as distinct manifestations of a larger pattern of "gnosis-centered" religious thought. To recognize such a larger pattern of thought is not equivalent to constructing a single religious movement called "Gnosticism." It is important to acknowledge that such gnosis-centered patterns of thought did not exist in a vacuum or ethereal world of ideas, but in distinct social worlds, among human individuals and communities, both within early Christianity and in the larger cultural worlds of late antiquity.

The sources: anti-heretical writings and the texts of Nag Hammadi

Before the discovery of the Nag Hammadi library in 1945, the available evidence for the religious thought of ancient "Gnosis" derived almost exclusively from reports and excerpts found in the writings of the heresiologists, especially Irenaeus, Hippolytus, Clement, Tertullian, and Epiphanius. In the course of describing their opponents' beliefs and practices, these writers often provide valuable information, such as the names of individual teachers, schools, and sects; detailed accounts of their teachings; and occasional reports of social organization and ritual practice. Yet as valuable as these contemporary reports are, they must be seen within the context of the heresi-ologists' polemical goals which were neither to document nor illuminate the religious systems of their opponents but rather to undermine them by exposing their diversity and "error."

With the discovery of the Nag Hammadi library in 1945, a large and rich new body of primary-source material became available for investigation, but these sources, written by and for insiders, have proved challenging to understand,[14] and the evidence of the anti-heretical writers has remained a valuable resource, even as it has continued to complicate the problem of defining "Gnosis" and "Gnosticism."[15] Critical analysis of the Nag Hammadi texts, and the relation of their religious perspectives to those who produced and read them, remains one of the most challenging and important tasks in the study of early Christianity and other ancient religious traditions. While the identity of those who produced the Nag Hammadi texts remains uncertain, there has emerged a general recognition that at least four major types of gnosis-centered thought can be distinguished. This essay treats the first three of these "types," defined as follows:[16]

1 **Thomasine Christianity**, represented chiefly by the *Gospel of Thomas* and the *Book of Thomas the Contender*.[17] While generally excluded from the category of "Gnosticism,"[18] the *Gospel of Thomas* is included here because it exhibits a religious perspective in which "gnosis" figures prominently.
2 **The "Sethian," Barbelo-Gnostic, or classic "Gnostic" system**, represented by the *Apocryphon of John*, the *Hypostasis of the Archons*, and several other Nag Hammadi texts, as well as Irenaeus, *Against Heresies* 1.29; Epiphanius, *Refutation of All Heresies* 26, 39, and 40; and related heresiological reports.[19]
3 **The Valentinian tradition**, known from the reports of Justin, Irenaeus, and later heresiologists as one of the leading Christian varieties of "Gnosis"; the evidence for the Valentinian tradition includes the fragments of Valentinus himself, Ptolemy's *Letter to Flora*, and *Excerpts of Theodotus*, as well as several Nag Hammadi texts, including the *Gospel of Truth*, the *Gospel of Philip*, and the *Tripartite Tractate*.[20]

I approach these as distinct types of Christian Gnosis that exhibit shared patterns of thought across a varied body of material. In what follows, I offer a brief description of each type, and focus on the conceptions of the divine and of the processes of creation and redemption in one representative example of each group.[21]

1 Thomasine Christianity: the *Gospel of Thomas*

The *Gospel of Thomas* is perhaps the most widely known text of the Nag Hammadi library. This is in no small part because it is a sayings gospel that has proved extremely valuable to the study of Jesus' sayings in the New Testament Gospels.[22] It presents the teachings of Jesus in ways that are both similar to and yet surprisingly different from the canonical Gospels. Many sayings in the *Gospel of Thomas* are extremely close to apocalyptic and wisdom traditions of the Q tradition.[23] Others reflect esoteric Jewish and early Christian traditions of Genesis interpretation, while several exhibit a more mystical theology and realized eschatology than those found in other known Jesus traditions.[24]

Valuable as the *Gospel of Thomas* has been for comparative gospel studies, it has also proved to be an extremely valuable text in its own right, especially for the evidence it provides of a distinctively Thomasine variety of Christianity, which is widely regarded as having its origins in the region of Syria and north-west Mesopotamia, and as having a distinctively ascetic character.[25] The gospel's overarching theological perspective is centered around the promise of salvation through a process of seeking, finding, and understanding the message of Jesus. Unlike the canonical Gospels, which blend Jesus' sayings into a narrative account, the *Gospel of Thomas* is a collection of sayings with no narrative or historical frame. For it, the significance of Jesus resides not in the events of his life, death, or resurrection, but rather in the meaning of his sayings.

The *Gospel of Thomas* opens with a saying that acknowledges the obscurity of the sayings and places salvific importance on finding their *hermeneia* or meaning:

> These are the hidden sayings that the living Jesus spoke and Didymus Judas Thomas wrote down. And he said, "Whoever finds the meaning (*hermeneia*) of these sayings will not taste death."
>
> (*Gospel of Thomas*, Prologue and Logion 1)[26]

Finding the *hermeneia* of Jesus' utterances, overcoming the state of "death," seeing the Light,[27] returning to the beginning, entering the Kingdom, and reigning are among the many images that the gospel employs to describe salvation: "Let one who seeks not stop seeking until one finds; and upon finding, one will be disturbed; and being disturbed, one will be astounded, and will reign over all."[28] While seeking and finding may refer to the *hermeneia* or meaning of Jesus' sayings, the ambiguous wording of this and other sayings in the *Gospel of Thomas* allows the reader to consider other hidden treasures that can be discovered through the interpretation of Jesus' teachings. These include the Kingdom of God, the identity of "the Living Jesus," the nature of the true self, and the divine itself.[29] Finding, seeing, or knowing these is closely connected to the gospel's images of salvation and becoming like the Living Jesus. Indeed, Logion 108 proclaims that "He who will drink from my mouth will become like me."[30]

In various passages, the *Gospel of Thomas* expresses its religious perspectives in binary oppositions or dualisms. These include Life and Death,[31] Spirit and Flesh,[32] Light and Darkness,[33] and Kingdom and Cosmos. Several sayings suggest that such opposed pairs represent two hierarchically ordered realms or states of existence and two ways of being human. It has been suggested that the thought patterns of the gospel, including its dualisms, may reflect traditions of Genesis interpretation that developed a distinctive Adamic typology in relation to baptismal practice and visionary mysticism.[34] This typology may have been based upon a mythic narrative of creation and redemption that involves three stages:[35] (1) a state of perfection in which the Spirit/primordial Adam existed as Light in perfect unity with the divine; (2) a moment of corruption or loss, in which the Light Adam is cast into darkness/the body/the cosmos; and (3) a salvific restoration or return to the beginning, in which the "Light" of Genesis 1:3 or the primordial human being of Genesis 1:26–27 is recovered within the self and the individual is redemptively transformed.

Within this mythic framework, the *Gospel of Thomas* may be said to reflect the notion that ritual initiation or visionary ascent effects a restoration of the primordial human being, the "Adam of great power and wealth," "the one who came into being before coming into being."[36] Recovering this primordial "Adam before Adam" is compared to standing at the beginning and knowing the end.[37] Paradoxically, the newly redeemed human being shares an identity with the original Adam, the primordial self which existed from before the creation of the world, an uncreated, divine self hidden within or behind the visible self.[38] Restoring or being transformed into this pre-created self may also figure into the interpretation of Logion 22, which compares nursing infants to those who enter the Kingdom. In response to his disciples' question whether they too must become "little ones," Jesus replies that they will enter the Kingdom when a series of transformations and substitutions have taken place:

> Jesus said to them, "When you make the two one and when you make the inside like the outside and the outside like the inside, and the above like the below, and when you make the male (*hooyt*) and the female (*shime*) into a single one, so that the male will not be male nor the female be female, when you make eyes in place of an eye, and a hand in place of a hand, and a foot in place of a foot, an image in place of an image, then you will enter the Kingdom."
>
> (*Gospel of Thomas*, Logion 22)[39]

With each of these images, something new comes into being, replacing what was: duality becomes unity, as two become one; opposing spatial categories undergo a reciprocal or two-way exchange ("inside–outside," "above–below"); the two genders become a single one;[40] new body parts (eyes, hand, foot) replace old; and a new image is made in place of another image. The old, created self gives way to a new self, a new identity or way of being human, for female and male alike.[41]

To return to the state of the pure Light that was "in the beginning" is to revert to a state superior even to that of humankind created in the image of God, male and female (Gen. 1:26–27). Those who enter the Kingdom have come to be like "the Living Jesus," having attained the "Gnosis" of seeing and understanding the hidden treasures of the Light, the Kingdom, the true self, the Living Jesus, and his words. Although these treasures, like the Kingdom, are hidden and invisible,[42] the Jesus of the *Gospel of Thomas* announces their availability to those who seek them, as he promises that those who seek will find and be transformed. As they come to know the meaning of his sayings, they will become like him, a Living one, a being of Light and Spirit, and will thus be restored to the state of union with the Kingdom and their original selfhood as children of the divine. In presenting its collection of Jesus' teachings, the *Gospel of Thomas* offers its reader a way to salvation through gnosis, knowing, and understanding the message and identity of Jesus, the divine, and the true self, as it provides contemporary readers an invaluable piece of evidence for Thomasine Christian thought.

2 The Sethian, Barbelo-Gnostic, or "classic Gnostic" system: the *Hypostasis of the Archons*

The Genesis accounts of creation also provide a rich source for the religious specu-lation of the "Sethian," Barbelo-Gnostic, or "classic Gnostic" tradition. This variety of Gnosis was first defined by Hans-Martin Schenke and closely parallels Bentley Layton's category of "classic Gnosticism."[43] The starting point for Schenke's construction of the "Sethian system" and "Sethian corpus of texts" is the brief description of Sethians in Epiphanius,[44] together with the parallels in Pseudo-Tertullian[45] and Philastrius,[46] as well as Irenaeus's report about the teachings of the "Barbelo Gnostics."[47] In Schenke's view, the Nag Hammadi texts which represent a "Sethian corpus" and provide the basis for any inquiry into what is Sethian include: *Apocryphon of John*, *Hypostasis of the Archons* (or *The Reality of the Rulers*), *Gospel of the Egyptians*, *Apocalypse of Adam*, *Three Steles of Seth*, *Zostrianos*, *Melchizedek*, *Thought of Norea*, *Trimorphic Protennoia*.[48]

All of these texts, Schenke argued, are closely related to one another, and "all of them represent or presuppose one and the same Gnostic system," with variations.[49] *The Apocryphon of John*, which exists in four Coptic translations (three in the Nag Hammadi library, and one in the Berlin Codex), is generally recognized as the most important representative text of Sethian Gnosis.[50] I have chosen to focus here on the similar, but less complex *Hypostasis of the Archons* (or *The Reality of the Rulers*), as a Sethian text that illustrates the religious, philosophical, and literary characteristics of Sethian Gnosis.

Among the features of the "Sethian system" identified by Schenke and shared, to varying degrees, by the texts of the Sethian corpus are the following ideas:

1 the belief that "Sethians" are the spiritual posterity or seed of Seth;
2 the conception of the heavenly/earthly Seth and/or Adam as Savior figures;
3 the notion of Four Aeons and Light-Givers, named Harmozel, Oroiael, Daveithe, and Eleleth, as heavenly places of rest for Adam, Seth, and the seed of Seth;
4 a divine Triad of Father, his consort Barbelo, and their son Autogenes (the Self-Generated), also known as the Anointed;
5 the depiction of the realm of Ialdabaoth, the Creator, and his offspring, the Archons or Rulers, as outside of and below that of the divine; and
6 speculation about distinct historical epochs, in which Ialdabaoth and his Archons try unsuccessfully to annihilate the seed of Seth.[51]

While further study of individual "Sethian" texts has led to some revision of Schenke's reconstruction of the "Sethian system,"[52] there has been general support for the hypothesis that there exists a Sethian corpus of texts and that its shared religious themes were spun from a rich, intertextual blend of sources drawn from Middle Platonism, Genesis interpretation, and certain strands of early Christian thought. Perhaps even more important, the literature of Sethian Gnosis displays a clear preference for mythic narrative as a mode of theological discourse.

In its present form, *Hypostasis of the Archons* is a composite of two genres: a narrative of creation and a revelation or apocalypse, delivered from the angelic Illuminator Eleleth to Norea, spiritual daughter of Adam and Eve. These are introduced by a brief letter in which the narrator informs an unnamed recipient that his purpose in writing is to provide an account of "the *hypostasis* (reality or nature) of the authorities" about whom the "great apostle" Paul wrote.[53] The narrative portions of *Hypostasis of the Archons* offer a retelling of the early chapters of Genesis as a story of confrontation between two modes of power: the Archons or Rulers of this world, led by the chief Archon Ialdabaoth, and multiple divine personae, including the Father, the Spirit, and the Illuminator Eleleth. Human beings enter the narrative as composite creatures, made of matter, soul, and Spirit, caught between these two opposed forces. The revelation from Eleleth to Norea promises salvation when the "True Human Being" comes and frees the spiritual children of Norea from the bondage of the Rulers.

The narrative begins abruptly with a brief episode that characterizes the chief Ruler Ialdabaoth as blind and arrogant, as he claims: "It is I who am god; there is none [apart from me]."[54] The Ruler's claim to be the only God elicits a voice of rebuke from Incorruptibility that exposes his error and sets in motion a process that leads to the creation of the first human beings. The origin of Ialdabaoth and his Archons is narrated later in the text, within Eleleth's revelation to Norea. According to this account, Ialdabaoth came into being when Sophia, a personified female element of the divine, "wished to create something, alone without her consort." Her solo effort brought forth Ialdabaoth, "an arrogant androgynous beast resembling a lion,"[55] grossly deficient because he lacks the generative principle of form which comes only from the male parent.[56] He becomes the "Chief Ruler" and Creator of the cosmos,[57] and makes himself a vast realm after the pattern of the divine realms, complete with seven offspring of his own, who are "androgynous just like their father."[58] In their presence, Ialdabaoth claims to be "the god of the Entirety." This false claim brings a rebuke from Zoe, the spiritual daughter of Sophia. Zoe breathes into his face and casts him down "into Tartaros, below the abyss."[59] Sabaoth, one of Ialdabaoth's offspring, seeing the power of that angel, repents and is raised by Sophia and Zoe to the seventh heaven, where he reigns as Sabaoth, God of the Forces.[60] Ialdabaoth's envy at seeing his offspring's splendor engenders envy, death, and further offspring, until "all the heavens of chaos became full of their multitudes." Even this, the narrator insists, took place "by the will of the Father" so that "the sum of chaos might be attained."[61]

Contrary to popular notions that "Gnostic" theology identifies the God of the biblical tradition with the deficient Creator of the world, *Hypostasis of the Archons* and other Sethian texts in fact identify different aspects of the biblical God with several distinct characters – some divine, some archontic. The creators of Sethian myth divided the attributes of the biblical God among several distinct personae: (1) the divine Father of the Entirety; (2) members of the divine Entirety – Sophia, Zoe, the Holy Spirit, and other personae that constitute the spiritual realm of Incorruptibility; (3) Ialdabaoth, the Chief Ruler of the cosmos; (4) his righteous son Sabaoth, who rules from the seventh heaven; and (5) the remaining Archons.

According to *Hypostasis of the Archons*, the attributes of humankind are assigned to three distinct categories of being: matter, soul, and Spirit. The Rulers seek to create the first human being as a "male counterpart" to the beautiful Voice from Incorruptibility that appears in the waters below. The Rulers, however, fail to understand their utter inability to grasp the divine – for they are made only of matter and soul (*psychikos*), while the Voice is of Spirit (*pneumatike*).[62] Formed from soil, Adam becomes *psychikos*, from the soul (*psyche*) breathed in by the Rulers. But it is only when the Spirit comes "to dwell within him" that the first human creature became "a *living* soul."[63] It is this Spirit, not the soul, that gives Life. Adam is thus created as a composite of matter and soul from the Archons and Spirit from the divine realm.

The Rulers extract the life-giving Spirit from Adam when they open "his side like a living woman," and Adam comes to be entirely of soul.[64] The Spiritual Woman appears before Adam as "the Mother of the Living (Gen. 3:20), the physician, the woman, and she who has given birth."[65] Adam's praise of the Spiritual Woman is interrupted as the Rulers, aroused once again by the female Spirit, conspire to sow their seed in her.[66] The Spirit evades the Rulers' attempts to grasp her by turning herself into a Tree, but leaves behind the carnal Eve, who is raped by the Rulers. When the Spirit later enters the Serpent, "the Instructor," and encourages Adam and Eve to eat from the Tree of Knowledge, they come to recognize that they are naked of the spiritual element.[67] The Ruler curses them, expels them from the garden, and casts humankind into great distraction and pain.[68]

The bodily Eve, deprived of Spirit, gives birth to Cain and Abel,[69] and later to Seth and Norea. The births of Seth and Norea mark a decisive improvement in the situation of humankind. Two epithets associated with Norea – "an assistance for many generations" and "the virgin whom the Forces did not defile"[70] – link her immediately to the spiritual realm and point to her ability to resist the Rulers' efforts to "lead her astray" and "render service" to them.[71] Norea cries out in a powerful voice and summons assistance from above.[72] Eleleth, "the great angel who stands in the presence of the Holy Spirit," comes to her and provides an account of the origin of the Rulers,[73] her own origin in the realm above, and the future of her "offspring." Eleleth assures Norea that she and her children belong to the Father and the imperishable Light. In three generations, Eleleth promises, "the True Human Being" will come "in a modeled form" to teach Norea's offspring and anoint them in the chrism of eternal life. They will be freed from error and gain *gnosis* of "the Truth, their root, the Father of the entirety, and the Holy Spirit."[74]

For ancient Christian readers of *Hypostasis of the Archons*, of course, the True Human Being had already come in the "modeled form" of Jesus, and the eschatological promises of Eleleth had already begun to be fulfilled. They had been anointed from the chrism of eternal life and gained gnosis of the divine realm, the reality or nature of the Rulers, and their own identity. As the spiritual children of Norea, they already exist "immortal in the midst of dying humankind," and the Rulers "cannot approach them because of the spirit of truth within them."[75]

Rather than approaching this narrative as "Platonism gone wild," or absurd fantasy, scholars of the Sethian tradition have suggested that *Hypostasis of the Archons* and other Sethian texts were not to be interpreted literally, but as mythic narratives, imaginative retellings of Genesis, New Testament traditions, and Platonic thought, encouraging their readers to struggle against the false "hypostasis" of the Rulers and align themselves with the true "hypostasis" of the divine realm.[76] While such readings would lead readers to construct sharp boundaries between the polarized and hierarchically ordered categories of Spirit–Flesh, Living–Dying, Knowing–Ignorant, and Redeemed–Unredeemed,[77] they would not necessarily lead to outright rejection of those assigned to the latter categories.[78] Indeed, the text suggests, those who enter into the text's theological perspectives and thereby gain gnosis of "the Truth" may well have been regarded as capable of moving higher and joining the redeemed, spiritual children of Norea, in the midst of "dying humankind." In this way, *Hypostasis of the Archons* creates a dualistic system that remains open to the possibility of movement or conversion for those "others," previously assigned to the category of "dying humankind."

3 The Valentinian tradition: Irenaeus's account and the *Gospel of Philip*

The Valentinian tradition is the best known of all the varieties of Christian Gnosis, and appears to have been the most successful in attracting followers throughout the Roman Empire. According to ancient reports, Valentinus was active in Rome from around CE 140 to 160. His school developed into "Western" and "Eastern" branches, and communities of Valentinians still existed in the eastern part of the empire in the fourth century, despite active opposition from Irenaeus and later anti-heretical writers.[79] Those whom we call "Valentinians" never used the term as a self-designation. Rather, the sources show that they were more likely to have called themselves "Christians," "the church (*ekklesia*),"[80] or "the spiritual seed,"[81] reflecting their self-understanding as both spiritual offspring of the divine and spiritual members of the Christian community.

The surviving fragments of Valentinus's writings, preserved mostly in the writings of Clement and Epiphanius, bear witness to a Christian thinker and writer of significant literary ability, who blended Platonic, biblical, and gnosis-centered themes to create a body of hymns, homilies, and letters with a distinctive mythopoetic rhetorical style.[82] His conceptual and literary legacy lived on in the work of his followers, in the anti-heretical writers' reports on Valentinian teaching, and in such texts as the *Excerpts of Theodotus, Letter of Ptolemy to Flora, Tripartite Tractate*, and *Gospel of Philip*.[83]

For the Valentinians, the redemptive work accomplished by Jesus Christ is understood within the framework of a Sophia myth similar to that of *Hypostasis of the Archons* and the Sethian tradition.[84] The processes of creation and redemption are set in motion by Sophia and culminate in a redemptive cure that overcomes the deficiency of the cosmos and reconnects dispersed spiritual elements in the cosmos to their divine source. This reconnection, accomplished in the activity of Jesus Christ, in language, and in ritual action, effects a redemptive movement from deficiency to fullness, incompleteness to completion, ignorance to gnosis of the self and the divine. Most characteristic of Valentinian thought is the notion that these redemptive movements occur in parallel moments within the divine, within episodes of the mythic narrative, and in the ritual processes by which members of the Valentinian community understood themselves to participate in the work of salvation.

Scholars distinguish between eastern and western branches of Valentinian thought, with crucial theological differences in conceptions of the divine, Sophia, and Christ. According to the eastern branch (represented in part by *Tripartite Tractate*, *Gospel of Truth*, *Gospel of Philip*, and *Excerpts of Theodotus* 1–42), the divine realm consists of an unlimited number of aeons existing in a hidden and seminal state within the Father which gradually become manifest as independent or discrete beings within the divine. According to this branch, Sophia desires to know the unknowable Father and is separated from the Pleroma. Outside the divine realm she gives birth to a son, usually called Christ. He retreats to the Pleroma, while Sophia remains outside.

By contrast, the western branch (represented in part by the reports of Irenaeus and Hippolytus, and *Excerpts of Theodotus* 43–65) describes the Pleroma as a system of thirty aeons, arranged in male–female pairs or syzygies, with Sophia appearing as the last and youngest of the aeons. The western branch further distinguishes between an upper Sophia and a lower Sophia, Achamoth, who remains outside the divine Pleroma. In Christology, the eastern branch views the Savior as having a spiritual body and being incarnated in a material body. The western branch holds that the Savior neither suffered nor assumed a material body, but rather put on a "psychical Christ," and it was this part alone that was crucified and suffered.

For the purposes of illustrating Valentinian thought in this section, I have chosen to highlight Irenaeus's account of Valentinian myth in *Against Heresies* 1 and excerpts from the *Gospel of Philip* from Nag Hammadi.

Irenaeus on the teachings of the Valentinians, *Against Heresies* **1.1–8**

Irenaeus's account of the teachings of the Valentinians in *Against Heresies* 1.1–8 provides a particularly detailed summary of Valentinian myth.[85] In this account, the divine is represented as a fullness or Pleroma of male (m.) and female (f.) spiritual beings, organized in male–female pairs or syzygies. These aeons come forth through a process of emanation, beginning with the invisible, pre-existent Father or Source (*Bythos*, m.), coexisting with Thought or Silence (*Sige*, f.). From them come forth Intellect (*Nous*, m.) and Truth (*Aletheia*, f.); Word (*Logos*, m.) and Life (*Zoe*, f.); Human Being (*Anthropos*, m.) and Church (*Ekklesia*, f.). From these eight come forth twenty-two more aeons, concluding with Wisdom or *Sophia* (f.), the last and youngest of the thirty aeons of the divine Pleroma.[86]

As in Sethian myth, it is Sophia who sets in motion the processes of world creation and redemption. Though narratives of Sophia's actions vary among the sources,[87] in the major strand of Irenaeus's account,[88] Sophia suffers passion apart from the embrace of her male consort, Desired (*Theletos*, m.), as she seeks to know the first male principle, "*Bythos*," who can be known only by the second male principle, "*Nous.*" In her misguided and passionate search, Sophia is restrained by a power called Boundary or Limit (*Horos*), which preserves the ineffability of the Father by holding back Sophia and restoring her to herself.[89] The Boundary separates the "formless, weak, and female fruit" of Sophia (her thinking and passions), and establishes them outside the divine realm.[90] Sophia's thinking, called "Achamoth," is given "a fragrance of incorruptibility" by the Anointed (Christ) and the Holy Spirit, but as she searches for "the Light that had left her" (the Anointed), she again experiences passions: grief, fear, uncertainty, lack of gnosis, and "turning back (or conversion) toward the one who had made her alive."[91] The distraught Achamoth, or lower Sophia, is visited by yet another male figure, "the Savior," who cures her of her passions by turning them from "incorporeal passions" into "incorporeal matter."[92] The lower Sophia becomes "pregnant with the contemplation of the lights," or angels, that accompanied the Savior, and produces "spiritual offspring" after their image.[93]

According to Irenaeus, then, Valentinian cosmology is based upon this myth of creation and Sophia's pivotal role within it. On one hand, Sophia was both the source, the Mother, of the divine, spiritual (*pneumatikos*) essence as well as a mediator who links the divine and cosmic and who is active in the perfection and redemption of this spiritual essence. On the other hand, it was Sophia's inappropriate emotions or "passions" which created the need within the cosmos for redemption in the first place. She was not only the source of the spiritual essence but also of the non-divine – material (*hylikos*) and animate (*psychikos*) – essences. Moreover, it was Sophia who was responsible for the dispersing (and therefore entrapping) of the spiritual elements within the non-divine elements of the cosmos.[94] In the final act of the eschatological drama, Irenaeus reports:

> When all the seed has grown to maturity, Achamoth their mother will – they say – leave the place of the midpoint, enter the Fullness, and receive as her bridegroom the Savior, who derives from all (the aeons), so that a pair is produced consisting of the Savior and Sophia who is Achamoth: they are the bridegroom and bride, and the entire fullness is the bridal chamber. And the spirituals are supposed to put off their souls; become intellectual spirits; unrestrainably and invisibly enter the fullness; and become brides of the angels that are with the Savior.
>
> (Irenaeus, *Against Heresies* 1.7.1)[95]

The Valentinian myth of Sophia thus conceptualizes redemption as coming about through the union of male and female as bridegroom and bride in the "bridal chamber." At the same time, it depicts the calamitous consequences of inappropriate emotion and the desire to step beyond one's boundaries, as well as the salvific benefits of restoring the rebellious, emotion-driven female to her proper place. In the end, the independent and rebellious Sophia-Achamoth is redeemed and restored precisely by returning to her proper place as the subordinate female bride of Christ.[96]

It is not surprising, as Clement of Alexandria reports, that the Valentinians approved of marriage as a reflection of the union of male and female emanations in the divine realm.[97] But perhaps even more important, as Ismo Dunderberg has argued, the Valentinian myth of Sophia provided a way of salvific knowledge and a therapy of emotions:

> What Valentinians had to offer in the intellectual marketplace of their time was a distinctly Christian theory of how desire can be cured. For them, Christ was the healer who "came to restore the emotions of the soul." Or, seen from another perspective, Valentinians contextualized their faith in Christ by expressing it in terms that made it seem more understandable, and more readily acceptable, to those having received a philosophical education.[98]

The myth of Sophia was offered, then, not only to account for the origin of the cosmos and its elements, but to serve as a christocentric therapy of the emotions, a way to rid oneself of inappropriate or "noxious emotions" through repentance, prayer, and the saving work of Christ the healer.[99] The myth of Sophia was equally crucial to the Valentinian theory and practice of ritual. The Marcosian deathbed ritual of redemption (*apolytrosis*), described by Irenaeus,[100] and paralleled by material in *The First Apocalypse of James* (NHC 5.3), shows that some Valentinians regarded knowledge (*gnosis*) and ritual performance of the Sophia myth as "necessary for their salvation."[101] Even more instructive for understanding the Valentinian theory and practice of ritual, however, is the rich collection of excerpts in the *Gospel of Philip* from Nag Hammadi.

Union as an image of salvation: excerpts from the *Gospel of Philip*

The *Gospel of Philip* from Nag Hammadi (NHC 2.3) provides further evidence of Valentinian uses of sexual imagery, symbolic language, and ritual. There is no narrative myth in the *Gospel of Philip*. As a collection of various excerpts from different works, the gospel represents no single strand of Valentinian thought, but it can be seen to have theoretical and theological coherence as Valentinian, once its complex metaphors and symbols are related to Valentinian conceptions of language, ritual, and the redemptive work of Christ.

The following series of quotations from the *Gospel of Philip* illustrates some essential features of this Valentinian theory of redemption through a process of reunification in language, ritual, and the work of Christ.

> Truth did not come to the world nakedly: rather, it came in prototypes and images: the world will not accept it in any other form. Rebirth exists along with an image of rebirth: by means of this image one must be truly reborn. Which image? Resurrection. And image must arise by means of image. By means of this image, the bridal chamber and the image must embark upon the realm of truth, that is, embark upon the return.
>
> (*Gospel of Philip* 67.9–27)

> The Lord did all things by means of a mystery: baptism, chrism, eucharist, ransom, and bridal chamber … […] said, "I have come to make [the lower]

like the [upper and the] outer like the [inner, and to join] them in [...] by means of prototypes [...] ... Now what is innermost of all is the fullness. Beyond that, there is nothing further within. This is what is called the uppermost.

(*Gospel of Philip* 67.27–29)

Before the anointed Christ, certain beings came from a realm that they could not re-enter, and went to a realm that they could not yet leave. Then the anointed (Christ) came: he brought out those who had entered and brought in those who had left.

(*Gospel of Philip* 68.17–21)

In the days when Eve was [in] Adam, death did not exist. When she was separated from him, death came into existence. If he [re-enters] and takes it unto himself, death will not exist.

(*Gospel of Philip* 68.22–26)

We are reborn by the holy spirit. And we are born by the anointed (Christ) through two things. We are anointed by the spirit. When we were born we were joined. No one can see himself in the water or in a mirror without light. Nor again can you see by the light without water or a mirror. For this reason it is necessary to baptize with two things – light and water. And light means chrism.

(*Gospel of Philip* 69.4–14)

While the topics treated in these passages may seem disconnected, one can in fact perceive a theory of redemption through the unification of cosmic realities or symbols (images, words, male and female, water, mirror, light) with their prototypes in the divine realm or aeon (Truth), of the individual initiate with his/her divine counterpart, and of the male with female.

E. Thomassen's discussion of the "dialectics of mutual participation" in the *Gospel of Philip* allows one to understand the ritual system of the Valentinians as one in which the initiate participated mutually with the Savior in several salvific moments at once: he or she was reborn and participated in the Savior's experiences of incarnation and baptism, scorn, death, resurrection, and reception of "the name that is above every name." In the gospel's reflections on the sacraments, such as baptism and chrism, several seemingly distinct moments are brought together in polysemic symbols and actions: the Savior's incarnation, baptism, crucifixion, and resurrection may be collapsed into one single act,[102] or the incarnation may be fused with references to the crucifixion, the garden narrative of Genesis 2–3, and the sacramental ointment or chrism of ritual practice. Thomassen interprets this to mean that within the thought world of the gospel, these referents are less significant as moments in a sequential narrative, and more significant in their common and mutually illuminated symbolism. As Thomassen points out, the logic of the text's symbolic parallelism between the redemptive acts performed by the Savior and the ritual acts of baptism, anointing, eucharist, redemption, and bridal chamber, carries with it the following implications: the acts of the Savior are in reality one single act, so each of the ritual acts will potentially reflect all of the components of the Savior's acts. Thus, Valentinian theory and practice come together with salvific effect as the community recalls or recites the crucial moments of the myth, from the union of the Father with Sophia which produces the Savior's spiritual body, through his descent in that body, his incarnation and birth, his baptism and anointing, the crucifixion, the separation from the cross, the resurrection, and the final unification in the bridal chamber. This series of successive events is seen as a single, indissoluble event from the perspective of its redemptive significance, and the Valentinian can participate in the redemptive event/s through the rituals of the Valentinian community. This method of identifying events of the Savior's work and the various components of the ritual system creates a nearly inexhaustible source of symbolic multivalence.[103]

This conception and experience of mutual participation illuminates crucial aspects of the religious dimensions of the *Gospel of Philip*, especially the blurring or dissolution of distinct moments of linear historical narrative in the transcendence of temporality. As the initiate re-enacts the mythic moments of Christ's incarnation and redemptive work in her own baptism, she participates in a ritual moment that transcends and dissolves the ordinary boundaries of time and space. He or she is in the Jordan with Jesus, on the cross, in the resurrection, entering the Pleroma and receiving the Name – all at once, in the initiatory experience of her own individual baptism and in the continuing communal rites of the Valentinian community. This is a key feature of Valentinian thought, as it reveals the way language, symbols, and rituals work as "types and images" of the spiritual realm in the *Gospel of Philip*.[104]

We might illuminate this theory further not only by considering its relevance in the context of baptism, but by relating it to the performance of the initiate and the distinctive features of Valentinian writing, reading, and ritual performance. Indeed, this illustrates two crucially important points about Valentinian teaching: one, that any ritual event, word, or passage from scripture can bear multiple meanings and make reference to multiple moments or spiritual realities at once; and two, that the temporal distinction between paradigmatic moments in the Savior's narrative – from creation through incarnation, baptism, crucifixion, and resurrection – and those moments in the initiate's experience is dissolved in the experience of the ritual.

While references to baptism, chrism, and eucharist are relatively clear, the imagery of "the bridal chamber," so central to the theological perspectives of the *Gospel of Philip*, is less clear.[105] The bridal chamber has neither a single referent (such as marriage, sexual union, the bedroom) nor a specific ritual, but rather resonates simultaneously with multiple notions of union, most often involving the reunification of previously separated entities, such as the reunification of the divine aeon with its "types and images" in the world. Central to these, of course, is the notion of the separation of the female from the male in the creation of Eve from Adam in the second creation account of Genesis. Even more important is the notion of their salvific reunification through the work of

Christ. In this context, it is possible to make sense of the *Gospel of Philip's* reflections on the role of Mary Magdalene and the ritual kiss, expressed in the following passages:

> There were three who always used to walk with the Lord: Mary, his mother, and his sister, and Magdalene, the one who was called his companion (*koinonos*). For Mary is the name of his sister and his mother and it is the name of his companion.
>
> > (*Gospel of Philip* 59.6–11)

> The Sophia (Wisdom) who is called "the barren" is the mother [of the] angels. And the companion (*koinonos*) of the […] is Mary Magdalene. The [… loved] her more than [all] the disciples, and he used to kiss her often on her [… more] often than the rest of the disciples. … They said to him, "Why do you love her more than all of us?" The Savior answered, saying to them, "Why do I not love you like her? If a blind person and one with sight are both in the darkness, they are not different from one another. When the light comes, then the person with sight will see the light, and the blind person will remain in the darkness."
>
> > (*Gospel of Philip* 63.30–64.9)

> If the female had not separated from the male, she and the male would not die. His separation became the beginning of death. Because of this Christ came to repair the separation which was from the beginning and re-unite the two and to give life to those who had died by separation and join them together.
>
> > (*Gospel of Philip* 70.9–18)[106]

As female "companion" to Jesus, Mary Magdalene plays a role in the *Gospel of Philip* that is at once symbolic, spiritual, and salvific. Within the mythic context of the separation of Eve from Adam, the relationship of Mary Magdalene and Jesus represents a reunification of the separated female and male.[107] As the iconic or imaged bridal chamber is a symbolic site for union, so the companionship and kiss of Mary Magdalene and Jesus symbolize the salvific moment when two previously separated elements (male and female, image and divine prototype, cosmic and divine) are reunited and bring forth spiritual fruit.

In the first passage, Mary Magdalene is linked to two other Mary's, but it is she who is singled out as "the companion" (*koinonos*) of the Savior.[108] The second passage elucidates Mary's role as "companion" more fully as it includes references to Sophia, to the Savior's love for Mary, and the "kiss." This is not a kiss of romantic love or marriage, but a moment of mythic and ritual significance in the Valentinian community, for this kiss provided the mythic foundation for the ritual kiss in the religious life of the community: "For it is by a kiss that the perfect conceive and give birth. For this reason we also kiss one another. We receive conception from the grace which is in one another."[109] In this way, the kiss of Mary Magdalene and Jesus establishes a paradigm and originating moment for spiritual conception through the mouth, that is, for the production of spiritual utterances: prophecy, poetry, song, and other manifestations of the divine *Logos* in language and sound.[110] The kiss of Jesus and Mary Magdalene leads the rest of the disciples to recognize that Mary was not only loved more than all women, but that she was loved more than the other disciples as well because she, unlike the blind, has seen the light.

Even more important, the reference to Sophia at the beginning of this passage shows that the companionship of Mary and Jesus belongs within a mythic context as a symbol of the salvific reunification of female and male. Behind this image of salvific union lies a mythic narrative consisting of three stages: primordial union, separation, reunification.[111] The first stage, based on the Valentinian myth of Sophia and its retelling of Genesis 2–3, involves the separation of Sophia from her divine counterpart and of Eve from Adam, as the third passage makes clear. Within the *Gospel of Philip's* mythic narratives of union – separation – reunification, Christ is the savior who came to repair the separation and give life. In this Mary Magdalene plays a crucial role in the narrative of salvation. Their "kiss" signifies a spiritual relationship that effects salvation in two ways. First, the companionship and kiss of Mary Magdalene and Jesus represent the salvific moment when female and male are reunited.[112] They undo the separation and restore the union of male and female among humans and, ultimately, within the divine. Second, their kiss establishes a mythic paradigm for the ritual kiss in the religious community, by which "the perfect conceive and give birth"[113] to spiritual utterances, prophecy, poetry, song, and other manifestations of the divine Logos in language and sound.[114]

As the female *koinonos* or spiritual partner of Jesus, Mary Magdalene plays a crucial role in the *Gospel of Philip*. Their companionship and kiss symbolize the sacred union of female and male that comes from spiritual insight or gnosis, and brings forth spiritual fruit. It does not involve literal marriage, sexual intercourse, or offspring, yet it may, nonetheless, point to an important role for Mary Magdalene and other women in the Valentinian community. As female "companion" (*koinonos*), Mary Magdalene is the spiritual counterpart to Jesus, especially beloved for her insight and vision. This insight gives her spiritual authority and may have reflected and increased the spiritual authority of other women in the community of the text as well, even as it aroused controversy.

Conclusion

This essay only begins to touch upon the variety and richness in the texts of Gnosis at Nag Hammadi. These texts employed a variety of strategies, including biblical interpretation, philosophical speculation, and their own unique style of myth-making to give expression to their religious views on the nature of the divine, the relation between creation and redemption, and the redemptive significance of Jesus Christ. Even such a brief survey as this demonstrates that those who would unify these texts and traditions under a single category like "Gnosticism" run the risk of ignoring the diversity and complexity. We contemporary readers can begin to understand these texts more fully as we bring to them modes of reading that are both more critical and more sensitive to their symbolic richness than were those of the anti-heretical writers of the early church.

Further reading

Primary sources

In addition to the translations listed in the Notes, the following should be noted:

R. P. Casey (ed. and trans.), *The Excerpta ex Theodoto of Clement of Alexandria*, London: Christophers, 1934.

W. Foerster, *Gnosis: A Selection of Gnostic Texts*, 2 vols, English trans. ed. R. McL. Wilson, Oxford: Clarendon, 1972, 1974; originally published as W. Foerster, *Die Gnosis*, 2 vols, Zürich: Artemis, 1969, 1971.

M. M. Waldstein and F. Wisse (eds), *The Apocryphon of John: Synopsis of Nag Hammadi Codices II,1; III,1; and IV,1 with BG 8502,2*, Nag Hammadi and Manichaean Studies 33, Leiden: E. J. Brill, 1995.

Secondary sources

U. Bianchi (ed.), *Le Origini dello Gnosticismo. Colloquio di Messina 13–18 Aprile 1966*, Studies in the History of Religion 12, Leiden: E. J. Brill, 1967.

J. Culianu, *The Tree of Gnosis: Gnostic Mythology from Early Christianity to Modern Nihilism*, San Francisco: HarperSan Francisco, 1990.

J. M. Dillon, *The Middle Platonists: A Study of Platonism 80 B.C. to A.D. 220*, London: Duckworth, 1977.

H. Jonas, *The Gnostic Religion: The Message of the Alien God and the Beginnings of Christianity*, 2nd edn, Boston: Beacon, 1958.

K. L. King, *The Secret Revelation of John*, Cambridge, MA: Harvard University Press, 2006.

A. H. B. Logan, *Gnostic Truth and Christian Heresy: A Study in the History of Gnosticism*, Edinburgh: T&T Clark, 1996.

E. H. Pagels, *The Gnostic Gospels*, New York: Random House, 1979.

L. Painchaud and A. Pasquier (eds), *Les Textes de Nag Hammadi et le Problème de leur Classification: Actes du colloque tenu à Québec du 15 au 19 septembre 1993*, Bibliothèque copte de Nag Hammadi: Section Études 3, Quebec: Presses de l'Université Laval, 1995.

K. Rudolph, *Gnosis: The Nature and History of Gnosticism*, trans. and ed. R. McL. Wilson, San Francisco: Harper and Row, 1983. (Translation of K. Rudolph, *Die Gnosis: Wesen und Geschichte einer spätantiken Religion*, 2d revised and expanded edn, Leipzig: Koehler & Amelang, 1977.)

R. T. Wallis and J. Bregman (eds), *Neoplatonism and Gnosticism*, Studies in Neoplatonism: Ancient and Modern 6, Albany, NY: SUNY Press, 1992.

Notes

1 K. L. King, *What is Gnosticism?*, Cambridge, MA: Harvard University Press, 2003, esp. ch. 2, "Gnosticism as Heresy," pp. 20–54. As King points out, More's use of the term emerged in the context of Protestant anti-Catholic polemics, and ever since "Gnosticism" has been established as a term for heresy in church history. See also B. Pearson, *Ancient Gnosticism: Traditions and Literature*, Minneapolis: Fortress, 2007, pp. 8–12; C. Markschies, *Gnosis: An Introduction*, London: T&T Clark, 2003, p. 14.

2 See, for example, Plato, *Republic* 613c; Alexander of Aphrodisias, *Commentary on the Metaphysics of Aristotle* 1.307.27, discussed in Markschies, *Gnosis*, p. 2.

3 In 1 Cor. 1:5, for example, the Apostle Paul gives thanks for the Corinthians' enrichment "in speech and *gnosis*," but later in the letter challenges their arrogance and immaturity. "Gnosis," linked to particular conceptions of faith, is also highly prized in the Gospel of John and the writings of Clement of Alexandria, among others.

4 1 Tim. 6:20–21: "Timothy, guard what has been entrusted to you. Avoid the profane chatter and contradictions of falsely so-called knowledge; by professing it some have missed the mark as regards the faith."

5 Irenaeus of Lyons, *Against the Heresies*, written around CE 180, was originally entitled *Refutation and Overthrow of Falsely So-Called Gnosis*. For a recent English translation with notes, see *Against the Heresies, Book 1*, trans. and annot. D. Unger and J. J. Dillon, Ancient Christian Writers 55, New York: Paulist, 1992.

6 Irenaeus, *Against Heresies* 1.22. Acts of the Apostles 8:9–24 describes Simon as a magician who had amazed the people of Samaria, was baptized by Philip, and attempted to buy the power to convey the Holy Spirit from the apostles Peter and John. In the anti-heretical literature, Simon appears in Justin Martyr, *First Apology* 26.2–3 and *Dialogue with Trypho* 120.6, in T. B. Falls, *Writings of Justin Martyr*, The Fathers of the Church: A New Translation 6, Washington, DC: The Catholic University of America Press, 1948, and in Irenaeus, *Against Heresies* 1.23.

7 Irenaeus, *Against Heresies* 1.29–30.

8 Pearson, *Ancient Gnosticism*, pp. 12–14, provides a lucid example of one such definition.

9 M. A. Williams, *Rethinking "Gnosticism": An Argument for Dismantling a Dubious Category*, Princeton, NJ: Princeton University Press, 1996, and K. L. King, *What is Gnosticism?*, have amply demonstrated the ways in which the modern term "Gnosticism" carries with it the distortions of Irenaeus's polemical construction, as well as numerous other problems of historical description and classification.

10 M. Smith, "The History of the Term Gnostikos," in B. Layton (ed.), *The Rediscovery of Gnosticism: Proceedings of the International Conference on Gnosticism at Yale New Haven, Connecticut, March 28–31, 1978*, vol. 2: *Sethian Gnosticism*, Leiden: E. J. Brill, 1981, pp. 796–807. See also B. Layton, "Prolegomena to the Study of Ancient Gnosticism," in L. M. White and O. L. Yarbrough (eds), *The Social World of the First Christians: Essays in Honor of Wayne A. Meeks*, Minneapolis: Augsburg Fortress, 1995, pp. 334–50 (esp. 335).

11 For fuller discussion of this perspective, see King, *What is Gnosticism?* and Williams, *Rethinking "Gnosticism."*

12 So most strongly, Williams, *Rethinking "Gnosticism,"* whose proposal that "biblical demiurgical traditions" be used as an alternative to "Gnosticism" has not been widely adopted.

13 B. Layton, "Classic Gnostic Scripture," in *The Gnostic Scriptures: A New Translation with Annotations and Introductions*, New York: Doubleday, 1987, pp. 5–215; Pearson, *Ancient Gnosticism*; M. Meyer, *The Gnostic Discoveries: The Impact of the Nag Hammadi Library*, San Francisco: HarperSanFrancisco, 2005, pp. 38–43. Layton, "Prolegomena to the Study of Ancient Gnosticism," argues that the ancient self-designation of some as "Gnostikoi" should serve as the basis for a more narrow definition, closely related to Irenaeus's categories of the "*gnostike hairesis*" ("gnostic sect") of *Against Heresies* 1.11 and the "Gnostikoi" of *Against Heresies* 1.29, and the related systems of the *Apocryphon of John* and other similar texts. Layton's list, "Classic Gnostic Scripture," closely resembles the "Sethian corpus" identified by H.-M. Schenke, "Das sethianische System nach Nag-Hammadi-Handschriften," in P. Nagel (ed.), *Studia Coptica*, Berlin: Akademie Verlag, 1974, pp. 165–74. See also H.-M. Schenke, "The Phenomenon and Significance of Gnostic Sethianism," in Layton, *Rediscovery of Gnosticism*, pp. 588–616.

14 J. D. Turner and A. M. McGuire (eds), *The Nag Hammadi Library after Fifty Years: Proceedings of the Society of Biblical Literature Commemoration, November 17–21, 1995*, Nag Hammadi and Manichaean Studies 44, Leiden: E. J. Brill, 1997, a collection of essays exploring the significance of the discovery and the first fifty years of scholarship.

15 F. Wisse, "The Nag Hammadi Library and the Heresiologists," *Vigiliae Christianae* 25, 1971, pp. 205–23, remains one of the most valuable and critical perspectives on the relationship of Nag Hammadi and the anti-heretical writers.

16 M. Meyer, "Epilogue: Schools of Thought in the Nag Hammadi Scriptures," in M. Meyer (ed.), *The Nag Hammadi Scriptures: The International Edition*, New York: HarperCollins, 2007, pp. 777–98. I have chosen to omit the fourth, "Hermetic Religion," because it does not appear in explicitly Christian form.

17 M. Meyer, "Epilogue: Schools of Thought in the Nag Hammadi Scriptures," includes discussion of *Gospel of Thomas* (Nag Hammadi Codex [NHC] 2.2), *The Book of Thomas the Contender* (NHC

2.7), *Dialogue of the Savior* (NHC 3.5), and *The Acts of Thomas* under the category of "Thomas Christianity." Layton, *Gnostic Scriptures*, pp. 359–412, includes the *Hymn of the Pearl* from the *Acts of Thomas*, along with these two Nag Hammadi texts under the category of "the School of St. Thomas."

18 For example Layton, *Gnostic Scriptures*, pp. x–xvi, 357–409, presents these not as examples of "Gnosticism," but rather as a distinct variety of Christian scripture from the geographical region of northern Mesopotamia, exhibiting "a mystical conception of salvation through self-acquaintance," or gnosis of the self. Pearson, *Ancient Gnosticism*, pp. 256–72, entitles his section on the Thomas material "Thomas Christianity," and clearly excludes it from his category of "Gnosticism." Pearson writes: "The *Gospel of Thomas* is not a Gnostic text, though some scholars argue that it is. But there is no doctrine of pleromatic emanations in it, no Sophia myth, and no ignorant or malevolent Demiurge. What it does share in common with Gnosticism is the emphasis on self-knowledge, but that is not something specific to Gnosticism as we have defined it" (p. 257).

19 J. D. Turner, "The Sethian School of Thought," in Meyer, *Nag Hammadi Scriptures*, pp. 784–9, provides a very clear and concise account of "Sethian" as "a typological category" in modern scholarship. The Sethian materials are recognized as strongly connected to certain traditions of Jewish scriptural interpretation and apocalyptic thought, Greek philosophy (especially Middle Platonism), and certain early Christian traditions.

20 For the fullest and most recent treatments of the Valentinian tradition, see E. Thomassen, *The Spiritual Seed: The Church of the "Valentinians,"* Nag Hammadi and Manichaean Studies 60, Leiden: Brill, 2006; I. Dunderberg, *Beyond Gnosticism: Myth, Lifestyle and Society in the School of Valentinus,* New York: Columbia University Press, 2008.

21 Although the focus of this essay is on patterns of thought, I agree strongly with the argument of I. Dunderberg, *Beyond Gnosticism*, on the value of considering "moral exhortation, views about emotions, and critical analysis of power and society," in the study of Valentinian and other gnosis-centered traditions.

22 The bibliography on the relation of the *Gospel of Thomas* to the New Testament Gospels and Q is extensive. See, for example, R. Cameron, "The Gospel of Thomas: A Forschungsbericht and Analysis," in W. Haase and H. Temporini (eds), *Aufstieg und Niedergang der römischen Welt* 2.25.6, Berlin: de Gruyter, 1988, pp. 4195–251; J. Kloppenborg, M. Meyer, S. J. Patterson, and M. G. Steinhauser (eds), *The Q-Thomas Reader*, Sonoma, CA: Polebridge, 1990.

23 On the *Gospel of Thomas* and the oral traditions underlying the New Testament Gospels, for example, see R. Uro, "Thomas and Oral Gospel Tradition," in R. Uro (ed.), *Thomas at the Crossroads: Essays on the Gospel of Thomas*, Edinburgh: T&T Clark, 1998, pp. 8–32.

24 See, for example, A. DeConick, *Seek to See Him: Ascent and Vision Mysticism in the Gospel of Thomas*, Leiden: E. J. Brill, 1996.

25 Among recent studies of Thomas Christianity, see R. Uro, J. M. Asgeirsson, and A. D. DeConick (eds), *Thomasine Traditions in Antiquity: The Social and Cultural Worlds of the Gospel of Thomas*, Leiden: Brill, 2006; R. Uro, *Thomas: Seeking the Historical Context of the Gospel of Thomas*, London: T&T Clark, 2003; and A. DeConick, *The Original Gospel of Thomas: A History of the Gospel and its Growth*, Library of New Testament Studies 286, London: T&T Clark, 2005, who argues that the *Gospel of Thomas* reflects various levels of composition and redaction. In her view, an apocalyptic core of sayings ("the kernel gospel") represents the earliest layer of sayings, with three later stages of accretions, increasingly less apocalyptic and more mystical.

26 Adapted from trans. M. Meyer, *The Gospel of Thomas: The Hidden Sayings of Jesus*, San Francisco: HarperSanFrancisco, 1992, p. 23.

27 On light imagery in the *Gospel of Thomas*, see especially Logia 24, 50, 77, 83. For the relation of the *Gospel of Thomas*'s light imagery to the interpretation of Genesis 1, see especially E. H. Pagels, "Exegesis of Genesis 1 in the Gospels of Thomas and John," *Journal of Biblical Literature* 118, 1999, pp. 477–96.

28 *Gospel of Thomas*, Logion 2; adapted from trans. Meyer, *Gospel of Thomas*, p. 23.

29 *Gospel of Thomas*, Logion 3, brings together the themes of Kingdom and knowledge, and implies a connection between knowledge of self as a child of the "living Father" and knowledge of the identity of Jesus: "When you know yourselves, then you will be known, and you will understand that you are children of the living Father." Adapted from trans. Meyer, *Gospel of Thomas*, p. 23.

30 Adapted from trans. Meyer, *Gospel of Thomas*, p. 63.

31 *Gospel of Thomas*, Logia 111 and 59, contrast the realms of Death and Life and suggest that one who lives from or looks to the Living One will not see death and becomes superior to the world.

32 *Gospel of Thomas*, Logion 29, for example, illustrates the opposition between Flesh and Spirit, as Jesus declares his amazement that the great wealth of Spirit has come to dwell in the poverty of the body.

33 *Gospel of Thomas*, Logia 24 and 61, show that the dualism of Light and Darkness corresponds to two types of people: those who are "undivided," having made the two one, are filled with Light and shine upon the *kosmos*; those, on the other hand, who exist in duality are dominated by darkness.

34 So S. Davies, *The Gospel of Thomas and Christian Wisdom*, New York: Seabury, 1983, and DeConick, *Seek to See Him*, respectively. For fuller discussion of Adamic typology in the *Gospel of Thomas* see H. Bloom, "'Whoever Discovers the Interpretation of These Sayings … ': A Reading by Harold Bloom," in Meyer, *Gospel of Thomas*, pp. 125–36; Pagels, "Exegesis of Genesis 1 in the Gospels of Thomas and John."

35 The imagery of becoming "little children" "is also part of a general Adamic typology, for the little child, the baptized person, was thought to be as innocent and sinless as Adam and Eve were before the fall" (Davies, *Gospel of Thomas*, p. 119). Such innocence has not to do only with sexuality, but also with ignorance of the distinction between good and evil.

36 *Gospel of Thomas*, Logia 85 and 19; adapted from trans. Meyer, *Gospel of Thomas*, pp. 57, 31.

37 *Gospel of Thomas*, Logion 18.

38 Bloom, "'Whoever Discovers the Interpretation of These Sayings … ',," in Meyer, *Gospel of Thomas*, appropriates a trope from W. B. Yeats to describe this pre-Adamic self: "Like William Blake, like Jakob Böhme, this Jesus is looking for the face he had before the world was made" (p. 136).

39 Adapted from trans. Meyer, *Gospel of Thomas*, p. 35.

40 When "the male and the female" are made into "a single one," this saying suggests, the distinction of the two genders is transformed, but not abandoned. There is still a "male" and a "female," but they are not "male" and "female" as they once were: "the [new] male" will not be "male" in the old sense and "the [new] female" will not be "female" in the old sense. Yet in contrast to the differences between the "old," untransformed states of male and female, the "new" male and female become one and the same.

41 These images of "old" and "new" human being (*anthropos*) are strikingly similar to the Pauline notions of "old anthropos" and "new anthropos" (see especially Rom. 6:6, Col. 3:9–10, Eph. 4:22–24), and similarly share connections to both Genesis interpretation and baptismal practice.

42 *Gospel of Thomas*, Logion 113: "The Father's Kingdom is spread out upon the earth and people do not see it." Adapted from trans. Meyer, *Gospel of Thomas*, p. 65.

43 Schenke, "Das sethianische System nach Nag-Hammadi-Handschriften"; "The Phenomenon and Significance of Gnostic Sethianism," in Layton, *Rediscovery of Gnosticism*, vol. 2; Layton, "Prolegomena to the Study of Ancient Gnosticism."

44 Epiphanius, *Refutation of All Heresies* 39 (cf. also 40.7.1–5).

45 Pseudo-Tertullian, *Against All Heresies* 2.

46 Philastrius, *Catalogue of Heresies* 3.

47 Irenaeus, *Against Heresies* 1.29.

48 These texts with their sources: *Apocryphon of John* (Berlin Codex, 2; NHC II.1, III.1, IV.1; together with the parallels in Irenaeus, *Against Heresies* 1.29), *Hypostasis of the Archons* (NHC II.4), *Gospel of the Egyptians* (NCH II.4, IV.2), *Apocalypse of Adam* (NHC V.5), *Three Steles of Seth* (NHC VII.5), *Zostrianos* (NHC VIII.1), *Melchizedek* (NHC IX.1), *Thought of Norea* (NHC IX.2), *Trimorphic Protennoia* (NHC XIII.1B). Layton, *Gnostic Scriptures*, pp. 5–214, includes in his collection of "Classic Gnostic Scripture" these nine texts from Schenke's Sethian corpus, as well as *Thunder, Perfect Mind* (NHC VI.2), *Allogenes* (NHC XI.3), as well as the reports of Irenaeus on Satorninos and the Gnostics (*Against Heresies* 1.29 and 1.30), of Porphyry on "the Gnostics" (*The Life of Plotinus*), and of Epiphanius on the Sethians, the Archontics, and the Gnostics (*Refutation of All Heresies*).

49 Schenke, "Das sethianische System nach Nag-Hammadi-Handschriften," p. 166.

50 K. L. King describes this text as "the first writing to formulate a comprehensive narrative of Christian theology, cosmology, and salvation" in her *The Secret Revelation of John*, Cambridge, MA: Harvard University Press, 2006, p. 2.

51 This notion has deep roots in Jewish and Christian apocalyptic traditions. On the apocalyptic traditions in Sethian texts, see especially H. W. Attridge, "Valentinian and Sethian Apocalyptic Traditions," *Journal of Early Christian Studies* 8, 2000, pp. 173–211.

52 For example, J. D. Turner has refined Schenke's hypothesis by highlighting evidence for diversity and historical development of Sethian thought. J. D. Turner, *Sethian Gnosticism and Platonic Tradition*, Bibliothèque copte de Nag Hammadi: Section Études 6, Québec, Canada: Presses de l'Université Laval; Louvain/Paris: Peeters, 2001.

53 *Hypostasis of the Archons* 86.20–27, quoting from Ephesians and Colossians. Translations of the text are my own. For published English translations, see B. Layton, "The Reality of the Rulers," in Layton, *Gnostic Scriptures*, pp. 65–76; "The Hypostasis of the Archons," in J. M. Robinson (ed.), *The Nag Hammadi Library*, 3rd completely revised edn, San Francisco: HarperCollins, pp. 161–9.

54 *Hypostasis of the Archons* 86.30–31. As noted by N. A. Dahl, this claim echoes the language of God in Isa. 45–46; N. A. Dahl, "The Arrogant Archon and the Lewd Sophia: Jewish Traditions in Gnostic Revolt," in Layton, *Rediscovery of Gnosticism*, vol. 2, pp. 689–712 (esp. 693).

55 *Hypostasis of the Archons* 94.2–19.

56 On ancient reproductive theory in Gnostic myth, see R. Smith, "Sex Education in Gnostic Schools," in K. L. King (ed.), *Images of the Feminine in Gnosticism*, Philadelphia: Fortress, 1988, pp. 345–60.

57 *Hypostasis of the Archons* 93.32–94.2. On the origins of the "Sophia myth" see, for example, G. W. MacRae, "The Jewish Background of the Gnostic Sophia Myth," *Novum Testamentum* 12, 1970, pp. 86–101. Similar but varying accounts of the "Sophia myth" occur in both Sethian and Valentinian texts. See below for further discussion of the Valentinian accounts.

58 *Hypostasis of the Archons* 94.34–95.4.

59 *Hypostasis of the Archons* 95.4–12.

60 For further analysis, see F. Fallon, *The Enthronement of Sabaoth: Jewish Elements in Gnostic Creation Myths*, Nag Hammadi Studies 10, Leiden: E. J. Brill, 1978.

61 *Hypostasis of the Archons* 96.3–16.

62 This distinction clearly resonates with one made by Paul in 1 Cor. 2:14–16: "that which is of *psyche/* soul (*psychikos*) cannot grasp the things of the spirit (*ta pneumatika*)."

63 *Hypostasis of the Archons* 88.10–16.

64 *Hypostasis of the Archons* 89.3–11.

65 *Hypostasis of the Archons* 89.11–17.

66 *Hypostasis of the Archons* 89.17–27.

67 *Hypostasis of the Archons* 90.13–19.

68 *Hypostasis of the Archons* 91.7–11.

69 *Hypostasis of the Archons* 91.11–21. There is some ambiguity about the paternity of Cain. Described as "their son," Cain could be the child either of the Rulers' rape or of Adam.

70 *Hypostasis of the Archons* 91.34–92.3.

71 *Hypostasis of the Archons* 92.18–92.32.

72 *Hypostasis of the Archons* 92.32–93.2.

73 In *Hypostasis of the Archons* 94.32–96.11, Eleleth narrates the myth of Sophia down to the creation of the full number of chaos "after the pattern of the things above," as taking place "by the will of the Father of the Entirety" (96.11–15).

74 *Hypostasis of the Archons* 96.27–97.20.

75 *Hypostasis of the Archons* 96.19–26.

76 A. McGuire, "Virginity and Subversion: Norea against the Powers in the Hypostasis of the Archons," in King, *Images of the Feminine*, pp. 239–58; K. L. King, "Ridicule and Rape, Rule and Rebellion: The Hypostasis of the Archons," in J. E. Goehring, C. W. Hedrick, J. T. Sanders, with H. D. Betz (eds), *Gnosticism and the Early Christian World: In Honor of James M. Robinson*, Sonoma, CA: Polebridge, 1990, pp. 3–24.

77 Such dualisms create hierarchical oppositions in which the first pole is esteemed, while the second is devalued and demeaned. It should be noted that the narrative uses sexual metaphors to represent both redemptive and non-redemptive states. Metaphors of virginity, conception, and birth ennoble the categories of the female and the Spirit, while metaphors of sexual desire and rape criticize the Archontic and the androgynous. For further analysis, see A. McGuire, "Women, Gender, and Gnosis

in Gnostic Texts and Traditions," in R. Kraemer and M. R. D'Angelo (eds), *Women and Christian Origins*, Oxford: Oxford University Press, 1999, pp. 257–99.

78 Close analysis of *Hypostasis of the Archons* and other texts of the Sethian corpus has produced different positions on the extent to which Sethian views of salvation were "open" or "closed." See, for example, M. A. Williams, "Deterministic Elitism? or Inclusive Theories of Conversion?," in his *Rethinking Gnosticism*, pp. 191–212. In the majority of texts, even those that would seem to have the most deterministic world view, persons without *gnosis* would appear to be capable of transformation or conversion.

79 C. Markschies, "Valentinian Gnosticism: Toward the Anatomy of a School," in Turner and McGuire, *Nag Hammadi Library after Fifty Years*, pp. 401–38. E. Thomassen offers a concise summary of Valentinian thought of the eastern and western branches in "The Valentinian School of Gnostic Thought," in Meyer, *Nag Hammadi Scriptures*, pp. 790–4. For a more complete account, see Thomassen, *Spiritual Seed*. See also L. Hurtado, *Lord Jesus Christ*, Grand Rapids, MI: Eerdmans, 2003, pp. 523–62, on Valentinian views of Jesus Christ.

80 *Tripartite Tractate* 125:4–5; Heracleon, frg. 37; Irenaeus, *Against Heresies* 1.5.6, and not insignificantly, the fragments of Valentinus.

81 *Excerpts of Theodotus*; Irenaeus, *Against Heresies* 1.5.6–6.1; and *Tripartite Tractate* 115.23–116.5.

82 Layton, *Gnostic Scriptures*, pp. 221–22, aptly distinguishes three sides of Valentinus's literary personality: (1) the mythmaker; (2) the Platonizing biblical theologian; and (3) the mystical poet.

83 Thomassen discusses these differences in more detail in her *Spiritual Seed*; and "The Valentinian School of Gnostic Thought," in Meyer, *Nag Hammadi Scriptures*, p. 793.

84 C. Markschies, *Valentinus Gnosticus?*, Tübingen: Mohr, 1992, and others have pointed out quite rightly that the fragments of Valentinus themselves exhibit no explicit traces of the Sophia myth itself. Nonetheless, Layton, *Gnostic Scriptures*, pp. 217–22, and others have argued that there may well have been some connection between Sethian myth and later developments of the Valentinian tradition.

85 For English translation of the entire account, see Unger and Dillon, *Against the Heresies, Book 1*, pp. 23–45. For a slightly abbreviated translation with detailed introduction and notes, see B. Layton, "Ptolemy's Version of the Gnostic Myth," in *Gnostic Scriptures*, pp. 276–302.

86 Irenaeus, *Against Heresies* 1.1.1–3.

87 There are significant variants included even in Irenaeus, *Against Heresies* 1.1–8. See G. C. Stead, "The Valentinian Myth of Sophia," *Journal of Theological Studies* 20, 1969, pp. 75–104, for a detailed analysis of the variations in the anti-heretical accounts of the Sophia myth. For more recent discussion, see Dunderberg, *Beyond Gnosticism*, pp. 97–118.

88 Irenaeus, *Against Heresies* 1.2.2. In what is usually designated the B strand, it is Sophia's desire to create something alone, apart from her male consort, that brings the Demiurge and his cosmos into being.

89 Irenaeus, *Against Heresies* 1.2.3–4.

90 Irenaeus, *Against Heresies* 1.2.5. *Against Heresies* 1.2.4 in Layton, *Gnostic Scriptures*: "For, thinking and its consequent passion were separated from her; she remained inside the fullness; but her thinking and the passion were bounded apart by the boundary, were fenced off with a palisade, and existed outside the fullness. This (thinking) was a spiritual essence, since it was a natural impulse to action on the part of an aeon. Yet it was without form and imageless because she had not comprehended anything. And – they say – for this reason it was a weak and female fruit" (p. 285).

91 Irenaeus, *Against Heresies* 1.4.1.

92 Irenaeus, *Against Heresies* 1.4.5.

93 Ibid.

94 Sophia's redemptive roles, however, pale in comparison to those of the male figures who come to redeem her, the Creator, and humankind alike: the Boundary or Limit; the Anointed; Jesus; and the Savior, who becomes Achamoth's "bridegroom" in the final, eschatological redemption – *Against Heresies* 1.7.1.

95 Trans. Layton, *Gnostic Scriptures*, pp. 294–5.

96 For further analysis of the images of Sophia, see J. J. Buckley, *Female Fault and Fulfilment in Gnosticism*, Studies in Religion, Chapel Hill, NC: University of North Carolina Press, 1986, esp. pp. 39–48

(*Apocrypha of John*), 61–70 (*Excerpts of Theodotus*), 116–20 (*Gospel of Philip*), 126–36 (conclusions); D. Good, *Reconstructing the Tradition of Sophia*, Atlanta: Scholars, 1987; K. L. King, "Sophia and Christ in the Apocryphon of John," in King, *Images of the Feminine in Gnosticism*, Philadelphia: Fortress, 1988, pp. 158–76. Dunderberg brilliantly illuminates the social and ethical implications of Valentinian myth and ritual for its community of practitioners in *Beyond Gnosticism*.

97 Clement of Alexandria, *Miscellanies* 3.1, reports that the Valentinians "hold that the union of man and woman is derived from the divine emanation in heaven above" and "approve of marriage."

98 Dunderberg, *Beyond Gnosticism*, p. 97.

99 Dunderberg, *Beyond Gnosticism*, p. 117–18.

100 Irenaeus, *Against Heresies* 1.21.1–5. For lucid discussion, see Dunderberg, *Beyond Gnosticism*, pp. 113–17.

101 Dunderberg, *Beyond Gnosticism*, p. 114.

102 Thomassen, *Spiritual Seed*, pp. 94–5.

103 Thomassen, *Spiritual Seed*, p. 95.

104 As Thomassen points out, *Spiritual Seed*, p. 101, sharing in the redemptive event provided by the ritual/s does not imply a simple identity between the Savior and the saved acting in the ritual, but a relationship of model and image. On the other hand, the relationship remains an ambiguous one of simultaneous identity and difference, with the Savior acquiring properties of the *salvandus* in the model narrative itself and the *salvandi* becoming Christs and fathers of spiritual offspring through the image of the ritual (*Gospel of Philip* 67.26–27; 61:20–35).

105 "Bridal chamber" appears as a central symbol throughout the gospel; in *Gospel of Philip* 65.11–12, it is modified by *eikonikos*, iconic or imaged, the adjective formed from the Greek noun *eikon* (image).

106 See also *Gospel of Philip* 68.22–26: "When Eve was still in Adam death did not exist. When she was separated from him death came into being. If he enters again and attains his former self, death will be no more."

107 Their companionship may also parallel the union of Light with Holy Spirit and of angels with images. *Gospel of Philip* 58.10–14: "He said on that day in the thanksgiving, 'You who have joined the perfect Light with the Holy Spirit, unite the angels also with us, as images'."

108 *Gospel of Philip* 59.6–11, my own translation. Contrast with trans. W. W. Isenberg, "The Gospel according to Philip," in B. Layton (ed.), *Nag Hammadi Codices II,2–7*, Leiden: E. J. Brill, 1989, p. 159: "His sister and his mother and his companion were each a Mary."

109 *Gospel of Philip* 58.30–59.6.

110 See P. C. Miller, "In Praise of Nonsense," in A. H. Armstrong (ed.), *Classical Mediterranean Spirituality*, New York: Crossroad, 1986, pp. 481–505, for an insightful study of theories of language and divine speech in late antiquity.

111 E. Pagels, "Adam and Eve, Christ and the Church: A Survey of Second Century Controversies Concerning Marriage," in A. Logan and A. Wedderbrun (eds), *New Testament and Gnosis*, Edinburgh: T&T Clark, 1983, pp. 146–75; and E. Pagels, "The 'Mystery of Marriage' in the *Gospel of Philip* Revisited," in B. Pearson (ed.), *The Future of Early Christianity*, Minneapolis: Fortress, 1991, pp. 442–54.

112 Their companionship may also parallel the union of Light with Holy Spirit and of angels with images. *Gospel of Philip* 58.10–14: He said on that day in the thanksgiving, "You who have joined (*hotr*) the perfect Light with the Holy Spirit, unite the angels also with us, as images."

113 *Gospel of Philip* 58.30–59.6.

114 See P. C. Miller, "In Praise of Nonsense," in A. H. Armstrong (ed.), *Classical Mediterranean Spirituality*, New York: Crossroad, 1986, pp. 481–505, for an insightful study of theories of language and divine speech in late antiquity.

13
SCHISM AND HERESY
Identity, cracks, and canyons in early Christianity

Pheme Perkins

While I stood staring into his misery,
he looked at me and with both hands he opened
his chest and said: "See how I tear myself!"

(Dante, *Inferno*)[1]

Divided beginnings

Dante's terrible *contrapasso* for schism depicts perpetrators endlessly cleft from head to bowels as they make their eternal circle in the depths of hell. One can imagine that the author of 1 John who tarred those who had left his fellowship with his newly invented label "Antichrists" would have considered such punishment well-deserved.[2] The lofty recognition – which also drives Dante's poem – that "God is love" and the associated command to imitate that love in relationships with one another (1 John 4:1–21) only applies to those who remain within the bounds of fellowship. Second John 9–10 instructs members of another house church gathering in the Johannine fellowship to treat those associated with the secessionists as complete outsiders: no hospitality, not even a greeting. What provoked such a rupture? The author alludes to both incorrect belief, failing to acknowledge Jesus coming "in the flesh," and incorrect conduct, a misguided understanding of sin. Beyond that, scholars have difficulty fitting the pieces together. Raymond Brown suggested that the result of this schism among Johannine churches in the Ephesus region led those connected with the evangelist to seek common cause with other communities that revered Peter as shepherd. Despite the spiritual insight of their founder, the Beloved Disciple, these Christians accepted Peter as shepherd of Jesus' flock (John 21:15–25).[3]

The mix of Christian teaching and practice in churches centered on Ephesus at the beginning of the second century becomes even more complicated when one includes the communities in the Pauline tradition, addressed in 1–2 Timothy and

Titus, as well as the Jewish Christian visionaries represented by John, the seer of Revelation. Trebilco suggests that some of their differences can be traced to the extent to which particular churches had assimilated to or resisted the Greco-Roman culture of this prosperous city.[4] Though some of the names and positions may be different, a history of Christianity in Rome from Paul in the mid-first century to Valentinus in the mid-second century exhibits the same complexity.[5] Origen, the third-century theologian from Alexandria, wrote a major work in response to a pagan critique of Christianity by the philosopher Celsus near the end of the second century. Celsus lumps orthodox Christian views together with those of Gnostics and Marcionites. He paints a picture of a fractious movement that encompasses widely different views about its key figure Jesus and yet maintains a bond of mutual love among its members.[6]

Negotiating diversity

These examples highlight the difficulties faced by students of second- and third-century Christianity. The movement comes out of its first century as a loosely connected network of house churches and local communities with different patterns of authority and organization. Nor is it possible to sort the observed diversity out by appealing to regional origins since the mobility of its adherents and missionary impulses leads to the presence of diverse forms of Christianity in its larger urban centers.[7] Lampe traces the phenomenon which he calls "fractionation" among Roman Christians back to its origins. Relying upon Romans 16, which designates as "church" individual groups, not believers in the city as a whole, he concludes that there were seven such circles, with an eighth created once Paul arrives.[8] However one describes the core beliefs in Jesus, baptism, the fellowship meal, and the Spirit that were shared across geographical and communal boundaries, one cannot imagine Christians of the second and third century as heirs to a fully articulated set of beliefs (doctrine) and practice (liturgy, ethics).[9]

Nor was there an organizational structure that gave a particular individual (such as Peter's successor as bishop in Rome) or group (such as a regional gathering of bishops or presbyters) uncontested authority to resolve the inevitable disputes. However, it is possible to observe the operation of informal networks in which a prominent bishop in one community would intervene to resolve conflicts in another. Two familiar examples from the Roman church will illustrate the point. It is important to remember that individuals referred to as "bishop of Rome" in the second century did not exercise direct, juridical control over all of the city's congregations. In the first case (c. 95), a Roman bishop, Clement, seeks to restore the original presbyters ousted in a factional revolt in Corinth. And in the fourth century, Eusebius reports that Clement's letter was still being read aloud in Christian assemblies in his own day.[10] Lampe's detailed study of clues as to the background and educational level of the author, who writes in the name of the Roman community, has produced important insights about the work. Its author was not highly educated in either rhetoric or philosophy. Its assemblage of diverse traditions makes 1 Clement an example of what Lampe calls "the collective process of education" by which Roman Christians assimilated traditions of the Hellenistic Jewish synagogues. Thus he proposes that the epistle is best understood as a communal work.[11]

This striking picture of the representative of the communal education of one community intervening to call another back to its apostolic heritage is not limited to Rome as authority. A controversy over the proper date for the celebration of Easter has Irenaeus, bishop of Lyons, bring a letter to the bishop of Rome, Victor (c. 189–99), on behalf of the churches in Asia Minor who followed the Jewish calendar in determining the date of Easter. He was able to persuade Victor to rescind his intention of breaking fellowship with all churches who followed this eastern practice. According to Eusebius considerable correspondence between various bishops as well as the personal negotiating skills of Irenaeus were required to forge this "agree to disagree" policy and permit those groups of eastern origins in the city of Rome to follow their own calendar.[12] These interventions at the end of the second century are set in an ecclesiastical context that has changed considerably since the time of Clement. Victor's initial decrees show that the episcopate now enjoys "monarchic authority." Lampe suggests that this tradition emerges by 160 when Bishop Anicetus represents himself as "the authoritative caretaker of the apostolic tradition in Rome."[13]

Opposing schools of Christianity

Development of succession lists for the bishops of major cities that could be tied to apostolic founders, made it possible to identify persons responsible for maintaining the tradition. In some respects, the cultural model was much like the succession of authorized heads of the ancient philosophical schools. However, for most of the second century, Christians in Rome had a wide array of congregations and of private teachers, who offered students deeper understanding of the faith than the preliminary catechesis. It was possible to refer to these private study circles as "heresies," distinct and often competing teachings, along the model of the philosophical schools. Despite Justin Martyr's clear disdain for the Gnostic teacher, Valentinus, he along with others such as Marcion and Justin's pupil, Tatian, operated within the general boundaries of "Christian assemblies" in the mid-second century.[14]

Opposition to teachers whose views were considered heterodox led heresiologists like Justin Martyr, Irenaeus, Tertullian, Hippolytus, and Epiphanius to forge increasingly elaborate genealogies for such movements. If "orthodox" or acceptable teaching reflects an apostolic lineage, then "heterodox" teaching must also have its lineage. Simon Magus (Acts 8) becomes the founder of a chain of deviant teachings.[15] The genealogical approach creates the impression that schism and heresy are deformed versions of a true teaching and/or communal way of life that had existed in pure form from the beginning.[16] In the third century, Hippolytus's *Refutation of All Heresies* blamed such doctrinal deviations on contamination of the Christian truth by various forms of pagan philosophy. This perspective played a prominent role in modern church history thanks to the influence of Adolf von Harnack for whom not only "heresies" but patristic theology as a whole represented the corruption of biblical truth by philosophical categories.[17]

Contemporary studies of formative Christianity acknowledge that any particular conflict over teaching or practice involved complex cultural and social as well as intellectual factors. The development of Christianity gave the movement a distinctive shape in different regions.[18] Markus Vinzent sees Christianity in Rome as absorbing cross-currents from around the Christian world rather than developing or propagating a theology peculiarly its own.[19] Yet many of the individuals who would be tagged as "heretics" in the second century had some ties to circles in that city (e.g. Marcion; Apelles; Valentinus; Ptolemy, another teacher of "Valentinian" gnosis; Tatian; as well as a group of Montanists; and Theodotus, "the shoemaker," who taught an adoptionist Christology) as did their "orthodox" opponents, Justin Martyr and Hippolytus as teachers in Rome, and Irenaeus, bishop of Lyons, whose intervention in disputes at Rome we have already noted. Valentinus appears to have been actively teaching in Rome at the same time as Justin Martyr (c. 155–60), who also knew Marcionites, Satornilians, and Basilideans as heretics.[20] By 180, Irenaeus opposed Valentinian teachers active among churches in Lyons. Local adherents of Valentinian teachings probably provided Irenaeus with the summaries of Gnostic and Valentinian speculative mythology that he employs and ridicules in his *Against Heresies*.[21] Unlike Marcion, who was either expelled or excluded himself from the larger Christian fellowship, Valentinus and the teachers who followed after him remained within the larger community.[22] Hence the pressing need to expose their errors.[23] Thomassen suggests that the Roman community did not have local resources to debate with diverse views. Irenaeus claims that under Anicetus (c. 155–66), Polycarp of Smyrna debated Marcionites, Valentinians, and others in Rome.[24]

Exclusion from fellowship

By the third century, Tertullian acknowledges that teachings associated with Apelles, Marcion, and Valentinus were known in Carthage.[25] He presumes that both Marcion and Valentinus had been repeatedly thrown out of the church.[26] However, contradictory statements elsewhere in Tertullian's writings that blame "heretical" Valentinianism on later followers and are uncertain about his relationship to the Roman church suggest that he has no clear information. By the end of the second century, excluding "heretics" from communion had become possible. Montanists,[27] the "shoemaker" Theodotus,[28] and (on Irenaeus's recommendation) a Valentinian teacher Florinus[29] suffered that penalty.[30] These developments point to a shift in the context of theological disputes during the second century. What had been diversity in local patterns of expression and practice with the inevitable clashes between the followers of different teachers, had become the focus of polemical struggles to define the boundaries of the larger Christian fellowship itself.[31] Similar transitions may be suggested for other urban centers which served as nodes in the network of communication that one observes passing through Rome. The alleged "catechetical school" which Eusebius projects back into the history of Alexandrian Christianity is largely the product of a fourth-century imagination.[32] Clement of Alexandria, Gnostic teachers like Basilides and Heracleon, and Eusebius's hero, Origen, all functioned as private teachers, whose instruction provided deeper insights into Christian scriptures for an educated elite.[33]

Origen's fate telegraphs conflicts over authority and correct doctrine which will embroil Alexandria during the christological controversies of the fourth century. Like Victor in Rome, Demetrius of Alexandria sought to consolidate episcopal authority over teaching and praxis. Expelled from the city, Origen moved to Caesarea where he was welcomed and ordained presbyter. There he addressed very different constituencies, ordinary believers, bishops not skilled in theological discourse as well as wealthy patrons.[34] Endowing local bishops with authority over the diverse Christian communities in a city did not eradicate theological diversity or even conflict between Christians who otherwise held to the accepted identity marks of belief in the God of the Jewish scriptures as the Father who sent Jesus (against Gnostics and Marcionites); Jesus' death on the cross for our salvation (against Docetists and Gnostics); typological or allegorical reading of the Jewish scriptures as referring to Christ (against Marcion and some Gnostics); participation in the sacraments of baptism and Eucharist.[35] Although the parameters of the Christian canon of "old" and "new" testaments would have some uncertainties at the edges for another two centuries, the Jewish scriptures of "law, prophets and writings" along with the four Gospels, Acts, and apostolic letters have been generally accepted as authoritative by the end of the second century.[36]

Christology and the Christian canon

The interpretation of the Christian writings takes on a new importance in the third century. The "orthodoxy" or "heresy" of particular teachers was to be measured by both the communal standard of acceptable belief as in 1 John and later the "rule of truth," their interpretation of the written Gospels, was also suspect.[37] Irenaeus opened his multi-volume refutation of heresies with a summary of the false genealogy and teachings followed by evidence that they abuse Scriptures to make them fit speculation that has no basis in the prophets, the Lord, or the apostles.[38] Later third-century authors presumed that the Gnostic Basilides (c. 130 in Alexandria) must have composed exegetical works on the Gospels or composed his own gospel, even though what survives in references to his writings is not commentary. Basilides uses "gospel" in the early second-century meaning of "oral preaching" or teaching about Jesus as savior.[39] Because Basilides taught that the good God permits evil only as just punishment for sins in this or a past life, he had to deny that Jesus suffered on the cross. Irenaeus reports that he supported that claim by "shape-shifting" Jesus with Simon of Cyrene. Simon died while Jesus stood by mocking the vain efforts of the rulers.[40] How much of that statement is Basilides and how much Irenaeus's assumption that Basilides was interpreting the passion story known from the Gospels can be debated.[41]

By the third century, theological debate centered on the interpretation of Scripture. The Monarchian controversy played out in both Rome and North Africa. To preserve the unity of God, various theologians in the Roman school insisted that the "God" united with or active in Jesus was none other than the Father. They thought that the incarnate Logos Christology favored by eastern theologians amounted to belief in two gods. As in many of the second-century cases, polemic reports by later parties to the dispute make it difficult to recreate the various lines of allegiance. In the gap created by Bishop Fabian's martyrdom two distinct "monarchian" factions are associated with Novatian (d. 258), who argued for the Word as a distinct person communicating the Father's divinity to the Son, and Cornelius.[42] The two also squared off in a disciplinary controversy over whether and under what conditions those who had denied their faith during the Decian persecution could be reconciled. Though siding with a rigorist policy in North Africa, Cyprian of Carthage supported Cornelius who advocated readmittance after a moderate penance. In that instance, he favored unity around the acknowledged bishop over communal purity.[43]

Earlier an intraschool rivalry pitted the Bishop Callistus, a monarchian, against Hippolytus, representing eastern Logos Christology, which may have influenced Novatian's Christology.[44] Both sides had been appealing to the Fourth Gospel in support of their position.[45] John 14:10 allowed the modalists to insist that what came to be as divine in the Son was the Father.[46] From their perspective, use of terms such as "person" or "substance" (*hypostasis*) for the Logos or the Son was equivalent to postulating a second divine being.[47] Thus there is no distinction within God prior to the incarnation of the "Father" as "Son." To their opponents, the flashpoint was the death of Christ. How could they assert that God fully participates in the Son when the verb, *sympaschein*, "suffer with," apparently commits the Father to dying. Hippolytus admits that Zephyrinus held that only the Son, not the Father, died but the charge of "Patripassianism" would become a key slogan employed against all forms of monarchian theology.[48] That accusation was coupled with the assertion that for monarchian theologians neither Son nor Spirit have real existence. The terms simply designate modes in which the Father acts. This accusation does not appear adequate to the real distinction between Father and Son which modalists attach to the incarnation. Heine suggests that at least from Callistus on, Roman modalists employed a Stoic explanation of the soul and body as two substances thoroughly blended, yet retaining their individual characteristics to explain the incarnation. In that framework it was possible to envisage the divine substance both experiencing and being disengaged from the suffering of the physical body. Consequently the monarchian theologians had an explanation for the Father "suffering with" the Son that did not involve patripassianism.[49] It may have been the case that the Asian teacher, Noetus, originally taught a less sophisticated form of monarchianism in Rome. Sabellius, another third-century teacher, apparently taught a form of modalism that could be labeled patripassianism.[50] Apparently Callistus refused fellowship to Sabellius and his followers.[51]

The issues raised in these third-century debates over how God is present in, to, or as the Son who became man, died, and was raised show that the "rule of faith" and the plain sense of the Scriptures were not sufficient to answer all questions. Sabellius may well have enlisted the common-sense beliefs of a less educated populace and tradition that had been the base of Roman Christianity since its founding. Though Hippolytus presents Callistus as an intellectual flyweight of lower-class, commercial origins, Callistus has accepted the need for a philosophical clarification in articulating Christian theology. Thus his reading of the relevant biblical texts sought to take on Logos christologies on the same ground. These arguments will pale beside the vigorous polemics surrounding the Arian controversies of the fourth and fifth centuries;

"Sabellianism" then becomes a broad label to stick on any opposition to the "hypostasis" and person language of Nicene parties.

External challenges

These intellectual divisions were not the only theological challenges to come out of the third century. A young devotee of a Jewish Christian baptismal sect, Mani (c. 214–76), would found a new religious movement. His personal revelations, elements of Christianity, of earlier gnostic speculations, Zoroastrianism, and the other religious currents to be met in Persia. This aggressively missionary movement to spread a universal faith both west into the Roman Empire and east beyond its boundaries posed a major challenge to fourth-century Christianity. Mani claimed to be the Paraclete of John 14:16 and may have inspired the first generation of believers with the apocalyptic expectation of living in the last days.[52] But unlike the Gnostic teachers, the followers of Basilides and of Valentinus, and the Marcionites of the previous century, Mani's followers had their own sacred texts. Mani broke with the rites of the cult in which he had been raised. His followers had their own cultic system so its theological and religious challenge to Christian believers comes from outside, not within as is the case with heresies.

Other disputes which divided Christians in the third-century churches involved practice, not theological speculation. With the severe persecution of any professed Christians under Decius in mid-century, festering divisions over readmitting those who had denied their faith came to the surface. Scriptural texts such as 1 John 5:16–17, Hebrews 6:4–8, and 10:26–27 supported the view that apostates could not be restored to communion. Even before the Decian persecution, Roman bishops held that such persons could be forgiven and return to fellowship after a moderate penance. To further confuse the issue, Christians imprisoned for confessing their faith claimed the spiritual authority to forgive the sin of erring brothers and sisters.[53] Since martyrs could be found among the adherents of both the Catholic and schismatic groups, readiness to die for the faith was not itself a mark of membership in the true church.[54] Where bishops were martyred or in hiding during persecution, individuals could receive sacraments from dissident clergy. Some bishops refused to accept such persons into communion without re-baptism. Others adopted a more lenient policy.[55] A bitter dispute over the issue set the lenient views of the bishop of Rome, Cornelius, against the presbyter, Novatian, who was excommunicated by a synod in approximately 251.[56] Eusebius alleges that Novatian had gone into hiding during the persecution and refused to visit believers in prison, thus he deserved that fate.[57]

Toward the end of the century, a longtime presbyter at Antioch, Paul of Samosata, was condemned by three synods (c. 269). Eusebius asserts that Paul had kept his heretical opinions hidden.[58] He quotes a long letter from the synod to the bishops of Rome and Alexandria that was also circulated around the various provinces. Allegedly records of an interrogation conducted by another presbyter schooled in rhetoric had been kept. However, the letter does not reflect a doctrinal or philosophical split but alleged sins of ambition and arrogance that included liturgical innovations. A brief suggestion that Paul denied the divine origins of Christ does not fit the ritual emphasis on the celebrant as "an angel come down from heaven." Consequently Mendels considers both of these cases more social or political divisions than theological ones. Remove the assumption that early Christians were divided over doctrine, and any third-century reader would infer that Novatian and Paul of Samosata led populist factions.[59]

Conclusion: the way forward

Dante's first example of a schismatic was not one of the many ecclesiastical sinners who are destroying Peter's flock but the prophet Mohammed. The medieval legend that Mohammed had created his heresy after failing in his ambition to become pope is yet another variant of the story Christians had used to explain heresy since the third century.[60] Failed ambition spawned malicious deformation of teaching and practice or so the story was told about the arch-heretic Simon Magus, Valentinus, Marcion, Novatian, Paul of Samosata, and many others. If that account is unfair to the complex history of Christians in the first three centuries, so is the modern tendency to view the emerging Christian orthodoxy as the achievement of victors in a factional struggle for power. The church is often said to have lost out on the creative speculation or "enlightened" openness to innovative practice of those forced outside the fellowship of Christians. The true complexity of forging an identity that will unite this global network of Christian believers is not well served by the modern reductionism to struggles for power either.

Without the shift from individual schools of Christian teachers to the theological exchange between regional bishops charged with overseeing the churches, the fourth-century move from private religious cult groups at the social margins to imperial religion would not have been possible. The second-century debates with the likes of Marcion and Valentinus consolidated the Christian commitment to the Scriptures and creator God of its Jewish heritage. (The problematic of Christian identity in relationship to Judaism of the second and third centuries and the increasingly marginal status of Jewish Christianity requires a separate essay.) Emergence of a widely shared Christian canon of four Gospels, Acts, and apostolic letters by the end of the second century not only unseated the claims of speculative mythologies to be the higher Christian teaching, it provided a new direction for theological reflection. Who is the one God, the Creator of heaven and earth? How is that God, the Father of the Son, present in Jesus of Nazareth? Such questions cannot be answered by simply repeating short formulae or by mere appeal to words of Scripture. Third-century debates focus on the problem of finding an appropriate language to resolve such questions.

Going forward to the great christological and Trinitarian conflicts of the fourth and fifth centuries, little remained of many of the initial efforts in our period beyond slogans that could be slung at the opposition such as Sabellian, monarchian, patri-passian. The move to imperial status erased the danger of persecution for those who adhered to recognized Christian congregations but not for others at the margins. As any reader of St Augustine's *Confessions* knows, Mani's new world religion continued to mount a powerful challenge to Christianity in the fourth century. What private teachers like Justin Martyr, Clement of Alexandria, and Origen did for the small groups of educated believers seeking to deepen their knowledge of the faith in the second and third centuries, bishops would be expected to accomplish from the public pulpits. And the great theologian bishops like Augustine would prove equal to the task.

Further reading

Primary sources

Eusebius, *Eusebius: The History of the Church from Christ to Constantine*, trans. G. A. Williamson, rev. and ed. with a new introduction by A. Louth, London: Penguin, 1989.

Secondary sources

H. Chadwick, *The Church in Ancient Society: From Galilee to Gregory the Great*, Oxford: Clarendon, 2001.

P. Lampe, *From Paul to Valentinus. Christians at Rome in the First Two Centuries*, Minneapolis: Fortress, 2003.

G. Lüdemann, *Heretics: The Other Side of Early Christianity*, trans. J. Bowden, Louisville, KY: Westminster John Knox, 1996; originally published as G. L. Lüdemann, *Ketzer: Die andere Seite des frühen Christentums*, Stuttgart: Radius-Verlag, 1995.

A. Marjanen and P. Luomanen (eds), *A Companion to Second Century Christian "Heretics,"* Supplements to Vigiliae Christianae 76, Leiden: Brill 2005.

M. M. Mitchell and F. M. Young (eds), *The Cambridge History of Christianity*, vol. 1: *Origins to Constantine*, Cambridge: Cambridge University Press, 2006.

E. Osborn, *The Emergence of Christian Theology*, Cambridge: Cambridge University Press, 1993.

B. A. Pearson, *Ancient Gnosticism: Traditions and Literature*, Minneapolis: Fortress, 2007.

Notes

1 Dante, *Inferno* 28.28–30; trans. M. Musa, *The Divine Comedy*, vol. 1: *Inferno*, New York: Penguin, 2003, p. 326.

2 1 John 2:18–19. See the extensive discussion of this passage in R. E. Brown, *The Epistles of John*, Anchor Bible 30, New York: Doubleday, 1982, pp. 330–71. Brown points out that however outsiders might have apportioned blame, the author places responsibility on the adversaries and adopts the rhetoric of the Old Testament for rebels against God, false prophets (Deut. 13:2–6, 13–14), "for the author his adversaries are apostates, and apostasy is a sign of the last times. By leaving, the secessionists were not making a mistake but were acting consistently according to their internal principle of darkness" (p. 367).

3 Brown, *Epistles of John*, pp. 69–115. On the Johannine churches as one strain of varied forms of Christianity, especially churches of Pauline origin, in the Ephesus region, see P. Trebilco, *The Early Christians in Ephesus from Paul to Ignatius*, Grand Rapids, MI: Eerdmans, 2007, pp. 268–92. Trebilco points out that there is no reason to think that the secessionist group ceased to exist in Ephesus after the circulation of 1–2 John (p. 292).

4 Trebilco, *Early Christians in Ephesus from Paul to Ignatius*, pp. 351–403.

5 P. Lampe, *From Paul to Valentinus: Christians at Rome in the First Two Centuries*, Minneapolis: Fortress, 2003; E. Thomassen, "Orthodoxy and Heresy in Second-Century Rome," *Harvard Theological Review* 97, 2004, pp. 241–56.

6 Origen, *Against Celsus* 1.1; H. Chadwick, *The Church in Ancient Society: From Galilee to Gregory the Great*, Oxford: Clarendon, 2001, pp. 110–13.

7 Walter Bauer's ground-breaking proposal that Christianity took shape differently in various regions, making what would become "heretical" beliefs its original form in regions like Alexandria or Syria,

does not account for this early local diversity. W. Bauer, *Orthodoxy and Heresy in Earliest Christianity*, ed. R. A. Kraft and G. Krodel, Philadelphia: Fortress, 1971; originally published as W. Bauer, *Rechtgläubigkeit und Ketzerie im ältesten Christentum*, Beiträge zur historischen Theologie 10, Tübingen: Mohr/Siebeck, 1934.

8 According to Acts 28:30–31; P. Lampe, *From Paul to Valentinus*, p. 359. Lampe's careful investigation of the material remains of Christianity in the city (as well as proposals for locating Christian groups in particular districts) indicates that one should take care in use of the term "house church." For the first two centuries, Christians assembled for worship and meals in rooms used for ordinary life. By the third century, they begin to have "cultic places," rooms set aside solely for religious functions (Minucius Felix, *Octavius* 9.1; Lampe, *From Paul to Valentinus*, pp. 368–69).

9 Such core beliefs are represented by the pre-Pauline hymnic and formulaic passages found in Paul's letters such as Phil. 2:6–11; Gal. 3:26–28; 1 Cor. 11:23–26, 15:3–5; Rom. 1:3–4, 3:24b–26; Col. 1:15–20. For a general discussion of unity and diversity across the New Testament canon see J. D. G. Dunn, *Unity and Diversity in the New Testament*, Philadelphia: Westminster, 1977.

10 Eusebius, *Ecclesiastical History* 2.16. In some cases it was even counted as part of the NT canon, though Eusebius recognizes in its use of a range of Pauline letters and of Hebrews the distinction between Clement's letter and authoritative scripture (3.38). The fifth-century Codex Alexandrinus copies it immediately after Revelation.

11 Lampe, *From Paul to Valentinus*, pp. 206–17.

12 Eusebius, *Ecclesiastical History* 5.23–25.

13 Eusebius, *Ecclesiastical History* 4.22; Lampe, *From Paul to Valentinus*, p. 403.

14 Thomassen, "Orthodoxy and Heresy in Second-Century Rome," pp. 241–56. Some scholars, relying on the few fragments from Valentinus, himself, preserved in patristic sources, claim that he never held the heterodox views about God, the aeons of creation, the fall of Wisdom, and the demonic creator of the Valentinian Gnostic myth so roundly attacked as heretical in Irenaeus (c. 180). However, Birger Pearson's judicious judgment seems more apt: "We see reflected in these precious fragments not only a learned Gnostic teacher, but also a devout Christian pastor of souls, a mystic visionary, and a gifted poet," *Ancient Gnosticism: Traditions and Literature*, Minneapolis: Fortress, 2007, p. 152.

15 Irenaeus, *Against Heresies* 1.23; Pearson, *Ancient Gnosticism*, pp. 25–33. Simon Magus's hold on the Christian imagination was also secured by the spectacular miracle-working contests between this figure and Peter in the *Acts of Peter* and his presentation as the archetypal opponent (= Paul) in the *Preaching of Peter*.

16 For the use of such genealogies to authorize one view of Christian teaching and practice against others called heretical in the broad debate over what is required for a group to claim the identity of "Christian" see D. Buell, *Making Christians: Clement of Alexandria and the Rhetoric of Legitimacy*, Princeton, NJ: Princeton University Press, 1999, pp. 5–9.

17 A. Harnack, *History of Dogma*, trans. N. Buchanan, 7 vols, trans. of 3rd German edn, New York: Dover, 1961; repr. Eugene, OR: Wipf & Stock, 1997; originally published as *Lehrbuch der Dogmageschichte*, 3 vols, Leipzig: Mohr, 1886–90. For an account of how those assumptions have led to a misunderstanding of the debates over divine impassibility and suffering see P. Gavrilyuk, *The Suffering of the Impassible God: The Dialectics of Patristic Thought*, Oxford: Oxford University Press, 2004.

18 Consequently sections on Christianity in different regions coupled with sections on particular issues in theology or practice have replaced the chronological style of writing church history, as in M. M. Mitchell and F. M. Young (eds), *The Cambridge History of Christianity*, vol. 1: *Origins to Constantine*, Cambridge: Cambridge University Press, 2006.

19 M. Vinzent, "Rome," in Mitchell and Young, *Cambridge History of Christianity*, vol. 1, pp. 397–412 (esp. 397–401). He agrees that social factionalism best describes Christianity in the city during the second and third centuries, though the decline of Christianity there during the third century may have been a consequence of state persecution (p. 401).

20 Thomassen, "Orthodoxy and Heresy in Second-Century Rome," 241.

21 Irenaeus, *Against Heresies* 1.1–7; 3.4.

22 I. Dunderberg, "The School of Valentinus," in A. Marjanen and P. Luomanen (eds), *A Companion to Second Century Christian "Heretics,"* Supplements to Vigiliae Christianae 76, Leiden: Brill 2005, pp. 64–99 (esp. 72); Thomassen, "Orthodoxy and Heresy in Second-Century Rome," pp. 342–3, claims

that Marcion was not expelled from the Roman church either. Rather, he infers, Marcion broke with that community and went on to found his own church after returning home to Pontus. As late as the fourth century, Cyril of Jerusalem warns that not all buildings that appear to be churches are orthodox (*Catechesis* 18.26; see H. Räisänen, "Marcion," in Marjanen and Luomanen [eds], *Companion to Second Century Christian "Heretics,"* pp. 100–24 [esp. 119]).

23 Irenaeus, *Against Heresies* 1.11.

24 Irenaeus, *Against Heresies* 3.3.

25 Tertullian, *Prescription against Heretics* 30.5–12; K. Greschat, *Apelles und Hermogenes: Zwei theologische Lehrer des zweiten Jahrhunderts*, Supplements to Vigiliae Christianae 48, Leiden: Brill, 2000, pp. 20–38.

26 Tertullian, *Prescription against Heretics* 30.2.

27 Eusebius, *Ecclesiastical History* 5.3–4; Tertullian, *Against Praxeas* 1.

28 Eusebius, *Ecclesiastical History* 5.28.

29 Eusebius, *Ecclesiastical History* 5.15.

30 Thomassen, "Orthodoxy and Heresy in Second-Century Rome," pp. 244–5. Thomassen points to a Syrian fragment of Irenaeus (*Syr. frg.* 28) as evidence that Victor's action against Florinus did not occur until after Irenaeus had written a letter exposing Florinus as a heretic.

31 Thomassen imagines three phases in Roman churches of the second century: (a) an initial period marked by decentralizing forces that supported the widespread diversity one observes in early sources; (b) groups which reacted against this divisiveness, seeking a more unified Christianity that produced such factional offshoots as *Shepherd of Hermas*, Marcion, and Valentinus; (c) a centralizing force that led to a single bishop with authority over the separate groups of Christians in the city ("Orthodoxy and Heresy in Second-Century Rome," 255). This model does not incorporate the contribution to developments in Rome which resulted from the city's position as a node in an intersecting web of relationships between it and churches elsewhere in the empire.

32 Eusebius, *Ecclesiastical History* 6.3–7.

33 D. Brakke, "Self-definition among Christian Groups: The Gnostics and Their Opponents," in Mitchell and Young, *Cambridge History of Christianity*, vol. 1, pp. 245–60 (esp. 246–58).

34 Brakke points out that Origen distinguishes the "charismatic" authority of spiritually adept teachers from the episcopal authority of the bishop ("Self-definition among Christian Groups," in Mitchell and Young, *Cambridge History of Christianity*, p. 259). In his *Homilies on Numbers* (2.1) Origen suggests that the "real bishop," the spiritually enlightened individual, is not necessarily the person who occupies the office of bishop.

35 Valentinians apparently participated in the sacramental rites of the larger Christian community but had both elaborate interpretations of those rituals as well as additional sacraments celebrated within their own groups. See Herbert Schmid, *Die Eucharistie ist Jesus: Anfänge einer Theorie des Sakraments im koptishcen Philippusevangelium (NHC II 3)*, Supplements to Vigiliae Christianae 88, Leiden: Brill, 2007. Schmid points out that Irenaeus's slanderous description of the communion rites initiated by the teacher Markus (*Against Heresies* 1.13.2) acknowledges that some might consider them to be equivalent to the eucharistic celebration in other Christian communities (pp. 400–401).

36 The expression "new testament" is rarely used for a collection of Christian writings in the second century. Kinzig's survey of the evidence shows that "new covenant" cannot be found as a book title before the end of the second century at which point it appears almost simultaneously in Alexandria, North Africa, and somewhat later at Rome (Novatian). W. Kinzig, "Καινὴ διαθήκη: The Title of the New Testament in the Second and Third Centuries," *Journal of Theological Studies* 45, 1994, pp. 514–44. However, leading theologians remain cautious about the expression. It appears to have been created by Marcion to refer to his "Christian scripture" (cf. Tertullian, *Prescription Against Heretics* 30.8–10; W. Kinzig, "Καινὴ διαθήκη," pp. 534–43).

37 Irenaeus, *Against Heresies* 1.10, 22.

38 Irenaeus, *Against Heresies* 1.1–7; 1.8–9. T. C. K. Ferguson, "The Rule of Truth and Irenaean Rhetoric in Book I of *Against Heresies*," *Vigiliae Christianae* 55, 2001, pp. 368–71.

39 J. A. Kelhoffer, "Basilides's Gospel and *Exegetica* (Treatises)," *Vigiliae Christianae* 59, 2005, pp. 115–29. Kelhoffer concludes that the term "exegetica" was not used for commentaries on Scripture before Origen in the mid-third century (p. 130); for a survey of Basilides' teaching see Pearson, *Ancient Gnosticism*, pp. 134–44. Pearson concludes that Basilides should be considered the first example of a

Christian philosopher (p. 144). He was particularly concerned with the problems of evil, free will and determinism; B. Pearson, "Basilides the Gnostic," in Marjanen and Luomanen, *Companion to Second Century Christian "Heretics,"* pp. 1–31 (esp. 18–22).

40 Cf. Ps. 2:4; Irenaeus, *Against Heresies* 1.24.4.

41 Kelhoffer, "Basilides's Gospel and *Exegetica* (Treatises)," pp. 118–20.

42 Vinzent, "Rome," p. 406.

43 Vinzent, "Rome," pp. 411–12; Cyprian's argument attaches the promise of Matt. 16:18–19 to the Roman bishop (*The Unity of the Catholic Church* 4); M. Simonetti, "Beginnings of Theological Reflection in the West," in A. Di Berardino and B. Studer (eds), *History of Theology*, vol. 1: *The Patristic Period*, Collegeville, MN: Liturgical, 1996, pp. 205–24 (esp. 216–23).

44 Although Novatian may have been familiar with Tertullian (*Against Praxeas*), he does not engage in Trinitarian reflection on the Holy Spirit as distinct person. Simonetti, "Beginnings of Theological Reflection in the West," in Di Berardino and Studer, *History of Theology*, p. 217.

45 R. E. Heine, "The Christology of Callistus," *Journal of Theological Studies* 49, 1998, pp. 56–91 (esp. 57–58), employs the first two books of Origen's *Commentary on John* as a control when evaluating the reports about monarchian opponents in *Against Noetus*, Hippolytus, *Refutation of All Heresies*, and Tertullian, *Against Praxeas*. Origen had visited Rome in the first decade of the third century; Hippolytus appears to deliberately omit or downplay the role of Scripture in formulating the monarchian arguments (p. 60).

46 Tertullian, *Against Praxeas* 27; Hippolytus, *Refutation of All Heresies* 9.2; 9.10–12; 10.27.

47 Tertullian, *Against Praxeas* 2.

48 Hippolytus, *Refutation of All Heresies* 9.11; Heine, "Christology of Callistus," pp. 66–77.

49 Heine, "Christology of Callistus," pp. 76–7.

50 Epiphanius, *Refutation of All Heresies* 62.1–2.

51 Heine, "The Christology of Callistus," pp. 90–91; Gavrilyuk, *Suffering of the Impassible God*, pp. 95–9.

52 I. Gardner and S. N. C. Lieu, *Manichaean Texts from the Roman Empire*, Cambridge: Cambridge University Press, 2004, pp. 1–45.

53 Throughout this period the relationships between Christian groups which differed in doctrine and/or practice were more tangled than the labels "heresy" or "schismatic" would suggest. It is implied in 1 John that those considered false teachers had deserted the fellowship of churches because they did not love their fellow believers. From a fourth-century perspective, Eusebius views heresy as the corruption of the originally pure church. Maureen Tilley argues that even in the fourth-century African church, it would have been difficult to determine whether the "Catholics" or Donatists represented the true lineage of Christianity. Each side claimed to be the true church, elected bishops, and celebrated Eucharist. Government approval for one side or the other might further muddy the waters if some Christians were reluctant to be incorporated into such congregations. M. Tilley, "When Schism Becomes Heresy in Late Antiquity: Developing Doctrinal Deviance in the Wounded Body of Christ," *Journal of Early Christian Studies* 15, 2007, pp. 1–21 (esp. 7–18).

54 Eusebius avoids describing the martyrs of groups considered heretical in the fourth century (see D. Mendels, *The Media Revolution of Early Christianity*, Minneapolis: Eerdmans, 1999, p. 107).

55 Eusebius, *Ecclesiastical History* 7.2–5.

56 Eusebius, *Ecclesiastical History* 6.43.

57 Mendels, *Media Revolution of Early Christianity*, pp. 151–77. Dionysius of Alexandria was drawn into the dispute. He wrote asking Novatian not to cause schism in the church (p. 172).

58 Eusebius, *Ecclesiastical History* 7.28–30.

59 Mendels, *Media Revolution of Early Christianity*, p. 170.

60 Musa, *Divine Comedy*, vol. 1, p. 331.

Part III
THOUGHT

14
GOD

M. C. Steenberg

When Jesus Christ ascended in glory from the midst of his disciples forty days after his resurrection, a people's vision of God was forever changed. Ten days later, when the Spirit came upon them "as divided tongues" at Pentecost (cf. Acts 2:3), their experience of the risen Lord was enflamed with a missionary zeal that would see it spread throughout the known world in a dramatically short span. Yet from the very moment that St Peter emerged from that upper room and preached the church's first homily to the people (cf. Acts 2:14–41), there came to the fore a tension that had been stirring since the archangel first announced to Mary that she would bear a child to be called "Son of the Highest" (Luke 1:32). The Father is confessed to have a Son. God is perceived in a dramatic, new way. St Peter put the matter directly to his hearers in Jerusalem: "Let all the house of Israel know assuredly that God has made this Jesus, whom you crucified, both Lord and Christ" (Acts 2:36).

Jesus, the man of Galilee, is "both Lord and Christ," and the people's confession of belief "in God" is forever altered. Further, the Spirit of God, long confessed but often in impersonal terms, was now seen to dwell in the very hearts of the Lord's faithful – the "Advocate" the Messiah, had promised (cf. John 15:26). Even the name of God himself – which since the time of David had been sung out, "Blessed be the Lord God, the God of Israel … and blessed be his glorious name forever" (Psalm 72:18, 19) – was given a new dimension in the great charge of the Lord, retaining its singularity yet expressing a mysterious communion: "Go therefore and make disciples of all nations, baptizing them in the Name of the Father, Son and the Holy Spirit" (Matthew 28:19).

St Peter's hearers (and at the pilgrimage feast of *Shavuot*, Pentecost, in Jerusalem they would have been almost exclusively Jews) are reported as being "cut to the heart" by his words (Acts 2:37), and the immediate effect of his preaching is that many are converted and believe; yet there lies behind this "mass conversion" of the first Christian Pentecost a tension that will have a long life in the church. The gathered faithful are moved by the compassion of the self-sacrificial Christ and eager to receive the salvation "from this perverse generation" (Acts 2:40) that he offers, yet the very confession that the Messiah is the Father's *Son*, acknowledged here in receipt of the Spirit, represents a powerful new theological vision – one which the newly baptized, rather like the apostles before them, would require time to absorb fully.

What was the "doctrine of God" amongst those first Christians, as well as amongst those of the second and third centuries, prior to the advent of the great doctrinal statements of the fourth and fifth? The question might well be complex enough, were Christianity to have remained solely in the religious world of the Jews (for its relationship to a "Jewish doctrine of God" was not simple, as Judaism itself was theologically diverse in those initial decades of the first millennium CE, and so questions of continuity and distinction from "Judaistic roots" are intrinsically amorphous); but with the extensive missionary labours that would follow the Pentecost, summed up perhaps most famously in the apostolic missions of the converted Jew, St Paul, the "Gentiles" too would bring their theological and religious presuppositions into early Christian discussion. How did the particularly Christian confession of God, grounded in the full revelation of the apostolic encounter with Christ, come to be articulated in this diverse milieu?

I would like to explore an answer, not from the approach of a defined "doctrine" of God (systematic theological explanations were hardly the focus of most early Christian discussions, particularly in our centuries); rather, through a consideration of the major questions about God that emerged from the increasingly complex and nuanced theological discussions of the second and third centuries. Particularly, I would like to focus on three such questions, in the mix of which the articulation of God took place: (1) Can there be multiplicity in unity? (2) Did God create? and (3) Has God changed? – or rather, has the Christian confession demanded an unacceptable "change" in conceptions of truth and divinity? Each of these questions, posed from the vantage point of a confession of Christ as the Father's Son, together with the Spirit whom he sent to the disciples, framed-in the Christian confession of "God" in these critical centuries, shaped in response to external events as well as internal reflections, demonstrating both continuity with the past and the creative expression of the reality fully revealed in Christ.

Can there be multiplicity in unity?

The most basic ramification of a particularly Christian confession is that God is in some sense "multiple." When St Peter confessed of Jesus, "Thou art the Christ, Son of the living God" (Matthew 16:16), he proclaimed both that Jesus was the anticipated Messiah (Christ), but also – and here, something unanticipated to most – that he was the Father's own Son. Similarly, when Christ informed the apostles that he would send the Spirit, when he charged a threefold baptism in the name of "Father, Son and Spirit," a multiplicity was confessed; and particularly in this latter baptismal commission, that multiplicity was mingled with unity. The Father, Son, and Spirit are each mentioned, but theirs is a singular "name." Unity is met with multiplicity. How can this be?

Jews had long confessed God as what in Greek would be called *monos theos*, "the one God" (whence our "monotheism") and – particularly when surrounded by the intently polytheistic Greeks and Romans – emphasized the oneness of God as a foundation of right belief revealed through the Law. The early Christians, too, knew and confessed God as unquestionably one; yet in the experience of Christ they had beheld one who was this God's Son. Ancient proclamations of God as "Father" in him met their correlate; and when the Son sent the Spirit, this "multiplicity" was fulfilled. Yet despite beginning with the experienced reality of these three, Christians maintained confession in "One God": a phrase that found its way into almost all early creedal formulae. Giving a title to this multiplicity-in-unity was not easy (for no other religion or philosophical system confessed such an idea, and as such language did not exist to articulate it precisely), yet attempts were nonetheless made. Theophilus of Antioch famously gave us the Greek *trias*, or "Triad";[1] whereas it was the Latin-speaking Tertullian of Carthage who eventually gave us *trinitas*, "Trinity" – a word that sounds far from unusual to ears today, since it has been in constant use since then, but one which nonetheless is a creative compression of "triad" and "unity" that tries to give articulation to precisely this divine mystery.[2]

Not surprisingly, most of the comments from the earliest centuries that deal with this "doctrinal" question are framed in pastoral contexts. St Ignatius of Antioch, writing a series of letters that were not principally doctrinal in nature, nonetheless gives us a significant glimpse of Christian reflection at the turn of the first century. Concerned for unity amongst Christians, and particularly for right ecclesiastical order, Ignatius delineates these matters with reference to the greater unity on which they are modelled: the unity of Christ with his Father. Writing to the Magnesians, he instructs:

> Do ye therefore all run together as into one temple of God, as to one altar, as to one Jesus Christ, who came forth from one Father, and is with and has gone to one.
>
> (Ignatius, *To the Magnesians* 7)

This echoes his language to the Ephesians, to whom St Paul had also written:

> I reckon you happy who are so joined to him [the bishop] as the Church is to Jesus Christ, and as Jesus Christ is to the Father, that so all things may agree in unity.
>
> (Ignatius, *To the Ephesians* 5)

Such passages, along with a host of others,[3] demonstrate Ignatius's firm conviction that the Father and the Son abide in an eternal unity, which the church is called to emulate in its unity around the bishop. None of these statements is a coherent articulation of "trinity," nor even a decisive doctrinal statement on the eternal relation of Father and Son (and, in other contexts, Spirit[4]); but such are not, of course, Ignatius's aims. His is chiefly a pastoral intention to build up ecclesiastical order and stability in an increasingly turbulent era of church life. Still, amidst his intentionally pastoral focus, dimensions of what would later be defined as Trinitarian confession already emerge. Jesus as Son is the *eternal* Word of the Father;[5] he has *come forth* from him and returned to him; he is "*joined*" to him – perhaps in some ways a problematic analogy for the abiding union of Father and Son, but one which nonetheless shows forth a real interconnection, and not simply a moral comparability or external similarity.

Slightly later than Ignatius, St Justin the Philosopher and Martyr would demonstrate the manner in which similar concerns were manifest in a rather different type of early Christian theological discourse. In his apologetic, Justin's chief concern was to establish the reasonableness of Christian faith and life in the broader social and intellectual sphere, and thereby to quell some of the chief grounds on which bias and even persecution were being levelled against Christian communities. In this context, where logical analysis was more called for than in St Ignatius's pastoral epistles, a different set of linguistic tools and metaphysical images could be and was deployed, refining the way the Christian confession might be articulated to others.

In a vein similar to Ignatius, who had insisted that Christians run to worship "as to one altar, as to one Jesus Christ," Justin argues to the general readership of his *First Apology* (nominally addressed to the emperor and senate) that Christians see Father, Son, and Spirit as divine and worthy of worship:

> But both him [the most true God the Father], and the Son – who came forth from him and taught us these things, and the host of the other good angels who follow and are made like to him – and the prophetic Spirit, we worship and adore, knowing them in reason and truth.[6]
>
> (Justin, *First Apology* 6)

Aware that the strangeness of this confession struck his Roman hearers just as much as the Jewish hearers (though for different reasons: Romans had little issue with the idea of multiple divinities, espousing themselves a diverse state pantheon; but the intellectual idea of what seemed "many gods being one" was a puzzle, and an apparent betrayal of fundamental philosophical common sense), Justin made ready comparisons with older Greco-Roman mythologies that suggested divine unity amongst multiple deities, as well as instances of divine sonship: even Jupiter was said to have sons.[7] Setting out, then, that even amongst pagan mythologies these ideas were not as foreign and strange as they might at first seem, Justin confesses a "truly reasonable" basis to a belief in Father, Son, and Spirit, which he feels comfortable describing in terms of a basic *taxis*, or ordering:

> [That we reasonably worship Christ,] having learned that he is the Son of the true God himself, and holding him in the second place, and the prophetic Spirit in the third, we will prove. For they proclaim our madness to consist in this, that we give to a crucified man a place second to the unchangeable and eternal God, the Creator of all; for they do not discern the mystery that is herein, to which, as we make it plain to you, we pray you to give heed.
>
> (Justin, *First Apology* 13)

This passage is sometimes regarded as more infamous than famous, as it seems to rank the Father, Son, and Spirit in a distinctly hierarchical manner (a concern that would be much in the air from the third to fourth centuries); yet Justin – and here he bears a certain continuity with Ignatius – is not so much determined to give an exacting explanation of their relationships, as he is to show that Father, Son, and Spirit, while eternal, are nonetheless distinct and have differing roles in the cosmos, in history.[8]

In this, he bears testimony to the degree to which confession of multiplicity-in-unity in God influenced Christian theological understanding from the earliest days: not simply in the realm of abstract reflection on God, but in the "practical" contexts of pastoral and ecclesiastical ordering (*à la* Ignatius), as well as scriptural exegesis and developments in broader theological articulation. Justin readily identifies (and extensively catalogues) different prophetic utterances of the Old Testament as originating distinctly, some from the Father, some from the Son, some from the Spirit;[9] and in his *Dialogue with Trypho the Jew*, declares that various appearances of God to the prophets and patriarchs were appearances of the Word, not of the Father (most famously in the visitation of the Word and two angels to Abraham (cf. Genesis 18);[10] but also in God's conversing with Moses and other theophanies).[11] The same vision also allows Justin to consider, like many to follow him, that the "Let *us* create … " language of Genesis 1–2 bespeaks this very multiplicity of the one God.[12] So the Father, Son, and Spirit are distinct and carry out different roles in the economy; yet they remain one, united, and eternal. As St Justin says of the Son:

> He appears arrayed in such forms as the Father pleases; and they call him the Word, because he carries tidings from the Father to men: but maintain that this power is indivisible and inseparable from the Father, just as they say that the light of the sun on the earth is indivisible and inseparable from the sun in the heavens.
>
> (Justin, *Dialogue with Trypho* 128)

What becomes clear, in the writings of these early centuries, is not simply that the confession of Jesus as "Son of the living God" meant that Christians somehow had to admit of and accept a multiplicity to God; but beyond this, that such multiplicity-in-unity proved a foundational and significant dimension of the Christian vision of God, influencing pastoral counsel, scriptural interpretation, intellectual dialogue, etc. Confession that *the one* God is at one and the same time *Father, Son, and Spirit* is more than merely a dogmatic point in an early Christian "doctrine of God": it is the very foundation of Christian life, thought, and experience in these earliest centuries.

This is perhaps most famously summed up in the period in a statement by St Irenaeus of Lyons, speaking of Christ:

> When we obey him, we do always learn that there is so great a God, and that it is he who by himself has established, fashioned, adorned and does contain all things – and among the "all things," are both this world of ours and our own selves. We also, then, were made, along with those things which are contained by him. And this is he of whom the scripture says, "and God formed man, taking dust of the earth, and breathed into his face the breath of life" (cf. Genesis 2.7). It was not angels, therefore, who made or formed us, nor had angels power to make an image of God, nor any one else except the true God, nor any power remotely distant from the Father of all things. For God did not stand in need of these [beings], in order to accomplish what he had

determined with himself beforehand should be done, as if he did not possess his own hands. For with him were always present the Word and Wisdom, the Son and the Spirit, by whom and in whom, freely and spontaneously, he made all things, and to whom he speaks, saying, "Let us make man after our image and likeness," taking from himself the substance of the creatures formed and the pattern of things made, and the type of all the adornments of the world.

(Irenaeus, Against Heresies 4.20.1)

In this passage we see the extent to which God, perceived as multiple-yet-one (that is, the one Father, inconceivable apart from his Word and Wisdom), was at the heart of multiple realms of early Christian theological discussion. It is precisely the fact that God is understood as the Father *with His Son and Spirit* that enables Irenaeus to articulate the creation of the cosmos; humankind bearing the divine image and likeness; a right perception of angels and angelic powers; etc. In using his famous analogy of "hands," he has made the relation of Father, Son, and Spirit so foundational to the "doctrine" of God, that the Father can no longer be conceived in any other way than together with them – "for with him *were always present* the Word and Wisdom."

In these early centuries, confession of "God" was – from the first – a confession of this mystery of multiplicity-in-unity. Readers of literature from the period are often surprised to discover the degree to which this is not only confessed, but to which it grounds all other discussion amongst Christian theologians of the period, challenging our common habit of suggesting that "Trinity" was not discussed until the late-third or fourth centuries. The language may have been quite different and the specific points of focus distinct (and if by "Trinity" we mean narrowly the specific dimensions of Trinitarian exegesis and vocabulary that were dominant in the post-Nicene debates, then clearly any talk of this in terms of the second and third centuries would be anachronistic); yet the second and third centuries alike are replete with Christians confessing that the "one God" of the cosmos is, in his divine unity, Father, Son, and Spirit.

Did God create?

The quotation, above, from St Irenaeus's *Against Heresies*, raises the second main question posed in the period regarding the Christian understanding of God, and links it directly to the first. The question of God's creative role in cosmic history was a driving concern in the second and third centuries, and the theological air was thick with various groups that offered alternative explanations as to whether and to what extent God was involved in the creation of what was patently a sinful and suffering world. Did God create such a world? And if so, what had this to say of God himself?

The Christian response to the question of God's creative activity was an unabashed "yes." The ancient scriptures' first revelation is that God "created the heavens and the earth" (Genesis 1:1); and, taking this foundational scriptural proclamation as the basis of articulating God's nature, nearly every tract and treatise of the early period treats, in some way or another, of God's creative work. Unsurprisingly, this creative dimension was often explored in pastoral terms – relating the re-creation of man to the initial creation of the cosmos – reflecting the primary concerns of the early centuries in particular.

From the second century, the emphasis begins to shift towards a theological reclamation of creation from the various groups that were seen to pervert it in one way or another (the "Gnostics," the Marcionites, etc.). Christianity's insistence on the creative nature of God meant that it was required to face the challenge posed by such a position: namely, articulating a reason and rhyme to the existence of evil and suffering, if one could not indulge in the somewhat simpler gnosticizing method of attributing it to creation itself, or to some manner of fallen creator-demiurge. In the midst of this exchange – often quite heated in the second and third centuries – the unique articulation of Christianity's Creator/creation dialectic begins to gain clearer expression: God's creative work, exemplified in his healing and restoration of the human creature in the person of the Son, reveals the true nature of the cosmos's first creation and discloses the Creator-God as one and the same with the healing, restoring Christ. It is the particularly Christian experience of the Father *through the Son*, perfected in the Spirit, that allows discussion of creation to be, for the early church, simultaneously a discussion of the triune nature of God himself.

Some attention was paid in the period to large-scale treatments of the creation narratives distinctly: Theophilus of Antioch, for example, wrote the detailed *To Autolycus*, treating of the Genesis creation saga in fairly minute detail. Works such as his are highly polemical (that is, in this case, that they attempt to disprove and discredit those perceived to view creation wrongly) and textual/exegetical, and some might argue they offer little in the way of profound theological reflections on the nature of God as Creator. Yet such works as *To Autolycus* have to be seen as part of a broader spectrum of writings in the second century, in which God's creative designs are explored in various ways and manners so as to disclose and articulate a vision of Father, Son, and Spirit that sees this One God directly responsible for creation and redemption as a single act of divine love.

This had been the brunt of Irenaeus's focus as evidenced across both his extant writings. God creates, and this creation discloses an essential characteristic of his nature. When creation is disrupted through sin, God works a re-creation, restoring what has fallen to the potential for new life and perfection.[13] The incarnation, then, and the healing wrought by the incarnate Christ, are the keys for understanding both creation and God as Creator. As Iain MacKenzie would write of Irenaeus's overarching theological emphasis:

> It is the overflowing love of God bringing into being an entity other than himself which may, in the relation of the respective integrities of that which is made and of him who is the Maker, share his eternal life in a "community of union" with him. It is this love of God which means that creation and redemption are so closely bound for Irenaeus. Creation and incarnation are but the two sides of the one act of the love of God towards what He makes.[14]

As we have already seen, this is cause for Irenaeus to understand God-as-Creator as foundational for perceiving God himself: even his analogy of Son and Spirit as "hands" of the Father is one that draws creation into view from the first. Hands exist to work, to act; and so the revelation that God is the Father with his two "hands" is simultaneously a confession that God is active, creative; and, in a directly related way, that a perception of creation reveals something of the nature and being of the divine.

This said, the attention paid to articulating God in the first Christian centuries was not chiefly concerned with broad categories, even if they be as significant as creation. Creation, and God as Creator, were of relevance in so much as perceiving God as Creator was part-and-parcel of seeing man as redeemed. So the locus of God's creative work was not addressed as the cosmos *writ large*, but the human person. God is seen in man (Christ); and in the human creature, redeemed by the Lord, God as Creator is seen in salvific terms. The stress placed on the fact of man as "after the image and likeness of God" in these centuries, bears out the observation that humanity's condition in the cosmos reveals the nature of its God; and so the very life of man revealed a God of "vitality," of creativity, of life-giving power. As was written by Tertullian at the beginning of the third century: "The divine creator fashioned this very flesh with his own hands in the image of God; which he animated with his own breath, after the likeness of his own vitality."[15]

God – Father with the Son and Spirit – was beheld to be creative and active (and not a removed or abstracted "divine principle"), self-communicative (hence it is not a generic "life-force" that animates man, but God's own breath),[16] and intimately associated with his creation, which bears, in the human creature, his own image and likeness (and so God was not a "removed creator," much less a divine pleroma utterly divided from creation by a demiurge, as certain "Gnostic" groups of the period were wont to suggest). These dimensions to God's nature were articulated in the early centuries, not through any dogmatic treatise on a doctrine of God, but through the radical insistence on God's creativity demanded by the polemical and rhetorical needs of the age. Similarly, it was in the confession of God as Father with his Son and Spirit that this creative reality was explored and expressed – something which set the Christian confession apart from various Jewish interlocutors of the period, who also wished to maintain a creative God but who did not express that confession in terms of the Father's Word, experienced as re-creative in human history, perfecting creation through the Spirit (an approach exemplified, for example, in Irenaeus's chief paradigm of God's authentic creation of the cosmos: the vision of Christ healing the man born blind in John 9, not through a "supernatural" force, but through the natural elements of dust and mud – proving the Son's creative power over matter itself).[17]

The question of God as Creator further reveals the degree to which issues that would, in later centuries, often be extracted into the realm of fairly abstract metaphysical discussion (e.g. the nature of God, God's eternal triadic relations, the question of "immanence or economy" in Trinitarian relations) were in the second and third centuries addressed primarily in terms of direct soteriological reflection. It is the need to understand the human creature – the one who sins, the one who is redeemed – that grounds articulation of God the Creator always in triadic terms, since the healing of man is experienced as triune act: the Spirit drawing man to Christ, who leads him to the Father.

Has God changed? Or rather, does Christianity's confession force change upon God as truth?

It was only to be expected that the Christian confession of God, rooted in the experience of Jesus Christ and the proclamation that he is Son of the Father, would rouse concern amongst various parties as to the "novelty" of the theology being espoused by the young church. The concept of God as eternal and unchanging was a theological and philosophical foundation-stone for most religious cultures of the era; and even beyond the strictly religious, where the philosophical contexts of the period saw truth, by and large, in equally unchanging and eternal terms. While the principal concern in articulating a Christian vision of God to Jews may have been the question of God as multiple yet one, in the broader milieu the question of "Christian novelty" was almost more pressing.

In later decades and centuries, the question "Has God changed?" would come more definitively to be asked in terms of the incarnational "becoming" of the Word, as expressed in the Gospel: "The word *became flesh* and dwelt amongst us" (John 1:14).[18] In our earliest centuries, however, this is not the primary focus of concern over change. Rather, we find the concern centring in the more basic question of whether a God, "suddenly" confessed as Father, Son, and Spirit, "newly" perceived as working a salvation "different" from that of the ancient covenants, proclaiming as truth something "different" from the ancient religious and philosophical perceptions of the same – whether such a confession of God could be held as credible in the face of so much apparent novelty. Or did not the very newness of the Christian confession mean that God had been "changed," and thus what was being confessed could not possibly be true (since ultimate truth was not perceived as changeable)?

Justin the Martyr was amongst the writers of our period to offer detailed response to such charges, asserting that the apparent novelty of the coming of Christ was in fact no new reality but the full expression of the divine nature that had always been active and present in the world, known in part. We have already made mention of his assertion that Christ is "the Word of whom every race of men were partakers" – that is, that Jesus' "recent" nativity and advent did not reveal his beginnings in existence, but rather his beginning as man. He is eternal and has always been with humankind, as Justin elaborates:

> We have been taught that Christ is the first-born of God, and we have declared above that he is the Word of whom every race of men were partakers; and those who lived reasonably are Christians, even though they have been thought atheists. … But who, through the power of the Word, according to the will of God the Father and Lord of all, was born of a Virgin as a man, and was named Jesus, and was crucified, and died, and rose again, and ascended

into heaven, an intelligent man will be able to comprehend from what has been already so largely said.

(Justin, *First Apology* 46)

Thus Justin was able to articulate Christ's eternity as Word, as Son, whilst at the same time affirming his new work in being born as man of the Virgin. His explanation could become somewhat fanciful at times (e.g. in his assertion that Plato read a copy of Moses),[19] and at others extremely detailed (e.g. his language of *Logos/logikos*, as well as his famous discussions of *logos spermatikos*);[20] but throughout he maintains the essential heart of his confession: that the Christian confession of the Father's Son, of the incarnation, does not make God into something "new," but rather confirms the ancient testimony of God's true nature, expressed in prophecy as well as through reason.[21]

A few years later, St Irenaeus would affirm the same points through utterly different means. Focused less on the philosophical arguments for God's universal and eternal nature, he framed his consideration in terms of the human creature bearing God's image, and who discovers that image fully in Christ:

For in times long past, it was said that man was created after the image of God, but it was not [actually] shown; for the Word was as yet invisible, after whose image man was created; wherefore also he did easily lose the likeness. When, however, the Word of God became flesh, he confirmed both these: for he both showed forth the image truly, since he became himself what was his image; and he re-established the likeness after a sure manner, by assimilating man to the invisible Father through means of the visible Word.

(Irenaeus, *Against Heresies* 5.16.2)

Here the Word's incarnation, which enables the Image to be seen directly and thus restores the potential for man to attain to God's likeness, confirms the eternity of the Word himself – the novelty of the incarnation is the assurance of the eternity not simply of God, but God as Father with his Son (and elsewhere in Irenaeus, his Spirit).[22]

The same basic confession is made in numerous ways throughout the second and third centuries, each in the unique context of different writers and theologians, but grounded in the same insistence on the changing nature of the *economy* of God's work in creation, but the unchanging nature of God himself. So, for example, Melito of Sardis would write in his poetic stanzas on the resurrection:

He [Christ] is the Pascha of our salvation.
It is he who in many endured many things:
It is he that was in Abel murdered,
and in Isaac bound,
and in Jacob exiled,
and in Joseph sold,

and in Moses exposed,
and in the lamb slain,
and in David persecuted,
and in the prophets dishonoured.
It is he that was enfleshed in a Virgin,
that was hanged on a tree.

(Melito of Sardis, *On the Resurrection* 69, 70)

Here the christological confession of the incarnation is framed in a manner that explicitly draws out the eternity of the Word who is "enfleshed in a virgin," that sees him active in the whole of human history in different ways, one and the same Lord. Melito is dealing in at least partially liturgical, poetic imagery here, rather than careful theological articulation, and so we should not take his statements on the Word being "in Joseph sold" as more than typological; but even this is demonstrative. The eternal nature of God as Father *with his Son and Spirit* is not just the interest of dogmatic or polemical tracts: the liturgical and expressive life of the early Christian communities is equally shaped by this central confession of the nature of God.

We have not, in these examples or really in any works of the first centuries, detailed metaphysical discussions of God's eternity and immutability; nor in the particularly christological responses to the question of "change" do we have intricate address of the matter of "becoming" that would so consume later generations. Christians of the second and third centuries, turning their attention to the first articulations of doctrinal questions posed most often in the fora of direct attack or challenge rather than the more open intellectual environments that would be possible and prominent in later centuries, tended to speak – even of squarely dogmatic questions – in eminently practical, pastoral terms. Yet in these varied discussions, a consistent confession is clear: God as the Father with his Son and Spirit, active in the cosmos since he himself set his "hands" to the work of creation itself, is one and the same throughout history. It is the same God who spoke in the prophets, who is present as Christ; and the novelty of the incarnation affirms, rather than challenges, this eternal and unchanging nature to the Christian God.

Later reflections

In the above, I have focused primarily on second-century texts and authors. I have avoided some of the looming figures of the third (particularly Origen), at least in part out of a desire to emphasize that the basic issues that consume their interests are anything but new when they arrive in the great dogmatic tracts of the third and fourth centuries. Figures such as Origen, Cyprian, Gregory Thaumaturgos and others may dedicate substantially more space to addressing questions of Trinity than their forebears, but they can hardly be seen to assign any more substantial a place to the *confession* of the triune nature of God – and indeed, in some ways the increasingly metaphysical language of their writings at times distances third-century Trinitarian discussion from its eminently practical, pastoral roots seen in earlier generations.

The third century began to give rise to a different kind of theological writing: the initial need to explain Christianity's basic beliefs to the "outside world" having diminished (to a degree) with time, the call for strict apologetic had also decreased (though it did not disappear, as the extant writings of Arnobius bear out); and the passage of time also gave Christians the opportunity to reflect further upon, and question, the nuance of many of the expressions used in the outward-facing polemical and early theological tracts of the first and second centuries. Theological articulations that had proven effective in asserting the basic contours of the faith to the pagans, or to the "Gnostics," could now be examined in more detail on their own merits.

It is this period that marks a kind of transition from earliest Christian "doctrinal" discussion, to the deep and often complex theological conversations and controversies exemplified in the fourth and fifth centuries. The third is home to such monumental figures as Clement and Origen in Alexandria, and Cyprian in Carthage, who, like Gregory Thaumaturgos (contemporary to the latter two), would leave indelible marks on the discussions to dominate the coming generation – a generation consumed by what R. P. C. Hanson famously called "the search for the Christian doctrine of God." In a chapter such as this, we could not possibly do justice to the full complexity of the theologians and thinkers of this age; yet for our purposes of discerning the doctrine of God in the period, what is of primary interest is the basic continuity with the discussions of the first and second centuries. While the third century will see much more nuanced metaphysical and philosophical investigations and expressions, the essential confessions of God are markedly consistent with the past. Figures such as Origen continue to wish to express, as "first principles," the fact that God is the Father with his Son and Spirit; that this God creates and redemptively re-creates; and that the salvific work of this God can and must be confessed as revealing his unchanging, eternal divine nature. This is echoed in Gregory Thaumaturgos, from his brief Declaration of Faith:

> There is one God, the Father of the living Word, who is his subsistent Wisdom and Power and Eternal Image: perfect Begetter of the perfect Begotten, Father of the only-begotten Son. There is one Lord, Only of the Only, God of God, Image and Likeness of Deity, Efficient Word, Wisdom comprehensive of the constitution of all things, and Power formative of the whole creation, true Son of true Father, Invisible of Invisible, Incorruptible of Incorruptible, and Immortal of Immortal, Eternal of Eternal. And there is one Holy Spirit, having his subsistence from God and being made manifest by the Son, to wit to men.
>
> (Gregory Thaumaturgos, *Declaration of Faith*)[23]

We certainly see here language that is reticent of Origen's, as well as a foreshadowing of that of the later Cappadocians; and the vocabulary speaks in metaphysical terms that would perhaps have been inconceivable to an Irenaeus, an Ignatius or a Theophilus (though perhaps not entirely to a Justin). Yet this reflection bears the same basic contours as the majority of articulations from the previous century, parcelled and analysed in the developing language of a new generation. What Irenaeus had been happy to announce as God the Father always working with his two "hands," the Word and Wisdom, Gregory is inclined to expound in terms of the subsistent realities of each of these three – the latter two grounded in the being of the Father. Between Irenaeus and Gregory had stood figures such as Athenagoras, expounding this relationship in terms – perhaps building on Justin – of mutual indwelling and the relationship of thought and mind:

> The Son of God is the Logos of the Father, in idea and in operation … the Father and the Son being one. And, the Son being in the Father and the Father in the Son, in oneness and power of spirit, the understanding and reason of the Father is the Son of God.
>
> (Athenagoras, *Plea for Christians* 10)

But here, too, we see attention paid to the same basic precepts. God is proclaimed as Father with Son and Spirit; this God is Creator, both in terms of his responsibility for the economy as well as with respect to his own nature ("He himself is uncreated … but has made all things by the Logos which is from him"[24]); and this God is the abiding, eternal and unchanging God of all power and truth.

The primary shift in third-century discussion is toward discreet address of the Father, Son, and Spirit as subsisting persons, with a consequent focus how they are unified and exist as the one God. The vocabulary of "hypostasis" and "person" (*prosopon*), together with that of "nature" (*physis*) and "essence" (*ousia*), begin to be utilized to give more substantial definition to the confessionally clear but metaphysically ambiguous claims of an earlier age, that the Son and Spirit were "always with the Father." Once introduced, such language would pose new challenges of its own, particularly in its diverse and often contradictory employment by different writers; and by the end of the third century Christian discussion had reached a certain tipping point in terms of its ability to carry on without some agreed approach to its own vocabulary and expression. The age of the great councils emerged out of this century with the heavy task of refining Christianity's articulation of its ancient confession with the apparatus of a new and developing vocabulary – a vocabulary that had the potential to express it with new and creative nuance, but which could, sometimes at the shift of a single word (or, in the case of the famous *homoousion/homoiousion* debates of the fourth century, a single letter) threaten to destroy a centuries-old confession of the Creator-God as eternally Father, Son, and Spirit.

Summary

It is tempting to try to see "Trinitarian" expressions in the second and third centuries, though scholarship has now long been wary of anachronistically reading back Trinitarian expressions (by which we normally mean expressions and articulations of the post-Nicene theological era) to periods that simply did not speak or think in such terms. This is a fair and valid concern, and prevents any number of misreadings of statements from our earliest centuries. Yet the fact that the early centuries did not speak of "The Trinity" in the same way as would later generations, does not mean that God was not perceived as a true Trinity of Father, Son, and Spirit. What is abundantly clear, across not only the second and third centuries, but even as far back as the first, is that the Christian confession of God, for all the variety of its earliest articulations and expressions, was consistent in its maintenance of God's multiplicity-in-unity. The experience of the first Christian Pentecost confirmed the apostles' previous confession: that Jesus of Galilee was Son of the Father, who had sent his promised Spirit. From this moment, the monotheism of the Christians was firmly established as something distinct from that of its Judaistic roots – roots now seen as prophetic of the triune mystery of Father, Son, and Spirit, established by this one God as the preparation for his full self-revelation in the incarnation of the Son.

Further reading

J. Behr, *The Formation of Christian Theology*, vol. 1, *The Way to Nicaea*, New York: St Vladimir's Seminary Press, 2001.

H. Chadwick, *Early Christian Thought and the Classical Tradition – Studies in Justin, Clement, and Origen*, Oxford: Clarendon, 1966.

J. Daniélou, *The Theology of Jewish Christianity*, vol. 1 of *The Development of Christian Doctrine Before the Council of Nicaea*, trans. and ed. John A. Baker, London: Darton, Longman & Todd, 1964; translation of *Théologie du judéo-christianisme*, vol. 1 of *Histoire des doctrines chrétiennes avant Nicée*, 2nd edn, Paris: Desclée, 1958.

P. Gavrilyuk, *The Suffering of the Impassible God: The Dialectics of Patristic Thought*, Oxford: Oxford University Press, 2004.

R. P. C. Hanson, *The Search for the Christian Doctrine of God – The Arian Controversy 318–381*, Edinburgh: T&T Clark, 1988.

M. C. Steenberg, *Of God and Man: Theology as Anthropology from Irenaeus to Athanasius*, Edinburgh: Continuum/T&T Clark, 2009.

T. G. Weinandy, *Does God Change? The Word's Becoming in the Incarnation*, Petersham: St Bede's, 1985. *Does God Suffer?*, Edinburgh: T&T Clark, 2000.

Notes

1 So in Theophilus of Antioch, *To Autolycus* 2.15, on the fourth day of creation: "In like manner also the three days which were before the luminaries are types of the Triad (Gr. *Triados*), of God, and his Word, and his Wisdom."

2 E.g. Tertullian, *Modesty* 21: "For the very Church itself is, properly and principally, the Spirit himself in whom is the trinity of the one divinity: Father, Son and Holy Spirit (*in quo est trinitas unius diuinitatis, Pater et Filius et Spiritus sanctus*)."

3 E.g. Ignatius, *To the Ephesians* 3 ("For even Jesus Christ, our inseparable life, is the manifested will of the Father; as also bishops, settled everywhere to the utmost bounds of the earth are so by the will of Jesus Christ"); *To the Magnesians* 7 ("As therefore the Lord did nothing without the Father, being united to him, neither by himself nor by the apostles, so neither do ye anything without the bishop and the presbyters"); *To the Magnesians* 8 ("On this account they were persecuted, being inspired by his grace fully to convince the unbelieving that there is one God, who has manifested himself by Jesus Christ his Son, who is his eternal Word, not proceeding forth from silence, and who in all things pleased him that sent him").

4 See, e.g., Ignatius, *To the Ephesians* 9.

5 Cf. Ignatius, *To the Magnesians* 8.

6 On the question of the Word as "Angel," which Justin inherits from Philo, see E. R. Goodenough, *The Theology of Justin Martyr: An Investigation into the Conceptions of Early Christian Literature and its Hellenistic and Judaistic Influences*, Jena: Frommann, 1923; repr. Amsterdam: Philo, 1968, pp. 156–7.

7 Cf. Justin, *First Apology* 21 and esp. 22.

8 On their eternity, see Justin's famous comment at *First Apology* 46: "[Lest people think the Word is new:] We have been taught that Christ is the first-born of God, and we have declared above that he is the Word of whom every race of men were partakers; and those who lived reasonably (*meta logou*) are Christians, even though they have been thought atheists; as, among the Greeks, Socrates and Heraclitus, and men like them."

9 See Justin, *First Apology* 37–39.

10 See Justin, *Dialogue with Trypho the Jew* 56.

11 See Justin, *Dialogue with Trypho the Jew* 58, 59.

12 See Justin, *Dialogue with Trypho the Jew* 62.

13 A line of thought that would later be exemplified in the writings of St Athanasius, much indebted to Irenaeus; see *On the Incarnation of the Word* 1.4; 6.4–8.3; etc.

14 I. M. MacKenzie, *Irenaeus's Demonstration of the Apostolic Preaching: A Theological Commentary and Translation*, Aldershot: Ashgate, 2002, p. 94.

15 Tertullian, *The Resurrection of the Flesh* 9.

16 Which Tertullian links directly to the Holy Spirit (see e.g. *Against Marcion* 2.9.2, 3; *Patience* 13), as had also Irenaeus (see *Against Heresies* 2.34.4).

17 See Irenaeus, *Against Heresies* 5.15.2.

18 On this debate, see P. Gavrilyuk, *The Suffering of the Impassible God: The Dialectics of Patristic Thought*, Oxford: Oxford University Press, 2004; and T. G. Weinandy, *Does God Change? The Word's Becoming in the Incarnation*, Petersham: St Bede's, 1985; *Does God Suffer?*, Edinburgh: T&T Clark, 2000.

19 Cf. Justin, *First Apology* 59. This is echoed in Clement of Alexandria, though in a slightly different manner; see *Miscellanies* 5.14.

20 See, e.g., Justin, *Second Apology* 8, 10.

21 And while the philosophical dimensions of Justin's explanations are often given more treatment in studies than the prophetic (undoubtedly because they are the more creative), it should be remembered that it is the fulfilment of ancient prophecies of the coming of Christ that is the chief affirmation of this fact for the martyr, and which makes up by far the bulk of his written focus.

22 For similar treatments in Irenaeus, see *Against Heresies* 3.18.1; 4.33.4.

23 Trans. S. D. F. Salmond, *A Declaration of Faith*, in A. Roberts and J. Donaldson (eds), *Gregory Thaumaturgos, Dionysius the Great, Julius Africanus, Anatolius and Minor Writers, Methodius, Arnobius*, vol. 6 in *The Ante-Nicene Fathers*, 10 vols, Edinburgh: T&T Clark, 1885–7; repr. Grand Rapids, MI: Wm. B. Eerdmans, 1987; repr. Peabody, MA: Hendrickson, 1994, p. 7.

24 Athenagoras, *Plea for Christians* 4.

15

CHRIST

The Apostolic Fathers to the third century

J. A. McGuckin

The second and third centuries were a profoundly important and uniquely fertile period for the early church in terms of the manner in which it assessed and re-articulated the evangelical and apostolic data it had received about Jesus. The Christology of this era has customarily commanded less attention than that given to the theologies of the New Testament, or to those of the fourth century or "Golden Age" of patristic christological thought. Often the transitional age of the second and third centuries was regarded as disappointingly vague. Scholars, alert to the deep subtleties of the New Testament literature, tended to feel it was an era of decline. It was generally regarded by Protestant scholarship up to the twentieth century as an age which continued the falling off in inspirational quality characteristic of the later Catholic Epistles, as compared with the evangelical or Pauline materials. In this same period, Catholic patristic scholarship found these ancient writings relevant only insofar as they could provide the apologetic materials of a defense of eucharistic realism, or the antiquity of episcopal governance, or evidence in support of Roman primacy. Twentieth-century scholars repaired some of the neglect, but even so, still tended to look upon the second and third centuries as simply an antechamber for the more important patristic epochs that would follow, especially seeing the christological formulae of this time as "undeveloped" except when they tended to have an afterlife. By this notion of being theologically undeveloped or even defective, scholars usually, and anachronistically, almost always meant "not in line with" or "up to the standard of" classical Nicene orthodoxy. On both counts, the Christology of these centuries seemed doubly enigmatic to commentators and was often passed over too quickly. Perhaps of all ages, it is our own, with its recent and remarkable advances in genetics, that is in a position to reaffirm the significance of embryology as important for what it reveals *in se* and not merely for that which it adumbrates. If so, these centuries should rightly be looked at once more, not solely to judge them for how they "bridged" eras before and after, but particularly for what they had to say on their own terms.

The Christology of this time was undoubtedly in flux, as it was faced with the monumentally important task of correlating a biblical matrix of thought with the more forensically focused concern of a now mainly Gentile movement that was fast moving along the intellectual roads of systematization. The former had been cast in heavily semiticized poetic forms, while the latter sought out more spacious metaphysical horizons than those provided by late Jewish apocalypticism. In terms of the first, not only the scriptural record was in course of being collated, coordinated, and read in the light of its totality, but the accumulation of teaching that the record contained as to the person and work of Jesus was now being carefully scrutinized and set out as "First Principles" of a coherent Christology. The church's confession of its faith in Jesus was no longer merely being expressed as a doxological element of its prayer, but was more and more being applied as the foundation of its advancing soteriology. In terms of the second, the evangelical statements of Jesus' saving acts and his glorification by the Father were being developed out of their original biblical eschatological matrix. While they would never cease to be charged with eschatological meaning, they were now reassessed in terms of a more Hellenistically conceived metaphysical backcloth. The Gnostic crisis was certainly one of the major force-fields that account for this, though it was a tendency already witnessed in the trajectory of the biblical record. The universal metaphysical scope of John 1:18, Colossians 1:15–20, and Ephesians 1:9–14 (3:9–13), for example, shows the movement of thought most clearly, across the span of the late first and early second centuries. This understanding of the exaltation of Jesus not simply as the reward of the suffering martyr (cf. Acts 2:32–33, 36), but rather as the in-breaking of the Eschaton, that is, the epiphany of the return of the Lord of the Cosmos to his status as Universal Benefactor after spending a time on earth as suffering pedagogue among a race that needed redemption and rescue.

Today we might sum up this intellectual movement that characterizes the second and third centuries in a threefold manner. First, it was a theology that re-expressed deep eschatology in metaphysical terms. Second, it made soteriological thought, based on a Wisdom- and Logos-Christology of redemptive Paideia, into the dominant motif. Finally, it increasingly sought to clarify the details of the relation between God's eternal being and the historical acts of his redemptive love, especially as this intimate conjunction of eternal and temporal was manifested in the person and work of Jesus. It is easy, perhaps, to sum it up so forensically and succinctly in such a manner. But one must recall that these achievements were being accomplished theoretically in a community which still lacked an extensive technical vocabulary, an established tradition of schools and teachers, and even a commonly agreed canon of scripture. In short, it was the achievement of these early centuries to set most of these things into place. Thereafter, the Christology of these centuries was further shaped and advanced by two other predominant forces, acting in their own turn, almost like fields of energy.

The first was the increasing specificity of Christian biblical interpretation. The second was the increasing rate at which Christianity produced insightful theologians and philosophers who turned their attention towards clarifying their religious tradition, and who often read one another carefully. In relation to the first of these energy fields, the late second to third centuries witness the Christians moving away from a generic use of scripture, initially meaning only the Old Testament, as if it were a form of illustration or decoration of an argument. The use of Scripture in this antique sense can still be witnessed in many of the Apostolic Fathers, where it is brought into an argument in the form of "proof texts" that might advance or clarify an argument. Scriptural stories are alluded to rather than single verses. The stories themselves tended to be valued as types or prefigurements of other stories about Jesus. But as the concept of the precedence of the New Testament took shape with the evangelical evidence assuming the role of a lens of interpretation over all other scriptural forms, this broad liturgical-narrative approach to scripture gave way to a different sense of the coherence of the whole scriptural mystery. Now the Old Testament was increasingly seen to be opened up by the New, and all together was "organized" in terms of how they were made coherent by reference to the focal story of Jesus' redemption of the cosmos. By the time the third century was well under way, the twin foci of an increasing "collation" of all the biblical evidence to a single narrative, and the dwelling on the theme of cosmic salvation as the key evangelical message, can both be seen to have resolved into one. Now, Christology itself had taken on the character of being a primary key to the interpretation of all scripture precisely as the story of cosmic redemption in and by Jesus.

It is abundantly clear that by the middle of the third century a revolution had taken place in the church's approach to, and use of, its scriptural record. This massive change in hermeneutics also explains the acceleration of its christological sophisti-cation at the end of the third century. In relation to the second of those energy fields we mentioned, some of the same thinkers who witness the change in exegetical style are those who specifically turn their attention to two issues in Christology. The issues are how Jesus of Nazareth ought to be described (Christology as the doctrine of his person), and how his significance should be summarized (Christology as the doctrine of salvation achieved in the death and resurrection of the Redeemer). This movement takes place inexorably, though it cannot be presumed to develop coherently, from one author to another in this period. This chapter, therefore, will henceforward follow a methodology of looking chiefly at the second and third centuries through the lenses of some of the major protagonists who wrote during this period, and predominantly studying them with reference to their biblically based christological theories.

What the method of using great writers as our guides lacks, of course, is the sense of what the *ordinary* Christian bishop of the day thought about things. But more often than not, our record is silent as to such things, leaving these exceptional writers, *faute de mieux*, having to stand as our developmental guides for Christology in this era. We must be aware that their evidence is not necessarily "typical" of every church in all areas of the Christian world. Some scholars have seized on this character of the diversity of early christological teaching to claim, without serious warrant, that there was no such thing as a standard of "apostolic doctrine" in the earliest churches, a concept to which such writers as Irenaeus or Tertullian appeal strongly. That is a tendentious conclusion which it is not the place of such an article as this to address. Suffice it to say that the writers that form the backbone of the second and third centuries are closely concerned with the notion of apostolic coherence, precisely because they work within the force-field of the twin patterns I have sketched out above. Additionally, they are concerned with the pastoral charge of the communities as a whole, as distinct from the Gnostic *magistri* of the same eras, who are more concerned with the gathering in of an illuminated elite.

Several among our authors clearly had the task of preaching at the Christian assemblies and so were *de facto* the archetypal theologians of the age. The "average preacher" of the time is undoubtedly more representative of the wider church of this era than the *literati* who survive for us, the latter being moved by their intellectual passion and/or controversies affecting their churches. But these less famous rhetors were non-writers in the main, and when one comes across them, their works give us a general flavor rather than specific "memorabilia." Being representative and being intellectual are not incompatible things, of course, but the paschal sermon of Melito of Sardis suggests to the reader more of a "normal type" sermon of the age than, say, an exegetical work by the great Origen a generation later. It is something of a surprise to find the Arabian bishop Heracleides arguing with Origen (*Dialogue with Heracleides*) in the mid-third century that "the soul is the blood," on the basis of a rather literalist understanding of the Levitical prescriptions. But he might not have been so odd in terms of the general way scripture was approached in the ordinary class of provincial churches, and by bishops who were not as brilliant as Origen. It is the theological writers however, while not always setting the agenda, who recognize the need for re-articulations of the faith of the churches in light of current questions. By and large, the Christian writers were very much aware of their main predecessors, and conscious of their relative strengths and defects. It would be the end of the fourth century before a workable theory of "patristic theology" would be in place among the Christians, but long before that the Christian intelligentsia had a lively sense of their own distinct biblical heritage, and who were the chief writers among them who had responded to it. Many had, for that very reason, also assumed the sacred mantle of the martyr.

Let this be enough to say, then, that a sketch of some of the main writers among these theologians still has its merits as a method. Each of them adds his own specific contribution, but is also part of a collective "attitude" that can be taken as an authentic sounding of the Christianity of the era. Nowhere is that more true than of our first set of protagonists known as the Apostolic Fathers, because they were the first who emerged as the post-New Testament theologians. In some cases they were contemporary with the later strata of writings that made it into the canon of the New Testament.

The Apostolic Fathers

The diverse group of second-century writers known, from the seventeenth century onwards, as the Apostolic Fathers, are so designated to distinguish them from the "apostolic authors" who were the writers of New Testament literature. Chief among them are the theologians: Clement of Rome, Ignatius of Antioch, Hermas, Polycarp of Smyrna, Papias of Hierapolis, as well as the authors of the *Letter of Barnabas*, the *Letter to Diognetus*, and *Second Clement*. The (anonymous) author of the *Didache* is also traditionally included in this group.[1] The Apostolic Fathers are immensely important for the understanding of the formation of the earliest Christian communities, but were relatively neglected by the post-Nicene church because they were so very different in form and style to current interests in theology.

The Nicene age, caught up in its own whirl of controversies, did not find their writings to be especially illuminating. They generally belonged to the antique world of the house church or the incipient rise of the monarchical bishops, and were frequently concerned with moral encouragement of the faithful from the perspective of a deeply eschatological outlook. The Christology of the Apostolic Fathers shows a deeply biblical inspiration that is still predominantly poetic in style. The eschatological matrix heavily conditions their christological understanding. The *parousia* of the Lord is felt among them to be close at hand. His vindication of the just, especially the suffering martyrs, is a powerful source of hope for the church. This hope gives the theme of victory an especially important place in their theology. Christ's ministry and passion is often read as a hero's endurance of the pains of battle, in order to enter into the glorious acclaim of his King and Father, bringing spoils of victory to the faithful.

Between CE 88–97, Clement was one of the presiding leaders of the Roman Christians and his words carried weight throughout the Mediterranean church. His letter to the Corinthians was occasioned by turmoil over leadership that occurred in Greece in the time of Domitian's persecution. In this letter, Clement's Christology is unreflective but, for that reason, none the less revealing. He binds himself by an oath to God, invoking Him as Father, Son, and Spirit.[2] He appeals for the church to be a mimesis of the divine unity, for, "Have we not," he says, "one God, and one Christ, and one Spirit of Grace poured out upon us?"[3] Clement gives evidence of what has for a long while been described as the theme of Spirit-Christology in the pre-Nicene Church. It is a vague and dubiously unhelpful concept, but it indicates the way in which there is a readiness among these early writers to synthesize the roles of the Word of God and the Spirit of Grace. Fourth-century Trinitarianism, after the acute clarification of Nicene Christology, will keep a clear distinction where the Apostolic Fathers are more fluid. For Clement, Christ is the pre-existent divine Word who has spoken in the scriptures. He is the "scepter" in the hand of God, the instrument through which God the Father has exercised majesty on this earth, noting once again the theme of the victory, and through whom God receives the acclamation of the church. Clement understands Christ as "the Way by which we have found salvation, the high priest of our offering," and it is through him (again evoking the theology of the Letter to the Hebrews) "that we are enabled to gaze up into the heights of heaven."[4]

Second Clement is a very early Christian homily based on Isaiah 54:1.[5] Here, the victory of Christ has made the Gentiles into the people of God. Christ is the joy of the church, the cause of its heavenly election. The author tells his congregation simply to "think of Jesus Christ as of God; as Judge of the living and the dead."[6] He is the Savior and "through him we have come to know the Father of Truth."[7] The author sees the Word as pre-existent divine Spirit, who, in history and for the salvation of a people, came to earth in fleshly form. He also shows Trinitarian patterns in his work (not precluded in the Apostolic Fathers' Spirit-Christology), as when he envisages the Divine Spirit, who is with God alongside the Word, as an archetype of the Heavenly Church.[8] While the obscurity and "untied ends" of the doctrine of God will cause puzzlement to later generations trying to bring clarity and systematic order into the church's Trinitarian theology, the two authors of the Clementine literature are nevertheless clear enough in their understanding that the appearance of Christ was a radical epiphany of Divine Spirit into the world, an incarnation of the Word for the cause of the salvation and election of a new people of God. As such, they see Christ as the High Priest of the church, and his earthly career as the symbol of his supreme eschatological victory.

The author of the *Letter of Barnabas*, composed in Alexandria circa 130, was concerned with apologetical arguments against the Jewish community who had criticized Christian doctrine. In a generic appeal for simple faith among the believers, he nevertheless demonstrates some of the basic axioms of his community's creed. Christ is the making visible of the invisible Godhead;[9] and he who came into the world did not become Son of God at that point, but was the Son of God even before the creation of the world.[10] For Barnabas, Christ is the "Lord of the whole world"[11] and came into the cosmos as the eschatological crisis of God; "that he might recapitulate the fulfillment of the sins of those who had persecuted his prophets to the death."[12] He came into this world precisely that he might destroy death and manifest the power of resurrection. The Lord of the end-time is thus the vindicator of all the blood of the righteous, including the present generation of suffering saints. His victory constitutes their salvation, their gathering together around him, and their gift of life. For these teachers, Christ is the savior not simply because of what he has done, but also for who he is.

Ignatius of Antioch (35–107), in a dossier of letters he wrote to various churches that lay on his route as a prisoner of faith from Asia Minor to Rome, is an important witness to the episcopal theology of one of the largest Christian communities of the early second century. His Christology is again based on the twofold pattern of New Testament confession: One Christ who is flesh and spirit (human and divine), and who saves humanity by his heroic fidelity. Ignatius loves to express the concept in dense antitheses: "There is one physician, composed of flesh and spirit, generate and ingenerate, God in man, true life in death, from Mary and from God, first passible, then impassible, Jesus Christ our Lord."[13] His sense of the importance of the fleshly commitment of the heavenly Lord (strikingly anti-Gnostic in tonality and intent) is brought out in rhetorical paradoxes such as: "the blood of God,"[14] "the sufferings of my God,"[15] and "God himself conceived by Mary."[16] Ignatius clearly witnesses to a faith in Jesus as the divine Son of God, and savior of the world who effects salvation through his sufferings in the flesh. He calls Jesus "our God,"[17] and says by this he means he is the "God who came in the flesh."[18] It is possible that he envisaged the divinity, until the time of the incarnation, as "indistinguishable" (or unable to be internally specified, which may be just another way to say that his Trinitarian theology is still unelaborated) after which point the "Sonship" was then manifested historically.[19] He also clearly presumes that this faith in the divinity of the Lord Jesus is the "standard faith" of the Christian communities of the Near East. His episcopal leaders call upon these communities to defend it against those who would separate the divinity from the material world (presumably Gnostic elements in the communities), whose Christology he characterizes as essentially "docetic," that is refusing the reality of the fleshly existence of the heavenly Lord.

This pattern of "Spirit-Christology" in the Apostolic Fathers is witnessed again in the theologian Hermas. He was possibly a captive Jewish priest from the Roman war of the first century, brought to Rome as a slave, and functioning as a prophet in the Roman Christian communities, while serving in the Christian household of a wealthy mistress. His theological thought is deeply eschatological. Many, even in antiquity, thought him strange and obscure. His writings are conceived in a visionary and ecstatic manner, and represent the last stages of the active era of prophets in early Christian worship. Hermas's theological goals are different to those of the bishop Ignatius. He is overwhelmed by the need to call the church to repentance and submission to the authority of the One Father. He describes Jesus as the vehicle for the "holy pre-existent Spirit" indwelling him.[20] His flesh cooperated so faithfully with the work of God's Spirit that it was promoted "to be a partner with Holy Spirit." Many interpreters have been greatly puzzled by the question of Hermas's binitarianism or trinitarianism. Did he believe in the Father, the Holy Spirit who was himself the eternal Son, and the Servant Jesus who was elevated to glory in an adoptionist sense? It is always better in his work, however, to translate "Holy Spirit" without the definite article, as meaning a close approximation to what later Christian generations would mean by divine status and energy, what theologians after Tertullian and Origen would describe as "divine nature." Like Ignatius, Hermas seems to be teaching that the pre-existent Son descended to work for the salvation of the world through the incarnate servant Jesus. He expresses himself inconsistently from time to time in his writings, and cannot be counted as confident a theologian as some of the other Apostolic Fathers. Nevertheless, he puts the main argument dramatically enough in this way: "God caused holy pre-existent Spirit, that which created all the cosmos, to dwell in flesh that he had desired."[21] His stress, however, is on the mediation of the Lord Jesus, and the supreme authority of God the Father. The looseness of many of the elements of the Apostolic Fathers' Christology, especially this aspect of the unspecified nature of the divine relations of Father and Son and Spirit, were to be the main reason the later generation of theologians sharpened their discourse considerably. The immediately succeeding generation of the church witnessed a marked elevation of theological thought, and combined with it a great effort to make theological language more precise. This era is known as the time of the Apologists.

Irenaeus of Lyons

The most important writer who serves as the bridge between the Apostolic Fathers and the Apologists is Irenaeus (c. 135–200). Originally from Smyrna, he studied at Rome before becoming a presbyter, and later bishop, of the church at Lyons. His community was disturbed by Gnostic teachers, a context that drew out from his pen an extensive apologia of the "norms" of Christian theology. These were established by Christian custom (he is an important advocate of tradition in theology), sober biblical exegesis (albeit of a highly symbolic form as it would strike the modern reader), the habitual forms of prayer and liturgy that had been accepted in the majority churches, and not least by cautious and conservative pastoral episcopal guidance. His theological work established patterns of Christian thought and administration which became constitutive for later catholic orthodoxy. His major work was the five-volume tractate *Against Heresies* (*Adversus Haereses*) in which he reviewed and contradicted Gnostic theological systems. His anti-Gnostic agenda led Irenaeus to emphasize the unity of God, his profound involvement with the material order, and to posit both these ideas as the essence of the principle of salvation. From them followed his central christological principles: that the Christ was one and the same, both flesh and eternal spirit seamlessly united, and that thus the Gnostic and Docetic teachers who wished to make a radical separation between the flesh and the spirit were fundamentally misguided.[22]

Irenaeus affirmed the sacramentality of the world as a gift of God the Father and elaborated a theory, based on Paul, of the recapitulation (*anakephalaiosis*) of human destiny in the person (and flesh) of Christ. Just as Christ sums up the whole cosmos in his divine and human person, so mankind is liberated from sin and death, and restored to a divine destiny. His achievement, theologically speaking, is that cosmology is now presented as seamlessly integrated with soteriology, making his writing the first major patristic elaboration of the theology of deification (*theosis*) which will become so important later. His insistence that Christ was both truly God and truly man would become a key element of later classical theology.[23] Precisely because the Lord assumed flesh, the fallen nature of humankind was enabled to be lifted up again to God's favor.[24] In his teaching that all the divine epiphanies of the Old Testament were manifestations of the eternal Logos (the same who eventually became man), Irenaeus set the foundation for rendering all Scripture into christological raw material. He thus transfigures the entire theology of biblical revelation by making it wholly christocentric. This was a major achievement in which he prefigured the great Origen of Alexandria, and set the tone for all subsequent patristic exegesis.

The Greek Apologists

After Irenaeus, Christian theology seems to speed up and deepen its level of reflection, a factor that characterizes the era between the middle of the second century and the beginning of the third. This is the time of the Apologists. It is a collective title of the theologians whose concern was largely with making a reasoned defense (or *apologia*) of the Christian faith before outsiders who were now taking note in a hostile way of the nascent Christian movement. The main writers of this group were Aristides, Justin Martyr, Tatian, Athenagoras, Theophilus, Minucius Felix, Tertullian, and Lactantius. Apart from their specific apologetic work of trying to present Christianity as worthy of being regarded as a "licit religion" in Roman terms, they also give interesting sidelights on the early form of pre-Nicene Christology. Many of them elaborate Christianity's first reflections on metaphysics, cultural theology, and cosmology. The greatest of them are Justin, Tertullian, and Lactantius. Justin Martyr offers rare insights on the earliest form of liturgy. Writers such as Tertullian and Lactantius begin to sketch out the basis of Christian systematic and political theology, though Theophilus was one of the first to elaborate a technical terminology for the doctrine of the Trinity. Generally speaking, the Apologists' enthusiasm for Logos-Christology led to the predominance of that scheme of thought in later Christianity.

Justin Martyr (Christian convert c. 132, martyred c. 165) describes the church as the community of those devoted to the Logos, or reason of God. The creative Logos had put a germinative seed of truth (*logos spermatikos*) in all hearts and had incarnated in the person of Jesus within history to reconcile all lovers of the truth in a single school of divine sophistry. For Justin, Christianity is the summation and fulfillment of all human searching for truth. His *First Apology*, therefore, sets out to prove the divinity of Jesus, for the benefit of pagans, from the venerable and antique prophecies of the Old Testament.[25] Similarly in his work addressed to Jewish readers he elaborates a central argument that the Christian worship of Jesus is no dilution of monotheism, but rather its refinement.[26] Ancient schools of philosophy shared a common vocabulary of principles, especially turning around the central notions of *logos* and *nomos*. The first term signified wisdom, both divine and human, which was germinally within the deepest recesses of the human mind and heart. This was the case because it had been gifted to mankind by the beneficence of Supreme Being. The second term signified the search for moral norms understood as the springs of the pattern of truth on earth. Justin and Lactantius are most concerned to argue that, in Christ, religion and wisdom are reconciled: worship and philosophy become one and the same thing in the Christian church.

Justin reaffirms the basic concept of the Son of God as eternal, the divine wisdom personified, who came to earth to save a failing race.[27] The incarnation was the supreme act of a salvific revelation that had been prefigured in other epiphanies of the Logos throughout human history.[28] His special merit as a theologian is found in the way he insists that the divine being of the Son is not merely a temporary "form" of the revelation of the Father, but an everlasting aspect of the very divinity, that makes of the Son the one supreme mediator of all truth and of the divine presence.[29] All that human seeking after the truth discovered laboriously in times past is now here, in Christ, presented to humanity full, complete, and in essence. It is nothing other than the life the world has been seeking after throughout history, now given to it as a grace.[30] Justin's combination of soteriological Logos thought, with this remarkably universalist sense of Christ's summation of all human history, will become an important influence (along with Irenaeus's theology) on the work of Origen, who will synthesize these ideas and bring them to a systematic clarity in the middle of the next century.

Early Latin theology

So far it has clearly been the Greek-speaking Christian world that has had the edge in theological reflection. The first great Latin thinker was Tertullian (c. 160–225), a convert from North Africa, whose work established a technical Latin Christian vocabulary. He devoted a brilliant and pugnacious legal mindset to the service of the church in the era of persecutions. He composed a series of works attacking the docetic ideas of the Gnostics and the dualism of Marcion (*Against Marcion, Against Hermogenes, The Resurrection of the Flesh, The Flesh of Christ*). His central theme was that Christ's incarnation was a true material reality, one that sacramentally vindicated the goodness of the material world, and gave the promise of true resurrection to believers. His work *Against Praxeas* set out the foundations for what would become the Latin doctrine of the Trinity, shaped by the main lines of Greek Logos theology. Here he shows how Modalism (the Spirit and Son as temporary "forms" of the being of the Father) is unscriptural, and no true defense of monotheism. His treatise sets out to explain how the Word and Spirit emanate as distinct persons from the Father, all possessing the same nature. His approach to Christology understood natures in the sense of legal possessions, which set Latin thought on a long path: Christ possesses two natures, but is only one person.

Another important western theologian was the Roman presbyter Hippolytus (170–236); although he wrote in Greek, which was still the language of the Christians of the capital. In his writing we see the final ascent of the Logos theology which would dominate the whole Christian world from then on. In most respects he follows the earlier Apologists in his understanding of the Logos as having been extrapolated from the divine Monad for the purpose of creation and salvation. Justin and Irenaeus are his masters, and in some respects he does not go beyond them, being more representative of the second century than the third. His context, however, pressed him to new things, for he felt it incumbent on him to demonstrate that the antique and often unreflecting Monarchianism could not longer go unchallenged. Monarchianism, with its insistence that the Father and Son are different names for different processes within the Godhead, an idea still prevalent in the communities, was inherently inferior to the Logos theology he espoused as more faithful to the Pauline and Johannine teachings on Christ the Divine Wisdom.

For Hippolytus (following Theophilus of Alexandria's teachings) the Logos was at first immanent (*endiathetos*) in the Divine Monad, then became the emitted word (*prophorikos*) in the process of Creation, and finally was the incarnate word (*ensarkos*) in the economy of salvation. In his spacious soteriology, Hippolytus follows Irenaeus's concept of salvation as recapitulation, whereby Christ assumes flesh to reverse the damage caused by Adam and restore immortality to the human race. Historically Hippolytus was important, for after him no theologian could unreflectively use language that suggested Father, Son, and Spirit were interchangeable designations in the Godhead. He underscored that the personal titles of Father and Logos manifested personal, hypostatic, distinctions of an eternal order. Certain christological formulae emerge with Hippolytus that will shape the thought of generations to come. Not least it consists of the image that occurs in his work of the Logos clothing himself with flesh out of a motive of love. He also sees the Logos becoming true man (not a mere manifestation of human form) and the Logos dwelling within his own flesh as the godhead within its temple, as "one and the same Son of God incarnate."[31]

Third-century Logos theology

The highest form of the Logos theology in the third century, however, is indisputably found in the works of two master theologians from Alexandria: Clement (150–215) and Origen (186–255). These two, and especially the latter, dominated the christological thought of all who came after them, even those who lamented the extent of their influence. Both theologians were influenced by the Jewish philosopher Philo who had shown them a pattern of a holistic and Logo-centric manner of interpreting the scriptures. The scriptures became a vast and all-encompassing story of how the Divine Wisdom set about the salvation of the human race through teaching it the paths of righteous behavior (Paideia Christology). In Clement's treatise *Christ the Educator* (*Paedagogus*), the incarnation of the Divine Wisdom is the ultimate act of embodied demonstration (*endeixis*) on the part of the divine teacher for the salvific re-education of a race that had gone astray. Christ sums up and perfects endless generations of human progress to the good through philosophy and ethics. Christ is the *telos*, or goal, to which all human culture and aspiration has been wending.

Origen's genius was to take that central idea and make it the driving force of a massive system of the theology of salvation. He saw all things (especially the scriptures that demonstrated this teaching in symbolic form) as witnesses to the manner in which the Divine Logos stood at the center of a great cosmic movement of the ascent of creation to the invisible Father. His Christology is scattered over a massive amount of treatises and biblical commentaries, and is not always concisely and coherently presented. But overall its magnificent architecture presented a vision of a creation that had emanated from the Logos itself, as a purely spiritual order. The world of created souls (*psychai*) fell from the meaning of their being (the contemplation of the unapproachable Godhead of the Father through the imagistic mediation of the Logos) in a pre-cosmic cataclysm. The material world was created as a result of the fall, in order to house these once great spirits who had fallen from the vision of God (a "cooling off"), having become alienated from God. Now psychic creation was composed of three orders of being: the angels who remained faithful, the rebel spirits whose rehabilitation was cast aside and who remained in enmity to God, and the fallen spirits who had been sent for remedial punishment to earth as embodied souls (the human race). The Logos, who had once formed the perfect vision of beauty and meaning for all these souls, still yearned to aid their ascent back to spiritual enlightenment and perfection. This ascent would be communion with the Logos, beginning in the material order, but passing beyond it to a state when the fallen souls could be progressively purified so as to ascend to clearer vision and more exalted states of being.

In suggesting this large scheme of salvation, Origen had put at the core of theology this mystical Christology of loving communion and Paideia. He had also alarmed many more simple believers by fusing biblical language and symbolism of the fall, with ideas of pre-existent psychic being, and pre-temporal lapsarianism. His bishop, Demetrios of Alexandria, was so alarmed at the publication of the treatise *On First Principles*, where many of these ideas were first sketched out, that he initiated the condemnation of Origen (then a layman) as a gnosticizing heretic. Even though the episcopate of Palestine supported Origen, and admitted him into the clergy, encouraging his emergence as an internationally recognized theologian, for the rest of his life he would have problems establishing his credentials as a "traditionalist" thinker in harmony with the wider church. The fourth century would take most of the architecture of his Christology, but the elements it would choose to jettison would also be determinative of most of the bitter arguments over orthodoxy that racked the church in what has come to be known as the Arian crisis.

The main frame of this Origenian Christology was to be treasured by the church, such as the vision of the Logos of God ever active, like a "Hound of Heaven" to seek out the lost souls in the cosmos and restore them to their former glory. However, many of the details of his speculations were to be jettisoned. One of these problematic aspects was the notion of the Logos's distinction from Jesus as the Son of God. The "becoming flesh" was simply an ontological impossibility for Origen. Logos is pure spirit and could never become flesh in the common understanding of that notion. If scripture seemed to suggest that contradiction, it was because the reader had misinterpreted a symbol simplistically. Spirit, or rather souls (pre-existent psychic being), could certainly become flesh. The pre-temporal fall of the rebellious souls (you and I who now constitute the human race, but were once part of the entourage of the Divine Logos and equals of the angels) proved the peculiar fact that souls could become enfleshed. But for the Logos, this was never a possibility. So it was that, despite the yearning of the Logos to redeem and rescue fallen *psychai* on earth, his plan to come among them as a teacher in the flesh, and work their education from out of a fleshly medium, could not happen – unless a medium presented itself to resolve the ontological dilemma. This, for Origen, is where the Great Soul Jesus entered into the schema. While most of the souls on earth fell there as a punishment, Origen believed that some (certain of the prophets such as Malachi – whose name "My Angel" gives the clue – also John the Baptist, and the Virgin Mary, for example) came down from a motive of altruistic love, in emulation of their master the Divine Logos. Of all the souls who had fallen, or slipped away from the primeval communion with the Logos which was established in the original making of the souls as a heavenly circle, one soul had, over aeons, never fallen but entered even deeper into communion with the Master, so as to form a perfect communion with him. It was this pre-existent soul, Jesus, who volunteered to come down to earth, be incarnate, and stand as the living medium (both physical and spiritual) of the presence of the Divine Logos, historically and concretely on earth.[32]

The Logos, as Origen understood it, was thus perfectly one with the humanity of Jesus, but not related to it directly, rather in a mediated, spiritual way, through his most perfect communion with the soul of Jesus. Origen's theoretical pursuit of the details of how this could be, marks a christological advance on all who had come before him. For him, the union of Godhead and flesh is no mere association but a "true union," something he even calls a "mingling" (*anakrasis*).[33] He points out the gospel's authority for calling the incarnation a union, not a correlation such as that which might be thought to be descriptive of the Word's inhabitation of a saint or prophet.[34] For Origen, it is an intimate relation of Godhead and humanity that even deifies the flesh of Jesus, but one in which the proper characteristics of each nature (divinity and humanity) need to be attributed precisely. The Logos does not suffer the experiences of the body or the soul.[35] This is the human lot which the Soul Jesus has assumed for itself on being born into material creation.[36]

The aftermath of Origen

This is a theory which is almost peculiar to Origen himself and often overlooked, but it was never to be accepted as standard in later Christian thought, and had little precedent to justify it. But for Origen it explained how Jesus could be the incarnation of the Divine Logos, without involving the perfection of Divine Spirit in the temporalities and limitations of the material order. Many of the intractable problems of fourth-century Christology (was Jesus the Son of God the direct personal incarnation of the Logos? was he ensouled? was he truly human as other men are?) derive from the manner in which Origen had thus set the christological agenda to run along these tracks. On the one hand, Origen strongly affirmed the existence and purpose of a soul in the Incarnate Lord, thus articulating an important christological principle that Gregory of Nazianzus would later repeat and canonize: "What was not assumed, was not healed." But it also has to be remembered that he distanced the Logos from the incarnation by inserting the mediation of another psychic subject altogether, the Great Psyche Jesus (who was not the Logos but an elevated creature of the Logos). The polarities of this problem, commonly known as the issue of christological ensoulment, were to haunt all the fourth century.

Despite its peculiarities of detail, the main outline of Origen's christological vision seized the imagination of later theologians. Logos theology became the undoubted core of almost all christological thought henceforth in Christian antiquity. The immense skill of Origen's biblical philosophy demonstrated a dazzling way of making all biblical revelation Logo-centric. Moreover, he did it in a manner that was clearly a simple and direct soteriology of Paideia. Origen made his theory of all cosmic life as the yearning of the Logos to re-educate his fallen creation into a story that was not only vastly metaphysical and stunning in its dimensions, but something that was also tender, loving, and intimately understandable. Origen had made Christology into the universal clearing house of all Christian theological thought. He ultimately translated it as the plan of the Logos to cause all souls to ascend on high once more, so as to enjoy his communion, and in that to discover the life-giving vision of God. Origen made Christology into a mysticism of love, and for all his defects, this fiery vision was to set the tone of most of what was to come in the fertile generation that followed, that is, the fourth and fifth centuries in which Christology came into its classical maturity through so many vicissitudes.

Further reading

L. W. Barnard, *Studies in the Apostolic Fathers*, Oxford: Blackwell, 1961.
T. D. Barnes, *Tertullian: A Historical and Literary Study*, Oxford: Oxford University Press, 1971.

F. L. Battles, *The Apologists*, Allison Park, PA: Pickwick, 1991.

R. M. Grant, *The Greek Apologists of the Second Century*, Philadelphia: Westminster, 1988.

A. Grillmeier, *Christ in Christian Tradition*, vol. 1: *From the Apostolic Age to Chalcedon (451)*, 2nd revised edn, London: John Knox, 1975.

J. N. D. Kelly, *Early Christian Doctrines*, London: A&C Black, 1958; 5th rev. edn, 1977; repr. London: Continuum, 2007.

J. Lawson, *The Biblical Theology of St. Irenaeus*, London: Epworth, 1948, A *Theological and Historical Introduction to the Apostolic Fathers and their Background*, New York: Macmillan, 1966.

J. A. McGuckin (ed.), *The Westminster Handbook to Origen of Alexandria*, Louisville, KY: Westminster John Knox, 2004.

J. Morgan, *The Importance of Tertullian in the Development of Christian Dogma*, London: Kegan Paul, Trench, Trubner, 1928.

J. T. Nielsen, *Adam and Christ in the Theology of Irenaeus of Lyons*, Assen: Van Gorcum, 1968.

E. Osborn, *Tertullian: First Theologian of the West*, Cambridge: Cambridge University Press, 1977.

R. Roberts, *The Theology of Tertullian*, London: Epworth, 1924.

S. Tugwell, *The Apostolic Fathers*, London: Continuum, 1989.

Notes

1 Two books known as the *Apostolic Church Order* (written somewhere in Egypt around the year 300) and the *Apostolic Constitutions* (written in Constantinople sometime in the late fourth century) have been often classed among the Apostolic Fathers, but they do not belong here. These works show that even in antiquity some Christian writers were deliberately archaizing so as to be included in this company.
2 Clement of Rome, *1 Clement* 58.2.
3 Clement of Rome, *1 Clement* 48.6.
4 Clement of Rome, *1 Clement* 36.1.
5 *Second Clement* is generally considered to have been written by someone other than Clement.
6 *2 Clement* 1.1.
7 *2 Clement* 3.1.
8 *2 Clement* 14.3.
9 *Barnabas* 5.10.
10 *Barnabas* 6.12.
11 *Barnabas* 5.5.
12 *Barnabas* 5.11.
13 Ignatius, *Letter to the Ephesians* 7.2.
14 Ignatius, *Letter to the Ephesians* 1.1.
15 Ignatius, *Letter to the Ephesians* 18.2.
16 Ignatius, *Letter to the Romans* 6.3.
17 Ignatius, *Letter to the Ephesians* 18.2; *Letter to the Trallians* 7.1.
18 Ignatius, *Letter to the Ephesians* 7.2, 19.3.
19 Ignatius, *Letter to the Smyrnaeans* 1.1.
20 *Shepherd of Hermas*, *Similitude* 5.6.
21 *Shepherd of Hermas*, *Similitude* 5.6, 5.7.
22 Irenaeus, *Against Heresies* 1.9.2; 3.16.2; 3.16.8; 3.17.4.
23 Irenaeus, *Against Heresies* 4.6.7.
24 Irenaeus, *Against Heresies* 5.14.2; 3.21ff.
25 Justin, *First Apology* 30–53.
26 Justin, *Dialogue with Trypho* 48–108.
27 Justin, *First Apology* 33.1; 13.3; 35.9.
28 Justin, *Dialogue with Trypho* 14.8.
29 Justin, *First Apology* 63.13; *Dialogue with Trypho* 128.1.
30 Justin, *Second Apology* 10.1.
31 Hippolytus, *Refutation of All Heresies* 15, 17; *On Christ and Antichrist* 4.

32 Origen, *On First Principles* 2.6.3–6.
33 Origen, *Against Celsus* 1.66; 2.9; 6.47.
34 Origen, *Commentary on John* 1.28.96.
35 Origen, *Against Celsus* 4.15.
36 Origen, *Against Celsus* 2.23; *On First Principles* 4.4.4; *Homilies on Jeremiah* 14.6.

16
REDEMPTION

James D. Ernest

The engine powering the spread of Christianity across ethnic and geographical boundaries in the early centuries was the proclamation of what the God of Israel had done in the death and exaltation of the Jewish teacher and healer Jesus – called by his followers "Christ" (Messiah) – to bring salvation to all peoples. Evidence – literary and otherwise – surviving from that period shows that this salvation was depicted as a redemption (buying back or ransoming) of people from a situation of bondage to sin and evil powers, to decay and death. His triumph could rescue them from their defeat. That, very broadly speaking, was the gospel Christians proclaimed. Precisely how they described the situation from which people needed redeeming, how they accounted for the ability of Jesus to redeem them, what response they believed was required from the redeemed, and what future they foresaw as the goal of redemption varied across times and places. All this depended on the religious, social, economic, political, and philosophical background and situation of the hearers and of the Christian teachers who addressed them. These teachers primarily derived an overarching narrative of redemption and a conceptual vocabulary for its further elaboration from evolving Christian interpretation of the scriptures of Israel, oral tradition deriving from Christ and his earlier followers, gospels and letters that had become or were in the process of becoming Christian scripture, and from evolving Christian practices pertaining to worship and ministry. Bringing these narrative, conceptual, and practical resources into conversation with the variegated traditions, concepts, and practices of the larger Greco-Roman world, they adapted the gospel of redemption to multiple new contexts. The result, from our vantage point, is a potentially bewildering complex of diverging and converging, contrasting yet intermingling, accounts of redemption. This complexity defeats any simplistic attempt to represent in a single pure generalization "what the early church taught" about redemption. But many of the competing accounts came to complementary expression through voices that participated together in a network of living communities which in fact were, and were becoming, one institutional church, while other voices and their accounts were coming to be seen as irreconcilable with the larger community and its discourse of salvation. Therefore it is possible to discern a coherent pattern of teaching.

But where to begin, and how to proceed? A strictly chronological organization of the material would be frustrated by the way in which alternative motifs and themes travel together and separately across the decades and centuries. Instead, the approach taken here is of a thematic nature. An opening section will focus on what remained the central symbol of redemption for the Apostle Paul: the cross of Christ. The cross is a good case study in the unity and diversity of early Christian teaching, because even this key symbol was susceptible of diverse interpretations – some of which flowed into ongoing church tradition, while others (some of which are highlighted below) were set aside as heterodox. A second section opens into a broader panorama by sketching strands of teaching and practice that connect with various stages in the narrative of the Redeemer. A third and final section sums up from the perspective of the story of the redeemed, considered individually and in community.

The sign of the cross

The centrality of the cross in the accomplishment of redemption is acknowledged in a backhanded way even in quarters where actual crucifixion was disdained. According to Irenaeus, the Valentinians claimed that when Paul said that the teaching about the cross is the power of God, and that he would never glory in anything but the cross, the cross he was talking about was none other than the high-level principle that they called Horos (limit). They said that in its supporting function it is called Horos, but in its dividing or separating function it is called Stauros (cross).[1] Related is a revelation of Christ described in the *Acts of John*, where the apostle, witnessing the apparent crucifixion of his Lord on a cross of wood, is drawn aside into a nearby cave where the Lord himself shows him a cross of light which he says is also called *logos*, mind, Jesus, Christ, door, way, bread, seed, resurrection, son, father, spirit, life, truth, faith, and grace.[2] Here "cross" becomes synonymous with the entire Johannine vocabulary of Christ and salvation – it becomes everything but the locus of real redemptive suffering, as the Lord says he has actually "suffered none of those things which they will say of me" and the apostle goes his way laughing at the gullible. For Paul, the wooden cross is an indispensable and highly significant prop in the drama of salvation; in Gnostic transformation it is a red herring – a deception and diversion.

For believers of a docetic or gnostic bent, the heightened symbolic force of the cross replaces its painful and offensive original meaning. Such a strategy has obvious value, given that for Jews and Gentiles alike crucifixion was the ultimate humiliation, signifying utter abandonment by God or the gods. But others explored the symbolism of the cross expansively without denying the Lord's suffering. Thus in the *Acts of Peter*, when the apostle is about to be crucified, he tells onlooking believers that the real cross is not that which is visible; but he goes on to embrace his own actual crucifixion (upside down for symbolic reasons) on a real cross.[3] And perhaps more convincingly anti-docetic than the Peter story is the insistence of Ignatius of Antioch on the real suffering of Jesus Christ, nailed in the flesh to a wooden cross at a particular juncture in history.[4] The participation of Christians in their Lord's suffering might be metaphorical or sacramental, or it might also be imitative and actual, as in the cases of Peter and Ignatius. In any event, Christ's own crucifixion was actual.

Early Christians explored deepened meanings of the cross along several dimensions. Reaching back into the textual archives of Jewish faith, they found the cross prefigured in texts similarly exploited in the New Testament, such as the serpent lifted up in the wilderness for the healing of all who would gaze upon it,[5] and in rather obvious additional passages, such as Exodus 17:8–13, where, in what would otherwise be a losing battle, the saving power of God becomes and remains effective when Moses assumes and holds a cruciform posture.[6] But they also found prefigurement in cases requiring greater ingenuity, such as the assertion that we can see that circumcision looks forward to the Lord from the fact that the male householders circumcised by Abraham at the first instance of the rite were 318 in number: the number 318 equals 10 + 8 + 300, in Greek writing *iota* plus *eta* plus *tau*; the letter combination *iota–eta* abbreviates the name of Jesus; and the letter *tau* is written in the shape of a cross.[7] Again, the wood of the cross is prefigured in a whole series of biblical objects: the rod used in various ways by Moses, Aaron's rod that budded, the tree planted by the waters in Psalm 1, the rod and the staff of Psalm 23, and the stick that Elijah cast upon the water in order to float the sunken ax-head.[8] The assertion of these and other types constituted so many stitches whereby the cross of Christ was sewn into the fabric of the Hebrew Scriptures, making the point that the whole history of God's saving intervention in the history of Israel anticipates and is completed in what happened on the cross. The directionality of the intertextual control is highlighted starkly when Ignatius of Antioch, responding to interlocutors who appealed to the (Old Testament) Scriptures as the indispensable basis and criterion of Christian teaching, points rather to the cross, death, and resurrection of Jesus Christ: the cross is the canon according to which the "archives" are interpreted rather than vice versa.[9]

Early Christians also found the cross figuratively present in many artifacts of common human culture: the mast of a ship, the plow, various tools, and the military ensign.[10] Unlike the biblical "types," these pointers to the cross appeal universally, to Gentiles as well as Jews. Ignatius drew a similar artifact into a word-picture evoking the early Christian portrayal of salvation as incorporation into a holy structure: the cross is the crane that uses the rope of the Holy Spirit to lift up believers, individual stones being built into a temple.[11] The cross thus becomes a prop in the enactment of the drama of salvation in the life of each believer. The theme of incorporation or actualization links this usage to the sign of the cross as executed in Christian worship (whether in gathered cult or in the course of everyday life), as when an early Syrian Christian poet has the believer approach the Lord with hands stretched out because "my extension is the common cross, that was lifted up on the way of the Righteous One."[12]

The cosmic projection of the cross noted above in Gnostic sources has analogies in mainstream authors who connect the effects of the cross with its shape. Noting Plato's indication of the role of the Greek letter *chi* in the formation of the cosmos,[13] which he identifies as a borrowing from Moses, Justin found the shape of the cross stamped into the universe.[14] This monogram could indicate limiting or separating, as in Gnostic usage, or it could indicate comprehending or embracing. Whereas the Gnostic writer Theodotus saw the cross as separating the faithful from the unfaithful and excluding the latter from the Pleroma,[15] Irenaeus takes up the embracing function, indicating that the crucified Son of God, inscribed crosswise on the universe, embraces north, south, east, and west, heights and depths, calling everyone everywhere to knowledge of the Father.[16] More particularly, the cross brings together the two previously separated populations of the world – Jews and Gentiles.[17] Thus redemption brings about both vertical and horizontal reconciliation. Clement of Alexandria brings the separating function of the cross down to earth in the separation of the soul from the pleasures of this life; the true gnostic is crucified to the world, thus following in the footsteps of Christ, and so becomes a Holy of Holies (i.e., is sanctified).[18]

If typological exegesis sites the cross everywhere in the history of salvation, and cosmic and shape-based readings explore its implications synchronically, early writers also found the cross inscribed in the future of redemption. In the *Gospel of Peter*, the cross follows the resurrected Jesus and the two accompanying angels from the tomb, and when the voice from heaven asks, "Have you preached to those who sleep?" it is the cross that answers yes. So the cross has accompanied Jesus to the abode of the dead, and since Jesus and the angels are prodigiously tall, this episode may indicate not only the resurrection but also the ascension.[19] At any rate, the tradition clearly associates the cross with the future return of Christ. Evidently taking the "sign of the Son of Man" that Matthew 24:30 says will appear in the heavens, heralding his return, to be the cross, the *Epistle of the Apostles* represents the Lord as saying that the sign of the cross will precede him when he comes down to judge the living and the dead. Other early apocalyptic works say the same.[20]

If this brief sketch were more fully filled out, we might find that in various sources the central emblem of redemption – the cross – points to all the variant elements of the narrative.[21] The story is about God's people Israel, about individual believers, even the whole cosmos. The redeemed are recalled from death, sin, and alienation variously conceived. Their response involves a process of sanctification. Their future entails participation in the glory of the Redeemer as they have participated through baptism in his death.

Tracking the career of the Redeemer

If the cross is the central symbol and prop in the drama of redemption, the Redeemer himself is the chief protagonist, and tracing his story-within-the-story, as generally summarized in the evolving "rule of faith," is one way to organize other elements that need to be mentioned. The following survey accordingly proceeds through the Redeemer's descent, incarnation, life, death, descent to the realm of the dead, resurrection, ascension and session, and future return.[22]

Descent

Noting the descent of the Redeemer to earth as a separate stage permits us to observe that the descent without the following stages does not yet provide a basis for a Christian idea of redemption. Complex Gnostic cosmologies involving multiple levels of intermediaries between the unknowable high god and humans share common-alities with apocalyptic conceptions of the universe such as those found in the New Testament and in the Christian (or Christianized) Pseudepigrapha, not to mention the more speculative soteriological ruminations of Origen. Apocalypticism in the world of Jesus did feature speculation on the identity and activity of angelic powers, good and evil, and the earthly effects of their doings. Evil, rampant on earth, had its champions also in realms above and below, but God was good, powerful, and interested and would eventually set all things right. The goodness of the creator guaranteed the ultimate goodness of the creation. In *The Ascension of Isaiah*, the prophet sees the Beloved descend through the seven heavens, past their angelic denizens, to the firmament for the purpose of being hanged on a tree so that he may plunder the angel of death, rise, and ascend again, bearing up the righteous with himself.[23] In the Gnostic schemes, the Redeemer descends in order to remind those who bear the Gnostic spark, and who in their captivity in the evil material realm have forgotten their true identity, of knowledge required for their ascent; but he does not die for them, rise, and lead them through life to glory after death.

Christian teachers who did know the subsequent stages nevertheless sometimes placed the greatest stress on the teaching and law-giving activities of Jesus – activities enabled by his descent with no necessary dependence on the remaining stages. Anti-Gnostic Christians were not opposed to revealed knowledge per se; they were opposed to esoteric knowledge, supposedly transmitted secretly by Christ to selected insiders, that supplanted or replaced the publicly proclaimed knowledge handed down from the Lord's apostles through those appointed to oversee the churches in major cities across the empire and recorded in the four Gospels that were universally accepted in the churches well before the end of the second century. That apostolic knowledge did have saving efficacy. The work of the Son included illuminating humankind by revealing the Father and clarifying the divine law, and pre-Nicene Christian teachers emphasized these aspects.[24] Jesus was the teacher par excellence, even the only teacher.[25] Such, the apologists sometimes seem to believe, is the meaning of his title *Logos*. His teaching office is at times presented as the goal even of his incarnation and death (as in the eventual "moral influence" understanding of the atonement; Jesus teaches by example as well as by word).[26] Clement of Alexandria, opposed as he was to Gnosticism, could present Christ as the Teacher (as in his treatise *Christ the Educator*) and reclaim the label "gnostic" for believers according to the canons of the Great Church. "Enlightenment" could become a virtual synonym for "baptism."[27] But for none of these writers was Christian redemption reducible without remainder to teaching and enlightenment or commanding and obedience; as other considerations in their writings show, these were in service to union with or assimilation to Christ.[28]

Incarnation

Incarnation – or to translate the usual Greek term more precisely, inhomini-zation – denotes a more distinctive claim. The Greek gods, who never had quite the transcendent character of the God of Israel anyway, could walk the earth in human form, but they did not really become fully human. Irenaeus, in the same sentence in which he hails Christ as "the one secure and true teacher, the Logos of God," says that "on account of his surpassing love he became what we are in order to equip us to become what he is" – a sentence that would echo through later elaborations of the *theosis* understanding of salvation.[29] What he means by "became what we are" is clarified over against the Gnostic contention that the demiurge produced a son of animal (psychic) nature who was born by "passing through Mary just as water flows through a pipe," that is, without acquiring anything of her substance, and that the Savior (a separate entity, belonging to the Pleroma) descended upon him at his baptism.[30] This Gnostic Christ, then, is neither truly God nor truly human and is therefore not the "one Christ Jesus, the Son of God, who became incarnate for our salvation" as Irenaeus says the church throughout the whole world believes.[31] The Word became human in order to accomplish, as a human and for humankind, what humans in their disobedient state could by no means accomplish for themselves: recovery of the lost image and likeness of God and victory over death.[32] The incarnate Christ unites God's incorruptibility and immortality to humanity, summing up or "recapitulating" in his own person the essential history of humankind's existence under God in order to do over correctly what Adam and his progeny got fatally wrong.[33] The union of believers with Christ begins with gracious and efficacious divine initiative. As a well-known patristic dictum holds, "The whole human would not have been saved if he had not assumed the whole human."[34]

Over against Gnostic beliefs that salvation was automatic, regardless of behavior, for the "spiritual" elite, who needed knowledge only for perfecting, while the merely "soulish" remainder of humankind needed works for salvation, Irenaeus says that humankind as a whole is redeemed, and indeed deified, through the gracious intervention of the Word.[35] But salvation is not automatic and determined: people must exercise their free will to maintain themselves in that which God freely gives.[36] So in practice redemption is a matter of incremental progress.[37] Again over against Gnostic teaching, the salvation not only of the spirit but also of the flesh is guaranteed by the shedding of Christ's blood and by eucharistic participation in his body and blood.[38] In the future lie bodily resurrection and a millennial earthly kingdom. So while Irenaeus is, because of the Gnostic challenge, mainly a theologian of the incarnation, he is not a reductionist but strives to incorporate the whole of traditional church teaching and practice in his presentation of the narrative of human redemption.

Life

While the canonical Gospels lay special stress on the death and resurrection of Christ, they also spend considerable time on his life, meaning not only his teaching, and not only his obedience as a reversal of human disobedience (as Irenaeus, building on Paul, would see it), but his effective works for others, especially the exorcisms and healings. This stage of the career of the Redeemer, though noted in some early summaries of apostolic preaching,[39] is missing in the later creeds and apparently also the earlier baptismal creeds that informed them. But in the world of the early church, where much physical and psychic suffering was attributed to the malevolent influence of celestial powers and other spiritual beings, demonstrable authority over demons was a powerful argument. Looking back from the fourth century, Athanasius saw that the spread of the gospel had brought the silencing of pagan oracles, central institutions of Gentile religious and civic life that Christians believed to be the voices of demons.[40] Additionally, Emperor Julian regretted that the Christians had overwhelmingly outperformed the pagans in charitable care for the sick and the poor. Christian imitation of the life of Jesus, whether through exorcisms and miracles or through religiously motivated deeds of human kindness and compassion, especially during epidemics, worked a ministry of practical redemption that furthered the numerical growth of Christianity.[41]

Death

In Judaism under Macedonian and Roman domination, to be executed by the authorities because of one's loyalty to God was already the highest expression of obedience and trust, and carried the expectation of reward in the life to come.[42] Jesus had suffered such a death, and for some of his disciples following him in martyrdom, this was the surest path to saving union with him – which was precisely the point of martyrdom. This is suggested by the only recorded words of some of the martyrs in the earliest preserved account, namely, "I am a Christian."[43] A larger number of words remain from the martyr Ignatius, but the central point is the same: he is *called* a Christian, but in order to *be* one he must follow his Lord in death.[44] Ignatius expresses a judgment that distinguished early catholic Christianity from all forms of docetism and Gnosticism, namely, that it was unacceptable to say that Christ merely *seemed* to suffer.[45]

Though Ignatius does not theorize about Christ's suffering, he acknowledges that Jesus died not simply or exclusively as an example but "on our behalf."[46] Other early Christian writers found various ways of saying why or how the death of Jesus could be of benefit to others, providing precedents for several "theories of the atonement" that have been elaborated and differentiated through the history of Christian thought down to the present. The New Testament writings offer several models, centrally including sacrificial images,[47] and *Barnabas*, where we find several types of the cross as noted above, says that the Lord offered himself as a sacrifice for our sins, identifying Jesus with both the scapegoat of the Yom Kippur ritual and the sacrificial red heifer of Leviticus 19.[48] The apologists in general are concerned with matters other than exploring the logic of the atonement, but Justin tells the Jew Trypho that the Passover lamb and the Yom Kippur goats were types of Christ.[49] A related term applied to Jesus in our literature is "ransom" (*lytron*, also sometimes translated "redemption"). In Matthew 20:28 Jesus already applies this term to himself, and several second-century texts echo the usage.[50] Irenaeus indicates that Jesus took on flesh in order to offer it up as a sacrifice, and in several places the surviving Latin rendering of *Against Heresies* uses propitiation language.[51] In the early fourth century Eusebius explains that Christians do not perform animal sacrifices, because the sacrifice of Christ has provided "the great and precious ransom of both Jews and Greeks," binding into one elaborate package the language of sacrifice, ransom, cleansing, and life given for life (*antipsychon*).[52] The word recalls a phrase constantly associated with sacrifices in the Greek version of Leviticus.[53] Later writers, picking up on language used by Tertullian in the context of penance, would say that Christ's sacrifice makes "satisfaction" for sin. If some pre-Nicene authors seem to say surprisingly little about how Christ's death saves, it may be because the paschal mystery lay at the heart of the faith and, like the eucharistic observance in which it was re-enacted weekly, was not to be disclosed carelessly to non-believers while Christianity remained a minority cult in a hostile environment.[54]

In the world in which Christianity was born, animal sacrifice was a visible and constant feature of most religions. It was only natural and indeed inevitable that Christians would describe both the death of Jesus and their own religious practices using sacrificial language. But neither in paganism nor (perhaps more importantly) in Judaism did sacrifice always mean a propitiatory sin-offering. It might mean some other kind of sin-offering, or it might be connected with worship, thanksgiving, or communion with God in some other or more general way.[55] For the author of Hebrews, Jesus offered himself once for all as a sacrifice for sin; no further sacrifice in that literal sense was necessary or possible. But Paul urged disciples to offer themselves as living sacrifices, i.e., to make their whole lives acts of worship, and spoke of his own suffering in sacrificial terms.[56] Analogies to both Hebrews and Paul can be found in later early Christian writers. So while penal substitution is at least one aspect of the meaning of Christ's sacrifice in early Christian sources, it is not dominant or even necessarily present every time the motif of sacrifice is invoked. "Sacrifice" may sometimes simply serve as a shorthand for cultic or ethical action vis-à-vis God, i.e., for the practice of religion.

In what sense, then, do Christians offer sacrifice to God? Ignatius speaks of becoming a "sacrifice of God."[57] He has narrowed down Paul's offering of one's whole life to martyrdom.[58] The *Martyrdom of Polycarp* compares the old saint to a splendid sacrificial ram, and in his final prayer he calls himself a sacrifice.[59] Justin, who sees Christ's sacrifice as the antitype of Israel's Passover lamb, also presents the eucharistic bread as the antitype of an Israelite grain offering.[60] But others used the concept more broadly, describing ethical and spiritual exertions other than martyrdom as sacrifice or as ransom for one's sins.[61] Since the temple is the locus of sacrifice, descriptions of Christians as stones being built into a temple (see above) should be recalled here: not only ethical life but cultic worship is sacrifice. Early on, the language of sacrifice is applied to the Eucharist.[62] Christian worship in general, with "offerings" (*prosphorai*) and "services" (*leitourgiai*) implied Christian counterparts to Israel's priests and Levites.[63] Even when the Eucharist specifically is mentioned, the emphasis may be on various elements of worship, including prayers, praise, and thanksgiving.[64] Thus the sacrifice of early Christians was the totality of their response to God, including the moral or ethical "offering" of their lives as well as their acts of cultic worship, including centrally the Eucharist.[65]

Saving union of believers with Christ is the point both of Christ's sacrifice in death for them and of the imitative sacrifice they offer in response, whether as martyrdom, praise, Eucharist, or service to others. Christ does not die as their substitute in a way that makes no response necessary. His gracious descent, teaching, incarnation, recapitulation of their history, and practical acts of liberating mercy enabled them, through imitation and obedience, to bind themselves closely to his sacrifice on their behalf.

Descent to the realm of the dead

Christ's post-crucifixion descent into hades or sheol, the realm of the dead, is not a dispensable mythological doublet of the death account. It advances the story of redemption by showing that the sacrificial victim, far from being passive, intrudes actively into enemy territory in order to announce and effect the release of those held captive. Here the question of the enemy, not yet broached in the foregoing, becomes pressing.

The descending Redeemer brings revelation to the benighted and alienated – did someone mislead them? The incarnate Redeemer establishes contact with ruined human nature – ruined by whom? The healing and exorcizing life of the Redeemer sets an example to follow but also begins an assault on the oppressive demonic forces, which then mount a counter-attack resulting in his martyrdom, which also, unbeknownst to them, has atoning efficacy: it cleanses those for whom he dies, and (seen as ransom) it purchases their freedom. When the writers noted above referred to ransom, they did not press the image to the point of asking to whom the ransom was paid, but when Origen comments on Matthew 22:28, he does raise that question. Flatly ruling God out of consideration, he asks gingerly, with the air of one who knows his suggestion may be shocking to some: could it be the evil one?[66] By the time of Gregory of Nyssa in the late fourth century, this suggestion would flower into a narrative in which Satan, tricked into pouncing on the one human Life to which he was not entitled, loses his rightful claim on the whole race.[67] By this stratagem Christ conquers the devil. So goes one development of the Christus Victor motif identified by Gustaf Aulén as the "classic" model of the atonement.[68]

On one level, the descent into hades is an attempt to answer the question regarding the salvation specifically of the Old Testament saints. In the *Ascension of Isaiah*, the prophet sees the spirits of Abel, Enoch, and all the righteous standing in the seventh heaven, robed but not crowned and not seated on their thrones. He is told that they will not receive their crowns until the Beloved descends into the world, incognito, to be hanged on a tree. He will then "plunder the angel of death," rise, and ascend, taking "many righteous" with him. Then they will receive their crowns and thrones.[69] Origen makes explicit the conflict with Satan and pushes it back to the cross: his *Commentary on Romans* says that Christ bound the devil on the cross, then entered his house (hell) in order to take the captives with him.[70] In earlier versions, such an apocryphon attributed by Justin to Jeremiah and the scene described above in the *Gospel of Peter*, proclamation is made to the dead but their actual release is not narrated.[71]

More generally, the descent into hades marks the nadir in the *upsilon* vector traced by the Son, who pre-exists in heaven, descends to rescue humans, then reascends, bearing them up to heaven. In the *Odes of Solomon*, Christ descends from on high to the regions below so that those in the middle are gathered to him.[72] Given the cosmology of the day, a redeemer who descended merely to the earth but not into the regions beneath the earth would have failed to span the cosmos and so would have left part of it beyond reach of redemption. Then again, perhaps some *are* beyond redemption: *The Ascension of Isaiah* explicitly stops the Beloved's descent short of "haguel," the pit of perdition.[73]

Liturgically speaking, the descent into hades provides a point of attachment in the career of Christ for the believer's descent beneath the waters of baptism. Once again imitation provides a means of union with the Redeemer.

Resurrection

If the early Christian story of Christ had been expressed always purely in terms of descent and ascent – even descent as far as hades – then the resurrection would perhaps not have been a critically important moment. Indeed, the Gospel of John's identification of the Son's "lifting up" in crucifixion as his glorification might tend to collapse death, resurrection, and ascension into one moment; and in John the ascension is implied, not narrated.[74] But in fact all four canonical Gospels narrate the discovery at the tomb on the first day of the week, and the resurrection is central to the gospel proclamation in Acts and in Paul's epistles. For the antidocetic and antignostic believers in the mainstream of early Christianity, the death of Christ was as real as the death of their own martyrs and loved ones, however gracefully and even triumphantly they accepted it, and so had to be his resurrection.[75] Like other key moments of his career, it was foretold in Scripture.[76]

As the most straightforward sign of Christ's victory over death and the devil, the resurrection functioned in the salvation of his followers as the basis for the full assurance with which his apostles and succeeding generations preached, and it had a correspondingly powerful persuasive effect on their hearers.[77] Ignatius saw the resurrection functioning, for believers of all ages to come, similarly to the banner that military units followed into battle.[78] Cross, death, and resurrection of Christ were the "archives" in which Christianity was grounded.[79] If the resurrection had been amenable to simple graphic representation, its emblem might perhaps have approached the pre-eminence of the cross among Christian symbols.

At any rate, early Christianity in general followed Paul in reasoning that the resurrection of Christ pointed to, and provided a firm basis of confidence in, their own future resurrection.[80] So in his final prayer before his martyrdom, Polycarp asks both that he may share in the resurrection to eternal life and that he may be in the Lord's presence "today." Like Paul, Polycarp (or his hagiographer) was apparently untroubled by questions of timing.[81] Papias, Justin, and Irenaeus expected a future resurrection to be followed by a millennial kingdom on earth,[82] so it is clear that, at least for some, resurrection was not reducible to a purely spiritual ascent following death. Ignatius points out that Jesus was "in the flesh even after the resurrection."[83]

Ascension and session

In the New Testament, only Luke and Acts narrate the physical ascension of Jesus at a particular time and place (in Luke, apparently on the day of resurrection; in Acts, forty days later). Elsewhere his ascension is implied. The resurrected Jesus of Matthew 28:18 not only has been vested with all earthly authority (like the "one like a son of man" of Dan. 7:13–14) but also explicitly claims authority in heaven; that authority grounds the work of the disciples who take salvation to the nations in his name. Acts encourages those who suffer for the gospel with the knowledge that their Lord stands at God's right hand in heaven.[84] Hebrews teaches that Jesus is "a great high priest who has passed through the heavens" with salvific consequences for those who hold fast to him.[85] Offering his own blood, he enters the true, heavenly sanctuary and obtains eternal redemption.[86] So already in these other first-century sources the presence of Jesus Christ in heaven contributes to his redeeming work; but the ascension itself is not narrated.

That reticence might be thought partly responsible for the delay until the fourth century of the separation of the ascension from the passion in Greek creeds and in liturgical observance. But separate liturgical observance of the resurrection was likewise delayed. In some earlier sources, the resurrection is portrayed in terms of ascension.[87] In others, the ascension is the completion or fulfillment of the resurrection.[88]

Nevertheless, the ascension, like the resurrection, does have its own manifold redemption-historical significance in pre-Nicene thought. Cyprian sees the resurrection not only as a manifestation of power but also as the transportation of saved humanity up to the Father, and further as the cue for the disciples to scatter and take the gospel to the nations.[89] Along similar lines, Lactantius notes that Christ ascended only after preparing his disciples to preach in his name, and on his departure he endowed them with the power to do so.[90] In an early work, Eusebius says the purpose of Jesus' preliminary ascent and re-descent in John 20:17 was to obtain and bring back the spiritual gifts.[91] He is clearly following Origen's *Commentary on John*, though Origen, characteristically, also has other reasons for that same ascent.[92] For example, Origen is the earliest patristic author to make explicit and repeated use of the Letter to the Hebrews, where he finds the ascended Jesus depicted as the heavenly high priest who mediates between humans and God. Having himself ascended through the heavens, he is able to lead the saints through its spheres to the abode of the Father.[93] Elsewhere, he connects Christ's priestly role with his atoning sacrifice of his own flesh in order to destroy the power of death over humans, so that those who take up their cross and follow him will be enabled to follow him from earth to heaven.[94]

Future return

In the end, though, believers expected Jesus to return from heaven to earth. The first-century Letter to Titus references the "blessed hope" of the early Christians, namely, the "manifestation of the glory of our great God and Savior, Jesus Christ"; this appearing would consummate his self-sacrificial work of redeeming from iniquity and purifying for himself "a people of his own."[95] The Redeemer's identity (as disclosed in the narratives of his descent, incarnation, and exaltation) and his hitherto finished work (as summed up in the narrative of his life, death, descent to hades, resurrection, and ascension) said most of what needed to be said regarding redemption, but so long as God's people remained subject to persecution, sickness, temptation, and death, the last enemy had not yet been defeated.[96] In the apocalyptic temporal framework, grounded in Jesus' own teaching, that was elaborated in the letters of Paul, in Luke and Acts, and in other early Christian writings, the final completion of the work of salvation was connected with the promise that the same Jesus who had ascended would in the end return.[97] As decades and centuries passed, Christian teachers repeated predictions of the "second coming" similar to those found in the New Testament,[98] including the imminence of this return.[99] As noted above, the expectation was that at his return, the redeemed who had died would be resurrected to eternal life. In some of his writings, Tertullian specified a subterranean intermediate state after death, followed by a post-resurrection judgment, on the basis of which some would be consigned to eternal hellfire.[100] In some writers (including Justin and Irenaeus), the literal character of this expectation was further elaborated in descriptions of an earthly millennial kingdom. Justin himself notes that many pious Christians did not share the millennial expectation.[101] Origen's framework was not apocalyptic, evidencing more kinship to that of the Gnostics whom he opposed: the souls of humans had fallen in a pre-existent state, and their restoration would coincide with the restoration (*apokatastasis*) of all things to their pre-fall condition. Tensions between (apocalyptic) materialistic and (post-apocalyptic) spiritualizing interpretations of the Christian hope, corresponding to philosophical outlook in general and anthropology in particular, would recur through Christian thought.

The life of the redeemed

In the framework of apocalyptic Second Temple Jewish thought, which is the matrix in which Christianity was born, salvation had both national and individual aspects, but the ethnic-national dimension was paramount. God's people Israel, in exile both abroad and in its own patrimonial territory, awaited redemption from the effects of its history (as narrated especially in the Deuteronomistic History) of failure to abide by the terms of the covenant. While the oppressor had the upper hand, individual martyrs could hope for ultimate vindication through resurrection, and the nation as a whole could expect eschatological restoration. Both sides of this hope survive in early Christian transformation. Witness Paul's Letter to the Romans, which after exploring the dynamics of salvation in terms that apply easily on the individual level, returns in chapters 9–11 to agonizing reconsideration of the question of national salvation. So while it was clear that the *subject* – the protagonist – in the Christian story of redemption was Jesus Christ, the question of the identity of the *object* of his redemption was ambiguous and could lead to revolutionary exploration. Paul's answer – "the Jew first, and also the Greek" – states in a nutshell a major dynamic of the pre-Nicene history of redemption.[102] The Jewish people did not flock to Jesus and his apostles *en masse*; it was individuals and sometimes their households, first Jewish and then increasingly and eventually almost exclusively Gentile, that became Christian. Gentile converts were effectively grafted into the biblical narrative, but their own story of redemption began not with a history of declension from a covenant but a history of subjugation to oppressive powers, prominently including demons masquerading as gods.

Eschatological considerations aside, their redemption had conditions and consequences in the here and now. Catechesis, baptism, and Eucharist brought them into membership in the body of Christ. The moral or ethical content of much of the surviving second- and third-century literature indicates that behavioral corollaries were central in the catechesis of the day. Second-century writers were aware of and sometimes quoted Paul's dictum that "by grace you have been saved, through faith … not by works," but we find no sustained reflection on the relation of works and faith in justification.[103] When Origen and later writers did raise that question, they tended to conclude that both in tandem were necessary. Origen was especially concerned to clarify (over against gnostic and astral determinism) that individuals had free will and were responsible for their deeds.[104] In the West, Tertullian maintained a strong emphasis on free will even while teaching that each new human soul inherits a nature that is predisposed to sin. He emphasizes that Christ's death is important to our redemption, but never fully develops an account of how; meanwhile, he often characterizes Christ as giver of a new law. As a gross generalization, then, the dominant second- and third-century perspective may seem to have been that believers were saved through following the way of life that Christ taught them.[105] In view of the variegated indications reviewed above, however, it would be fairer to say that writers in this period had not yet confronted the synthetic questions that were sharpened and answered by theologians in later centuries. Those who mine early Christian teaching in quest of later doctrines of grace, predestination, atonement, and justification may find both more and less than they seek: copious hints, beginnings, and isolated clear statements of all kinds of later positions, but less extensive, integrated, and focused reflection on how all these threads hang together in a coherent account of the salvation of an individual believer.

But the moral discourse, whether prescriptive or descriptive, in the second- and third-century writings, whether exoteric (like that of the apologists, at least putatively) or addressed to believers, was not intended as a theoretical account of redemption; it aimed to construct a concrete practice of Christian community – a community whereby Christians participated in and were united with Christ and with each other – and it pointed to that practice as a sign of the victory of God in Jesus Christ over all contrary powers and principalities. Thus Justin points to the conversion of believers from sexual immorality to chastity, from magical arts to the love of God, from greed for possessions to willingness to share with the needy, from internecine strife to a spirit of harmony and reconciliation.[106] Justin's putative aim was to win the emperor's admiration, and thus the protection or at least toleration of the Christian movement, but the broader claim is akin to the point in the famous passage of the *Epistle to Diognetus* that claims Christians are to the world what the soul is to the body, namely, that the charity lived out in the community of the redeemed represents the highest potential and the intended destiny of the human race as a whole.[107] The *disciplina arcana* that prevented some of our writers from disclosing their sacramental practices and the doctrinal understandings pertaining to them in exoteric writings does not entirely conceal from our view the fact that for them this practice of charity was not a purely human moral accomplishment but a participation in the career of the Redeemer who became human, abasing himself to the point of crucifixion, in order to elevate humanity to fellowship with the divine.

Further reading

Primary sources

J. H. Charlesworth, *The Old Testament Pseudepigrapha*, 2 vols, Garden City, NY: Doubleday, 1983–5. (Includes numerous early Christian, Jewish-Christian, or Christianized Jewish works such as the *Martyrdom and Ascension of Isaiah*, *Odes of Solomon*, and *Testaments of the Twelve Patriarchs*.)

M. W. Holmes (ed. and trans.), *The Apostolic Fathers: Greek Texts and English Translations*, 3rd edn, Grand Rapids, MI: Baker Academic, 2007. Also available without the original-language texts: *The Apostolic Fathers in English*, 3rd edn, Grand Rapids, MI: Baker Academic, 2006. (Includes *Didache*, 1 and 2 *Clement*, the letters of Ignatius, *Epistle to Diognetus*, *Barnabas*, and *Shepherd of Hermas*.)

A. Roberts and J. Donaldson (eds), *The Ante-Nicene Fathers*, 10 vols, Edinburgh: T&T Clark, 1885–7; repr. Grand Rapids, MI: Wm. B. Eerdmans, 1987; repr. Peabody, MA: Hendrickson, 1994. (The translations and introductions are dated, but this is still the most comprehensive collection of pre-Nicene Christian literature in English.)

J. M. Robinson, *The Nag Hammadi Library*, 3rd edn, New York: HarperCollins, 1990. (Translations of the Gnostic documents discovered at Nag Hammadi in Egypt in 1945.)

W. Schneemelcher, *New Testament Apocrypha*, rev. edn, trans. R. McL. Wilson, 2 vols, Louisville, KY: Westminster John Knox, 1991. (Includes translations of numerous non-canonical early Christian writings, including apocryphal gospels and acts.)

Secondary sources

G. Aulén, *Christus Victor: An Historical Study of the Three Main Types of the Idea of Atonement*, trans. A. G. Hebert, London: SPCK, 1931; repr. Eugene, OR: Wipf & Stock, 2003. (An influential set of lectures originally published in Swedish as *Den kristna försoningstankenin*, 1930.)

J. Daniélou, *The Development of Christian Doctrine before the Council of Nicaea*, vol. 1: *The Theology of Jewish Christianity*, trans. and ed. J. A. Baker, London: Darton, Longman & Todd, 1964. (Chapters 8 and 9 cover the theology of redemption.) Vol. 2: *Gospel Message and Hellenistic Culture*, trans. and ed. J. A. Baker, London: Darton, Longman & Todd, 1973. (Chapter 7, on the content of early catechesis, is especially pertinent.)

J. N. D. Kelly, *Early Christian Doctrines*, London: A&C Black, 1958; 5th rev. edn, 1977; repr. London: Continuum, 2007. (A standard account. See esp. chapter 7 on pre-Nicene soteriology.)

J. Pelikan, "The Meaning of Salvation," in *The Emergence of the Catholic Tradition (100–600)*, vol. 1 of *The Christian Tradition: A History of the Development of Doctrine*, Chicago: University of Chicago Press, 1971, pp. 141–55.

B. Sesboüét, *Le Dieu du salut*, vol. 1 of B. Sesboüét and J. Wolinski, *Histoire des dogmes*, Paris: Desclée, 1994. (An introductory general survey of the development of Christian doctrine through the patristic period, with soteriological material throughout.)

H. E. W. Turner, *The Patristic Doctrine of Redemption: A Study of the Development of Doctrine during the First Five Centuries*, London: A. R. Mowbray, 1952; repr. Eugene, OR: Wipf & Stock, 2004. (More balanced than Aulén.)

Notes

1 1 Cor. 1:18; Gal. 6:4; Irenaeus, *Against Heresies* 1.3.5.

2 *Acts of John* 97–102.

3 *Acts of Peter* 36–8.

4 Ignatius, *To the Smyrnaeans* 1.2.

5 *Barnabas* 12.5–7; Justin, *Dialogue with Trypho* 90; cf. John 3:14, alluding to Num. 21:9.

6 *Barnabas* 12.2; Justin, *Dialogue with Trypho* 91.4.

7 *Barnabas* 9.7–8, referring to Gen. 17:23.

8 Justin, *Dialogue with Trypho* 86.

9 Ignatius, *To the Philadelphians* 8.2.

10 Justin, *First Apology* 55.

11 1 Pet. 2:5; *Shepherd of Hermas, Similitudes* 9.

12 *Odes of Solomon* 42.1–2.

13 Plato, *Phaedrus* 36b.

14 Justin, *First Apology* 60.

15 Clement of Alexandria, *Excerpts from Theodotus* 2.42.1; 1.22.4.

16 Irenaeus, *Demonstration of the Apostolic Preaching* 34.

17 Irenaeus, *Against Heresies* 5.17.4, referring to Eph. 2:14–16.

18 Clement of Alexandria, *Miscellanies* 2.20.

19 *Gospel of Peter* 39–42. For this interpretation, see J. Daniélou, *The Theology of Jewish Christianity*, trans. and ed. J. A. Baker, London: Darton, Longman & Todd, 1964, pp. 249–50, 266–8.

20 *Epistle of the Apostles* 16; *Apocalypse of Peter* 1; *Apocalypse of Elijah* 3.2.

21 For a survey of appearances of the cross of Christ (i.e., the cross itself, not the cross as a general symbol) through the fourth century, see J.-M. Prieur, *La croix chez les Pères (du IIe au début du IVe siècle)*, Cahiers de Biblia patristica 8, Strasbourg: Université Marc Bloch, 2006.

22 J. Pelikan, *The Emergence of the Catholic Tradition (100–600)*, vol. 1 of *The Christian Tradition: A History of the Development of Doctrine*, Chicago: University of Chicago Press, 1971, p. 142, organizes his discussion of salvation around (1) the life and teachings, (2) the suffering and death, and (3) the resurrection and exaltation of Jesus.

23 *Ascension of Isaiah* 9.6–18.

24 Matt. 11:27; John 1:9, 17:3; Matt. 5–7.

25 Ignatius, *To the Ephesians* 15.1; 9.1.

26 Irenaeus, *Against Heresies* 5.1.1.

27 H. E. W. Turner, "Christ as Illuminator," in *The Patristic Doctrine of Redemption*, Eugene, OR: Wipf & Stock, 2004, pp. 29–46.

28 Pelikan, *Emergence of the Catholic Tradition*, pp. 142–6.

29 Irenaeus, *Against Heresies* 5.Pref. Theosis is sometimes said to be the dominant Eastern image of salvation, but Andrew Louth points out that *theosis* (the completion or fulfillment of the human creation) and redemption (repair or restoration of the damage of the fall) are two different things. See A. Louth, "The Place of *Theosis* in Orthodox Theology," in M. J. Christensen and J. A. Wittung (eds), *Partakers of the Divine Nature: The History and Development of Deification in the Christian Traditions*, Grand Rapids, MI: Baker Academic, 2008, pp. 32–44.

30 Irenaeus, *Against Heresies* 1.7.2.

31 Irenaeus, *Against Heresies* 1.10.1; cf. 3.11.3.

32 Irenaeus, *Against Heresies* 3.18.1–3.

33 Irenaeus, *Against Heresies* 3.19.1.

34 Origen, *Dialogue with Heraclides* 7.

35 Irenaeus, *Against Heresies* 1.6.

36 Irenaeus, *Against Heresies* 4.37.

37 Irenaeus, *Against Heresies* 4.38.3.

38 Irenaeus, *Against Heresies* 5.2.2.

39 Acts 2:22, 10:38.

40 Athanasius, *On the Incarnation* 46.

41 See R. Stark, *The Rise of Christianity: How the Obscure, Marginal Jesus Movement Became the Dominant Religious Force in the Western World in a Few Centuries*, San Francisco: HarperSanFrancisco, 1997, pp. 73–94.

42 4 Macc.; Dan. 12.

43 *Acts of the Scillitan Martyrs.*

44 Ignatius, *To the Romans* 3.2.

45 Ignatius, *To the Trallians* 10; *To the Smyrnaeans* 4.2.

46 Ignatius, *To the Romans* 6.1.

47 On sacrifice in early Christianity, see R. J. Daly, *Christian Sacrifice: The Judaeo-Christian Background before Origen*, Washington, DC: Catholic University of America Press, 1978; *The Origins of the Christian Doctrine of Sacrifice*, Philadelphia: Fortress, 1978 (which concisely distills the results fully documented in *Christian Sacrifice*); F. M. Young, *The Use of Sacrificial Ideas in Greek Christian Writers from the New Testament to John Chrysostom*, Cambridge, MA: Philadelphia Patristic Foundation, 1979.

48 *Barnabas* 7.3; 7.10; 8.

49 Justin, *Dialogue with Trypho* 40.

50 *Diognetus* 9.2; *Protevangelium of James* 7.2 = 16.8–10; Melito, *Pascha* 789.

51 Irenaeus, *Against Heresies* 4.16, 4.29.1, 4.29.2; *Demonstration of the Apostolic Preaching* 31. See Daly, *Origins of the Christian Doctrine of Sacrifice*, pp. 93–4.

52 Eusebius, *Demonstration of the Gospel* 1.10.8

53 Daly, *Origins of the Christian Doctrine of Sacrifice*, pp. 3–4.

54 Cf. Pelikan, *Emergence of the Catholic Tradition*, p.148.

55 See Young, *Use of Sacrificial Ideas in Greek Christian Writers*, pp. 1–3.

56 Phil. 2:7; cf. 2 Tim. 4:6.

57 Ignatius, *To the Romans* 4.2 (*thysia*); cf. *To the Ephesians* 8.1 and 18.1(*peripsēma*).

58 Daly, *Origins of the Christian Doctrine of Sacrifice*, pp. 86–7.

59 *Martyrdom of Polycarp* 14.1; 14.2 (*thysia*).

60 Justin, *Dialogue with Trypho* 40.1–2 and 72.1; 41.

61 *Shepherd of Hermas*, *Similitudes* 5.3.8; *Barnabas* 19.10.

62 See *Didache* 14.1; cf. Cyprian, *Letter* 63.

63 *1 Clement* 40; Daly, *Origins of the Christian Doctrine of Sacrifice*, p. 85.

64 Irenaeus, *Against Heresies* 4.29.5.

65 Daly, *Origins of the Christian Doctrine of Sacrifice*, p. 140.

66 Origen, *Commentary on Matthew* 16.8.300–321.

67 Gregory of Nyssa, *Great Catechetical Oration* 24.

68 G. Aulén, *Christus Victor: An Historical Study of the Three Main Types of the Idea of Atonement*, trans. A. G. Hebert, Eugene, OR: Wipf & Stock, 2003.

69 *Ascension of Isaiah* 9.6–18.

70 Origen, *Commentary on Romans* 5.10, cited in Daniélou, *The Theology of Jewish Christianity*, pp. 241–2.

71 Justin, *Dialogue with Trypho* 72.4; cf. Daniélou, *The Theology of Jewish Christianity*, pp. 235–6.

72 *Odes of Solomon* 22.1–2.

73 *Ascension of Isaiah* 10.8–14.

74 John 20:17.

75 E.g., Ignatius, *To the Magnesians* 11, links the factual reality of the birth, the suffering, and the resurrection of Christ.

76 E.g., Justin, *Dialogue with Trypho* 106.

77 *1 Clement* 42.3; Ignatius, *To the Philadelphians*, Salutation; Eusebius, *Divine Manifestation* 3.74.

78 Ignatius, *To the Smyrnaeans* 1.2.

79 Ignatius, *To the Philadelphians* 8.2.

80 1 Cor 15; *Barnabas* 5.6; so also, with additional signs of resurrection in nature, *1 Clement* 24–5.

81 *Martyrdom of Polycarp* 14.2. To take another example, Origen also speaks both of the survival of the soul beyond the death of the body (*On First Principles* Preface, 5) and of the resurrection of the body (*On First Principles* 2.10.1–2).

82 *Fragments of Papias* 3.12; 7.7; 16; 27; Justin, *Dialogue with Trypho* 8.

83 Ignatius, *To the Smyrnaeans* 3.2.

84 Acts 7:56.

85 Heb. 4:14.

86 Heb. 9:12.

87 *Testament of Benjamin* 9.5; *Gospel of Peter* 36–40.

88 Origen, *Commentary on John* 10.37.245.

89 Cyprian, *That Idols Are Not Gods* 6.14.

90 Lactantius, *The Divine Institutes* 21; *Epitome of the Divine Institutes* 47.

91 Eusebius, *General Elementary Introduction*, in T. Gaisford (ed.), *Eusebii Pamphili episcopi Caesariensis Eclogae propheticae*, Oxford: Oxford University Press, 1842, p. 102.

92 Origen, *Commentary on John* 6.56.288–6.57.292.

93 Origen, *Against Celsus* 6.20.

94 Origen, *Homily on Numbers* 9.5; *Exhortation to Martyrdom* 13. See R. A. Greer, *The Captain of Our Salvation: A Study in the Patristic Exegesis of Hebrews*, Tübingen: Mohr Siebeck, 1973, pp. 58–60.

95 Titus 2:13–14. For early Christian eschatology in detail, see B. E. Daly, *The Hope of the Early Church: A Handbook of Patristic Eschatology*, Cambridge: Cambridge University Press, 1992; repr. Peabody, MA: Hendrickson, 2003.

96 For an overview of patristic soteriology concluding that "the soteriology of the early church … most commonly understands redemption or salvation as being achieved in Jesus' identity rather than accomplished as his work," see B. E. Daley, "He Himself Is Our Peace," in S. Davis, D. Kendall, and G. O'Collins (eds), *The Redemption: An Interdisciplinary Symposium on Christ as Redeemer*, Oxford: Oxford University Press, 2004, pp. 149–76. For death as the last enemy, see 1 Cor. 15:26.

97 For Jesus and the New Testament, see works like D. C. Allison, *Jesus of Nazareth, Millenarian Prophet*, Minneapolis: Fortress, 1998, and standard NT theologies. Acts 1:11 indicates that Jesus will return in the same way that he ascended.

98 E.g., *Didache* 16.8; *2 Clement* 17.4–5; Justin, *Dialogue with Trypho* 110; Irenaeus, *Against Heresies* 4.33.1;

99 E.g., Cyprian, *Letter* 63.18.

100 Tertullian, *The Soul's Testimony* 55; *The Resurrection of the Flesh* 35; *The Shows* 30.

101 Justin, *Dialogue with Trypho* 80.2.

102 Rom. 1:16, 2:9, 2:10. The same movement is indicated in various forms, narrative and otherwise, in the Gospels, in Acts, and in most of the New Testament.

103 Polycarp, *To the Philippians* 1.3, quotes Eph. 2:8. Cf. *1 Clement* 32.4. For a quick survey from a post-Reformation perspective, see D. H. Williams, *Evangelicals and Tradition*, Grand Rapids, MI: Baker Academic, 2005, pp. 129–32.

104 Williams, *Evangelicals and Tradition*, pp. 133–4.

105 J. N. D. Kelly, *Early Christian Doctrines*, rev. edn, New York: Harper Collins, 1976, pp. 164–83.

106 Justin, *First Apology* 14.

107 *Diognetus* 6.

17
SCRIPTURE
Peter W. Martens

Sacred writings left an indelible mark upon pre-Nicene Christianity. These writings were energetically copied by scribes, translated into several languages, and widely disseminated throughout Christian networks. They were read and expounded upon in the setting of the liturgy, studied privately, and on occasion examined with a keen scholarly eye. Despite their fluid boundaries, these Scriptures were unmistakably woven into the oral and written discourses of early Christianity. There are hints that early Christians committed parts of these writings to memory, and the surviving literature from this period abounds in allusions, paraphrases, quotations, re-tellings, and explicit interpretations of Scripture. While such direct interpretation (reference to a passage followed by its analysis) was usually episodic, the two leading scriptural scholars in our period, Hippolytus and Origen, inaugurated a long-standing literary genre characterized by such interpretation: the commentary. This vigorous interest in the Scriptures flowed from an overarching conviction: that these writings mapped religiously. The Scriptures were thought to express the Christian message of salvation and guide those who read and heard them well along the journey of salvation. The earnestness with which these writings permeated the church's mission of catechesis, moral exhortation, and advanced instruction; the zeal with which they were marshaled into the arena of competing interpretations and religious debate; and the precision with which they were targeted by imperial persecution: all point to the divine or holy status Christians ascribed these writings.

This essay provides an orientation to the Scriptures in pre-Nicene Christianity by exploring five interrelated topics: the physical form these Scriptures took and how they were transmitted and stored; their scope; in what translations they circulated; how they were examined with the Greco-Roman philological apparatus; and finally, the characteristics of their message.

Scripture as artifact: format, dissemination, and storage

When we think of Christian Scripture today, we tend to think of a single codex: a collection of sheets folded in half, gathered together at the spine and protected by a cover. This was not, however, the customary format of Scripture in early Christianity. Whole Bibles that included the Old and New Testaments (*pandects*) were rare – none were constructed in the pre-Nicene period, and it was not until the ninth century that the Bible took this physical form with any frequency.[1] In early Christianity, when someone spoke of the Scriptures, what invariably came to mind was, rather, a series of physical books. Moreover, these books did not necessarily take the form of books as they typically circulate today (codices). They also circulated as scrolls. The roll book, or scroll, was the standard format for a book in the Greco-Roman world, and in Jewish circles Scriptures were inscribed on scrolls, even after the development of the codex. From the second to fourth centuries CE there was, however, a significant change in the physical configuration of books: the scroll was gradually replaced by the codex. Christians – for reasons still not well known today – did not hesitate to transmit their writings, including their Scriptures, in this new format.[2]

Codices came in varying sizes, which meant that a sacred writing could circulate either on its own in a small codex, or in a collection of writings within a larger codex. For instance, a relatively small codex running to thirty-two leaves in length accommodates our earliest copy of the Apocalypse (P 47).[3] Larger codices, however, could contain collections of writings. Extant manuscripts of the Septuagint are often collections, whether of the Pentateuch, Octateuch, a dossier of historical books, the three or five books ascribed to Solomon, the Minor Prophets or Major Prophets.[4] It is similar with the New Testament. Of particular importance are the two anthologies that emerge in the second century: collections of Paul's letters at the beginning of the century, and toward the middle, collections of the Gospels.[5] As we will shortly see, a book technology that facilitated collections of writings played a role in the emergence of the canon of Christian Scriptures.

These Scriptures, moreover, did not always circulate unabridged. They were also transmitted in excerpts, usually in the form of citations (in varying degrees of length and precision) within larger literary works, but also in the form of self-standing anthologies that strung a number of quotations together. These anthologies ("testimony books") contained excerpted scriptural passages, usually from the Old Testament, that were then used as proof-texts by Christian writers within the context of a Jewish polemic to help demonstrate their faith's commitment to Jesus as Messiah, the irrelevance of the Jewish cult, and the church as the new people of God. In our period there are two examples of this testimony book. Cyprian's *To Quirinius* is the earliest extant document, a three-book abridgement of select scriptural passages. A century earlier, however, Melito offered the first explicit reference to such a collection when he spoke of creating "extracts" from the Old Testament "concerning the Savior and our faith" and putting them into six (no longer extant) books.[6]

In whatever format the Scriptures were preserved, they needed to be copied for the purposes of preservation and transmission. Prior to the invention of the printing press, scribes painstakingly copied books line-by-line, word-by-word.[7] In the pre-Nicene period, most of this duplication took place privately. Replication also transpired through collaborative enterprises, though scholars debate whether we ought to envision something as formal as a scriptorium in the pre-Nicene period.[8]

As scriptural writings were copied and then disseminated in the second and third centuries, some fell into the hands of individual scholars with their own private collections, though the evidence for this is admittedly thin.[9] Most Scriptures found their way into ecclesiastical libraries that stored the texts supporting these churches' liturgical, catechetical, and archival needs.[10] While not all churches had dedicated spaces for their libraries, some certainly did. There is an illuminating anecdote from the Diocletian persecution that called for the destruction of copies of Scripture.[11] An official record from 19 May 303 details the search of a church in Cirta, Numidia, where we learn that the building where the congregation met had a library, several (empty) cupboards, and "one very large codex" – other sections of its Scriptures, totaling thirty-seven items, were distributed among several liturgical readers.[12]

Mention should also be made of two substantial libraries that sprang up in the early third century and that served the research interests of early Christian scholars. Presumably neither of these libraries operated with significant independence of its local church, though whether they were larger ecclesiastical archives or separate collections remains unclear.[13] Alexander, the bishop of Jerusalem, founded one of these libraries in Jerusalem, probably during his episcopate (212–50).[14] Origen established the other after he had settled in nearby Caesarea (Maritima) in 231/232. This collection was probably developed around Origen's personal library. Subsequent Caesarean ecclesiastical leaders, most notably its presbyter Pamphilus and its later bishop and scholar Eusebius, expanded it.[15]

The scope of Scripture in pre-Nicene Christianity

The topic of canonicity has attracted prolific scholarly interest over the last century and it remains one of the more vexing topics in early Christian studies today.[16] One of the sources for confusion is the term "canon," which is defined inconsistently in the scholarly literature. I will mean something very specific by the term: a "canon" refers (1) to a list of sacred writings that was final (i.e. a list that comprehensively identified every scriptural writing, and by extension, excluded every other writing not on this list), as well as (2) to a list that was accepted by a majority of congregations.[17] With this working definition in mind, we can sketch out the phases that preceded the emergence of such a canon of Christian Scriptures in pre-Nicene Christianity.

Since Christianity emerged from within Judaism, the earliest followers of Jesus already acknowledged a number of sacred writings – as a whole, this collection would have been very similar to those writings thought to be scriptural by other first-century Jews. Moreover, at the beginning of the second century, a growing body of more recent literature had emerged (and was still emerging) that was beginning to be viewed as a supplement to, and on par with, this older collection. All these writings together could be demarcated from other literature by modifying them with adjectives like "holy," "heavenly," "sacred," or "divine."

But it was not entirely clear what writings met the requirements of Scripture. We see any number of disputes, disagreements, and uncertainties about the status of particular writings throughout the pre-Nicene period. Indeed, in the early fourth century Eusebius still divided books vying for scriptural status into three categories: "accepted," "disputed," and "rejected"[18] – the "disputed" category is telling, since it confirms that a fixed or final list of sacred writings was not yet established, at least in Caesarea. It is in the fourth century that we begin to see a proliferation of scriptural lists that lack the "disputed" category of writings – such lists were, for their authors at least, final and unambiguous. However, the presence of such lists still does not testify to a canon, since the lists of individual authors and congregations often did not agree with one another and were little more than parochial.[19] It was not until the fifth century that something approaching the canon, as defined above, began to emerge: a final list of Scriptures that also achieved widespread acceptance.

This brief narrative clarifies the sorts of questions that are pertinent to discussions of the scope of Scripture in pre-Nicene Christianity: (1) what were the hallmarks of a divine or holy writing?; (2) what circumstances would have precipitated a decision about whether a writing was scriptural?; and finally (3), what particular writings were thought to meet the requirements of Scripture?

For early Christians, most of the characteristics of a sacred writing could be traced back to its provenance. These Christians believed (and argued) that their Scriptures enjoyed a dual authorship: divine and human agents collaborated in their production.[20] On the one hand, divine authorship could be attributed to God, though more frequently to the Word and Holy Spirit; human authorship, on the other hand, was traced back to Moses and the prophets for Israel's Scriptures, and for the New Testament, the apostles, or those who had been their associates.[21] All of these human authors had been "moved," "illumined," "enlightened," or "inspired" by the divine authors.[22] Closely tied to this conviction about authorship was the issue of antiquity. By the standards of late antique Christians, Moses and the prophets were ancient. Moreover, even for the New Testament writings there were corresponding expectations of antiquity, since the apostles and their associates were thought to have composed their texts within a generation or so of Jesus' death.[23] In the minds of early Christians, the provenance of Scripture – its authorship and antiquity – led to a series of additional convictions about its authority (trustworthy), applicability (catholic), and content (salubrious). More on these characteristics below.

There were several circumstances already in play in the second and third centuries that would have expedited decisions about the scriptural status of any given writing. Some of these were endemic to the codex and the transmission of texts. Both the phenomenon of a larger codex that could accommodate a collection (does such-and-such a writing merit inclusion within a larger collection of acknowledged sacred writings?), as well as the expenditure of effort associated with copying writings would have raised questions about the scriptural status of any given writing. The liturgical and scholarly activities of Christians no doubt also played a role in this process. Decisions had to be made about what passages would be publicly read and expounded upon in the liturgy, as well as about the writings that deserved close scholarly scrutiny. Several figures and movements also played a role in precipitating decisions about the scriptural status of writings: Marcion contentiously challenged the sacred status of writings already widely regarded as scriptural; the Montanist movement emphasized the continuous gift of the inspiring Spirit, thus pulling in the opposite direction of Marcion, since it compelled Christians to emphasize the final authority of apostolic writings; the "Gnostic" coalition asserted dependence upon secret, unwritten apostolic traditions; the production of literature that resembled, and in some cases, competed with New Testament texts (the so-called "New Testament apocrypha") also raised questions about what counted as Scripture and what did not. Another factor that played a decisive role in this process were persecutions, as already seen above, since some of these required Christians to hand over their Scriptures, thereby catalyzing the identification of these writings.[24] What is intriguing, finally, about all these factors is that while they undoubtedly elicited decisions about the scriptural status of particular writings, early Christian authors often protested that they did not make these decisions themselves. Invariably they deferred to precedent, namely, to the decisions already made by churches. Authors repeatedly adjudicated the scriptural status of a particular work by noting its contemporary use, or lack thereof, in early Christian congregations.[25]

When we look at the scope of the Scriptures in pre-Nicene Christianity we find the situation fluid. Writers expressed uncertainty about the scriptural status of select writings and could disagree with one another (sometimes knowingly, sometimes unknowingly) about what writings counted as Scripture. Moreover, lists of any sort were rare.[26] A precise account of what writings were considered scriptural in the pre-Nicene period would require a case-by-case inquiry into particular authors and congregations. While this lies beyond the scope of this essay, a rough outline can be sketched.

As already noted above, the earliest followers of Jesus possessed charter documents. In the second and third centuries Christians designated these writings in any number of ways: "our Scriptures,"[27] "books,"[28] "law,"[29] and sometimes "Old Testament."[30] Far more common were the designations "prophets"[31] or "law and prophets"[32] – in the latter case, the law referred specifically to the Pentateuch and the prophets more ambiguously to most anything else thought to be scriptural. The prophets would certainly have included Joshua, Judges, Samuel, Kings, Ezekiel, Jeremiah, Isaiah, and the shorter prophets, but also works like the Psalms, Job, Daniel, and Wisdom. In fact, the three most frequently cited scriptural books in the second and third centuries came from this "Old Testament": Genesis, Isaiah, and the Psalms.[33] While indeterminacy did surround the scriptural status of several writings (some of which would later achieve canonical status, and others which would not), a collection of sacred writings was already emerging that would have found widespread consent.[34]

The writings that would supplement this collection went by several names: "apostles,"[35] "New Testament,"[36] but particularly prominent, some variation of "the gospels and apostolic writings."[37] Already in the first century there is evidence that Jesus' words and the apostolic writings could be juxtaposed to Israel's Scriptures, thereby suggesting a similar status with these writings.[38] While there were, as with the Old Testament, indeterminacies,[39] by the middle of the second century the shape of the contemporary New Testament canon was emerging: the four Gospels, the letters of Paul, 1 Peter, and 1 John were widely held as scriptural.[40]

The contours of the New Testament were, then, analogous to the Old Testament in the pre-Nicene period. By the middle of the second century there was widespread agreement about a core scriptural collection for both groups of literature, while a number of writings resided nebulously on the periphery and would continue to do so through the fourth and fifth centuries. Before turning to the translations in which these Scriptures circulated, there is one final point worth keeping in mind: we should not assume that individual congregations would have possessed all the writings they acknowledged to be sacred. The episode noted above, where Melito, bishop of Sardis, needed to travel to Jerusalem in order to compile an anthology of excerpts from the Old Testament, suggests that this bishop did not have in his possession all the writings he thought counted as Scripture.[41]

Pre-Nicene translations of the Scriptures

At the birth of Christianity the Jewish Bible circulated in a variety of Hebrew recensions as well as in a Greek translation that would later be called the "Septuagint" (LXX).[42] This translation would become the official translation endorsed by the Greek-speaking Christian churches. The *Letter of Aristeas* relays the miraculous rendering into Greek of the Torah in the third century BCE. While this story was regularly told in early Christian literature (with some important variations), much of it is regarded as legendary today.[43] Scholarly consensus attributes the translation of the Pentateuch in the third century BCE to Greek-speaking Jewish communities of the Diaspora. The translation of additional Hebrew Scriptures into Greek continued into the first century CE and was the work of multiple translators, while additional, native-Greek writings could be included in septuagintal collections.[44] A particularly pressing problem for some early Christian scholars was the phenomenon of multiple recensions of septuagintal books, combined with the presence of additional, and often discrepant, Greek translations produced in the second century: the translations of Aquila, Symmachus, and Theodotian.[45] These translations, combined with variations within the septuagintal textual tradition, elicited important text-critical work (more on this below).

Toward the end of the second century, writings from the LXX and the Greek New Testament began to be translated into Latin. The first translations appeared in the Roman province of Africa, and by the third century, many Old Latin versions circulated in Europe as well. It is not clear to what extent the first major Latin Christian writer, Tertullian, had everything he would have considered Scripture available in Latin translation – it is possible that he himself translated several texts from Greek. By the middle of the third century, Cyprian probably enjoyed most of the Scriptures in Latin translation, though this text was itself a revision of earlier translations. The Old Latin versions were a living document, revised many times and highly diverse.[46]

The main Syriac translation of the Hebrew Old Testament was the Peshitta. Like the LXX and the Old Latin versions, it too had multiple translators. This translation was finished by the third century CE.[47] Scholars term the oldest Syriac translation of the New Testament the "Old Syriac." By the end of the third century the four Gospels, Acts of the Apostles, and Paul's fourteen letters (Hebrews included) had been translated.[48]

The other pre-Nicene translation was into the various Egyptian dialects grouped under the heading "Coptic." In the pre-Constantinian period, the scholarly consensus is that numerous translators working independently of one another and in various dialects began translating various books of the Old and New Testaments. By the end of the third century, certainly the Gospels and select Old Testament writings (translated mostly from the LXX) had been rendered into Coptic dialects.[49]

Reading and study

How, and in what settings, did people become familiar with these Scriptures? In late antiquity, books (including the Christian Scriptures) were usually read out loud.[50] Only a small fraction of Christians could read (estimates of literacy rates in late antiquity, including early Christians, range from as low as 5 per cent to as high as 20 per cent),[51] but there is solid evidence for the private reading of Scripture in the second and third centuries.[52] It was primarily within the liturgy, however, that most Christians, particularly the majority who could not read, became familiar with their sacred writings. The practice of scriptural reading in the context of worship is already attested in the first century and there are several references to the practice of the public reading of Scripture in the liturgy in the middle of the second century.[53] A particularly important second-century reference to this practice in Rome comes from Justin:

> And on the day called Sunday, all who live in cities or in the country gather together to one place, and the memoirs of the apostles or the writings of the prophets are read, as long as time permits; then, when the reader has ceased, the president verbally instructs, and exhorts to the imitation of these good things.
>
> (Justin, *First Apology* 67)[54]

Toward the end of the second century the office of the reader emerged. The earliest evidence for this office comes from Tertullian, and Cyprian speaks frequently of it,[55] as well as indicating that the lector read on a raised platform.[56] By the middle of the third century this office was widespread: Eusebius, for instance, provides us with a list of third-century Roman clergy that includes numerous readers.[57]

Alongside this basic act of reading, we detect in the second and third centuries a burgeoning interest in the closer examination of Scripture within a variety of institutional settings.[58] On the whole, it was the writings of the law and prophets that garnered the most attention in our period, though toward the end of the second century we detect a growing interest in the study of New Testament literature as well. The following is a list of some of the landmark scriptural scholars and their writings: *1 Clement* (c. 96), *Barnabas* (before 140), and Melito's *On Pascha* (second half of second century) – all offered dedicated commentary on portions of the Old Testament.[59] Melito's *Extracts* (an anthology of Old Testament texts referring to Jesus) no longer survives, as do only fragments of Papias's five-book treatise, *Expositions of the Sayings of the Lord* (early second century). There was an interest in the Scriptures, particularly the opening chapters of Genesis, within the broad Gnostic coalition. Mention should be made of Valentinus, Ptolemy, and Heracleon (middle- to late-second-century figures). Heracleon's *Exegetical Notes on the Gospel of John* was the first dedicated exposition of a particular scriptural book. Justin's writings, especially the *First Apology* (c. 153–7) and *Dialogue with Trypho* (c. 160), and Theophilus of Antioch's second book of *To Autolycus* (after 180), evince more than a rudimentary knowledge of the Old Testament. Both of Irenaeus's surviving works, *Against Heresies* (book three written during the pontificate of Eleutherus, 174–89), as well as the later *Demonstration of the Apostolic Preaching*, indicate a substantial acquaintance with the Old and New Testaments. Clement of Alexandria (who flourished in the 190s) wrote a book, now nearly completely lost, the *Hypotyposes*, that apparently offered a summary of the whole of Scripture; he also wrote *Extracts from the Prophets*, brief annotations that often take a biblical text as the point of departure, as well as a homily on Mark 10:17–30, *Who Is the Rich Man That Shall Be Saved?*[60] Dionysius of Alexandria (d. 264–5) investigated the Apocalypse in his *On the Promises*; Gregory Thaumaturgos (mid-third century) composed the *Paraphrase of Ecclesiastes* into classical Greek. Several scholars, including Julius Africanus (c. 160 – c. 210), Origen (c. 185–254), Pamphilus (d. 310), and Lucian of Antioch (d. 312), had a keen eye for discrepancies in biblical manuscripts. Among early Latin writers, Tertullian (born c. 160) wove extensive biblical exegesis into *Against the Jews*, *Against Marcion*, and *Against Praxeas*. Novatian's (c. 200–57) exegetical interests surfaced clearly in *On the Trinity* and *On Jewish Foods*, and Cyprian (c. 200–58) interspersed his exegetical reflections throughout his writings, and also composed the three books of testimonies *To Quirinus*.

The two pre-Nicene figures, however, who merit most attention for their commitment to biblical scholarship are Hippolytus (first half of third century) and his near contemporary, Origen. Prior to these two scholars, biblical exegesis was usually episodic. With Hippolytus and Origen, however, there was a heightened commitment to exegetical inquiry, and to the presentation of this inquiry in scholia, exegetical homilies, and commentaries. Hippolytus authored several exegetical works on the Old Testament: extant are the *Commentary on Daniel*, *Commentary on the Song of Songs*, *Homily on David and Goliath*, and *The Blessings of Isaac and Jacob and Moses*.[61] With Origen we have, by all accounts, the first professional Christian philologist who made scholarly inquiry into most, if not all, of the books he considered scriptural.[62] Moreover, Origen offered a program for students to study Scripture in Alexandria[63] and embarked upon an even more ambitious program in Caesarea: a broad curriculum that culminated in the interpretation of Scripture.[64]

One of the most important advances in scholarship in the latter half of the twentieth century has been the contextualization of early Christian exegesis within the world of late antique literary analysis.[65] Scholars have demonstrated with increasing specificity how early Christian exegetes already in the second and third centuries drew in varying degrees upon the general education (*enkyklios paideia*), including the exegetical practices cultivated by the Greco-Roman philologist (*grammatikos*), in their attempts to study Scripture carefully. Origen explicitly counseled such an approach to scriptural study in his famous *Letter to Gregory*:

For this reason, I pray that you productively draw from Greek philosophy those things that are able to become, as it were, general teachings or preparatory teachings for Christianity, as well as those from geometry and astronomy which will be useful for the interpretation of the holy writings, in order that what the philosophers say about geometry and music and philology and rhetoric and astronomy – that these are philosophy's helpmates – that this too we might say concerning philosophy itself as it relates to Christianity.

(Origen, *Letter to Gregory* 1)

In what follows I will discuss the early Christian exegetical enterprise by subdividing it into three procedural moments (text criticism, historical examination, and literary analysis) before turning to the two referents these procedures sought to identify (the literal and the nonliteral).

As already noted above, prior to the printing press, books were painstakingly copied word-by-word. This laborious process not surprisingly led to the introduction of errors into manuscripts. Most of these errors were probably unintentional, the result of fatigue, carelessness or incompetence, though some were purposeful. In his *Commentary on Matthew* Origen offers a representative lament, that "the differences among the copies [of the Gospels] have become great either through the negligence of some copyists, or through the perverse audacity of others, or through those who are careless in the correction of the exemplars."[66] Scribes were frequently accused of purposefully corrupting biblical manuscripts – it was a charge often specifically leveled against Jews and schismatic Christians.[67]

Before Justin few interpreters knew of or were concerned with variant readings in the biblical manuscripts. With Justin and a number of subsequent authors, we detect a growing concern for a correct scriptural text.[68] We are best informed of Origen's text-critical work on the Old Testament. He possessed the major Greek translations of the Hebrew Bible – the translations of Aquila, Symmachus, the LXX (the church's adopted version), and Theodotian, along with several others he found in Palestine[69] – and even had Hebrew manuscripts in his possession. To illuminate and correct many of the discrepancies in the LXX copies, Origen created the *Hexapla*, a monumental six-column work. This work would have been consulted by reading from top to bottom: each row was dedicated to a single Hebrew word or phrase. The reader could then pause at any word and read from left to right, moving through each of the six columns: the first column on the left margin contained the Hebrew text in Hebrew characters; it was followed by a column with the Hebrew text transliterated into Greek characters and then the four Greek translations of Aquila, Symmachus, the LXX, and Theodotian. There are a number of scholarly debates surrounding the *Hexapla*, including the purposes this massive work would have served Origen (by some estimates, it reached forty codices).[70] There seem to be at least two reasons for its construction: it helped Origen correct the discrepancies between the variants in the multiple copies of the LXX; it also alerted him to the differences between the church's Greek copies of Scripture and those Hebrew copies in circulation among the Jews, with whom Origen interacted throughout his scholarly career.[71]

Two other prominent branches of the exegetical enterprise in late antiquity were historical inquiry and literary analysis. At a basic level, historical inquiry began with the refutation or confirmation of people, sayings, and events narrated in biblical passages: could such-and-such have existed, been spoken, or happened, or were these fictions?[72] Beyond this preliminary historical inquiry, early Christian authors applied a range of knowledge drawn from the *enkyklios paideia* to biblical passages. There are any number of instances where geography,[73] ancient history,[74] natural sciences,[75] geometry,[76] philosophy,[77] or even previous exegetical work, Christian and Jewish,[78] facilitated commentary on biblical passages.

Literary analysis was probably the most prevalent concern of late antique biblical exegesis. It included, at the level of words: definitions,[79] etymological analyses of proper nouns,[80] and numerological analysis.[81] Figures of speech were parsed as well.[82] For larger syntactical units, authors paid particular attention to grammatical issues,[83] the sequencing of a passage,[84] and the person(s) speaking in a passage.[85] Probably the most pervasive literary technique was using clearer passages to illuminate opaque passages.[86]

While this basic sketch of exegetical procedures ushers us into the world of early Christian literary analysis, it certainly does not exhaust its philological apparatus. Arguably the most debated feature of the early Christian exegetical enterprise today is its allegorical moment. Within the parameters of this essay it is impossible to address all of the debates in the scholarship, so what follows is a series of signposts that hopefully guide readers through the complexities that swirl around the literal and allegorical interpretations of Scripture in pre-Nicene Christianity.

(1) It is misleading to speak of literal and allegorical exegesis as "techniques" or "methods," since they identified, not philological procedures *per se*, but rather the sorts of *referents* the aforementioned historical and literary procedures could uncover.[87] Contrary to some scholarly constructs, in early Christianity philological scholarship lay as much at the root of literal interpretation as it did nonliteral interpretation.[88]

(2) Interpreters sought two exegetical referents: the literal and the nonliteral.

Literal interpretations aimed for the "letter" or "history," what could variously be called the "obvious," "first-hand," "proper," "surface," or "immediate" referent. Nonliteral interpretations, designated by terms like "allegorical," "figurative," "philo-sophical," "ascending," "mystical," and "spiritual," sought after the "other," "lofty," "deeper," or "hidden" referent. In short, literal interpretation identified the immediate referent, whereas allegorical interpretation cast about for the "other" referent.[89]

It is important to stress that exegetical vocabulary could be used fluidly in the second and third centuries. Hard distinctions, for instance, between *theoria* and allegory emerged later, in the fourth-century critique of Origen's exegesis (esp. in Diodore of Tarsus and Theodore of Mopsuestia). Similarly, expressions like "anagogical" or "tropological" exegesis should not be read anachronistically as signifying something distinct from "allegorical" exegesis since it is, again, only in the early fifth century with John Cassian that a distinction between these sorts of interpretations was made.[90]

It is also important not to confuse the literal and nonliteral referents with the multiple senses of Scripture. In Origen's famous discussion of the three senses of

Scripture in *On First Principles* 4.2.4 he speaks of the "body," "soul," and "spirit" of Scripture. Here he means one literal referent (body) and two nonliteral referents (soul and spirit), the latter two differentiated from one another by their content (the moral life and doctrine respectively).[91]

"Typology" is a largely unhelpful term not only because it does not translate an ancient Greek or Latin word, but also because it suggests in modern treatments a conflict with allegory (where "typology" equates to successful nonliteral exegesis and "allegory" to its unsuccessful nonliteral twin). While there was plenty of talk in pre-Nicene Christianity about scriptural figures (*tupoi*) and how to read them nonliterally, there was no special vocabulary to signify the nonliteral reading of *tupoi*. The terms used to express this nonliteral interpretation included "spiritual," "mystical," and "ascending" exegesis, the very expressions that could often be used interchangeably with "allegorical."[92] Indeed, in book two of his *Miscellanies*, Clement of Alexandria referred to "allegorizing (*allégorésas*) Isaac as consecrated sacrifice," since he was "a type (*tupon*) for us of the coming economy of salvation."[93]

(3) When we canvass the pre-Nicene period we see a willingness to read *both* the Old and New Testaments literally and nonliterally. Christians read Old Testament passages literally and New Testament passages as well, so long as the literal referent proved instructive and edifying.[94]

Of course, the Scriptures could also be read nonliterally, and as a general rule the allegorical referent was some facet of the church's teaching, usually pertaining to Jesus Christ, the ethical life of Christians, and on occasion the cosmos as God's creation. Early Christians repeatedly allegorized Old Testament figures, events, and institutions (i.e. the Jewish cult including circumcision, the Sabbath, the tabernacle and temple, sacrificial system, etc.).[95] Jesus' parables were often analyzed nonliterally.[96]

For particular passages, some were consistently read literally (such as the Pauline corpus), others nonliterally (the events pertaining to the Jewish cult), and still others both literally and nonliterally.[97]

(4) The spirit of the allegorical enterprise was both flexible and principled. It was, on the one hand, open-ended: scholars could offer multiple nonliteral interpretations of a given passage[98] and could happily concede that they did not have the last word.[99] On the other hand, these same scholars expressed a concern for criteria that demarcated proper from improper allegorical interpretations.[100]

(5) Finally, there was awareness, at least in certain circles, of how contentious nonliteral interpretation could be. Origen was often put on the defensive in his homilies when he embarked upon his allegorical readings, which suggests unease with this approach to Scripture in his congregations.[101] He felt the need to respond at length to Celsus's critique of Christians who allegorized Scripture,[102] his allegorical readings would later draw the ire of Porphyry,[103] and two of his staunchest supporters, Pamphilus and Eusebius, specifically undertook a defense of his allegory in their *Apology for Origen*.[104]

Scripture's message

We gather a more complete sense of how, and why, the Scriptures were studied in early Christianity when we examine a few additional convictions about their message. As already noted above, early Christians believed that their scriptures enjoyed a dual authorship and that these authors had collaborated to communicate a message. But where could this message be found? There were two widely repeated and shared patterns of responses to this question. On the one hand, interpreters could speak of the Scriptures as either "closed" or "open." Scripture's meanings could be hidden – buried intentionally by the authors in enigmas, parables, allegories, etc., so as to provide the few who were capable of delving more deeply into the text with challenges.[105] But the Scriptures could also convey meanings plainly and openly to the larger public, especially those teachings that were central to its saving message.[106] If this first pattern of responses to the question, "Where could this message be found?" had *accessibility* as its motif, the other pattern was centered upon the theme of *scope*: the message of Scripture could be born by the smallest details of the text (thereby justifying a pains-taking analysis of its minutiae[107]), but at the same time, it could also be discovered "macroscopically," as it were, throughout all of Scripture.

One of the leading debates in pre-Nicene Christianity centered upon this macro-scopic message of Scripture. Those Christians committed to the authority of both the Old and New Testaments (however fluid these collections might have been) found themselves in a debate with two communities, the Jews and Gnostics, who each defined the breadth of Scripture's harmonious and saving message more narrowly. On the one hand, these Christians shared with the Jews a common set of Scriptures, yet needed to make a case for Jesus and the church as reflected in New Testament writings. The basic motif in the sprawling *adversus Iudaeos* literature of the second and third centuries was that the prophecies in Israel's Scriptures, whether in the form of written oracles or figurative events,[108] pointed to Jesus as the promised Messiah, the replacement of Israel's ceremonial cult, and the church as the new people of God.[109] Early Christian exegetes defended such a style of reading by turning back to the precedent set by Paul, or even Jesus,[110] and in turn, charged the Jews with an ignorance of their own Scriptures and sometimes with literalism.[111]

On the other hand, these same Christians shared a commitment to Jesus with Marcion and the Gnostic coalition, even if this allegiance was expressed in patently different ways.[112] Yet a case had to be made for the continuity of the message in the Old Testament with that in the New.[113] The strategy of response to the Gnostic coalition was very similar to the responses formulated in debate with the Jews: to demonstrate the accord between the two testaments – the same God, the same story of salvation, linked by prophecies that found their fulfillment in Jesus and the church.[114] In both of these debates, the argument for the harmonious, single message of Scripture running through both testaments resulted in a reciprocal transference of authority: on the one hand, the life and mission of Jesus was validated by its location with the narrative of the Old Testament; on the other hand, Jesus confirmed the authority of Israel's Scriptures.[115]

In both of these conversations the majority of Christians expressed the conviction that the Scriptures spoke with one voice from beginning to end. What, then, did Scripture's authors intend to communicate?[116] The answer we frequently hear is that they collaborated to speak a *saving message* to each and every reader. Irenaeus, for instance, could write:

> This, beloved, is the preaching of the truth, and this is the character of our salvation, and this is the way of life, which the prophets announced and Christ confirmed and the apostles handed over and the church, in the whole world, hands down to her children.
>
> (Irenaeus, *Demonstration of the Apostolic Preaching* 98)[117]

Or Clement:

> It is now time ... to go to the prophetic Scriptures; for the oracles present us with the appliances necessary for the attainment of piety, and so establish the truth. The divine Scriptures and institutions of wisdom form the short road to salvation. Devoid of embellishment, of outward beauty of diction, of wordiness and seductiveness, they raise up humanity strangled by wickedness, teaching men to despise the casualties of life; and with one and the same voice remedying many evils, they at once dissuade us from pernicious deceit, and clearly exhort us to the attainment of the salvation set before us.
>
> (Clement of Alexandria, *Exhortation to the Greeks* 8.77)[118]

We can trace this remarkable claim about Scripture throughout pre-Nicene Christianity.[119] Moreover, we can also detect several attempts to specify the content of this saving message. At times, early Christian exegetes offered syntheses of Scripture's message that were decidedly christocentric, in keeping with the conviction that this one voice of Scripture was only clearly heard after the incarnation.[120] So, for instance, Origen could assert that there was a sense in which everything – the law, prophets, gospels, apostolic epistles – was in some way "gospel," since each part of Scripture announced Jesus.[121] More often, however, and particularly in the context of Gnostic polemic, several authors from the second century onward sketched summaries of the cardinal teachings of Christianity, i.e. "rules" of faith. Many of these were short, with articles on God the Father, Jesus Christ, and the Holy Spirit, whereas others were longer with several additional articles on creation, souls, angelic beings, and even Scripture.[122] What is interesting about these rules is that they not only served as a criterion for assessing the validity of competing interpretations of Scripture, but that they were also thought to be concise summaries of the scriptural message.[123]

This expectation that the Scriptures announced a saving message in turn colored the exegetical enterprise, so that it too was plotted on explicitly religious coordinates. For most early Christians, adherence to the church's rule of faith and allegiance to Jesus as the Messiah both characterized ideal interpreters of Scripture. These interpreters also needed to cultivate virtues that shaped inquiry into Scripture, such as attentiveness, curiosity, care, a love for truth, and persistence. Referring to Scripture, Irenaeus wrote:

A sound mind ... devoted to piety and the love of truth, will eagerly meditate upon those things which God has placed within the power of mankind, and has subjected to our knowledge, and will make advancement in them, rendering the knowledge of them easy to him by means of daily study.

(Irenaeus, *Against Heresies* 2.27.1)[124]

Theophilus advised: "But do you also, if you please, give reverential attention to the prophetic Scriptures."[125] And Origen exhorted a whole series of commitments:

You, then, my lord and son, apply yourself to the reading of the divine Scriptures, but do apply yourself. We need great application when we are reading divine things, so that we may not be precipitous in saying or understanding anything concerning them. Also, applying yourself to divine reading with the intention to believe and to please God, knock at what is closed in it, and it will be opened to you by the doorkeeper, concerning whom Jesus said, "To him the doorkeeper opens" [John 10:3]. As you apply yourself to divine reading, seek correctly and with unshakable faith in God the sense of the divine Scriptures hidden from the many. Do not be content with knocking and seeking, for prayer is most necessary for understanding divine matters. It was to exhort us to this very thing that the Savior did not only say, "Knock, and it shall be opened to you" and "Seek, and you shall find," but also, "Ask, and it shall be given to you" [Matt. 7:7; Luke 11:9].

(Origen, *Letter to Gregory* 4)[126]

Interpreters, as Origen does in this paragraph, spoke of the reading of Scripture as an encounter with God in prayer where the interpreter requested and also received from Scripture's divine author clues about its message. "There is a veil of ignorance lying upon the heart of those who read and do not understand" the Scriptures, Origen wrote.

This veil is taken away by God's gift, when He perceives a man who has done everything in his own power, and by use has exercised his senses to distinguish good and evil, and has unceasingly said in his prayer, "Open thou mine eyes, that I may understand thy wonders out of thy law" [Ps. 118:18].

(Origen, *Against Celsus* 4.50)[127]

While there were several Christian intellectuals in our period who modeled scholarly proficiency in the interpretation of Scripture, what was not lost or seen as conflicting with this ideal was the awareness that the exegetical enterprise was a deeply religious affair. At its core, interpreters, and those for whom they interpreted, sought to discern in Scripture a life-giving message; Scripture offered more than information, it offered salvation. Passages like those cited above make clear that the interpreter's task was not simply to discern with technical proficiency the Christian drama of salvation inscribed in Scripture's pages. Rather, the exercise of interpretation already afforded the interpreter an opportunity to participate in this living drama, an exercise by which interpreters could express their Christian commitments – be they adherence to the church's rule, discipleship to Jesus, cultivating reading virtues, or embarking on the life of prayer – and thereby make their return to God through the still shifting collection of sacred writings.

It comes as no surprise, then, that we see such energetic activity pulsating around the Scriptures in early Christianity: these writings were copied, translated and disseminated, and they played a prominent role in religious disputes, persecution, and in the religious life of the individual interpreter. While these Scriptures were subjected to private scholarly scrutiny, they were also ushered into the public domain when they were read within the liturgy, expounded upon in the homily, and woven in a variety of ways into early Christian literature. Consistently, these writings were used to support the ongoing life of Christian churches, advancing a range of liturgical, catechetical and apologetical interests. Ultimately, then, the role of Scripture for the larger Christian community was no different than its role for the individual interpreter. F. Young has put it well: "The Bible's principal function in the patristic period was the generation of a way of life, grounded in the truth about the way things are, as revealed by God's Word. Exegesis served this end. ... The heart of the matter lay in the many-faceted process of finding life's meaning portrayed in the pages of scripture."[128] Origen stated the matter concisely: "Scripture has been prepared by God to be given for humanity's salvation."[129]

Further reading

P. R. Ackroyd and C. F. Evans (eds), *The Cambridge History of the Bible*, vol. 1: *From the Beginnings to Jerome*, Cambridge: Cambridge University Press, 1970.

J. Daniélou, *From Shadows to Reality: Studies in Biblical Typology of the Fathers*, trans. W. Hibberd, London: Burns & Oates, 1960; originally published as *Sacramentum futuri: Études sur les origines de la typologie biblique*, Paris: Beauchesne, 1950.

H. Y. Gamble, *Books and Readers in the Early Church: A History of Early Christian Texts*, New Haven, CT: Yale University Press, 1995.

A. Harnack, *Bible Reading in the Early Church*, trans. J. R. Wilkinson, New York: Putnam, 1912; repr. Eugene, OR: Wipf & Stock, 2005; originally published as *Über den privaten Gebrauch der Heiligen Schriften in der alten Kirche*, Leipzig: Hinrich, 1912.

C. Kannengiesser, *Handbook of Patristic Exegesis: The Bible in Ancient Christianity*, 2 vols, Bible in Ancient Christianity 1, Leiden: Brill, 2004. (See especially volume 1 which covers up through the third century.)

N. F. Marcos, *The Septuagint in Context: Introduction to the Greek Versions of the Bible*, trans. W. G. E. Watson, Leiden: Brill, 2001.

C. Markschies, *Kaiserzeitliche christliche Theologie und ihre Institutionen: Prolegomena zu einer Geschichte der antiken christlichen Theologie*, Tübingen: Mohr Siebeck, 2007.

L. M. McDonald and J. A. Sanders (eds), *The Canon Debate*, Peabody, MA: Hendrickson, 2002.

B. Neuschäfer, *Origenes als Philologe*, Basil: Friedrich Reinhardt, 1987.

C. H. Roberts and T. C. Skeat, *The Birth of the Codex*, London: Oxford University Press, 1987.

F. Stuhlhofer, *Der Gebrauch der Bibel von Jesus bis Euseb: Eine statistische Untersuchung zur Kanonsgeschichte*, Wuppertal: R. Brockhaus, 1988.

F. M. Young, *Biblical Exegesis and the Formation of Christian Culture*, Cambridge: Cambridge University Press, 1997.

Notes

1 The earliest Greek *pandects*, Codex Vaticanus and Codex Sinaiticus, come from the fourth century. The etymological history of the term "Bible" illustrates well the shifting physical format of the Christian Scriptures. The English "Bible" derives from the late Latin *biblia* (fem. sg.), for the earlier *biblia* (neut. pl.). According to the *Oxford English Dictionary*, the "common change of a Latin neuter plural into a feminine singular … was in the case of *biblia* facilitated by the habit of regarding the Scriptures as one work" (*The Oxford English Dictionary*, 2nd edn, s.v. "Bible"). In the Middle Ages the sacred "books" of Christians are increasingly transmitted physically as *one* book, hence the singular *biblia* from which we get "Bible." To trace the etymology further, the earlier Latin plural *biblia* was adopted from the Greek *ta biblia*, the plural of *biblion*, the customary Greek word for "book." Justin (*Dialogue with Trypho* 75) uses the singular noun to refer to an individual book of the Bible. In the plural, it can refer to the Old Testament writings (*2 Clement* 14.2; Origen, *Homilies on Jeremiah* 14.12) or to the whole Christian Scriptures (Origen, *Commentary on John* 6.8).

2 Of the approximately 172 biblical manuscripts or fragments written before the turn of the fifth century (98 from the Old Testament and 74 from the New), roughly 158 come from codices and only 14 from scrolls. Statistics from C. H. Roberts and T. C. Skeat, *The Birth of the Codex*, London: Oxford University Press, 1987, p. 38. For a concise discussion of the hypotheses that attempt to explain why Christians preferred the codex to the scroll, see *Birth of the Codex*, pp. 45–61. For a more substantial discussion of the early Christian book, see H. Y. Gamble, *Books and Readers in the Early Church: A History of Early Christian Texts*, New Haven, CT: Yale University Press, 1995, pp. 42–81.

3 B. M. Metzger and B. D. Ehrman, *The Text of the New Testament: Its Transmission, Corruption, and Restoration*, 4th edn, New York: Oxford University Press, 2005, p. 55.

4 H. B. Swete, *An Introduction to the Old Testament in Greek*, Cambridge: Cambridge University Press, 1902; repr. Eugene, OR: Wipf & Stock, 2003, p. 123. Not only did the order of writings *within* these collections vary, so too did the order *between* them – the general pattern, however, divided books according to genre or content: historical, poetic, followed by prophetic writings (cf. pp. 216–20).

5 For example, Chester Beatty Papyrus 46 is dated *c.* CE 200 and comprised originally 104 leaves: it contained ten letters of Paul in the following order: Rom., Heb., 1 and 2 Cor., Eph., Gal., Phil., Col., 1 and 2 Thess. Chester Beatty Papyrus 45 dates to the early third century and contained the four Gospels and the Acts of the Apostles on originally 220 leaves (Metzger and Ehrman, *Text of the New Testament*, pp. 54–5). Within these collections the order of writings was variable, though Paul's letters tended to be subdivided into two categories, those addressed to churches on the one hand, and those addressed to individuals on the other, and within each of these lists the letters were collected in order of descending length. More complete NT manuscripts often have the sequence: Gospels, Acts of the Apostles, Catholic Epistles, Pauline Epistles, and finally the Apocalypse. On the sequencing of NT writings, see "Appendix II: Variations in the Sequence of the Books of the New Testament," in B. M. Metzger, *The Canon of the New Testament: Its Origin, Development and Significance*, Oxford: Clarendon, 1987, pp. 295–300.

6 Eusebius, *Ecclesiastical History* 4.26.12–14. There is scholarly debate about when testimony collections were first used, and in what formats they circulated. As O. Skarsaune has argued, it is probably misleading to think that testimony passages circulated exclusively in anthologies, such as those mentioned above. There was more likely a "testimony tradition" that was passed along in a variety of literary formats (including citations embedded in earlier Christian literature, such as Matt., Rom., and *1 Clem.*), and was also transmitted orally (O. Skarsaune, "Scriptural Interpretation in the Second and Third Centuries," in M. Sæbø [ed.], *Hebrew Bible/Old Testament: The History of Its Interpretation*, vol. 1: *From the Beginnings to the Middle Ages (Until 1300)*, Göttingen: Vandenhoeck & Ruprecht, 1996, pp. 418–21). Important second-century writings that rely on some sort of testimony tradition include *Barnabas*, Justin's *First Apology* and *Dialogue with Trypho*, and the no longer extant work, *A Controversy between Jason and Papiscus about Christ*. Also see M. C. Albl, *"And Scripture Cannot Be Broken": The Form and Function of the Early Christian Testimonia Collections*, Leiden: Brill, 1999, pp. 97–158.

7 See K. Haines-Eitzen, *Guardians of Letters: Literacy, Power and the Transmitters of Early Christian Literature*, New York: Oxford University Press, 2000, for a social history of the scribes who copied Christian texts during the second and third centuries.

8 There are hints of scriptoria surrounding the figure of Origen in both his Alexandrian and Caesarean periods. Eusebius tells us that Origen's patron, Ambrose, provided him with a staff of shorthand writers who took down his dictations, as well as copyists and young women trained in fine writing. These helped not only in the preparation of Origen's scriptural commentaries, but also in the transmission of the "biblical oracles" themselves (*Ecclesiastical History* 6.23.1–2). Also note a fragment from an undated letter, in which Origen writes: "we who are compelled to study and correct *ta antigrapha*," i.e. copies of manuscripts. The letter does not specify whether these are *scriptural* manuscripts, though the reference to Origen and his fellow philologists studying and correcting copies seems to suggest the Scriptures (P. Nautin, *Lettres et écrivains chrétiens des IIe et IIIe siècles*, Paris: Cerf, 1961, pp. 250.7–251.12).

  The strongest evidence for a *scriptorium* comes from the early fourth century in Caesarea. Constantine commissioned this city's bishop, Eusebius, to furnish the new churches in Constantinople "with fifty copies of the sacred Scriptures" (Eusebius, *Life of Constantine* 4.36). It is difficult to imagine the fluid completion of this task without some sort of scriptorium (so also G. Cavallo, "Scuola, scriptorium, biblioteca a Cesarea," in G. Cavallo [ed.], *Le biblioteche nel mondo antico e medievala*, Bari: Laterza 1988, pp. 67–70; Gamble, *Books and Readers in the Early Church*, pp. 121, 158) though some still contest the idea of this institution in Caesarea (K. Haines-Eitzen, *Guardians of Letters*, pp. 89–91; T. C. Skeat, "Codex Sinaiticus," *Journal of Theological Studies* 50, 1999, 607). This debate depends, of course, upon how ambitiously we define the term "scriptorium."

9 See C. Markschies, *Kaiserzeitliche christliche Theologie und ihre Institutionen: Prolegomena zu einer Geschichte der antiken christlichen Theologie*, Tübingen: Mohr Siebeck, 2007, pp. 311–14.

10 To be clear, these libraries were not housed in discrete buildings. In the pre-Constantinian period, most congregations gathered in an unmodified house church or *domus ecclesiae* ("house of the church"), i.e. a domestic setting that had undergone basic renovations to make the house more suitable for basic liturgical purposes. See L. Michael White, *Building God's House in the Roman World: Architectural Adaptation among Pagans, Jews, and Christians*, Baltimore: Johns Hopkins University Press, 1990, pp. 102–39.

11 See Eusebius, *Ecclesiastical History* 8.2.4–5; *Martyrs of Palestine* [short] Preface; *Life of Constantine* 3.1. Also see W. Speyer, *Büchervernichtung und Zensur des Geistes bei Heiden, Juden und Christen*, Stuttgart: Hiersmann, 1981.

12 For a translation of the *Deeds of Zenophilus*, see M. Edwards (ed. and trans.), *Optatus: Against the Donatists*, Liverpool: Liverpool University Press, 1997, pp. 150–69. See also Gamble, *Books and Readers in the Early Church*, pp. 145–54.

13 H. Y. Gamble and A. J. Carriker distinguish these two libraries more softly from the archival collections than C. Markschies. For Gamble, they are distinguished by serving purposes beyond the liturgical and archival, i.e. research (*Books and Readers in the Early Church*, p. 154); for Carriker, by offering more substantial works of literature and scholarship (*The Library of Eusebius of Caesarea*, Leiden: Brill, 2003, pp. 2–3). Markschies, however, draws a sharper demarcation, contending that these larger libraries, unlike the archives, were open to the public (*Kaiserzeitliche christliche Theologie und ihre Institutionen*, p. 311).

14 Eusebius briefly mentions this library, and his use of it in the composition of his *Ecclesiastical History* 6.20.1–2. See A. Ehrhardt, "Die griechische Patriarchal-Bibliothek von Jerusalem," *Römische Quartalschrift* 5, 1891, pp. 217–65; 6, 1892, pp. 339–65.

15 On Pamphilus and this library, see Eusebius, *Ecclesiastical History* 6.32.3; Jerome, *Letter* 34.1; Jerome, *On Illustrious Men* 75. For a fuller discussion of this library, see Carriker, *Library of Eusebius of Caesarea*.

16 Several essays in L. M. McDonald and J. A. Sanders (eds), *The Canon Debate*, Peabody, MA: Hendrickson, 2002, provide helpful orientation to the topic.

17 There are basically two different definitions of "canon" in the scholarly literature. The broader definition renders it as a list of scriptural books, where a writing is "canonical" if it functioned as scripture. According to this definition, there was certainly a canon in pre-Nicene Christianity, since there were Scriptures in pre-Nicene Christianity. Moreover, since this canon was subject to revision, both expansions and contractions as debates and uncertainties swirled around the scriptural status of any given book, scholars can talk about the canon as "open" until the fourth and fifth centuries when

it finally began to "close." The increasing trend in the literature, however, is to render "canon" more narrowly. Such a "canon" is a *closed* or *fixed* list of Scriptures, i.e. a list that comprehensively identifies every scriptural writing (and by extension, excludes every other writing from this list). I follow this, but also make explicit what is often tacitly assumed in this narrower definition: that this fixed list must also achieve widespread acceptance. Thus, when a scriptural writing is called "canonical" on this definition, it is because it is part of a widely accepted and final collection. On this definition, then, while the earliest followers of Jesus possessed Scriptures, they did not possess a "canon" of Scriptures. On these different definitions of "canon" in the scholarship, see A. C. Sundberg Jr, "Toward a Revised History of the New Testament Canon," *Studia Evangelica* 4, 1968, pp. 452–61; J. Barton, *Holy Writings, Sacred Texts: The Canon in Early Christianity*, Louisville: Westminster John Knox, 1997, pp. 1–14; H. Y. Gamble, "The New Testament Canon: Recent Research and the Status Quaestionis," McDonald and Sanders, *Canon Debate*, pp. 267–71.

It is, moreover, a different question to ask what early Christian writers meant when they used the term *kanon* in reference to scriptural writings (this only happens in the second half of the fourth century). For a brief discussion of this term and the debates surrounding its use in antiquity, see Metzger, *Canon of the New Testament*, pp. 289–93; more substantially, see H. Ohme, *Kanon Ekklesiastikos: Die Bedeutung des Altkirchlichen Kanonbegriffs*, New York: Walter de Gruyter, 1998.

18 Eusebius, *Ecclesiastical History* 3.25.1–7.

19 For instance, when Augustine was writing *Christian Instruction* (c. 396) we still have a picture of indeterminacy – at 2.12 he suggests that individual churches have their own final lists, but that these do not always agree with one another.

20 Irenaeus, *Against Heresies* 2.28.2; Theophilus, *To Autolycus* 2.22; for an extended argument for Scripture's inspiration, see Origen, *On First Principles* 4.1.1–7; for a Valentinian account of the inspiration of the Mosaic law, see Ptolemy, *Letter to Flora*.

21 Eusebius, *Ecclesiastical History* 3.25.1–7; 3.28.2; 6.25.11–14. On apostolicity as a criterion, see W. H. Ohlig, *Die theologische Begründung des neutestamentlichen Kanons in der alten Kirche*, Dusseldorf: Patmos, 1972, pp. 57–156.

22 Athenagoras describes God inspiring the prophets as a flute player plays a flute (*Plea on Behalf of Christians* 9; pseudo-Justin, *Hortatory Address to Greeks* 8 for the image of a harp or lyre). Note Origen's defense of the consciousness of those inspired (*On First Principles* 3.3.4; *Against Celsus* 7.3–4; *Homilies on Ezekiel* 6.1).

23 On antiquity as a characteristic of Scripture, see Irenaeus, *Against Heresies* 3.11.9, 5.20.1; Hegesippus (Eusebius, *Ecclesiastical History* 4.22.8); Clement of Alexandria, *Miscellanies* 7.17; Tertullian, *Prescription against Heretics* 32, *Against Marcion* 4.5; Origen, *Commentary on Matthew Ser* 47; Eusebius, *Ecclesiastical History* 3.38.1–2; Muratorian Canon on *Shepherd of Hermas*. In several of these passages antiquity is said to safeguard the orthodoxy of a particular writing. The antiquity of Scripture also played a leading role in the polemic with Greco-Roman critics of Christianity who contended that the Scriptures were insufficiently antique. One of the responses that we find scattered throughout pre-Nicene writings was that Moses and the prophets antedated the Greek poets and philosophers, and that when the latter spoke well, they were dependent upon the former or directly dependent upon the God of Christians (e.g. Justin, *First Apology* 54; pseudo-Justin, *Hortatory Address to Greeks* 8, *passim*; Tatian, *Address to Greeks* 31; Theophilus, *To Autolycus* 3.20–30; Clement of Alexandria, *Miscellanies* 1.25; Origen, *Against Celsus* 4.11, 4.21, 6.7). See A. J. Droge, *Homer or Moses? Early Christian Interpretations of the History of Culture*, Tübingen: Mohr Siebeck, 1989.

24 The standard histories of the canon discuss these factors. See, for instance, Ohlig, *Die theologische Begründung*, pp. 34–53; Metzger, *Canon of the New Testament*, pp. 75–112.

25 Eusebius, *Ecclesiastical History* 3.3.2, 3.24.17–18, 3.25.6. See W. H. Ohlig, *Die theologische Begründung*, pp. 269–95.

26 Depending upon how one dates the Muratorian canon – it has been traditionally dated to the late second century, though A. C. Sundberg, "Canon Muratori: A Fourth Century List," *Harvard Theological Review* 66, 1973, pp. 1–41; and G. Hahneman, *The Muratorian Fragment and the Development of the Canon*, Oxford: Clarendon, 1992, locate it in the fourth century. The two pre-Nicene lists of OT writings come from Melito (Eusebius, *Ecclesiastical History* 4.26.13–14) and Origen (Eusebius, *Ecclesiastical History* 6.25.2). The three pre-Nicene NT lists are: Irenaeus (Eusebius,

Ecclesiastical History 5.8.2–8); Clement of Alexandria (Eusebius, *Ecclesiastical History* 6.14.1–7); Origen (Eusebius, *Ecclesiastical History* 6.25.3–14).

27 Theophilus, *To Autolycus* 3.29.

28 *2 Clement* 14.2.

29 Irenaeus, *Against Heresies* 3.12.11, 4.9.1; Tertullian, *Against Marcion* 1.19, 4.1, 4.11.

30 Melito is the first to link the idea of covenant with Scriptures when he spoke of the "books of the old covenant" (Eusebius, *Ecclesiastical History* 4.26.13); Irenaeus, *Against Heresies* 4.9.1; Clement of Alexandria clearly links the idea of covenant with authoritative Jewish and Christian Scriptures (*Miscellanies* 3.6; 4.21); Tertullian, *Against Praxeas* 15; and Origen, though with reluctance, speaks of "Old" and "New Testaments": see *On First Principles* 4.1.1; *Commentary on John* 5.8; *Prayer* 22.1; and *Homilies on Numbers* 9.4 where the Old Testament is only "old" if it is understood carnally; it is "new" if it is understood spiritually; likewise, the NT becomes "old" when it is read in a fleshly manner.

31 Polycarp, *To the Philippians* 6.3; *Barnabas* 6; Justin, *First Apology* 67; Irenaeus, *Against Heresies* 2.2.5, 5.Pref.; Clement of Alexandria, *Exhortation to the Greeks* 8; Origen, *Commentary on John* 1.32.

32 Ignatius, *To the Smyrnaeans* 5.1; Irenaeus, *Against Heresies* 1.3.6, 4.2.1; *Diognetus* 11.6; Clement of Alexandria, *Miscellanies* 6.11; Tertullian, *Prescription against Heretics* 36; Hippolytus, *Commentary on Daniel* 4.12; Origen, *On First Principles* 1.Pref.4, 1.3.1.

33 For a helpful table of OT citations in the second and third centuries, see F. Stuhlhofer, *Der Gebrauch der Bible von Jesus bis Euseb: Eine statistische Untersuchung zur Kanonsgeschichte*, Wuppertal: R. Brockhaus, 1988, pp. 59–60.

34 It is important to note that the early church's endorsement of the LXX, the oldest Greek translation of Hebrew Scriptures, did not imply the endorsement of a fixed table of contents. The few extant complete LXX manuscripts, along with lists of OT books, confirm that LXX copies did not circulate with identical contents (see Swete, *Introduction to the Old Testament in Greek*, pp. 197–230).

35 Polycarp, *To the Philippians* 6.3; *2 Clement* 14.2; Justin, *First Apology* 67.

36 Irenaeus, *Against Heresies* 3.12.11–12, 4.15.2; Clement of Alexandria, *Miscellanies* 5.13; Tertullian, *Against Marcion* 4.1; Origen, *On First Principles* 4.1.1, *Commentary on John* 5.8. See Kinzig, "Καινὴ διαθήνκη: The Title of the New Testament in the Second and Third Centuries," *Journal of Theological Studies* 45, 1994, pp. 519–44.

37 Irenaeus, *Against Heresies* 2.2.5, 3.9.1; *Demonstration of the Apostolic Preaching* 98; Theophilus, *To Autolycus* 3.12; Tertullian, *Prescription against Heretics* 36; Clement of Alexandria, *Miscellanies* 7.16; Origen, *On First Principles* Pref.1, 1.3.1.

38 Jesus' words had scriptural status in the first century (see 1 Cor. 7:10, 9:14, 11:23–26; and esp. 1 Tim. 5:18 where, along with Deut. 25:4, Jesus' words count as "Scripture"); Paul's writings also count as Scripture (see 2 Pet. 3:16). In the second century, this juxtaposition is frequent: for example, *2 Clement* 2.1–4, 14.2; *Barnabas* 4; Athenagoras, *Resurrection* 18; Theophilus, *To Autolycus* 2.22; Ptolemy, *Letter to Flora* 3.5–8, 4.1, 4.4, 7.5, 7.10, etc.

39 Particularly surrounding the *Shepherd of Hermas*, *Barnabas*, *Didache*, *1 Clement*, 2 Pet. 2–3, John, Heb., James, the Apocalypse. See H. Y. Gamble, "Status Quaestionis," in McDonald and Sanders, *Canon Debate*, pp. 287–90 for a more detailed discussion.

40 For patterns of citation, see Stuhlhofer, *Der Gebrauch der Bible von Jesus bis Euseb*, p. 41.

41 Eusebius, *Ecclesiastical History* 4.26.12–14.

42 "Septuagint" is from the Latin for "seventy" (*septuaginta*). The earliest designation of this Greek translation as the "seventy" probably occurs at Eusebius, *Ecclesiastical History* 6.16.1, 4 (*hebdome-konta*); Augustine appears to have been the first Latin writer to refer to this translation by the Latin *septuaginta* (*City of God* 18.42).

43 See Justin, *First Apology* 31; Pseudo-Justin, *Exhortation to the Greeks* 13; Irenaeus, *Against Heresies* 3.21.2; Clement of Alexandria, *Miscellanies* 1.22; Tertullian, *Apology* 18. For a full list, see S. Jellicoe, *The Septuagint and Modern Study*, Oxford: Clarendon, 1968, pp. 33–5.

44 N. F. Marcos, *The Septuagint in Context: Introduction to the Greek Versions of the Bible*, trans. W. G. E. Watson, Leiden: Brill, 2001, pp. 53–66.

45 On these and other Greek translations, see Marcos, *Septuagint in Context*, pp. 109–73.

46 Augustine's comment about the Latin translations is telling: "Those who translated the Scriptures from Hebrew into Greek can be counted; this is certainly not true of Latin translators. The fact is that

whenever in the early days of the faith a Greek codex came into anybody's hands, and he felt that he had the slightest familiarity with each language, he rushed in with a translation" (*Christian Instruction* 2.16; trans. E. Hill, *Teaching Christianity: De Doctrina Christiana*, vol. 11 of *The Works of Augustine: A Translation for the 21st Century*, Hyde Park, NY: New City, 1996, p. 136).

47 See M. P. Weitzman, *The Syriac Version of the Old Testament: An Introduction*, Cambridge: Cambridge University Press, 1999.

48 Mention should also be made of Tatian's *Diatessaron* (*c.* 170), a harmony of the four Gospels woven together into a single narrative. There is debate, however, about whether this harmony was first composed in Syriac or Greek. See W. L. Petersen, *Tatian's Diatessaron: Its Creation, Dissemination, Significance and History in Scholarship*, Leiden: Brill, 1994.

49 On the Coptic translations of the OT, see P. Nagel, "Old Testament, Coptic Translations of," in A. S. Atiya (ed.), *The Coptic Encyclopedia*, vol. 6, New York, 1991, pp. 1836–40.

50 Though silent reading was not as rare as scholars have customarily thought. See B. M. W. Knox, "Silent Reading in Antiquity," *Greek, Roman and Byzantine Studies* 9, 1968, pp. 421–35; A. K. Gavrilov, "Reading Techniques in Classical Antiquity," *Classical Quarterly* 47, 1997, pp. 56–73; M. Burnyeat, "Postscript on Silent Reading," *Classical Quarterly* 47, 1997, pp. 74–6.

51 The most extensive discussion of literacy in the ancient world is by W.V. Harris, *Ancient Literacy*, Cambridge, MA: Harvard University Press, 1989. The study offers low estimates of literacy rates in the ancient world. See also the respondents to Harris in J. H. Humphrey (ed.), *Literacy in the Roman World*, Journal of Roman Archaeology Supplementary Series 3, Ann Arbor, MI: Journal of Roman Archeology, 1991.

52 Perhaps Polycarp, *To the Philippians* 12.1; Eusebius, *Ecclesiastical History* 4.26.13; Ptolemy, *Letter to Flora* 3.1; Clement of Alexandria, *Miscellanies* 1.7; Tertullian, *Apology* 31; Origen and his father (Eusebius, *Ecclesiastical History* 6.2.7–11); Origen, *Homilies on Genesis* 10.1, 11.3, 12.5; *Homilies on Exodus* 12.2, 12.27; *Homilies on Leviticus* 11.7; *Homilies on Numbers* 2.1, 27.1; *Homilies on Joshua* 20.1, etc. Also note the anecdote relayed by Jerome (*Apology against Rufinus* 1.9) where, quoting from Eusebius's *Life of Pamphilus*, he notes how Pamphilus would eagerly lend copies of Scripture to men and women who could read. For a more complete dossier of evidence, see A. Harnack, *Bible Reading in the Early Church*, trans. J. R. Wilkinson, Eugene, OR: Wipf & Stock, 2005, pp. 32–89.

53 There are several scattered references to this practice already in the NT (1 Tim. 4:13; Rev. 1:3).

54 Trans. and ed. A. Roberts and W. H. Rambaut, *The Apostolic Fathers with Justin Martyr and Irenaeus*, rev. edn, in *The Ante-Nicene Fathers*, vol. 1, Edinburgh: T&T Clark, 1885–7; repr. Grand Rapids, MI: Wm. B. Eerdmans, 1987; repr. Peabody, MA: Hendrickson, 1994, p. 186.

55 Tertullian, *Prescription against Heretics* 41; *Apology* 39; Cyprian, *Letters* 29, 38.2, 39.4–5. See H. Leclercq, "Lecteur," in F. Cabrol and H. Leclercq (eds), *Dictionnaire d'archéologie chrétienne et de liturgie*, vol. 8, Paris: Librairie Letouzey et Ané, 1929, pp. 2241–69.

56 Cyprian, *Letters* 38.2, 39.5.

57 Eusebius, *Ecclesiastical History* 6.43.11.

58 See Markschies, *Kaiserzeitliche christliche Theologie und ihre Institutionen*, pp. 43–213, for the institutional settings in which Christian theology was practiced in the second and third centuries.

59 The dates that follow are taken from C. Moreschini and E. Norelli, *Early Christian Greek and Latin Literature: A Literary History*, vol. 1: *From Paul to the Age of Constantine*, trans. M. J. O'Connell, Peabody, MA: Hendrickson, 2005.

60 Also known as *Salvation of the Rich*.

61 There are significant debates about the identity of Hippolytus, whether we ought to maintain a single author for the large Hippolytean corpus, or maintain two different authors. For orientation, see Moreschini and Norelli, *Early Christian Greek and Latin Literature*, vol. 1, pp. 232–8; J. A. Cerrato, *Hippolytus between East and West: The Commentaries and the Provenance of the Corpus*, Oxford: Oxford University Press, 2002.

62 For a list of his specifically exegetical works, see M. Geerard (ed.), *Clavis Patrum Graecorum*, vol. 1: *Patres Antenicaeni*, Turnhout, Belgium: Brepols, 1983, pp. 1410–68, 1500.

63 Eusebius, *Ecclesiastical History* 6.3.1–9, 13. There are several debates about the character of this school. For a recent overview (with bibliography), see Markschies, *Kaiserzeitliche christliche Theologie und ihre Institutionen*, pp. 97–102.

64 See Gregory, *Address of Thanksgiving*, esp. ch. 15. For a preliminary orientation to this school, including its history after Origen, see Carriker, *Library of Eusebius*, pp. 6–17.

65 The important English studies here are R. M. Grant, *The Letter and the Spirit*, London: SPCK, 1957; *The Earliest Lives of Jesus*, London: SPCK, 1961, ch. 2. The two most substantial investigations of this topic are: C. Schäublin, *Untersuchungen zu Methode und Herkunft der Antiochenischen Exegese*, Cologne: P. Hanstein, 1974; and B. Neuschäfer, *Origenes als Philologe*, Basil: Friedrich Reinhardt, 1987. For a quick sketch of the philological commitments of early Christian scriptural scholars, see F. Young, *Biblical Exegesis and the Formation of Christian Culture*, Cambridge: Cambridge University Press, 1997, pp. 76–96. Standard accounts of the antique literary scholarship include: J. E. Sandys, *A History of Classical Scholarship*, vol. 1: *From the Sixth Century BC to the End of the Middle Ages*, 3rd edn, New York: Hafner, 1967; R. Pfeiffer, *A History of Classical Scholarship*, vol. 1: *From the Beginnings to the Hellenistic Age*, New York: Oxford University Press, 1968. Much of the attention that now follows will be directed to Origen, whose achievements in pre-Nicene biblical scholarship tower over other scholars.

66 Origen, *Commentary on Matthew* 15.14. Irenaeus on copyists' errors: *Against Heresies* 5.30.1.

67 For examples of the charge of scribal corruption without theological motivation, see Irenaeus, *Against Heresies* 5.30.1; Origen, *Commentary on Matthew* 16.19; *Homilies on Jeremiah* 16.5.2. For scribal corruption under theological influence, see: Irenaeus, *Against Heresies* 1.27.2, perhaps 4.33.8; Justin, *Dialogue with Trypho* 72–3; Tertullian, *Prescription against Heretics* 38, *Against Marcion* books 4 and 5 passim, *On the Flesh of Christ* 19; Dionysius (Eusebius, *Ecclesiastical History* 4.23.12); and Eusebius, *Ecclesiastical History* 5.28.15–19. See A. Bludau, *Die Schriftsfälschungen der Häretiker: Ein Beitrag zur Textkritik der Bibel*, Munster: Aschendorf, 1925; B. Ehrman, *The Orthodox Corruption of Scripture: the Effect of Early Christological Controversies on the Text of the New Testament*, New York: Oxford University Press, 1993, who argues that the "proto-orthodox" writers of the second and third century also corrupted biblical manuscripts to preserve their vision of Jesus.

68 For example, Justin, *Dialogue with Trypho* 120, 131 (see O. Skarsaune, *The Proof from Prophecy: A Study in Justin Martyr's Proof-Text Tradition: Text-Type, Provenance, Theological Profile*, Leiden: Brill, 1987, pp. 25–46).

69 There is the anecdote of Origen discovering three additional Greek translations for the Psalms, one of these in a jar in Jericho (Eusebius, *Ecclesiastical History* 6.26.2–3).

70 The estimate is provided by A. Grafton and M. Williams, *Christianity and the Transformation of the Book: Origen, Eusebius, and the Library of Caesarea*, Cambridge, MA: Belknap, 2006, p. 105. They also offer a good first orientation to the *Hexapla* on pp. 86–132. For a more detailed investigation of the *Hexapla*, see A. Salvesen (ed.), *Origen's Hexapla and Fragments: Papers presented at the Rich Seminar on the Hexapla, Oxford Centre for Hebrew and Jewish Studies, 25th–3rd August 1994*, Texte und Studien zum Antiken Judentum 58, Tübingen: Mohr Siebeck, 1998.

71 The former reason articulated at *Commentary on Matthew* 15.4; the latter in the *Letter to Africanus* 5.

72 See Grant, *Earliest Lives of Jesus*, pp. 38–49 for a brief discussion of this concern in Greco-Roman rhetorical handbooks, and pp. 62–79 for Origen's concern with this same issue. See Origen, *Commentary on John* 10.119–22, 10.129–30; *Against Celsus*, 1.42; *On First Principles* 4.2.8–4.3.5.

73 Origen on place names (*Commentary on John* 6.204–16; *Commentary on Matthew* 11.18; *Against Celsus* 4.44).

74 Hippolytus, *Commentary on Daniel* 1.1–5 for a discussion of the Babylonian exile as the setting for the book of Daniel; Origen uses Josephus's *Antiquities* (*Against Celsus* 1.47) and Phlegon's *Chronicle* (*Commentary on Matthew Ser* 40, 134; *Against Celsus* 2.14, 2.33, 2.59) to help fix dates.

75 See Hippolytus's comments on the four beasts of Daniel 7 (*Commentary on Daniel* 4.2 for how the first beast symbolizes Nebuchadnezzar); Origen on various animals (*Against Celsus* 2.48; *Homilies on Jeremiah* 17.1–3); Origen reflects on the nature of stones (*Commentary on Matthew* 10.7); on lightning (*Homilies on Jeremiah* 8.4); on the soul–body relationship (*Against Celsus* 1.33); on the schools of medicine (*Against Celsus* 3.12); on medicinal treatments (*Homilies on Leviticus* 8.10; *Homilies on Numbers* 17.1); on physiology (*On First Principles* 2.10.4; *Commentary on Matthew* 13.6); on astronomy (*Against Celsus* 1.58–59); on the status of various celestial bodies (*On First Principles* 2.3.6).

76 Origen, *Homilies on Genesis* 2.2 on the geometrical cubits with which Noah's ark was constructed.

77 Stoic moral philosophy and Lot's daughters at Origen, *Against Celsus* 4.45; *Letter to Gregory* 1.

78 For a helpful overview, see O. Skarsaune, "The Development of Scriptural Interpretation in the Second and Third Centuries," in Saebø, *Hebrew Bible/Old Testament*, vol. 1, pp. 373–442, for interdependencies among Christian authors in their readings of the prophets; on the use of Philo in early Christian literature, see D. T. Runia, *Philo in Early Christian Literature: A Survey*, Minneapolis: Fortress, 1993.

79 Origen is often defining terms in Scripture: "daily" in Lord's Prayer (*On Prayer* 27.7); "thanksgiving" (*Commentary on Ephesians* 23); on the difference between "wonders and signs" (*Commentary on John* 13.450); on "beginning" (*Commentary on John* 1.90–124).

80 Hippolytus, *Blessings of Isaac, Jacob and Moses* 1.24; Clement of Alexandria, *Christ the Educator* 1.6; Origen, *Commentary on John* 2.4; *Homilies on Jeremiah* 10.4; *Against Celsus* 5.30. Origen refers to his dependence upon an onomasticon at *Homilies on Numbers* 20.3 and *Commentary on John* 2.197.

81 Valentinians do so according to Irenaeus, *Against Heresies* 1.1.3; *Barnabas* 9; Clement of Alexandria, *Miscellanies* 6.11; Origen, *Homilies on Genesis* 2.2; *Homilies on Exodus* 9.3; *Homilies on Numbers* 22.1.

82 Origen on the difference between a parable and a similitude (*Commentary on Matthew* 10.4); he identifies onomatopia (*Commentary on Ephesians* 3), metaphor (*Commentary on John* 10.221), synecdoche (*Against Celsus* 4.77; *Commentary on Matthew* 12.38), hyperbole (*Commentary on 1 Corinthians* 49), etc.

83 Origen discusses the use of the article in John 1:1 (*Commentary on John* 2.12–18); how ambiguous sentences ought to be read (interrogative or imperative at *Commentary on John* 32.113); ambiguous grammatical forms (*Homilies on the Psalms* 4.5); on solecisms (*Commentary on John* 4; extract from the *Commentary on Hosea* [*Philocalia* 8]).

84 Irenaeus is particularly concerned with the order and sequence of Scripture in his debate with Valentinians (*Against Heresies* 1.8.1); Origen, *Homilies on Joshua* 25.1; *Commentary on Matthew* 17.26; *Against Celsus* 4.40; *On First Principles* 4.2.9.

85 Sometimes termed "prosopological" exegesis. *1 Clement* 22 on Christ speaking in Ps. 33; Justin, *First Apology* 36, 38; *Dialogue with Trypho* 56, 62; Theophilus, *To Autolycus* 2.22; Irenaeus, *Demonstration of the Apostolic Preaching* 48–49; Origen, *Homily 5 on 1 Samuel* 4, *Commentary on John* 6.53.

86 Irenaeus, *Against Heresies* 2.27.1, 2.28.3; Clement of Alexandria, *Miscellanies* 7.16; Tertullian, *Against Praxeas* 20; Origen, *Commentary on Psalms 1–25*, Preface; *Commentary on 1 Corinthians* 11; *Against Celsus* 7.11; *Homilies on Jeremiah* 27.1.

87 For instance, arguably the prized literary technique, reading unclear passages in light of clearer ones ("clarifying Homer with Homer"), could yield both literal (Origen, *Homilies on Jeremiah* 4.1) and nonliteral referents (Origen, *Commentary on Matthew* 10.1; *Commentary on John* 13.361).

88 *Pace* Neuschäfer, who has the tendency to separate Origen the philologist from Origen the allegorist (*Origenes als Philologe*, p. 292).

89 Important discussions of allegory (or its synonyms) include: Tertullian, *Against Marcion* 3.14; Clement of Alexandria, *Miscellanies* 5.4; Origen, *Against Celsus* 2.69; *On First Principles* 4.2.2; 4.2.6; *Commentary on Matthew* 12.3. Recall Heraclitus's definition of compositional allegory in his *Homeric Problems*: "Allegory is named eponymously, for it is the trope which proclaims one set of things but in fact signifies other things different from what it says" (Félix Buffière [ed.], *Héraclite: Allégories d'Homère*, 2nd edn, Paris: Les Belles Lettres, 1989, frg. 5.2).

90 For exegetical terminology, see C. Curti et al. (eds), *La terminologia esegetica nell'antichità: Atti del Primo Seminario di antichità christiane, Bari, 25 ottobre 1984*, Bari: Edipuglia, 1987.

91 Or for that matter the multiple ways of reading the law for Clement of Alexandria (*Miscellanies* 1.28). For a discussion of Origen's multiple senses, see E. A. D. Lauro, *The Soul and Spirit of Scripture within Origen's Exegesis*, Leiden: Brill, 2005.

92 See P. W. Martens, "Revisiting the Allegory/Typology Distinction: The Case of Origen," *Journal of Early Christian Studies* 16.3, 2008, 283–317.

93 Clement of Alexandria, *Miscellanies* 2.5.

94 There are numerous examples of the literal reading of the Old Testament: see the moral exempla of prominent Israelites in *1 Clement* 4, 9–12, 17–18; Clement of Alexandria on taking the Mosaic laws literally (*Miscellanies* 1.26–27; *Christ the Educator* 3.12); Origen, *On First Principles* 4.3.3; *Homilies on Genesis* 2, 5, 8; *Homilies on Numbers* 11.1. For the NT, most of the exegesis of the Pauline corpus is literal.

95 Still useful in this regard, J. Daniélou, *From Shadows to Reality: Studies in Biblical Typology of the Fathers*, trans. W. Hibberd, London: Burns & Oates, 1960. See texts at n. 109 below.

96 Irenaeus, *Against Heresies* 3.17.3, 4.22.2, 4.36.1–2, 5.25.4; *Gospel of Philip* 111b; Clement of Alexandria writes: "But well knowing that the Saviour teaches nothing in a merely human way, but teaches all things to His own with divine and mystic wisdom, we must not listen to His utterances carnally; but with due investigation and intelligence must search out and learn the meaning hidden in them"; Clement of Alexandria, *Salvation of the Rich* 5; trans. W. Wilson, *Clemen Alexandrinus On the Salvation of the Rich Man*, in A. Roberts and W. H. Rambaut (eds), *Fathers of the Second Century: Hermas, Tatian, Athenagoras, Theophilus, and Clement of Alexandria (Entire)*, in *The Ante-Nicene Fathers*, 10 vols, Edinburgh: T&T Clark, 1885–7; repr. Grand Rapids, MI: Wm. B. Eerdmans, 1987; repr. Peabody, MA: Hendrickson, 1994, p. 592; Origen, *Commentary on Matthew* 13.16; *Commentary on John* 1.45 ("the task before us now is to translate the gospel perceptible to the senses into the spiritual gospel").

97 For examples of literal and allegorical exegesis applied to the same passage, see Irenaeus on the garden of Eden (literally at *Against Heresies* 5.23.1, and figuratively at *Against Heresies* 5.20.2); Origen too offers literal and nonliteral readings of particular passages – see *Homilies on Genesis* 2 for literal and nonliteral readings of Noah's ark.

98 See Clement of Alexandria's multiple nonliteral interpretations of the appurtenances in the temple (*Miscellanies* 5.6); Origen, *Homilies on Genesis* 2.6, 12.3; *Homilies on Exodus* 3.3; *Homilies on Leviticus* 1; *Homilies on Numbers* 27; and the discussion in Lauro, *Soul and Spirit within Origen's Exegesis*, esp. ch. 4.

99 On the impossibility of a perfect understanding of Scripture in this life: Origen, *On First Principles* 4.3.15; and how Scripture will only be fully understood in the eschatological paradise: *On First Principles* 2.11.5.

100 See Martens, "Revisiting the Allegory/Typology Distinction."

101 Origen, *Homilies on Genesis* 13.3; *Homilies on Exodus* 5.1.

102 See Origen, *Against Celsus* 1.20, 4.39, 4.42.

103 As cited in Eusebius, *Ecclesiastical History* 6.19.4–8.

104 See the *Apology for Origen*, sections 87, 122–6.

105 According to Eusebius, Tatian's *Problems* (no longer extant) explained "the obscure and hidden parts of the divine Scriptures" (*Ecclesiastical History* 5.13.8); Justin, *Dialogue with Trypho* 90; Irenaeus, *Against Heresies* 4.26.1; Clement of Alexandria: "It would be tedious to go over all the prophets and the law specifying what is spoken in enigmas; for almost the whole of Scripture gives its utterance in this way" (*Miscellanies* 5.6); or: "All then, in a word, who have spoken of divine things, both Barbarians and Greeks, have veiled the first principles of things, and delivered the truth in enigmas, and symbols, and allegories, and metaphors, and such like tropes" (*Miscellanies* 5.4); Hippolytus, *Blessings of Isaac, Jacob and Moses* 1.6 and 1.9 on how the OT conceals with its literal sense the mysteries of Christ; Origen, *On First Principles* 3.6.1, 4.1.6, 4.2.2–3, 4.2.8; Scriptures have difficulties/stumbling blocks: *On First Principles* 4.2.9–4.3.5; *Against Celsus* 4.38, 4.44; *Homilies on Ezekiel* 14.2.

106 Irenaeus, *Against Heresies* 2.27.1, 2.28.3; Origen, *On First Principles* 1.Pref.3.

107 Origen, *Philocalia* 1.28, 2.4, 8; *Commentary on the Psalms 1–25*, fragment from Pref.4; *Homilies on Numbers* 27.1; *On First Principles* 4.3.12.

108 Most authors draw upon both sorts of prophetic communication, though some show tendencies for one over the other: Justin focuses upon the prophetic oracles, whereas in Melito's *On Pascha* there is a focus upon prophetic events. Justin (*Dialogue with Trypho* 114) and Irenaeus (*Against Heresies* 4.20.8) both make this distinction between prophetic oracles and events.

109 Only a brief indication of this enormous motif: *1 Clement* 12; *Epistle of Barnabas, passim*; Justin, *Dialogue with Trypho, passim*; Irenaeus, *Against Heresies* 4.14.2–3, 4.9.3, 4.20.5, 8; *Demonstration of the Apostolic Preaching* 43–97; Melito, *On Pascha*; Clement of Alexandria, *Miscellanies* 6.15–16; repeatedly in Hippolytus and Origen, and for point of comparison, both of their *Commentaries on the Song of Songs*; Origen, *Homilies on Genesis* 2.3, 8.8–9, 15.7; *Homilies on Exodus* 5; *Homilies on Leviticus* 2.6, etc.

110 Justin turns to Jesus as "the interpreter of unrecognized prophecies" (*First Apology* 32); Tertullian, *Against Marcion* 3.14; Origen, *Against Celsus* 2.2, 4.49; *Homilies on Exodus* 5.1; *Homilies on Joshua* 15.1.

111 Origen, *On First Principles* 4.2.1–2. On this vexing charge, see P. W. Martens, "Why Does Origen Accuse the Jews of 'Literalism'? A Case Study of Christian Identity and Biblical Exegesis in Antiquity," *Adamantius: The International Journal of Origen and the Alexandrian Tradition* 13, 2007, pp. 218–30.

112 As Origen himself stated: *On First Principles* 1.Pref.2.

113 In his *Antitheses* Marcion argued for a series of contradictions within the Old Testament, as well as between the OT and his Jesus and Paul. Ptolemy, a Valentinian, took a decidedly middle view between total rejection of the Mosaic law (Marcion) and total acceptance of it in his *Letter to Flora*. According to him, the Mosaic law was threefold in that it contained: unjust legislation, which was abolished by Savior; imperfect legislation, which needed to be perfected; and legislation with merely a symbolic value. Marcion and those in the Gnostic coalition with exegetical interests certainly read the Old Testament, but did so in such a way as to generate a religious system that sharply demarcated the God of the OT from the God of the NT.

114 Against Marcion and the Gnostic coalition, authors like Irenaeus (*Against Heresies* 4.34.3, 5), Tertullian (*Against Marcion* 3.20), Clement of Alexandria (*Miscellanies* 2.18), and Origen (*On First Principles* 1.Pref.4) explicitly argue for the authority of the OT. Clement speaks of the Old and New as "one in power" (*Miscellanies* 2.6) or simply "one Testament" (*Miscellanies* 7.17) and Origen echoes this: "So then, the power of the Gospel is found in the Law, and the Gospels are understood as being supported by the foundation of the Law; I do not give the name 'Old Testament' to the Law, if I understand it spiritually. The Law becomes an 'Old Testament' only for those who want to understand it in a fleshly way. … But for us, who understand and explain it spiritually and according to the Gospel meaning, it is always new. Indeed both are 'New Testaments' for us" (*Homilies on Numbers* 9.4.1–2; trans. T. Scheck, *Origen: Homilies on Numbers*, forthcoming).

115 On the single, harmonious voice of Scripture: Irenaeus, *Against Heresies* 2.28.3; Origen, *Philocalia* 6.2; *Commentary on Matthew* fragment 3.

116 On the language of intent (*skopos*), see Origen, *On First Principles* 4.2.7 and 4.2.8.

117 Trans. John Behr, *St Irenaeus of Lyon: On the Apostolic Preaching*, Crestwood, NY: St Vladimir's Seminary Press, 1997, p. 100.

118 Trans. in *Exhortation to the Heathen*, in Roberts and Rambaut, *Fathers of the Second Century*, 1885–7; repr. Grand Rapids: Wm. B. Eerdmans, 1987; repr. Peabody, MA: Hendrickson, 1994, pp. 193–4.

119 "All Scripture is inspired by God and is useful for teaching, for reproof, for correction, and for training in righteousness" (2 Tim. 3:16). "Very truly, I tell you, anyone who hears my word and believes him who sent me has eternal life, and does not come under judgment, but has passed from death to life" (John 4:24 – New Revised Standard Version). See also: "These are the secret sayings which the living Jesus spoke … 'Whoever finds the interpretation of these sayings will not experience death'" (*Gospel of Thomas* Prologue.1). Also note Clement of Alexandria's reference to the "Sicilian bee" (probably Pantaenus), who "gathered the spoil of the flowers of the prophetic and apostolic meadow engendered in the souls of his hearers a deathless element of knowledge" (*Miscellanies* 1.1). Hippolytus, *Commentary on Daniel* 1.7 on nothing useless in Scripture; Origen claims that human souls "cannot otherwise reach perfection except through the rich and wise truth about God" (*On First Principles* 4.2.7).

120 Justin, *Dialogue with Trypho* 100; Irenaeus, *Against Heresies* 4.26.1; Origen, *Commentary on John* 1.33, *On First Principles* 4.1.6.

121 *Commentary on John* 1.27–46; or, the opening of *On First Principles* where Origen writes: "All who believe and are convinced that grace and truth came by Jesus Christ and that Christ is the truth … derive the knowledge which calls men to lead a good and blessed life from no other source but the very words and teaching of Christ." As Origen continues, he insists that by the "words of Christ" he means not only what is recorded in the Gospels, but also Moses, the prophets, and apostolic writings (*On First Principles* 1.Pref.1; trans. G. W. Butterworth, *Origen: On First Principles*, Gloucester, MA: Peter Smith, 1973, p. 1).

122 Rules are offered by Irenaeus, *Demonstration of Apostolic Preaching* 6; *Against Heresies* 1.10.1, 1.22.1, 3.4.2, 4.35.4; Tertullian, *Prescription against Heretics* 13; *The Veiling of Virgins* 1.3; *Against Praxeas* 2; Polycrates (Eusebius, *Ecclesiastical History* 5.24.6); Origen, *On First Principles* 1.Pref.2–10; *Commentary on John* 32.186–97; Novatian, *On the Trinity* 1.1, 9.1, 11.10, 17.1, 22.1, 29.19. Origen's

On First Principles and Novatian's *On the Trinity*, can both be read as commentaries on the rule of faith.

123 See Irenaeus, *Against Heresies* 4.35.5; Tertullian, *Prescription against Heretics* 20–22; esp. Origen, *On First Principles* 1.Pref., where both of these functions of the rule – as a criterion for scriptural interpretation *and* as a synthesis of the clear apostolic teaching – are made clear.

124 Trans. A. Roberts and W. H. Rambaut in *Against Heresies, Books 1–5 and Fragments*, in *Apostolic Fathers with Justin Martyr*; repr. Grand Rapids, MI: Wm. B. Eerdmans, 1987; repr. Peabody, MA: Hendrickson, 1994, p. 398. Similarly, Hippolytus, *Commentary on Daniel* 4.15.

125 Theophilus, *To Autolycus* 1.14. Also on attentiveness when reading Scripture: Irenaeus, *Against Heresies* 4.26.1; Hippolytus *Commentary on Daniel* 4.18.

126 Trans. J. W. Trigg, *Origen*, London: Routledge, 1998, p. 212.

127 Trans. H. Chadwick, *Origen: Contra Celsum*, Cambridge: Cambridge University Press, 1953. Many authors will refer to the gracious work of the Holy Spirit or Word in aiding them in their interpretation of Scripture: Justin, *Dialogue with Trypho* 100; Irenaeus, *Against Heresies* 2.28.3; Hippolytus, *Blessings of Isaac, Jacob and Moses*, 1.Preamble.

128 Young, *Biblical Exegesis and the Formation of Christian Culture*, p. 215.

129 Origen, *On First Principles* 4.2.4.

18
COMMUNITY AND WORSHIP

Everett Ferguson

Christians shared with Jews, but unlike most other religious groups in Greco-Roman antiquity, a strong sense of community life. Others had a sense of common identity and shared rituals, but none, it seems, had the solidarity of a strong community organization exhibited in Judaism and Christianity. A possible exception is Mithraism, but it lacked the exclusiveness characteristic of the biblical religions. Some philosophical schools, like the Epicureans and possibly the Neopythagoreans, exhibited a community life built around adherence to a founder that included some practices characteristic of a religion. Nonetheless, the sense of "church" was a distinctive feature of early Christian faith and practice.

The communal appeal of Christianity

Scholars often note Christianity's communal dimension as a significant factor in its growth and spread. Adolf Harnack in his classic work on *The Mission and Expansion of Christianity in the First Three Centuries* devoted a chapter to "The Organisation of the Christian Community, as Bearing upon the Christian Mission," in which he developed Christian brotherhood as something unique in Greek and Roman life and even superior to the synagogues of Judaism from which it sprang. He declared, "We may take it for granted that the mere existence and persistent activity of the individual Christian communities did more than anything else to bring about the extension of the Christian religion."[1]

Martin P. Nilsson identified six features of Christianity important to its success. Two of these are relevant to my topic: self-government in a bureaucratic world, and the power of Christianity's organization.[2] Similarly, A. D. Nock referred to the success of Christianity "as the success of an institution which united the sacramentalism and the philosophy of the time"; "It satisfied also social needs and it secured men against loneliness."[3] Rodney Stark considers sociological factors in the rise of Christianity to the top of the Roman world, noting that "conversion to new, deviant religious groups occurs when ... people have or develop stronger attachments to members of the group than they have to nonmembers."[4]

More recently Helmut Koester in answering the question, "Why did Christianity succeed?" pointed to the Christian community. "One should not see the success of Christianity simply on the level of a great religious message; one has to see it also in the consistent and very well thought out establishment of institutions to serve the needs of the community." He continues, "What I think the Christians offer probably as well or better than anybody else in the Roman world is a sense of belonging."[5] His language here echoes, probably unknowingly, one of the three elements Alan Kreider identified as involved in conversion – belief, belonging, and behavior.[6] The strong sense of belonging (to the Lord Jesus and of his people to one another) as characteristic of the early Christian community is the theme of this article.

Images of the church

An indication of the importance of the community life of early Christians is the number and variety of images employed for the church. What is immediately evident is that the images all emphasize the communal aspect of Christian faith and life. This communal emphasis stands in contrast to the individualistic approach of so many of the expressions of Christianity in the modern Western world. Most of these images have their origin in biblical usage. They, furthermore, testify to the importance of the church in Christian thought and in addition to the relation of the church to key theological concepts.

There is a comprehensive collection of images for the church and its people in Origen with references to these images in other authors by F. Ledegang.[7] He groups the scores of images and related terminology in the writings of Origen into six categories: body of Christ, bride of Christ, family, house and sanctuary, people of God, and "the earth and all that is in it." I take representative samples from each of the categories and cite illustrative passages from Origen and his predecessors and contemporaries.

Body

The biblical basis of the imagery of the body for the church is 1 Corinthians 12:12–27 and Romans 12:4–5.[8] The homily known as *2 Clement* used the language of the church as the body of Christ to argue for the preexistence of the church. The author's high view of the church stresses its close identification with Christ, taking the body as the equivalent of the flesh of Christ.

> So then, brothers, if we do the will of God our Father, we will belong to the first church, the spiritual one that was created before the sun and moon. ...
> So then, let us choose to belong to the church of life so that we may be saved. I do not think you are ignorant that the church is the living body of Christ. For Scripture says, "God made the human being male and female" [Gen. 1:27]. The male is Christ, and the female is the church. And you know that the Books and the Apostles say that the church is not [only] of the present time but is from the beginning. For it existed spiritually, as also did our Jesus.

But he was manifested in these last days in order to save us. And the church, being spiritual, was manifested in the flesh of Christ. ... But if we say that the flesh is the church and the Spirit is Christ, then the one who abuses the flesh abuses Christ.

(*2 Clement* 14.2–3, 4)[9]

The author may secondarily be warning against those who disparaged the flesh.[10]

Origen makes extensive use of the body imagery; the following passage explicitly refers to its scriptural basis.

We say that the divine Scriptures declare the body of Christ, animated by the Son of God, to be the whole church of God, and the members of this body – considered as a whole – to consist of those who are believers. Since, as a soul vivifies and moves the body ... , so the Word, arousing and moving the whole body, the church, to the things that need to be done, moves also each individual member belonging to the church, so that they do nothing apart from the Word.

(Origen, *Against Celsus* 6.48)[11]

Origen uses the analogy of the church to a body, animated by a soul, to support the union of the soul of Jesus, perfect man, with the eternal Word, Son of God; but he is drawing on 1 Corinthians 12:12 and 27 as well as Romans 12:4–5.[12]

Paul's image of the church as the body of Christ must have worked itself deeply into the Christian consciousness for it to be used so early for such different purposes from Paul's as to argue for the nature of Christ (Origen) and for the preexistence of the church (*2 Clement*).

Bride

The biblical basis of the imagery of the church as the bride of Christ goes back to the Old Testament picture of Israel as married to God that was then applied to Christ and the church (2 Cor. 11:2; Eph. 5:25–28; Rev. 19:7, 21:2). Clement of Alexandria interprets Romans 7:2, 4 to mean Christians belong to Christ as "bride and church, which must be pure both from inner thoughts contrary to the truth and from outward temptations [heresies]."[13] Tertullian stresses that the church is the virgin bride of Christ. Against a bishop's proclamation of forgiveness for the sins of adultery and fornication, the rigorist Tertullian, who considered these sins unforgivable by the church, protests, "The church is a virgin! Far from Christ's betrothed be such a proclamation."[14]

Origen applies the imagery of the bride to the church in his *Commentary on the Song of Songs*. He connects the language of body with that of a bride. Commenting on Paul's words, "Our bodies are members of Christ," he explains,

For when he says "our bodies," he shows that these bodies are the body of the bride; but when he mentions the "members of Christ," he indicates that these same bodies are the body of the Bridegroom.

(Origen, *Commentary on the Song of Songs* 3.2 on 1:16)[15]

Methodius was a critic of Origen on some points of doctrine, but he shared with him the image of church as bride. Those who embrace the truth and are delivered from the evils of the flesh become "a church and help-meet of Christ, betrothed and given in marriage to him as a virgin, according to the apostle" (2 Cor. 11:2).[16]

Mother

The most popular image drawn from the family that was applied to the church in early Christianity was that of a mother.[17] The maternal picture of the church lacks explicit New Testament precedent, but there are hints of it (Gal. 4:25–28). The *Letter of the Churches of Lyon and Vienne* provides one of the early uses of maternal imagery for the church. It speaks of those who in persecution had denied the faith and then came back to faith: "There was great joy to the Virgin Mother, who had miscarried with them as though dead, and was receiving them back alive."[18] Irenaeus in his catechetical work *Demonstration [or Proof] of the Apostolic Preaching* 94 contrasts the church and the synagogue in a similar way to Galatians 4:27 (= Isa. 54:1), "The Lord grants more children to the church than to the synagogue of the past."[19]

Clement of Alexandria said, "The mother draws to herself the children, and we seek our mother, the church."[20] He follows this with a striking statement combining the imagery of virgin and mother for the church:

> One is the universal Father, one also the universal Word, the Holy Spirit is one and the same everywhere, and one is the only virgin mother. I love to call her church. This one alone … is both virgin and mother, pure as a virgin, loving as a mother. She calls her children and nurses them with holy milk, the Word suited to infants.
> (Clement of Alexandria, *Christ the Educator* 1.6.42.1)

Clement seems to have Mary, the mother of Jesus, in mind with the language of virgin mother, but his reference is to the church. This passage is an early instance of adding the church to the usual Trinitarian confession. It is to be noted that the milk supplied by this mother to her children is not her own teachings but the universal Word. Origen gave an allegorical interpretation of Proverbs 17:25:

> The church is our mother, whom God the Father betrothed to himself as wife. For always through her he begets sons and daughters for himself. And such as are educated in the knowledge and wisdom of God are a joy to both God our Father and the mother church.
> (Origen, *Exposition on Proverbs*)[21]

Origen is precise here that the origin of the children is with God the Father and not with the church. Others were not always so careful and sometimes spoke, perhaps loosely, as if the children (Christians) derived from the church. Methodius said that the church "conceives believers and gives them new birth by the washing of regeneration [Titus 3:5]," because Christ implants the spiritual seed that "is conceived and formed by the church, as by a woman, so as to give birth and nourishment to virtue."[22] Methodius, like Origen, is careful not to ascribe the generating power to the mother, but unlike Origen he ascribes the implanting of the spiritual seed to Christ and not God (whose description as Father accords with Origen's language).[23]

Building/temple

The image of the church as a building, particularly a temple, is common in the New Testament (1 Cor. 3:10–17; Eph. 3:20–22; 1 Pet. 2:4–6). Hermas has two elaborate developments of the church as a tower.[24] The parallel is drawn between the creation of the world and the creation of the church, both the earth and the church being founded on the waters.[25] According to the parable of the tower "the rock and the gate are the Son of God."[26] "The tower is the church," and the stones placed in the building are those who take the name of the Son of God and are clothed with the appropriate virtues.[27]

More often the building used to describe the church is a temple. The theme of the spiritual temple replacing the physical temple in Jerusalem is expressed early in Christian literature by *Barnabas*, but the author applies it to the individual.[28] Other authors soon give a collective interpretation. Clement of Alexandria states the argument of early Christian apologists against material temples, while applying the terminology of temple to the church and the assembly of God's people.[29]

> Is it not the case that we do not rightly and truly circumscribe in any place the one who cannot be contained, nor do we confine in temples made with hands that which contains all things? What work of builders, stone cutters, and of handicraft can be holy? ... If the sacred [ιερα] is understood in a twofold way, of God himself and of a structure in his honor, is it not proper that we call holy the church, which is according to full knowledge for the honor of God, is of great worth, and is not constructed by human skill ... but is fashioned by the will of God into a temple? For I do not call the place but the assembly of the elect the church.
>
> (Clement of Alexandria, *Miscellanies* 7.5.28)[30]

So, for Clement, in accord with the New Testament, God's temple now is not a place but the people assembled, the church.

For Tertullian, Christ was the rejected stone that became "the chief corner-stone," "accepted and elevated to the top place of the temple, even his church."[31] Alternatively, Christ, in contrast to the Jewish temple that was destroyed, "is the true temple of God,"[32] but by extension Christians are "priests of the spiritual temple, that is of the church."[33] According to this imagery, it is the Holy Spirit who builds "the church, which is indeed the temple, household, and city of God."[34] The church is the spiritual temple, built upon Peter.[35]

Origen applies the language of the temple to the church mostly in biblical passages about the temple. His commentary on John 2:2:19–21 combines the images of body and of temple for the church:

> If the body of Jesus is said to be his temple, it is worth asking whether we must take this in a singular manner, or must endeavor to refer each of the things recorded about the temple anagogically to the saying about the body of Jesus, whether it be the body which he received from the virgin, or the church, which is said to be his body. ...
>
> One ... will say that the body, understood in either way, has been called the temple because as the temple had the glory of God dwelling in it, so the Firstborn of all creation, being the image and glory of God, is properly said to be the temple bearing the image of God in respect to his body or the church.[...]
>
> We shall attempt, however, to refer each of the statements which have reference to the temple anagogically to the church. ...
>
> Then each of the living stones, will be a stone of the temple according to the worth of its life here.
>
> (Origen, *Commentary on John* 10.263–4, 267–8)

Here, as is usual with him, Origen quickly moves from the corporate use of the image to the individual believer.

People of God

The New Testament picks up from the Hebrew Bible the language of the people of God, a race, and applies it to the Christian people (Rom. 2:28–29; 9:24–26; 1 Pet. 2:9–10).[36] Early apologists presented Christians as a third (or fourth) race. *The Epistle to Diognetus* says that Christians in their religion "neither acknowledge those considered to be gods by the Greeks nor observe the superstition of the Jews," but are a "new race or way of life."[37]

Justin Martyr uses the language of people and race in reference to the church in succession to Israel: "After that Righteous One was put to death, we flourished as another people." He continues, "We are not only a people but also a holy people" and a people chosen by God.[38]

In an extended discussion of different images for the children of God, Clement of Alexandria says that the Lord "calls us sometimes children, sometimes chickens, sometimes infants, and at other times sons and often little children, and a new people and a recent people."[39] He makes the contrast, "the old race [Israel] was perverse and hard hearted," but "we the new people are tender as a child."[40]

> Formerly the older people had an older covenant, and the law disciplined the people with fear ... but to the new and recent people a new covenant has been given, the Word has become flesh, and fear is turned into love.
>
> (Clement of Alexandria, *Christ the Educator* 1.7.59.1)[41]

The children of God "become a new, holy people, by regeneration."[42] Alongside the word "people" Clement also uses the word "race" for Christians. Out of the Greek and Jewish peoples "there are gathered into one race of the saved people those who come to faith."[43] Tertullian too develops the theme of the two peoples. He interpreted Genesis 25:23 about the two nations and two peoples in the womb of Rebekah as referring to the older people of Israel (the Jews) and the later or lesser people, the Christians.[44] In all the nations now "dwells the people of the name of Christ."[45]

Origen works with the theme of peoplehood quite extensively and in various ways. One passage illustrative of his approach, after contrasting the Egyptian people and the Israelite people and their respective priests, addresses the congregation:

> Examining yourself, consider to which people you belong and the priesthood of which order you hold. If you still serve the carnal senses ... , know that you are of the Egyptian people. But if you have before your eyes the Decalogue of the Law and the decade of the New Testament ... and from that you offer tithes ... , "you are a true Israelite in whom there is no guile" [John 1:47].
>
> (Origen, *Homilies on Genesis* 16.6)

Here as elsewhere Origen identifies the true Christian people with the true Israel of Old Testament scripture.

Ark/ship

First Peter 3:20–22 appealed to Noah's ark and the flood (Gen. 6–8) as prefiguring baptism and salvation. Early Christians continued to make use of this narrative as an image of deliverance.[46] Origen, although not the first to connect the ark with the church, was the first to work out the ark motif extensively in an ecclesiological sense.[47] In his *Homilies on Genesis* he drew lessons for the church from the instructions about the building of the ark. "This people, therefore, which is saved in the church, is compared to all those whether men or animals that are saved in the ark."[48] He continues by interpreting the different levels in the ark as degrees of progress in faith, and he takes Noah as an image of Christ.

> Therefore, Christ, the spiritual Noah, in his ark in which he frees the human race from destruction, that is, in his church, has established in its breadth the number fifty, the number of forgiveness.
>
> (Origen, *Homilies on Genesis* 2.5)[49]

Tertullian anticipated the theme of the ark as a type of the church in his treatment of the flood in Noah's day as a type of baptism: "The dove is the Holy Spirit, sent forth from heaven, where is the church, a figure of the ark."[50] And Latin Christianity made much use of the analogy of the ark and the church. Callistus of Rome argued that "the ark of Noah was a symbol of the church, in which were both dogs, wolves, and ravens," and so he alleged that those guilty of sin could remain in the church.[51] Cyprian too argued from the ark as a type of the church: First Peter 3:20–21 proves that "the one ark of Noah was a type of the one church" and so only the baptism administered in the church (and not by schismatics) is valid; on this analogy those outside the church will perish.[52] Thereafter the analogy of the ark and the church was common.

Different from the image of the ark was the non-biblical image of a ship. The earliest reference to a ship other than the ark as the church appears to be Tertullian, *Baptism* 12.7.[53] He was responding to those who suggested that "the apostles underwent a substitute for baptism when in the little ship they were engulfed by the waves [Matt. 8:23–27]." Tertullian replied that that was different from being "baptized by the rule of religion," and he then affirmed, "that little ship presented a type of the church, because on the sea, which means this present world, it is being tossed about by the waves, which mean persecutions and temptations." It has been argued that the ship as a symbol of the church is a recasting of an older conception of Israel in an eschatological storm at sea, perhaps drawn from a lost apocalyptic book.[54]

Hippolytus makes an elaborate development of the comparison of the church to a ship.

> The "wings of the vessels" [Isa. 18:1] are the churches; and the sea is the world, in which the church is set, like a ship tossed in the deep, but not destroyed; for she has with her the skilled pilot, Christ. And she bears in her midst also the trophy (which is erected) over death; for she carries with her the cross of the Lord. For … her tillers are the two Testaments; and the ropes that stretch around her are the love of Christ, which binds the church; and the net which she bears with her is the laver of the regeneration which renews believers. … As the wind the Spirit from heaven is present, by whom those who believe are sealed. She has also anchors of iron accompanying her, that is the holy commandments of Christ himself, which are strong as iron. She also has sailors on the right and the left, assessors like the holy angels, by whom the church is always governed and defended. The ladder in her leading up to the sailyard is an emblem of the passion of Christ, which brings the faithful to the ascent to heaven. And the top sails aloft upon the yard are the company of prophets, martyrs, and apostles, who have entered into their rest in the kingdom of Christ.
>
> (Hippolytus, *On Christ and Antichrist* 59)

A similarly elaborate but different comparison of the ship to the church occurs in the Pseudo-Clementine literature.[55]

This sampling of the rich variety of early Christian imagery for the church demonstrates the importance of the church in the experience and practice of early Christians.[56]

Entry into the church

Baptism was the line of demarcation between the church and the world. The second and third centuries saw an increasing formalization of the process of entry into the church, reaching a climax in the impressive baptismal liturgies of the fourth and fifth centuries. This elaboration of the baptismal ceremony served at least three purposes: (1) it gave an enacted expression to the meaning of baptism; (2) it separated the casual inquirers from the truly committed by impressing on the candidates the seriousness of becoming a Christian; and (3) it instructed and prepared them for a faithful life.

Faith and repentance were the prerequisites for baptism. In explaining Christian practices to the government authorities Justin Martyr states:

> We shall explain in what way we dedicated ourselves to God and were made new through Christ. ... As many as are persuaded and believe that the things taught and said by us are true and promise to be able to live accordingly are taught to fast, pray, and ask God for the forgiveness of past sins, while we pray and fast with them. Then they are led by us to where there is water, and in the manner of the regeneration by which we ourselves were regenerated they are regenerated. For at that time they obtain for themselves the washing in water in the name of God the Master of all and Father, and of our Savior Jesus Christ, and of the Holy Spirit. ... [In order that we might] obtain in the water the forgiveness of past sins, there is called upon the one who chooses to be born again and who repents of his sins the name of God the Master of all and Father.
>
> (Justin, *1 Apology* 61)

Justin indicates a period of prayer and fasting in preparation for the baptism.[57]

By the end of the second and beginning of the third century the instruction preparatory to baptism was being formalized in a catechumenate. The work known as the *Apostolic Tradition* gives the most information, including a normally three-year period of instruction.[58] Recent studies have raised questions about the connection of the work with Hippolytus of Rome and argued that it is "living literature" that in its surviving form contains layers of material over a period of time, so without outside confirmation we cannot be certain of the time before the fourth century for the practices included.[59]

The preaching and teaching given to inquirers and candidates for membership in the church were summarized in the "Rule of Faith" (*regula fidei*) or "Canon of Truth" (*kanón alétheias*).[60] These summaries were fluid in wording but had a similar content. They took a "history of salvation" approach emphasizing the earthly career of Jesus Christ from birth to resurrection as predicted by the Old Testament prophets and climaxing with his return in judgment.[61] They were often structured according to a Trinitarian pattern.

The Apostles Creed had its origin in baptismal confessions of faith.[62] These also early had a Trinitarian structure. The earliest confessions appear to have had an interrogatory form: "Do you believe … ?" with the response, "I believe." Declaratory confessions at baptism can be confirmed only from the fourth century. Baptism was administered "in the name of the Father, Son, and Holy Spirit" (Matt. 28:19; *Didache* 7.1). This practice may have given rise to a triple immersion, first attested by Tertullian.[63] The normal practice was immersion, with exceptions made in case of a lack of sufficient water[64] or for persons on their sickbed at the point of death.[65] Infant baptism is certainly mentioned for the first time by Tertullian.[66] Inscriptional evidence suggests that infant baptism began with cases of sick children whom it was desired to die baptized so as to be assured of entrance into heaven (John 3:5).[67]

An anointing found a place in the baptismal liturgy at an early date (at least by the late second century), either preceding the immersions (in Syria), following them, or often later in both positions. The anointing was variously associated with the biblical anointing of priests and with the bestowal of the Holy Spirit.[68]

The early church elaborated a rich doctrine of baptism.[69] Some of the principal terms used for baptism were regeneration (John 3:5 was the most quoted baptismal text in the second century), a grace gift, illumination, perfection, and bath.[70] Baptism was the time of receiving through God's grace new birth as children of God, enlightenment of spiritual truths (especially in the instruction accompanying baptism), completeness of new life, and the washing away (forgiveness) of sins. Another important term for baptism was "seal."[71] This word relates to baptism as the time of the bestowal of the Holy Spirit. All these blessings were because baptism was connected to the death of Christ on the cross, an association that made the paschal season the most appropriate time for baptism.[72]

Composition and organization of the community

Christianity began as a movement among Jews, but by the second century its adherents were already predominantly Gentiles, and Jewish Christianity was increasingly marginalized. Another significant change in the second and especially the third century was the move up the social and economic ladder. As Christianity spread geographically and numerically, so the number of Christians in the upper echelons of society increased significantly.[73] Christians included a literate elite from the beginning, as witnessed in the New Testament documents. Indeed the churches resembled "bookish communities" and could be characterized from a sociological perspective as Bible study groups, expressed in the intensive and high level of Bible study and interpretation. Thus the second and third centuries produced an extensive theological literature, both orthodox and deviant.

These Christian communities did not have a centralized organization. In the second and third centuries, however, the churches did strengthen their structures on a local and then regional level.[74] This development was an effort to give organizational expression to unity. Moreover, travel by representatives of the churches and exchange of writings gave a sense of being part of a worldwide community with similar faith commitments.

The earliest Christian writings reflect a plurality of presbyter-bishops assisted by deacons in the leadership of each church.[75] The terms presbyter, bishop, and pastor were originally interchangeable for the same group of men.[76] Clement of Rome affirmed the apostolic appointment of bishops and deacons and the provision that there should be a continuation of these functionaries in the churches.[77] This is often cited as establishing "apostolic succession," but one should avoid reading into the statement the meaning that "apostolic succession" came to have later, that is, a succession by bishops to certain functions of apostles.[78] Clement describes only a historical sequence (and he included the deacons in his statement). Gnostics claimed for their teachers a succession from the apostles through the latter's associates.[79] Apostolic succession of the bishops in the churches as a doctrine arose as an argument against the claims of heretical teachers to a secret tradition.

Ignatius offers the first evidence of distinguishing the offices of bishop and presbyter by limiting the term bishop to the chief or head of the presbytery.[80] Ignatius does not base the offices on apostolic appointment or apostolic succession but presents the bishop as an image of God the Father, the council of presbyters as corresponding to the college of apostles, and the deacons as representing the serving ministry of Christ.[81] Ignatius's central concern was unity. Borrowing the language of political concord, he saw obedience to one bishop as unifying the house churches of the city.[82] Basically the bishop is a congregational bishop (or pastor). Ignatius's correspondent Polycarp seems not to have shared his apparently sharp distinction between the one bishop and the body of presbyters. He spoke of the latter as his "fellow presbyters," and when he wrote to the church at Philippi he spoke only of deacons and presbyters.[83]

Ignatius's threefold ministry of bishop, presbyters, and deacons became the pattern throughout the church by the late second century.[84] The earlier association of the bishop and presbyters continued in the language of Irenaeus and Clement of Alexandria, for whom the term presbyter included the bishop but the term bishop no longer applied to presbyters.[85]

Appointed widows seem to have formed a distinct order in the church.[86] How early female deacons were recognized is not clear. They are certainly present with the designation deaconesses in the third century.[87]

Other functionaries were present in the second century but not so prominent by the third. Teachers functioned within the congregational organization, but those we know best established schools more or less independent of the local congregations. Justin Martyr represented the mainstream of emerging orthodoxy, but Marcion, Valentinus, and others presented alternative doctrinal viewpoints.

Prophets were still active in the *Didache* and Hermas but were soon less in evidence.[88] The revival of prophecy in the Montanist movement was resisted in the episcopally organized churches. Montanism brought women to prominence, even in the leadership of worship and administering sacraments.[89] Sociologically based studies of early Christianity have interpreted much of the conflict in the early church in terms of opposition between charisma and office. Examples such as Hermas, who was a householder[90] but functioned as a prophet (receiving the revelations in the *Visions*), and Ignatius, a bishop who appealed to his prophetic speech,[91] caution against a sharp dichotomy.[92]

Efforts to give organizational expression to inter-congregational unity began in the second century. Regional *ad hoc* councils met to consider a proper response to

Montanism and to discuss the proper time for an annual commemoration of the Lord's passion (the Pasch).[93] During the third century, regional meetings of bishops became regular.[94] These councils were presided over by the metropolitan bishop in the province, who was the bishop of the capital city or of the chief church in the province.

Worship of the community

The local Christian community found expression in and could be defined as those who assembled weekly for communion (eucharist).[95] This assembly occurred on Sunday, the day called by Jews "the first day of the week," and by early Christians "the Lord's day," because it was the day of Jesus' resurrection.[96] A combination of Jewish and Christian terminology continues in modern Greek, which follows Jewish practice in naming the days Monday through Thursday by the numerals two through five, Friday as Preparation day, and Saturday as Sabbath, and Christian practice in naming Sunday as Lord's (day). These names must go back to the earliest times of Christian Greek. The Christian week centered on the Lord's day. The importance of the weekly assembly was shown in that Christians continued meeting in spite of persecution.[97]

Justin Martyr provides the fullest, orderly account of an early Christian assembly. It was marked by the reading of the Scriptures (the Prophets and the Gospels) and a discourse on the readings by the "president" (bishop?), prayer, communion of bread and wine mixed with water, and a contribution.[98] Although this one account is not sufficient to establish a common liturgical structure in our period, it does incorporate the elements that have characterized Christian liturgy ever since.[99] Justin does not mention hymns, but other sources indicate their presence.[100] The hymns and hymnic-like passages that have come down to us are notable for their Christ-centered and almost confessional character.[101] The early prayers also are rich in their borrowing of biblical language and in their doctrinal content. The dominant note of the early prayers is praise, with which they begin (frequently a recitation of God's mighty acts) and end (a doxology – to God through Christ in the Holy Spirit). Other elements of prayer were confession of faith and of sin, thanksgiving, and petitions for others' needs. The liturgical prayers promoted a strong sense of community, ratified by the unison "Amen" of the congregation.[102]

The two foci of Christian worship are hearing the word of the Lord in scripture reading and preaching and partaking of the eucharist. Readings from the Jewish Bible were early complemented by readings from apostolic writings, and what was read in the assemblies was an important signal of canonicity. The earliest non-canonical account of the eucharist occurs in the *Didache* 9–10, 14 and reflects a setting in which the eucharist occurs in the context of a full meal. The prayers are very Jewish and unlike the main line of Christian development make no reference to the death of Christ. The main features are thanksgiving, fellowship, unity, and eschatology. The "sacrifice" of *Didache* 14 may be the eucharist itself, or more likely the prayers of thanksgiving, or possibly the way of life of the members of the community.[103]

The eucharist occasioned extensive doctrinal development.[104] The idea of "spiritual sacrifice" in contrast to material sacrifices[105] was soon extended from the prayers at the eucharist to include the elements of bread and fruit of the vine.[106] The idea, as capsuled in the name eucharist, was a sacrifice of thanksgiving and praise.[107] Malachi 1:11 was the most quoted eucharistic text in the second century. Cyprian pointed the way to fourth-century developments by associating not only the bread and cup with the sacrifice but also by connecting the eucharistic sacrifice with Christ's sacrifice on the cross.[108]

The material nature of the bread and wine in the eucharist was an important argument for the goodness of the created world and for the physical humanity of Christ against Docetists and Gnostics.[109] Even where authors use the language of symbol or figure for the elements, modern readers must remember that for the ancients there was a closer relation between the symbol and what was symbolized than is true for moderns.[110] The move from Hebraic (biblical) thought, where consecration changed the function of the elements, to Greek (philosophical) thought, where change affected the substance of the elements, contributed to a more realistic conception of the real presence of the body and blood of Christ in the eucharist. The benefits of the divine life of Christ, mediated by the Holy Spirit, exceeded the physical nourishment of bread and wine. One may describe the relation of symbolism and realism in these early descriptions of the eucharist as a symbolism of bread and wine as signs and a realism of the spiritual gift conveyed by the signs.[111] The congregational assemblies for worship gave identity and unity to the Christian communities. They established the sense of "belonging" that was so important to early Christian existence.

Further reading

Primary sources

P. F. Bradshaw, M. E. Johnson and L. E. Phillips (trans. and comm.), *The Apostolic Tradition*, Hermeneia, Minneapolis: Fortress, 2002. (Instructions for organization and worship that had enormous influence on modern liturgical renewal.)

Cyprian, *On the Unity of the Catholic Church*, trans. M. Bévenot, Ancient Christian Writers 25, Westminster, MD: Newman [New York: Paulist], 1957. (A response to schism, it is the first doctrinal treatise on the church.)

M. W. Holmes (ed. and trans.), *The Apostolic Fathers*, 3rd edn, Grand Rapids, MI: Baker, 2007, pp. 44–131, 138–65. (Earliest non-canonical writings acceptable to the mainstream of the church.)

Tertullian, *On Baptism*, ed. and trans. E. Evans, *Tertullian's Homily on Baptism*, London: SPCK, 1964. (The earliest surviving treatise on baptism.)

Secondary sources

P. F. Bradshaw, *The Search for the Origins of Christian Worship*, 2nd edn, Oxford: Oxford University Press, 2002. (Argues for diversity of liturgical practice in the early centuries and warns against reading later uniformity into the earliest sources.)

E. Ferguson, *Early Christians Speak*, 3rd edn, Abilene, TX: Abilene Christian University Press, 1999. (Collection of source passages with commentary on matters of faith, worship, organization, and life in the second and third centuries.)

A. F. Gregory and C. M. Tuckett (eds), *Trajectories through the New Testament and the Apostolic Fathers*, Oxford: Oxford University Press, 2005. (Articles tracing themes from the New Testament in the Apostolic Fathers.)

T. Halton, *The Church*, Message of the Fathers of the Church 4, Wilmington, DE: Michael Glazier [Collegeville, MN: Liturgical], 1985. (Passages from the early centuries, some as late as seventh and eighth centuries, topically arranged on aspects of the church.)

F. Ledegang, *Mysterium ecclesiae: Images of the Church and Its Members in Origen*, Leuven: Leuven University Press, 2001. (An exhaustive treatment of various images of the church in Origen with frequent note of parallels in other authors.)

J. D. Zizioulas, *Eucharist, Bishop, Church: The Unity of the Church in the Divine Eucharist and the Bishop during the First Three Centuries*, Brookline, MA: Holy Cross Orthodox Press, 2001. (Eastern Orthodox doctrinal perspective.)

Notes

1 A. Harnack, *The Mission and Expansion of Christianity in the First Three Centuries*, trans. and ed. by James Moffatt, New York: Harper Torchbooks, 1961, p. 434.

2 M. P. Nilsson, *Greek Piety*, Oxford: Clarendon, 1948, pp. 182–83.

3 A. D. Nock, *Conversion: The Old and the New in Religion from Alexander the Great to Augustine of Hippo*, Oxford: Clarendon, 1933, pp. 210–11 and note his summary on p. xii.

4 R. Stark, *The Rise of Christianity: A Sociologist Reconsiders History*, Princeton, NJ: Princeton University Press, 1996, p. 18.

5 H. Koester, "Why Did Christianity Succeed? The Great Appeal," in *From Jesus to Christ: The First Christians*, Frontline Series, Public Broadcasting Service, 6 and 7 April 1998, accessed online 10 June 2009 at http://www.pbs.org/wgbh/pages/frontline/shows/religion/why/appeal.html.

6 A. Kreider, *The Change of Conversion and the Origin of Christendom*, Harrisburg: Trinity Press International, 1999, p. 92; A. Kreider, "Changing Patterns of Conversion in the West," in A. Kreider (ed.), *The Origins of Christendom in the West*, Edinburgh: T&T Clark, 2001, p. 3.

7 F. Ledegang, *Mysterium ecclesiae: Images of the Church and Its Members in Origen*, Leuven: Leuven University Press, 2001; L. Pernveden, *The Concept of the Church in the Shepherd of Hermas*, Lund: Gleerup, 1966. D. Rankin, *Tertullian and the Church*, Cambridge: Cambridge University Press, 1995, has a chapter on "Tertullian's Ecclesiological Images" (pp. 65–90): ark, ship, camp, body of Christ, Trinity, Spirit, mother, bride, virgin, school, and sect. For a later patristic figure there is G. D. Christo, *The Church's Identity Established through Images according to Saint John Chrysostom*, Rolli, NH: Orthodox Research Institute, 2006.

8 An early reflection of the Pauline argument in 1 Cor. 12 but without use of the word church is Clement, *1 Clement* 37.5–38.1. Justin, *Dialogue* 42.3, speaks of "the church, being many persons in number" as like "the many members" that make up "one body."

9 J. Muddiman, "The Church in Ephesians, 2 Clement, and the *Shepherd of Hermas*," in A. F. Gregory and C. M. Tuckett (eds), *Trajectories through the New Testament and the Apostolic Fathers*, Oxford: Oxford University Press, 2005, pp. 114–16, discusses the preexistence of the church as a reapplication of the themes of the preexistence of Wisdom and of Israel in Jewish thought. Cf. *Shepherd of Hermas*, Vision 2.4 (2.8), for the church created first of all things. Ignatius, *To the Magnesians* 1, has a prayer that in the churches there may be a unity of the flesh and spirit of Jesus Christ.

10 Clement of Alexandria, *Miscellanies* 7.14.87.3, after identifying the "holy church" with the "spiritual body" of Christ, cites 1 Cor. 6:13 that it "is not for fornication."

11 Cf. Clement of Alexandria, *Christ the Educator* 1.5.22, "Believers are members of Christ."

12 Clement of Alexandria, *Christ the Educator* 1.6.42, supports the incarnation on the basis that as a human being is a combination of body and soul so the Lord is of flesh and blood. In his *Extracts from the Prophets* 56, he cites the alternative interpretations of Ps. 19:4–6 that the "Lord's tabernacle is his body," or "it is the church of the faithful."

13 Clement of Alexandria, *Miscellanies* 3.12.80.

14 Tertullian, *Modesty* 1.

15 Note also 3.15 on 2:13–14 and 3.1 on 1:15.

16 Methodius, *Banquet of the Ten Virgins* 3.8.

17 The major study of the image is J. C. Plumpe, *Mater Ecclesia: An Inquiry into the Concept of the Church as Mother in Early Christianity*, Washington, DC: Catholic University of America Press, 1943.

18 Eusebius, *Ecclesiastical History* 5.1.45; cf. the allusion in 5.1.49.

19 In chapter 98 Irenaeus says that the church throughout the world hands down the preaching of the truth to her children. In *Against Heresies* 3.24.1 he says against heretics that those "who do not partake of the Spirit [of God] are not nourished into life from the mother's breasts."

20 Clement of Alexandria, *Christ the Educator* 1.5.21; *Christ the Educator* 3.12.99 says the same with reference to the church, "Let us children run to our good mother."

21 *Patrologia Graeca* 17.201B.

22 Methodius, *Banquet of the Ten Virgins* 3.8.

23 Again, Methodius says that when the Word (Christ) begets in each one a true knowledge and faith, Christ is spiritually born in them: "Therefore, the church swells and travails in birth until Christ is formed in us [Gal. 4:19]" – *Banquet of the Ten Virgins* 8.8.

24 *Shepherd of Hermas*, Vision 3.2.4–3.9.10 (10–17) and *Parables* 9.2.1–9.16.7 (79–93).

25 *Shepherd of Hermas*, Vision 1.3.4 (3) for the earth "founded upon the waters" and 3.3.3 and 5 (11) for the tower, identified as the church, "built upon the waters" of baptism and "founded on the word of the almighty and glorious name." J. Muddiman, "The Church in Ephesians, 2 Clement, and the *Shepherd of Hermas*," pp. 119–20.

26 *Shepherd of Hermas*, Parables 9.12.1 (89).

27 *Shepherd of Hermas*, Parables 9.13.1 (89); 9.12.4–15.6 (89–92).

28 *Barnabas* 16, especially verse 8.

29 Minucius Felix, *Octavius* 33. Clement employs the philosophical principle that God encompasses all things and is contained by nothing – Theophilus, *To Autolycus* 1.5, 2.3; Athenagoras, *Plea on Behalf of Christians* 8; see W. R. Schoedel, "Enclosing, Not Enclosed: The Early Christian Doctrine of God," in W. R. Schoedel and R. L Wilken (eds), *Early Christian Literature and the Classical Intellectual Tradition: In Honorem Robert M. Grant*, Paris: Beauchesne, 1979, pp. 75–86; repr. in E. Ferguson (ed.), *Doctrines of God and Christ in the Early Church*, Studies in Early Christianity 9, New York: Garland [Taylor & Francis], 1993, pp. 1–12.

30 *Miscellanies* 7.13.82 says with reference to 1 Cor. 3:16 that "The temple is large, as the church, but small, as the human being." F. Ledegang, *Mysterium ecclesiae*, p. 320, lists Clement's varied use of the temple imagery: the cosmos, the soul of the Gnostic, the body, the body of Jesus, as well as the church.

31 Tertullian, *Against Marcion* 3.7.

32 Tertullian, *Against the Jews* 13. In *Against Marcion* 3.24 Christ is "the temple of God, and also the gate by whom heaven is entered."

33 Tertullian, *Against the Jews* 14. Individual Christians are themselves "temples of God, and altars, and lights, and sacred vessels" according to *The Crown* 9.

34 Tertullian, *Against Marcion* 3.23.

35 Tertullian, *Monogamy* 8.

36 On the general theme, D. K. Buell, *Why This New Race: Ethnic Reasoning in Early Christianity*, New York: Columbia University Press, 2005.

37 *Diognetus* 1. Aristides divided humanity into the worshippers of pagan gods (the Syriac version gives four classes by dividing these into barbarians and Greeks), Jews, and Christians – *Apology* 2. The *Preaching of Peter* said, "Do not worship as the Greeks," "neither worship as the Jews," but "worship in a new way by Christ" – quoted by Clement of Alexandria, *Miscellanies* 6.5. Tertullian, however, assigns the designation "third race" to pagan critics and rejects it (*To the Heathen* 8).

38 Justin, *Dialogue with Trypho* 119.3–4. In 123 Justin quotes Old Testament passages to show that the church of the Gentiles is a new Israel, "counted worthy to be called a people" (123.1). He affirms of Christians that "We are the true high priestly race of God" (116.3).

39 Clement of Alexandria, *Christ the Educator* 1.5.14.

40 Clement of Alexandria, *Christ the Educator* 1.5.19.4.

41 Cf. *Christ the Educator* 1.5.20.3, "In contrast to the older people, the new and recent people have learned new blessings."

42 Clement of Alexandria, *Christ the Educator* 1.6.32.4.

43 Clement of Alexandria, *Miscellanies* 6.5.42.

44 Tertullian, *Against the Jews* 1.

45 Tertullian, *Against the Jews* 7.

46 Note Justin, *Dialogue with Trypho* 138 and the frequency of Noah in the ark in early Christian funerary art.

47 Ledegang, *Mysterium ecclesiae*, pp. 371–6.

48 Origen, *Homilies on Genesis* 2.3.

49 Fifty has the significance of forgiveness from the year of Jubilee and the release from debts.

50 Tertullian, *On Baptism* 8.4.

51 Hippolytus, *Refutation of All Heresies* 9.12(7).23. Tertullian in *Idolatry* 24.4 alludes to this argument, referring to the different kinds of animals (raven, kite, dog, and serpent) in the ark as representing different types of people in the church, but he insists that no idolater was in the ark, so "Let there not be in the church what was not in the ark."

52 Cyprian, *Letters* 69.2.2; 75.15.

53 An unspecified ship in *Modesty* 13.20.

54 E. Peterson, "Das Schiff als Symbol der Kirche: Die Tat des Messias im eschatologischen Meerssturm in der jüdischen und altchristlichen Ueberlieferung," *Theologische Zeitschrift* 6, 1950, pp. 77–9.

55 Pseudo-Clement, *Letter of Clement to James* 14. Chapter 15 applies the comparison with specific exhortations to the different members of the church.

56 An indirect testimony to the importance of the church for early Christians is that in the elaboration of Valentinianism by Ptolemy *ekklesia* (church) is one of the eight aeons in the ogdoad, the highest part of the *Pleroma* – Irenaeus, *Against Heresies* 1.1.1.

57 For fasting in preparation for baptism see *Didache* 7.4. For the sequence, fasting, praying, and being baptized. cf. Acts 9:9, 11, 18.

58 *Apostolic Tradition* 17. The requirements include sponsors to vouch for a person's readiness (15.2), inquiries about marital status (15.6–7; 16.15–16), rejection of an extensive list of crafts and professions associated with immorality or idolatry (16), prayer (18–19.1), living virtuously and practicing good works (20.1–2), being exorcized (20.3), and fasting (20.7).

59 M. Metzger, "Nouvelles perspective pour le prétendue *Tradition apostolique*," *Ecclesia Orans* 5, 1988, pp. 241–59; "Enquêtes autour de la prétendue *Tradition apostolique*," *Ecclesia Orans* 9, 1992, pp. 7–36; "A propos des règlements écclesiastique et de la prétendue *Tradition apostolique*," *Revue des sciences religieuses* 66, 1992, pp. 249–61; A. Brent, *Hippolytus and the Roman Church in the Third Century: Communities in Tension Before the Emergence of a Monarch-Bishop*, Leiden: Brill, 1995; J. A. Cerrato, *Hippolytus between East and West: The Commentaries and the Provenance of the Corpus*, New York: Oxford University Press, 2002; P. Bradshaw, M. E. Johnson, and L. E. Phillips, *The Apostolic Tradition: A Commentary*, Hermeneia, Minneapolis: Fortress, 2002.

60 Some of the early statements with commentary are given in E. Ferguson, *Early Christians Speak*, 3rd edn, Abilene, TX: Abilene Christian University Press, 1999, pp. 19–28.

61 M. J. Svigel, "Second Century Incarnational Christology and Early Catholic Christianity," PhD diss., Dallas Theological Seminary, 2008, argues that the pattern of pre-incarnate existence, union of the Son with fleshly humanity, real birth and life, real suffering and death, bodily resurrection, and heavenly assumption were the distinguishing marks of catholic Christianity in contrast to other christologies.

62 Recent studies are surveyed by E. Ferguson, "Creeds, Councils, and Canons," in S. Harvey and D. Hunter (eds), *Oxford Handbook of Early Christian Studies*, Oxford: Oxford University Press, 2008, pp. 427–45.

63 Tertullian, *The Crown* 3.

64 *Didache* 7.3.

65 Cyprian, *Letters* 69 [75].12.1–3.

66 Tertullian, *Baptism* 18. The major contributions of D. F. Wright to the history of infant baptism are brought together in D. F. Wright, *Infant Baptism in Historical Perspective: Collected Studies*, Milton Keynes: Paternoster, 2007.

67 E. Ferguson, "Inscriptions and the Origin of Infant Baptism," *Journal of Theological Studies* 30, 1979, pp. 37–46; repr. in E. Ferguson (ed.), *Conversion, Catechumenate, and Baptism in the Early Church*, Studies in Early Christianity 11, New York: Garland [Taylor & Francis], 1993, pp. 391–400.

68 G. W. H. Lampe, *The Seal of the Spirit*, 2nd edn, London: SPCK, 1967; M. Dudley and G. Rowell (eds), *The Oil of Gladness: Anointing in the Christian Tradition*, London: SPCK, 1993.

69 E. Ferguson, *Baptism in the Early Church: History, Theology, and Liturgy in the First Five Centuries*, Grand Rapids, MI: Eerdmans, 2009.

70 Clement of Alexandria, *Christ the Educator* 1.6.26.2.

71 *Shepherd of Hermas, Parables* 9.16.3–6 [93.3–6]; *2 Clement* 6.9; 7.6; 8.6.

72 Tertullian, *Baptism* 19.

73 For an introduction to the study of early Christianity as a social phenomenon see L. M. White, "Sociological Interpretation," in E. Ferguson (ed.), *Encyclopedia of Early Christianity*, 2nd edn, New York: Garland [Taylor & Francis], 1997, pp. 1070–2.

74 E. Ferguson (ed.), *Church, Ministry, and Organization in the Early Church Era*, Studies in Early Christianity 13, New York: Garland [Taylor & Francis], 1993, contains a collection of articles on organization and theology of ministry in the early church.

75 Acts 14:23; Phil. 1:1; *Didache* 15.1; Polycarp, *Philippians* 6.1; *Shepherd of Hermas, Vision* 2.4.2–3 (8.2–3). Ferguson, *Early Christians Speak*, pp. 163–75, translates and comments on some of the principal passages bearing on the organization of the early church.

76 Acts 20:17, 28; 1 Pet. 5:1–2; Clement of Rome, *1 Clement* 42, 44.

77 Clement of Rome, *1 Clement* 42; 44. For his statement that the apostles appointed the tested men among their first-fruits as bishops and deacons, compare 1 Cor. 16:15–16. With reference to Hermas and Clement, P. S. Jeffers, *Conflict at Rome: Social Order and Hierarchy in Early Christianity*, Minneapolis: Fortress, 1991, studies the diversity in the church at Rome.

78 Perhaps implied in Hippolytus, *Refutation of All Heresies* Preface; explicit in Cyprian, *Letters* 64.3; 66.4.

79 Irenaeus, *Against Heresies* 3.2.1.

80 Ignatius, *To the Trallians* 3; *To the Smyrnaeans* 8; *To Polycarp* 6.

81 In addition to the passages in the preceding note, see the parallels he makes between God and the bishop in *To the Ephesians* 3.2 and 4.1; cf. 5.3.

82 D. M. Reis, "Following in Paul's Footsteps: *Mimésis* and Power in Ignatius of Antioch," and H. O. Maier, "The Politics and Rhetoric of Discord and Concord in Paul and Ignatius," in Gregory and Tuckett, *Trajectories through the New Testament and the Apostolic Fathers*, pp. 287–305 (esp. 302–4), 307–24 (esp. 316).

83 Polycarp, *Philippians* Preface; 5.2–3; 6.1.

84 E. G. Jay, "From Presbyter-Bishops to Bishops and Presbyters," *Second Century* 1, 1981, pp. 125–62. For deacons see J. M. Barnett, *The Diaconate: A Full and Equal Order*, rev. edn, New York: Seabury, 1994.

85 Irenaeus, *Against Heresies* 3.2.2, 4.26.2; Clement of Alexandria, *Miscellanies* 3.12.90.1, 7.1.3.3; *Salvation of the Rich* 42.

86 1 Tim. 5:9–11; *Didascalia* 14–15; Origen, *Commentary on John* 32.7. B. Thurston, *The Widows – A Woman's Ministry in the Early Church*, Minneapolis: Fortress, 1989.

87 *Didascalia* 16. K. Madigan and C. Osiek (eds), *Ordained Women in the Early Church: A Documentary History*, Baltimore: Johns Hopkins University Press, 2005; J. Wijngaards, *Women Deacons in the Early Church*, New York: Crossroad, 2006.

88 *Didache* 11.10–12, 13.1–6; *Shepherd of Hermas, Mandate* 11.1–21 (43.1–21); Eusebius, *Ecclesiastical History* 3.37.1, 5.17.3–4.

89 Firmillian in Cyprian, *Letters* 75[74].10 presumably had in mind a Montanist woman who celebrated the Eucharist and baptized; cf. Tertullian, *Prescription against Heretics* 41.5 for unspecified heretics, but contrast *The Soul* 9 for a woman who reported her visions only after the sacred services.

90 *Shepherd of Hermas, Parables* 7.1–3.

91 Ignatius, *To the Philadelphians* 7.1.

92 A. Stewart-Sykes, "Prophecy and Patronage: The Relationship between Charismatic Functionaries and Household Officers in Early Christianity," in Gregory and Tuckett, *Trajectories through the New Testament and the Apostolic Fathers*, pp. 165–89.

93 Eusebius, *Ecclesiastical History* 5.16.10 for Montanism; 5.23.2–4, for the paschal controversy.

94 Best known is the situation in North Africa – Cyprian, *Letters* 55; 67.1.

95 E. Ferguson (ed.), *Worship in Early Christianity*, Studies in Early Christianity 15, New York: Garland [Taylor & Francis], 1993.

96 W. Rordorf, *Sunday: The History of the Day of Rest and Worship in the Earliest Centuries of the Christian Church*, Philadelphia: Westminster, 1968; texts collected in *Sabbat und Sonntag in der Alten Kirche*, Traditio Christiana, Zurich: Theologischer, 1972; a shorter collection in Ferguson, *Early Christians Speak*, pp. 65–7, with commentary, pp. 69–73; D. A. Carson (ed.), *From Sabbath to Lord's Day: A Biblical, Historical and Theological Investigation*, Grand Rapids, MI: Zondervan, 1982.

97 Tertullian, *Flight in Persecution* 3; 14.

98 Justin, *1 Apology* 67. See Ferguson, *Early Christians Speak*, pp. 79–89; and "Justin Martyr and the Liturgy," *Restoration Quarterly* 36, 1994, pp. 267–78.

99 P. F. Bradshaw, *The Search for the Origins of Christian Worship*, 2nd edn, Oxford: Oxford University Press, 2002, concludes there was much more diversity than uniformity in the early centuries.

100 Pliny, *Letters* 10.96; Clement of Alexandria, *Christ the Educator* 3.11.80.3; Tertullian, *Soul* 9.4.

101 Ferguson, *Early Christians Speak*, pp. 145–62 (esp. 152).

102 Ferguson, *Early Christians Speak*, pp. 133–44.

103 C. Claussen, "The Eucharist in the Gospel of John and in the *Didache*," in Gregory and Tuckett, *Trajectories through the New Testament and the Apostolic Fathers*, pp. 135–63 (esp. 156–7, 162).

104 J. D. Zizioulas, *Eucharist, Bishop, Church: The Unity of the Church in the Divine Eucharist and the Bishop during the First Three Centuries*, Brookline, MA: Holy Cross Orthodox Press, 2001; P. F. Bradshaw, *Eucharistic Origins*, Oxford: Oxford University Press, 2004.

105 E. Ferguson, "Spiritual Sacrifice in Early Christianity and Its Environment," in H. Temporini and W. Haase (eds), *Aufstieg und Niedergang der römischen Welt* 2.23.1, Berlin: de Gruyter, 1980, pp. 1151–89.

106 The important texts are translated and commented on in Ferguson, *Early Christians Speak*, pp. 115–23.

107 W. Rordorf, "Le Sacrifice eucharistique," *Theologische Zeitschrift* 25, 1969, pp. 335–53; repr. in Ferguson, *Worship in Early Christianity*, pp. 193–211.

108 Cyprian, *Letter* 63 [62].14, 17.

109 Ferguson, *Early Christians Speak*, pp. 103–14, translates and comments on texts pertinent to the real presence of Christ in the Eucharist.

110 For symbol and allegory for the bread and wine – Clement of Alexandria, *Christ the Educator* 1.6.43; 2.2.10–20; Origen, *Commentary on Matthew* 11.14; *Homilies on Leviticus* 7.5. For figure – Tertullian, *Against Marcion* 4.40. For antitype – *Apostolic Tradition* 23.1.

111 C. W. Dugmore, "Sacrament and Sacrifice in the Early Fathers," *Journal of Ecclesiastical History* 2, 1951, pp. 24–37; repr. in Ferguson, *Worship in Early Christianity*, pp. 178–91. As this statement applies especially to Augustine see pp. 33–4 = pp.187–8.

INDEX